PROFESSOR BLAIKLOCK'S
HANDBOOK OF BIBLE PEOPLE

Scripture Union
130 City Road, London EC1V 2NJ

© E. M. Blaiklock 1979

ISBN 0 85421 810 6

Printed and bound in Great Britain by
Billing & Sons Limited, Guildford, London and Worcester

The 740 studies of Biblical Characters which follow appeared originally in small paperbacks from the Scripture Union, published in connection with a parallel survey of Biblical doctrines. It has been thought that readers would like to have them in this separate form.

The men and women of the Bible were people like ourselves. In my teaching years at the University of Auckland, I always begged my students in Greek and Roman literature and Ancient History, not to speak of 'the ancients', as if those who lived in an earlier world and another century were a race apart. They were not. They, like the characters of the Bible, were men and women of 'like passions with ourselves', the same joys and sorrows, loves and hatreds, desires and aspirations.

The story of humanity set out in the Bible, if we begin with Abraham, the first person to whom an historical date can, with some precision, be attached, cover over two thousand years of history, almost as long a tract of time as lies between us and John the Apostle, last of all the people of the Bible to live and write within its context.

Over that period, life offered the same challenges, the same temptations, the same paths for courage, hope, heroism, sacrifice. Abraham, David, Paul faced the same tensions, the same human situations—and met them with the same resources of the spirit. Their God was the same God, clearer, sharper, deeper though their conception of Him, in its culmination in the New Testament, became.

So why should we at the other end of history, not also find in both Testaments our brethren and sisters? We do. That is why there is illumination for us, sometimes warning, sometimes vital clues to living, and clarity of guidance in the study of how other men and women, in triumph and disaster, in peace and strife, faced what life offered and all that life could do to them.

Read with an eye on the Bible. Relevant passages are prescribed, and their words according to the reader's experience, may appear differently than they do to the one who writes. This need cause no surprise. There is no dogmatism, no finality in what is written here. These characters take shape and form from the one who sets out to describe them, and another may quite well see them in another light. Meanwhile let each be pondered, considered slowly, and made the theme of admiration, pity, understanding or what the reader will.

E. M. Blaiklock

Titirangi
  Auckland N.Z.
    August 29, 1978

1 : Adam the First Man

Genesis 1.26–31

No one knows how many thousands of years ago it was, but at some point in time Man appeared in an earthly Paradise. He was Adam, and he moves into the first pages of the Bible, a true human being, recognizably one of us, innocent, at peace with God, and happy. God, says the Bible, with sublime simplicity, 'created man in His own image'. Man still, even in his fallen state, finds within himself the same sort of reason which expresses itself in the universe. Without that assumption all scientific investigation would be impossible. The first mark of Adam in the plain, brief pages which open the Bible is intelligence. At his first appearance he is without all arts and crafts, but is challenged to an intelligent obedience to God (Gen. **2**.15–17); he is entrusted with responsibility, on the assumption that he is able intelligently to bear it (Gen. **1**.28–30); he has the gift of language, in which man gives expression not only to his reason, but also to his imagination (Gen. **2**.19). Here quite obviously is man endowed with all that which makes man unique. Man's distinctive being consists in knowing himself to be God's creation, known of God and knowing Him. In his very creation is a summons to listen, to understand, and to believe. Unlike all else in the created universe, man is a citizen of two worlds. Though part of God's creation, and participating in it, man stands, like God, over against the physical world and is, in consequence, its divinely appointed master. He is in the world but something other than the world. That is why he can create within the physical world that which is other than the

1

world-culture, the work of his mind and spirit. That is why man can rule. Man's distinctiveness is not in the power of his body, or the acuteness of his senses, in both of which he falls notably short of other creatures, but in the fact that he stands 'in God's image', having understanding of God's thought, purpose and will. This is precisely how Adam is described. Nothing so far has marred the beauty of his life. His happiness flows from unclouded fellowship. God takes joy in him, and he in God. It is a picture soon to fade.

2 : Adam's Responsibility

Genesis 2.7–15

Every man is a volume, someone has remarked, if we know how to read it. This is eminently true of Adam. All man's potentialities, all his vast opportunity, and all his capacity for failure, are to be read in him. He is given dominion over all the created world, and all subordinate creatures. Concerning the Garden, he is told 'to till it and keep it'. The two words go together, and measure man's responsibility. Adam no doubt understood it quite literally. He was to give back to the earth what he took from it. Man, and it is part of the Fall which is now looming large in the tragic Genesis story, has learned that part of his task which feeds his pride. He has tilled the earth, bent Nature to his ends, and tamed her. Perhaps in the process he has already destroyed her. Read the first half of Isa. 24. The earth, says the prophet, is defiled under its own inhabitants, because they have broken eternal laws. One such law is that man gives in proportion as he receives, that duty and privilege go together. God put Adam in his earthy Eden, 'to *serve* and *keep* it' (Gen. 2.15). Adam was master, but, like any true master, he ruled only in proportion as he served; he had to keep the garden, i.e. 'care for it' (NEB). How many long years Adam lived in happiness, seeking to serve God and God's creation, and discovering in the process that the created world, on such terms, served him, we do not know. The brief account, in the language of far centuries, tells us no more than we need to know. We are, none the less, left with the impression of Adam's unique Godlikeness, his easy bearing of the load of a lordship unknown on the earth

2

before. 'The most important thought I ever had,' wrote Daniel Webster, 'was that of my individual responsibility to God.' Adam bore the load joyously and well while obedience was in the forefront of his life. 'No man doth safely rule,' said Thomas à Kempis, 'but he that hath learned gladly to obey.' Such was Adam, God's regent on earth, in the years of his innocence. The time of that innocence extended into the years of fellowship with Eve. Chapter 2 closes with God's image still visible in Adam.

3 : Adam's Rebellion

Genesis 2.16–20

Part of God's image in man is moral. This does not mean that fallen man is morally like God. It simply maintains that to be aware of the ethical imperative is part of man's constitution. Reason leads man not only to principles of knowledge but also to laws of conduct. He also possesses the power of self-decision. It is this which most clearly constituted Adam a Person. Alone in Creation man is faced constantly with the call to moral decision. It is a condition born of his responsibility. No one can deprive him of his power of deciding for himself. The only Power which could force him to say 'yes' will not do so, because the act of compulsion would alter the constitution of man, and deny the fundamental principle of his creation. God left Adam free to make his choice. Man's present constitution, for all the arguments of modern sophistry, is clear. Man is free. The power to decide has been conferred upon him, and that power is continually stirred and renewed by God's call. Inescapable, more than the air we breathe, is the law that man must decide, as long as he lives, and at every moment of his life. If man could escape that necessity he would cease to be man.

Adam was the second human being to be faced with temptation. Eve was the first, and to that subject we shall return in the next study. He was called to decide, wavered before the right decision, and made the wrong one. The act loosed sin upon the human race. It visibly loosed sin in Adam. He allowed his love for Eve to lead him astray (Gen. 3.6), and yet was small enough to blame Eve for

3

the seduction (12), and even to turn, with argument perilously close to modern theories which diminish or deny free-will, to blaming God. It was 'the woman God gave him' which initiated harm. It was, in other words, a situation for which God was responsible! With broken fellowship came loss of innocence, and shame (10). What opportunity Adam, at this point of failure, lost, for, as Penn said, 'to be innocent is to be not guilty, but to be virtuous is to overcome our evil inclinations'. It could have been, as all victory is, a great leap forward for his humanity.

4 : Eve the First Woman
Genesis 2.21–3.6

If Adam is recognizably man, Eve is as recognizably woman. The fellowship of the first couple is complete. Their sin and their shame are mutual, and there is pathos in this. In the untold pages of the story, some of them magnificently imagined by Milton in *Paradise Lost,* joy, worship and fellowship with God must have been equally shared. Part of the deep sadness of their story is the real worth of Adam's and Eve's love, each for the other.

It is easy to trace the steps which led to sin. Curiosity was roused by the temptation. Eve stopped and looked. She reflected and talked, when she should have fled. John, in some of the last pages of the Bible to be written, speaks of temptation, and they throw vivid light on aspects of human character. Eve was human and had the wherewithal to sin. 'Everything in the world,' wrote John, 'the lust of the flesh, the lust of the eyes, and the proud glory of life, is not of the Father, but of the world' (1 John 2.16). The 'lust which the flesh feels', to paraphrase the word, is the desire for unlawful indulgence. The eyes, undisciplined, treacherous, minister to this inward urge. Then comes 'the pride of life', 'the braggart boast of life', or however the difficult phrase may be rendered, the ostentation of the human heart, its desire for eminence not earned by goodness, its self-exaltation.

To all these sides of man's or woman's nature the Tempter made appeal. Eve need not have fallen. She was under no compulsion, for, as commentators have pointed out, the three-

4

fold classification includes all sources of sin, and finds parallel illustration in the temptations of Eve and the Lord. First, 'the lust of the flesh'. Compare, 'the tree was good for food', and 'command that these stones become bread'. Compare secondly, 'it was a delight to the eyes', with the spectacular display of 'cast yourself down'. Lastly, 'the tree was to be desired to make one wise'. Satan offered 'all the kingdoms of the world and the glory of them' . . .

A fateful and fatal moment. When woman stands firm, evil cringes. Wrote Milton:

> *Abash'd the Devil stood,*
> *And felt how awful goodness is, and saw*
> *Virtue in her shape how lovely . . .*

When woman fell:

> *Earth felt the wound, and Nature from her seat*
> *Sighing through all her works gave sign of woe*
> *That all was lost . . .*

5 : Adam and Eve
Genesis 3.7–4.2

The last chapter of the story of Adam and Eve is a sad one, yet, if we look with live imagination at the few brief words which tell it, a story shot through with beauty. Much survived moral disaster, for atonement had been made. Their mutual love is still evident, and Milton, in his magnificent story of the event, stresses this fact. To face all life can bring of exile, pain and toil, with someone faithful at one's side, is one of God's vast benedictions. This blessing Adam and Eve knew:

> *The world was all before them, where to choose*
> *Their place of rest, and Providence their guide :*
> *They hand in hand with wandering steps and slow*
> *Through Eden took their solitary way.*

Eden was lost, but not **God**. God's guidance, the fruit of His combined wisdom and love, as Milton's insight saw, was still theirs. They were now more recognizably like us, their fallen posterity, than ever. They knew good and evil, and the price of that knowledge is the understanding of sorrow and harsh toil. Nature now, once the ally, was hostile (Gen. 3.17 f.). It demanded labour to surrender that which, in the Golden Age, it had given spontaneously.

Knowing evil, they also knew the tension of strife with evil. There was 'enmity between the seed of the serpent and the seed of the woman', that ancient battle which we all know every day. In the brief story there is no evidence that Adam, and also Eve, did not win in the conflict which sprang from their first disobedience. They had known God in close and wondrous intimacy, and the memory, if not some continuance of its reality, must have coloured life, and given them, even in their exile, a graciousness beyond the ordinary.

> *Like the vase in which roses*
> *Have once been distilled,*
> *You may break, you may shatter*
> *The vase if you will,*
> *But the scent of the roses*
> *Will cling to it still.*

And knowing evil, they were to know too, in eternal fellowship with all who have known the anguish of evil in their own household, the fact that sin is not confined to one generation. They saw the Fall, and lived long enough to see the Fall continue its blight upon mankind. They gave life to Abel, but also to Cain.

6 : Cain the First Killer

Genesis 4.3–15

The first death in the world was murder. Abel, the victim of Cain's violence, is a shadowy figure. He was the first shepherd, that ancient stock of the nomad hinterlands which was to produce some of the best men of the Bible, and whose age-old calling was to provide imagery in Scripture from the days of Moses' desert training to Psa. 23, and the Lord Himself (John 10). Like some humble shepherd of the wilderness, Abel slips into the story, makes his offering, and meets his fate.

6

Cain stands full length. Jealousy is the first mark of him. It is commonly stated that Abel's offering found acceptance because it contained the symbolism of death for sin, which was to be so prominent a feature of the Law, and this may indeed be true. But such offerings as Cain brought are not without a place in the system yet to be, and is not the likelier reason for Cain's rejection Cain himself? 'The acceptance of the offering,' wrote Marcus Dods, 'depends on the acceptance of the offerer . . . God looks through the offering to the state of the soul from which it proceeds.'

Cain was probably already hostile to his brother. The quarrel between them merely found a focus in religion. Jealousy always grows from fear of another's superiority, and Cain saw his brother, a gentler soul, as a challenge to some form of untamed and unsurrendered violence in himself. There is some evidence that the murder was premeditated. In translating v. 8 the NEB makes Cain say: 'Let us go into the open country.' There Abel would have little fear. It was his own native sheepland. And there, unsuspecting, he was attacked and killed. Jealousy begat anger, and anger is a form of madness. And anger, as the Lord pointed out, is the seedbed of violence and murder Matt. 5.21 f.).

Cain was the first hard and unrepentant man. He went out from God's presence with something less than the punishment which he first feared (4.14 f.), but with dull resentment about the consequences of the deed which he had done. Such is the unreasoning response of rebels. No deed is complete in itself. No evil act can be confined to the hour of its doing. Sin is eminently productive. Each act of wickedness forms a link in a chain, which, unless God breaks it in grace, tangles with eternity.

7 : Lamech the Second Killer

Genesis 4.17–25

Sin, we have remarked, cannot be confined to its place and time. The brief record of Cain's line shows how it endures 'to the third and fourth generation'. The line of Cain was a line of able men. Lamech had the advantage of an emerging technology. There is only one recorded utterance of this arrogant man, one deed in the record. The deed is murder, the utterance is one of godless pride.

Verses 23 and 24 show how the tradition of Cain was maintained. Out of Cain's story was extracted one detail, the protection which was, in God's grace accorded to him, in spite of his dire sin. And now, presuming on that, as though it was some special privilege earned and granted, Lamech professes a greater immunity, doubtless through the working of metals which was becoming the monopoly of his tribe (22).

In his words, Lamech's character emerges in its completeness—violent, self-reliant, godless. He has slain a man for wounding him. He puts the boast in poetry, for the Hebrew is rhythmic and contains that parallelism of ideas which is the feature of such poetry.

> I have slain a man for wounding me,
> A young man for striking me,
> If Cain is avenged sevenfold,
> Truly Lamech seventy-sevenfold.

This is chanted to his wives, perhaps to the musical accompaniment of Jubal's lyre and pipes (21).

Let the world, and his wives, the threat implies, beware. It is to be blow for blow, eleven times more effective than God's guarantee of Cain. Cain at least felt some need of God. Lamech feels none. His swift right hand, and his tribe's power will protect him,

> . . . all valiant dust that builds on dust
> And guarding calls not Thee to guard . . .

'The pride of life', which Eve sensed in the first temptation, and which prompted the ancestor to murder, prompts the descendant to the second murder, compounded with blasphemous self-sufficiency. The story horrified the parallel line of Seth, and the insolent Lamech's words were preserved in the oral record, which perhaps with Abraham became the written one.

So Lamech passes from the page of history. If 'they that take the sword perish by the sword', we can be sure that he reaped the harvest of his defiance, arrogance and violent pride. The story does not consider his end worth recording. It turns to Seth, whose descendant Enoch, contemporaneous with Lamech of Cain's line, 'walked with God'.

8 : Enoch, who Walked with God
Genesis 5.18–24

With Enoch, whose whole biography is compassed likewise in four verses, we find Paradise Regained. Lamech's character stood out, lurid and unrelieved by any tint of goodness, in his taunt-song. Enoch is known to us in four words: 'Enoch walked with God.' That brief sentence merits a good man a place in any study of the characters of the Bible. It is not often that a man passes from this earth and leaves behind him nothing but a testimony of good. In most men there is the damaging exception—

> *They have much wisdom, yet they are not wise,*
> *They have much goodness, yet they do not well.*
> *Much valour, yet life mocks it with some spell.*

'Naaman, commander of the army of the king of Syria, was a great man with his master and in high favour . . . *but* he was a leper.' Some such adversative clause caps all eulogy of man. Nor is the glum ending confined to the statements of theology. It is apparent in history. The Greeks invented democracy, *but* their history illustrates and documents democracy's decay and fall. Rome was given to rule the world, *but* was unable to save her empire. The Jews gave us the Old Testament, *but* crucified Christ. The twentieth century was heralded with guns and bells as the coming golden age of progress and plenty *but* . . .

Doubtless Enoch bore the scars of the Fall. The record does not claim that Enoch was sinless. All, however, that men remembered of him was the unruffled tranquillity of one whose whole life was lived in awareness that he was not alone, that One walked beside him 'every step, every mile of the way'. When the life is committed to God, and God's Spirit indwells the core of one's being, then, and only then, is one led 'in the paths of righteousness for his name's sake'.

9

Enoch had learned the secret. Perhaps a store of spiritual truth, a heritage of deep wisdom from Adam and Eve who had also walked with God, found fruitful harbourage in the life of Adam's descendant. Suddenly Enoch was gone, and men remembered how he had never done other than seek God's will, and had been before them the very image and pattern of his Friend. They could draw only one conclusion. The intimacy begun was consummated. The path trodden so consistently and well had turned upwards and disappeared.

Questions and themes for study and discussion on Studies 1–8

1. What recognizable traces of 'the image of God' are visible in man?
2. What do you find in the story of Eden to support 'conservation'?
3. Why and how is 'responsibility' an essential facet of character?
4. In what way was Adam a 'reasonable being'?
5. What did (a) the Lord, (b) Paul, teach about temptation?
6. What do Adam and Eve teach us about marriage?
7. What is the basis of jealousy?
8. What is the attitude of the Bible to violence?
9. How do we walk with God? Scan the Epistle to the Ephesians.

9 : Noah, who Obeyed God

Genesis 6.9–8.19

In one of his essays Montaigne remarked: 'The first law that ever God gave to man was a law of obedience, a commandment pure and simple, wherein man had nothing to enquire after or to dispute, forasmuch as to obey is the proper office of a rational soul acknowledging a heavenly benefactor.'

The memory of the first command, and what had flowed from its flouting by their first parents, must have been a firm tradition with Adam's posterity, passed, after the ancient fashion, from mouth to mouth, and inculcated in each succeeding generation. It is evident that in Noah the tradition held fast, for plain obedience is the hall-mark of his character.

The Euphrates plain was no stranger to floods. The flat river-valley drains a vast watershed of mountains, and archaeology finds abundant evidence of floods. The inundation of God's judgement, which was part of a warning and a command which came to Noah, was, however, something beyond all human experience. Noah was in the line of Enoch. He, too, 'walked with God' (6.9), and was blameless in God's sight. It is in such uncluttered hearts that awareness and conviction of God's will and purposes can grow.

Noah was called, by faith, to prepare. The great chapter on faith in Hebrews sets him thus in the lineage of his two great ancestors (Heb. 11.4–7). Abraham was to be the next in the noble line. The ark was no doubt long in building. No one else heeded the warning. Noah had his carpenters and shipwrights, for the project was far beyond the resources of one family. He was, it seems, an influential chief, for the gathering of ship-timber from remote forests for the task in the almost treeless plain must have been a vast undertaking. Noah must have incurred ridicule, but faith implies obedience, as the writer to the Hebrews continually stresses. Steadfastly he continued. There was some virtue in the huge preoccupations of the work. 'Doing the will of God leaves me no time for disputing about His plans,' said George Macdonald, and Noah had little time to question the still cloudless sky, and the continuing evidence that the carefree and corrupt society about him was right. He had been told to build. He obeyed. Obedience, first-fruit of trust, must have been an habitual part of him, for how true it is that obedience is not truly performed by the body, if the heart is dissatisfied.

10 : Noah's Lapse

Genesis 9

Faith was the mark of Noah's character, and it had new testings to endure. 'God remembered Noah,' says a revealing verse (8.1), and the words are full of meaning. Alone on the wide waters, with all the world they had known drowned and destroyed beneath them, the survivors must have endured anxiety and utter loneliness. No hint is given in the story of what went on in Noah's mind, but his faith is still apparent. Had God forgotten him? The question could have been a strong insistent one. He releases the raven and then the dove, putting thus a symbol of peace into the imagery and vocabulary of mankind. In due course faith found that for which it looked—the dry land, a new life, and a renewed covenant with God.

Then came Noah's strange lapse. The man who had earned a place in the honour roll of the faithful is seen drunk on the floor of his tent. We could well have been spared this picture, but the Bible is impartially frank in its revelation of the truth about the men and women who made its story. Perhaps there are circumstances unknown to us, as there always are in any spectacular demonstration of human failure. Tensions, sadness, joy, we might speculate endlessly concerning what lay behind Noah's excess. We do not know.

But look at the sorry situation without such speculation. Here was a good man defeated, a sight of shame which brought out the coarseness of one of his sons, and the delicacy and honour of the other two. Noah had lived through years of tension, over which his faith had triumphed. He failed and fell, like Elijah, in a moment of victory. Perhaps, indeed, the hour of triumph, when the long-borne burden is suddenly lifted, is the time of most dangerous assault. The mind relaxes from its long guard, and evil finds a new chink in the armour. So it was with Noah, and the curse on Canaan does nothing to enhance Noah in our eyes. He was called to suffer for Ham's conduct, and Ham may indeed have proved himself unworthy of trust, but the sad fact remains that Noah's carnality provided the context and occasion for Ham's sin. Let us pray that we may end well.

11 : Abraham of Ur

Hebrews 11.8–22

Environment and heredity both play their part in forming the character of a man, and of Abraham's environment we know a great deal. Of his ancestry, and its contribution to the shaping of one of the great men of all time, we know very little. Joshua (Josh. 24.2) described Terah, Abraham's father, as a pagan, and his name seems to be connected with that of the moon-goddess, who was worshipped at Ur. This may mean very little, and Ur was no congenial dwelling-place for Terah, or he would not have so readily abandoned it with his son. But Terah's influence, by relationship or instruction, upon Abraham can only be a subject of speculation.

The port of Ur, however, and what it signified to its lively inhabitants, is closer to our knowledge. The ruins are not far from the confluence of the two great Mesopotamian rivers, and four millennia of river silt have built a plain which now separates Ur from the Sea by many miles. Harbour-works may be identified in the ruins of the town, and in ancient times it was obviously the gateway to the Middle East, and therefore to the caravan routes which wound up the Euphrates, curved round what is called the Fertile Crescent to Damascus, and down to the other river-valley civilization, that of Egypt on the Nile. And Egypt's delta looked to the Mediterranean where sailed the ships of Caphtor, Minoan Crete, and other cultures of prehistoric Europe.

Looking East, Ur faced the sealanes of the Persian Gulf, where man first learned to sail the high seas. The dhows coasted to the third of the river civilizations, that of the Indus Valley, where, in the ruins of the amazingly modern town of Mohenjo-Daro, pottery remains from Ur have been found. The traders doubtless penetrated much further east and touched Taprobane or Ceylon. There they met the junks from China and made contact with all the complex of Far Eastern trade.

Ur lay at the very centre of this vast web of human activity. It was a stimulating place for a man of intellect. Nowhere, more than at this nodal point of the ancient world's communications, could a man gain a greater and more detailed knowledge of the inhabited globe. From Crete, to Egypt, to Syria, and east to India and the Indies the long chain of Abraham's information stretched. It proved a mighty challenge.

12 : Abraham and God

Genesis 12.1–3; Acts 7.1–8

God prepares the heart and mind of man for His self-revelation. As he surveyed the wide world from his unique vantage-

13

point, Abraham must have found one thought obtrusive. Ur, with its corrupt and idolatrous worship, was no exception. The world was lost in degrading views of God. From the bull-worship of Crete, to the animal deities of brilliant Egypt, from the worship of the Sun-god on the Phoenician coast, to the sadistic and sensual deities of which the sailors who traded to the Indus and the Malabar coast could tell, it was one wide story of burdensome corruption.

Some search for something purer, better, holier must have stirred in the heart of Abraham of Ur, because, at his first entrance on the story, he is described as knowing God (12.1). God meets those who seek Him, grants His grace to out-reaching faith, and speaks to those who listen (Acts 17.26–28). Abraham, brooding over benighted mankind, had found the only God. That discovery inspired, as it always will and must, a longing to share the saving and sanctifying truth.

All this must have taken place before Abraham appears in the Bible story. The great man knew, as few others in his age knew, the far-flung mass of humankind. His yearning, like his knowledge, must have embraced them all. He was the first man with the missionary urge within him. How could he impart the tremendous truth, which had become clear to him, to an audience so vast? He knew how long it took to ride on camel-back, or sail on shipboard, to the scattered nations of whose existence and need he had become aware. He knew that no one man could reach them all, and no one generation see their enlightenment.

But what if a nation could be founded, away from the corrupt centres of man, in the clean wilderness, a nation dedicated to the One God, and prepared to be the custodian and propagator of His truth? That is the vision in which the Hebrew nation began. God had moved in a questing and willing heart. God had prompted and led. A great soul had sought, heard, found and followed. That is perhaps how the call came to rise and march. So 'the glory of God appeared', as Stephen told the Sanhedrin, 'to Abraham, when he was in Mesopotamia, before he dwelt in Haran'.

13 : Abraham's Father

Joshua 24.1–5

At this point it might be profitable to return briefly to Terah, whose enigmatic person must be, as was earlier remarked, a matter of speculation only. There are, however, one or two pointers to reality. Stephen, in his historic address to the Sanhedrin, says quite clearly that the call to migrate and to found a people in the wilderness came not to the father, Terah, but to his son, Abraham, while the family still lived at Ur—a point not made clear in Genesis. Joshua speaks of the clan as worshippers of alien gods.

The picture which seems to emerge is that of a patriarchal clan, with major acts of policy still firmly in the hands of the chief, Terah, but with large trust and acceptance given to his eldest son, Abraham. Conviction lays hold of the son, and a clear call comes to leave Ur, and its corruptions. For no other motive, perhaps, than his respect for his son's deep convictions, the head of the family agrees to migrate, but is strongly enough in control to dictate a pause at Haran, the Carrhae of Roman history, and the scene of the Parthians' spectacular victory over Crassus' three legions in 53 B.C.

Abraham was unwilling, in his father's lifetime, to oppose this pause in his fortunes. This was but limited obedience to the great call, and points to Terah's own limited under-standing and faith. It was only after his father's death that Abraham felt free to move. In Gen. 12.1 comes the call which Stephen says was clearly given in Ur. On Terah's death it was repeated, if the sequence of Gen. 11.32; 12.1 is chronological. It is more likely that the sequence is psychological, and that the two succeeding verses suggest a renewal of purpose, now that the impediment of Terah's imperfect faith was removed. It is thus that a father can muffle his son's call, impede his progress in the work of God, or, by his caution and unbelief, hold back the outworking of a divine plan in his son's life. Terah seems, as we peer back through history, to have been a man not without vision, not lacking a desire to abandon an inadequate life, or a corrupt environment, but for lack of bravery or conviction, to have fallen short of the best, and held his family back with him.

15

14 : Abraham's Retreat

Genesis 12.10–20

In Gen. 14.13 there is a curious phrase—'Abraham the Hebrew'. The word appears to mean 'the Wanderer', the person who, in the modern world, is called 'the stateless man'. Read again the tribute in Heb. 11. Abraham had left the environment which denied him his life's purpose, but he had left it at some cost. Terah had revealed, and Lot was to repeat the demonstration, that attachment to city life was strong in the tribe. Abraham left his city, and those who could not share his faith. And now Haran, like Ur, lay over the rim of the desert. Terah was dead, and however much the son may have deplored the father's tardiness, these were patriarchal days, and Abraham must have felt alone, and found the load of his responsibility heavy.

That, perhaps, is why caution overwhelmed faith at the first impact of famine. Abraham withdrew to Egypt, where the regular flooding of the Nile, fed by the vast reservoirs of the interior, protected agriculture, for the most part, from the effects of drought, disastrous in more exposed lands. Faith, in thoughtful and sensitive minds, is ever dogged by doubt. Thus it grows, in strife and contest. As Tennyson put it in his *In Memoriam* (*XCVI*):

> *'He fought his doubts and gathered strength,*
> *He would not make his judgement blind.*
> *He faced the spectres of the mind*
> *And laid them; thus he came at length*
> *To find a stronger faith his own . . .'*

But such final victory is not always won in a single fight. Abraham knew defeat. He retreated to a land as corrupt as that which he had left, and ran straight into its pollution. Sarai, his wife, was the first to confront the peril. Abraham's half-truth—for Sarai was, in fact, a half-sister—reveals the dilemmas into which a man runs when he leaves the circle of God's will. He lied, and was rebuked by a pagan. Perhaps, too, it was in the course of this deviant adventure that Sarai acquired Hagar, her Egyptian maid, and set in motion those events which, linked each to each, were to influence Abraham's whole life and heritage, and to extend down through posterity to today's headlines. It is impossible,

16

as Macbeth remarked, 'with the deed to trammel up the consequences'. Abraham was what Virgil called 'a hinge of fate'. Great events turned on him. None of us knows when we may be called to assume such a role. Faith treads valiantly and carefully.

15 : Abraham's Return
Genesis 13.1–7; Romans 4.1–8

No doubt chastened and relieved, Abraham passed through the barren Negev, and came to the place 'where his altar was in the beginning'. Here he 'called on the name of the Lord' (4). This, surely, is restoration. He had passed through a period of barrenness and alienation. His vision was dim. It is not impossible that his wife's continued childlessness was already beginning to impose some strain upon his faith, and to make his mighty concept of a people of God appear a little absurd. It all depended upon a simple sequence, the birth of an heir. Deepening anxiety on this score had played, perhaps, a part in the lapse of faith which had taken him to Egypt. There his very consciousness of God had dimmed.

The danger from which Sarai had been so wonderfully rescued, and the consequent peril to the purity of his whole eagerly desired line, may have awakened Abraham to the reality of God's continuing care, and called him to re-dedication. He traced his long path back to the sacred spot of his first worship in the land which had been promised to him, and in a new act of committal sought again the freshness of his faith.

It is a common enough experience in life to find each new act of faith and surrender challenged. No sooner had his heart been set right with God, than a fresh testing confronted him—strife in his own clan. Abraham's nephew Lot, since Terah's death, may have functioned as the deputy sheikh of the desert tribe. They had prospered in men and cattle. The limited grazing lands of the hill country, to which the sedentary city populations of the coastal plain and the Jordan valley tended to confine them, were inadequate for the common grazing of their herds and flocks. Strife broke out as strife does where human beings, eager for their own rights and advantage, are pressed too closely upon each other.

17

The final verse is significant. The alien dwelt in the land, and the words must mean that Abraham was jealous for the integrity of his tribe and its testimony before the corrupt society which was so closely observing him. He had found anew his peace with God. He was anxious now not to dishonour God by a spectacle of disunity and conflict within the group which had professed a new and greater loyalty to a God so different from the pagan deities worshipped commonly about them.

16 : Abraham's Faith
Genesis 13.8–18

Determined that there was to be no strife in the family of God, Abraham gave Lot the choice of dwelling-place. He had learned a deep lesson of faith in Egypt, and now he left the whole matter in the hands of God, though, in truth, as the patriarch, it was in his right to decide (Phil. 2.5–8). The two chiefs stood on some eminence on the mountain spine of Palestine, from which the whole Jordan plain was visible. That deep rift valley runs down to the steaming Dead Sea, whose southern end appears today to cover the sites of Sodom and Gomorrah. Its seventy-mile length is traversed by the Jordan, whose convolutions make a stream almost four times as long as the river plain through which it winds its tortuous way. Lush tropical vegetation filled it (10) before the great eruption, which collapsed the southern end of the valley bottom, and spoiled some of the rich wealth of the long plain.

Set against this was the gaunt wilderness of the Judean uplands. From the point of view of material advantage, and human social contact, the choice for a worldly-minded man was quite obviously the Jordan valley. The wilderness held only loneliness, the harsh living of shepherds, the daily search for meagre pasture in the more sheltered vales, and all the stern testings of adverse environment of which Abraham was as aware as Lot. And yet Abraham, in quiet and sublime faith, allowed Lot to choose. Lot chose, and went his way. He 'moved his tent as far as Sodom' (12).

Observe now the pattern, setting these eleven verses side by side with those which told of Abraham's descent to Egypt, in search of those same advantages as Lot sought, as he moved towards the fertile and comfortable haunts of men. Moral peril quickly followed the great man's mistake, as it was to follow his nephew's similar error. But now Abraham had chosen the wise course, and left the outcome in the hands of God. After Lot had gone his way, God spoke to Abraham. From the high country of his camp, the length and breadth of the land was visible, from distant segments of the Mediterranean, to the blue walls of the Moab hills, from the far skylines which masked Galilee, to the southern haze where the Negev desert lay. This, said the Voice, was to be his land. Abraham built an altar near Hebron to remind himself of the covenant renewed.

Questions and themes for study and discussion on Studies 9–16

1. Define obedience. Is it reasonable?
2. What does Noah teach of parenthood?
3. How does environment shape character?
4. How is doubt best dealt with?
5. Look up Heb. 11.1 in various translations, and define faith.
6. How is faith commonly tested? Illustrate from the Psalms.
7. How does the pursuit of material advantage corrupt faith?
8. How do we still 'build an altar'?

17 : Lot

Luke 17.22–32

We may pause for a moment to look down the river plain and consider Lot. Faith sets the future above the present, the unseen above the seen, God's will above all things. Lot had not done this. Why? 'Living in tents' (Heb. 11.9) had been hard. Had the sojourn in Egypt given the family a renewed taste for city life? Where to locate one's family is sometimes an important question in a parent's endeavour to ensure their salvation.

And did Lot, having observed Abraham's own long frustration under Terah, think that, in terms of his own personal honour and advantage, a subordinate post under the patriarch had little to offer? He became a judge in Sodom, and the fact may be a glimpse of unexpressed ambitions (Gen. **19**.1; 'to sit in the gate' was a technical expression for a judge). The city in the plain seemed to offer much to 'the lust of the eyes', for it was the old temptation over again, pressing hard on a character which did not look for a 'city without foundations'. The unseen, which Lot did not consider, was shocking —the corruption beneath the bright surface of Sodom's wealth, and the sure judgement of God upon its sin, and upon those who shared its sin. He could not see that a prayerless, hasty, carnal choice was destined to lead to the death of his wife, the loss of his possessions, the corruption of his family, and the foundation of a pagan posterity. We should beware of what we choose.

We saw two men standing at the place of decision. Such moments, like some persistent eddy in a stream, come in life, and determine its texture. There is a dual tug—the eternal pull of evil, and the eternal pull of God's spirit. As James Russell Lowell put it:

> Once to every man and nation comes the moment
>   to decide,
> In the strife of Truth and Falsehood, for the good
>   or evil side;
> Some great cause, God's new Messiah, offering each
>   the bloom or blight,
> Parts the goats upon the left hand, and the sheep
>   upon the right,
> And the choice goes by forever 'twixt that darkness
>   and that light.

We never know amid the flow of life's choices, which will be final and irreversible. The 'great cause' which faced the two men on the hill-top was the founding of a nation for God. They both chose and the moment passed. So men seal their destiny.

18 : Abraham's Raid
Genesis 14.1–16; 2 Corinthians 6.11–18

The story of Abraham's rescue of Lot breaks unexpectedly into the narrative. The reader hardly expects to meet the patriarch in the role of desert guerrilla fighter. It was a task thrust upon him. A small confederation of chiefs from the Euphrates valley had sent a punitive expedition down to Sodom, and had sacked the plain. Lot shared the misfortune of his associates.

The story must have come from Abraham, who, it may be guessed, was careful to preserve the records of a family on which such a destiny rested. If so, we must ascribe the brevity of a notable historical document to the modesty of the writer, who saw the hand of God in a victory so complete.

Abraham's decision and initiative, none the less, and the strength of his growing household, show clearly in the story (14). His men knew all the paths and byways of the wilderness, and the forces from the north were no doubt as prone to panic as Eastern armies were. They had, in fact, good reason to be afraid. Palestine was an Egyptian sphere of influence. The Nile empire, through all her history and on to the present day, has regarded the narrow land to the north of her as a buffer against the powers which, from the Hittites to Persia, constituted a threat to Egyptian security. At the same time, Egypt seldom held more than the long coastal plain with any vigour or completeness. Hence the possibility of petty war and raiding in the hilly hinterland, a border plague which even the Romans found it difficult to control.

Raiding parties like the one in the story would risk an inroad, but would be anxious to retreat into the desert, and would be in some apprehension of pursuit. For all they knew, any attack from behind them could only be a task-force of the Egyptians. Hence the rapid success of Abraham's well-planned, and sudden night-attack, and the impunity of his withdrawal.

Lot was saved by the bold and competent leadership of the uncle whom he had abandoned, and restored to his chosen environment without reproach. The fact that, after a lesson so sharp, he returned to Sodom, is indication enough of how deeply the life he had adopted had penetrated him. Faith,

21

observe, is not quietism. In this story Abraham acts with the speed of a Bedu raider.

19 : Abraham's Friend
Genesis 14.17–20; Hebrews 7.1–10

Melchizedek, king of Salem, is an intriguing person. Like Moses' princess, he steps with dignity into half a page of Bible history, and then is gone. His significance, however, is out of all proportion to the amount of space his story fills. He came down from the hills when Abraham returned from his night raid, heavy with the spoils of Sodom, then stepped back out of the story, leaving us hungry to know him. His character left a deep impression, for the writer of Psa. 110 and the writer of the Epistle to the Hebrews found him a fascinating figure of Christ.

Psa. 110 looks forward to one who combines the offices of king and priest, but a priest of no common order, apart from the line of Aaron. Preoccupied as he was with the O.T., the writer of Hebrews also finds the mysterious priest of Genesis significant. As the first chapter of the epistle shows (1.3), Psa. 110 was prominent in the author's mind, and in Chs. 5-7 he expounds his difficult theme of one who foreshadowed the Lord before Aaron. Aaron's priesthood and the law.

Archaeology has something to say on the theme. The passage in Hebrews says that Melchizedek was 'without father and mother', which simply means that he founded his dynasty. It was also a 'king of Salem', who boasts in the famous Tell-el-Amarna letters of 1380 B.C.: Behold this land, neither my father nor my mother gave it me—the hand of the mighty King gave it me.' The words explain the text from Hebrews.

Archaeology can thus, strangely enough, produce another person not dissimilar to the good priest-king of Salem. It emerges that, although the Bible speaks of the line of revelation which found consummation in Christ, the truth was known and cherished elsewhere. Perhaps there lies in the fact some anticipation of the universal gospel which Paul was to preach.

22

20 : Abraham and the King of Sodom
Genesis 14.21–24

We lingered over the most puzzling character in *Genesis,* Melchizedek of Jerusalem, because it is evident that Abraham recognized his superiority. This chapter is rich in facets of the patriarch's character. We noted his modesty, his firm decisiveness and action in face of crisis, his graciousness towards erring Lot, his humility and courtesy to the stately king . . . Observe now his upright determination to be separate from unclean gain (23).

Sodom was sunk in the corruption which put a base word into the languages of the world. People generally get the rulers they deserve, and the ruler of Sodom, no doubt, reflected the vices which he permitted or was powerless to prevent, in the community he governed. Abraham revealed something of the man's character when he mentioned, with a touch of irony, the peril he was eager to shun. He did not wish to hear, in the gossip of the land, that 'the king of Sodom made Abraham rich'.

Perhaps this was a reflection of talk commonly heard about Lot, who had demeaned himself to accept the hospitality of Sodom, and the honour of office at their hands. In a corrupt society such boons are too often conferred in the hope that the recipient will be compromised, and Sodom must have regarded their sojourner from the increasingly powerful desert tribe, a worthwhile asset. Indeed the events of the raid clearly demonstrated the fact. But for the guerrilla campaign of the shepherds, Sodom would have remained stripped and forlorn.

Abraham wanted no compromising alliance. When he left Ur and Haran, and retired from the ill-starred expedition into Egypt, Abraham had divested himself of the urban entanglements which might have compromised his plan for a clean society. He had conferred a boon on the ungodly, but wanted to be under no obligation to them. Observe how he was inspired and aided in this wise and upright decision. He met the good Melchizedek, and was able to view the man of Sodom side by side with the man of Jerusalem. To meet good men and women on the Lord's day often aids us when we are confronted with a lesser world throughout the week. To commune with Christ every morning, is to steady mind and heart

23

when we meet, in the rush and press of life, those who will have none of Him. But note that history was outworking through Abraham, faulty but faithful, not through the statuesque king of Salem.

21 : Reaction

Genesis 15

'Courage,' said Plutarch, 'consists not in hazarding without fear, but being resolutely minded in a just cause.' Abraham had demonstrated this when, with his band of young men, he attacked an army. But in the weariness which follows resolute action there is sometimes a rebound, and sudden fear. We see Elijah, at the peak of his brave career, succumb to that sudden and most human reaction. And so did Abraham.

It was probably the following night, and it is in night's murk and loneliness that courage most commonly ebbs. With the need for action over, and time to think, Abraham began to fear that courage had been rashness, and swift valour foolhardiness. He could well imagine what the raiders from the river would think and do when full day dawned and they recovered from their panic-stricken flight. A fast reconnaissance on camel-back would establish the fact that there was no regular Egyptian force in the vicinity. The desert nomads are uncanny in their ability to read the signs in the sand, and it is likely enough that the size and nature of the attacking guerrilla-force were plain for skilled trackers' eyes to assess.

Abraham would imagine all this and pass on to the dire conclusion that, by the middle of the day, his enemies would know who had attacked them, and where he lived. Then would come the revengeful raid. And it was all for backslidden Lot. Then, too, he might continue, in the sick reasonings of the night, was it common sense to rebuff the ruler of Sodom in the exaltation which followed the conversation with the saintly Melchizedek?

At which, clear in Abraham's inner being, came the voice which he had learned to recognize as the voice of his God: 'Fear not, Abram, I am your shield; your reward shall be very great.'

With a great surge of faith renewed, the patriarch, calmed now and at peace, went out into the night. The cold sand was under his feet, the stars shone in uncovered splendour in the chill night (5). So should his offspring be—and v. 6 put a great text into the Bible.

22 : Abraham and Hagar

Genesis 16

The events of this chapter were as repugnant to later ideas of the Hebrews as they are to us, but they conformed to the Code of Hammurabi, and to laws familiar to Abraham in Ur and Haran. Two relevant provisions, both of which Sarai had in mind, run: 'If a man marries a wife, and she has not given him children, if that man marries his concubine and brings her into his house, then that concubine shall not rank with his wife.' And again: 'If a man has married a wife, and she has given her husband a female slave who bears him children, and afterwards that slave ranks herself with her mistress, because she has borne children, her mistress shall not sell her for silver . . . The concubine shall be fettered and counted among the slaves.' From which provisions it appears that, in the terms of the secular law, Sarai did not treat Hagar as harshly as she was permitted to do.

It is, however, at the personalities of the story that we are looking principally, and the question arises why Abraham had recourse to a secular and pagan law, when he found himself still without an heir. Sarai may have marked and pitied his anxiety, for he had staked his whole life on this venture of faith. He had, at great sacrifice, and at the cost of lonely exile, provided an unencumbered environment for his posterity—but what if posterity were denied him?

It was without doubt a failure of a sorely tried faith which persuaded Abraham to descend to this permitted subterfuge— a failure perhaps aided by a breath of carnality of the sort to which the flesh is prone. Abraham was not perfect, and it is important to remember Paul's insistent emphasis on the fact that he was not perfect. He was a fallible man but he believed God, and that was counted to him for righteousness. And whose faith is perfect? Faith grows with the assaults

25

upon it. Doubt dogs its exercise, and the great patriarch was no exception. But no such mistake goes without its consequences. The line of Ishmael still opposes Isaac and continues to multiply the pain one step of faithlessness can cause.

23 : Abraham and the Covenant
Genesis 17

We have called the patriarch by his common name throughout because it is under the nomenclature of the Abrahamic Covenant that he is known in the New Testament. Strictly, up to this point in the narrative, he was known as Abram. It is popularly believed that Abram means 'exalted father', and Abraham 'father of a multitude', and these translations could be correct, but in actual fact the etymology of both names is far from certain. One point is sure, 'ab' signifies father, and it was only the birth of Ishmael which rescued either name from taunt and ridicule.

Hence the remark in v. 18, and the pathos embedded in it. The old promise, almost forgotten over the thirteen years since the stormy events of Ishmael's birth, was convincingly renewed. But Abraham was old, and the covenant proposed seemed more and more to mock his virtually childless state. He clung with some desperation to the one chance of posterity, the son of the Egyptian servant-girl. 'Oh that Ishmael might live in thy sight', is a yearning prayer to have done with testing and further waiting, and to have the one son born to him, for all the blemish on the lineage, declared the heir. Such a promise would break the tension in which he lived.

It was natural enough. Time-bound man chafes at God's long delays. 'O Lord, make haste to help us' is the most human of man's prayers. And the Lord Himself permitted us, in the prayer which was given to be a model for all prayers, to ask to be delivered from temptation. It is not always God's will that we should be so delivered, and that is a theme Paul takes up in the first five verses of Rom. 5. Abraham was establishing the pattern of saving faith. He did not know the part which he and his belief were to play in plans yet unrevealed for man, and among that other posterity which were to be 'as the stars of heaven'. There was purpose in God's delays, and Abraham, still puzzled and desperately perplexed, believed, and fulfilled the obligations of the new covenant made with him. It is a strong faith which continues to march when there is no light at all upon the way, and does not doubt in the darkness what God told when it was light.

24 : Abraham the Host
Genesis 18

'If a man be gracious to strangers, it shows that he is a citizen of the world,' said Francis Bacon, 'and that his heart is no island, cut off from other islands, but a continent that joins them.' Abraham was not embittered by the vast disappointment which, to this very date, had held his life in tension. In his human relationships he retained his Eastern courtesy and hospitality. 'Do not neglect to show hospitality to strangers,' runs a famous verse in Hebrews (13.1), 'for thereby some have entertained angels unawares.' The reference was to this scene. From his noonday rest in the door of his tent, Abraham was stirred to action by the arrival of strange and unrecognized guests. It was only with dawning insight that the patriarch realized that they were no ordinary messengers, and somehow succeeded in conveying to Sarah, in the seclusion of the tent, that the entertainment of that afternoon was no common experience. With a woman's live curiosity she was keenly listening, and heard words which surprised and embarrassed her.

But there was apprehension, too, as well as exultation in the great elusive promise renewed. The strangers rose, and set off towards Sodom, and Abraham heard the tale of coming catastrophe. There follows the moving story of intercessory prayer, which put a potent and consoling text into the speculation of man upon God's judgements, and the last things: 'Shall not the Judge of all the earth do right?' (25). Indeed He will—beyond our imagining, satisfying all our loftiest and most refined ideas of justice, with equity complete and overwhelming . . .

Abraham's line of thought is clear. Peter's testimony preserves an ancient tradition that Lot had not surrendered to the abominations of his environment (2 Pet. 2.7). Abraham was aware of this, and for all the retreat of Lot, which he must have deplored, he must have been confident that the renegade had kept his household pure. Surely, in the small den of iniquity down on the plain, there was one island of righteous life? Ten was no doubt the number at which Abraham assessed the small urban household of his departed nephew. At that point he stopped praying. Here begins the doctrine of the Remnant, the 'salt of the earth', which from then till now has preserved corrupt societies from final disintegration.

Questions and themes for study and discussion on Studies 17–24

1. Trace the imagery of the shield through Scripture.
2. What has Hebrews to say of Melchizedek?
3. How can God be a reward? Consider Heb. 11.6.
4. What is a 'covenant'?
5. What significance lies in a name in Hebrew belief?
6. What have you learned from the character of Abraham?
7. Consider the frankness of Scripture about human faults.

25 : Lot's Last Chapter

Genesis 19.1–30

Lot chose the way which led to Sodom. He pitched his tent toward the city, and like a magnet the city drew him. He became a citizen, and 'sat in the gate' as a magistrate. His family were immersed in the wickedness of the dark, luxurious little town as their sombre ending shows.

And disaster fell on the valley floor. A fanciful Russian has suggested that space visitors exploded surplus atomic fuel there, and left a record of supernatural visitants to Sodom and grim retribution. The city's fate needs no such interpretation. Warning certainly came to Sodom, and Lot was urged to flee. He did, reluctantly, as the volcanic fountains broke their bonds, and Sodom rocked under the combined assault of earthquake and volcano. Lot's wife looked back, lingering no doubt in anguish, as the scene of the life she had come to cherish flamed amid the spouting gas. Caught in some red hot mass flung from the buried seabed of some earlier salt sea, she became a 'pillar of salt' and a perennial warning for those who fail to make good a prompt escape when catastrophe threatens a corrupt, disintegrating world.

In the hills, safe on his upland pastures, Abraham looked south, and the smoke of Sodom rose 'like the smoke of a furnace'. Some mighty spectacle of ascending conflagration held him spellbound. Perhaps some great mushroom cloud arose from the valley, as oil, freed deep in the earth's scar, flared in the volcanic fires. Certain it is that the whole area is burned and scorched to this distant day, and that the great rift in the globe's skin must bring the surface down near the beds of fuel which are rich throughout the Middle East. No great shock would break open the old wound and set the world bleeding its inflammable oil.

So perished the 'cities of the plain', and with them the land's fertility, its tropic wealth and garden green. And like Lot's wife, the towns became a proverb, and one of them a name for perversion, a 'hissing', as the later prophets of the Hebrews say.

Peter says a good word about Lot (2 Pet. 2.7), but 'just' though the backslider may have been, he had no influence among those with whom he had chosen to link his destiny, and in his lamentable weakness lost his wife, his daughters, and his place in history. Much evil can flow from weakness, from one carnal choice, from one failure to grasp God's opportunity. It was a vital day when Lot and Abraham stood together on the ridge.

26 : Abraham's Lapse

Genesis 20

A map will add significant details to this story. Abraham at the time was dwelling in the Negev, and his nomadic life was dependent upon water, upon rainfall in a word, and the periodic variations of climate. The coastal plain, agricultural, and commonly the first recipient of the Mediterranean rainbelts, was a natural refuge when the hill-country suffered from a spell of drought.

Gerar lay at the foot of the hills, and was in the hands of the Philistines, those European colonists from Crete, who had a colony on the coast long centuries before the disasters which befell their homeland swelled the settlement to the size of a nation. The ruler of Gerar, some tribal prince, bears a Hebrew name both in Abraham's and Isaac's time (Gen. **26**), and Abimelech is probably a Hebrew translation of a royal title, so that the ruler who encountered both father and son in similar circumstances is not necessarily the same person.

Abraham, long years before, had learned the lesson of such subterfuge as he now practises again, but it is the way of men to repeat their mistakes—'the burned fool's bandaged finger,' as Kipling put it, 'goes wobbling back to the fire.' The patriarch, in a moment of panic, under some stress of testing, again earned the rebuke of an alien. Curiously enough, he retained for his family the respect of the community he had wronged, and this fact is testimony to the completeness and honesty of the repentance which healed the fault. The next chapter shows Abimelech manifesting deep confidence in Abraham and trust in his plighted word (**21**.22–34). A lapse of faith can only be remedied, as Abraham had remedied it after his lamentable retreat to Egypt, by a wholehearted return to the position abandoned in fear, doubt, or transient disillusionment. 'It is the greatest and dearest blessing God ever gave to man,' said the good Jeremy Taylor, 'that they may repent; and therefore to deny or to delay repentance is to refuse health when brought by the skill of the physician—to refuse liberty offered to us by our gracious Lord.' And this applies to the old, equally with the young. No age is exempt from temptation, fortified against all failure, or immune from man's old infidelity—backsliding. Such is the lesson taught in the language of his pain by 'the Father of the Faithful'.

27 : Abraham's Sacrifice

Genesis 22.1–19

In a case in the British Museum stands a small statue of a goat caught by its large horns in a flowering tree. There is a small oblong base, decorated with silver plate and mosaic in pink and white, and on it, erect on its hind legs, stands the goat. The front legs are bound by silver chains to the delicate golden branches of a tree which rises in front of him, a stylized object with a short firm trunk and two geometrical boughs.

The leaves and flowers, all in gold, rise higher than the goat's golden head. There is hair of lapis lazuli, the blue silicate which figured widely in Sumerian art. The sculptor has contrived to represent the hair or wool of the body in shell. This little work of curiously fussy art throws some light on the tale of Abraham.

To Abraham, in the grip of his great idea, one common feature bound mankind together, the baseness of a universal polytheism, and the horror of the world's sanguinary cults. Obeying a Voice within which had become a part of his faith, he had left the busy town and set out to found, as we have seen, in the clean desert, a race dedicated to the service of the One God.

No man pursues a project of faith without his days of doubt, and there came a time when Abraham became obsessed with an awful thought. The Voice which had so surely governed his conscience took on strange tones. Unbelievably, it bade him to sacrifice his son, even as he had seen children die in the pagan city from which he had retreated in loathing. Abraham, convinced that this terrible pressure on the mind must have a meaning, set out to obey. He set up the altar, he placed the wood, he bound his son . . .

Then, unmistakably, all was clear. There was 'a ram caught in a thicket' hard by. The Voice was strong in command. God, even as Abraham had told his son, had provided the sacrifice. Part of Sumerian belief must have been that an animal so imprisoned had been claimed of heaven as a sacrifice. Abraham recognized the Divine provision, performed the ritual, and found his mind for ever freed from the fear that God might indeed demand a parent's ultimate sacrifice. His obedience had been complete. The race he founded was commanded to write that salutary liberty into the law which became their way of life (Exod. 20.13). To those who read the Old Testament in the light of the New, another meaning emerges—the substitutionary death of Christ. Abraham knew nothing of this.

31

28 : Abraham the Businessman

Genesis 23

The Bible does not pretend to present a consecutive history of the men and women who made its story. It did not set out to provide the raw materials of history for historians unborn. It selected its incidents, and families such as Abraham's preserved the record of events necessary for their future guidance. The chapter is by way of being a record of the title to the cemetery of the clan at Hebron, bought from the tough Hittites.

Abraham was obviously a wealthy man. Hebron, Beersheba and Gerar were key points on the caravan routes, and although there is no mention of such business and trade transactions, it is obvious that the patriarchal community were engaged in the legitimate commerce of the trade-routes of Palestine. From what other source could have come the considerable amount of silver with which Abraham lightly paid for one small lot of ground? James Kelso points out that 400 silver shekels 'the current market rate' (16), was an exorbitant price, when, 'for similar Palestinian real estate' Jeremiah paid only 17 silver shekels. Perhaps it is not legitimate to compare land values separated by such a lapse of time, especially when the latter took place during a period of war and enemy occupation, when land prices would have fallen heavily, but it does seem clear that the shrewd Hittite, after the elaborate Eastern interchange of courtesies, took from the rich desert-chief an inordinately large sum of money.

Observe Abraham's courtesy. A person's character is sometimes best observed from its reflection in the lives or attitudes of others. The previous chapter reveals the polished deference of the prince of Gerar towards the man who, on their first encounter, had disappointed and harmed him. The present scene is similarly instructive. Abraham knew that he was being overcharged. That was one reason why he had the document of sale drawn up with elaborate detail (17), and with proper witnesses (18). He judged haggling beneath his dignity, and, in its ancient context, discourteous. He was a stranger in the land. He had God's word that the land should belong to his descendants. Until such consummation he recognized the rights of its occupants, observed their laws,

32

and conformed to their courtesies. A testimony is worth some outlay in cash and it was a testimony that Abraham sought to establish in the alien's land. There is no outward sign of true courtesy, said Goethe rightly, 'which does not rest on a deep moral foundation'. The grace of God is in courtesy.

29 : Abraham's Servant
Genesis 24

We have spoken of the mirror-image of a person's life which can be seen in the character of another. The servant of this charming chapter, besides being a gracious person in his own right, reflects very vividly the fine master he serves. 'We become willing servants to the good by the bonds their virtues lay upon us,' said Sir Philip Sidney, and in Eliezer of Damascus Abraham had a willing servant of the sort which only goodness could produce.

Abraham had done more than inspire the loyalty and faithfulness which enabled him to entrust a delicate and vital mission, together with a considerable sum of money, to a steward's care. He had transmitted his faith to his man. And yet a faith which was no mechanical lip-service to a God imposed upon him. No one can doubt, in the words of the servant's prayer, the reality and personal understanding of the faith he cherished. He sought guidance with a plain simplicity of language, observed with wonder the working of God's hand in circumstance, and gave thanks for the miracle. Abraham, the man of faith, had proved the reality of his faith by passing it so potently to one who served him.

Observe his loyalty. The servant, we have reasonably assumed, was the Eliezer of 15.2, named heir of Abraham, according to well-attested custom. Such adoption was null and void on the birth subsequently of an heir, and Eliezer had been supplanted, it would appear, by Isaac. His loyalty was in no wise diminished. If the assumption is mistaken, and the envoy to Bethuel was not Abraham's one-time heir, his loyalty is still a shining virtue. Loyalty, ran a Roman saying, is the holiest good in the human heart. It is the test of love, for loyalty is steadfastness in performing love's obligations. Loyalty is the chief mark of unselfishness, for it must disregard personal advantages in furthering the interests of its object. It is a jewel in a treacherous world. So Milton pictures the seraph Abdiel:

> ... *Abdiel, faithful found*
> *Among the faithless, faithful only he;*
> *Unshaken, unseduced, unterrified,*
> *His loyalty he kept, his love, his zeal.*

Love, zeal, piety mark the servant who took the caravan train to Haran. He is a good man to know. With his act of efficient, sensitive and selfless service he disappears from history, but not from the approval of God—'Well done, good and faithful servant.'

30 : Rebekah
Genesis 24.15–67

Rebekah, or Rebecca as the New Testament, following the Vulgate, spells her name in its only reference (Rom. 9.10), was the daughter of Bethuel, Abraham's nephew. She moves gracefully into the charming story of this chapter, like some maiden, exquisitely carved, from the frieze of the Parthenon. Yet such a simile falls short, for Rebekah is no marble figure, but warm and vital. We meet her busy about the tasks of the household, spontaneously courteous and hospitable, and ready to go a second mile in generosity (19 f.). Active and vigorous, she added eager energy to her natural attractiveness, no withdrawn, proud, and self-conscious beauty, but ready to display, at some cost in time and in strength, the hospitality of desert peoples to the wanderer and the stranger in the land. It is a good daughter who reflects the virtues of her house (25).

There are days in life which are a hinge of our fortunes, and it is well to treat each day as if it contained eternal consequence. This was Rebekah's day. Abraham's dignified and devoted servant was taken home to the house of Bethuel, and stated his errand. Bravely Rebekah recognized the movement of God's hand, and faced calmly the unknown future. She had, as a girl should, prepared her heart and mind for the fulfilment of marriage. It is a natural ambition, a worthy goal for which the normal man or woman plans. It involves

34

a major choice in life, a choice faced and made with small experience, and under the urge and thrust of the deepest of the heart's emotions. Cold reason takes second place, and it is well for those who move into life's longest partnership to do so with the consciousness of God's guidance, and with passion disciplined by virtue, unselfishness, and a desire for God's will. Rebekah seemed taught in such matters, made her choice with calm decisiveness and simplicity (58), and departed on her high adventure.

And yet there is sadness in the story, for the idyll ended. Disappointment was to try Rebekah sorely, and perhaps a certain rift of understanding came between the young wife and a husband twice her age. Was love complete when loyalty died, and husband and wife were sundered in their lamentable favouritism? Life has no more sombre sight than promise faded, than first love grown cold, and later years which disappoint and fall short of all that might have been. Testing and trial, borne together and in mutual trust, need not spoil and weaken.

31 : Isaac
Genesis 24.62–67; 25.19–26; Psalm 105.1–11

Isaac is a somewhat elusive and colourless character among the patriarchs. It is almost as if he had lived so long under the shadow of Abraham that he had failed somehow to develop a sharp and decisive individuality. His virtues are passive ones. We meet him at the close of the romantic story of Rebekah walking in quiet meditation on the desert sand as the stars come out. We met him earlier in the grim story of Abraham's temptation on Moriah, where the marks of his character, seen behind the words of the narrative, are vivid —utter obedience to his father, complete faith (Abraham had passed this quality well and truly to his son), and full surrender to God's will. Isaac emerged from that ordeal 'born again'. He had lost his life to find it again.

Isaac was forty years of age when he married. There is no reason at all why a marriage between a man of that age and a girl like Rebekah should not be happy and successful, but it

35

calls for adjustment and understanding of a sort to which, perhaps, judging by the sequel, Isaac and his bride did not rise. We are told that Isaac loved Rebekah (**24**.67), and in the briefly traversed story of their early years of union (**25**.20 f.) Isaac's concern for his wife's great disappointment is evident. But was the gulf, in their case, bridged?

A stronger man might have bridged it, but Isaac, faithful, devout and submissive, had not, perhaps, those more active qualities which could have compassed this end. Abraham may have been to blame for some fault here. We have seen his anxiety for the line of his descent, upon which his whole vision for God's new race depended. He may have delayed too long his son's marriage in this live concern, a delay meekly and characteristically endured by Isaac. Parental dominance can be too overpowering. To protect one's sons is good and godly. To stunt their growth, like that of a plant that grows in the shade of a tree, is disservice.

Matthew Arnold touched the thought in *Rugby Chapel*, when he wrote of his great father's death:

> *For fifteen years,*
> *We who till then in thy shade,*
> *Rested as under the boughs*
> *Of a mighty oak, have endured*
> *Sunshine and rain as we might,*
> *Bare, unshaded, alone,*
> *Lacking the shelter of thee.*

Did Isaac wilt in the sun and rain when the great oak of Mamre fell?

32 : Abraham's Son

Genesis 26

This is a very sad chapter. Isaac's folly in falsely describing Rebekah as his sister is psychologically true to form. This is no mistaken repetition of an old tradition. It illustrates too exactly, and too sadly, Isaac's subservience to his father, and the unhealthy dominance of a great man over his weaker son. Abraham had done precisely this, and, in a moment of apprehension and of stress, his son followed the same pattern of deceit, and earned the same embarrassing reproof from a pagan.

Isaac was weak, and it is not long before the arrogant recognize weakness and take advantage of it. Colonists from Crete, as we have already seen, had a foothold on the southern coast of Palestine. They were called Philistines, a cultured European people, and had actually given Palestine its name. There is a perennial hostility between Lowlander and Highlander, and the shepherds of the hills were often at odds with the townsmen of the plain. It is evident from the story of the disputed wells that the plainsmen were on the offensive, and were actively pushing the Hebrews back into their hill-country and wilderness hinterlands. Such was history's first confrontation of Asian and European.

Isaac, typically, retreated, and at last, in the deep desert, found rest. Rehoboth means 'broad places', or 'room'. The Israelis have a dry-farming research-centre on the site. Here Isaac felt he could breathe unmolested. And God demonstrated His care for the man of peace. So to move out of an atmosphere of hostility and strife was manifestly His will. He renewed His covenant with Isaac, and so blessed him that the alien sought his friendship and alliance.

But catch the note of pain at the chapter's end. Esau, demonstrating his lack of sympathy with his family's ideals, married a Hittite, and gave her the Hebrew name of Judith. To give a name does not change a character, and the intruder 'made life bitter' for her parents-in-law. There are few sins more contemptible. To be a good son or daughter to the parents of a wife or husband is no betrayal of one's own people, but a source of satisfaction, a cementing of friendship and a rich reward. This situation should have been demonstration enough to the head of the clan that Esau was not likely to be a suitable successor. But we shall see the sequel.

Questions and themes for study and discussion on Studies 25–32

1. What was Lot's basic fault?
2. Is there anything to learn from Abraham about prayer?
3. What did the Lord mean by: 'Consider Lot's wife'?
4. Are lies ever justified?

5. What has the New Testament to say of Abraham in three epistles?

6. List Abraham's testings.

7. How does religion enter business?

8. What are the chief qualities of 'a good and faithful servant'?

9. What place has loyalty in marriage?

10. To what extent is protectiveness a parental virtue?

33 : Esau the Profane

Genesis 25.29–34; Hebrews 12.16, 17

Esau was a 'profane' person (Heb. 12.16, AV). Profane, in fact, is a good translation, if the word is taken in its literal sense. Its basic meaning is 'outside the temple', therefore 'removed from the sacred', 'unconsecrated'. It applies exactly to Esau. He was outside the circle of his family's faith, aspirations, desires. He was outside the will of God. He had chosen, in his self-will, to stand outside the plan.

The story in Gen. 25, to which we have returned, is abundant illustration of his gross, unsanctified personality. The story of the 'mess of pottage' put a metaphor into the languages of the world, but does not mean that the destiny of Israel was decided over a corrupt bargain and the sale of a dish of lentil soup in a nomad camp in the Negev. The real reason why the birthright passed to Jacob was that, with all his lamentable faults, he did not despise it. Esau did, as the last verse of the chapter points out.

Esau was completely unsuitable for the high task of leadership. He was an earthy, carnal character without finer sensibilities or spiritual insight of any sort. The bargain with Jacob was, in his eyes, a joke. He had no idea what 'the birthright' signified, beyond that it was a formal recognition of tribal leadership. He had no intention of keeping a bargain so ridiculously made, as his later plaint to his father, when Jacob, again deceitfully, had confirmed the transaction, amply shows.

Esau was a man of the flesh, and a slave to strong and violent appetites. To such characters, consequences, responsibilities, decency, the standing and testimony of the family, God's will and morality, matter nothing when the flesh is calling. They never resist its demands, never recognize a higher calling which enjoins self-control, and the taming of the desires of the flesh.

The end of the story comes two chapters later. To such personalities comes sometimes the realization of what has been done in the heat of passion, the confidence of prosperity, the arrogance of youth, the pride of the heart, or the greed of the body. A 'great and bitter cry' (27.34) does not then avail. Life can become a 'mess of pottage' by our folly and wilfulness. It does not satisfy, is transient, and destroys the beauty of God's plan. As the Persian Omar said:

> The earthly hopes men set their hearts upon
> Turn ashes, or they prosper, and anon,
> Like snow upon the dusty desert's face
> Lighting a little hour or two, are gone.

34 : Isaac's Family

Genesis 27

The family life of the aged Isaac is an unpleasant picture. Here is the unwholesome revelation of a wife disloyal to a weakening husband, of a man and wife perniciously cherishing their favourites, of an old man who had lost his vision, and of a strong wife who appears never really to have had one.

We have discussed the carnal Esau. His brother was scarcely better. He was self-seeking, crafty, and ready, for his own advantage, to exploit a brother's manifest weakness. His one redeeming feature was that he did, in a dim, perverted way, have some realization of what 'the birthright' meant.

Rebekah had little of such understanding when she sought to secure it for her cunning son. A mother's supreme task is to lead her sons and daughters to God. Her darkest sin is to turn them away from God and uprightness. And no mother can expect her children to rise higher than herself. A Jezebel produces an Athaliah. Jacob matched the treachery of Rebekah, and his regard for his father was no greater than his mother's regard for her husband. She prompts her son to lie and to deceive, and the vast irony of the situation is that they secure corruptly, and at infinite cost in suffering, what they would have won in any case, had they waited for God's time, and the outworking of God's plan. So, many a 'birthright' of happiness, joy, fulfilment, in more spheres of life than one, is soiled and spoiled by premature and hasty grasping with lustful hands, what God Himself will give, crowned with His blessing.

To 'do evil that good may come' is a vicious doctrine. Evil produces 'after its kind'. Success, in the worldly sense of the word, is not the supreme good of life. Rebekah lost her son. As far as the record goes, there is no evidence that she ever saw Jacob again. Misfortune dogged Jacob's life, and it was only long years later that he found his peace with God. Amiel, the Swiss philosopher of the ninteenth century, rightly said : 'Woman is the salvation or destruction of the family. She carries its destiny in the folds of her robe.' The obligation lay more heavily on Rebekah in Isaac's time of obvious decrepitude.

35 : The Aged Isaac
Genesis 27

We must read this fascinating chapter again, because a broken old man sits in the camel-hair tent, of whom we have said little. Isaac, however, is the key to this situation. We have noted his strain of weakness, and this was an element in the sad fortunes of his family. He is old now, somewhat deaf, and totally blind, and a web of intrigue is spun about him by his clever wife, and subtle son.

For himself, Isaac preferred his vivacious, uncomplicated son Esau, who brought good meat into the camp from his hunting in the wilderness. He did not see, or care, that such genial qualities are often shallow and fickle. He had fallen into selfishness in his lonely old age, solitary because fellowship with his wife had faded. Preoccupied with her son Jacob, Rebekah had no doubt neglected him and he had become more and more withdrawn.

He had taken to measuring worthiness by what advantage accrued to himself, and vision had so faded and judgement

40

so tragically weakened, that he could bring himself to propose Esau as his heir. He felt no call of God, but sought the stimulus of wine and meat in order to rise to that high level of poetry and prophecy which was the Eastern context of such a ceremonial.

So tenuous was now the thread of God's purpose which had begun with Abraham's call from Ur. So sad was the last chapter of a life which God had once sealed for His own. We should make it our prayer to end well. To know how to grow old is a task for wisdom, the most difficult chapter in the book of living.

There was something, none the less, of the truth inherited from his father left flickering but alive in him. The tragic story of the great deception runs to its base conclusion and at v. 33 Isaac awakes, with a burning blaze of realization, to the fact that the course of folly which he had chosen in self-will, without confiding in Rebekah, and in pure pursuit of favouritism, was not only wrong, but had been taken from his hands. He finds that God has restrained him and produced an end he had not intended. His strong words : 'Yes, and he shall be blessed', mark his repentance for frightful tampering with God's plan. And a frightful thing it is to tamper with God's purpose for our lives—or for the lives of others.

36 : Jacob's Journey

Genesis 28

With typical deception Rebekah secures the safety of her favourite son. She never saw him again. There is a touch of pathos in v. 9. Left alone now with his parents, Esau seeks to please them, and perhaps clumsily to remedy his earlier error by marrying a girl less alien to their kin (26.34).

Jacob sped north, following the mountain spine of Palestine. For all his treachery and double dealing, he had 'the root of the matter in him', as Bunyan put it of another. He was on his way to the old homeland of his family, and the memory of his grandfather Abraham was alive in his mind.

This is surely demonstrated by his dream. He had heard perhaps tales of the ziggurat of Ur, the great artificial hill

41

of cubed masses of brick, topped by the temple of Ur's chief goddess, and housing some of the priestly corporation which controlled much of Ur's irrigated farmland. Up the side climbed a steep stairway, the remains of which are still to be seen. Perhaps Abraham's last view of his hometown across the level desert, in the clear air, was the ziggurat, with the far specks of distant humanity visible on the stair.

Did this become a child's imagery of heaven and the way up and down thereto? It was still a living image in Nathanael's prayer almost two millennia later, when the Lord uttered a mysterious word to him, only to be understood in the terminology of the prayer under the fig-tree, of which only Christ and Nathanael knew (John 1.51).

Jacob needed help. There was enough of reality in him to cause him to turn to the one-time source of help. He sought the God of Abraham, and from the depths of his mind the dream drew the image of the way to heaven. No one reaches for God without God reaching in strong response to him, and Jacob, for all his unworthiness, was granted a renewal of the ancient covenant.

Like the followers of the Lord Himself he misconstrued the proffered Kingdom in terms of his own advantage. He bargained foolishly with God, but he was determined to return to the land of destiny. Fortunately, God's guidance and God's blessing do not depend on the clarity or the unselfishness of our understanding. The spark was dimly burning. Over long years, and through manifold suffering, God fanned it to a flame.

37 : Jacob in Exile
Genesis 29

This is a strangely touching and human chapter. Jacob's love for Rachel, and the pathos of Leah's unmerited rejection, make a moving story. There is also the dark threat of Laban's deceit.

Observe the old-world hospitality which was part of the character of the peoples of the wilderness, the river plain and the ancient caravan trails. Hospitality is a mark of character, for it is fed by graciousness, activated by unselfishness, and adorned by courtesy. We have seen Abraham dispense it, and Abraham's servant receive it, in the very place where Jacob is now so generously received.

'The polite of every country,' said Goldsmith, 'have but one character. A gentleman of Sweden differs but little, except in trifles, from one of any other country . . .' Jacob comes very near to us in these moments of polished courtesy. Courtesy is the patina of culture. It is the first casualty when culture decays.

But there was another sphere, not so heartening, in which Jacob also received that which he had himself bestowed. He had dealt deceitfully with Esau, and now, at a high and vital moment of his life, he is himself the victim of an act of cruel deception. It was bitter pain for both the girls. It was a blow for Jacob, who must have remembered and recognized the misery he had himself inflicted. Commonly in life double-dealing returns upon itself. The continuing story shows that Jacob was far from purged of his old fault. In Laban, however, he had met another who was his match.

The worst of all frauds is to deceive oneself. All sin comes more easily after that, and Jacob was perilously near the point where he was his own victim. There is one safe course only in life, and constitutional deceivers like Jacob find it difficult to accept the fact. That course was well laid down by Ruskin: 'Do not let us lie at all. Do not think of one falsity as harmless, and another as slight, and another as unintended. Cast them all aside. They may be light and accidental, but they are ugly soot from the smoke of the pit, and it is better that our hearts should be swept clean of them, without one care as to which is largest or blackest.'

38 : Jacob's Prosperity

Genesis 30

Like the nation which was to spring from him, Jacob had to endure a long period of servitude. It is not possible to disguise the fact that Jacob was little more than a bond servant of his father-in-law for a full twenty years. It was in God's plan. Spoiled and protected by his mother, Jacob needed this weathering of character. He needed the taste of his own brew of duplicity. Laban was a harsh burden, but, like many people, Jacob needed the experience of such a man about him.

His family-life was a sad one, and a grim indictment of any other system of marriage than that which owns and reveres Christian values. Poor Leah poured her grief into the names of her first three sons. Reuben (Look! A son), Simeon (he—presumably Gòd—hears) and Levi (meaning doubtful, but possibly 'joined'). Later Levitical law forbade such bigamy of jointly living sisters (Lev. **18**.18). The hate-filled rivalry of Jacob's household provides a reason for the prohibition. The disgraceful rivalry in child-bearing extended to the 'giving' of servant maids, as secondary breeders, doubtless with Jacob's base compliance, and reference to the folly of his own grandfather, who had similarly invoked old Sumerian law. The rill of God's purposes through the race of Abraham was again tenuous. And yet this Jacob was to be Israel.

The device which Jacob employed to gain material advantage at Laban's expense was superstition. There is no genetical basis for the practice, and the increase of Jacob's holdings over those of Laban must have been due to some providence of God to provide the wherewithal for the exodus to Palestine. So often men attribute to their own clever devising that which is in fact the gift of God's grace.

Jacob's swindling was none the less true to form. That Laban richly deserved such disloyalty was no excuse. In fact the wheel had come full circle again. 'Man never fastened one end of a chain around the neck of his brother,' said Lamartine, 'that God did not fasten the other end round the neck of the oppressor.' Laban was now to feel the tug of the chain with which he had bound Jacob. Jacob might have awaited rescue by worthier means, but he had not yet learned to 'leave it all quietly to God' (Psa. **62**.5 in Moffatt's rendering. The whole psalm is a comment on Jacob's adventures).

39 : Jacob's Return
Genesis 31

There is little new in this chapter, but it is a vital link with the next great movement in Jacob's life. He had deceived Laban, and there was hot anger in the tribe. It was well to have out upon the surface that which was active underneath, and the hostile atmosphere around him decided Jacob that the time was ripe for a return to the Promised Land.

Perhaps there was little noble in his motives. The territory of Laban had become a difficult place, and like the Prodigal Son Jacob sought the father's house. But it was a move in the right direction, and God seems, in His grace, to accept the smallest of motives for action in the right direction. Besides, we have seen that there was, deep down beneath all the clutter of selfishness and sham in Jacob's life, some knowledge of the purpose of God in His people and in the land. He seemed conscious of the pull of God's will, and could hear God's voice—when it suited him to hear.

The memory of Bethel remained with him, and Bethel may be thought of as Jacob's experience of conversion. He could not but see the purpose of God in sending him into exile. After his cynical deception of Isaac he had been pulled up by the roots, and God sometimes does this to shake the dirt from the roots. The process had not been notably complete in Jacob's case. Bethel could have been the beginning of a changed and ennobled life. Conversion, notwithstanding experiences of a 'second blessing', can and should be an embracing experience of transformation. In too many cases, and Jacob's was among them, the divine encounter effected but a partial change.

He brought more useless trash back from the Euphrates than Laban's stolen idols. He still bore the load of his deceitfulness. It had paid him well in the sort of advantage that Jacob understood. He was still fond of material things. He had won them in abundance. Men commonly get out of life what they seek with all their heart. The question is what those things are worth in the end. Read 1 Cor. 3.11-20. Jacob was very soon after Laban's departure to have a striking illustration of this truth.

Questions and themes for study and discussion on Studies 33–39

1. How far and when should evil be actively resisted?

2. What has the New Testament to say about 'alien' marriage?

3. What of favouritism in a family? Are there other Biblical examples?

45

4. List some other mothers of Scripture, notable for good or ill.

5. What is our 'birthright'?

6. How is it possible 'to tamper with God's purpose'?

7. How much is faith a prerequisite for God's guidance?

8. What place has hospitality in a Christian's testimony?

9. 'To have done with lying is the beginning of all virtue.' Discuss this.

40 : Jacob and Esau

Genesis 32.1–21

It is worthwhile to look at a map. Laban had pursued the fugitive caravan southward, and come upon it in the highlands east of Jordan called Gilead. It was rough country and there was rougher still beyond. South of Gilead lay one of the eastern tributaries of the Jordan, the Jabbok stream, which flowed in a deep dark gorge under the shadow of the Gilead uplands down to the river. It was probably the gorge up which David struggled in the last lap of his retreat from Absalom centuries later. David was to make his headquarters at Mahanaim (Twin Camps), which Jacob named next day. It was here, after Barzillai's feast, that David probably wrote Psa. 23, and it was no doubt the dark Jabbok ravine which gave him the imagery of the 'valley of the shadow of death'.

It was such a valley to Jacob. From the northern slopes, with Laban gone, Jacob looked south to a new life and the land of his birth. His projected path was probably along the route of the present highway from the Dead Sea to Amman, for Jacob seems to have purposed crossing the Jordan where the Allenby Bridge crosses it today, near Jericho. But between Jacob and the life he hoped to renew was a looming obstacle. He had seen it rising on the skyline for some days—the blue mass of the Mountains of Moab, which flanked the road, the river and the salt Dead Sea. And this was Esau's territory.

Jacob was mortally afraid—

The ghosts of forgotten actions,
Came floating before his sight,

46

And things that he thought were dead things,
Were alive with a terrible might . . .

It is one of the penalties of evil that its consequences lie in ambush down the path of life.

Note Jacob's action. His whole subtle mind was active in his self-defence. He approached Esau with polite diplomacy (3 f.), but was dismayed to hear that his wronged brother was on his way to meet him with a considerable force. He arranged his company for rapid dispersal and flight. Then, with all his organization complete, having the assurance of God's presence (1 f.), he turned to prayer (9–12). In spite of his own unworthiness (10), he knew that God honours obedience (9) and fulfils His promises (12).

41 : Jacob's Wrestling
Genesis 32.22–33.17

Jacob had his 'mess of pottage' back. He knew how fragile was all material prosperity. In one hour it could all belong to Esau, with his own life forfeited, or spared for penury and slavery. He was alone in his suffering, for he had achieved no fellowship with his wives. In the hour of his mind's agony he could only send them away (32.23).

Left alone by the Jabbok, Jacob met the Guardian of the Land, identified in Hos. 12.3 f. The whole terrible struggle was God's battle with Jacob to bring him to surrender. He had just been shown in stark horror how weak, how little, he was, and how worthless all those goods he had striven for with subtlety and selfishness over many years. But there was to be no entry into the promised land for the old, soiled Jacob. God was presenting His ultimatum. Jacob had made his typically clever and deceitful arrangements to impress his brother with his might and wealth, but God did not intend to allow Jacob to begin a new chapter of his life on the slim foundations of trickery.

There comes a time in the life of those who inadequately follow God when He demands reality. He tolerates half-

47

heartedness and carnal discipleship to a certain point, and then suddenly He confronts the selfish follower with the challenge which tests sincerity. God had long enough been pressing hard upon Jacob's uncommitted life. Conscience, riding beside him, had been calling ever louder to him, 'Surrender!' Now, with crisis in the morning, the time had come for the last struggle. Jacob, like many another, had wondrous power in resisting God.

The way to win in any wrestling with God is to surrender. God won. Jacob, calm now, and prepared still to trust and follow, whatever Esau did, is given a new name (2 Cor. 5.17). When wrestling with God changes to clinging to God, God will act.

Day dawned. Esau came. None of Jacob's fears materialized. It was a facet of Esau's earthy personality that he bore no grudge. Jacob, like some Christians, was shamed before the greater worth of one who made no high pretensions. The caravan moved on. Silent, humble, subdued, Jacob rode in its midst. He crossed the river a cleaner man.

42 : Jacob's Harvest
Genesis 34

It is part of the frankness of the Bible that it speaks of the sins and the follies of those that make its story, as well as of their qualities of good. This chapter is an ugly tale, and one which the reader might gladly pass by, but it is part of Scripture and must be faced. This was the material with which God was compelled to work. Is it much better today?

In the old Scofield Reference Bible this chapter was headed: 'Jacob reaps the harvest of his evil years' (Gal. 6.7 f.). It is sombrely appropriate. Here is our first contact with Jacob's sons. Over the next fifteen chapters we come to know them as strong, ruthless men, whose path to God was as rough, twisting, and difficult as their father's had been.

Jacob was in many ways to blame. No man can expect his sons to be better than he is himself. By the mercy of God they sometimes are, but it is not in human power to lift another beyond the level of one's own attainment in spiritual matters. For long, vital and impressionable years these men had watched their father's life. They had seen his reliance on subtle dealing, and their own brutal and sanguinary treatment of their neighbours was nothing more than a version of their father's trickery. A family sometimes has its own way of applying to circumstances the principles it has picked up in rudimentary form from its parents' conduct and example.

Complete obedience on Jacob's part might have preserved the men from the temptation, for it was his choice which determined the circumstances of the atrocity which they committed. Jacob was Israel now, and a full understanding of the Covenant might have dictated a return to the clean Judean hills where the separate life of the tribe and its Abrahamic faith could have been developed free and apart from the contaminating influence of pagan neighbours, and the presence of the Canaanitish towns.

Old nature died hard, and lifelong habit had taught Jacob to seek advantage. The fertile vale of Shechem was better grazing, and more comfortable country than the harsh uplands of Judea which Abraham had chosen when Lot moved down to Sodom, or the southern desert round Beersheba where Isaac sought refuge. Shechem and its perils need never have entered the lives of Jacob's sons had it not been for Jacob's choice of a dwelling place.

Hence tragedy, and a stain upon Jacob's name among the inhabitants of the land. Remember Abraham's care for their presence. The phrase of his grandfather, uttered to Lot, stuck in Jacob's mind. The situation was a grim reminder (13.7).

43 : Back to Bethel

Genesis 35

The crime of Jacob's sons had roused the hostility of the land, and it was only the restraining hand of God which quelled the movement which rose against the intruding tribe (5), now on its way back to the place of blessing. Bethel was a symbol in Jacob's life. His return to it was a renewal and a recommittal. It is sometimes necessary in human experience for the soul to seek the old sources of its strength and vision. Abraham did.

Jacob began with some determination. We begin to see in him the marks of the new life which began when he surrendered completely to God on the banks of the Jabbok in the night encounter. God re-emphasizes to him that his name is new (10). This is no repetition of a story. It is psychologically apt, and no sign of the clumsy editing of some old corpus of Hebrew tales. Jacob was given his new name by the Gilead stream. All deep experience needs feeding. Jacob was a better man but no man attains perfection in sudden flight. We too commonly 'wrestle on towards heaven 'gainst storm and wind and tide', and Jacob, even in his new role as Israel, had already made one major error. He was, like many of those who read about him, to make more. The task, for those who fall, is to rise again.

It was a good beginning, none the less, to cleanse his camp of the remaining vestiges of idolatry. His women, notably Rachel, had retained remnants of old paganism. All spiritual advance begins properly with such cleansing. The 'strange gods' of such a purging are unearthed in numbers by Palestinian archaeologists. They are the common fertility symbols of sex-ridden and perverted cults.

They have their modern counterparts. If a parent purposes to lead his family 'back to Bethel', the place of renewal, rededication and old vigour, it is sometimes necessary to get rid of the family idols. 'Little children, keep yourselves from idols' (1 John 5.21), are probably the last words to be written in the Bible. And 'idols' are not always obscene figurines of baked and painted clay. They can be possessions of more than one form, pursuits and preoccupations, ideas, and pleasures—anything, in a word, which usurps the supreme place in a life. They block the path to Bethel and at all costs must be cast aside.

44 : Esau Again

Genesis 36

This chapter might easily be passed by in a study of the characters of Scripture were it not for a tragedy embedded in two verses. Esau has been dismissed as a profane, an irreligious and carnal man, and in his early years the record has shown him insensitive to his privilege, and to the great purposes of God working out in Abraham's children.

And yet there is also evidence that Easu contained good human material, had someone known how truly to love him. Isaac's love was selfish. Rebekah, in her blind favouritism, did not love him at all. Jacob saw him as a rival. (The phrase, 'I have hated Esau' [Mal. 1.2 f., cf. Rom. 9.13], was not, of course, a denial of God's own nature. In Semitic thought the phrase only means: 'To Esau have I given second place in my purposes'—and that was Esau's choice.)

There are several hints at Esau's hidden worth. His cry of pain, when he found that Isaac had given the blessing to another, is an indication of a sensitive heart behind the bluff and unrevealing exterior. When he met Jacob south of the Jabbok, he was a generous brother, with no revengeful spirit harbouring the rankling memory of old wrongs. He makes a pleasant impression.

The first of the two significant verses mentioned is v. 6 in this chapter. Esau retreated from his brother's presence. He could have remained in the land, even if, with the gentler out-working of God's purposes, he had at last been brought to see that Jacob should be the spiritual leader of the tribe. Esau would have doubtlessly been given a noble role to play. Jacob had made it impossible for him to remain in the place of blessing.

Verse 6 again shows the sensitivity of Esau's character under the rugged façade. Here was a life damaged by another, a 'drop-out', if that word may be used, from the plans and purposes of God. But no one can so withdraw without becoming a menace. Verse 43 is the second verse which, we have suggested, is significant in this chapter. Read, in some Bible dictionary, what harm the people of Edom did to Israel. List prominent Edomites. It is a sad pity that, through the clumsy selfishness of an unconsecrated mother and brother, a man of worth and ability was harmed and spoiled, and driven from the place he might have occupied, and the usefulness he might have known.

Questions and themes for study and discussion on Studies 40–44

1. What five things are most worth seeking in life?
2. What is 'carnal' Christianity?

3. How do prayer and organization mingle?

4. Consider the last view of Esau. What of unlikeable Christians?

5. What is the secret of parental influence? What of heredity and environment?

6. What are 'strange gods', 'idols', in modern experience?

7. Name some prominent Edomites.

45 : The Boy Joseph

Genesis 37.1–4

Joseph moves actively into the story at the age of seventeen. Among his older brothers, pasturing the sheep, he appears immediately as the odd man, ill-received, and outside the circle. It was partly his father's folly. Joseph received from the bereaved Jacob all the affection he held for the dead Rachel, and Rachel was the great love of Jacob's stormy life. Jacob made his favourite son a 'long-sleeved robe', as the word appears to be correctly rendered, setting him thus apart from his brothers. Jacob had no excuse for favouritism. He had seen the fruits of such foolishness in his own parental home. He had seen what it had done to him and to Esau. Worse than this—Jacob made the lad his confidant, and listened to his tales of the others' misconduct. Misconduct there may have been, but to the elder brothers Joseph became a spy, while the distinctive dress he wore was a constant reminder to rough and earthy men that, in their father's eyes, the favoured lad was too good for the hard work they were called upon to do.

They hated him. Hate is a vice of narrow souls, and it feeds like a cancer on its host. It is a madness of the spirit, which quenches all pity, and corrupts all judgement. Envy breeds hatred, for hatred is envy's active form, and Jacob had sown the seeds of envy. It was the Roman historian Tacitus who said that hatred of those who are most nearly connected with us is likely to be the most inveterate. He might have found prime illlustration in this story, outworked in the Judean wilderness, seventeen centuries before Christ.

52

It is quite clear that the ageing Jacob had grown apart from his sons. They had bitterly disappointed him, by their crudity, their cruelty, and their carnality. He had little reason to reproach them, for they were the product of his own years of wandering. He had now all but lost control, the grazing lands were wide, and the roaming of the shepherds took the men far beyond the camp's discipline. It is clear from a later remark in the story (13) that Jacob used Joseph as his messenger and overseer. The story reeks from its beginnings with all the ingredients of tragedy. So much of life's misfortune is built of our own folly. We set the stage for our sorrow, and write the first chapter of our book of pain.

46 : Joseph the Dreamer

Genesis 37.5–11

The O.T. has little to say of dreams, apart from Joseph's story and Daniel's, though it recognizes that a message from God can come in this way. Eccl. 5.3 states that dreams arise from the pressure of the day's events, and an explanation of the mind's activity in sleep could hardly be more modern. Joseph's dream is a light upon his own naïve self-esteem. Such pride was hardly the fault of a seventeen-year-old boy. He had been encouraged to look upon himself as a special person, and in some position of advantage over his brothers. Joseph had a brilliant and a subtle mind, as all the rest of his career demonstrates, and it was not difficult for him to anticipate Jacob's plans for him. The unsuspecting simplicity with which he revealed to his resentful brothers the imaginative dream which his sleeping mind had woven out of such ambitions, is also a light on his guileless character. At the same time it demonstrates how completely Jacob had spoilt him.

The second dream was woven out of imagery from the night sky, a real presence for shepherds 'who watch their flocks by night', as Psa. 8 demonstrates. Observe that the details of the dream, even on Jacob's interpretation, were never fulfilled. Joseph's mother never went to Egypt, and Jacob never did formal obeisance to his son. The dream revealed Joseph rather than Joseph's destiny, and Jacob, like Mary in the story of Jesus in the Temple, 'hid the saying in his heart' (11). Perhaps he sensed a warning in words so precocious. It could hardly have missed his notice that the older men 'could not speak peaceably' (4) to the boy.

Jacob's evident determination to favour Joseph may have arisen from his own interpretation of the past. He had tricked Esau, but could not fail to realize that it was he who stood in Abraham's succession. The curious incident of the blessing of Joseph's sons years later (Gen. 48) shows the same preoccupation. Indeed a thread of such inverted succession runs through Bible history. David, youngest of the sons of Jesse, was not the only example. At the same time, this does not relieve Jacob of unwisdom. It was the same old fault of not waiting for God, and God's good time.

47 : Joseph's Journey

Genesis 37.11–20

And so Joseph's brethren envied their young brother. Envy, said Pliny, wisely, 'always implies conscious inferiority, wherever it abides', and the older sons of Jacob lived under the sense of their father's disapproval. They had doubtless earned such disapprobation by their violence and carnal conduct, and Jacob was an irascible character who was deeply disappointed in his sons. Part of his disappointment was, as we have already seen, traceable to faults in his own life, but, human nature being faulty, this does not always make a parent humble. It can lead to irritation with the son who reveals so painfully the faults of the past. A mirror can show our faults too truthfully for comfort.

Jacob, nevertheless, cared more for his sons than they cared for him. The story reveals their lack of concern. A glance at the map will show how far they had wandered with their flocks, up through the hilly sheep-country of Palestine to Shechem, and then to Dothan. Jacob had not heard of them for a considerable time, so decided to send Joseph, a big decision on his part, to discover their whereabouts. Joseph became lost many miles from home, and a friendly stranger gave him the news that the shepherds had shifted camp to Dothan. He followed them.

In the clean, clear air of the hill-country, the brethren saw and recognized their hated brother from some distance. Innocently, he was wearing his distinctive dress, and on his camel may have made a striking figure. Their contempt is audible in their words. 'The dreamer' must have been their nickname for him, and the measure of their dislike. Joseph's foolishly-reported dreams had bitten deep into their resentful natures, and provided a pivot for hostile action. It is the fashion of men to give a nickname to one whose superiority, real or imagined, they refuse to accept. It aids a feeling of inferiority to give a derisive or bitter name to someone feared, disliked or resented. 'This dreamer' was to be brought low and comfort sought for their hurt spirits by a demonstration of the folly of Joseph's dreams. But often, in the prosecution of his aims, sinful man, by his own act, brings about the very opposite of his intention. That principle, as Aristotle pointed out, is a consistent element in Greek tragedy.

48 : Reuben

Genesis 37.21–36

Reuben, Leah's eldest son, and the natural leader of the brethren, appears in the story of Joseph as a weak but well-intentioned man, the best, save for one grave lapse, of a difficult and harsh company. He was unable to control his brothers, and too fearful of their rebellion to take a firm stand against their crime. He spoke against their action, as he was years later to remind them (42.22), and the incident left a deep mark of guilt and grief upon him. He was too cowardly, none the less, to take a clear stand, though he knew the right, and remained silent when the act of cruelty was committed, and when the foul lie was told to Jacob, along with the accompanying act of cynical evil, the bloodstained garment, which had long since become a symbol of their hate and bitterness. Reuben had intended to return secretly and release Joseph. Virtue which lacks courage lacks its chief constituent, and goodness which acts thus in secret contains small merit.

Reuben also knew that he ran a terrible risk with his brother's life when the boy was placed in what was no doubt a cracked and disused cistern, of the sort which abounded in Palestine, and provided Jeremiah with both a potent word-picture and also a shocking personal experience (Jer. 2.13; 38). Reuben was the Pilate of the situation, too compromised by past feebleness and moral surrender to act with decision and bravery in the hour of crisis.

For Joseph, as Reuben himself later confessed, the event was agonizing. He pleaded in vain with the brutal men. They sinned twice against him. First they left him in the pit, deep as Jeremiah's 'prison' in mire and débris, then they sold him into slavery. A conflation of two accounts has been alleged here. Perhaps there actually were two accounts, one of them Joseph's own. Ishmaelites are more closely defined as Midianites in the 'second' account. There is no reason at all to suppose that Moses did not have many primary sources to work upon. In fact, this possibility enhances the ancient authority of the documents. Nor is there any shadow of contradiction in the story . . . And so Joseph came to sorrow and servitude in a foreign land. It must have been difficult to believe that there was any purpose in what appeared dire disaster.

49 : Joseph's Testing
Genesis 39.1–9

Joseph was a sensitive, intelligent young man and his position in the household of Potiphar held no illusions for him. He knew that he was a slave. At the same time note the resilience and the courage of the youth. He was a trained manager. His office under his father had already shown his ability, and a natural gift in the boy for organization and administration may have been a reason for Jacob's thus employing him, as well as the father's tenderness towards Rachel's elder son.

Joseph could see no future. There was nothing to encourage any hope. There was only a task to be done, commingled though the obligation was with injustice. Potiphar, however, must have been, within his social context, a worthy man, and he was at least shrewd enough to recognize consummate ability when he saw it. Perhaps he was also indolent, and finding himself fortunate enough to secure the services of a vigorous young man, who was able to lift all the load of management and organization from his shoulders, he left him to do it, and took life easily.

Joseph did it, and did it well. But success, ability and personal charm themselves constitute a pathway for temptation. Herodotus, the Greek historian who visited Egypt, had a low opinion of the morals of the women of the land, but there never has been a land where the sudden temptation which confronted Joseph is beyond experience. The woman was immoral, drunk perhaps, treacherous and mendacious. Such situations can arise with fearful abruptness. The web of circumstances inevitably turns the mind to the thought of an active and malign intelligence behind evil.

It was a day like any other day. Life's crises often come without warning. The temptation came in the moment of loneliness with every adjunct of enticement. Here, for the Hebrew slave, could be 'spoiling the Egyptians' indeed, and revenge, 'the fume of little minds', could be glutted. Flattery, the feeding of self-esteem, the establishment of social position, all these lay in the situation. The affection, the love of the lady of the house, discreetly played as Joseph knew his ability could play such an advantage, could lead to unimagined advantage. Was not a Semite on the throne of Egypt? This was probably the age of the Hyksos kings, those intruders from the wilderness whose ascendancy was in Joseph's day.

50 : Joseph's Crisis

Genesis 39.10–20

Joseph had done his best to avoid temptation. He shunned the presence of the temptress (10), and this is sound policy. Peril, moral as well as physical, can often be located, anticipated, and in consequence avoided. It is folly not to do so.

The crisis, none the less, was sudden, and in a sudden vicious assault it is training, the automatic reaction, which counts. The swift and unexpected attack reveals the hidden weakness, the soft and easily penetrated point in the defences,

It was at this point that Joseph showed his worth. He had cultivated that which David saw, in his blinding moment of self-understanding, he so lamentably lacked, 'truth in the inward being' (Psa. 51.6). He had never cherished sin and prepared the way for moral catastrophe. 'How then *can* I do this great wickedness, and sin against God?' had been his answer (9). There is no other.

The sex-ridden day in which we live is a time of tense and unremitting temptation, and Joseph's shining example and simple word stand as the answer to beleaguered young men and women. How *can* those for whom Christ died, who have accepted, in His name, the old canons of chastity, how *can* they cast aside the treasures of purity, uprightness and holiness by undisciplined conduct and wanton sin?

Observe that Joseph called sin by its proper name. There is the prime requirement of holiness. He also stated that a sin against the person of another is a sin against God. So did the Prodigal Son when he 'came to himself' (Luke 15.17). Sin thrives on soft terminology and avoiding the issues of plain truth. Let us be accurate in definition.

Potiphar's 'anger was kindled', but his action in imprisoning the boy was curiously mild. Perhaps in his heart he distrusted his wife, or even guessed her infatuation, and was preoccupied only in saving face before his scandalized household, when he thrust Joseph into prison. It was surely in his power to kill his errant slave.

Here was multiple disaster. Another world had fallen apart. An act of righteousness produced not immediate reward but what appeared to be irremediable disaster. First unmerited slavery, then undeserved imprisonment, had befallen the innocent. 'Truth for ever on the scaffold, wrong forever on the throne . . .' but, as Lowell's verse continues, 'Standeth God within the shadows, keeping watch upon His own.'

51 : Joseph in Prison

Genesis 39.21—40.23

Joseph's whole career in Egypt throws a curious light upon the Egyptians. He met three men in authority, Potiphar, the keeper of the prison, and Pharaoh. All three were ready at a moment's notice to surrender their power and authority to a man of proven ability and integrity. The willingness to delegate is a secret of firm and good leadership, and perhaps it was an ingrained quality among the leading men of the great Nile empire. Once again Joseph found himself in a responsible position, trusted and useful. The fact reveals that he must have been conspicuously able, but it also shows his strength of character. Once more he had won the victory over despair, and the natural temptation to surrender. The young man had recognized a basic truth—there is always a task to be done, and it is always fruitful to do it.

Joseph was trusted by the prisoners as well as by the keeper of the prison, or 'the captain of the guard', as the same officer is called. Hence the confidences of the baker and the butler. It is possible to explain their dreams in psychological terms and symbols. They knew of the coming event of Pharaoh's birthday, and the custom of amnesty and final punishment involved. One man was conscious of innocence, the other of his guilt in some palace plot. Apprehension and hope played a part in the subconscious structure of the mind's imagining in sleep. Joseph had a life-long interest in the theme, and gave the interpretation, helped perhaps by his own knowledge of the nature of the charges against the two prisoners. If we understand the event thus we must not forget that his use of such knowledge was the method God employed —we cannot exclude God from the interpretation (40.8).

The butler forgot what he owed. It is a common fault of men. Swift was savage on this sin. 'He that calls a man ungrateful,' he said, 'sums up all the evil of which one can be guilty.' Animals leave ingratitude to man. It is part of our fallen nature, and can ruin the soul. It should be spurned as a thing most contemptible. The mordant French epigrammatist, Rochefoucauld, remarked drily: 'We seldom find people ungrateful so long as we are in a position to render them services.' The butler was in no further need of Joseph. When he found that a longer memory gave him advantage in Pharaoh's eyes, the hypocrite was able to remember (41.9). There is one last bitter and most damnable extension of ingratitude, and that is to feel actual resentment against the person whose goodness has put us under an obligation.

52 : Joseph's Pharaoh

Genesis 41.1–33

It seems most likely that Joseph's captivity in Egypt fell during that prolonged period when a Semite dynasty, the Hyksos, the hated 'Shepherd Kings', controlled the land. We would gladly know more of this succession of monarchs, but the Egyptians so loathed the memory of the alien rule that records were destroyed and history deliberately suppressed.

Hence the value of this one intimate glimpse of a Semite Pharaoh. Curiously, some details of history escaped the Egyptian iconoclasts, and one papyrus reveals how common in lists of servants' names and even those of prison inmates, were Semitic words. Perhaps the fact that the baker mentioned that Joseph was a Hebrew had something to do with the promptitude of his release and summoning to the royal presence. Equally, the butler and the baker may have been elements from the native Egyptian Establishment which the new dynasty took over as a going concern, and which may conceivably have contained elements of disloyalty and potential conspiracy, of which the ruling monarch was wise to take continual account. It was natural that he should be inclined to favour a Hebrew, a fellow-Semite, for any high office or position of confidence or intimacy.

Consider, too, the strange little confirmation of history in the very imagery of Pharaoh's dreams. Dreams are built out of the stuff of the mind's preoccupations, and on the throne of the land was a man with a live concern for his country's agricultural economy, and with an eye for good cattle. The Pharaoh had also noted the dependence of the land upon the rhythmic rise and fall of the Nile. Egypt, said Herodotus, is 'the gift of the Nile'. It is a strip of fertile river valley, hemmed from East and West by arid deserts, and dependent upon irrigation by the river whose annual silt deposit built its very territory.

Pharaoh sensed trouble for Egypt, and the concern was altogether to his credit. Nor was he a man who scorned instruction and advice. He sought what he needed in the place where he thought he might well find it, and when that project failed, he turned to another suggested source. It was a dramatic moment when Joseph, observing all the accepted proprieties, appeared in the palace. He did not neglect the obligation to humility. To God alone he ascribed any salutary insight which he had demonstrated.

53 : Joseph in Power
Genesis 41.34–57

Everything suddenly began to fall into place. Life is sometimes like that. God's plans are long maturing, and timebound man is sometimes irked by the seeming tardiness of the movements of God's hand. Many circumstances must synchronize, and that is why 'the mills of God grind slowly'. At the same time 'they grind exceeding small', and we might add—'sure'.

Joseph did not know that, when he sought to manage Jacob's affairs, when he took the right course and did his best for Potiphar and the head gaoler, God was in fact preparing him for the organization of Egypt, and that Egypt thus preserved was to be a place of refuge for Joseph's own family. Faithfulness in small things, as the Parable of the Talents has it, is often the prerequisite for a wider trust.

It is a magnificent success-story. Abraham, as Professor James Kelso has cogently demonstrated, was a very considerable business man, and here was the first patriarch's great-grandson, showing in the management of the whole economy of the world's most powerful nation, that same easy movement from agriculture into business which has always been the achievement of the able Jew. Joseph was the first example of the successful Jewish statesman and businessman. From Babylon of the post-exilic centuries, on through all history, they have been legion.

Joseph was now a happy man. He married, and had cause to thank God that he came to that great event in life unspoiled and unsoiled by sexual misconduct. Those who come to marriage tarnished and damaged by a premature snatching of life's joys with unsanctified and unclean hands do not realize how much they miss of what the good God intended them, in His own good time, to have and to hold.

Joseph served his master well. He brought all Egypt into the hands of Pharaoh, and those who naturally deplore this totalitarian and political use of economic power must realize that much of Egypt, especially the south, was disaffected towards the northern-based rule of the dynasty. Joseph sought to stabilize Semitic power in the land by this clever piece of organization. A huge increase in export trade went along with it, for the abnormal drought-conditions, which had harmed the Nile watershed, were due to one of those periodic shifts of the Sahara rainbelts which Elijah's day experienced, and which affected, it seems to be shown from recent historical and climatological theories, a far wider area than the Nile valley.

Questions and themes for study and discussion on Studies 45–53

1. Is popularity always possible or desirable?

2. Consider some of the other situations in Scripture where brother meets brother.

3. Hatred as a political doctrine.

4. 'Spoiling' children.

5. Define and study in a Christian context, envy, jealousy and emulation.

6. Cowardice and virtue : Are the two consistent?

7. Temptation is not sin.

8. Sin begins in the mind.

9. Chastity and marriage.

10. How is sin minimized in definition?

11. Ingratitude, its reasons, and its deadliness in religion.

12. Love and wisdom as the basis of God's planning.

54 : Joseph's Family

Genesis 42.1–35

The scene shifts back to Palestine, and the story rings with reality. Jacob is old and peppery (1), but in control of his family, and clear in his plans for the feeding of his growing household. There was plenty of hard cash in hand, another indication that James Kelso is correct in his belief that the patriarchs were business-men drawing considerable income from their dominating position on the trade-routes of the Fertile Crescent.

An Egyptian fresco shows a caravan of Semites moving into Egypt, and this was the journey which the brothers, under Jacob's sharp command, now undertook. They came to the great depot where the export wheat was distributed, and found Joseph, unrecognized, in command. He knew them immediately.

In attempting to understand Joseph's treatment of his brothers, it is at first necessary to look at the historical context. Many men in his place of power would have richly avenged old wrongs. Secondly, it is fruitful to endeavour to penetrate Joseph's motives, and the best explanation to be found for his policy towards them is to see that his basic aim was to forgive and to restore fellowship.

He wanted fellowship to be real, and not based upon fear, or abject surrender on the part of the rough persecutors of his youth. He had not seen them or known them for very many years, and he desired, above all, to explore their minds, and to see whether time or the long pressures of life had brought any salutary change in them. It is well to remember Joseph's supreme intelligence, and the powers of psychological insight he has already demonstrated in his human relationships. The naïve and simple-minded boy is long since past. Here is a man of penetrating understanding.

An injection of salutary fear was a good piece of probing and of therapy. He accused them of spying. Egypt, with its alien dynasty, was a fine field for disaffection. She had corn, too, in a hungry world, and the one perilous highroad for invasion was down the route which the Hebrews must have traversed. Joseph's treatment produced its immediate result. He knew now that Reuben was innocent of the major crime against him (22), and that their common conscience nagged over their cruel wrongdoings (21). Joseph was deeply moved (24). He left Reuben, in consequence, to lead the party back, and retained Simeon, the next in order of age. Other elements of mystery (28) deepened their unease. We, like Joseph, are beginning to see the signs of healthy change in

63

these earthy men. They still feared God, and while that abides there is hope.

55 : Jacob Again

Genesis 42.36—43.14

Old Jacob's dark view of his circumstances (42.36—43.14) seemed justified. He had set his life right with God and received his new name, but the years had been filled, not with joy and triumph, but with seeming disaster. He was disappointed with his sons. Scan the preceding chapters. They tell the story ruthlessly—the personal sins of Reuben and Judah, the collective sins of the group against Shechem and Joseph. Only Rachel's sons seemed true, and in the old tradition. And now Joseph, in his father's conviction, was dead, and the boy Benjamin, last relic of the beloved wife, was under dire menace.

It was natural to think that he was heavily besieged, and that the whole scheme of things was against him. There are times of darkness in life, as many an agonized psalm bears witness, and as more than one biography in the Bible illustrates—Elijah, for a prime example. Nor is it a service to one so burdened to prattle about 'the sin of worry', and to exhort to cheerfulness. Such crude mishandling can break the few threads by which crushed spirits hold to faith and balance.

Jacob took the proper course. He refused to be thrust into premature action (38), or to be over-persuaded by those whose judgement was far from being beyond reproach. With the passing months the course became more clear. At Hebron Jacob's tribe had considerable flocks and cultivation. The land was becoming a dustbowl as the famine bore more and more heavily upon the whole region. Jacob, as the patriarch, was fully aware of his duty to the whole of his family and their dependants. He steeled himself to send another caravan down to the one market where food in plenty was still for sale.

Judah, who, perhaps because of Reuben's shame (35.22), and Simeon's incarceration, had assumed, for all his own unworthiness (38.12–26), the position of spokesman, raised the question of Benjamin. It must have wrung Jacob's heart

(43.14), but duty won the day and the boy went south with the wagon-train.

Jacob little knew what the real shape of circumstances was. It is so in life. God builds the pattern of His purposes out of dark threads and light. Jacob's spirit needed purging, and the wider plan of history had need of his suffering. Paul has a strange phrase which hints that the Christian is sometimes called to share the sufferings of Christ in order to attain a similar godly fruitfulness (Col. 1.24). Such now was Jacob's role.

56 : Joseph's Banquet

Genesis 43.15—44.12

Whoever first wrote this story, and it was probably Joseph himself, wrote brilliantly. The narrative catches the air of innocence with which the brethren present themselves at Joseph's door, their carefully accurate account of their adventure on the former journey, and the nervous fears which haunted them. It was good for their souls, no doubt, that they should learn what terror can mean. The elaborate courtesies with which Joseph increased their apprehension, and the slips of the tongue (27, 29) by which he almost betrayed himself, are admirably described.

The banquet followed, with Egyptians and Hebrews set apart in a species of racial segregation. Two matters puzzled the bewildered men still more. Joseph sat them in order of age. Then he favoured Benjamin. The vastly larger portion sent by Joseph to his favourite brother may indeed reflect an Eastern custom of honour, but elaborate explanations can often be set aside. Joseph remembered Benjamin as a small boy with an enormous appetite. Perhaps he was simply joking.

He was not yet sure. He was hoping against hope that the harsh and brutal men were changed. His was a God-given love which sought to bless, but could not act unless hands of penitence reached out to receive it. He thought he could see a change. He knew that they had spoken truthfully to him. He was determined now to test them in the matter of Benjamin. Would they sacrifice the lad for their own safety? Would

65

they pity their father's stricken old age? This was to be the final demonstration.

Hence the elaborate plot and the silver cup in Benjamin's sack. A difficulty has been found in the statement that the cup was used for divination by Joseph. Either this is a statement related to the plot (5), and designed to give verisimilitude to the allegation, or else Joseph actually held to this fragment of superstition. He had, after all, no Bible, save perhaps his own written recollections of the family tradition. He had lived, too, in a pagan environment. No character is perfect. None is free from mistaken concepts of God's ways. Witness ourselves. Observe the misuse of Scripture in 'promise box' and random snatching of texts, for nothing else than 'divination'.

57 : Joseph Convinced

Genesis 44.13—45.15

The brothers surely were changed men. Without a moment's hesitation they saddled their beasts and turned back to Egypt to accompany their brother into peril. Judah's nobility is outstanding. There were heroism and self-sacrifice in his prompt offer to give his own life for the rest, and to keep his compact with a broken and aged man.

The spectacle of a man so transformed broke Joseph completely. He was convinced that God had done His work with the men who had so grievously wronged him. To forgive is divine, and Joseph nobly forgave. It is a lesson we must learn. General Oglethorpe said to John Wesley: 'I never forgive.' 'Then I hope, sir,' replied Wesley, 'that you never sin.' It is only the mean and narrow soul which does not know the glory of forgiving. Implacable hatred is diabolic.

Joseph had richly learned the lessons of apparent disaster. God has a plan for the life which is committed to Him. Any evil unreservedly placed in His creative hands can be transformed into good, and Joseph had seen abundant illustration of this divine truth in the household and the prison of his slavery. Had he failed then, in bitterness, or paralysed despair, the grand consummation by which he was to play a part in history might never have taken place. He saw God's hand in this. The crime of his elder brothers, which he now so generously dismisses (45.5), was woven into a great plan of divine blessing. Joseph's faith enabled God thus to transform it.

The comforting word offered thus to those guilty of such crime, was inspired by the fact that they were quite obviously penitent. They had demonstrated the fact in their loyalty to Benjamin. Like God himself, whose grace he demonstrated, Joseph had no hankering for their remorse. We are free to forgive ourselves for the sins God has forgiven us. And forgiveness, truly conceived, is an act whereby sin is made to disappear from out of the sinner's conscience, as good medicine makes a malady disappear from the body. So Joseph found joy, for to forgive is to know one of the great solaces of life.

58 : Jacob's Migration
Genesis 45.16—46.7; 46.28—47.12

Pharaoh was a generous man but his advice to Joseph was not altogether bereft of self-interest. His was an alien dynasty, and for one of the 'Shepherd Kings' it was of some military advantage to welcome a substantial Semitic migration into the northern parts of Egypt. It helped to hold the land's communications.

But observe Jacob. His turbulent career and his complicated character have occupied almost half the book, and he is now seen in tried and tested old age. After the ancestral mistake of Abraham, doubtless written into the records of the tribe, a retreat from the land of blessing and of promise was a serious step. Jacob remembered his own withdrawal, and with what strife by the Jabbok stream the Guardian of the Land had conceded new entry. And now, in the words of his beloved and rediscovered son, came the charge to go to Egypt, and to abandon the considerable pasturelands at Hebron where the family's dead lay buried, and where roots of habitation were striking deep and satisfyingly.

It is significant that Jacob seeks God's will. Too often he had loved to pick and choose his path but now, 'lead Thou me on'. He moved south to the very borders of the Negev, a sort of frontier, beyond which lay the desert approaches to the isthmus, and the vestibule of the Nile Valley. To Beersheba he could go without abandoning the land given to his grandfather, and sanctified by his presence. The famine, none the less, lay heavy on the hungry land, and Jacob's perplexity may be easily imagined. It was one of those occasions when human judgement falters, and a word from God is dire necessity.

Hence the sacrifices at Beersheba (46.1). Jacob was urgent in his search for guidance, and he received the sanction which he sought. On the strength of God's word, Jacob made the momentous step. He was a subdued and humble man. When he stood before the ruler of Egypt he spoke of his stormy days (47.9), for he could now look back and in a long perspective see the course of his mistakes. It is well to live in quiet anticipation of such a day. It comes inevitably with the mounting years.

59 : Jacob's Ending

Genesis 47.27—48.22

'An old man's past's a strange thing,' said John Masefield, 'for it never leaves his mind.' Jacob is nearing his end, and is urgent in his pleading that Egypt shall not be Israel's final abode. Hence the strong hint of 47.30 f. Where the family's honoured dead were resting, there too Jacob wished to rest, and this was sign enough in the eyes of all that Egypt was but a place of sojourning. In his final charge to Joseph, which makes the moving and human story in the next chapter, Jacob lives in the deeply significant past, and v. 4 is surely as near to command that a dying man in an alien land could come, when he was speaking to that land's second citizen. The chapter ends, too, with compelling prophecy (21), itself a virtual command to emigrate.

The incident of the blessing of Joseph's two sons is curious. Jacob is living vividly in his past. It is the blessing of the Guardian of the Land, which he invokes upon the boys (16), for that incident of testing on the stream-bank, in which Jacob grew into the maturity of Israel, is bulking large in his mind. It sometimes happens that the years bring clarity, and the backward look shows the real significance of life, and reveals what truly mattered and what did not. Perhaps also the principle of the succession whereby he had displaced Esau, as Isaac had succeeded Ishmael, and as Joseph had overtopped his brothers, thus confirming the ancient portent of his dreams, was becoming obsessive in his mind.

To Joseph's distress, he carries the principle into the ritual of blessing. It seems that, in his determination so to act, the old man ended with his arms *crossed* on the boys' heads. The fact is not significant, beyond its emphasis on Jacob's indomitable will. That will had carried him far. It had not always sought the aid and dominance of Another's Will. For some folk such surrender is difficult, but the great example of Christ abides: 'Nevertheless not my will, but thine, be done . . .' And so Tennyson:

> *Our wills are ours, we know not how;*
> *Our wills are ours, TO MAKE THEM THINE.*

To do just that had been a hard task for Jacob, and now the end was near—with a last flutter of his old stubbornness.

60 : Joseph's Ending

Genesis 49 and 50

In a poetic passage which reads like Virgil's pageant of heroes in his great poem of an unborn Rome, Jacob covers the future of his sons. Reuben and Simeon must have found the last flare of their father's anger searing. The old man had little tenderness for them, and perhaps this is the last flicker of a Jacob which still refused to die . . .

The sting and pain of such surviving disapproval was probably the source of the renewed apprehension which the brothers suffered after the funeral, and the amazing spectacle of lamentation at Hebron, whither Jacob's body was borne. Pharaoh must have held Palestine with some strength at the time, in one of those waxing phases of Egyptian influence which form a pattern of history in the land. The large band of Egyptians which accompanied the cortège, had a possible double purpose. Not in the cruel sense of his later and alien successor, but in some care for his own stability in Egypt, Pharaoh was perhaps not disposed to allow so loyal and strong a minority to depart from the land. Hence the beginnings of the Egyptian captivity, which Israel should have broken before it became too strong and hostile.

The brothers, under tacit compulsion to return, now feared that their old sin might discover them. The morbid revival of guilt for sin dealt with and forgiven is sometimes a symptom of an insecurity bred of circumstances and sudden alarming change. Joseph was noble to the last, and still fulfilling the high words of assurance (50.19). It was not his, he said, to harm where God had obviously blessed. A principle of human forgiveness is involved. When God has forgiven it is not for man to hold and nourish a grudge or seek reprisal.

So Joseph died, and it was not his fault if the descendants of Israel tarried unduly in the land, as others, centuries later, tarried in pagan Babylon. He died, and Genesis, which began with Adam in a garden, ended with Joseph in a coffin in Egypt. But God's purpose was unfolding, and history was being made or marred by the deeds and the thoughts of men.

Questions and themes for study and discussion on Studies 54–60

1. Forgiveness. Trace its incidence in Scripture. Should forgiveness be unconditional?

2. 'The dark hours of the soul.' How should we deal with anxiety?

3. What qualities of good are visible in Joseph's brothers?

4. Two must play a part in all acts of forgiveness.

5. How does remorse differ from repentance?

6. How did Jacob come by his final qualities of character?

7. Will is the key to personality, character, and standing with God. Why is this so? Illustrate from Scripture.

8. The 'guilt complex'.

61 : Pharaoh

Exodus 1

The Bible is not preoccupied with Egyptian history, but the situation in the land of the Nile when its second book opens is consonant with the course of events when the invading Semitic rulers were expelled, and the Egyptian Pharaohs resumed their interrupted government of the land. Who the grim tyrant of this chapter was, however, is uncertain. Dates assigned to the departure of Israel from Egypt vary between 1440 and 1290 B.C., and the ruler who sought to control the population in the Delta, where a hated pocket of Semites, once protected by the overthrown Hyksos, still remained, will, of course, be determined by the date of the Exodus.

The king, 'who did not know Joseph' (8), like his successor of later chapters, must, then, be simply Pharaoh. He was a frightened man. All tyrants are, and this man's fear was that a dissident group of shepherds lay across or beside vital northern communications out of Egypt to the Middle East, that old reservoir of invaders of the Nile Valley from ancient on to modern times. 'Necessity,' said William Pitt, 'is the argument of tyrants, but it is the creed of slaves.' Pharaoh was a greater slave than those whose numbers he sought murderously to control. Tyranny is weakness, and Pharaoh's limits are visible in the chapter. The two Hebrew midwives, fearing God rather than the person of the ruler, frustrated the savage decree and outfaced him. Outfaced, he did nothing, thus declaring his limitations.

'Tyrants,' said Hazlitt, 'forgo all respect of humanity in proportion as they are sunk beneath it. Taught to believe themselves of a different species, they really become so, lose their participation with their kind, and in mimicking the god, dwindle into the brute.' The remark could be sombrely illustrated from this old story on to Chaka the Zulu, and Hitler and Stalin of our own grisly century. It is a curious fact that such men of sin have always succeeded, against their will, in bringing to visibility some of the choice virtues of mankind in those they have sought to dominate and subdue. But hateful is the power and pitiable the life of those who wish to be feared rather than loved. They are invariably defied.

71

62 : Jochebed, Miriam and Pharaoh's Daughter

Exodus 2.1–10

Three women fill the first ten verses of this chapter, and make
pleasant reading. In two later contexts (Exod. 6.20; Num.
26.59) we learn that the name of Moses' mother was Jochebed,
and the second context gives the name of Moses' sister as
Miriam. Inventive and bold in her love for her child, Jochebed
made a tiny papyrus boat, a miniature of the reed-boats which
the Egyptians used for fowling in the marshes, also of the *Ra*,
Thor Heyerdahl's Atlantic craft, and sent the child down a
backwater of the Nile upon it.

The virtues of the mother are sometimes visited upon the
children, and the quick-witted little girl who was sent to
watch the frail craft saw the rescue at the hands of Pharaoh's
daughter. Her swift intervention, possibly part of the mother's
plot to secure royal protection and immunity for her child,
was eminently successful, and Moses became the ward of the
palace, and was returned to his mother to nurse for pay. It
was an ironical situation.

The princess, so coolly scornful of the royal decree against
the male children of the Hebrews, is an unknown person. The
dates are quite uncertain, though some have sought to make
a case for her being the redoubtable Hatshepsut, one of the
most powerful and remarkable women of all Egyptian history.
The cavalier fashion in which a directive of Pharaoh himself
is dismissed by the princess would eminently fit the dominating character of this woman who, through the reigns of three
Pharaohs, was a mighty power in Egypt, but such slight
evidence is far from being enough for certain identification.
The princess does, however, reveal that good can be discovered in most unlikely places, and that a tyrant need not
expect respect or obedience even from those nearest to him.
She was a kindly woman, whether a princess of the royal line,
or, as others say, a daughter of a harem woman of Pharaoh's
polygamous house. In the right place at the right time, her
goodness served history. Pity is the straightest path to a
woman's love, and it was pity, itself a noble virtue, which
showed the true humanity of Pharaoh's daughter. It is love
which unites the three women of this story, so varied otherwise in age and in condition.

63 : Moses' Renunciation

Acts 7.20-29; Hebrews 11.23-27

The brevity of the Bible is sometimes disconcerting. Stephen, in his remarkable historical survey before the Jewish Sanhedrin, follows the same rabbinical source as the writer to the Hebrews, which had considerable traditional information about Moses' life in the royal tutelage. Several facts seem obvious. First, Moses had a standard Egyptian education. He passed through this pagan training without in any way losing his faith in God, and this leads obviously to the second fact. Somehow his own people must have maintained influential contact with him. He thus forms a prime example of a person brought up in an alien intellectual environment, who, in spite of a powerful personality, maintains the simplicity of an ancestral faith.

His Egyptian training was, in fact, an ideal preparation. He must have been made aware of codes of law and ritual, such as the code of the Hittites and Egypt's own, and he was to be the divinely appointed legislator through whom the laws of the Israelite theocracy were to be given, and its standards of austere morality established.

There came the moment of decision, one of those 'sharp agate points on which destiny turns', as Churchill once put it, a 'hinge of fate', as the same perceptive voice had it, quoting Roman Virgil without acknowledgement! Whether Moses' princess-patron was still alive at this moment of decision and renunciation, it is impossible to say, but if she was, it must have been a stern moment of tension. The appearance of ingratitude had to be faced, also what appeared to common sense the quixotic renunciation of comfort, high condition, bright prospects, and even such possibilities of supreme power in Egypt as the great Joseph had held. Moses must have faced such a temptation as that which was thrust upon Christ Himself, when he saw the wide and salutary benefit which such power contains. To abandon it all for the sake of utter integrity, and the complete identification with an outcast people for which his conscience called, must have seemed to his friends the peak of folly. But integrity, and confidence in God are the first prerequisites of any true service. And so Moses 'refused to be called the son of Pharaoh's daughter' . . .

64 : Moses' Disappointment

Exodus 2.11-15

It is the common testimony of most men who have counted much for God that somewhere in their early experience lies a soul-searching disappointment. Moses, the polished prince of Egypt, made his great act of self-renunciation, and after the fashion of man, pictured himself as the acclaimed and accepted saviour of the Hebrew slaves, proudly and victoriously leading them out of their humiliation and servitude.

He found double rejection. Pharaoh's resentment towards the ungrateful rebel against his house and its generosity is obvious. A prince of the land normally would have had nothing to fear about striking down an overseer of slaves, and the fact that Moses had to flee the country after his act of violence shows that Pharaoh was waiting for a chance to deal with him, but also playing the situation with some care. He wanted no full-scale rising among the slaves.

Moses had begun his new role in all the arrogance of the flesh. He expected his show of strength to win him acclaim among those whom he sought to aid. Instead it won betrayal. It was Moses' first great lesson in human nature. To lead a nation he needed much finer training than the palace could ever give him. The base and contemptible man that awakened him to reality was his first teacher in the new school. No self-sufficient and violent man can properly lead in God's name.

So Moses escaped to Midian, his great projects in ruin. His sense of failure must have been overwhelming. He could not possibly foresee how the situation could be remedied or reversed. Those who face a catastrophic collapse of all their hopes should study this story very carefully. Failure is not final, and that truth haunts the Bible. A forgotten essay of Winston Churchill, from the days of his own political rejection, deals with Moses, and shows how that remarkable leader saw analogy in Moses' rejection. We must learn in life, as Kipling put it, to deal with triumph and disaster, 'and treat those two imposters just the same'. It was the saintly Fenelon who said : 'In the light of eternity we shall see that what we desired would have been fatal to us, and that which we would have avoided as essential to our wellbeing.'

65 : Moses' Withdrawal

Exodus 2.16–22; Psalm 90

For those rejected of men, God prepares a place of retreat. Elijah was nursed to healing on Horeb, Mark, rejected by Paul, found solace in his spiritual father, Peter. Moses withdrew to the wilderness, found a kindly welcome and a home with Jethro, and learned the lessons he put into the poetry of Psa. 90 and perhaps Psa. 91.

His schooling was beginning. Toynbee, in his great *Study of History*, lists among the phenomena of the human story the principle of Withdrawal and Return. He finds that, again and again in history, a person, a group, or even a nation (Israel is an example) withdraws from the visible stage of events, to return to it transformed, strengthened and cleansed, to play a vital part.

Moses could see none of this at the time. He who had aspired to lead a nation was called instead to shepherd sheep. Perhaps, on the whole, this is not a bad training for the shepherding of the human flock. Nor is there a better place than the wilderness for the self-examination and the meditation which lead, if the surrendered spirit would have it so, to the knowledge of self and of God, which must precede all usefulness.

Moses was not embittered by his stern experience. He turned from the high, proud projects which he had set before himself, the rapid and spectacular success, to the slow and humdrum task of the nomad's unchanging life. There is always some task obviously at hand to do, and when we cannot see through the obscurities of the future and God's wise design, it is well to turn to the doing of what lies before the feet. Nothing else will happen until that small demand has been met. In God's plan there is nothing small or great. We are unable to estimate the relative importance of our tasks. All that is commonly possible is to see the task awaiting, and to do it, leaving the final outcome, which could be of incalculable worth, to God, and the revelation of the future. Loneliness is the God-given opportunity to cut adrift, and discover oneself—and God. Moses was engaged on a wider reconnaissance than he knew. This was the land through which he was to lead Israel. But God was also explaining the by-ways of the spirit and the highroads of Heaven.

66 : Moses at the Bush

Exodus 3.1–14

It is again not uncommonly the experience of those whom God calls to some great task to find that the experience of testing ends with dramatic suddenness. Moses was resigned now to a lifetime of obscurity. He had learned the meekness which was to be remembered as the hallmark of his character (Num. 12.1–3). And then the burning bush! It was a day like any other day, and the landscape was the brown desert, which was the scene each morning of Moses' quiet unchanging life . . . It is well to be alert.

Moses spoke later (Deut. 33.16) of 'him that dwelt in the bush'. In the story, as J. A. Motyer points out, the words 'holy', 'living' and 'indwelling', predominate. 'The bush', he writes, 'is not consumed because the flame needs no fuel, being self-sufficient . . . equally it is the unapproachable holiness of God . . .'

Perhaps Moses, next great figure in the line of Abraham's monotheism, needed the deep lesson which culminated in God's revelation of His holy name (14). Israel, as the incident under Mount Sinai was to show, had become contaminated with Egyptian idolatry and polytheism. No people were more gross in their conception of deity. The animal and bird-headed creatures which passed for gods in the base conception of the dwellers by the Nile must have haunted the thoughts of the persecuted slaves. After all, the bleak evidence of circumstances did appear to make the gods of Egypt seem a stronger power than the unseen deity which left them to toil in their labour camps.

It is possible that Moses' own mind, powerful though it was, lay in need of such a purging. He had discovered in the wilderness that 'the Most High' was 'his habitation', and 'underneath were the everlasting arms'. He was never to waver in that faith, and now God, alive and shining in the strangely blazing bush, confirmed to Moses the long lessons of his exile. In such fashion, too, was his own weakness to be indwelt, and his own person possessed during the years of service so unexpectedly dawning upon him.

Moses was never to forget. It behoves us similarly to remember. The bush ablaze was a common bush, the ground where Moses was bidden stand, reverently unshod, was the

76

common floor of the valley. He saw now that his shepherding was holy, and the daily monotony divine. So, too, with all we do, and seek to do for God.

67 : Moses' Reluctance

Exodus 4

It is sometimes the way with men to overcorrect a fault. Human nature so easily falls into extremes. The Greeks observed the fact and placed in their list of virtues a word which the N.T. usually translates in the sense of 'sobriety'. The word is *sophrosyne,* and signifies a sane and saving balance between extremes. It is the balanced self-control which, while saving courage from cowardice, holds it back from the extreme of rashness, or, while exalting chastity, preserves it from prudery.

All virtues are properly infused with such self-discipline. It is a good and salutary quality to know well that which we are not fitted to do. At the same time it is good to avoid the over-exaggerated modesty which holds back from doing that which is within reach of native ability and contains an obligation.

Moses had been over-confident in the goodwill of his people, too eager in his trust of them, and had met disillusionment at the crude treachery of one or two. Now he is sceptical of their acceptance. He was hasty and talkative, no doubt, but now he holds back from the Lord's clear call, and distrusts his native powers of speech. The silences of the great and empty wilderness, and the quiet camp or farmstead where the weary shepherd family gathered at night, ready more for sleep than conversation, might well have dampened any youthful eloquence or sparkle of speech.

Note that Moses does not describe the weird experience of the burning bush, or his commission from God. Some events go too deep for speech (18). Those too ready to babble about personal spiritual experience might note the fact. Similarly Peter said no word in public about a vital interview with the Lord (1 Cor. 15.5). Perhaps Moses went too far in his reticence, and failed to confide adequately in his wife Zipporah. She was outside Moses' Hebrew tradition, and failed to understand the ancient sign, which an expression of Divine wrath (perhaps some deadly illness) had brought back to her husband's mind. There should be complete understanding between those so linked together.

And so it came about that Moses moved out to his great enterprise in self-distrust, and with the strain of tension between himself and Jethro's daughter. It was a sad beginning, its burden lightened a little by the renewed fellowship with his brother Aaron and his competent help.

68 : Pharaoh

Exodus 7

This is the third ruler of Egypt to appear in this book and the imprint is the same. Few sayings are as well known as Lord Acton's word: 'All power corrupts, and absolute power corrupts absolutely.' Pharaoh was unable to recognize justice, or the right of another to freedom. The statement that the Lord hardened Pharaoh's heart is sometimes a difficulty to those who approach the fashions of Hebrew thought with minds too rigidly western in their logic. Hebrew thinks directly, and does not distinguish between primary and secondary action, or between God's directive and His permissive will. God set in order and operation those laws of the mind which bring judgement on evil obstinacy, decree that each wilful act of sin makes it easier to commit the next, and that resistance to God quenches conscience and dulls the soul to the voice of God.

If God decreed such laws, says the Hebrew, He therefore constructed the situation. But God cannot, by His very nature, be the author of any evil, and the western mind must think of this matter in another way. God 'hardened Pharaoh's heart' only in the sense that He was the giver of the command which brought Pharaoh's obstinacy to the point of revelation. Pharaoh hardened his own heart (as the Biblical account itself recognizes, 8.15), and by God's decree it became more and more easy for Pharaoh to continue in his folly.

'An obstinate man,' said Frances Ann Butler, a century ago, 'does not hold opinions, they hold him, for when he is

78

once possessed with an error it is like a devil, only cast out with great difficulty.' Obstinacy is, of course, a will asserting itself without being able to justify itself, and the will of Egypt's Pharaoh was corrupt. Pharaoh was a stupid man, for obstinacy is as much the sign of the stupid as it is of the fundamentally weak. So Pharaoh's understanding became hardened, proof against all persuasion, argument or appeal. It is a sorry state for a man to find himself in, a prerequisite for the ruin of the mind and of the soul.

Meanwhile the props were knocked from under him. Each plague attacked something in which Egypt trusted, the divine river, the sun, worshipped as a god . . . But this fascinating study must be set aside. In these comments we follow the personalities and minds of men at grips with life and circumstances.

Questions and themes for study and discussion on Studies 61–68

1. What forms of secular training are of advantage in God's work?

2. What good things had Egypt to offer Moses?

3. How do men 'harden the heart'?

4. 'Withdrawal and Return' in human experience.

5. 'The wilderness' as a training ground.

6. What did Egypt do for Israel?

7. What are the essential qualities of leadership?

8. Violence.

9. Patience.

69 : Pharaoh Weakens

Exodus 8

Under the pressure of trouble it is the common fashion of men to make large promises. Pharaoh's land and no doubt his authority were heavily imperilled by the strange visitations which fell upon both. The plagues were generally phenomena of which Egypt had some experience, and it was probably easy for sceptical Egyptians to convince themselves that the country was in the grip of a series of interrelated natural catastrophes, which, in course of time, would pass as such visitations commonly do. A mind determined to disbelieve can find reasons for any scepticism, and Pharaoh was not a man to change mind or outlook if he could find pretext or excuse to remain unbelieving.

Twice he wavers. The evil passes, and, being a man without regard for his word or his honour, he goes back upon an undertaking. Bemused by the divine honours which surrounded his person, and buttressed about by sycophants, the god-king of the most powerful land in the world saw little call to bow to a subject tribe which he despised, or to the deity which people so abandoned professed to serve and to invoke.

Pharaoh was also a cunning man. Hence his two suggested compromises (25, 28), one rejected outright, and the other tentatively met (26, 29). There is no virtue in cunning. Discretion is a part of wisdom, and to be found in men of reason and sound sense. Cunning is a species of instinct, which baser men share with the brutes themselves. Moses goes so far as to charge Pharaoh with deceit. There could be few more serious charges. No one ever deceives in a good cause. It is well always to remember this simple truth. In the first great work of European literature, the *Iliad* of Homer, Achilles tells the deputation which had come to plead with him, and beg him to aid the wavering Greek army:

> *Who dares think one thing and another tell,*
> *My heart mistrusts him as the gates of Hell.*

The judgement which falls upon deceit is inability to see or to apprehend the truth. Pharaoh became the sorry victim of his own lying. He was unable to grasp the smallness of his person before Almighty God, or the imminence of judgement. It is difficult to humble vanity and self-esteem, and the whole condition of Egyptian monarchy fed these vices. Read Shelley's poem *Ozymandias*.

70 : Pharaoh Blunders On
Exodus 9 and 10

In all unbelief there is necessarily a large opinion of self and a small opinion of God. Ironically enough, the mighty catastrophes which had befallen Egypt were sufficient to make a normal, intelligent man aware of his smallness, weakness and helplessness. At the same time the cymbal-beating priests, the worshippers of animal deities, and the great hierarchical corporations, which held the land in their grip, were quite unable, by ritual, by prayer, or by sacrifice, to relieve the stricken country of its disasters.

It was therefore simultaneously obvious that the God of Moses was in action against those who sought to defy His decree. It required some steadfastness of unbelief to carry on in pride and obstinacy. Unbelief can only darken and destroy. Egypt was suffering from the madness of its king, preoccupied with maintaining his high estate, untaught, unwilling, and unready to surrender to any power. Thereby he would admit the existence of that which was greater than himself.

Pharaoh wavers once or twice. He suggests more compromises (**10**.7–11, 24). He even takes the word 'sin' upon his lips, and at that moment was the nearest he came to salvation (**9**.27). To observe the struggles of the man is to have no doubt that he was not the puppet of a judgement against which he had no chance of resistance. He was the victim of an obstinacy which he utterly refused to surrender, of a pride and self-esteem, which he was determined at all costs to maintain.

Even in his moment of near-enlightenment he cannot accept in all completeness the full blame, certain though it is that he was the key to the whole deadly tangle of events. He drags his people into the orbit of his own guilt (**9**.27). Certain it is that they lay within the orbit of his judgement. The land was polluted under his feet, for in this world no man is able to sin by himself. Somehow, somewhere, all sin escapes abroad, and infects. It cannot be contained within any restricted context of time or place. Nor can we 'with the deed trammel up the consequences', as we have already seen.

The last grim verse of ch. **9** contains a sombre truth. To turn the face from blessing is to have the face of blessing turn away. Rejected truth is dangerous. A ghastly last illustration was looming.

81

71 : Moses as Leader

Exodus 11 and 12

Consider Moses at the peak of his career. This is his 'finest hour'. Without flinching he has outfaced the angry king and endured his treacheries. His own anger (11.8) was natural enough. There is, no doubt, such a phenomenon as righteous anger. In Matt. 23 the 'wrath of God' moves in the words of Christ. It was loosed against false leadership, against self-advancement which, feeding its own desires, cared nothing for the sufferings of those whose helplessness meets the consequences of their leaders' sins. The land of Egypt was to endure again the results of the royal obstinacy.

Coolly and sternly Moses carried out God's commands. Note that in the command to the departing slaves to collect material recompense from the nation that had for such weary years enslaved them, there was no abating of God's righteousness. Neither Moses, nor the multitude which carried out his directions, committed any act of deception or theft. The 'borrow' and 'lent' of the AV[KJV] (12.35 f.) are one of those clumsy renderings which have so lamentably distorted meaning. To be consistent, Judg. 5.25, where the same word occurs, would require the rendering: 'He borrowed water and she gave him milk.' And 1 Kings 3.11 would appear: 'Because you have borrowed this, and have not borrowed for yourself long life . . .' Or take 2 Kings 2.10, which, incorporating the same perverse rendering, would read: 'And Elijah said to Elisha: You have borrowed a hard thing.'

Is it not clear enough from such contexts that the word should be translated 'ask'? The Israelites did no more than collect a tiny fragment of the vast compensation due to an emancipated nation from their overlords. Much of the collected wealth went later into the adornment of the tabernacle. Moses, at the height of his power, was called to no deception (11.3). His prestige, if one combs the record of his dangerous diplomacy, will be seen to be that of a man who is under orders and obeys. No false move could be made now. Step by step, Moses disentangled the great caravan of the freed slaves from society and the land. It demanded steady nerves, confident faith, and a certainty of goal—three prime requisites of leadership.

72 : Moses' Courage
Exodus 14

The mighty wind drove back the waters which covered, it is thought, more of the Suez isthmus in those days, and left the sea a defence ('a wall' does not imply visibly upstanding water) on both flanks. But this is by the way; we are looking at the man, not the event. It does seem evident that both Israel and the Egyptians saw what seemed an abnormal tidal phenomenon. As with the ten plagues, which were exaggerations of natural phenomena, there was room for the sceptical to doubt, and for 'hardening of heart'.

It was an uncanny situation, none the less, and the mass of the people needed above all an infusion of courage. And the one who led them, at this moment, needed above all to be brave. Moses' situation was exactly that of Isaiah, centuries later, when he called Hezekiah's Jerusalem to 'quietness and confidence'. Linger over 14.13. Courage consists not in overlooking danger, but in facing it in God's name. All true courage is cool and calm. It is not a brutal defiance which constitutes real bravery but a certain serenity of strength. It is a firm resolve. It was a time of crisis—a 'hinge of fate'.

The way out of a difficulty is seldom retreat, never retreat when the path of duty, God's will, or righteousness, goes straight ahead. The path to safety for the harassed host was through the formidable barrier that lay across their path. They had no means of knowing that it would melt away in front of their resolution to advance. There are times when faith alone avails. Hence the exhortation of 14.13 to courage and quietness. There was nothing at the moment which anyone could do. It was the time when God alone could devise a means of salvation. Such intervention sometimes waits for faith to act.

It was a lonely moment for Moses. Alfred de Vigny, in his magnificent poem on Moses, catches this thought. Preeminence has this penalty, as Elijah found. It can be friendless, exalted beyond the common fellowship of men, and painfully sundered. The rank and file of the Church might remember this. Leaders sometimes crave for something more than honour. They yearn for fellowship, the familiar warmth of ordinary men.

73 : Moses the Poet

Exodus 15; Psalms 90; 91

Psa. **90** was traditionally ascribed to Moses, and the next psalm stands in a natural sequence significant for those who respect the insight of the editors of the psalter. It is very probable that Moses was the writer of both poems, and that the closing verses of Psa. **91** refer to this very event.

In the formed and mature poetry, already showing the parallel rhythms of thought characteristic of Hebrew verse, we see another facet of the character of the man. His education among the aristocracy of Egypt made him, no doubt, aware of literary artistry, but whence the characteristically Hebrew form? It seems evident that he kept his contact with his own people so jealously that he was able, in the hour of his triumph and exultation, to slip into their national modes of poetry and song.

Some of the world's greatest poetry has flowed from the joy of a triumphant faith. The prophets, especially Isaiah, are an illustration. The poems in the opening chapters of Luke, rescued by him from oblivion, are examples. So are multitudes of great hymns. We should never sing in worship with unworthy, mean and insipid words.

Observe in four words in Exod. **15**.20 a flash of light on Moses' loneliness, that burden of which de Vigny wrote. Miriam was 'Aaron's sister'. She was also Moses' sister, but Israel knew her otherwise. Moses had grown up in the princess' palace. His way of life was remote from that of the enslaved Hebrews. However frequently he managed to visit the family of which he had become aware, nothing could prevent his seeming one of another world. His stature, for all the meekness which had become a part of him, was such that his brother and sister were quite unable to bridge the gap which lay between them. In Num. **12**.1 f. we find the two united against their great brother. It is a sad situation. People are lonely, said someone, because they build walls and not bridges. This is not always so. It seems to take two to build a bridge. Christ was lonely. Read how He 'walked ahead' on His last journey up from Jericho to Jerusalem. If we must pay this price for leadership, let it be remembered that One is 'with us always' (Matt. **28**.20; Mark **10**.32; Luke **18**.31–34).

74 : Moses' Loneliness
Exodus 17

The remoteness and isolation of the great leader is repeatedly evident in the story. There is something almost anticipatory of Christ Himself in his experience, and that perhaps is a fact of life for all who seek to tread the path of Christ. The restless, fickle multitude blamed the leader (2), almost to the point of pelting him with stones (4). There is little that is more difficult to bear than ingratitude. Such a return for benefit conferred is, as Shakespeare once put it, harsher than the blast of any winter wind. Moses had given up rank, wealth, a career, the ease and comfort of life among the great and powerful, to serve this battered multitude of emancipated slaves, at the cost of hardship, rejection, misunderstanding, and all the advantages this world has to offer. The least recompense he might have expected was some show of realization on the part of those he sought, at such cost, to help, some measure, in short, of gratitude.

He found none. He was blamed for the labour of the desert march, in positive danger when water failed. God vindicated him, as God will. The fact that water behind a thin veil of rock, which can yield to a sharp blow, is a phenomenon of Sinai is no diminution of the miracle which took place. In his extremity Moses was aided, and then called upon to pray for the graceless multitude in their next conflict. Perhaps the most significant feature of the story of the battle with the desert dwellers is that a new character appears in the story.

Moses has been too harassed, too much alone. His burdens were beginning to produce their wear and tear. It is interesting then to note, in this chapter and the next, the coming of aid, unobtrusive, unlooked for. Joshua makes his unheralded appearance, and Moses finds fellowship from Aaron and Hur in the place of prayer. Perhaps Moses is learning a lesson which he found it a little difficult to learn, and at which we shall look again in the next section—the need to share the load of leadership, and to call in others, especially younger men, to aid and fortify. There are those who withhold the help that man should give to man. There are also those who find it difficult to receive it.

75 : Jethro
Exodus 18

It was remarked of Joseph's Egypt (Study 51) that those in high authority seemed to be able to choose reliable subordinates and successfully to delegate to them their functions. It is a supreme requirement of all leadership to be able thus to hand down control, to be able to pick reliable helpers and to trust them. Perhaps the court in which Moses had learned the ways of rule lacked this facility, perhaps Moses, a known alien, was himself excluded from all office, or perhaps, by some quirk of character, he found it difficult to delegate authority.

To be sure, a vast cultural and social gulf yawned between him and the enslaved tribes whom he sought to lead to freedom. He appears to have trusted Aaron, but even that confidence was not destined to stand the strain and tension of events. He was one of history's mighty law-givers, and was to be the agent of God in giving His people a judicial code.

Meanwhile Moses himself was the sole fount of law and justice. His loneliness perhaps found yet another form of expression here. The task was overwhelming him, and the arrival of Jethro, his father-in-law, was providential. There is something touching in Moses' welcome (7), which throws a fine light on the old man's worth and graciousness in Moses' eyes. He comes into the camp like a breeze of common sense. Clearly he, too, was in the line of God's people, and had high and noble concepts of religion and faith. The testimony of his son-in-law was a blessing to him, and he repaid the enlivenment and clarification of his faith (11) by practical advice in the dispensation of justice in the camp (17-23). It is a testimony to Moses' respect for the Midianite priest that he gave heed, and found, when called upon to act, that the people beneath him were not entirely without ability. Those willing to divest themselves of authority not infrequently encounter this surprise. Jethro departed (27), having in a few sane words played a constructive part in history. He had anticipated the Law of Moses (20), and given God a voice.

Moses was strengthened by his delegation of rule. Nothing more impairs authority than too frequent use of it, and he now had a buffer. He sat now not as a rower but steersman, seldom seen to stir.

76 : Moses the Lawgiver

Exodus 19 and 20

Moses was a teachable man. All meek men are. We learn from Deut. 1.9–15 that he allowed the people to elect their own officers. But it is possible to surrender authority upwards, as well as downwards, and it is not without some significance that the giving of the Law follows Jethro's departure from the camp. The story shows this movement of history to rest upon a divine initiative, but it is also a law of spiritual progress that God acts when His outreaching grace encounters the outreaching hands of faith.

There is a certain significance in the fact that Moses' code is not the first in history. We have already in the story of Abraham (Study 22) had occasion to mention the code of Hammurabi. Other codes of law are also known, and certain features of the Mosaic ordinances are not without parallel in earlier legislation. The Hebrew law is unique in its purity, its theocratic basis, the divine authority it claims, and for its place in the whole complex of Scripture.

Moses was a learned man (Acts 7.22). He knew that society was founded on law, and he was undoubtedly conscious, not only of Egypt's law, but of the codes of other Middle Eastern nations. It may be presumed that he thought on these matters when he found himself the leader of a nation without such benefits. And it sometimes happens in life that a turn of events will bring a project into focus, and canalize a half-formed purpose. God guides thus. If a man is committed to the doing of God's will, the slow moulding of events, the long pondering and meditation of a mind that does not simply seek its own advantages, lead suddenly to moments of compulsion, and calls to action.

Jethro was a catalyst. His sharp, lucid counsel brought Moses to one of those points of readiness which mark the crises of God in a human life. God called in this way. Sinai awaited Moses. Note the new ease with which the leader slips into the new pattern of leadership. He calls the elders (19.7) to whom he has passed a measure of his authority. The ready response of the people, who seemed supremely conscious of the great moment that was approaching, must have appeared to Moses the final confirmation.

87

1. Courage as a virtue. What of rashness?
2. The uses of loneliness. Need we be lonely?
3. Consider Psa. **91** over against Psa. **90**, and Moses' words and experience.
4. The cost of leadership. How can the rank and file help?
5. Delegation. Why do leaders hesitate to delegate?
6. The 'practical man' in God's work.
7. Why is law necessary?

77 : Bezaleel
Exodus 28.1–11; 35.30–35; 37.1–29

It should not surprise us to find an artist among the characters of Scripture. Bezaleel, the son of Uri, the son of Hur, must have been a very young man, if he was the grandson of Moses' still-active colleague. Of his colleague, Aholiab (31.6), we have not even this tenuous clue. These were men of skilful hands and cultivated minds, demonstrations, both of them, that in the harshest conditions of life the divinely given love of beauty can survive. Their indomitable spirits had been able to extract the essence from the majesty of Egypt's art which stood around their slavery. Their training in the working of wood and metal must have been, like Joseph's, in the place and time of servitude.

It was Jacques Maritain who remarked that all art is a creative effort of which the well-springs lie in the spirit, 'and which brings us at once the most intimate self of the artist and the secret concurrences which he has perceived in things by means of a vision or intuition all his own'. This surely is what the saying of **31.3** means. A soul prepared by its own cherished love of beauty in colour, material, line and form, was touched by the Spirit of God to deeper understanding.

The object which the artist shapes, vase, picture, vestment, or any work of the hands, must, if it is truly a work of art, express something other than itself. It must be a sign as well as an object. A meaning must lie within it, containing a message for man. The Tabernacle and all its furnishings had precisely this significance. It is wrong to elaborate too far and standardize meanings. The whole impact of the lovely tent and its instruments of worship is meaningful, and the particular meaning of some of its aspects may vary with the viewer. Above all it showed God's presence, holy but accessible, in the camp of His people. If the highest function of art is to make man aware of a higher reality, Bezaleel and his men, by their consecration to the task, were preachers of the first order.

It is the perversion of art by evil which so often obtrudes today, when literature, music and other forms of the spirit's symbolic self-expression, are devoted to causing awareness of *lower* realities. C. S. Lewis makes a powerful point in *That Hideous Strength,* when he shows corrupt forms of art used to break down the mind's perception of the true and the ordered. Poetry without rhythm, music in shattered forms, are an expression of a disordered spirit in revolt against the discipline of the universe. We glimpse Bezaleel through these truths, a serene man, seeing deeply into the meaning of things. The 'skilfulness of his hands' reflected God (Psa. 78.72).

78 : Aaron and the Elders
Exodus 24.9–15; 32.1–6

The two passages must be read side by side. They are a vivid light on Aaron's lack of leadership. The elders of Israel, along with the priestly family (24.9), were privileged to see a vision of God. What this means exactly we do not know. Sinai was the scene of strange phenomena, and, as always in the dealings of man with God, faith was no doubt demanded. There was, if this situation is like that which is experienced so often in life, room for the determined sceptic to doubt. Otherwise how could men so enlightened and privileged, have sinned so grievously and idolatrously as they did (32.1–6)? There were those who saw 'no beauty' in Christ.

When Moses and Joshua moved further up the mountain, Aaron and the seventy elders were bidden remain on the lower foothill (still known as the Mount of the Elders) until Moses returned. When Moses finally did return, Joshua alone was with him. The rest, led by Aaron, or unrestrained by Aaron, had abandoned the post of duty and disobeyed instructions. And Aaron's sons were watching.

It thus came about that Aaron faced the tense situation in

the camp. The people, corrupted and soiled by long slavery, had not risen to Moses' purity of worship, and they received no enlightenment from the weak and perhaps frightened Aaron. They demanded vociferously and disloyally that which they had seen in Egypt, some visible representation of the deity who had brought them out of bondage. Instead of resisting the popular clamour, which he would not have been forced to face had he remained where Moses had directed him to stay, Aaron produced some golden representation of the Egyptian calf-god Apis, and called it Yahweh. There were craftsmen in the camp, as we have seen, and he must have deflected some of them from their nobler tasks to turn them to this idol-making.

The people then fell into a base pagan orgy (6), with such obscenities of carnal worship as took place in Egypt at the celebration of more than one fertility cult. Aaron said no word. Cowards cannot lead. Crowds can be terrifying, but brave men can face them out. Aaron could speak well. He had little else.

79 : Moses the Intercessor

Exodus 32.7–18

Moses is never more Christlike than he appears at this moment (11–13). He has suffered much ingratitude and much stupidity at the hands of the horde of slaves which he had sought, at immense cost, to lead into freedom and nationhood. He had been engaged in giving them a code of law, and a system of worship which should meet the deep needs which found crass, hasty and unsanctified expression in the demand for the golden calf. His first reaction, none the less, was to stand in the breach, 'two arms outstretched to save'.

Consider the theme of his prayer. He recalls the past, deepest ground of confidence for all petition and intercession. He is urgent for the honour of God before a watching and cynical pagan world. He pleads in the name of the honoured dead, and falls back upon the known and sacred words of the ancient covenant. This must have been the prayer of a man of prayer, habituated to converse with God, and living in the light of divine promises.

But again observe how promptly he turned to this supreme resource. Abraham Lincoln once said that he frequently found himself driven to his knees by the overwhelming conviction that he had nowhere else to go. 'My own wisdom', he said, 'and that of all about me, seemed insufficient for the day.' Somewhere up the rugged screes of darkened Sinai, with Joshua alone there to see, Moses, still not in full knowledge of the disaster which had taken place in the camp, thus fell to intercession.

God heard him, for prayer is not overcoming God's reluctance to save, it is rather a laying hold of His vast willingness to do so. The love of God for the rebel people was not to be surpassed by Moses' own yearning over them . . . The prayer over, Moses strode on, the Law in his hands. He knew now that he must act. It was Jeremy Taylor who said : 'The body of our prayer is the sum of our duty, and as we must ask of God whatsoever we need, so we must watch and labour for all that which we ask.' There are times, as Moses knew, to 'be still, and know that I am God'. There are also times to be up and doing. Strengthened in this firm conviction, without a fear, accompanied by his one faithful henchman, Moses moved down towards the sounds of revelry which marked the camp.

80 : Prince of Egypt

Exodus 32.19–35

Moses was a meek man, but all meekness left him when he entered the riotous camp. It was a case, if ever there was a case, for righteous indignation. It was an occasion for the prince of Egypt, which Moses was trained to be. That hidden person was to appear again, more disastrously, at the end of Moses' career. On this more justifiable occasion, anger still made him overact to the vast provocation. There was no need for the terrible gesture of dashing to destruction the tablets of the Law, the crown of his work for Israel. The fearful symbolism of the pulverized calf scattered on the water of the host was another reaction of the wrath which held him, and that perhaps had justification. So, too, in the context of rebellion so massive, had the swift surgery in the camp. A long process of history might have been severed at this point had weakness allowed disaffection to survive, smoulder, and later rekindle. Time was to show that the roots remained.

Aaron might well have been terrified. Before the flaming

majesty of his brother, he appears again the weak and contemptible man he could, on occasion, be. He cringes (22), lapsing into the address observed towards Egyptian royalty. He shifts all blame on to the rebel mob (23). Worse than this, he lies. He gives the impression that no fashioning, no labour of creative hands or human workmanship, attended the making of the golden calf. It was a miracle, a mystery, for he had merely cast in the surrendered gold, 'and there came out this calf' (24).

It was only after the telling of Aaron's lie that Moses looked more closely at the crowd, and saw the evidences of the tempest of debauchery which had swept the camp. The sons of Levi had remained uncontaminated. They would have stood loyally by the feeble Aaron in the moment of his testing, had he called boldly on their aid. It was his ultimate shame to stand rebuked by the rank and file of the priestly tribe of which he was the leader. Levi was loyal to Moses, and would have stood by Moses' brother. Their aid had not been sought in the hour of crisis—a common fault of man . . .

The storm in the heart and mind was over. With broken words (32) Moses, again the intercessor, pleads for them. It is a touching close to the tale of disappointment and swift, decisive wrath.

81 : Moses in Triumph
Exodus 33; 34; 40

Moses, at this point in the story, stood at the peak of his career, and some basic features of his character become visible. The incident of pagan backsliding under the Mount of the Law was a crisis. Moses dealt with it in a manner which foreshadows the very work of Christ. He was never more intimate with God, and never more identified with Israel. He took the sins of his people on his own shoulders, and suffered for them.

The mysterious events on Sinai at least teach that the great man who led Israel advanced at this time to the heights of his worth. No man can associate with God without carrying some aura of that fellowship. A deep and compelling realization of his utter dependence fell on Moses (33.15). It is possible only to guess, in a man so taciturn, what profound work had been done in the soul throughout these awesome weeks. The glow upon Moses' countenance, which daunted the people who saw him as he returned from the mountain, was the expression of an inner sanctification which proceeded from the indwelling spirit of his life.

Moses had, in fact, passed all the tests. He had refused the prospect of personal power, a new race with him as founder. He had chosen instead the role of advocate and intercessor, almost of sin-bearer. He had wrought to completion the project which God had laid on his heart, the giving of a Law to a mass of slaves whom he led to liberty. He had thrown into the scale his personal happiness, the quietude he had learned at last in the long desert years to love, he had stood alone, or in a place where he thought he might be alone, save for one faithful young man . . . Scan the studies and see what Moses had endured.

Such times are times of recommissioning. When the ready and surrendered spirit of man is open to receive and hold the ever available, enabling and empowering grace of God, a blessed conjunction is effected. Observe in the closing chapter of Exodus Moses' serenity, command and quiet, confident leadership. The babe in the papyrus boat of the opening of the book has become one of the strong men of history.

Questions and themes for study and discussion on Studies 77–81

1. The function of art.
2. Evil in art.
3. Aaron's failure. His reasons.
4. The power of the mob.
5. When should we pray?
6. 'Be angry and sin not'.
7. The man God uses.
8. Serenity.

82 : Moses' Weariness

Numbers 11

Moses was made, like any one of us, of flesh and blood. The burden of his task was bearing heavily upon him. He was weary to death with the load of leadership, loneliness, and the daily ingratitude of those whom he sought to aid. All this can be read in his complaints (11–15). Much is smugly said by some preachers about complaining. It ranks with anxiety as a target for heavy moralizing. It is, none the less, a human reaction, not perhaps admirable, but to be understood only by those who have borne the burden of the day.

Elijah, as we shall later see, was broken nervously by the strain of carrying a people's fault, and Moses carried a load as heavy. Elijah, like Moses, hid nothing of his pain, but put it into plain words in the presence of God. To look through the psalms is to receive similar instruction. Again and again, especially in the early psalms, some deep trouble afflicts the spirit of the writer, and the psalm of his complaint is full of frank and vivid words giving voice and expression to distress.

This is how to deal with the malady. Life has its tensions under which, at times, the spirit of man is likely to break. To cover and conceal the pain is only to drive its poison deeper into the spirit. It is sound therapy both viewed spiritually, and viewed psychologically, to have the matter out of its damaging concealment, and put it into the language of prayer. So did Elijah, so does Moses. And in the process of confession the first step towards healing has been taken. What harms and hurts is what Coleridge called

> *A grief without a pang, void, dark and drear,*
> *A stifled, drowsy, unimpassioned grief,*
> *Which finds no natural outlet, no relief,*
> *In word, or sigh, or tear.*

Read the opening verses of Psa. **22**: 'My God, my God, look upon me; why hast thou forsaken me: and art so far from my health, and the words of my complaint . . ?' (*Book of Common Prayer*). It was part of Moses' faith that he came thus to God with his weariness of soul. God's response was to aid him in his trouble, and to give him the joy of seeing that his example was not in vain. His spirit has fallen upon others too. So Elijah was told that God had still a remnant, who had not bowed the knee to Baal.

83 : Moses' Trouble

Numbers 12

Zipporah was probably dead. The last mention of Moses' Midianite wife was in Exodus **18**, where Jethro brought her to the camp. Moses, if this is the case, married a second time, a woman of Cush, no doubt one of the mixed host which had come out of Egyptian bondage along with the departing people of Israel. Of the woman herself we are told nothing, but it must have been a person of some standing who could satisfy the mind of a man of Moses' stature. This was the whole point of the criticism of Aaron and Miriam. They had cause to fear that Moses had taken a confidant in his wife. What fuller and more necessary function has a wife to give than this? To be sure, wives are taken by men who cannot provide this aid and comfort, but a man schooled in loneliness like Moses would not be likely to make so fundamental a mistake, nor would a woman ill-equipped for the intimacy of the mind be likely to stir anger so deep in the brother and sister who, to this point, had shared a little of Moses' counsel.

But note the reality of the narrative. The prohibition of Exod. 34.16 and of Deut. 7.3 did not cover cases such as this —accepted proselytes of Israel. It was only after the Exile that mixed marriage of any sort was looked upon with horror. And if, as some would have it, the pentateuchal narratives were a priestly fiction of this later age, how could it come about that the great Lawgiver himself is credited with an action abominable in the eyes of later Jewry?

Miriam must have taken the lead, and earned the deeper reproach. In the same event, Moses reveals the 'meekness', which was his highest spiritual achievement. The narrative seems to suggest that such a quality of character is best illustrated in moments of stress and provocation by doing what Moses did—leaving it all to God. Moffatt renders the opening verse of Psa. 62 : 'Leave it all quietly to God, my soul.' Moses did precisely that.

84 : The Prince Once More

Numbers 20

The lesson of this story is a sad one. Worn down again by the pressing burden of the discontented multitude, Moses broke, and lost the quiet self-control he had built up over the long and arduous years. The prince of Egypt leaped out again from the depths in which it had lain hidden. Look at his hot words in v. 10. The reverence, which had long since learned to ascribe all to the God who had guided him, melted away, and the old aristocrat shouted his contempt for the querulous canaille.

Moses, in fact, had fallen short of the meekness which had become the chief mark of his character. Meekness, in perfection, might have borne this day's fearful irritation. Meekness is not insensibility or servility, and there was no call to demean himself before the crowd. Meekness does not cringe. It is benevolent, patient, forbearing, quiet. Like love, its basic element, it 'bears all things'. Meekness has its active and its passive elements. It leads to the subduing of wrath and resentment, and bearing the resentments of others. On both counts the great leader failed.

But why so severe a punishment? Peter likewise failed, allowing, at a moment of pressure and crisis, the old subdued spirit to burst through the crust of long self-discipline and control. Peter was forgiven and recommissioned. Why not Moses? In fact, Moses' rejection for the coming task of leading Israel over the Jordan was not only a punishment. A moment was chosen to allow an ageing leader to see why he would be required to hand over an arduous command to a younger and more vigorous successor.

Moses had demonstrated his limitations. The task ahead demanded a man of iron control and cool determination. Joshua's training had been in a different school, far other than the imperious and lordly ways of Pharaoh's household. Moses had finished his work. It was a great work, nobly done, but he had shown, in the moment of blinding anger, that he was not qualified to perform what lay ahead. Hence his rejection. He lost none of his standing with God, or his worth. He lost the command for the next movement of history, and he knew why.

85 : Moses Prepares
Numbers 27.12–23

An astonishing career is coming to an end. Death is shadowing the great leader, and death in those days held none of the clear hope which came with the risen Christ. Survival was generally taken for granted among all peoples, and it is quite certain that Moses, who had known God so well, had no doubts about another dimension of life beyond the grave.

A vast anthology of faith could be collected from ancient literature on this theme. Whence this consensus of all peoples, were immortality not planted in man's inner being? Emerson was correct when he said that we are much better believers in immortality than we can give grounds for. The real evidence is too subtle, or is higher than we can write down in propositions.

Indeed, could Moses have sustained the unselfish burden that he did, were not the deep instinctive faith as strong in him as it has been in hosts of great men, that purpose is not bounded by the tomb, and all aspiration quenched in dissolution? A belief in the justice of God, and who more firmly than Moses held to this noble thought, demanded then as now the conclusion that life was not a cheating of mankind, and all hope a farce. This was a thought dear to Tennyson:

> *Thou wilt not leave us in the dust,*
> *Thou madest man, he knows not why;*
> *He thinks he was not made to die;*
> *And Thou hast made him: Thou art just,*
> > *—In Memoriam.*

> *Truth for Truth and Good for Good! The Good,*
> *the True, the Pure, the Just—*
> *Take the charm 'For ever' from them, and they*
> *crumble into dust.*
> > *—Sixty Years After.*

But note Moses' calmness. He knows that the end is near, but his first concern is to make sure that the work at which he has toiled for so long, and which stands so critically poised by Jordan, should find worthy hands to continue it. Death is looming but Moses carries on. It is a test of ultimate conviction how man confronts the last enemy. In the ultimate hour Moses 'did as the Lord commanded him' (22). If death is defeated, as the Christian believes, the close of life should find him at his work. Says the old negro song: 'He'll find me picking cotton when He comes.' There is no better armour against the arrows of death than to be busy in the service of God.

86 : Moses Sums Up
Deuteronomy 1

Deuteronomy has suffered much at the hands of the critics, and this is not the place to survey the theories, which range from the fantastic to the plausible, which seek to date and allocate the book. What these studies are seeking is character, and the varied features of humanity which move through the pages of the Bible. We are still in quest of Moses, and, with what is known of the antiquity of literature, there is nothing absurd in accepting a tradition as old as rabbinical scholarship, and accepted by Christ Himself (Matt. **19**.8), that Deuteronomy was the work of Moses, his last will and testament, part of the preparation enjoined upon him as the end drew near.

A man's preoccupations, as life's evening deepens, are some indication of the man. Moses set diligently to work, not only to make certain the succession in the post of leadership, but to make the path for the new leader safe. Judaism, like Christianity, was based on history, and rooted in God's revelation of Himself to man. Moses saw an urgent task in making apparent to the people the story of their call and destiny, and the moral principles inherent in the birth and progress of their race. In the first chapter of Deuteronomy he opens the great story, and sets such a pattern as Joshua followed long years later when his call came, as Stephen followed before the Sanhedrin on the eve of his martyrdom, and which was Paul's constant resource.

Faith and patriotism are vibrant in the story (11). So too is honesty. Observe the tragic close of verse 19: 'and we came to Kadesh-barnea.' That obscure place-name was written on Moses' heart as a term of anguish, the place and time when Israel frustrated his dreams, abandoned their own destiny, and turned obstinate ears to the summons of God. It is a great man who can see all he has worked and longed for shattered in the hands of gross or foolish men, and then can turn, gather up the fragments and begin to build again. That is what Moses did. He loved the errant people through 'the day of provocation', and led them on.

'The style is the man,' as the French saying has it, and Moses is visible in this quiet and measured prose, traversing days and years which were difficult to remember, days of hope deferred in which no one saw the sickness of his heart, days of grinding toil in which none was permitted to see his utter weariness. It was thus that Moses learned to know his God.

87 : Moses and the Future
Deuteronomy 4.1–40

More than one chapter in Deuteronomy might illustrate the theme which Moses stresses here. Read chs. 28 to 32, and consider the story of Jeshurun in 32.15. Moses understood as well as any of the prophets who were to follow him and build the structure of the O.T., that the rise and fall of nations depend upon moral laws. All great movements of mankind have at their core some grand idea. When that central faith decays, then with it the people perish. No nation is destroyed from without which has not first destroyed itself from within.

Moses' education here reveals itself. He becomes strangely like Paul of Tarsus, who was chosen from a context where cultures met and who understood on a wider front than ever Gamaliel alone could have opened to him, the reach of mankind and the task involved in grafting on to the tree of sacred history a new branch, with new fruit.

The urgency of such warnings are light upon the man, light upon the strength of his intellect and of his understanding, light upon the deep yearning and concern which he felt for his people. Moses was conscious of the deeper insight, the loftier comprehension of God and man, of the past and the future, which had been granted him, but unlike some who were to speak for Jewry, this was not transmuted into arrogant superiority, but into responsibility. He saw the truth, and was alarmed lest others should not see it with his clarity. Again he reminds us of Paul, and passage after passage of that great Christian's urgent argument, as he bore 'the load of all the churches'.

How true is the word of the historian J. A. Froude: 'History is a voice forever sounding across the centuries the laws of right and wrong. Opinions alter, manners change, but the moral law is written on the tables of eternity.' Moses would have agreed. He is sounding the note which makes the refrain of chs. 4–6. And he sought, with what success and with what failure history was to show, to pass the truth on, woven with salutary tradition, to his people. Here is the first great prophet-historian speaking. Moses' 'eye was not dim' when he came to life's ending (34.7). Neither was his mind.

88 : Moses the Theologian
Deuteronomy 6; 10.17–21; Mark 12.28–34

John won the title of Theologian, tradition says, because of the penetrating and fundamental statements he made about God—'God is Love', 'God is Light', 'God is Spirit'. Moses might have deserved the same honour by his reduction of the essence of the Law to the fundamental truth of 6.4 f.

It was the great glory of Israel, and it goes back to the primitive revelation accorded Abraham, to grasp the truth that God is One. In a world of gross polytheism this was miracle indeed, and points to something more than the insight of a human mind, however brilliant, however upright, it may have been.

Moses took up the thread of thought from Abraham. It was the patriarch's grasp of essential truth that set the thought of faith, and the uplift of the trusting heart, at the centre of religion. Moses saw that love was also the response God sought. He had called history to witness that such a response was logical. Ponder v. 12, which speaks of history, of Moses' own experience, and then, after the fashion of Scripture, assumes a significance beyond that of the writer's first intent. There is more than one house of bondage from which God gives emancipation.

To love God truly is to keep the Law, and it was this thought which the Lord Jesus caught up from Moses, applied and extended. And if the love of God is a real experience, no portion of life or activity is divorced from that preoccupation (8 f.). Herein lay the saving thought for Judaism, but what did Judaism do? Verse 8 illustrates. It was shining poetry. The legalists took the words as dullest prose, and literally festooned hand and forehead with written, ornamented fragments of the Law.

But it is Moses we seek, as the last rays of his life's sun rest on him. And what a mind and spirit was this, so to penetrate the centre of God's grace and man's reaction to it! Here are assembled in one chapter the holy triad of 1 Cor. 13, faith, hope and love. Love cannot be exclusively 'beamed'. Moses loved God for God's deliverance. He was quite unable, in the same reaction, to do other than love his fellow men. We again meet the yearning care, that not only for one enlightened generation, but for all time the tremendous thought should hold in its first power (20–25).

89 : Moses the Intercessor
Deuteronomy 9

It is a tender light on Moses' character that in these last days he moved back in vivid memory to the day he bore the Christ-like burden of his people's sin. If one hour must be picked from a life so sacrificial, as Moses' finest, it was surely the hour under Horeb when the multitude had touched the depths and their leader became their intercessor. He bore the scars upon his heart of that day's testing.

We remarked that, if a man loves God in truth, he must of spiritual necessity demonstrate that love by love towards his fellows. 'Love,' Luther remarked, 'is an image of God, and not a lifeless image, but the living essence of the divine nature . . . Faith, like light, should be simple and unbending; while love, like warmth, should beam forth on every side and bend to every necessity of our brethren.'

Moses, to be sure, had been unsparing in the stern severity with which he suppressed that dire rebellion. All history for his people swung on that day's hinge. But the man's real heart was shown in his agony of pleading for the people, which he remembers now in poignant terms (25–29).

There is a line of fruitful study here, for intercession was one of the strongest notes in prayer in this period. Witness Abraham pleading for Sodom. In Moses' prayers this feature was prominent (Exod. 32.11 ff., 31 f., 33.12–16; 34.9; Num. 11.11–15; 14.13–19; 21.7; Deut. 9.18–21; 10.10). It is taken for granted that great souls availed with God to win blessing for others, and in that very fact is part of the preparation for Christ.

There is no diviner task for the Christian today than to make others think of his Lord. The greater characters of the O.T. performed a similar function. The image of the Coming One takes form and shape in them. We have observed this spiritual phenomenon in Abraham (Study 11f.) Joseph, and now in Moses. Christ is the supreme Intercessor (Isa. 53.12). The function is one in which the aged can find unbroken usefulness. Moses was old, and the old may still pray. Prayer fulfils some law. It is a privilege of participation in His work which God grants to His own. It is an imitation of Christ. We need know no more.

90 : Moses the Poet

Deuteronomy 32 and 33

Moses closed his life with poetry. The first poem in the Bible, as Professor D. J. Wiseman pointed out to me as we drove one crystal day through New Zealand's Waipoua Forest, is a poem of married love. Adam uttered the ecstatic words for Eve (Gen. 2.23 f.). It is fitting that the Pentateuch, the first great movement of the Bible, should similarly end with poetry. Like David and Isaiah, Moses was a poet, and if poetry, as Shelley said, is 'the record of the best and happiest moments of the happiest and best minds', then Moses' twilight was blessed indeed.

Moses had learned in suffering what he taught in song. Look at Psa. 90, which is also ascribed to the great Lawgiver, and also Psa. 91, placed next to it in hint of similar origin. Both psalms illustrate what has been said. Distilled from life's strife and testing came truth which clothed itself in imagery and words charged with emotion. In Moses' last song trace the richness of the word-pictures—the rain, with the brown desert growing green under its cool beneficence, the rock, in the shadow of which the weary found rest in the ruthless heat of the midday sun, the eagle, which nested on the high crags, and covered her nestlings with mighty wings, the vine, one of the fruits of the land, and the everlasting arms of God, like the arms of parent or shepherd carrying the helpless to safety.

This is a side of Moses' character which might have dried and withered in the aridity of legislation and administration. He might easily have become a man of cold intellect, wary of the emotions, and suspicious of the movements of the heart. It was his faith and his love for God which preserved him from such atrophy. True religion must satisfy the mind, but it also enlivens the heart, for love, and its children, pity, compassion and mercy, are not the products of cold thought, but the fruit of the deeper understanding of the heart.

Moses had now only to bid farewell. Alone he climbed the mountainside. The broad green ribbon of the Jordan river plain widened to his view. The stream wound deviously through the fertile valley floor. The foursquare keep of Jericho showed afar amid its smudge of palm trees. But Moses, as he had said in poetry, was not alone.

Questions and themes for study and discussion on Studies 82-90

1. Frankness in prayer.
2. The duty of fellowship in prayer.
3. Confession. Where should it be made?
4. In what ways was Moses disqualified for further leadership?
5. Courage and death.
6. With six months to live, what would you seek to do?
7. What significance has the history of your own people?
8. What spiritual significance does the Epistle to the Hebrews discover in the story of Kadesh-barnea?
9. In what sense did Moses understand Jewish 'exclusiveness'?
10. Consider 'freedom' and 'bondage' in N.T. contexts.
11. Intercession as part of prayer.
12. What hints of Moses' authorship are contained in Pss. 90 and 91?

91 : Nadab and Abihu

Leviticus 10.1–11

No one knows the exact nature of the 'unholy fire' mentioned in this passage. The sharp judgement which fell on those who used it finds its moral justification in the nature of the task Aaron's two sons were called to perform. They stood at a critical point in the religious history of mankind, and those who hold the belief that a process of revelation was going on must grant the need for sharp lessons in matters vital to that revelation and its security.

Whatever Nadab and Abihu did, it was some act of irreverence, some error which revealed the lightness with which they held the intensely meaningful law and ritual committed to

103

their hands. That which does present a greater problem to the modern reader of the Old Testament is Moses' command to Aaron to withdraw from the whole process and ritual of mourning for the two dead men. Is this a trait of hardness on Moses' part, or is it designed as a reinforcement of the sanctity of the Tabernacle, which had been violated by Nadab and Abihu?

The second suggestion may have some weight, but only if it is associated with Aaron's own fault. Aaron was responsible for the attitude of the two men which had led them to disaster. He had by his faulty and craven example encouraged their casual attitude towards divine things. When Moses ordered Aaron and the elders to wait in a certain place on Sinai (Exod. 24.12–14), the two sons of Aaron saw their father give way to some pressure, perhaps from the Seventy, and abandon the post of duty (Exod. 32.1). When the multitude arose with impatient shouts of ingratitude towards the man who had led them out of Egypt, Nadab and Abihu saw their father quail before popular clamour and fail to exercise the authority which might have saved the people from the horrible situation into which they fell. When Aaron lied to Moses about the origin of the golden calf, Nadab and Abihu heard their father lie. It is little wonder that, so faultily trained, they themselves failed to obey the letter of some unrecorded ordinance. Hence the stern prohibition on their father.

92 : Caleb

Numbers 13, 14; Deuteronomy 1; Joshua 14.6–15

The geography of the reconnaissance into Palestine is a little difficult to follow, and it could be that two separate parties covered the land, one much further to the north than the other. If this is so it would be a fair guess that Caleb led one party, and Joshua the other, and that Caleb's party returned first and gave its report. This would account for what appears to be a certain repetition between chs. 13 and 14.

This is not of great importance. What matters is the reaction of the men of the two parties. The leaders, Caleb and Joshua, did not carry their men with them. We shall meet Joshua frequently in these chapters of biography. Caleb deserves a special look. But for the one fine hour of his return from the probe into Palestine he might never have been known.

Let it be promptly admitted that there was much to daunt the desert-tribes. Palestine was crowded. It lay across one of the great highways of trade and travel in the ancient world. It still does, and the news of almost every day, with Israel as a pawn and prize of East and West, as a barrier on the road to Africa, as a bridgehead into the Arab world, clearly demonstrates a truth of geography and of history.

The spies saw much to fill them with misgivings. Caleb, a quiet, simple, faithful man, if a guess may be hazarded about him, saw beyond the difficulties. He saw, like the rest, the sturdy little fortresses which studded the land. He was conscious, like the rest, of the power of Egypt which penetrated the area, ready to take a hand against all incursion from the hinterland. The vast difficulties which lay in the task of conquest were as obvious to him as to his timid companions. He simply had faith in the old promises made to the patriarchs.

Courage and faith overlap in the experience of the human personality. One feeds the other. If faith is lacking courage loses its tap-root. If courage is lacking no one can claim to possess faith. We should be glad of a closer look at this strong and valiant man. Our clearest glimpse is of many years later when the land was overrun and Caleb asks, strong as ever in old age, to be permitted to claim his inheritance. Courage in him proved itself in action. Faith, in a manner which would have delighted James, demonstrated its reality in deeds. So must it ever be.

93 : Korah

Numbers 16

Those confident enough to divide an ancient document, on highly doubtful assumptions, into a composite story of several sources, imagine a threefold narrative in this chapter. There is no need, nor indeed, solid grounds, for this conjecture. Three bases of revolt are stated—first, that Moses and Aaron have usurped authority beyond their due, second, that the whole march was a failure, for the comparative security and plenty of their Egyptian bondage had been exchanged for the penury of the wilderness, on the promise of illusory prosperity, and thirdly, that the priesthood was no monopoly of the two brothers, but should be shared.

Admittedly, these three complaints sit awkwardly together, but the very fact throws what light the story may upon the character of Korah. He was obviously the typical demagogue, determined, if one charge failed or did not appeal, to be ready with another. It was a situation like that in Aesop's fable, where the wolf and the lamb drink from the same stream. Korah hoped to gain advantage. Protest is not always wrong, but a remark of Sir Thomas More often applies to such movements: 'Who does more earnestly long for change than he who is uneasy in his present circumstances? And who run to create confusions with so desperate a boldness, as those who, having nothing to lose, hope to gain by them?'

The eminence of Moses was visible, and it is the way of some lesser spirits to envy all who stand above them. Korah had no sincerity, or the rabble-rousing charge of leading Israel into poverty and hardship would not have been added to the political complaints of Moses' autocracy and assumption of authority. Korah, encouraged by the adherence of the petty group who always gather round the disaffected, each for reasons of his own, and commonly for reasons less than honest, sought eminence for himself, not basic justice. Such people are one of the blights of democratic society. The envious man, said Horace, grows lean at his neighbour's success. Moses was no seeker of what men call success. His meekness and compassion are evident in this chapter. But Korah read others by his own preoccupations, and became, in the Bible, a warning for self-seekers. (Num. **26**.9; Psa. **106**.17; Jude 11; cf. Deut. **11**.6.)

94 : Balaam

Numbers 22.1–31

The writers of the New Testament, with wider access to rabbinical tradition than we have, knew more of Balaam than the Old Testament reveals. For that reason it will be a good introduction to this strange story to read 2 Pet. **2**.15; Jude 11; Jas. **4**.4 and Rev. **2**.14. These passages imply that Balaam was a hireling, selling spiritual things for money, and at the same time a cunning and effective diplomatist, who taught the foes of Israel those subtle devices of temptation and corruption by which the moral and spiritual strength of the people might be undermined. On such qualities the vigour of a nation depends, and the insight shown, albeit basely directed, is a pointer to the ability of this foreigner.

He came, significantly enough, from Pethor on the Euphrates, an old area of civilization, where some tradition of Abraham may still have lingered. He was no Canaanite, purveyor of grim superstitions, no wizard of some depraved pagan cult, but more likely, a man conscious of the obligations of higher religion, who knew God, had some regard for His guidance, was conscious of good, and the obligations of his spiritual calling. He sinned, in other words, against the light.

Hence the horror with which the New Testament writers regarded him. They saw his posterity in those who, for their own gain, for the ease of conformity, or in perversity, set out to modify Christianity, and to work out a compromise with the surrounding pagan world of the first century.

Up to v. 14 in the story of this chapter, Balaam has acted without obvious fault. He saw the right, sought God's will, and hearkened to the voice of his conscience. He had, nevertheless, his price, his weak point, and something in his message to Balak, or perhaps in the messengers' own report, betrayed this inherent weakness to a clever man. Hence the second embassy, and hence, it would appear, God's permission to accompany the envoys. God does not change His mind, and Balaam knew God's will in the matter. But Balaam was trying to cover that which he desired in self-will to do, with a convenient veil of piety. It was therefore in judgement upon him that God dismissed him on his way. Even then he was given, like Judas, a last chance to retreat to that which he knew was right. Dumb things have a voice, and an ass was used to call Balaam to heed his conscience.

95 : Balaam's Conscience
Numbers 22.32–41

Even an ass, such is the irony of this passage, could see the stern presence which stood in Balaam's path. He was no doubt moving on in some trepidation, for at the outset of such pernicious enterprises, when an enlightened man moves obstinately forward in despite of conscience, the mind is apprehensive, and fear gnaws the heart. 'Half the wrong things men do,' wrote Robert Watson, 'are done, not in spite of conscience but with its dubious consent, when the first clear decision has been set aside.'

The remark is acute and fits the situation of Balaam exactly. He forced himself forward against the sharp verdict of his first clear enlightenment and found himself in the hands of God, compelled to face the consequences of his chosen course. This is the clearest reading of the story, and takes into account the patterns of Hebrew thought in which God is regarded as the prime mover, because He established the complex of psychological laws which find expression in the situation. This was a matter glanced at when 'the hardening of Pharaoh's heart' was discussed in an earlier study (Study 68).

Balaam's confession of sin (34) was no deep repentance. He was simply baffled in his hireling's course. A crafty programme sometimes escapes from the control of its initiator. God so governs that the very subterfuges and self-seeking of men can be woven into the plan of His purposes. That which a cunning and self-seeking man like Balaam begins to do in self-will cannot always be arrested at the point which the sinner determines. It is always wise to watch the beginnings of sin. We cannot 'with the deed trammel up the consequences', as we have already quoted, or contain in time and place that which we do amiss. Sin is like fire, apt to spread beyond control. Balaam's fundamental greed had landed him in the position which Judas found beyond all management. He was rent between Almighty God, into whose hands he had fallen, and the prince in whose power his life was placed.

96 : Balaam the Prophet

Numbers 23.1–26

Balak no doubt offered his sacrifices to Chemosh, sun-god of Moab, and now Balaam demands like sacrifice to Jehovah. He is the true type of the man who is well conscious of the truth, but unwilling, for love of some cherished advantage, to break his association with corrupt men. There is a pompousness about him which points to this damaging trait of character. With a royal air he bids the prince abide by the altar, and he himself withdraws with mysterious dignity to a vantage-point on the hills to meet his God.

From his high peak the hireling prophet could see the smudge of smoke from Balak's pitiable altar fires behind him, and far away to the east, in the clear desert air, he could look over the sea of Israel's encampment. It required little insight or special revelation to see with whom the future lay—with the broken mountain tribe, or the advancing flood of sternly moral nomads (22.41). This perhaps is why he was willing to listen to the words which formed in his heart, and ready to deliver Jehovah's message. His advantage obviously lay with the newcomers, but the situation in which he found himself was one which required some delicate handling. Balaam had one advantage—his vast prestige with Balak. He played it well, and thought in his base heart to win credit with God for his self-interested faithfulness. Perhaps he had even heard of Moses' advancing years, and envisaged the possibility of stepping into so august a place. For those eaten by ambition, the far skies are no limit. News travels fast among desert tribes, and Balaam may have counted on the words of his prophecy filtering down to the Hebrew camp. Certain it is that the rich poetic words of his utterance brought him no credit nor reward. They rose from evil motives.

Observe how in the very words notes of egotism and self-defence break through. Balaam was none the less a man of keen intellect, and caught, through all the fog of his self-seeking, some vision of the great work God was beginning to do in the deserts behind Jordan. God's words of himself, in spite rose to his lips, and here again was a moment in which he might have reached out and found salvation. It was like the moment when Jesus washed Judas' feet.

97 : Balak
Numbers 23.27–30

Read the whole chapter again, because here is a confrontation indeed. Obtuse superstition is set over against inspired insight. And yet the victim of obtuse paganism is less blame-worthy than the clever man who saw with perfect clarity the shining truth, and yet failed to translate the vision into salutary deeds. The mummeries of heathendom are set in contrast with a breath of genuine prophecy, albeit on the lips of one unworthy of uttering the words.

Observe Balak. He was the ruler of a poverty-stricken land. The rain-laden winds from the Mediterranean had dropped most of their beneficence by the time they reached the purple hill-country between Jordan and the wilderness, and the sacrifices of animals on the altars demanded by the expensive 'holy man' were not of the sort an indigent highland chieftain was likely to look on without thought of the cost. Animals were Balak's wealth.

The whole pathetic simplicity of the man is in view in the closing verses of the chapter. His conception of God determined his outlook. He had built himself a deity in his own image, making him, as the psalmist puts it, altogether like himself (Psa. 50.21). He thought of all beings as having their price. Balak was willing to meet all genuine accounts. In return he expected the goods for which he paid. And God was reckoned among his customers. The proper sacrifices had been made, but with no eye to any deeper meaning than that attaching to any business transaction. God must surely deliver the goods for which such payment had been faithfully made.

Balak's people had known defeat at the hands of the Amorites (21.26–30). Israel had defeated the Amorites, and had refrained from overrunning a broken Moab. Traverse had been refused, and now Balak was harvesting his folly. In the wretched hope that some return might yet be made for his outlay, he took Balaam to yet another eminence and had him prophesy. That is what Balaam did.

There is a lesson in the man. Even with the light of Christ before them there are those who regard their religion as a business transaction, and who 'tithe' to win prosperity, and trust God to rescue from self-chosen folly, and answer prayer according to specifications.

98 : Balaam Again
Numbers 24

Regardless of expense, Balaam demanded similar sacrifices. Either this high-handedness was part of his self-exaltation before the chief, or perhaps he clung blindly to the thought that he might see some way out of his unsatisfactory performance. Or perhaps he still played the desperate double-game of favouring Israel in the guise of doing Moab's will. He was in a highly perilous situation, whichever way the truth lies, and whatever were the thoughts and motives in the subtle shaman's brain, no good clings to them, and no credit is owing to him.

Balaam, at this point, seems overwhelmed by God. Now, with no note of conciliation or excuse in mind for what to Balak appeared the basest of betrayals, Balaam spoke in wild poetry. Here again poured out the words which showed what Balaam might have been, had his life been clean, and had the genuine understanding which he had of the ways of God commanded his personal allegiance. He was, in fact, singularly well-informed about Israel, and even put into striking words a Messianic oracle (17).

Balak was utterly disconcerted. He clapped his hands, the common signal of despots for the devoted bodyguard to appear. No defender appears to have sprung to his master's side at the sound of the imperious signal. No doubt Balaam had been clever enough to take his royal employer to the eminence alone, and without the armed men who might, at the whim of the moment, have been ordered to deal with him. Helpless to order some incantation of cursing, Balak weakly bids the disobedient prophet be gone, and hears in return more self-righteous words, and another burst of prophecy.

Apparently Balaam did not permanently go. It might have been to his advantage to do so. The sequel shows that Balak was still under his influence, and he remained with base and consciously evil advice to win the advantage which Balak had in mind to confer upon him (11). The closing verse of the chapter appears to speak of separation. If so, it was temporary and the hireling returned to give nefarious advice. He may still have had in mind some liaison with Israel. Instead he won a name of infamy.

99 : Balaam's Baseness

Numbers 25

Chapter 31 contains eight verses which round off the story of Balaam, and justify the traditions about the prophet which appear to have been known to the writers of the New Testament. He must have returned from his home to Moab neglecting yet another opportunity to extricate himself from a compromising and evil association. He was drawn back, by his own cupidity, to the place of temptation and disaster. God's patience went unregarded.

The chapter before us and its brief sequels make grim reading. Balaam, familiar with the base sexualities of the fertility cults of the land, cults which, with his genuine knowledge of the true God, he may well have despised, suggested to Balak that the promiscuity of some pagan ritual of the fields be used to seduce the men of Israel. Under Sinai the tribes had fallen into the temptation which such carnality could bring, and the stern code of separation, imposed upon the Hebrews, was primarily designed to form a barrier in such a world against the social and personal evils which the contemporary cults of obscenity and sexual perversion contained.

Hence the sanguinary repression of the popular outbreak. Moabite women, on some Dionysiac revel, must have invaded the camp. The weaker men among the people were drawn into the celebration. They were not the men among whom the destiny of Israel was safe. Hence the stern measures. But Balaam well understood the effectiveness of such an intrusion. To break the walls of morality which surrounded Israel, would ultimately be to break the nation. That law of decadence still functions. Therein lies the deep peril which confronts Christendom today. The walls are crumbling, and the only hope for Western Civilization is in the possible survival of a fortress in the midst, the Christian Church, not compromising, not tolerating the sundry Balaams who speak unctuously of another ethic than that which stands in Christ, but maintaining chastity and separation from the world's evil —such is the only hope for the race.

Balaam died as he had lived. To throw in one's lot with evil and evil men is to invite the fate which falls on such rebellion. It is poetic justice. Balaam had it in him to be a great man, a poet and a prophet. He might have found a place in history and a citizenship among the tribes. He desired this, in all probability, but he wanted it upon his terms, not God's.

1. In what does irreverence consist?
2. Courage, cowardice, rashness and faith. Define each in relation to difficulty.
3. Rebellion. Is it ever justifiable?
4. Conscience and the Holy Spirit.
5. The self-defeat of obstinacy.
6. 'Sin and well-doing cannot be unfruitful.'
7. Balaam and Balak in their modern setting.
8. Christianity and prosperity.
9. False shepherds. See Milton's 'Lycidas' and John 10.
10. What barriers preserve the Christian in an age of exaggerated sexuality?

100 : Joshua Son of Nun

Exodus 17.13, 14; 24.13; 32.17, 18; 33.7–11

An unobtrusive person has appeared five times in the closing chapters of Exodus. He is described only once, and with the utmost brevity: 'Joshua the Son of Nun, a young man . . .' (33.11). He appears in that same context to have been the guardian or keeper of the Tabernacle. We would be glad to know what went on in the mind of Moses' henchman during his lonely vigil in the beautiful place. It was, in fact, his second vigil. When Moses left the elders to wait and watch on the lower slope of Sinai, he moved up into the murk on the mountain with Joshua alone for company (24.13). It seems clear enough from the continuing narrative that Moses was alone on the mountain-top. When he came down to the disordered camp, Joshua was again in his company. The situation, therefore, appears to have been that Joshua waited alone for his master at some point higher up the slopes.

There may have been purpose in all this. Youth, for all the restless cries of the present century, is not in possession of all the answers. From immemorial time, man has sought to hand on his accumulated stocks of wisdom to the next generation.

Youth must lay hold of the heritage, and age must learn when it is appropriate to stand aside and allow youth to take over. And, save in changeless tribal communities, like those of the Australian aborigines, youth commonly takes what age gives, and interprets it in the light of new experience, but youth must beware lest, in its natural impatience, it changes tradition too soon and in the light of experience too tenuous and too brief.

Joshua speaks only once in the few passages of narrative in which he appears. He knew that Moses prayed for him. He knew that Moses was seeking to pass on his immense experience. It is an enormous privilege for a young man to serve an apprenticeship of service under a man of surpassing strength, goodness and knowledge. They are wise who recognize the worth of such a rare tutelage, and make every endeavour to learn. The passing years terminate all things, and nothing more rapidly than that brief phase of life called youth. Joshua recognized this fact, and in his silence and, at times, enforced withdrawal, allowed the lessons of his fellowship with the great to sink deep into his spirit. We shall follow Joshua's progress, and it will be interesting to observe those traits of character which came to him from Israel's first chief and legislator.

101 : Joshua Takes Over

Deuteronomy 3.21–29; 34.1–12; Joshua 1

'Show me the man you honour,' said Thomas Carlyle, 'and I will show you the man you are, for it shows me what your ideal of manhood is, and what kind of a man you long to be.' Through the story of the desert wanderings of Israel, Joshua has appeared consistently and unobtrusively at Moses' side. He is the very image and ideal of the faithful servant and loyal officer. It is obvious that in Moses, Joshua saw greatness. It is equally obvious that he would measure himself against Moses' superb equipment of mind and spirit, his education in all the culture of a great imperial race, trained in a royal household for the tasks of leadership, and divinely commissioned in his office.

Inevitably, Joshua would learn to rely on his hero and his leader. He would draw into the fabric of his own personality traits of Moses' character which would aid and steady him, but which at the same time would check the free and full development of his own characteristic attitudes and personal worth. He would find dependence upon the older man's wisdom and swift insight becoming a part of his daily habit.

In such situations there comes the moment of loneliness and challenge. A parent dies, a leader is removed, and the next generation stands suddenly in the front rank, with no one to command, no one to lead, and a task demanding action awaiting.

Hence the word to Joshua. The word 'success' occurs in Josh. 1.8. It is said that this is its only appearance in all the vocabulary of the Authorised Version (KJV). The word suggests what was the nagging question in Joshua's mind: 'Can I do it?' 'Is the task beyond me?' Montesquieu remarked once that 'success depends on knowing how long it takes to succeed'. Joshua had at least the clear indication that it was going to demand concentration (8) and perseverance, and both, in the conquest of any land set before us, are worth more than talent and opportunity. Not that Joshua was without talent and opportunity. He was an able and a mature soldier. His host stood poised on the frontier of conquest, desert-hardened. He needed, none the less, a strengthening of spirit, and above all a sharp awareness that the leader who had gone from the camp was not the only source of command, direction and guidance. We shall look at this matter more closely in the next study.

102 : Joshua's Encouragement
Deuteronomy 31.7, 8, 22, 23; 1 Corinthians 16.13

Read Joshua 1.1–8 again. It is possible to see in what was said to Joshua, the attitude of mind in which, at this dawn of a new day in his people's history, he looked across the twisting river to the blur of green where Jericho's fortress walls stood among the palms.

He felt weak, fearful and untaught. Then came, the very

echo of the dead Moses' voice, the command to be strong (cf. Deut. **31**.22 f. with Josh. **1**.6). Joshua was no weakling. No man can answer for his courage who has never been in danger, but a trumpet call can nerve the spirit, and Joshua's call came from a Voice he knew to be the word of God for him, and which quite uncannily took up the very words of the one who was never far from Joshua's memory at this hour of crisis. The task was so similar. The Jordan lay across the path as the Red Sea once had lain. Unknown tracts lay ahead, and nothing so tries courage as the unknown. Joshua felt the pull of fear.

'What is strength,' Milton asked, 'without a double share of wisdom?' Milton, scholar as he was, probably had a verse of Horace, the Roman poet, in his mind: 'Force, reft of counsel, falls of its own weight.' To storm across the river, and in a rush of fanatic bravery to assault the walls of Jericho, was no answer to the problems of the day. Joshua needed supremely what he had known so long—wisdom. Moses was gone, but Moses' law remained, and it was Moses, as much as God, which Joshua found in the code which was now the possession of the people.

And so emerges the clear outline of a good man's character —a man conscious of his needs, and of the qualities he lacked, a man who was aware of weakness and inadequacy, and of his own defects of wisdom and judgement, but a man utterly committed to the vast work in hand, prepared to listen, to obey his God, to study to do all things according to God's will. God asks no more of man. Such a man He can use. Josh. **3** and **4**, which should be read, clearly show the steadied personality of the leader of Israel, the new man taking shape.

103 : Nun

Deuteronomy 4.9, 10; 6.7, 20–24; 11.18–21; 32.46

A character too likely to be forgotten must find a place, if not in our study, at least in our imagination, before we leave the first pages of the story of Joshua. Joshua was 'the son of Nun'. The influence of Moses in the life of his faithful deputy is rightly stressed, but long before Moses picked Joshua to be his lieutenant, another man, and perhaps a woman, played a decisive part in the life of the youth who was to lead Israel.

116

Observe the passages from Deuteronomy set out above. It was almost an obsession with Moses to hand on the great tradition. It may have been a memory of his own parents, or of whoever it was who saw to it that the prince in Pharaoh's household should not be cut off from the memory and calling of the race to which his blood belonged, which God used to prompt this deep preoccupation. At any rate, Nun, the father of Joshua, must have obeyed.

We know nothing about him. He is a mere name, like the parents of many another man, who, for good or ill, have left a mark upon the pages of human history. We can only judge Nun by Joshua his son. Francis Quarles wrote three and a half centuries ago: 'In early life I had nearly been betrayed into the principles of infidelity; but there was one argument in favour of Christianity which I could not refute, and that was the consistent character and example of my own father.'

Parents are sometimes unaware of how deep and abiding an influence they have on the character of their children. It is a fair guess that Nun, for all the obscurity which surrounded his earthly life, was a faithful man. So it is with life. It is not given to all to stand in the blaze of prominence. The occasion makes for fame, but does not produce the worth on which fame rests, as Gray remarked to those that lay in Stoke Poges churchyard:

> *Some village Hampden, that with dauntless breast*
> *The little tyrant of his fields withstood;*
> *Some mute, inglorious Milton here may rest,*
> *Some Cromwell guiltless of his country's blood.*

The great men of the world do their deeds and win their laurels. Again and again, it is a wife, a parent, a teacher, a friend, unknown to the record, who has made them what they are.

104 : Rahab

Joshua 2.1–24; 6.17, 22–25; Hebrews 11.31; James 2.25

Rahab had a house which was part of the town wall of Jericho. She may have been an inn-keeper, and 'harlot' could be a pejorative term used for people engaged in this tavern trade, a term, no doubt, at times justified. Jericho lay on a trade-route, and it seems likely enough that the spies who came in with the jostling crowds would wear some fashion of disguise, and follow the itinerant merchants and tradesmen to such hostelries and accommodation as catered for the passing visitors to the valley.

Or Rahab could also have been a temple courtesan whose spirit sickened of the base religions of Canaan which demanded her body's service as a ritual of some foul fertility cult. The fact that Rahab knew all about the great movement of nomadic tribesmen across the Jordan reveals two facts—first, that there was considerable traffic in and out of Jericho, and secondly, that a woman of Jericho was accurately enough informed about the God of the strangers to find in her own mind the pull and urgency of a call to nobler living.

Rahab was a woman of resource and intelligence. She knew how to outwit the royal police, and bravely risked her all in hiding the spies on her flat roof beneath the bundles of flax. She drove a shrewd bargain with the fugitives. It was to include all her family. Her scheme of retreat similarly showed her intelligence. She had sent the pursuers off to the fords of Jordan five miles away across the valley floor. She directed the spies westwards towards the wall of hills which define the Jordan plain towards Judea. Visible from the mound of Jericho is the traditional Mount of the Temptation, an arid wall of rock which was probably 'the hills' of Rahab's phrase.

Rahab had given the spies priceless information. 'What is the use of concrete if the will is weak,' sneered Hitler after Munich in 1938 when his staff marvelled at the toughness of the abandoned Czechoslovakian fortifications. Rahab had shown a Jericho in no condition to withstand the Hebrew onslaught. Battles are won and lost in the minds of men. In all the strife of life it is morale which counts. Now look and wonder at Matt. 1.5.

105 : The New Joshua

Joshua 3 and 4

To read these chapters attentively is to gain a conception of some toughening in the spirit of Israel's leader. There is a dash of Moses' decisiveness about him. He had been bidden 'be strong and of a good courage', and has obeyed the behest. 'There is nothing,' said Hazlitt, 'more to be esteemed than a manly firmness and decision of character. I like a person who knows his mind and sticks to it, who sees at once what, in given circumstances, is to be done and does it.' This is Joshua exactly, as he organizes the crossing of Jordan. He has his host under perfect discipline. The Jordan runs dry, and the machinery of this provision was such as has been seen in the present century, the damming of the stream by earthfalls in a narrow ravine through which the course cuts, further to the north.

Then there was the strange and silent marching round the city, an uncanny proceeding, which could have been spoiled by one man breaking rank, or replying to the shouts of derision and insult which would undoubtedly come from the watching Canaanites on the wall. Joshua could risk the strange manoeuvre only if he knew that his army could be trusted to carry out a command which it was impossible to explain to them, and which to many hard-headed soldiers in the ranks must have appeared the folly and absurdity which the watching Canaanites probably described it in ribald terms.

Joshua had clearly been accepted by a people accustomed to obey the commands of Moses, a 'stiff-necked' people, not given to an easy docility. It must betoken a quality in the man himself which commanded obedience. Sir Philip Sidney said: 'A brave captain is as a root out of which, as branches, the courage of the soldiers doth spring.' Here are the captain and the army which take shape before us in those chapters of strife. Moses' labours were bearing fruit. Moses' successor was 'entering into his labours'.

Note 4.24. It explains a good deal in Joshua's stormy story. A dominant idea held his mind. He wished to magnify God— in a word, to make God, and not himself, appear great in the eyes of the people. Joshua was a man of briefer speech than his old chief Moses, but the purport of his message was the same. No people prospers who degrades or dims the image of God.

106 : King of Jericho
Joshua 5 and 6

We may allow ourselves the liberty, as we look at the men and women of the Bible, to probe in imagination a little behind the text, and picture those who do not stand clear cut in the story, and visible in their detail. We sought in this way to see Nun, the father of Joshua. What of Joshua's enemy, the prince who ruled Jericho?

There is little said about this petty Canaanite chief. He was obviously alert for peril, and in some command of the situation inside the walls of his fortress-town. He was immediately informed of the arrival of the strangers at Rahab's house, and promptly despatched an investigating team. Beyond the recording of these details of promptitude and decision, the Bible has nothing to say.

Palestine was an Egyptian buffer area. From time immemorial until today, the power on the Nile has sought control over the long narrow strip of territory between the Rift Valley and the sea, and these centuries were a period of dominant, though fluctuating, Egyptian influence. The small fortress towns of Palestine were in the hands of chiefs who owed allegiance to Pharaoh.

In the Tell el Amarna letters are numerous communications from places in Palestine begging for help from Egypt against some form of nomad invasion. If Garstang's earlier date for the Exodus and the invasion of Palestine could be otherwise established, these pleas could undoubtedly be referred to the dilemma of chiefs like the ruler of Jericho, left without resource against the Hebrew attack during a period of Egyptian preoccupation at home.

We cannot here go into the question of the date, but the letters from Palestine do speak of the fear which must have been abroad in southern Canaan, whatever the date. For example, Arad-Hiba, king of Jerusalem, writes of people called 'the Habiru', who are on the move: 'They are capturing the fortresses of the Pharaoh,' he says. 'Not a single governor remains. All have perished. Zimrida of Lachish has been killed. Let Pharaoh send help.' And so on. Such was the dilemma in Jericho, whether these strange documents refer to the actual attack of Joshua on the land, or to some similar inroad a century and a half earlier. The king of Jericho, in his small heat-ridden town, amid a servile population, cursed by sombre and sanguinary gods, must have felt a wretched man indeed.

107 : Achan

Joshua 7; 1 Chronicles 2.7

Example, said Edmund Burke, 'is the school of mankind. They will learn in no other.' And it was Kant who set down the ethical principle: 'So act that your principle of action might safely be made a law for the whole world.' Achan cared nothing for principle or example. He set his family a grim pattern of covetousness, and disobedience. At this crisis in the nation's history, discipline, and absolute willingness to obey, were vital. Achan could not see it so. No man is so insignificant as to be sure that his example will do no harm.

Moreover, Israel was moving into the forefront of history with a moral law superior to anything the world had so far known. True, in the Euphrates Valley, Hammurabi had codified the law. The people of Haran and the Hittites had their legal codes. No people had anything quite like the Ten Commandments, nor a Law which referred all sin and righteousness to God alone. And here, on the very threshold of a great move forward in the nation's history, when, as the word to the leader had it (1.8, 9), all success depended on the moral stamina which social righteousness could give, one man opts out, and abandons the very source of all the nation's hope for strength and victory. Achan knew better, he thought, than Joshua and Moses' Law.

He had no care for the future, no concern for his family, involved, as he had seen in the desert and at the time of Korah's rebellion, in the parent's sin. A corrupt environment lay across the people's path. A culture, shocking in its decadence, was symbolized by the material wealth of Jericho. Joshua sought a ritual of separation to which all those who went forward to battle were called to commit themselves. Hence, as with Ananias and Sapphira, the stern punishment. There are high moments of history when all is at stake.

The Septuagint translation of 7.25, 26, which, of course, could represent an ancient text, omits reference to the

121

destruction of family and goods, and since also the pronouns 'him' and 'them' can easily be confused in Hebrew, some have thought that the instructions of 7.15 were not, in the end, carried out. The story, whatever the end was, is vivid evidence of the deep feeling for the solidarity of the community held by Israel at this point of history.

Questions and themes for study and discussion on Studies 100–107

1. What can youth learn from old age?
2. 'When I am weak, then I am strong.'
3. 'Like father, like son.'
4. Defeat accepted is defeat assured.
5. Does the job make the man or the man the job?

108 : Joshua Relives the Past

Joshua 8

The future of a country is secure only in the hands of those who hold a regard for the past. It was Washington who once said: 'We ought not to look back unless it is to derive useful lessons from past errors, and for the purpose of profiting by dearly bought experience.' There is, in the Bible, a dual attitude towards the past. Paul bids us forget that which lies behind, and press on to the future in Christ, but again and again we are bidden with equal authority to consider God's dealing in past days, and build upon the foundations there laid.

It was part of Joshua's strength that he understood these obligations. It is the way of small, weak men to try to destroy the work of those who went before, as though their achievement provoked some invidious comparison with their own doings. Men of moral strength and confidence make every endeavour to weave what others have done into the texture of their own performance.

Joshua must have been mightily conscious of the fact that he captained a new movement of history. The Jordan river was a frontier in time as well as in place. He might easily have been tempted, like those who are unhealthily conscious of a

122

rift called the 'generation gap', to work on entirely new principles, to carve a new path, with new attitudes, new ways. Instead of such damaging folly, he knew that the moral laws on which the present and the future depended had been grasped, applied, and written on tablets of enduring stone in Moses' day.

Hence his action after the next forward movement in the conquest of Canaan. He reaffirmed (30–35) the great principles on which Moses had worked. In a stage-setting deliberately evocative of the past, and recalling the very situation of a great challenge of his predecessor, Joshua reinstituted the ceremony of the blessings and the cursings. He revived and reiterated (35) the lawgiver's words, to the last syllable. It was an act of greatness. Israel was always conscious of its history, and built much hope, much courage, much endeavour upon the knowledge and understanding of it. Joshua set such a course when he took over the work of one of the greatest figures of all time and sought to construct his own contribution upon its solid base.

109 : Adonizedek

Joshua 10

We are tracing in these studies the character and personality of men and women. Hundreds of human beings move through the pages of the Bible for good or for ill. Their words and deeds are woven with the message of the book to teach us what lessons they may. It will be a good practice for those who follow these notes to read the story as a continuous whole, though the specific reading may be only one portion.

In this chapter the person of a Canaanitish chief is chosen as typical of the whole group. This part of Joshua's story is grim reading. The words mingle with the clash of sword and spear, and the reek of burning villages. Adonizedek was one of the small feudal rulers of Palestine who had played his part, like the other petty despots of the land, in spreading the corruption and sanguinary religion which the flood of the Hebrew conquest swept away. It was a day of reckoning.

The land was 'defiled under its inhabitants' (cf. Isa. 24.5), and the men who held authority in town and countryside were morally responsible for the blood and sadism, the cultic murder of infants, and all the other horrors of corrupt humanity which soiled the clean earth. The calamity which befell the 'kings' of Canaan must be judged in the light of these historic facts.

The story is briefly told. Much would be clearer were more words available. Consider the case of another ruler of similar name, Adonibezek, whose story is told with one revealing detail in the first seven verses of the story of the judges (Judg. 1.1–7). The incident happens to record the sombre cruelty of the man which found just retribution at the hands of the Israelites. Cruelty shows utter corruption, and the archaeological evidence from the little towns of Canaan reveals the nature of the communities which the kings who meet their end in this chapter ruled over.

It is a principle of human history that men and nations reap what they sow. It is certain enough that the solid retribution which fell upon the defeated enemies of Joshua was nothing more than the dark harvest of their own deeds. Joshua must not therefore, as Israel's ruler, be regarded as a stony monumental figure, hard and merciless, but a man hot with anger at evil, and deeply conscious that he cleansed a land. The 'iniquity of the Amorites' (Gen. 15.16) was at last full.

110 : Joshua's Success

Joshua 11

Joshua had been promised success (1.8) and the conditions of winning it had been laid down. He had fulfilled the conditions completely, as the closing verses of ch. 10 show. He had obeyed the law. It was a terrible task, that of leading Israel to victory in the land, but as a soldier and administrator he served his country well.

It is appropriate here to mention a factor in that success. 'A successful man,' said Albert Einstein, 'is he who receives a great deal from his fellow men, usually incomparably more than corresponds to his service to them.' This is not always true. Joshua gave himself. He always had given himself without thought of personal advantage. He had provided leadership, and, by his faithfulness, an indispensable link with the past. The great scientist's remark, however, does touch one point of truth. Israel's multitude had played its part in the making of history.

A host of unnamed men and women were a part of the history of these years. They move dimly through the murk and the noise which fill these chapters, but bravery, endurance and readiness to follow and obey must have been common marks of the men and women of the Hebrew host. We glimpse them in the long march round Jericho, circling the little fortress by the Jordan, and perhaps not understanding the purpose of what seemed an aimless manoeuvre. They maintained the ban of silence imposed upon them under the invective from the walls. Such were the people who backed Joshua's success and made it possible.

Those who are led reflect the qualities of the leader. A riotous and undisciplined army is an indication of undisciplined weakness in the man at the head. An ordered, self-controlled host, is a sure reflection of the stern and sturdy character of the leader. The nature of authority inevitably filters down and shows itself in the morale of the organization which that authority controls or fails to control. Joshua had his success. He owed it to his nation, but his nation had equal debt to him. 'Nothing fails like success,' someone has said. Joshua bore success with dignity. He knew to whom he owed it and it never tempted him to arrogance or to self-esteem. He had learned Moses' lessons well. It was all 'by faith'.

111 : Caleb

Joshua 14

We are permitted to meet one of the multitude who contributed to the triumph of Joshua. Caleb appears again in the next chapter and briefly in Judg. 1. It is good to meet the old man again. 'An old man's past's a strange thing,' said John Masefield, 'for it never leaves his mind.' Not so with Caleb. He can, to be sure, speak of the brave days when he served Moses, but he is forward-looking, eager to accomplish something more before the end. Writing his famous essay on old age, at the age of 63, Cicero remarked: 'As I approve of the youth who has something of the old man in him, so I am no less pleased with the old man that has something of the youth. He that follows this rule may be old in body but can never be so in mind.' Tennyson touched the same theme in his magnificent *Ulysses*:

> *How dull it is to pause and make an end,*
> *To rust unburnish'd, not to shine in use!*
> *As though to breathe were life . . .*
>
> . . . .
>
> *Old age hath yet his honour and his toil.*
>
> . . . .
>
> *Tho' much is taken, much abides; and tho'*
> *We are not now that strength which in old days*
> *Moved earth and heaven; that which we are, we are;*
> *One equal temper of heroic hearts,*
> *Made weak by time and fate, but strong in will*
> *To strive, to seek, to find, and not to yield.*

Caleb would have agreed. He is among the valiant old men of the Bible—Barzillai, Simeon, John, are others—and he sets the tone; 'and not to yield'. Clement Attlee quoted those words in tribute to Winston Churchill, and it is difficult to imagine a better motto as the years pile up behind . . . 'We shall never surrender.'

But the time arrives for certain resolutions. Unyieldingness should not hold the old man to tasks another can do better. He must learn gracefully to retire before he irks and burdens those whose respect he wishes to retain. He must learn to listen more and talk less, to avoid the temptation of capping every tale. Above all, let the future remain a challenge, as Caleb found it, a time to claim the unclaimed promise, to finish the unfinished task. Said Ulysses:

> *Vile it were to store and hoard myself,*
> *With this grey spirit yearning in desire*
> *To follow Knowledge like a sinking star . . .*

There is still a path to tread. John wrote his Gospel in his nineties.

112 : Phinehas

Joshua 22

Said John Foster Dulles once: 'When the world thermometer registers "not war, not peace" it is hard to decide whether to follow military or political judgements.' It is perhaps easier to follow spiritual judgements, and to do that requires a diplomat of deep understanding and insight. In Phinehas we meet such a man. He cuts a fine figure.

There was a real danger lest the Jordan should become a divisive frontier through the very body of Israel. The twisting river is no great military obstacle, but it easily becomes a line in the minds of men, and there was some peril lest the tribes which had petitioned for a portion on the desert side of Jordan should become dissociated from those who occupied the land west of the river, Israel's heart-land.

It was obvious that the faith which Abraham had brought from Ur of the Chaldees, and the Law which Moses had given as the form and organization of that faith, were the cement which held the tribes of Israel together. When the trans-Jordanian segments set up their altar, it appeared that division, and the sundering of a hard-won unity, was on the way. It was to come thus in later centuries.

Phinehas was the very man for the task of protest and investigation. He speaks with frankness, but a frankness seasoned with tact and courtesy. He delivers his warning faithfully, with appeal to historic precedents. He approaches those to whom he was sent with dignity and clarity of speech. Of an ambassador no one can expect more.

Hence, in chief measure, his success. The language of the reply reflects the language of the protest and the appeal—courteous, earnest, sincere. Their altar, they said, was not schismatic and in no sense intended to replace the altar which symbolized the unity of Israel. It was a mere memorial cairn, designed, not to divide, but to recall a unity which Jordan might have challenged.

Phinehas was no man of war. He came to his task cool, open-minded, ready to believe the best. An ambassador must be a man of peace, and lay hold of peace, if peace may be had on terms of honour. This was the peace which Phinehas brought back from across the great Rift Valley. It is a reflection of his worth and his wisdom, no less than of his eloquence.

113 : Joshua's Charge
Joshua 23.1—24.28

Joshua saw his final task in a brave reminder. The old see more truly the significance of history because they see the meaning of their own life's experience. With rugged courage he faced the people with their past. Man was man even in that ancient century, and the 'generation gap' was no doubt apparent and exaggerated. Those were rising who knew nothing of the blood and toil, and sweat and tears, which had bought the good they knew and the peace they now enjoyed.

Each generation must choose, because although the past has its dire lessons as well as its inspiration and encouragement, it is fatal to live in the past. Paul himself is witness to that (Phil. **3.**13), and the experience of the first disciples (John **6.**66). An equal list of Scripture texts could support the other lessons, that the past is neglected to our peril. A balanced life is lived if all the experience of the years that lie behind is interwoven with the needs, the movements and the tasks of the present.

And the choice, man's age-old choice, is between God and whatever stands against Him, be it the base heritage of Canaan, or Baal, or Antichrist. They ever tug, and the pull of the society in which we live is a tension to resolve. Paul wrote: 'I therefore implore you, brothers, in the name of God's mercies, to dedicate your bodies as a living sacrifice, consecrated to God, well-pleasing to Him, which is the worship proper to your nature. *And cease trying to adapt yourself to the age you live in, but continue your transformation by the renewing of your mind,* to the end that you may test out for yourselves the will of God, that, namely, which is good, well-pleasing to him, and perfect' (Rom. **12.**1 f. E.M.B.).

Note the closing words of **24.**15. The old man made no oratorical pause. There was no quick look to see which way the crowd was moving, no attempt to assess the mood of the people and adapt his words thereto. He was not a leader of that sort. He took his stand, and he took it for his house.

128

It is a notable fact that this is what produced the response of the people (16).

Joshua tested them further. Perhaps some unrecorded event of national backsliding lies behind the hard words of v. 19. Joshua took and bound them by a ritual act, especially sacred in that Eastern context. Brief, pungent, unyielding and without a syllable of compromise, he fixed their decision firmly in their minds.

114 : Joshua's Passing
Joshua 24.29–33; Judges 2.1–10

Here are two more lines to add to the quotation (Study 110) from Tennyson's *Ulysses* . . . They could have been written of Joshua :

> *Death closes and all: but something ere the end*
> *Some work of noble note may yet be done . . .*

How true indeed of the son of Nun. He had watched the green old age of Moses, perhaps, too, the last vigour of the unrecorded Nun. He had seen Caleb strong and valiant in his closing days. And now death was creeping also on him. He had not the clear view out beyond death which is the Christian's glorious privilege, though he no doubt took it for granted, as all ancient peoples did, that the grave was not the final terminus, life's utter end.

How a man faces the last enemy, tells much of his character through life. It matters 'how we all go out at journey's end'. And that last phrase was first coined by Dryden :

> *With equal mind what happens let us bear,*
> *Nor joy nor grieve too much for things beyond*
> *   our care,*
> *Like pilgrims to th'appointed place we tend;*
> *The world's an inn and death the journey's end.*

Resolution, dignity, care for those yet to be, valiant example, words of ripe wisdom—these all showed the man. That some heard him, and carried the banner on, is demonstrated by the fact that another generation stood true after his passing (2.10). Youth thinks the end remote, and life an endless journey. Life hurries on, appearing to accelerate with the years. It is a good and healthful thing to look at those who march to the boundary, like Joshua, unsoiled. There is jubilation in ending well. Said Saul Kane in Masefield's poem:

> *I wondered then why life should be,*
> *And what would be the end of me*
> *When youth and health and strength were gone*
> *And cold old age came creeping on.*

No need to wonder for those who hold fast to Christ, and watch men like Joshua—or Paul. For those who seek a New Testament reading turn now to the last words of the great apostle to the Gentiles which close the second of the two letters to young Timothy.

Questions and themes for study and discussion on Studies 108–114

1. The differing roles of tradition and creativity in the work of a leader.
2. The unnamed men and women of the Bible.
3. What are the prime qualities of good leadership?
4. What are the chief tasks of old age?
5. What are the dangers of diplomacy?
6. What is the finest service of old age?

115 : The Judges
Judges 1—3

The theme passes with the next book of the Old Testament into a sombre period of history, a time when 'startled faces flicker in the gloom', and the plan of God for His people became a mere rill in the wilderness of history.

It was an age of battle and of violence. Consider Othniel, Ehud and Shamgar of these early chapters. 'War,' wrote

130

Thucydides in one of the most penetrating chapters of Greek history, 'is a rough schoolmaster, and brings most men's characters to the level of their fortunes.' This was true of these grim years.

Moses was gone. Joshua was gone. Israel lacked a great leader. The men who rose to deliver and to guide, and moments of crisis seemed to bring them to the fore, were lesser men, with some rudiments of faith in God, but little insight into the character of God, to ennoble and to soften them. These strong and sometimes brutal men were called 'saviours' (3.9, 15), more because of the opportuneness of their leadership than its quality.

It was, in fact, a 'dark age' for Israel, with wide disorganization, tribal discord and defeat. To see in the judges who successively rose and ruled, from Othniel to Samson, a 'type of Christ' (in anything but their mere office), as one commentator puts it, is to distort exegesis beyond recognition. As the words of Thucydides, the Greek historian, had it in the above quotation, the times produced the men, and few could see in the treacherous Ehud, for all the political advantage of the murder he committed, much resembling Christ in actuality or symbol.

This is not to deny in any way that God overruled in such troubled times, but it is a principle of God's action in history that He works through such men as seek Him, and that quest is sometimes a fumbling and a groping in the dark by ignorant and confused people who know little of His ways. This is the lesson we shall have occasion again and again to learn as we read this sad book, and meet its primitive characters. Passion and determination they had. Witness Shamgar with his crude armament. Of these early three judges there is no mention of faith, goodness, or those great qualities we found in Moses and Joshua, and many of the men who caught their bright reflection. But 'God was in the shadows keeping watch upon His own'.

116 : Deborah and Barak

Judges 4, 5

It is strange, yet logical, to take these two persons together. Deborah is the most sharply drawn character we have so far met in the book. Barak is a mere shadow beside her, and one suspects some weakness and timidity in the man (4.8). There are those who are born to follow, but sometimes those who accept such a lowly role when higher honour beckons, lose in reputation what they gain in effectiveness, as Deborah warned her captain of the northern host (4.9). But she in no way despised him.

It was, to be sure, a perilous and terrifying situation. Hazor was a major stronghold, a Canaanitish city which had taken full advantage of the Iron Age, whose techniques were developing. And furthermore the Esdraelon plain was ideal terrain for armoured warfare. Sisera had 900 chariots, and it was the intervention of the flash-flood and vicious rain-storm (5.20 f.) which gave the ill-armed Israelitish tribesmen the victory. But we miss in Barak the dash and resolution with which true leaders of men face overwhelming odds. In the social context of that day it was shame to accept the leadership of a woman however able she had proved herself to be.

Of that ability there is no doubt. It was perhaps 1125 B.C. Deborah was a prophetess in the most ancient significance of that word. She was of great and recognized wisdom (4.4–8), and used her insight and understanding to dispense justice from a primitive court held under a palm tree which became an historic monument (4.5). To gain such acceptance among the rough tribesmen, distracted in their feuds, and amid the social disorganization of this early day, betokened a woman of great and noble character and charm. Observe that Barak obeys her swift, decisive commands, and that he claims the advantage of her presence because of the aura which surrounded her person as well as because of a certain hesitation, born of the timidity within him, to seize and hold the part which the prophetess was eager to grant him. Her willingness to send Barak on the campaign as sole commander, itself throws some light on Deborah's quality. There was no laying hold of authority, beyond that willingly ceded by her people, in her. Oddly enough, Hebrews 11.32 mentions only Barak among the heroes of faith.

132

117 : Deborah's Song

Judges 5

The songs sung by an age or a people teach much about the society from which they spring. So do the songs of men and women in the context of their personal experience. We have the song of Miriam (Exod. 15.21), but that was a response to the psalm of Moses, who was a lyrist in his own right.

Deborah's song is the song of a triumphant woman, to be set beside the psalms of women recorded by Luke in the early chapters of his Gospel. Historically it has its significance, for it teaches something of the relations between the tribes in the far twelfth century before Christ. It is also a source of information about the events at hand. Only from the song do we hear of the natural causes which frustrated Sisera and placed opportunity in Barak's hands, the flash-flood and the swollen Kishon.

Deborah, the authoress, is vividly evident in the words. She sounds a note of genuine praise to God, and from such allegiance flows her social conscience. She passes rapidly from the thought of God's providence to the conception of peace, justice and class harmony, which necessarily flow from such a faith and gratitude so real. She found a unity based in history, and the malediction on Meroz (5.23), the town which broke that unity in the day of stress, whips harshly into the paean of praise. Here was the stern side of Israel's Joan of Arc. Without that side to her character she could not have served such a day.

The same facet of character is shown in the praise of Jael, who killed Sisera. It was an act of war, and as such was accepted by the warrior-prophetess. 'A note of sympathy,' characteristic of a woman, says one commentator, is evident in the little vignette of Sisera's mother, looking out for her son's returning. It is difficult, however, to see anything in these grimly jubilant verses (28–30) of softness or sympathy. Deborah triumphs over the alien woman, and the gloating over Israel's spoil which the poem rightly imagines on the foreigner's lips, leaves little room to lament the bereavement she suffered, when Hazor's Guderian failed to reach his home. Upon the invader fell the retribution of the Law, and we have met a fierce, loyal and able woman of the Law.

118 : Gideon

Judges 6.1–27

Between the lines of Gideon's story may be read again the plight of Israel, their precarious tenure of the land, and their vulnerability to their foes. The Amalekites and the Midianites were tribes of desert nomads, Bedouin of sorts, who haunted the eastern borderlands, where the desert impinges on 'the sown'. Gideon's secret threshing of the wheat (11) reveals the helplessness of the people against the raiding from the wilderness. It was high time for a new leader, and Gideon, of all the men who have moved through the story since the death of Joshua, was most fitted for the role.

Observe that Hebrews (11.32) lists Gideon among the heroes of faith, but it is significant that the story itself stresses the caution and tentative approach which inhibited faith in the hero. It is not triumphant confidence alone which is honoured of God. He rewards 'the grain of mustard seed'. It is clear that Gideon was a harassed and discouraged man. He bore the burdens of long defeat. He was unaided by any strong surviving tradition. When the messenger of God first summoned him to the task of national deliverance, it was with bitter unbelief that he at first responded (13). The only explanation he found to offer for the sorry state of his nation was that God, who had once been at hand with present aid, had forsaken His people.

'And the Lord looked upon him' (14, AV[KJV]), says the text, and evidently saw more within him than the words upon his lips could show. It is not always possible to judge a man from what he says, and the penetrating glance of deeper understanding revealed in Gideon the reality of belief which could be used.

Note now two turns in the story. Gideon asked for confirmation. He was to do it again in the matter of the fleece and the dew. It is an indication of his character—a deep dislike of rash and hasty action. It is not always possible, indeed it is seldom right and good, to importune God for proof. Sometimes, however, divine grace meets us at the place and point of our feeble faith, and grants a demonstration of God's reality. Gideon had his demonstration (21).

Secondly, he was bidden himself to demonstrate his faith by works. It was essential for a man so cautious to commit himself, and to turn belief into salutary action. Gideon required no small courage to go forth against the apostate cults which were beginning to infiltrate the borderlands of Israel. Deliverance began as deliverance does by a cleansing act and a movement of consecration.

119 : Joash

Judges 6.28–32

Gideon had asked for signs. If his eyes were open to the movements of God's hand, he had a sign indeed in the loyalty of his own father. Brave old Joash moves into the story on the morrow of his son's idol-breaking. There are parents whose examples bring a son to a knowledge of God. In rarer instances the stream flows backward and a son is salvation to his father.

Joash is good to meet. No sooner had he seen the decisiveness of his son's action than he recognized its rectitude, and moved to his defence. Perhaps he had himself known long since what should have been done, but had hesitated to act. Now the deed was done, and, late though the hour was, Joash took his stand. Perhaps we can add a verse to Marianne Farningham's variation of Charlotte Elliott's well-known evangelistic hymn.

> *Just as I am, though youth is past,*
> *And the leaves grow brown in the autumn blast,*
> *Though few be the years I can give—at last,*
> *Lord of all life, I come.*

The appearance of Joash is brief but effective. He must have been one who had won the respect of his fellow villagers of Ophrah. It is no light matter to face a hostile crowd. Feelings ran high and violence was in the air when the old man stepped forward to address the crowd. They had lost their god—so be it—was he not the sun-god, and was his blazing sign not a witness to the scene, high in the heaven? Cannot Baal look after himself? *Dis iniuriae dis curae,* says Tacitus— 'wrongs done to the gods are the gods' concern'. Something like that is intended in the new name Joash gives now to his son. It is a taunt given in irony against Baal-worship, if its meaning is: 'Let Baal fight against him' (C. F. Kraft in the *Interpreter's Dictionary of the Bible*.)

The Hebrew peasantry were simple hard-headed men, and the plain common sense of Joash's argument seems to have appealed to them. The old man had something of Elijah in him, for the challenge in the name of Jerubaal was in the same spirit as Elijah's taunts on Carmel, three centuries later. The story of Joash is brief, and hardly rounded-off in the fast-moving narrative, but the end is clear. The people listened and Gideon survived to save them.

120 : Gideon's Testing
Judges 6.33–7.7

The Midianites were in the Esdraelon Plain, otherwise Jezreel, ideal terrain for armoured war like that of Sisera, but not the type of country for camel-borne Bedouin. Gideon, however, could see the extent of the twin forces from the hills, and took the precaution of calling a general rally. There was nothing wrong in this, but the tribal forces of Israel were not in a condition to fight. Gideon may have observed the signs of disorder, apprehension, lack of spirit and assurance. It was discouraging.

Hence his yearning for a 'sign', always a mark of feeble faith. The dew on the fleece was a not unnatural phenomenon. In the Negev, the phenomenon of v. 38 can be repeated on any dewy morning. Hence the revival of ancient farming methods, and stone mulching in the area. Hence Gideon's timid request for confirmation.

Gideon has presumed to test God. God now tests him (7.2). Did Shakespeare have v. 3 in mind when he made Henry cry before the clash at Agincourt?—

> *Rather proclaim it, Westmoreland, through all my host,*
> *That he which hath no stomach to this fight,*
> *Let him depart; his passport shall be made,*
> *And crowns for convoy put into his purse.*

It is a sorry comment on the state of the land that over two-thirds of the host departed.

Now came the further test. Gideon was camped on the slopes of the hills. The rank and file were desperate with thirst, for the water lay at the foot where the riders of the raiding tribes could sweep down on watering-parties. The test seems to have been devised to separate the few who, in a moment of physical stress, set their duty of alertness in the face of the foe before the alleviation of their bodily need. Those who kept their eyes forward, and lifted the water in their hand, were the men Gideon needed.

All through the Bible God works by the few. Gideon needed this lesson. That he accepted it, and the ludicrous odds with which he faced the enemy, shows that his faith was growing. This is a principle of life. While we grow we live. Gideon was attaining the stature God desired in him.

121 : Gideon's Victory
Judges 7.8—8.21

Gideon took his servant Purah to look more closely at the foe. God has tested him. He has faced the test. Now he is given some assurance. Add Purah to the list of worthy servants in the Bible. Some of them are well known—Joshua, for instance, and Timothy. Add those who are mere names, Jonathan's armourbearer, Elijah's servant, and others.

Gideon was not lacking in plain courage. It was an act of considerable daring to creep within hearing distance of the men in the nomad laager. The conversation thus overheard was of some significance. Wheat was grown on the fertile plain. Barley, the poorer crop, was grown on the less productive hill country. The barley loaf, which rolled destructively down into the camp of the Midianites, was a dream-symbol of a hillsmen's raid. It is a perfectly credible piece of psychology, the translation into phantasy of a genuine fear. Out of their proper element on the Jezreel Plain, the Midianites were afraid, and looking at the hills.

Gideon took intelligent advantage of the state of apprehension in which the invading tribesmen found themselves. He was a guerrilla leader of splendid resourcefulness, and his attack demonstrated what history has a hundred times revealed —that it is morale and confidence that matter, and that numbers are irrelevant. The coalition of the desert tribes was flung into confusion, and compelled to run the long and deadly gauntlet of the Jordan jungle and the trans-Jordan hill-country which separated them disastrously from the open desert which was their natural habitat. They were tangled in the land. Gideon had the victory.

'Reviewing the story of Gideon's life,' wrote Dr. Robert A. Watson, the leisurely Victorian commentator, 'we find this clear lesson, that within certain limits, he who trusts and obeys God has a quite irresistible efficiency.' This was his one lesson for Israel. The Mosaic law seems scarcely to have been known to him. But he did lay hold of God at the one point where his rudimentary faith could reach out and find Him—and God asks no more of any one of us . . . 'Yet,' Dr. Watson continues, 'seriously limited as he was, Gideon, when he had once laid hold of the fact that he was called by the unseen God to deliver Israel, went on step by step to the great victory which made the tribes free.'

122 : Gideon at Peace

Judges 8.22–28

Gideon was popular and, to his praise, rejected the temptation to found a royal dynasty on his popularity. This was greatly to his credit. We have noted earlier his touch of humility. It was one facet of the caution with which he moved towards the fulfilment of his call to lead Israel.

Surprisingly, that call seems to have evoked another sort of ambition. The Mosaic law, and the careful organization of the priesthood and the ritual of worship, were so obliterated in the common experience of Israel, that Gideon, having rejected royal estate, found the priesthood an acceptable aspiration. Weary of war, he desired holy office—an unexpected trait, and to be explained as a by-product of the deep experience of victory under God's hand which he had enjoyed in the Midian-Amalek war. 'A strong, but not spiritual religiousness,' writes the Victorian commentator, whom we have quoted, 'was the chief characteristic of Gideon's character.'

He was making a mistake. There are those who are drawn to the office of the priesthood or the ministry because of some

138

glamour they imagine therein, or because of some personal search for peace, power or position. It was no doubt the first named, a quest for peace, that moved Gideon, but he had no right or calling in this desire.

His 'religiousness' made much of signs and symbols—the dew for example, and the sign of the angel. He now translates this into a form of action, and makes a rich ephod as a sign of his self-appointed office. This led, such is the desire of man for concrete objects of worship, to a new idolatry (27). The sign and symbol usurped the place of the reality.

And so Gideon died, a primitive figure of faith, little comprehending the wider issues of his day, but faithfully fulfilling the one task to which he was called. He gave his country peace, but beyond that he had nothing to give, and when his strong presence was gone, the land lapsed once more into the half-paganism which paralysed it.

Questions and themes for study and discussion on Studies 115–122

1. Why is Barak only and not Deborah mentioned in Heb. 11.32?
2. 'The hardest task that I can tell, is to play the second fiddle well.'
3. Name six other great women of the Bible.
4. Study a map of the Esdraelon plain and find the places mentioned in the story of Deborah and Barak. Where else do we meet the Kishon? Locate Carmel.
5. What is faith?
6. 'The dearest idol I have known, whate'er that idol be. . . .' What are modern idols, and how can the problems they pose be tackled?

123 : Abimelech
Judges 8.29—9.57

Gideon's strength gave peace to the land for forty years, but it was a peace which ended when his personal influence was removed by death. It was based too feebly on the influence of a personality, with no roots in God's law. After Joshua's death a tradition endured for a generation. Not so when Gideon went the way of all flesh.

The horrifying division of the land became again apparent. The town of Shechem, with its mixed population, was jealous of the hill hamlet of Ophrah. The old hankering for a king, after the fashion of the heathen world, arose, and on the wave of popular demand, Abimelech was swept to power.

Abimelech was a base and evil character. Financed by funds from a heathen temple, he staged a villainous *coup d'état*. Hiring a band of desperadoes, he waded to power through a river of blood. Gideon's work had begun with the throwing down of Baal's altar. Abimelech's career began with Baal's money used for mass murder.

It is a grim story. There is nothing to commend Abimelech. He is the living example of the successful adventurer, a man of Jehu's or Absalom's mould, but with none of Jehu's intellectual power, or Absalom's personal charm, a bleak, evil criminal. Jotham's keen wit was of no avail against him, uncanny though Shechem must have found the voice ringing from the top of Mount Gerizim, and telling the parable of the trees and their king. Jotham deserved better of his people than the exile which befell him.

Shechem had lifted Abimelech to power. Shechem betrayed him. Gaal, one of the inconsiderable characters in the story, led the revolt and won wounds and defeat. Apparent chance killed the villainous Abimelech, a death which, in his ludicrous pride, he thought shameful. A woman fractured his skull with a broken fragment of a millstone hurled adroitly from the tower-top. Abimelech, like the town which had first sponsored and financed him, reaped the crop of his sowing. To this internecine strife had God's people come. It was a Dark Age in the story of the land.

The sorry theme runs on to the end of the next chapter. Another period of over forty years is compassed with figures of faceless men flitting through the smoke, Tola and Jair of whom little is said. The raiders from the desert frontiers, the Phoenicians from the coast, press hard, and under the pressure the land cries for a leader.

140

124 : Jephthah
Judges 11

A strange leader arose, a man of Gilead east of Jordan, a wild area of highland, the country of Jair, the last judge mentioned. Jephthah was no adventurer, thrusting himself, like the base Abimelech, into a vacant heritage. He was called to save his people from the pressure of the invaders, called from exile. It is not the only time in history that a rejected man has been summoned from the wilderness to lead his people. The list ranges from Moses and David to Churchill and De Gaulle.

Jephthah secured his guarantees, and began his leadership with an act of wise diplomacy. He gave Ammon a chance to withdraw, and in the approach he made demonstrated some knowledge of his nation's history. The tradition was not quite dead, in spite of the appalling ignorance which Jephthah was later to reveal. The Mosaic law was firm against human sacrifice. The consecration of the first-born had this for its aim and end. The story of Abraham and Isaac was designed to make clear, after the ancient dramatic fashion, that Jehovah was no Moloch, demanding a price of human blood.

Jephthah had no excuse for his foolish vow, and less for carrying it to its horrible conclusion. He demonstrates the folly and the evil into which a man can fall when the truth is not patently before his eyes. Jephthah had faith. He is honoured by a minor place in the list of Hebrews 11.32, and yet his life was marred by a culpable ignorance of the character of God. What sort of demon did the rough judge imagine God to be, when he did his daughter to death in pursuance of a vow no man is called upon to make?

And yet men, unable to grasp the truth about the love of God and the completeness of salvation by faith, have more than once followed Jephthah's path. There have been periods in the history of the Church when the thought that God required appeasement by self-inflicted woe took hold of men like a darkness of the mind. The fourth century was soiled by the heresy. Jerome tells of a monk who for forty years drank nothing but muddy water. For six months Macarius of Alexandria slept in a swamp, and he always carried with him a load of iron. Bessarion never lay down to sleep. Most hideous of all was the asceticism of Simeon. He lived with a rope tied

141

tightly round him, so that it cut into the festering flesh. He
crept with vermin, and slept in a dry well. At last he found
a pillar, one of the ruin remnants which strewed that falling
world, and for thirty years, exposed to the rigours of all
weathers, lived there incessantly bowing in prayer. Read
Tennyson's poem: *Saint Simeon Stylites*.

125 : Jephthah's End

Judges 12

Jephthah, for all the folly of his cruel sacrifice, must not be
too harshly judged. His was a hard and shadowed youth, but
he seems to have made an upright home, and it was tragedy
indeed that he should mar it with self-made sorrow. For six
years he lived with the memory of his murdered daughter,
like Agamemnon of the Greek legend, clouded by his folly
and his failure to understand the mind of God.

The civil war which was thrust upon him was none of his
own making. The river proved a frontier of strife. The word
'rivus' is the Latin for a stream, and 'rivales' means those who
share the same stream. That the word 'rival' should find such
derivation has social significance. It is clearly part of history's
experience that rivers form no divisive frontier like mountains and deserts, which keep hostile peoples apart. They
cause dangerous confrontations. Hence 'the watch on the
Rhine'.

Hence too, the clash between the tribes of Israel. Jephthah
was a fighting-man, but he was no lover of war. As with the
threatening people of Ammon, he did his best by diplomacy
to turn Ephraim's jealousy aside. Ephraim was the head tribe
of the house of Joseph. It occupied the heartland of Palestine,
and lived in jealous suspicion of all eminence outside its
borders. Ephraim challenged Gideon in his hour of triumph,
and now they picked a quarrel with Jephthah. They looked
upon the highlanders of trans-Jordan as a lesser breed to be
taught their place. Jephthah is shown in a most honourable
light. He did his best to avert strife. He reasoned and pleaded
with his arrogant foes, and found no response. 'War,' said
someone, 'is the continuation of diplomacy by other means,'
and there is a grim measure of truth in the words. Jephthah

was forced into the Jordan Valley civil war, and its subsequent horrors. Once in, he acquitted himself as Hamlet was
bidden do:

> *Of entrance to a quarrel, beware but, being in,*
> *Bear't that th' opposed may beware of thee.*

Jephthah fought in sorrow. Sorrow had dogged his days
from rejected youth to memory-ridden age. Age? Perhaps he
died in his forties, worn out by all that life and his own folly
had done to him.

126 : Samson's Parents

Judges 13

More shadowy figures flit and pass. The tenth, eleventh and
twelfth judges pass their undistinguished way. Few of them
are clear-cut figures, as we peer through the darkness of that
lamentable age in an endeavour to know them. With Samson
comes a change. Perhaps a new chronicler has taken over in
the Hebrew record. Perhaps the theme draws nearer to the
days of some stability, when men remembered more fully, or
had time for literature and the writing of history.

We know all we need to know: how thin and deviant had
become the stream of historical purpose which flowed through
Israel, how tragically the truth and its practice could be lost,
and how lamentably surrounding heathendom could press
upon the land . . .

With Samson comes something new, a sharply drawn and
complicated personality, a person like ourselves, and something more than a vague figure with a sword or torch, some
fierce-faced and alien man half glimpsed through the murk of
a Dark Age. The story enters recognizable territory.

As though to prepare the way there comes a glimpse of
Samson's parents. Manoah and his wife lived their lives of
peasant peace in the horrible years the story has described.
The Book of Ruth has a like story to tell of pockets of tranquillity among the sheltered hills, while the borders were
aflame with strife. The childless couple, like 'God's poor' in
Isaiah, like Amos, like Joseph and Mary, and a hundred

others in Scripture, show that, for all the sin, backsliding and apostasy in high places, God had always what was to be called His Remnant, His Faithful Few.

Manoah and his wife are humble and pious folk, eager to know how best to rear the child so strangely promised to them. The child was to bring them sorrow. He was to fall far short of what he might have been, but he could never, through all the turbulence of his days, accuse the simple folk who had sought so anxiously to order his childhood, of having failed in their duty towards him. They sought to teach him self-control.

Poor Manoah! He appears once more, perhaps a score of years later (14.3), with a word of sane and scorned advice, and he died before the tragic end of the son who might have been so great (16.31).

127 : Young Samson

Judges 14

A new enemy was on the borders. Down in what today is called the Gaza Strip, the Philistines had held a foothold and a colony since the days of Isaac, whose herdsmen clashed with theirs over water-rights. The Philistines were Europeans, a group of tribal expatriates from Crete, where what historians call the Minoan civilization had flourished for a full millennium. Originally, the group which gave Palestine (derived from Philistine) its name, may have been a trading-post. But Crete had fallen on evil days. Natural disaster and assault from the mainland, as far as it is possible from the findings of archaeology to fit the story together, had all but devastated the long island. At this time, in the twelfth century before Christ, and on into the days of Saul and David, there must have been a vast influx of people, with consequent search for living-space, and clashes with the occupiers of the hinterland.

It was a second invasion of the land. The Hebrew nomads had thrust in through the hill-country from the eastern wilderness. The Philistines drove in from the west and the Mediterranean. A clash, where the hills met the coastal plain, was inevitable. It was the first confrontation between Europe and Asia in history. And the Europeans brought

144

culture, the art which may still be seen in the Palace of Knossos and other places in Crete, and their fish-god Dagon.

Perhaps this is what seduced Samson. It is possible to conjecture that the splendid young Hebrew, magnificently strong and keenly intellectual, might have been a missionary to Philistia. The one advantage the Hebrews had over the intruders from the West, was a clear and noble view of God. Perhaps the thirteenth judge might have been a conqueror of a different sort. Jephthah had dimly shown that there could be alternatives to war.

But Samson was a fool with women, and perhaps was fascinated by the culture of the foe. It is a recognizable situation. Among the Philistines he had popularity. Their bullfighting, evident from the Cretan frescoes, shows evidence of their admiration for physical prowess. In this they were the forerunners of the Greeks. Samson was popular, and long tolerated in spite of the mischievous acts of vandalism in which he misused his strength.

Manoah was right. Samson had no right to marry outside the tribe. The chronicler's remark at (14.4) need mean no more than that out of Samson's folly God derived some military advantage for Israel. But surely God's first plan could rather have been that the fine young man should be a Jonah, an Amos, a prophet messenger who might have brought blessing rather than blood.

128 : Samson's Folly

Judges 15

Young men should read the story of Samson well. Bemused by the polished Philistines, despising the simple, chaste girls of the village community, where he had been born and taught, the young man Samson found a mate among the sophisticated young women of the alien. Curiously enough we know what the Philistine women were like from the frescoes of Crete. If they carried their national dress to Palestine, the women wore bustles and full-flounced skirts, contrasting with the bare-breasted cut of the bust. A greater contrast in appearance with the girls of the Hebrews could not well be imagined.

Milton's poem *Samson Agonistes* interprets the situation well. Samson had a first-class mind, as well as a magnificent body. He was of giant strength and superb daring, both qualities which women admire. He was no doubt under heavy siege from them, and the legends of Crete, which sometimes contain, as legends do, shreds of historical truth, suggest that the Philistine women had no great regard for moral purity.

Samson, too, had made friends among the people of the plain. One of them took his wife (**15**.2), for his marriage was, as he might have expected it to be, based as it was on a betrayal of ideals, a failure. Popularity, as well as his natural carnality, was his undoing. 'Like a petty god I walked about, admired by all,' Milton makes him say. He ended by betrayal right and left. The Philistines sought him to destroy him, and his own folk turned him over to the foe. No man can serve two masters (11–13). Samson learned that lesson in a bitter way.

Godless women, unholy fellowship with evil, compromising friendships, ruined Samson. It was as Milton makes the fallen hero say, 'through mine own default'. He betrayed his people, for it was a private war he fought with the Philistines, no crusade of national deliverance. He betrayed his God, for it was a dim faith and a travesty of Manoah's which he bore. The true values which might have enriched his life were found among the rough tribesmen, not among the cultured pagans. True joy, true pleasure, true renown, lay with his own folk. He wasted his life in riotous living, the Prodigal Son of the Old Testament, undisciplined, capricious, carnal, violent for violence' sake. But Samson was the prodigal who came home dead.

129 : Samson's Failure

2 Corinthians 6

We should pause at this point to review the eternal laws which explain Samson's failure. William Neil in his small commentary remarks inexplicably that 'there is no obvious religious or moral value in the Samson stories'. Surely the moral lessons crowd every sentence.

Samson's usefulness depended upon 'separation'. Separation is a real principle of spiritual victory. God, and Samson's parents working under divine command, had brought him up as a Nazirite. This was a special calling, under two orders. There were temporary Nazirites, and permanent ones. Only Samson, Samuel and John the Baptist belonged to the latter class (Num. 6.1–21). The Nazirite calling was to fortify the future judge against the fierce temptations which Philistia offered.

This is why the suggestion has been made that Samson's real calling was to take God to the heathen plainsmen. He was trained to go among them, 'unspotted by the world'. He could help the Philistines only if he was separate from them. Hence the prohibition against alcohol. The Philistines, if inference may be drawn from the beer mugs discovered among the remains, were prodigious drinkers.

Samson kept the long hair, which was the symbol of his separation, but he forgot the reality, for surely Delilah could hardly have cut his precious locks had he not been lying in her room in a drunken sleep. It was 'gracious living', to be sure, down in Gath, the social drink, the free flirtation, cheap sexuality, and in the midst of it all, in Milton's powerful words, 'God disglorified, blasphemed, and had in scorn'.

Selfish and uncontrolled passion, forgetfulness of sacred vows, led successively to loss of hair, the mere symbol, of power, the reality, of eyes and freedom. How many seek 'freedom' in a 'permissive society' and find bondage! The lessons which the commentator we have quoted failed to see? Simply these: Let youth commit to God the strength of mind and body, find a life-companion among God's people, learn early that love is God's gift and not to be soiled, keep separate from that which spoils, and stay in 'the Father's house'.

Let us close this note with Phillips' rendering of Rom. 13.12–14: 'The night is nearly over, the day has almost dawned. Let us therefore fling away the things that men do in the dark, let us arm ourselves for the fight of the day! Let us live cleanly, as in the daylight, not in the "delights" of getting drunk or playing with sex, nor yet in quarrelling or jealousies. Let us be Christ's men from head to foot, and give no chances to the flesh to have its fling.'

147

130 : Delilah

Judges 16.1–22

Delilah, Samson's second wife, 'that specious Monster my accomplished Snare', as Milton makes him call her, was one of the bad women of Scripture. Curiously enough, Samson could see her baseness. He allowed her to deceive him, not once, but more than once. Milton again, in his tragic inter-pretation of the sad story, catches the situation aright. The foolish man, trapped by his carnality, walked the same path of folly again and again—

> *each time perceiving*
> *How openly, and with what impudence*
> *She purposed to betray me, and (which was worse*
> *Than undissembl'd hate) with what contempt*
> *She sought to make me Traitor to myself.*

He goes on, in Milton's poem, to tell how the evil woman battered the weary man—

> *Who with a grain of manhood well resolv'd*
> *Might easily have shook off all her snares.*

The poet touches well a point of psychological truth. Continual surrender to carnal sin produces a paralysis of resolution. The sinner, again, to quote Milton's perceptive poem, becomes 'the dungeon of himself'.

There is always 'a way of escape' (1 Cor. **10**.13) but it demands an act of will on the part of the tempted to rise and 'shake off the snares'. Bunyan had a word about Samson: 'Temptations, when we meet them at first,' he said, 'are as the lion which roared upon Samson. But if we overcome them, the next time we see them we shall find a nest of honey within them.' How very true—but the Hebrew Hercules, who could tear a lion apart, was a weakling in the hands of a woman whom he knew to be a liar and an agent of his enemies.

Delilah has had a numberless posterity. Bruyère, that keen observer of human character, followed by Tennyson, remarked that women can be better than the best of men—and worse than the worst. It would be difficult to find a baser character than Delilah, wheedling, feline, treacherous . . . But what can be expected of one who uses love for evil ends?

Milton makes Delilah come pleading for pardon. The text of Scripture gives no hint of this. Samson will have none of her. He rejects her touch—

> At distance I forgive thee, go with that;
> Beware thy falsehood, and the pious works
> It hath brought forth to make thee memorable
> Among illustrious women, faithful wives :
> Cherish thy hastened widowhood with the gold
> Of matrimonial treason : so farewell.

Delilah, serpent to the last, turns on the blind, doomed man and rejoices in her deed.

131 : Samson's End

Judges 16.23–31

'Eyeless in Gaza, at the mill with slaves', Samson had time to think of what had befallen him :

> . . . restless thoughts, that like a deadly swarm
> Of hornets arm'd, no sooner found alone,
> Rush upon me thronging, and present
> Times past, what once I was, and what am now . . .

There can be no greater agony than the thought of irrevocable ill, the contrast past all remedy, between what might have been, and what turned out to be. Oscar Wilde's last poems, published after his early death in 1903, were contained in a volume significantly titled: Hélas (Alas). These lines occur—

> Surely there was a time I might have trod
> The sunlit heights, and from life's dissonance,
> Struck one clear chord to reach the ears of God.

This might also have been true of Samson, the blinded slave who might have led a nation. He did nothing for Israel save massacre thousands of Philistines. And the Philistine menace remained—and worsened. Dagon was no rival, only a fish-god,

149

born of the sick imagination of the maritime Cretans. Samson might have made peace by bringing Jehovah to the foe.

The end was service curtailed, and horrible death. House foundations in the area have revealed a pattern of building where the structure of a house rested on two adjacent pillars on a flat stone pediment. Samson sat between, and circled each pillar with an arm. Those who happened to look saw the ripple of mighty muscles in his back. They saw the great sinews of his arms start. They saw the crisped and blood-drained hands. They saw him give a fearsome lift, and 'bow himself' forward as he slid the two pillars, on which the structure of the roof depended, from their footing on the pediment on which he sat. In mighty ruin the roof caved in, and the walls fell outward. The crowded street without received the debris. In the packed eastern town adjacent structures were torn down with the falling ruin. It was sanguinary disaster. So Samson, the great 'might have been,' died. That God answered his last prayer does not prove its harmony with His highest purpose (cf. Psa. **106**.15). Dr Watson, the Victorian commentator, wrote: 'Not Milton's apology for Samson, not the authority of all who have likened Samson's sacrifice to Christ's, can keep us from deciding that this was a case of vengeance and self-murder, not of noble devotion.' If there was self-sacrifice in Samson, it was the sacrifice of a higher self to a lower. He destroyed Philistines—and deepened their hatred for Israel.

Questions and themes for study and discussion on Studies 123–131

1. What New Testament illustrations can you quote for the fact that God appears to meet man on the level of his available faith?

2. What constitutes a 'call' to God's service? In what sense can a 'call' be a special one?

3. How did tradition and Moses' law make it clear that no human sacrifice was right?

4. The sources of temptation in a social context, and a secular culture.

5. What evidence of mental quality do you find in Samson's story?

150

6. In what ways can Samson's mistake of confusing symbol with reality be repeated in a modern setting?

132 : Micah

Judges 17

The closing chapters of Judges seem designed to show the chaos of religious and civil confusion, the breakdown of worship and inter-tribal strife into which the land fell during this veritable Dark Age. Part of the story centres in the Ephraimite Micah, a man of means and position, who lived in the central hill-country.

The influence of Shiloh, the religious centre of Palestine, if any one place could, in such a time, boast that name, was so feeble that Micah conceived the idea of a family temple, complete with graven images (observe the plural) and a son of the household consecrated as a priest to serve them. To such a depth had the worship of Jehovah and the great Mosaic Code descended.

It was a great opportunity in Micah's eyes when a wandering Levite came that way. The fact that there were such mendicant priests on the road in Palestine is itself indicative of the collapse of centralized worship and authority. The man from Bethlehem was a type common in the European Middle Ages, a charlatan prepared to turn his reputation for sanctity to personal comfort and advantage.

The Levites had no special inheritance in the land, and in the general disorganization of religion were under heavy temptation to earn a living by their wits. The tithes that should have supported them were unpaid, and lesser men found some rational form of self-justification in preying on the community, and in meeting any popular demand which opened the way to such monetary and carnal advantage. To this had the heritage of Moses and Aaron descended.

And so the man from Bethlehem, for a wage of silver, a ration of clothes, and assured lodging (10), became the 'spiritual father' of Micah, who thought his wealth could secure him a private priest, access to God, and all the worldly

151

advantages which men through all time have found in the practice of a cult. They are not unknown today, inside and outside the fabric of the professing Church. There are odd birds nesting in the mustard tree.

Observe the pathos of the last verse. Poor Micah had a Levite of his own, and it followed that divine blessing would follow. For a cheap rate he had secured the best that religion could give. As an antidote to the thought read Rom. 12.1, 2.

133 : Moses' Descendant

Judges 18

The well-told story in this chapter is revealing. Dan had not secured its heritage, so sent out from the country of Zorah and Eshtaol, the old district of Samson, some spies to seek for living-space. The men made two discoveries. They found Micah's secluded estate, his private chapel, and the fraudulent priest. The base man actually bestowed his blessing on their predatory enterprise (6). The second discovery was an idyllic community in northern Palestine, a forgotten colony of Phoenician Sidon, where the land was fertile, and where crime was unknown (7). It was such a community as men have dreamed about but seldom achieved.

The five scoundrels came back to report to their tribesmen in Zorah and Eshtaol, and the Danites set out with arms and a wagon train to migrate north. Passing through Ephraim they remembered the farmstead of Micah and the Levite of Bethlehem, who was the private priest. Bethlehem, after all, is only a dozen miles from Zorah and Eshtaol, and many of them knew the man. They decided to appropriate him along with the cultic images in the temple, which Micah had built and maintained.

Micah protested, but he and his farm labourers were no match for six hundred armed men of Dan. It suited the Levite to function as a tribal priest, rather than a household chaplain, so the column moved on, equipped now with their medicine-man. Micah had lost his religion, for religions thus built are easily taken away.

The Danites moved on into the peaceful Phoenician town, murdered its unsuspecting inhabitants, and settled on the appropriated land. They set up their graven image, and the heathen worship which went along with it. The Levite from Bethlehem became their permanent priest, and founded a sort of sacerdotal dynasty (30). But then comes the surprise. For the first time the calculating Levite from Bethlehem is named. He is Jonathan, son of Gershom, and Gershom was the son of Moses and Zipporah (Exod. 2.22; 18.3). If 1280 B.C. is accepted as the date of the Exodus, chronology just allows the possibility that Jonathan was Moses' grandson. But genealogies are seldom complete (e.g. the Lord, as 'the son of David') and two or three generations may lie between Gershom and Jonathan. But how tragic that a noble line should so decay.

134 : Naomi

Ruth 1

The closing chapters of Judges are best passed over. They are recorded to reveal to those who read what can happen to a nation which forgets its God. They are history as Gibbon once described it: 'the register of the crimes, follies and misfortunes of mankind'.

The chronicler of the later chapters of Judges may easily have been a man of Bethlehem. That famous little town appears close to the events recorded. The Book of Ruth is also a tale of Bethlehem and probably comes from the same pen. It is vividly written and we sense the same capable hand which told the grim stories which close the major book. Ruth is also a tale of the Judges (1.1), and some instinct impelled the writer to make it a story apart.

That Elimelech should take his family across the Jordan and the Dead Sea into alien Moab, was perhaps the measure of his despair over the chaotic state of the land. The closing chapters of Judges give some indication of the evil which roved within a score of miles of his own home town. And there was always the menace of the raiding Philistines from the coastal lowlands.

It was, none the less, a tragic decision. Until quite recently a type of malaria was indigenous to the region, which fell with peculiar impact upon younger men. This may account for the deaths which widowed the gracious Naomi and took away her sons.

Perhaps Naomi's heart was never in the project. The history of more than one frontier has seen devoted women leave home and kindred with heavy hearts to follow an adventurous or restless family. Few have followed to tragedy more sad than that which fell to Naomi's lot. We have met citizens of Bethlehem in the story of the Judges, and they have not commanded admiration or respect. Naomi stands in contrast, and reveals that, in the most sombre times of a people's history, there can be godliness, sweetness and unselfishness among God's Few. Every word this woman utters is full of grace, thought for others, and godly simplicity. Naomi is the most womanly woman we have so far met since Eve—as Wordsworth put it:

> *A being breathing thoughtful breath,*
> *A traveller 'twixt life and death;*
> *The reason firm, the temperate will,*
> *Endurance, foresight, strength, and skill;*
> *A perfect woman, nobly planned*
> *To warn, to comfort and command,*
> *And yet a spirit still, and bright*
> *With something of angelic light.*

135 : Ruth

Ruth 1.15—2.23

The quality of Naomi is revealed by the love and devotion she was able to excite. With words which have been made a part of the spirit of man, Ruth refuses to go back to Moab, to Chemosh (Moab's god) and the past (16 f.). She faces the future confident in another's love. There is a significant picture in her act of anyone facing the unknown, confident that Christ's care will be unwavering.

In all such decisions there is a counting of the cost and a cost to be paid. There are moments of doubt and of loneliness. Keats was no doubt right in his *Ode to the Nightingale*, when he pictured:

154

The sad heart of Ruth, when sick for home
She stood in tears amid the alien corn.

The young woman of Moab knew that she courted rejection among the Hebrews, who hated her race. She went with Naomi because she could not be happy apart from the mother she loved. To win such affection shows the worth of the one who won it. Naomi had her compensatiòns.

Naomi returned to Bethlehem and, as so often happens, the old circle had closed. The place seemed different. She was hardly recognized, and the contrast between her present misfortune and her past felicity was made more painful and more keen by the sight of the familiar streets and the crowded houses on the ridge.

For Ruth, the whole environment must have been bitterly strange. There can be nothing more daunting than a foreign city where every word spoken reveals by turn of phrase and accent the gulf between the native and the stranger. Ruth met the situation with courage and hard work. Every instinct would suggest flight, and avoidance of confrontation. Instead, the young widow mastered herself and went out, as she was entitled by the Mosaic code of mercy to do, to glean in the harvest. The work was, no doubt, hard, and unrewarding. The Moabite was not welcome in the congregation of Israel, and it was only the marriage to a Hebrew, and the shield of Naomi's goodness, which covered her in her solitary task. Ruth had counted the cost and made her choice. And when choice òf such sort has been made, it is well to abide by it. Ruth did, and won the reward of faithfulness.

136 : Boaz
Ruth 3, 4

We have met a gracious woman. We now meet a good and generous man. Those who read French will find a beautiful poem on Boaz by Victor Hugo, who, with fidelity to Scripture, pictures the old man of Bethlehem going out of his way in simple kindness to aid the weary girl who lingered in his field.

Naomi's directions, and Ruth's compliance involved no immodesty. It was the way of the East to communicate in symbols. The threshing-floor was an open space. The workers slept in their cloaks. It was thus that Boaz was made aware of his obligations as a kinsman—to marry the widow of the deceased relative, and continue his line. In the case of Ruth that line was to be an important one, as the list of her posterity, from David to Christ, reveals.

It is evident that, in the midst of wide forgetfulness of the Mosaic law, there was some memory of its social provisions, and the good Boaz had no hesitation in obeying as he was required to do, and meeting all the requirements of the law.

So the story moved to its happy ending, Boaz, Ruth and Naomi, all rescued from their varied loneliness and bereavement, and the brave, good woman, who had sought her home again after sad and distant wandering, rewarded by the holding of Ruth's child in her arms.

From the ridges where Bethlehem stands, far to the east, can be seen the purple edge of the mountains of Moab. The girl who had been faithful to a woman who had loved her could now look at the far line of blue with no homesickness, but only joy for the discovery of a God who cared, guided and planned. The upward path from the floor of Jordan to the hills of Bethlehem had been hard upon the feet, but it was the path of love, decision and committal, and such paths lead home.

The book ends. We have met in its pages only love, goodness, faith, loyalty, kindness, obedience, generosity, mercy, fulfilment, courtesy—and never a deed or word of evil. And all these qualities and virtues have been shown only where they can be shown—in the persons of two women and a man.

Questions and themes for study and discussion on Studies 132–136

1. Discuss private interpretations of religion in the light of the authority of Scripture.
2. Collect from the Pentateuch the Law's provisions for foreigners.

3. Study the picture of the virtuous woman in Proverbs.
4. Collect from the Pentateuch the Law's requirements for the kinsman of a deceased person.
5. What historical principles may be derived from the narrative of the Judges?
6. What lessons arise from the story of Ruth?

137 : Elkanah

1 Samuel 1.1–23

The scene is set in the quiet hill-country hamlet of Ramathaim-Zophim. Like Bethlehem it is a backwater of the land, away from the turbulence of the invaders from the eastern desert and the western coastal strip, away too from much of the evil which haunted that century. The chapter might be a continuation of Ruth's story, with the spotlight of the historian changing from the farm of Boaz to the farm of Elkanah.

He was a quiet and somewhat complacent man, this farmer-father of the last of the judges of Israel, an obscure man made great by his son, or perhaps by the devotion of a good wife, whose prayers gave Samuel to his people. Elkanah fulfilled with annual precision the duties of his faith. He made his pilgrimage to the national shrine of Shiloh, where the ark of the covenant was kept, and no doubt felt that by this meticulous observance of the formalities of religion all his duty towards God was done. His was no corrupt worship, nor was his view of God a mean and unworthy one, but there was little of challenge in his faith, nothing to disturb his genial and somewhat shallow complacency.

For observe his household. Elkanah gives no evidence of awareness concerning the division in his house. Doubtless quoting Jacob as his precedent, he supports two wives, and does nothing to quench the venom of the wife who first had children, against her unfortunate partner. Elkanah had no conception of the pain in Hannah's heart, and of the hunger

157

for children of her own, which could not be satisfied by any gifts, by anything, in fact at all, short of the proper fulfilment.

There is a faint touch of the ludicrous in the good man's conviction that the blessing of having him for a husband was in itself compensation. He, surely, he tells the persecuted and distracted woman, is worth more than many sons. And what if Peninnah was harsh to her? Was he not most abundantly kind? He had no word of reproach for Peninnah, who marred a high religious occasion by her waspish attacks on the object of her jealousy. A harmless man, in short, notable for neither good nor ill, but more for good than ill, quietly pleased with himself, and with small concern for the deeper implications of religion.

138 : Peninnah

Proverbs 14.1; 17.1–5

Elkanah's wife Peninnah was an insecure and a tormented woman. The divided household reveals all the evils of anything other than, or short of, holy monogamy. And, as so often happens in life, justice seemed awry. A woman eminently fitted to bring up children, was without offspring. One whose bitter jealousy and hatred unfitted her for the task of motherhood had been entrusted with the rearing of a family.

That this responsibility did not make Peninnah gentle and humble is the measure of that evil which was eating her life away. Of all the passions which afflict man, jealousy is the hardest to bear, exacts the hardest service, and pays the bitterest of wages. It is condemned to watch the success of its enemy. Perhaps Peninnah was younger, less popular with the village, less beautiful than Hannah. Something took away all joy in her children. Merely to see Hannah accepted and high in Elkanah's affections, shallow though those affections were, was gall to her spirit. She was very unsure of her worth, and when the clumsy husband gave his childless wife 'a double portion' at the time of religious festival (1 Sam. 1.5, RV), Peninnah's hatred was stirred to its turbid depths.

Jealousy is the fear or realization of another's superiority, and Peninnah paid her rival this unsolicited compliment, but in entertaining the deadly visitant in her heart, she ruined her peace, and preyed upon herself. Envy, like anger, burns itself in its own fire. It has no other task than that of detracting from another's virtue, and in so doing quenches virtue in its host. As Franklin once remarked: 'Whoever feels pain at hearing of the good of his neighbour will feel a pleasure in the reverse. And those who despair to rise in distinction by their virtues, are happy if others can be depressed to a level with themselves.'

This was Peninnah's fate and her predicament. This was the poison which spoiled the household of Elkanah, without, as far as the evidence of the story goes, any reaction or attention from that self-centred man. The pathetic creature had much to make her contented and happy. Because she could not have more, the first unrivalled place, she destroyed the wealth she had in folly. To some extent she merits pity as the victim of a society which gave woman less than her due.

139 : Hannah

1 Samuel 1.21–2.11

Childlessness was a peculiar burden to a pious Hebrew woman. In such a fate she found herself excluded from the national destiny. ('In thee and in thy seed shall all the families of the earth be blessed' [Gen. 28.14, AV, KJV]). She could never become the ancestress of the One who should 'bruise the serpent's head'. Hence the peculiar bitterness of the assault Peninnah made upon Hannah's peace. It required a deep grief to attract the attention of Elkanah, but Hannah's distress was such that it brought out all the kindliness of that simply constructed man.

She must have felt that there was no one who truly under-stood her, and in that conviction is loneliness indeed. It was a further blow when the aged priest, accustomed to the loud and shallow prayers of many of the visitors to his shrine, was too obtuse to mark the distress which sought solitary com-munion with God for the deep petitions of the heart. The gentleness and moving eloquence of Hannah's reply to his clumsy assessment of her trouble (1.15 f.), is a clear indication of her gentleness of character, and the quiet ways she had learned in the hard school of Peninnah's jealousy and scorn.

Hannah was a woman of undemonstrative faith and deep committal, strong and quietly decisive. She makes up her own mind about visiting the Shiloh festival, and about the career of the child she had been given. Elkanah shows his easy-going acceptance of his wife in a manner which indicates the strength of character he found in her.

The psalm of praise which Hannah sings in Eli's presence (2.1–10) reveals her understanding of divine things in an age when men had small understanding of their God. It recognizes the power of God and the certainty of ultimate justice. It expresses faith in God's power to keep, and joy at answered prayer. It vibrates with gratitude.

Gratitude, this deep characteristic of Hannah's character, is a quality for consideration. Here are some words for consideration: . . . 'A humble mind is the soil out of which thanks naturally grow' (Henry Ward Beecher). . . . 'A thankful heart is not only the greatest virtue, but the parent of all other virtues' (Marcus Tullius Cicero) . . . 'Every virtue divorced from thankfulness is maimed and limps along the spiritual road' (John Henry Jowett) . . . 'O Lord that lends me life, lend me a heart replete with thankfulness' (William Shakespeare).

140 : Hophni and Phinehas

1 Samuel 2.12–36; 4.16–22

Hophni and Phinehas were 'sons of Belial', and the Old Testament has no darker word of reproach. Belial means literally and basically 'worthlessness', and is used of the dissolute, the reprobate and the uncouth. There have been many flashes of history in the story of the judges which illuminate the shocking degradation of the times, but few are more repulsive than that which shows the greed and lechery of the sons of Eli.

160

There was little enough in this age of divided weakness and infiltrating paganism to unite Israel around the Law and Moses' God, but the shrine of Shiloh, with its sacred memorials of the ancient Tabernacle, was one attempt to attain this end. If corruption found a home and centre there, the damage was grave indeed. In the sons of Eli, the high priest of Shiloh's shrine, it found such a harbourage.

Evil in the two men, who were probably middle-aged, since their father neared the age of ninety, was open, cynical and unconcealed. Nadab and Abihu died because of an act of gross irreverence (Lev. **10**). Hophni and Phinehas died also, though less immediately. The ritual for the securing of the priest's portion was established, but roughly disregarded by these uncouth men. Reverence is the first element of religion. It cannot but be felt by anyone who has correct views of the greatness and holiness of God, and of man in relation to God.

Through all time, since the Pharisees and their 'unpardonable sin', their 'blasphemy against the Holy Spirit', of which the Lord accused them, people whose life is lived close to the practice of the forms and rituals of religion have been exposed to the temptation of treating sacred things with levity. Blasphemy lies along that path. The significance of such ministry must be kept with care.

If such unholiness was visible and condoned in the central holy place of Israel, what hope was there for the proper training of the common folk who resorted there in 'the fear of the Lord'? Such was the wider significance of Hophni and Phinehas. Their sin, like all sin, was contagious, but with such carriers at large, what hope was there to contain and to quench the virus? The story is woven with the end of Eli and the beginning of Samuel to reveal the need for the destruction of the old, and the establishment of the new.

141 : Eli

1 Samuel 2.27–36; 4.1–22

Eli sprang, not from the eldest, but the youngest of the sons of Aaron in his descent. Since the older line was passed over in the choice of a priest for Shiloh's shrine, it would appear

161

that once, perhaps in his young manhood, Eli was a person of vigour and devotion.

We meet him only in his old age. In the first chapter of the book he is shown a trifle obtuse and impatient with a case of pathetic need, but rapidly adjusting to the situation when the real facts are courteously put before him. In the second chapter he is shown weakly protesting against the base iniquities of his carnal sons. In the third chapter he is seen in gentle humility receiving from the lips of a child a sombre confirmation of the sentence conveyed to him by 'the man of God'.

There is much therefore about Eli which we do not know. In the few verses which, in these chapters, form the substance of his biography, or at least the later years of it, Eli appears to us a pitiable, a weak, but a pious old man, unable to cope with a mounting wave of evil.

None the less, that evil was of his making. He was passive in days which demanded action, silent in days which called for speech, a weakling in days which cried for strength, and mild when God's name called for passionate defence. He set his family and their concupiscence above the honour of God, and, in his office, there could hardly have been a greater fault.

Verse 30, in the terrible indictment of the unnamed 'man of God', set an immortal verse into the annals of the faith, and put into words a promise which millions have discovered in their life experience to be true, but the same verse, taken in the context of the grim warning, defines and nails down Eli's sin. He had not honoured God. His sons had made themselves vile, and he restrained them not. He was called to exercise discipline, and had failed to exercise it. There was no excuse for his weakness. He stood in high office and the nation mattered more than his family. So Eli died with his last years shadowed by a mistake in his youth or middle age. It was too late.

142 : Temple-boy
1 Samuel 3

It is difficult to estimate the age of Samuel in this story. He must have been old enough to serve as the immediate servant of the aged Eli, strong enough to open the temple doors, and intelligent enough to deliver a detailed message. Shall we say twelve or thirteen years, the age of the Lord in Luke's story of His childhood?

The RSV might have been a little bolder in its translation of the first verse. The NEB puts the situation well: 'Now in those days the word of the Lord was seldom heard.' It was not an unrecognizable situation. Indeed, the whole story could be symbolic. The light in the dim sanctuary was dying down when the Lord spoke to Samuel. A generation had failed but, as John remarked, the darkness does not quench the word, and often when the old have failed He speaks to the young.

But when He does so, He still utters the substance of His own unchanging word. The message comes with new impact, and with new clarity, but Samuel is commissioned to communicate to the erring old man exactly the same penetrating truth as 'the man of God' of the earlier chapter had communicated to him. Truth does not change, but God sometimes finds it necessary to use new voices to carry its message.

The maturity of the boy is evident. He had grown up in the solemn precincts of the shrine of Shiloh, handling divine things, performing, with seeming delight, the divine offices. Hophni and Phinehas had been hardened and brutalized by their careless handling of God's vessels. Familiarity bred contempt. With Samuel the opposite process took place. It depends always with what reverence, and what devotion the work is undertaken. In the case of the little boy, the son of a devout mother, prepared by Hannah's ministrations and prayers for the task of the neophyte, the place of God had been sanctifying.

The story finds its climax in vs. 18 and 19. Samuel delivered the painful message word for word. That is why God confirmed his words. In a day when the faithful failed among the children of men (Psa. 12.1) Samuel was found to be faithful. We dismiss old Eli with a touch of sorrow. To hear his doom from a child he loved must have been pain indeed.

143 : Samuel the Judge

1 Samuel 7

Samuel was a judge in a wider sense of the word than any of his predecessors, who in general were men brought forward by some national crisis, and inspired to some act of patriotic deliverance. Verse 16 shows Samuel on circuit, dispensing justice in local courts, and in the act giving some unity to the perilously divided tribes. It was something of the same task as Henry II undertook for England in the Middle Ages.

Samuel's policy of unification was needed now that the sketchy cohesion which had made Shiloh its centre had been destroyed. The deep Philistine raiding, in which the house of Eli had perished, also overran Shiloh. The chronicler of Samuel does not mention this. The raid, the looting and the murder of the priests are mentioned by the psalmist (78.60–64) and Jeremiah (7.12; 26.9). The grim experience, and the escape from the raiders, may have been traumatic for the young boy who served the shrine. So, too, may have been the loss of that sacred talisman the Ark.

Had Shiloh stood, Samuel might have been tempted to follow the tradition of Eli, and function rather as pontiff than legislator. It was a legislator, rather than a high priest, which the situation in the land demanded, and the pressure of circumstances forced the role on Samuel. This is what faith should seek in life—a proper function in relation to events, and the meaning of those situations in which God places us or allows us to be placed. It is thus that He guides a mind alert to discover His will. Shiloh, and the priesthood associated with it, had seen their day.

Samuel, from the wealth of his experience, struck a more spiritual note than any other leader had done since Joshua. Observe the tenor of his address to assembled Israel. The old monotheistic tradition, with its rejection of idolatry, was not dead. It needed a voice, and Samuel gave it one. The people responded with vigour, as the reaction to the Philistine raid shows. It is a testimony to Samuel's leadership. He was no soldier, but he supplied what no soldier dare lack—a rank and file filled with belief in their cause.

144 : Samuel's Sons

1 Samuel 8.1–6; Deuteronomy 4.9, 10; 11.18–21

With all the shocking example of Eli before him Samuel failed to hold his children. He himself had set them no example of corruption or of unfairness. And yet the young men, Joel and Abijah, who held court on their father's behalf on the edge of the southern desert, became notorious for the taking of bribes and the perversion of justice.

How is this to be accounted for? Let it be stated immediately that it is not always the fault of parents if their children do not follow in their steps. At the same time, if visited by such a calamity, parents should search their life, their attitudes, their outlook, in earnest endeavour to discover, if possible, the cause of failure, and to put it right.

Wherein could a good man like Samuel have failed so lamentably? Perhaps he was too much absent from home, busy on the tasks of his national leadership. Perhaps, following the advice which Jethro gave once to Moses, he should have acquired the art of delegation, and brought again to life Moses' effective scheme of co-operative justice. Perhaps Samuel was too eager to hold the reins of power in his own hands, and, inevitably overworked, had not found time for that fellowship with his family which is such a vital element in the upbringing of the young. There are times when boys need their father, as a guide, a confidant and a friend. It is a primary duty for a father, and the successful leading of one's children to God must be a priority in all of life's activities.

Perhaps, in spite of the sombre warning of Eli's example, Samuel had been too eager to see his sons follow in his steps as legislators. No mistake produces such unfortunate results as misguided parental efforts to force children into a predetermined pattern of life. Parental ambitions do not matter. What does matter is that young men and women should find the career for which they are fitted and in which they can find true fulfilment and happiness. When Mark clashed with Paul, the fault may perhaps be traced to the desire of Mary his mother, or his uncle Barnabas, to see the young man take up a missionary career. His role was to write a Gospel, Joel and Abijah were not fitted to hold a

165

judicial role, and it was a disservice to them and to Israel to thrust them into such a position.

This is guesswork, but it is obvious that, in upbringing or in premature and unwise appointment, somewhere along the line of life, Samuel had failed.

145 : Samuel's Crisis

1 Samuel 8

Samuel took the demand for a king as a vote of no confidence. The fact confirms the suspicion that a basic fault in him was a certain infusion of pride. He was old. His sons had betrayed him. No one else was trained to succeed him. He had made no provision for the continuation of the magnificent work he had done save the unwise and abortive attempt to found a line of judges. This was a quite lamentable lack, and betokened a reprehensible measure of self-esteem.

In the united demand for the establishment of a monarchy, there was some indication of the effectiveness of Samuel's work. Here, after all, was Israel speaking with a united voice, and this unity was, without a doubt, a product of Samuel's judgeship, and his establishment of a system of justice. Had he, by the acceptable choice of a successor, in the way in which Moses chose Joshua, or alternatively, had he, in a wise system of delegation, after the same Mosaic pattern, left a framework of judicial power in the land, the demand for a monarchy might never have arisen. Samuel must be blamed for some of it.

Perhaps then, as we have remarked, a corner of Samuel's basic pride is seen when he takes the demand of the people as a rejection of himself. The people, in fact, had been notably patient. The leader was old. His sons were unsuitable to succeed him. It was becoming late, and many could remember the near-anarchy of the years before Samuel took power in the land. It is then pointed out to Samuel that it was not the judge who was rejected, but rather God Himself. The ideal constitution for Israel was a theocracy, with power administered through the priests. Failing this, a guided monarchy was the next best plan. This becomes clear to

Samuel, and it became clear because of his unbroken habit of seeking God's will, and faithfully telling the people what he had learned in the holy place of such communion. His experience as a child in the Temple set the pattern for old age. Life is not infrequently so ordained. Without reserve or trimming of words, the old judge explains the financial and religious implications of their demand. The people were unconvinced.

Questions and themes for study and discussion on Studies 137–145

1. What are the roots of jealousy? Consider Sarah, Rachel and Leah, and Joseph's brothers.

2. What is irreverence?

3. What is blasphemy?

4. How can parents best ensure their children's loyalty to their own ideals?

5. Why do some characters find delegation difficult?

146 : Saul

1 Samuel 9 and 10

Saul is not unlike the 'rich young ruler' who brought his shallow enthusiasm to Christ. He had much, but lacked the essential surrender to God. Saul appears in the ninth chapter in a humble role, the dutiful son of a rich family wandering the highlands of central Palestine in search of some valuable animals.

He must be pictured, therefore, as a man of some self-reliance and courage. It was no land, in those days, to wander through with impunity. Saul had a servant with him, who must be added to the list of faithful henchmen whom we have met, from Eliezer of Damascus to the servant of Gideon. Saul had a way with men, a gift of true leadership, and the servant moves confidently by the side of his stalwart young master, as much a friend and a counsellor as an underling.

There is much therefore to commend the man in whom old Samuel found the future king of Israel. The aged judge saw in the remarkable sequence of circumstances, which brought the son of Kish to the meeting place, a situation so unusual that he found in it the hand of God. Saul obviously had the physique and the presence which would commend him to the people who looked for a leader among the nations, a popular figure fitted to unite scattered and suspicious tribes round some symbol of unity. It is in mind and spirit that he lacked something.

Yet the hesitation which he shows in the face of Samuel's astonishing announcement is no mark against him. It is a **becoming diffidence, a true humility.** It was necessary for Samuel to talk long and earnestly to him, in unrecorded conversation, to convince the man of Benjamin that there was a genuine call to him to take up the burden of leadership and overcome reluctance.

How deeply Samuel influenced him is not clear. The tenth chapter shows Saul's need for confirmatory signs. Saul has what seems to have been a deep religious experience with a group of religious celebrants, but it is to be doubted whether he ever attained a rich, meaningful and sustaining faith. Prophets to him were 'seers', men of divine magic, and God a somewhat blurred idea. Hence the failure to carry the full approval of the land. He failed to win 'the worthless' (10.27), but accepted their scorn in humble silence. We feel a shadow upon Saul, and can understand how Samuel yearned over him.

147 : Saul the Soldier

1 Samuel 11

Saul went back to his daily tasks. His call had come, but not his moment. It was a month later, according to Josephus, that Israel was stirred by shocking news. The remnants of the nation who had chosen to remain to the east of Jordan had as their reward the well-watered uplands and valley pastures of Gilead, but at the price of some grave disadvantages. They were exposed to the people of the desert, and the tribes who, like the Ammonites, cultivated the desert edge.

Still remembering their old humiliation under Jephthah, the people of Ammon, strong and arrogant again, came in array against Jabesh and offered the unhappy Gileadites, as the price of peace, mutilation and sadistic humiliation. Messengers hurried through Israel, and it is a sign of the new unity that Samuel's judgeship had achieved, that a wave of horror and indignation went through the land. Saul saw that his hour was come. In many ways it was his finest hour, for shadows were to fall early across his reign. At this moment he shows himself decisive, ardent, a true leader of men, and wise enough to seize an occasion of national stress and unity to show his worth, and rally the people behind him.

Riding this wave of pity and concern for their sundered brethren across the Jordan, Saul collected his army and marched. It must have been forced and exhausting marching. David, in retreat from Absalom, seems to have taken three days to accomplish a comparable march. How long Saul took is not clear, though he appears to have promised a decisive intervention within twenty-four hours of the messengers' reporting back.

Such was the dynamism of his leadership that he did precisely this. It was no easy march from the central uplands of Israel down into the jungle tangle of the Jordan Rift Valley ('the swellings of Jordan' of the AV [KJV] phrase), up the trans-Jordan mountain slopes, and to Jabesh. Without pausing for breath, and achieving surprise by the threefold division of his forces, Saul fell upon the cruel invaders, and won a spectacular victory. The men of Jabesh never forgot it (1 Sam. 31.11).

The effect on Israel was equally spectacular. The tribes had their hero (12). On the surge of sudden and unifying popularity, Saul became the accepted monarch. It was a time of universal rejoicing, a sort of V Day (15). Saul is shown at his best (13). Perhaps he might always have been like this had he known God better. And was that lack partly Samuel's fault?

148 : Samuel's Testimony

1 Samuel 12; Job 8.8–10

Samuel appears to have been the only one of the judges who was deeply conscious of his nation's history. Perhaps his childhood as the temple-servant at Shiloh had given him access to the stored records of the past. Such records there certainly were, and where would they have been more appropriately housed than in the place where Israel's holy relics were kept?

At any rate, he shows in this encounter with the people a very wide knowledge of Israel's history and its significance. His whole approach, his speed of almost defiant challenge, his tone of authority and command are modelled on Joshua's last words. His rapid survey of history from the Exodus, on through the troubled story of the nation to Samson and the day of Saul's victory, shows a sense of the nation's destiny long lacking in the stormy characters who were called to her leadership.

The appeal to experience, and the endeavour to root the nation's faith in the realization of God's active hand in their affairs, was a sound and constant preoccupation with Samuel. He had struck that note when he set up the stone called Ebenezer, between Mizpah and Jeshanah [Shen] (1 Sam. 7.12). The word means: 'Stone of Help'—help, that is, from God. Furthermore, Samuel was prompted to the symbolic action by his own knowledge of history. Mizpah, the name of the Benjamite town (Josh. 18.26), means 'watchtower', and had perhaps reminded the judge that this was a name which Jacob had given to a cairn set up as a memorial of the agreement between him and Laban (Gen. 31.45–49). It was a significant memorial. 'Not to know what was done in former times,' said Cicero, 'is to be always a child. If no use is made of the toil and trouble of past ages, the world must remain for ever in the infancy of knowledge.'

Words of counsel could hardly be nobler than those which Samuel uttered before the assembled multitudes as the conclusion of his speech (20–24). Here was Israel's religion in brief, as Moses and Joshua might have put it. The worth of history is shown in the words. A nation loses contact with its past to its dire peril—a point to be considered by those who order education, or preach the message of the Christian faith—an historically grounded religion.

149 : Saul's Impatience

1 Samuel 13

Saul faced a grave military crisis at the end of the second year of his reign. The Philistines were on the march again, and Saul was finding it difficult to hold the people to their newly discovered unity. The threat, too, was grave, and the people followed Saul's leadership with much misgiving. The mood of confidence was gone (7).

It was at this point that Samuel, whose religious prestige was tremendous in the land, chose to delay his coming. Whereupon, as the heading in one popular reference Bible puts it, Saul 'intruded into the priests' office', and offered a sacrifice. It is difficult to be censorious over this act of haste. Saul saw the need for despatch. The army was melting away. Perhaps he should have remembered Gideon, but it was the business of Samuel, if he guarded jealously, as was just, the office of priest, to be at Gilgal in order to bring such significant history to Saul's and the people's remembrance.

Saul, as we have seen, had no deep spirituality. The sacrifice was a formality, and it is here perhaps that some truth and justice must be accorded the rebuke which Samuel gave.

It was not so much the 'intrusion into the priest's office' which condemned Saul's reign to failure or to inconclusiveness, but the impatience with delay, born of an inadequate view of his God, which prompted a perfunctory act of sacrifice.

It is probably quite true that Saul undertook the task of sacrifice with some reluctance (12), but apparently he had received a clear direction regarding the limitations of his royal prerogatives (13), and deliberately disobeyed them. Here was the weakness which was to prove disastrous.

The task of conflict, none the less, was faced with courage. The situation was interesting historically, for here, in a clear record, was the Bronze Age encountering the Iron Age (19–23). The weapon-gap could be closed only by faith, and the confidence and ardour which arise from utter dedication to a cause. This had been shown in the Jabesh-Gilead campaign. Saul could not see the same Spirit abroad when he faced the Philistines. But Saul had one immense and unappreciated advantage—a soldier for a son.

150 : Jonathan

1 Samuel 14.1–15

Jonathan is one of the great characters of the Old Testament, brave, loyal, gracious, a soldier and a friend. The story of his exploit at Michmash reveals much of his person. He was the stuff of which commandoes are made. He could inspire the absolute and unquestioning loyalty of his cool young armourbearer, worthily the theme of a Moody and Sankey hymn. He was simple in his faith and ready to act on it.

The details of Jonathan's manoeuvre are not clear. The Philistines held a commanding hill-position, but clearly one which could be turned, and itself outflanked by a force able to climb unseen and unopposed up a steep ascent. It is fairly obvious from accounts of Philistine reactions in earlier chapters that, as a people, they were prone to panic. This was the flaw of character that Jonathan was determined to turn to his advantage.

Suddenly the Philistine garrison on the hilltop saw two Hebrew warriors, in iron armour like their own, appear over the skyline above them, Jonathan may have been able to give the impression that an effective force was on the way up behind him. At the sight, the garrison on the plateau fled in panic. Their way of retreat was probably a narrow hill-path, so that the panic-stricken soldiers thrust one another to their deaths in their haste to reach safety. It was a piece of astounding bluff, which gave the prince his victory, but it required a courageous and a resourceful man to stage it.

Lest the situation appear unlikely, there is comparatively modern confirmation. A battalion of Allenby's London Regiment in 1917 was located where Saul held his six hundred on that occasion. The local place-name of Mukmas prompted the commander to read his Old Testament. He concluded that the Turks who barred his path were positioned like the Philistines. Reconnaissance showed that the lay of the land had not changed, and that the Turkish position could be turned after the ancient model. A platoon was sent out to occupy the superior position, and when dawn revealed their presence, the Turkish garrison withdrew.

So Jonathan, ill-starred and shadowed by his passionate father, enters the story. He is not destined to stay in it long, or to play the part he might, in happier circumstances, have played, but he is good to know.

151 : Saul and his Son

1 Samuel 14.16–46

On the heights of Michmash, Jonathan had the Philistines in flight. The distant noise roused Saul. In his excitement (19) he waved aside the priest. He was too busy to pray. It was the same impatience he had shown before (13.8–10). In his pagan folly he condemned his army to hunger. Consider the results. The victory was incomplete. In the evening the desperate people broke the law (32). Now, at last, Saul thought to pray, or to perform that mechanical ritual to which he reduced such an exercise. Like many who pray only at such times, and in such perfunctory fashion, he felt cold, rejected and unheard (37). Too unspiritual and obtuse to apprehend the true cause in himself and his sin, Saul remembered his foolish vow . . . God sometimes allows folly to work itself out. He allowed Jonathan to stand incongruously condemned. And Saul would actually have killed Jonathan! A surge of anger through the Hebrew host was all that saved the splendid young warrior. And so Saul, scrupulous of superstition, and so careless of obedience, blunders on to Endor. The chapter is rich in lessons, and the spoiling faults of Saul's character emerge again . . .

The contrast between Saul and his son is striking. Saul was a hot-headed and passionate man. This side of his character, properly ordered and controlled, might have led him far. It determined the ardour of his drive against the Ammonites before Jabesh-Gilead. But Saul never broke through to a lofty and dominating faith. God to him was an elemental power to be propitiated, or appeased and harnessed by some movements of formality. Jonathan, on the other hand, was as cool-headed as he was brave. He could assess his father's folly (29), and probably undertook his lonely exploit because he had no confidence in winning the jealous Saul's sanction. Had he been spared his sad ending he would have made a splendid king, but it is part of the tragedy of Saul that he dragged to ruin his fine son. Such involvement is inseparable from our humanity. The same basic fact worked through to tragedy in Achan's family (Jos. 7). The same truth can be rich and fruitful in joy.

152 : Saul and Samuel

1 Samuel 15

The modern world, weary of war and bloodshed, may find
this chapter, with Samuel's decree of destruction against the
Amalekites, disturbing to read. The Amalekites must first be
seen for what they were—a species of Bedouin tribe, ranging
the eastern borderlands of Israel from Sinai and the Arabah
northwards, harassing the frontier, raiding, looting, murdering. If peace was to reign in Palestine, their utter defeat was
necessary. The war must be seen in the context of war
such as this century has known, where beleagured nations
have had cruelty, aggression and the determination of desperate guerrilla groups cursing their borderlands and damaging all peace. Saul had a task such as the Emperor Augustus
had at the beginning of this era—the pacification of the
frontiers behind which peace and prosperity were to grow.
For a ruler of Israel it was a national duty.

So much for the task. Speaking of the corruption and
utter decadence of the pagan tribes of Canaan, one archaeologist has remarked that, to him, the wonder was not that a
sentence of elimination went out against such damaged stocks,
but that it was delayed so long. At any rate Saul had his
orders. He knew the facts which Ezra was to stress (Ezra
9.11). And Saul, as was his way, interpreted those orders as
he saw fit. It was not in mercy that he spared Agag, the
sadistic ruler of the desert tribes (33), but for some personal
satisfaction, a species of triumphal procession perhaps, with
the captive king walking before his chariot. It was an act
of royal pride.

He lied to Samuel. He blamed 'the people' (21) for what
he had himself sanctioned. He demonstrated once more, and
this time for the last time, his untrustworthiness. His was to
be no continuing monarchy. Such self-will contained the seeds
of its own final defeat. Samuel knew it, and grieved for Saul
(35), for he had loved the man whom his own hands had
anointed. He saw his face no more.

Samuel in his stern rebuke shows himself the forerunner
of the major prophets. His remark about obedience and
sacrifice (22) should be read in connection with the first call
of Isaiah to Israel (Isa. **1**.11–20), three centuries later. It
was the old lesson which Israel found it so difficult to learn.

Read Psa. 119 and observe the dominance of the theme of obedience.

Questions and themes for study and discussion on Studies 146–152

1. Was Saul a wrong choice?

2. What is popularity worth?

3. Saul's view of God.

4. The centrality of obedience in religion.

5. The purpose of waiting, and the folly of impatience.

153 : The Shepherd Boy

1 Samuel 16.1–13; Psalm 8

The secret visit of the aged prophet to Bethlehem is told with brevity, but much may be read between the lines. The old age of the prophet was a sad and shadowed one. The breach with Saul was absolute (2), and Saul himself was entering the last darkened era of his reign, a time of mental illness and fierce frustration.

The farming community of Bethlehem was full of solidity. We have walked on its high hills in earlier studies, and met some of its sturdy peasants and shepherds. We now meet the household of Jesse, Ruth's grandson. The strong young men paraded before the prophet, and he looked into the eyes of each. In no case did he feel that surge of conviction which he had learned to know as the voice of God.

David was forgotten, and when the messenger sent for him, out on the very slopes where, a millennium later, 'the shepherds watched their flocks by night', he came running. Hence perhaps his 'ruddy' countenance, hot from his race home. He was handsome, too, a boy with fine eyes (12). So David, of whose mind and heart more is revealed than of any other character in the Old Testament, enters the story of the Bible.

He was good to look upon, but also had a choice mind. These were the unspoiled days of which perhaps Psa. 8 is one of the echoes, days of poetry, music, love of the open hills and the countryside. He was soon to meet Saul, and the tasks and tests which life had in store for him.

175

Amid the flood of his self-revelation in the poetry which flowed from him, David never seems to mention the momentous event in the farmhouse at Bethlehem. Perhaps it was unwise to speak of it before jealous brothers (17.28). Jesse himself, such were the perilous times, may have imposed a bond of silence on his family. But in David's conduct, this day and its events most certainly reveal themselves. He lived, all through his greater days, on a mighty faith that he was destined for the throne. Hence his noble abstinence from all violence towards the hostile king. No haste, like Jacob's, was to rend for him the delicate web of God's outworking purposes. So here stood the youth who was to succeed gloriously, fall lamentably, rise again, and in all experience reveal more of God and man than any other figure before Isaiah.

154 : Darkened King

1 Samuel 16.14–23; Galatians 5

Verse 14 reads strangely, and raises again the question earlier discussed (See Study No. 68)—the 'hardening' of Pharaoh's heart. A Hebrew would not have thought the statement strange, or that it in any way made the Author of All Good the creator simultaneously of evil. God permitted Saul's affliction. To such malady of the mind had the tensions of obstinate self-will led. The end was to be a recognizable paranoia.

It is a solemn fact of human experience that the spirit which will not bend before God sometimes breaks before circumstance. The drive and dash were obviously departing from Saul. In the next chapter he sits helpless and afraid before the challenge of Goliath (17.11). This is not the warrior who led the relief expedition to Jabesh-Gilead. His memory also seems impaired. He knew David as the harp-player of his melancholic hours, but asks Abner who he is (17.55–58). Of course the question might merely be as to David's lineage, a detail naturally enough forgotten. Nor do we know the time lapse between the chapters.

But so it became the ironic lot of the anointed king of Israel to sit and soothe the wild passions of the one who now

176

unworthily sat upon the throne. Thus was David tested. God sometimes imposes strange tasks upon His servants. He calls upon them to serve the thankless and unworthy, to waste time —or so it appears—on fruitless duties, and consume energy and impair health on activities which bring no joy and seem to have little purpose.

The reason is that the fruits of the Spirit (they are listed in the letter to the Galatians) are measured only in the qualities of the soul. These are what God values. David had enormous trials ahead of him, and it was of the first importance that he should learn as a young man to wait, and continue waiting, to trust and to obey. A leader must be practised in obedience, and of all the lessons which man is called upon to learn, that of patience stands to the fore. Touching the strings of the harp in the gloomy presence of the tormented man, David was to learn self-control, pity, endurance . . . Read Browning's poem *Saul*, which magnificently evokes the scene of the king and the harpist.

155 : Goliath
1 Samuel 17

The enormous hoplite of the Philistines was possibly one of the scattered Rephaim (Deut. 2.20–23), a race of extraordinary physique, who had taken refuge with the Philistines, and served as a mercenary in their army. The Philistines were prone to admire a man of strength and stature. Witness their early acceptance of Samson. There is some evidence, from skeletal remains, of the presence of men of exceedingly large stature in Palestine. The length of the cubit is not sure. It depends upon the average size of the human body, an uncertain criterion. According to the measurements of the Siloam Tunnel, the cubit may have been near fifteen inches. Beings of comparable stature have been known. Such stature is sometimes due to an excess of a growth hormone produced by the pituitary gland, a rare but documented phenomenon. The Royal College of Surgeons is said to hold the skeleton of a nine-foot Irishman.

The character of the giant hoplite is clearly depicted, arrogant, blasphemous, mightily enjoying his popularity with his own folk and the fear of the foe. The fruit of such arrogance is over-confidence. Goliath committed the cardinal mistake of underestimating his foe, always a dangerous error.

The result which followed is true to a historical principle of warfare. It is even true to nature. The vast armoured reptiles, who once dominated creation, have all disappeared. The stegosaur, whose forty-foot skeletons may be seen in museum halls, was covered with horn and bone from its tiny head to its mighty tail. It and its like disappeared before new creations, unarmoured, but with greater mobility, greater striking-power, and greater intelligence. So in history. Heavier knights did not sweep the heavy knights away, but longbows at Crécy, and flights of arrows from unmailed bowmen. Not galleons, but swift corvettes, scuttled the Armada. Elephants (read it in the story of the Maccabees) were beaten not by bigger or better elephants, but by brave men with short stabbing spears. So with David. 'Am I a dog,' roared the Philistine, 'that you come to me with sticks?' He threw back his head to laugh. Under the helmet brim, which should have been kept low, the whistling slingstone found the exposed forehead. Greater mobility, and greater striking-power, in the hands of higher intelligence, and a higher morale based on a burning faith, had won the day. David always remembered that moment (Psa. 27.1–3).

156 : Saul's Jealousy

1 Samuel 18.5–22

'Jealousy is cruel as the grave,' says Solomon. 'Its flashes are flashes of fire, a most vehement flame' (Song of Sol. 8.6). We have met jealousy before in Scripture, and seen it for the base and vicious thing it is. Its source is pride and self-esteem, and it seeks to thrust others down that self may be exalted. It sees a threat to security in every success or achievement of another. In Saul's case the vice was fed by the growth of his psychological malady. His deepening paranoia saw rivals everywhere, even in the shepherd boy, who had struck down for him the warrior of Gath, the fearsome Goliath.

Jealousy began in this vivid story with a popular song, not meant to be taken literally, but built on Hebrew parallelism (7). Once entertained, the evil became a habit of thought with Saul, so that David became an object of obsessive hatred. Thought eventually issued in action, as all thought commonly does. All deeds, good or evil, begin in the mind, and Saul's attempt at murder began with thoughts and visions of murder, entertained and cherished in the person. The Lord's teaching in the Sermon on the Mount, that the guilt lies in cherishing and retaining the desire, finds confirmation in the javelin of Saul. He failed to kill David, but bore the load of the desire.

The attempt was unsuccessful, for in David Saul was dealing with a superbly trained athlete. So next came low cunning, another characteristic symptom of Saul's worsening malady. Saul becomes contemptible when he uses his daughter's affection to plot treachery against David, and covers a plot with a show of generosity.

Observe in the whole story David's self-control. Saul was 'raving' in his house (10), but David, obviously without relaxing his caution, bravely sought to calm him with his music. Twice it is remarked (14, 15) that the sorely tried young man behaved with wisdom. He made no attempt, as many a denizen of an Eastern Court might have done, to remove his tormentor by assassination. He ignored the wave of popularity which was running in his favour through the land. He abstained from all retaliation. Such reserve could arise only from a deep, quiet confidence that his times and his person were alike in God's hands. It was one of David's finest hours.

157 : Jonathan the Man

1 Samuel 18.1–5; 19.1–17; 20.1–16

Jonathan has a high place among the characters of the Old Testament. Good, true, valiant, he stands in that tense and corrupt court and household, and under the sad shadow of his father's madness, a figure of integrity and strength. It sometimes falls to a good man's lot to live out his life in dark and evil places, to find his desire for good met with daily frustration, and whose worth seems wasted.

179

Jonathan's brave championship of David had little abiding influence on Saul, who speedily lapsed into his corroding jealousy, but Jonathan left a noble story in Scripture, which has played its part in the annals of the human spirit. Nor can we guess how much the friendship of the good prince meant to the future king of Israel in his time of testing. Jonathan was well aware that David was to possess his father's kingdom. Nor did he ever question that he owed a debt of loyalty to his father, as well as to his friend. He must have been sombrely aware of the fact that his own life was tangled with his father's doom. Friendship cost him much, and he never used it to his own advantage, never lifted a hand against his father.

But look again at David in this same situation. The thought of Jonathan and his loyalty must have been a cleansing power in the exile's mind. Considering Saul, his madness and his cruelty, David might have been tempted to look with some satisfaction on his own integrity and greater suitability for royal power in Israel. God, he could secretly conclude, had chosen him as a proper substitute for the murderous king. To look at Jonathan was to see such a conclusion crumble. With a man like Jonathan as Saul's natural heir, the choice of David was not nearly apparent. Jonathan, popular with the people of the land, David's equal in military exploits, a nobleman in character as well as in rank, would have made a distinguished king. David was turned to the humbling thought that he was not chosen for any excellence he possessed beyond his friend. He faced the outworking of an inscrutable plan, and could only face it with a plea for help. God had chosen, he knew not why. It was his part to justify the choice.

158 : Jonathan the Friend

1 Samuel 20.17–42

'Never contract friendship,' said Confucius, 'with a man who is not better than yourself.' How this policy could mutually work out is difficult to see, but there is a certain wisdom in the advice. It is possible that, judged by the visible qualities of character, Jonathan was a better man than David.

180

But note Jonathan's final word: 'The Lord shall be between me and you . . .' (42). The words establish a principle of friendship, relevant in all relationships between one person and another. In all true patterns of human love and fellowship there is a trinity—two persons and their Lord. It is the presence of the Lord which softens all clash of personality and harmonizes differences between man and man, and man and woman. The influence of one person on another, if that influence is mediated through God in a common faith and loyalty, can only produce good. It can never promote evil. God, therefore, becomes the test of all true friendship. If He cannot form a third, any relationship between two people is unblest, unsteady and unhealthy. Jonathan, then, enunciated an eternal truth in his last words to his friend.

The closing words of the vivid story are infinitely sad. Like the Lord 'setting his face steadfastly' to go up to Jerusalem and all that was waiting for Him there, Jonathan turned away, and returned to his duty, and his fate. There was nothing to stop his going into the wilderness with his friend. Between them they could have headed a popular movement. It would have been easy to have rebelled against a father who had used him so ill. But he chose duty, when he chose the road back to the city, and that road led to death. It was a road of sorrow, but it held the peace of God. There is a sense in which Jonathan died for another, and in that choice foreshadowed the very Christ of God.

'We do not choose our own parts in life,' said Epictetus. 'Our simple duty is confined to playing them well.' In such a role the good Jonathan never faltered. And it was Carlyle who said truly: 'Our grand business is not to see what lies dimly in the distance, but to do what lies clearly to hand.' The only clear path for Jonathan at that sad moment was the one down which the lad with the bow and the quiver full of arrows had taken.

159 : David's Desperation

1 Samuel 21.1–9; 22.1–23; Psalm 52

David lied to Ahimelech the priest. He secured help from the innocent man of God by a subterfuge. It was, no doubt, a stratagem of war, and a desperate attempt at self-preservation, but it was none the less an unworthy falsehood, especially in one who knew the will of God, and had learned well some of the lessons of nobler living. In the last words of the story David accepts full responsibility for the grim disaster which fell upon the innocent community, and offers no excuse for himself. He dealt with his fault in the only way in which fault can properly be dealt with. He recognized it for what it was, confessed it, made no attempt to mitigate it, and made every effort to quench the continuing effects.

But it all arose from deception. 'O what a tangled web we weave,' wrote Scott, 'when first we practise to deceive.' It seemed so simple and obvious a piece of trickery, to secure food for his hungry men, and weapons for himself, by a piece of untruthfulness. But he wove a web which enmeshed the lives of a whole innocent little town. Sin is like some virus, entering unseen into a body and ravaging it throughout. 'Sin came into the world through one man' and incidentally by one lie (Gen. 3.4).

David poured some of his feelings into the poetry of a psalm. He had met an evil man, but he was bitterly aware that he had given that evil man an occasion for action. His horror at treachery and the wickedness of the tongue appears in many a psalm, and David must have been aware of how very difficult it is to draw a firm boundary line between the small falsehood which produced the massacre of Nob, and the information which Doeg gave to Saul. Doeg, in fact, spoke the truth, yet used his tongue for evil. Had an untruth not played disastrously into his hand, he would have been impotent to harm.

'Do not let us lie at all,' said Ruskin, 'do not let us think of one falsehood as harmless, another as slight, and another as unintended. Cast them all aside. They are all ugly smoke from the pit, and it is better that our heart should be swept clean of them.'

1. The fruits of the Spirit.

2. How should jealousy in self, or in others against us, be dealt with?

3. The bases of true friendship.

4. Priorities in loyalty.

5. Are there degrees in falsehood?

160 : David in Exile

1 Samuel 21.10–15; 27.1–12; 29.1–11

It is difficult to sort out the chronology of David's time among the Philistines. On the face of it the book seems to record two periods among them, and the matter is of no great historical importance. We are seeking the personalities of Scripture, and here, without doubt, is an unexpected facet of character revealed.

The months spent at Gath were among the darkest of David's life. He was leagued with his people's enemies. He could be described in very truth as a traitor to his own. But note that we are clearly told that this was David's day of hopelessness and despair (27.1). Like other characters in the Bible, he was walking after the devices of his own heart. Not David the godly, but David the backslider walks before us, for the Bible is ruthless in revealing the faults of those who have added the brightest chapters in its story. It never hides the truth. And who are we to cast a stone? Let us remember further that the outlaw of these unhappy days was the ruddy youth who once, in joy and innocence, kept his father's sheep. Hate and jealousy in the hearts of those who should have loved and honoured him had done this damage to him. Furthermore, he paid, as men always must pay, in the inevitable justice of things, for these backslidings. His hand was declared unfit to build the house of the Lord he so passionately desired to see. And let us also remember, in this and all such cases, that the One who knows the agony in the sinner's mind alone can truly judge his sin. David came back. He won the final victory.

This truth must be borne in mind in interpreting the many utterances of praise for David in Scripture. For example, 1 Kings 11.4 f. (AV[KJV]) speaks of David walking before God with a 'perfect' heart. How can this be justified in one so obviously faulty? 'Perfection' of heart does not, however, suggest sinlessness, but whole-heartedness and singleness of purpose. David is visibly imperfect, and the Bible is as ruthless with his imperfections as it is with those of Jacob and Peter. His story stands in Scripture as a warning, as well as an inspiration. David paid, and paid again, for his sin. David was a man after God's heart, because he knew repentance, because he could bow with humility beneath chastening, and because his life was fed on a faith in a grand unfolding Plan.

161 : David in Adullam

Psalm 34

Man, as old Samuel was warned in Jesse's farmhouse, looks on the outward appearance of a man (1 Sam. 16.7), God sees 'the hidden part'. It is easy to be harsh with David for his retreat to Gath, but fortunately, in his case, we have more than the story of events. David was a poet, and a man of prayer. He poured into his poetry both the jubilation and the agony of his heart.

Driven out with scorn by the enemies of his people, he found the clean wilderness again. In the cave with two openings and a spring of water, where he made his guerrilla headquarters in the rough Judean hills, the exile realized how good God has been to him. In this revealing psalm we can guess what happened in his distraught and tormented mind during the days of his humiliation. In it we see how his faith held beneath his dark backsliding, and what convictions stayed him from complete self-destruction.

Abimelech was, of course, Achish. Like Pharaoh and Caesar, the word had become a dynastic title. Achish had dismissed David with contempt. The shame turned to thankful joy. It was an answer to prayer (4), dim and fumbling though prayer must have been in those days of sad disgrace. David knew where to look (5), in other words, in whom to put his ultimate trust. And catch the note of pure confession in the next verse (6). David had failed because he had not 'looked' in the right direction. Circumstances, besetting trouble, the harsh treacheries of men, had held his eyes. There is one only to fear (9), and fear in such a context is no degrading terror, but a reverence compounded of love, loyalty, and faith. This is the emerging lesson from the dark experience of Gath (11). Men should fear not the malice or the machinations of men, but rather the peril of leaving the circle of God's protection. Back in the great cave, David could almost imagine God's messenger standing sentinel (7) at the cave's mouth. He had learned a lesson he was to learn again, in circumstances yet more bitter, that God can do nothing with pride and self-sufficiency (18; Psa. 51.17).

This is an alphabetical psalm. To aid in memorizing, each verse is made to begin with a letter of the Hebrew alphabet. David has two letters left, so he sets forth the two truths which had thrust themselves on his perceptive mind in the days of his humiliation—the suicidalness of evil (21), and the completeness of God's salvation (22; Rom. 8.1).

162 : David and the Ziphites
1 Samuel 23; Psalm 54

The chronicler describes a month of warfare, David's blow for the country he loved, though its king had rejected him, the brief reappearance of Jonathan in the story, Jonathan who had caught a breath of hope, and the treachery of the men of Ziph. Treachery, as many a psalm bears witness, stirred David to the depths. He was a man of deep loyalties, and found the vicious betrayal of men a difficult fault to understand or to forgive. He was to know much of it.

It was a close call for David. The guerrilla fighter avoids active confrontation, but Saul had David at bay, when the Philistine enemy came into the hill country on one of his perennial raids, and the king was compelled to pull back the experienced army units which his hatred had committed to the combing of the wilderness for the fugitive. David took the opportunity thus offered to withdraw deeper into the wild country towards the Dead Sea.

In the wilderness David knew his best days. Down among the wadis, crags and cliffs of the Judean ranges, David learned some of the deeper lessons of faith, patience and calm confidence in God which infuse his psalms. Adversity can be creative when prosperity benumbs. Adversity is often the straightest path to truth. 'Adversity is like the period of the former and the latter rain,' said Sir Walter Scott, 'cold, comfortless, unfriendly. Yet from that season have their birth the flower and the fruit, the date and the rose.' Sir Philip Sidney echoes from an earlier century: 'The truly great and good, in affliction bear a countenance more princely than they are wont. It is the temper of the highest hearts, like the palm tree, to strive most upward when most burdened.'

It is also a truth, evident from the psalms of David's creative years, that anything committed in complete faith to God can be transmuted into good. The psalm set down above sprang from the sombre experience of betrayal. Observe the complete surrender of the evil thing to God's transforming hands (1), the resort to prayer (2), the fact of experience (3) set over against a calm faith (4), and the emerging confidence which speaks of the objects of petition as already granted (6 f.). This is faith in its strength and its tranquillity. It was born of a day of trouble.

163 : David and Saul

1 Samuel 24

The cave could have been Adullam, for the geography of the chapter is vague. Saul was on his way to scour Engedi, but the cave where he met David was on the way there (3), and the encounter was unexpected. If the Adullam cave is correctly identified, it had two entrances, and this would account for the boldness of the guerrilla band in the presence of the enemy commando-force. They knew that they could rapidly melt away into the wild hills behind.

Observe David's sensitive mercy. Saul was the Lord's anointed. David knew that he was rejected and that he himself had been chosen to succeed to the royal throne. And yet such was his faith at this time of testing that he refused to lift a finger to promote his own manifest destiny. He had learned the lesson that time-bound man finds it most difficult to learn, that God acts in His own good time, that it is best to wait for that time, and that patience and endurance are qualities rich in good and blessing.

David's words (9–15) are full of grace and courtesy. They touched a responsive chord in the distraught enemy's heart. Sanity and peace return briefly to Saul, and he speaks with love and contrition. For a brief time he is near to God and to restoration. The scales fall from his eyes and he sees himself for what he is, and recognizes the worth of the man he was hunting in bitterness of soul. His speech is full of pathos.

David knew that such repentance was not likely to endure. He had seen the undulations of mood in the tormented man. He was aware that those whom he could trust were the rough and determined men who had gathered to him in the wilderness (22.2), and that the king would keep no covenant or pact. For the meantime the hunt was over. Saul, in brief penitence, withdrew his task-force, and David disappeared into the hills to await his day.

It is a sad chapter, but it shows David in one of his finest hours, sensitive to the movements of God's will, tranquil in his assurance, strong, forbearing, kind. Perhaps Shakespeare had the passage in mind when he said that mercy 'becomes the throned monarch better than his crown.' In David's mind the crown could wait.

164 : David's Faith (1)

Psalm 27

This period of David's life is rich in psalms. Some of them bear ancient rabbinical headings which link the utterance or prayer with some specific experience. Psa. 57 is thus identified, and the tradition behind the identification must be accorded the respect which tradition not uncommonly merits. In the case of other psalms we can only hazard a conjecture, but there are quite a handful which bear the marks of David's wilderness meditations. Of these we might pick out two or three for comment, as we seek to know the man who became the second and the greatest king of Israel, and also one of the great religious poets of all time.

Look at Psa. 27. Some great deliverance has taken place, and it has grown out of past triumph. Catch the echoes of Goliath (2; 1 Sam. 17.41–58). Similarly, David told Saul on that occasion about his prowess with the bear. Victory, as is commonly the case, was born of victory. In the moral sphere the first fight is the most important. If defeat comes there, it is likely to be permanent.

Mark the imagery of the opening words. First comes light. Faith knows what it is about (John 11.8–10). Its principles are sharp and clear (Gen. 39.9). Its goal is plain to see (Phil. 3.14). Second comes salvation, strong in the thought of one who had just escaped some net of evil, salvation from evil circumstance (5), despair (6), calumny (12). Third comes strength. Weakness spawns cowardice, frustration, defeat.

And all this flows from the grand thought that God cares, plans, loves. High on some crag (5), watching his baffled foes far below him in the ravine, David sees in one moment of dazzling truth the most important fact in life—there is a God who is love. The AV(KJV) is closer to the Hebrew than the RSV in v. 13, provided the unnecessary main clause in italics ('I had fainted') is omitted. Looking down on the trap he has evaded, David gasps without rounded syntax, and in an unfinished sentence: '. . . unless I had believed to see the goodness of the Lord in the land of the living.' The main clause can be filled in by each who can echo that prayer, according to his own circumstances.

Therefore, he concludes, wait for God, and he was soon to make that theme the subject of a whole psalm, which we shall look at in the next study.

165 : David's Faith (2)

Psalm 37

'Wait for the Lord,' David concluded in the closing verse of yesterday's reading, 'be strong and let your heart take courage; yea, wait for the Lord!' The wild jubilation of that psalm has passed. The psalm which forms today's reading conforms more closely to Wordsworth's definition of poetry: 'Poetry is the spontaneous overflow of powerful feelings. It takes its origin from emotion recollected in tranquillity.'

In this psalm David reaches the same firm conclusion (34) by a quieter path. Why must a man 'wait for the Lord'? Because God's blessings are the reward of faith. They tarry. God's blessings, too, are part of a wider pattern, which requires time to weave itself. Abraham's story is a rich illustration. Again, God's blessings come only when we are ready to understand them. Moses was an illustration.

David is writing here of absolute trust (2 Tim. 1.12), complete committal of mind, heart, life to God, believing that He can control, overrule, transmute circumstances and experience, and so enrich the life. It is not merely a passive state. It is active: 'Trust in the Lord, and do good' (3).

Thus the believer 'delights' in Him (4), and takes pleasure in doing His will. Service can be dour (Mal. 3.13–15) and sour (Luke 15.29). Unwilling service carries no promise. Willing service is rewarded with 'the desires of the heart'. And what are they? The 'heart' in the imagery of the Bible is the core of the personality. And what do we there, in the redeemed centre of our being, desire? Purity, peace, power, confidence, courage? What do we want when nearest to Christ, and in our most solemn moments? Surely nothing less than the will of God in our lives.

'Commit your way . . .' (5). Let us paraphrase vs. 5 f.: 'Trust God to take over career, home, work, circumstances, ambitions and all else, and He will so mould events that your deepest and purest desires shall find fulfilment beyond your dreams, and that life will be filled with the most glorious satisfaction.'

'Be still before the Lord . . .' (7). Thus resting involves the mind, the imagination, the will (Isa 26.3). It means sometimes taking our hands off events as David did in the cave. It means ceasing to strive and leaving vindication (6) and deliverance to God. And remember that this psalm was written by a harried, hunted fugitive.

166 : David's Faith (3)

Psalm 57

This psalm is dated. The heading might more exactly read: 'when he fled from Saul into the cave.' The cave was his guerrilla headquarters at Adullam. The wild place had its lessons. Some storm in the mountains (1), and a remembered word of Moses (Deut. **32**.11; cf. Matt. **23**.37), provide a train of thought. The storm in David's life was the threat of death (3), the violence of men (4), slander, to which he was always peculiarly sensitive (4), and treachery (6), which always horrified and depressed him.

The remedy was to rest in God. 'In thy strong hands I lay me down . . .' There is no parallel in all ancient literature, outside the Old Testament, for this thought of God as a refuge and a tender protector. Doggedly, steadfastly (7, 10), David holds to the thought that a purpose (2) is working out through all that takes place (Rom. **8**.28), a purpose no malice could defeat.

Steadfastness is the keyword of the psalm. 'Stead' is an old word in English for 'place'. 'In my stead'; 'instead of . . .'; 'bedstead'; 'homestead', all illustrate it. 'Steadfast' means, therefore, 'firm in its proper place'. Steadfastness of heart means unshakeable resolution, and immovable faith in the centre of the personality, a stance unassailable (Eph. **6**.13 f.).

Note how the psalm breaks through to jubilation. It was probably written close in time to the psalm which precedes it, for, as it may be often observed in the psalms, there are word-echoes and repetitions of theme. Look through the two psalms together and list these phenomena. Psa. **56** ends, to be sure, with a word of quiet victory, a moving prayer which is better read in the AV than in the RSV. This psalm bursts out like a mountain spring into a shout of triumph. The singer goes outside the cave, looks to the high sailing clouds, and sees God's love high as the dome of the sky, and 'steadfast' as his own faith. This is the fourth time in this psalm (RSV) that the adjective has occurred. 'Steady then—keep cool and pray' (1 Pet. **4**.7—Moffatt).

Questions and themes for study and discussion on Studies 160–166

1. 'A man after God's own heart.'

190

2. Deception in Philistia. Is it still practised?

3. 'Sweet are the uses of adversity'.

4. God's plan in our lives. Suppose we frustrate it?
   Has He alternatives?

5. 'God is Light'. What of guidance?

6. '. . . unless I had believed . . .' (Psa. **27**.13, AV [KJV]).
   Fill in several main clauses.

7. 'Lord, make haste to save us'. Consider this prayer in the
   light of Psa. **37**.

167 : Nabal

1 Samuel 25

Nabal was a descendant of old Caleb, but he was a drunken
churl (3, 36). The success of any guerrilla movement depends
upon the support of the countryside and the goodwill of the
population at large. This axiom may be illustrated from all
history. David and his men had sought to earn the goodwill
of the shepherds of the Shephelah. After all, they were a
police force (15 f.) against the perennial raiding from both
the desert hinterlands and the coastal plain. David did not
run Nabal into danger near the area where Saul was active.
He sought some sustenance from his plenty away to the north
in Carmel, where Nabal had property. But the man was a
boor (17), unworthy of his wife, a clever woman who had
the confidence of her husband's men.

Nabal died of heart failure (36–38), but he died as he had
lived. Lack of courtesy is lack of love, and lack of love is
lack of God. Courtesy is a Christian virtue. It is a gift of our
faith to our way of life, and boorish Nabal is a warning and
a lesson. 'The small courtesies of life', once hailed by Laur-
ence Sterne, are said to be on the wane.

The crowd, inseparable from urban living, can press hard
against the defences of life—on the congested road, in the
packed supermarket, in the inevitable queue and in the
hundred places where man impedes, and so frustrates, his
fellows. Delay, obstruction, inefficiency and a seeming un-
concern for others, try the patience, fray the temper and put

191

sharpness into the voice and impatience into action. Courtesy becomes a casualty, because courtesy requires serenity, and calls for self-command.

A decay of courtesy could have a cause more sinister than a deteriorating human environment. Perhaps the spirit of man betrays a certain weariness. Old standards of conduct, for more than one unhappy reason, have been abandoned. The Christian faith is under mindless assault.

There is a species of rebellion which finds a perverted satisfaction in damaging old traditions. Sometimes, for all the bandying of the word love in such social contexts, regard for the feelings, the ease and the ideals of others—and they are all elements of love—is the missing factor. It was Belloc who said:

> *Of Courtesy—it is much less*
> *Than courage of heart or holiness;*
> *Yet in my walks it seems to me*
> *That the Grace of God is in courtesy.*

Belloc had in mind Francis of Assisi, who said: 'Courtesy is one of the properties of God, who gives His rain to the just and unjust by courtesy. Courtesy is the sister of charity by which hatred is vanquished and love is cherished.' Churlish Nabal and gracious Abigail are worth a steady look.

168 : David and Saul Again

1 Samuel 26

Slander had been at work again. David hated it. Saul entertained it. David knew this. Hence his earlier distrust of Saul, now sadly justified. David's curse on slanderers (19) echoes through all time. He who by lies stirs another to evil action bears the burden of the guilt. David's magnificent forbearance is equally for our instruction. 'Devotion', wrote William Law relevantly, 'signifies a life given to God. He is a devout man who lives no longer to his own will, but to the sole will of God, who makes all the parts of his common life parts of piety by doing everything in the name of God.'

Abishai's advice (8) was no doubt a strong temptation. Saul had been spared, and had sinned again with arrogant disregard of mercy shown and the covenant implied. But David was living, in these stirring and momentous days, close to God. He wanted nothing less than the will of God in his life. At such moments he touches the grace of Christ. The lessons of Psa. 37 were being gloriously applied to difficult circumstances.

It is a splendidly told story, this account of the breathless raid on the sleeping camp. It was an act of astonishing courage, and should have stirred Saul to genuine and final repentance. But David still 'went his way' (25), withholding his trust. To trust God is not to abandon the salutary exercise of reason. God guides through the qualities with which He has endowed the mind. The land must have been seething with treachery. The old tribal jealousies and animosities were still just below the surface. They had bedevilled the days of the judges. In the next century they were to divide the land. The evil men of Ziph were not the only group willing to surrender David to Saul.

The Christian does well not to trust the world. He does well who insulates himself from the control of secular society. There are entanglements which turn to snares. The Christian cannot expect ultimate justice from a world which denied it to Christ. Like his Lord, he should not 'commit himself to them' (John 2.24).

169 : Saul's Twilight

1 Samuel 28.3–25

This attack was no common raid. The Philistines had often penetrated the hill-country, looting hamlets and driving off flocks. This time, they sought a wider conquest. The coastal strip was becoming too narrow for them, and they were obviously looking with covetous eyes on the rich plain of Esdraelon or Jezreel, scene of the old victories of Barak and Gideon. Watching the twinkling camp fires of the Philistines from the surrounding ramparts of the hills, Saul saw the coming of the end (4 f.).

The irony of the situation was that history gave clear direction. Had Saul risen to the vast occasion, Gideon's victory and Barak's too might have told him that, if God stood with him, the number of his men or their armaments was of small consequence. But was God with him? This was a question for which Saul, with his defective view of God, had no clear answer. God is not a power to be tapped at the whim of any man, and for long years Saul had scorned God's will in his life, and refused to acknowledge His control. That man's fate is a grim one to whom God says in the end: 'Thy will be done.' Saul was desperate.

Endor lay on the lip of the hills overlooking the plain, and a woman in the village practised the sinister arts of necromancy. It is impossible to explain Saul's vision of Samuel in the language of human experience. The woman, like all her kind, was a charlatan, but it does not seem possible to explain all the phenomena associated with such tamperings with psychic matters by the resources of trickery and deceit. Whatever lay behind the eerie experience, God used it to say His last word to Saul. He listened aghast.

He hears that the morrow is the end. He hears, too, that the nation and his sons shall fall. It is impossible to isolate evil. An act of wrong can be confined neither to time nor place. The lives of men are interwoven, and sin in any personality infects a wider area than that of the life which is its host.

The sight of her broken king stirred some human pity in the weird woman who had been used in this final tragedy. She hurried and prepared Saul's last meal. In the darkened hut on the hillside, the man who might have been a great man ate of the pathetic creature's meat and bread, and, like Judas, went out into the night.

170 : David's Raid

1 Samuel 30

Free from his disastrous entanglement with the Philistines which we have earlier discussed, David regained his old strength and vigour of mind. It is a little difficult to sort out the chronology of these chapters. The last verse of the earlier chapter seems to set David's emancipation from his compromising service just before the northern drive to Jezreel, in repelling which Saul was to lose his life.

The guerrilla band found immediate work at hand. It was a vast opportunity for the Amalekites of the southern desert. Saul had denuded the southern frontiers, and marched his available troops north to face the deep Philistine penetration. The Philistines, too, had stripped their borderlines. The Amalekite savages fell on Ziklag, and took away the families of David's fighting men. They were the nomads of the wilderness whom, long years before, Saul had been called upon to eliminate. The fate of the sick Egyptian (13) is a pointer to their inhumanity and baseness.

Perhaps it was an answer to desperate prayer from the captives that God intervened and plucked David and his band from their Philistine compromise. The callous raiders, directed by the victim of their cruelty, soon had the finest band of fighting-men in Israel on their tracks. In their camp was merrymaking. The wild Bedouin had raided successfully into both the territory of the coastal Philistines, and into the hill country of the Hebrews. David's commandoes fell on them and scattered them.

The real David, royal, generous, confident, seems to emerge in the division of the spoil from the successful raid. He established a principle of reward (24) which has its place in Christian service. It is the will to serve rather than the visible achievement of service which matters, and, as C. S. Lewis once remarked, it is part of the courtesy of Heaven to regard the desire as equal to the deed. Consciousness of a great deliverance, a sudden glow of recovered freedom, and fellowship with God renewed, brought David the mood of generosity and jubilation which seems to flash through the ending of this story. Ziklag was in ashes and it was well destroyed. It was the symbol of failure, retreat and compromise.

171 : Saul's Ending
1 Samuel 31

Archaeology has confirmed the deep northern penetration of the Philistines around this period. Altars bearing characteristic

Cretan features date from 1100 to 1050 B.C, and seem to mark at least a generation of Philistine occupation.

And on Mount Gilboa Saul fought his last fight, and fell with his sons under the Philistine arrows. Saul was a tragic figure. He had qualities of strength and heroism, and in his hour of shame and disaster the men of Jabesh-Gilead remembered what he had done for them, bravely raided Bethshan, and brought the bodies of the king and his sons home for burial.

It is the end which matters. It is the end which all should keep in view. Masefield makes this a haunting thought in Saul Kane's colourful mind. He pictured the 'white unwritten book'—

> *A book that God will take, my friend,*
> *As each goes out at journey's end . . .*
>
> . . . .
>
> *The book he lent is given back*
> *All blotted red and smutted black . . .*
>
> . . . .
>
> *I wondered then why life should be,*
> *And what would be the end of me*
> *When youth and health and strength were gone,*
> *And cold old age came creeping on.*

Such thoughts, as Masefield showed in his poem, soften a hard man for penitence, and bring him face to face with God.

Saul had been called to a high task and a noble enterprise. He lost the vision of it in self-will, arrogance and disobedience. He wasted his energies on hate. He was unable to keep his word. He was blessed with noble friends; Samuel who had once loved him, David who had sought to serve him, Jonathan his own son. He was unable to give himself to their affection, their guidance and their consistent loyalty.

To be sure there was a streak of madness in the man, but his mental disorder was fed by what he wilfully entertained in his heart. We become that which we choose to be in a very real way. Hold hate at the core of the being and it eats up the personality, until none can encounter the host without a confrontation with the evil which has come to dwell within him. The same is true of love, of Christ in the heart. That is why it should be life's chief concern how 'each goes out at journey's end'.

172 : The Amalekite
2 Samuel 1.1–16

David was back two days from his punitive campaign against the Amalekites. Had his tough fighting-force been with Saul, the disaster of Mount Gilboa might not have occurred, but it was not David's fault that his hardened warriors had no part in Saul's army.

He was camping in the ruins of Ziklag when a lone Amalekite came down the mountain trails, either making for home or, a less likely suggestion, seeking David, with advantage for himself in mind. The true account of Saul's death is found in the previous chapter. The Amalekite was a liar. He had no doubt been haunting the area of battle like a jackal, in order to strip the dead, or to pick up some useful weapons and armour. His encounter with David, himself just back from scattering and punishing his desert tribesmen, was perhaps the last meeting he desired. His quick-witted and most circumstantial lying was both his attempt to extricate himself from a perilous situation, and to secure the reward which, by the base standards of his own depraved people, would have certainly been forthcoming. Rent clothes and hair befouled was the adjustment of a moment.

It was ironical that an Amalekite should tell this story, after both Saul's and David's relations with that people. David was hardly likely to overlook a crime against the man whom he himself had twice spared in reverence for the unction of God which had once lain on him, and the liar paid the penalty for the death he had professed to deal. Crude evil overreached itself.

'A lie is troublesome,' wrote Joseph Addison, 'and sets a man's invention upon the rack, and one trick needs a great many to make it good. It is like building upon a false foundation which continually stands in need of props to shore it up.' The Amalekite had been at his scavenger's task in the night before the Philistines found Saul's body. He had looted crown and bracelet. The theft led to the invention, itself twisted to win an ignoble end, and complicated by the mistake so often made by vicious men—that of imagining that others are like themselves. Simon the sorcerer thought he could secure the benison of the Holy Spirit from the apostles for money. Such propositions add crudity to vice.

1. 'Reputation, reputation . . . O, I have lost my reputation. I have lost the immortal part of me, and what remains is bestial' (*Othello*). In what sense is this true of Nabal? Why is reputation of value?

2. Courtesy in the New Testament.

3. The Christian in worldly society. What rules govern participation?

4. Compromise, its cause and cure.

5. 'It is not the beginning of an enterprise but the ending thereof which bringeth true glory' (Drake).

6. Lying. What is the danger contained in the habit? See last paragraph of Study 171.

173 : David's Lament
2 Samuel 1.17–27; 1 Corinthians 13

It was the habit of David to turn the experiences of life into lyric poetry. Such poems, addressed to God, formed his psalms. This lament for the fallen does not quite fall into the category. It is not a prayer, nor specifically directed towards God, but it shows David's poetic power at its best.

It also reveals his character. Many versions retain the RV rendering which calls this poem 'the Song of the Bow'. The reason for the title would seem to be David's tender recollection of one of the last meetings with his friend, when Jonathan feigned archery practice to come to him secretly outside the town. The word 'bow' occurs in v. 22, a key line of the song.

It shows the deep strain of generosity in the singer. He ordered the learning of the song throughout all Israel. He was no small, mean-spirited man who feared the reputation of any predecessors. Jonathan might worthily have held the kingship. Saul had qualities which, as the men of Jabesh-Gilead had just movingly demonstrated, some folk vividly remembered.

David writes no 'taunt-song', no lyric of personal triumph.

There is no sour note of denunciation for the dead, nor any recollection of evil or suffering. Saul was God's anointed, and David could never forget that this carried some seal of divine calling. Hence the notes of praise for the unfortunate man.

The attitude was no act of calculated policy. David had demonstrated enough the grace which determined his forgiving spirit towards his persecutor. At the same time, such liberal magnanimity was likely to help solve the divisions of the land. David was about to found afresh a unified monarchy, and division might well find origin in a continuing rift between those who followed David and those who remembered Saul.

David, too, had a strong capacity for friendship. His love for Jonathan vibrates through his verse. So, too, does his patriotism. The death of Saul is to David no elimination of a personal foe, but a blow against the country over which the pagan foe might well indulge his ungodly glee. There is no reproach in patriotism. One who has not risen to the level of clean and simple patriotism is not likely to rise to the levels which other virtues demand.

174 : David's Summary
Psalm 18

Gratitude overwhelmed David when he looked back over the decade of his sufferings, and saw how worthwhile all his trials had been. David had learned vital lessons. He had proved the faithfulness of God. In crowded imagery (2), such as that found in Pss. 31 and 71, he extols the protection God had given him. He had seen the wild storm break over the Judean ranges (7–16), and thought how like the tempests of life the violence of Nature was . . . God keeps His promises (30). He gives strength (32, 39). He answers prayer (35).

After trial and tribulation, David could declare that life was worth the living. What is life? Man's life is warfare, said Job; 'a long fool's errand to the grave,' said Housman. 'Draw the curtain,' said dying Rabelais, 'the farce is played out.' 'Life is real, and life is earnest,' said Longfellow, who had suffered intensely, 'and the grave is not its goal.'

This psalm is David's answer, and the answer is very close to that of Paul: 'For me to live is Christ.' Amid calamitous events, betrayal, treachery, exile in the wilderness, frustration, misrepresentation and malice, David found a song to sing. If God was over all, permitting no suffering that He was not able to turn to usefulness, allowing no defeat which He was not certain to transmute into His own form of victory, then life was gladness, confidence, jubilant adventure. Even failure, backsliding and stumbling are not outside such transformation.

The outburst of the heart in the first words of the psalm shows David to be one with those who knew God in Christ, rather than in company with the judges and the men of dim and stumbling faith who had filled the annals of the preceding century. Such was the conclusion to which David came, on some quiet evening, perhaps in Hebron, as he looked back over the tumultuous years. They were to prove the greatest years of his life.

It is good thus to look back and trace the path of guidance. But life, as Kierkegaard said, 'though it can be only understood backwards must be lived forward.' There can be no pausing. 'Hitherto the Lord has helped us' (1 Sam. 7.12), is a stand of faith only when it is the basis of new committal and daily dedication. He gives His marching orders day by day.

175 : David Crowned

2 Samuel 2.1–7; Psalm 101

Much had been taken from David's path by the death of Saul. He sought counsel of God (1), and was sent up to Hebron, one of the ancient cities of the land. There Abraham had pitched his tent in the oak woods, there he had bought Sarah's burying-place. The place was tangled with history for a thousand years before David made it his first royal seat.

It is possible that Psa. 101 was his self-imposed charter of royalty at this momentous juncture of his life. He begins with an ideal of blameless conduct (2), using the same verb as is used in 1 Sam. 18.14 f., where David 'had success'. He is picking up the theme of Psa. 15, so that blameless conduct may reasonably be said to be the consistent objective of his life. It is sad to think that the bright ideal was to be so savagely assailed. The early years of his reign were, at any rate, beyond reproach.

Call the psalm, as one commentator does, 'the Moral Ideals of a King,' and observe the qualities he covets and the vices he abhors. The first is 'integrity of heart' (see Psa. **78**.72), explained by the next clause. The refusal to contemplate baseness fortifies the personality against evil. Integrity means absence of corruption, that completeness which God would have in His people.

Nor will he have the shallow and the apostate around him (3). He seeks steadfastness, a word we have already examined. 'Perverseness of heart' (4) means obstinate resistance to good, the dedication to evil which Christ found damnable in the Pharisees. Nor will he have liars and slanderers or arrogant men around him. We have seen how acutely David suffered in soul and in circumstances from such vicious foes. He swears to destroy them (5).

He wants faithful men about him (6), men at whose conduct none shall point reproach, no liars (7), no evildoers (8). The phrase 'morning by morning' refers, of course, to the Oriental royal custom of the matutinal audience (2 Sam. **15**.2). Little by little he purposed to eliminate bad men from the land. It was a grand ideal which the thirty-year-old (2 Sam. **5**.4) king set himself. He desired a pure land, as the writer of Psa. **104** desired a pure earth. The accomplishment has eluded good rulers of all ages but finds its last apocalyptic expression in Rev. **21**.27—'Nothing unclean shall enter it, nor anyone who practises abomination or falsehood.'

176 : The Soldiers

2 Samuel 2.12–32; 3.12–39

Saul was naturally popular in Gilead, and his marshal, Abner, an opportunist and a foe of David, took the opportunity to frustrate the Hebron régime and its hopes of national unity by setting up Saul's son as king at Mahanaim. Judah alone was loyal to David. The rest of the land was divided— bewildered by conflicting loyalties, or desperately following Abner's puppet. It was unlikely that a trans-Jordanian government could hold wide sway in territories west of the great valley. Nor was it likely that David was without support in Mahanaim. Some of his guerrilla activities had been based there, and a score of years later he found a safe refuge and support at Mahanaim when he retreated before Absalom.

Abner was a soldier of the worst type, accustomed to war and bloodshed, careless of the land's peace, a militarist who saw his way of life at an army's head and in troubled times. War did not brutalize David. Like Jephthah, who was curiously enlightened at this one point, he preferred the ways of peace. The High Command, the General Staff, and other groups exploiting military power, sometimes force the hand of governments.

This note is written as 1970 ends. In 1870, one century ago, Bismarck's editing of the Ems telegram began the series of events which ran on to 1914, 1939, and the tensions of today. The pressure of the oiled and efficient Prussian war machine was a factor in precipitating the war with France, which sparked the long hatred of Germany and her neighbour. The war-clouds were receding when Bismarck played his unscrupulous hand. The army chief, Helmut von Moltke, said Bismarck in his memoirs, looked 'quite old and frail,' when he thought the war with France was not going to break out. He took the 'old bloodletter', as he described him, to a table, and showed him how the abbreviation and distortion of the famous telegram would make war quite inevitable. Moltke looked quite spry and fresh again, when sure of the war, which was his trade. He showed how the soul can die.

Such a man was Abner, ready to cry peace when his cause collapsed (**2**.26), ready to change sides at need (**3**.12), and dying as he had lived. Joab, who killed him, was no better. He was David's nephew, and David's marshal, but a thorn in David's side.

177 : Ishbosheth

2 Samuel 4

Eshbaal was probably the real name of Saul's unfortunate son (1 Chron. **8**.33; **9**.39). During the period of the judges and on into the monarchy many names were compounded with 'baal', a word which means 'master', and could apply to Israel's God. It was the introduction of Phoenician idolatry, and the growing problem of the fertility cults (Hos. 2.16), which gave the name its pagan connotations, and banished it from nomenclature. Hence the substitution in retrospect, in this man's name, of 'bosheth' which means 'shame'. Ishbosheth was the 'man of shame'.

There are those in history and in life who are caught up in some catastrophic stream of events and driven to a fate not of their own making. Perhaps Pilate was one, but Pilate was able at any moment to break out of the encompassing tangle of circumstances by one heroic, if costly, act of will. Perhaps the pathetic Ishbosheth could have done the same. The record is brief, and has nothing to say of those conversations or compulsions by which Abner forced the prince's hand. He was forty years of age, no romantic, inexperienced youth. He had watched with adult eyes the development of his own father's tragedy. He must have talked with his brother Jonathan, whose eyes were open to the shape of coming events.

Perhaps he was a legalist, who stood upon what he considered the letter of the law, his right of succession. Curiously enough, Nelson Glueck, rabbi, historian and archaeologist, still stands by Ishbosheth's legal right, and, describing the Jabbok gorge, pictures David in hazardous retreat from Absalom up its wild course. Almost in the spirit of a Hebrew taunt-song, he writes: 'What thoughts weigh down the weary shoulders of this refugee? No Nathan is necessary this time to accuse him of having stolen the poor man's only ewe lamb. The rushing stream, the stabbing thorns, the frowning hills shout insistently, "The sin is thine, O David, and vengeance is the Lord's." Dark forebodings tugged at his heart strings.'

But David had nothing on his conscience concerning Ishbosheth. He avenged his murder. There was no right of absolute succession in the young monarchy. David was called of God to the kingship, and Jonathan, the eldest son of Saul, had recognized the fact. Nor would the weak and shadowy Ishbosheth have been other than Abner's tool in a new round of war, division and tension.

1. Why is patriotism out of fashion in some quarters today?
2. Perversity of heart. Define and consider.
3. Integrity. Define and illustrate.
4. Past, present and future in Christian experience.
5. Need anyone be used by bad men?

178 : David's Household
2 Samuel 3.1–6; 5

These events, briefly chronicled, and sometimes reaching back in time to resume a thread, may also be read in the Chronicles (e.g. 1 Chron. 11–14). Sometimes a relevant or interesting detail is added by the second narrative.

As we seek, however, to isolate the picture of David's person, and to understand his character, we can pass by the briefly told record of war, the capture of Jerusalem, and the renewed threat from the Philistines of the Gaza Strip. From the passages before us, one blemish on David's reign, the social reflection of a blemish in his character, springs out—his disordered and polygamous household.

It is a truth which can be abundantly illustrated from both literature and life, that good men can be blind to some aspects of evil. There were good Christians in the first century and in the nineteenth, who had no conscience about the evil and crime of slavery. Luther's writings abundantly illustrate the defectiveness of his social conscience in certain aspects of government and authority.

And David was a child of his age in matters of sex. The defect was to betray him twice, and lead to ruinous and agonizing sequences of events. The tensions and problems of the harem are obvious. No household is safe where polygamy forms a hotbed and breeding-ground for plot, counter-plot, and base intrigue. This was a legacy which David was to hand on to the brilliant Solomon, and which was to ruin his reign.

Was David responsible for this moral defect? David was a

man of deep insight into the mind of God. He was a man of understanding. He must have had misgivings. Moreover, he had before his eyes, knowing as he did the old history of his race, the example of the patriarchs. Abraham had one wife, and Abraham's one adventure in deviation, justified by Sumerian law though it was, produced disaster. Monogamy was implicit in the Creation story, and polygamy appeared first in the line of Cain. Through recorded history—Jacob, Moses, Gideon, and Elkanah, for example—trouble enough was generated in polygamous households. David had the information, the insight, and the intellect to know better. There was an unsanctified corner in his personality. Such a bridge-head of evil can be the source of inroads of catastrophe. Observe the process in the rest of David's story.

179 : David and the Ark

2 Samuel 6; Psalm 24

The strange story of David's bringing home the Ark of the Covenant should be read in the light of the triumph-song which celebrated its returning. The Ark was something more than a mere talisman, a sacred object, in David's mind, and this we learn only from the hymn which forms Psa. 24. Merely to read the story in the chronicler's account leaves the modern reader somewhat sympathetic towards Michal, who saw some despite to royal dignity and decency in David's ceremonial dancing before the Ark. He seems less than generous in his virtual divorce from her.

Psa. 24 reveals what was happening in heart and mind. To David the coming of the Ark to Jerusalem signified a return to pure worship. The lovely box containing the tablets of the Law, and, surmounted by the empty mercy-seat where the winged cherubim gazed down on abstract perfection, was a deeply significant object. Here was also a great historical event, and David sought to make the people to whom he had given a capital city, and now was giving a centre of divine worship, aware of Jehovah's greatness.

As the procession wound up the road to the citadel of

Zion, the antiphonal singing of the Levitical choirs echoed round the rocky heights. God, the hymn proclaims, is no tribal totem (1 f.), but the ruler of the whole world and all the races in it. This was the vision of Abraham. It was to be the vision of Isaiah and of Paul. Nor could such a God be worshipped by the impure (3 f.). Observe again David's preoccupation with candour, goodness, and love of truth. 'Clean hands' signifies righteousness in action and deed. The hands can be the tools of evil (Rom. **6**.12 f.). They should be the servants of Christ (Rom. **12**.1). A 'pure heart' signifies the desire for righteousness at the point of origin of all action— the centre of the personality.

The house of God is not an easy or a comfortable dwelling for those who have no desire for the One who reigns there (read C. S. Lewis' *Great Divorce*). The prerequisite of all blessing is not to 'lift up the soul to that which is false', those merchandise of Vanity Fair, the ephemeral, material objects of man's mistaken desires. Such are the children of God through all the ages—'those who seek Him'. And those who seek Him find blessing (Isa. **55**.6–9).

But here, indeed, is insight into the personality of the writer. No other man, right to the threshold of his day, had such a penetrating insight into spiritual truth. The procession wound round the rocky track. The Ark, carried high on its stout poles (Exod. **25**.10–22), passed through the gates. It was a great moment, spoiled, thought David, by proud Michal's sneer.

180 : David's Peace

2 Samuel 7

In human experience there is the valley of the shadow, and there are also, as David was to put it in a psalm, the still waters and the pleasant pastures. The embattled years were over, and the king lay in a patch of peace, and thought of God. There are those who call for help in the day of trouble, when the shadows are dark and the way perilous and rough. Then, with ease and prosperity, the heart, as Deuteronomy puts it (**31**.20), 'grows fat', and God is forgotten.

It is to David's honour that, when quietness came to his life, he thought of God and adornment for His worship. He sought to give God a worthy symbolic dwelling place, and the thought did him credit. We honour God still by worthy church buildings, for all the contrary notions of radical theologians. Nathan, who appears in the story for the first time, brought word that the gift was not to be, but also came with assurance of the continuity of David's house, a covenant to be strangely fulfilled in Christ.

David went in and 'sat before the Lord'. The phrase seems to occur nowhere else in Scripture, and betokens an intimacy in David's worship, a father and son relationship which prefigures the free entry of the Christian to the presence of his Lord (1 John 2.28). David prayed with heartfelt earnestness for the preservation of his line. It was a small desire seen in the perspective of God's larger plans. It was not answered on the plane on which David placed it, although a descendant of the son of Jesse did in truth sit upon Judah's throne for some four centuries.

It is the way of God to answer the heart's petitions (Psa. 37.4) on a level far beyond the fumbling words in which they are framed. We cannot know the future. God does. Our small wisdom cannot adequately define that which is best for us. God's wisdom is as complete and perfect as His love. 'His plans are not our plans', but His plans do not necessarily set our plans aside and frustrate them. God reinterprets, enlarges, sublimates and transforms. David would have prayed for a larger fulfilment, a more glorious kingdom, had he been able to conceive and to formulate the prayer. This was the answer given, and it was an answer built round the core of surrender and sincerity in the prayer the seeker prayed, as he sat before God in the dim shrine.

181 : David's Strife (1)
2 Samuel 8; Psalm 44

Much battling on the frontiers is compressed into this brief account. It is impossible to follow it in detail. It appears that major campaigns were undertaken in two directions, against

Moab in the east, and against Aram or Syria in the north. The aim of the former thrust was iron. The Philistines, as we have seen, were men of the Iron Age. The Hebrews still lived in the Bronze Age. They lacked a vital weaponry. David sought the iron ores of Edom. Solomon was to build refineries near the Gulf of Aqaba. To the north, David sought a stable frontier, and the passing reference to Damascus suggests that at this time Israel reached its widest and most imperial boundaries.

The chronicler's bald account leaves out the gusts of anxiety, the days of tension and of stress, the weariness of conflict and all the tumult of war which David knew, over what may have been a considerable span of years. Thanks to the psalms, we may catch some echoes of his feelings and his prayers. Identification, in the absence of headings, must be conjectural, but it seems possible that Psa. 44 is Davidic, and belongs to this period, though to be sure some, including Calvin, have referred it to the time of the Maccabees.

Read it with these assumptions in mind. The first eight verses show the suppliant banking on his reserves of divine salvation. 'Our fathers have told us . . .' God who did great things in the past can act again. But in vs. 9–16 the mood changes. On such stormy frontiers, with the heathen raging (Psa. 2), it was not possible to live in the continual light of victory. There befell days of disaster, and the psalmist searches his heart and the ways of his people to discover the reason. He finds himself bearing the burden of the nation's backsliding and its sin, and in protestation and confession falls before God's holiness, and pleads for pardon.

The remainder of the psalm, which is almost unrelieved in its gloom, calls for God to bless those who have thus humbled themselves before Him. God is pleased with well-worn prayers. Today is as full of Him as was yesterday. God's mercies are not withdrawn. The prayer is in God's hands.

182 : David's Strife (2)

1 Chronicles 18; Psalm 60

Psa. 60 may certainly be referred to this period. The old rabbinical headings represent an ancient tradition, not to be lightly set aside. The psalm was written on the morrow of a defeat, followed by unexpected victory. It is not to be supposed that David's wide reorganization of the complicated frontiers of Israel proceeded without fluctuations of military fortune. Edom and Moab appear to have attacked while David confronted the Syrians or Aramaeans in the north. Joab, David's rough soldier nephew, by some manoeuvre turned the tide.

The first three verses show what should be done with defeat in any sphere of life. The facts should be faced. Two courses are open in any sort of failure or defeat. The beaten man can lie down and submit, or he can rise and refuse to accept the situation. See Mic. 7.8 f. Note the pronoun: '. . . until *He* pleads my cause.' And see Rom. 8.31–39, especially in Phillips' translation.

Failure is not final. Failure confessed can be a stepping stone, a challenge, a spur, a stimulus to success. We have seen in the course of these studies, many failures turned to success —most notably Moses' failure. We shall see Mark and Peter.

Verse 4 ends obscurely in the RSV, and other versions differ widely over the same closing words, which are possibly corrupt in the text. The major portion of the verse is, however, clear. 'Thou hast set up a banner for those who fear thee, to rally to it . . .' The banner, in the dust and confusion of the battlefield, showed where the king was. A rallying point held hard-pressed men from scattering in rout. And so, as David had found in the days of life's defeats, when he was hemmed in he made for God, and God's truth. Experience of battle had woven his imagery.

The thought is, and David never wavered here, that God is near, involved, able and willing to help. There is no need for Job's despairing 'Oh, that I knew where I might find him . . .' And look at the closing words of Isa. 54. Here then is a secret of the psalmist's life. He was often defeated. We shall soon read of his most shocking defeat. And we shall see him rally from that defeat, moving back to where the banner stood—and God, ready to hold the broken line and give fresh courage.

1. Christian marriage, fidelity, and the so-called 'permissive society'.
2. The symbolism of the Ark.
3. 'Far more abundantly than all that we ask or think' (Eph. 3.20).
4. Is any failure final?

183 : Bathsheba

2 Samuel 11

Bathsheba was the daùghter of Eliam, probably one of David's Thirty-seven (2 Sam. 23.34). It was in this context that the brave Uriah met and married her, for the Hittite convert was also one of the chosen Thirty-seven. A romance between a fine soldier and the beautiful daughter of his comrade-in-arms might have run a life-long course of happiness, but for the happenings of one sad afternoon.

Who initiated this historic series of sinful events? It appears from the narrative that it was David looking down from his palace roof on the tangle of houses and courtyards below. But what was Bathsheba doing to be thus visible as she bathed? If she was in full view below, so was David above. From a later appearance in the story, a generation later (1 Kings 1), it is evident that Bathsheba was a resourceful and clever woman. Nor was David's weakness for women unknown. This is a fault of character which cannot long be hidden. Did the young wife construct the situation? There is more than a suspicion that she spread the net into which David so promptly fell.

Her husband was a fine man. David employed many mercenaries. Men of Cretan stock, no doubt mercenaries from the Philistines, followed him when he retreated before Absalom, and the Hittite, a convert to the worship of Yahweh on the evidence of his name, was one of these strong and trusted men. He was a man of resolution. Observing a taboo which was probably incorporated in the code of the select bodyguard in which he served the king (1 Sam. 21.4), Uriah was not tricked into a visit to his wife, and the subterfuge by which the sinner sought to cover up his sin. Perhaps also Uriah had his suspicions. David had made enquiries (3) about Bathsheba and rumour in an ancient city was not likely to run less fast than rumour runs today.

David himself should have been with his men. But middle-age brought ease. The flatteries of an urban court were undermining his old standards. He grew slack, arrogant, undisciplined, and the Enemy struck at that point in his defences where the victim was weak—an eventuality which is among the sure circumstances of life. He was either the victim of a scheming woman or of his own backsliding. In either case it was an unsanctified corner in his life which provided entrance for the evil which overwhelmed him.

184 : Nathan

2 Samuel 12

Nathan was a brave man. It was no light matter to face the wrath of an oriental despot, and that is what David had become. Power, as the saying has it, corrupts, and David had power, and used it ill. Courage consists, not in disregarding danger, but in looking danger in the face without flinching. True courage is cool and calm. It is not manifested in brutal force, but in the firm resolve which goodness and reason fortify. It does not imply absence of fear, but fearing the reproach of conscience, the shame of compromise, and the stigma of cowardice, more than the perils of right action. Moral courage, too, is a rarer virtue than physical courage, which is fed by the body's reaction, and often made easier by a blinding of the reason.

By all the tests Nathan was a man of rare courage. He had a task of some magnitude, as well as of danger. He was faced with a psychological and a spiritual problem. David had sought to quench his conscience in action. The attack on the citadel of Rabbah (the modern Amman), which is mentioned at the end of the chapter, probably took place before the events recorded in the first fifteen verses. It may have taken place during Bathsheba's hypocritical mourning for Uriah (**11.**26 f.). David, like Saul of Tarsus, sought to brain-wash himself by violent action and cruelty (**31**).

He had a measure of success. Joab, no doubt, did not make it too apparent that he had his uncle in his power. The land at large, which murmured its scorn (**14**), was remote from the monarch cushioned by his court. A strange numbness of spirit lay upon him. His mind and heart no longer leaped into action, jubilation, or even lamentation, at the touch of circumstance. The poet in him was dead.

After the careful manner of the Hebrew teacher, Nathan approached his task of enlightenment and condemnation with a parable. But such preamble does not preclude the point and the conclusion, and Nathan did not halt short of his solemn duty of firm rebuke. It reached its mark, and broke the sinner down. He was forgiven—but the consequences remained. No sin, as we have observed before, can be confined to the place and time of its committal. The same applies blessedly to every act of good.

185 : David the Penitent (1)
Psalm 51.1-17

There is one thing and one only to do with sin, and that is to commit it to God in penitence. If this is done some good can be wrought from it by God's creative hands. Psa. **51**, which has brought comfort and healing to multitudes, was the good which God brought from David's sin.

Psa. **51**, perhaps together with Pss. **32**, **38** and **143**, is David's act of public penitence. It was sung by the Levite choirs, and vs. 18 f, a liturgical addition perhaps from the days of the captivity, are indication that it continued to be sung. Such was the permanence of David's shame, but also of David's repentance and forgiveness. Like Henry the Second, scourged at Becket's tomb eight centuries ago, David let the nation see his sorrow,

The psalm should be studied in all solemnity. If David's carnal sin and sin of blood are not shared by all, he is a fortunate man (or perhaps an insensitive man) who does not feel the kinship of the sinner in more than one verse of this

212

prayer. It is a moving insight into David's mind—his deep sense of sin, the agonizing obsession (3) with his guilt, the sense of uncleanness (2) . . .

He appeals to God's mercy and there is no other plea (1). He makes no excuse. He uses three words for sin, represented by three words in English. First, 'transgression' (1). The Hebrew word means basically 'rebellion'. David was conscious that he had betrayed his God. Second, 'iniquity' (2). Basically the word implies a bending or a twisting of the straight and true. The word 'bent', which C. S. Lewis acquired from George Macdonald, draws near to this conception. Third, 'sin' (3). Like one of the common Greek New Testament words, this word implies a falling short of a goal, a missing of the mark.

Note the plural 'transgressions'. No sin stands alone. 'Wash me,' he calls and the word-picture is deeply embedded in Scripture and Christian ritual (Isa. 1.16; Jer. 2.22; 4.14; Mal. 3.2). 'My rebellion I recognize,' says v. 3. 'Against THEE, THEE only, have I sinned . . .' (4). He has sinned against Uriah, Bathsheba, Joab and his people, but all this was swallowed up in the thought of God outraged, His love scorned, and His plan cast aside.

And he knew, this man of splendid insight, where it had all begun—in the heart, in evil entertained by the mind (6). It is there that forgiveness, too, must find its base.

186 : David the Penitent (2)
Psalm 32

This theme should not be passed by without further contemplation of the shattered man. Two beatitudes open Psa. 32. The forgiven sinner is happy, blessed and at peace, because life's greatest problem is solved when a man is reconciled to God.

David had tried to cover his sin, and found it a principle of death in his deepest being (3). God does press hard on the sinner. The fact can be illustrated by the story of Paul, Bunyan, Bilney and Francis Thompson. (Read the vivid lines in *The Hound of Heaven* which begin: 'I fled Him down the nights and down the days'.) 'Give them no rest,' Donald

213

Barnhouse used to pray, 'until they find their rest in Thee' (4). Only surrender brings peace. (Read the last few hundred lines of John Masefield's *Everlasting Mercy*.)

The RSV correctly renders v. 6. The spirit of repentance should not be lost. Such sin as David had committed, as we have seen, can benumb the soul. Amid the storm and turmoil of distress it is sometimes hard to apprehend the truth, and lay hold on God. The image in the verse is of one swept away by a sudden flood. Man needs a refuge (7) from the sting of pursuing conscience, the power, and the doom of sin. Refuges can be false, and of no avail in the stress of the soul (Isa. **28**.15). God alone avails (Isa. **32**.2). No human philosophy, no attenuated and decayed religiosity, can take the place of the living God. 'Thou must save, and Thou alone.'

At v. 8 God takes over the utterance. He promises instruction, direction and guidance—but only to those docile under His hand, and moving willingly according to His will (9).

This is the way of blessedness with which the psalm began. Faith obtains mercy, the theme of **51**.1, mercy which garrisons the soul like a protecting army (10). Joy goes with righteousness, and righteousness is from God (11).

The small psalm contains a wealth of truth and reaches with understanding deep into the New Testament. Go carefully through Psa. **38** in similar fashion. It seems to fit the mood of this time in David's life.

187 : David's Household

2 Samuel 13; Psalm 143

The chapter is almost too painful to read. Nathan's verdict had been that, though the sin was forgiven, forces were loosed which changed life and changed history. David's example had been ruined. He might well pray that he might show sinners God's way (**51**.13). He was indeed used to 'teach transgressors God's ways', but he also taught transgressors the ways of sin.

214

Amnon merely did what, in another context, his father had done. So did Absalom, of whom much more will be heard in this disordered household. The whole evil sequence of events began, and ran on, because David had lost his moral hold on his household, and was in no position to rebuke anyone.

From this time, too, begins the political ascendancy of the brutal and murderous Joab. David had damaged the man's soul by inviting complicity in his sin, and lost, in consequence, any authority which he might have held over him.

Sin is infinitely prolific. Once planted, like some weed, it produces more sin, more unhappiness. Men and women are vastly more important than they imagine. For good or ill, they influence all those with whom they come into contact, and project their sin into other generations—as they also project good.

Psa. 143 seems, by its verbal echoes, to belong to this period of David's life, perhaps a little later in time than the cry of penitential agony of Psa. 51. It is more positive in its outlook, and sees the issues of righteousness with sharper clarity. The prayer of everyone should be in the words of vs. 6, 8, 9, 10. There should be a conscious reaching after God and good. 'If with all your hearts, ye truly seek me . . .' says Jer. 29.13 in the famous choral rendering, and no blessing attends half-hearted seeking. Trust is a 'lifting up of the soul' in such an eager quest, a retreat into God, and above all, a life-long preoccupation with God's will. Such was the wisdom which David learned in the school of his own self-inflicted catastrophe. He set it down in poetry and song, that others might learn from schooling less harsh and grievous. This was the one good he could snatch for God from calamitous events. For himself he moved on to face what might be. His enlightenment had increased the burden of his responsibility.

Questions and themes for study and discussion on Studies 183–187

1. 'No one ever became suddenly bad' (Juvenal).

2. What does repentance imply?

3. The heart as the fount out of which sinful acts flow.

4. The influence of sin upon others.

188 : Absalom

2 Samuel 13

This chapter is almost too horrible to read, but the Bible does not profess to be anything but a record of the truth, and it is bitter truth that evil was abroad in David's family. Of poor Tamar and the vile Amnon nothing need be said. Of Absalom, scourge of his father, much will be heard. In passion and in violence he enters the story; in passion and in violence he will leave it.

The roots of the evil which clustered round the prince went back deep into the past. Absalom should never have been born. To the north-west, on the edge of the desert along the road to Damascus, lay the sheikdom of Geshur. The wider conquests of David thrust far in that direction, and it was part of his settlement of the frontiers to cement buffer-areas by dynastic ties with the border princelings. This is no doubt the background of David's alliance in marriage with Maacah, the daughter of Geshur's ruler (2 Sam. 3.3).

We have already marked a fundamental fault in David's character, for which he paid dearly. It must have been a wilful fault. He knew enough of the old laws of his land to be well aware of ancient prohibitions against intermingling with pagans. He was also an enlightened man. The early psalms show deep awareness of God's ways, and reveal his own deep yearning to stand well with God. But David was a man of strong passions, polygamy was sanctioned, the alliance was necessary, and there was abundant motive and excuse for following the desires of the flesh. Maacah, probably beautiful, and passionate in her Bedouin way, was the king's temptation. And thus he fathered Absalom, misnamed Father of Peace, and so brought strife and bitter grief into his house.

For some unrevealed reason, perhaps for his wild mother's sake, David loved Absalom with unreasoning blindness. It is with some horror that the reader realizes, as the chapter closes, that the son for whom David mourns (37) is not the dead Amnon, but the living refugee, Absalom. It may well be imagined in what sort of an atmosphere the undisciplined young man had grown up. He was probably denied no wish or whim. He could hate fiercely. He could plot and hold his tongue. He was savagely proud. The wrong done

216

to his sister touched his honour, and revenge was part of his mother's desert code. And Absalom was his mother's son.

189 : Absalom's Father

Deuteronomy 8.11–14; John 15.1–6; Revelation 2.4, 5, 21–23

It is not true that parents are always to blame for the sins of their children, but it is a charge not to be denied in too many cases for our comfort. This point in the narrative cannot be passed without a glance at the condition of Absalom's father. Hence the readings on back-sliding, especially relevant to those of David's age and condition— successful, beginning to age, and a prey to that erosion of stern standards and weakening ideals which once tautened and sustained the spirit.

A grim picture of the royal court emerges from these chapters in the story. A household is so often what the head, by example or permissiveness, makes it. The court is a scene familiar to history, of mishandled affluence, power misused and abused, of suspicion, hatred and intrigue. The head of the household, unchallenged in the place of power, seemingly secure, had sadly deteriorated. The old hero of the people, the dashing guerrilla chief, able to win the love and devotion of men, the object of ready loyalty and self-sacrifice, had become the aloof and self-centred despot, the victim, as such men often are, óf the military men and the women around him.

And what of his own record of tyranny? The court knew, the people knew, of Uriah and Bathsheba. In agony and con-trition, that dual sin had been put right with God, but human malice, ever ready to bring down the proud, the uplifted, and the good, laid hold of the sin, and forgot the repentance. Nor was the attitude of the people at large entirely dictated by malice. Justice was a deep-seated passion in Israel. The Decalogue, too, was known in every home. David had trampled on two commandments, and scorned a third. He had been a great leader, but leadership depends on moral worth, and there were those who could no longer believe in David's moral worth. The old days of strife, through which

217

David's military genius had forged a united Israel, were receding into history. A new generation was rising, and tribal sin was rearing its divided head. It is common enough with the young to question established authority, especially when those who carry it forfeit the reverence upon which all authority must ultimately rest. David is a sorry sight, backslidden, falsely secure, obstinate, deceived—and about to be dealt with by the God he had known, and had so sadly forgotten.

190 : Absalom's Return

2 Samuel 14.1–15.12

The lamentable state of David's rule is evident in this story. He was weak, but obviously difficult to deal with and approach. Joab's subterfuge shows how the king had lost touch with his subjects and how incalculable his moods were. Absalom was allowed to return to Jerusalem with neither rebuke nor punishment.

'Not so had God taught David to forgive', runs a footnote in Dr. Scofield's well-known annotated Bible. 'It would seem,' he continues 'that had David at this time taken Absalom into intimacy, the rebellion might have been averted.' Few will agree with this view. Absalom deserved chastisement. He had murdered a brother, and gave no sign of repentance. Amnon, to be sure, had richly earned his fate, but royal authority, under royal law, should have exacted some satisfaction and requital.

David would have precipitated rebellion from some other quarter had Absalom been promoted to any sort of intimacy. The best fate would have been to leave him in his self-imposed exile. But in the whole incident, David's moral torpor is evident. It is the same mood as that in which Nathan found him after his great sin, dull and insensitive.

Absalom waited, obviously expecting some move from the palace. Seeing no intention either to chastise or to restore him, he began audaciously to plot under the very eyes of the languid king. He set himself up in ostentatious state, and impudently set out to win the affections of his own generation, and of the rebellious and disgruntled among the people. It is impossible to imagine that no one brought such treason to the

218

notice of the king. Perhaps the spirit of revolt lapped the very palace, or perhaps David was quite unable to believe such enormities about his pampered son.

A sort of paralysis lay upon him, as the land seethed. Older men in Israel would be wary of the young demagogue, but younger men found him attractive, and in a land where justice lacked adequate machinery (15.2–6), and the ruler, who should have dispensed justice, grew remote, there would be a host who nursed grievance, who desired change, or who saw advantage in revolt. They cohered round the young rebel.

191 : David's Flight
2 Samuel 15.7–37; Psalm 2

It required a shock to bring David back to life. The shock, in the mercy of God, came. It was to give a spiritually moribund man a new lease of life. Taking advantage of a religious festival in the old royal capital of Hebron, Absalom had himself proclaimed king. It was a piece of audacity in keeping with his wild, flamboyant character. Hebron is a bare twenty miles south of Jerusalem, along the land's central spine of hills, and the news must have reached the king in a matter of hours.

It galvanized him to life. In a moment he assessed the military situation. All the old warrior instincts in him revived. The wilderness was always a symbol of security in Hebrew thought. David had proved its reality over long years. The city was a trap. In the desert was hope. With bitter clarity David saw that Jerusalem was a snare. A guerrilla fighter must, as we have seen, have the countryside with him. Towns are his ruin. The choices, at that critical moment, were plain. It was obviously a matter of retreat in one of three directions. First, there was the coastal plain where the old Philistine foe offered small security. Second, there was the way north, where tribal disaffection lay. Since Absalom lay across the southern route, the only way left was down to the Jordan valley, and across to Mahanaim. This involved a tactical manoeuvre of great peril, a retreat across the front of the enemy. It reveals David's renewed vigour of mind that he saw, in swift decisiveness, that this is what he had to do.

He was a new man. The smell of the hot rocks and the sand of the old wilderness was in his nostrils. He was ready to trust God and risk all on firm, swift action. Perhaps Psa. 2 reflects one apprehension which he had to face. The border tribes had been subdued in David's wide stabilization of his borderlands. They would hear of dynamic strife in Israel, and be ready for advantage. On this issue David could only trust God. The raging heathen and the people of Israel, seduced by vain promises, both found a place in that psalm of confidence, and the verse reflects a new-born faith.

The little army crossed the Kedron and bore east. There were faithful mercenaries, some of them Philistines—the Cherethites and the men from Gath. Ittai the Gittite was such a man as David had destroyed in Uriah. And Ittai recognized a new David, or perhaps the old David come back to life,

192 : Shimei

2 Samuel 16

For a fearfully dangerous hour or two the column wound out of Jerusalem, over the Mount of Olives, and on to the long descent of the Jericho road. They intended to swing north-east from that long highway and make for the Jordan wilderness by a higher route. But this was Absalom's moment, and he cannot have lacked supporters to advise an immediate attack. Bemused by his own royal splendour and what he imagined victory, Absalom, the victim of his own arrogance, made for Jerusalem. David's column of refugees, travelling slowly with women and children, can have been hardly more than ten miles away.

Had David needed a demonstration that, even in the capital, the people were not all with him, Shimei provided it. Shimei stood for the house of Saul, whom David had displaced. The day of trouble brings out the hidden evil in a situation, and David was subject to abuse, in which he recognized some ring of truth, at his own city gate. It left its mark on his mind, as Psalm 3 reveals. On the level of human judgement, David had the blood of base murder on his conscience. The crude calumnies of Shimei were not without justification, but took no account of David's penitence, which was public enough.

Shimei himself is revealed in the act. Slander is the revenge of a coward. David dealt with it well. The way to check slander is to treat it with contempt. Try to overtake it, and it outruns the pursuer. David treated Shimei with grace, though the man must have been a burden to bear as he followed the small band on the other side of the Kedron ravine, shouting his curses, and throwing stones. So the king left his royal city.

But they had not been intercepted on the Mount of Olives, 'close thing' though it was, with Absalom on their right flank moving up from Hebron. It was of the utmost urgency to press on. It was beyond belief to every experienced soldier there that no cloud of dust rose down the road to Bethlehem and Hebron. They staggered on as fast as they dared, chose a camping-place, and bivouacked for the night. They slept, and woke, and the moods and trepidations of the next few days seem to be reflected in a handful of psalms which tell us much of David's character. Meanwhile Absalom and the scoundrel Ahithophel entered Jerusalem. It was a fatal blunder.

193 : Hushai

2 Samuel 17.1–22

Hushai was a loyal man, and it is all to his credit that Absalom was surprised to see him apparently throwing in his lot with the godless crew he had gathered round him. By the rough rules of warfare, Hushai's subtle part was a necessary one. He was fighting Absalom with the weapons which the dissolute prince himself had chosen. Absalom could ask no more. He had brought treachery and deceit to the contest. Treachery and deceit were to be the final cause of his failure.

Ahithophel's plan was the only militarily feasible one. David needed time to withdraw to his old guerrilla strongholds. A swift attack by a fast-moving body of chosen troops alone could prevent him and finish the war. Villain though he was, Ahithophel saw this with blinding clarity, and when his advice was rejected he knew with such conviction that the rebel cause was doomed that suicide seemed to him the only resource.

Hushai understood Absalom well. He had marked his delusions of grandeur. He played upon his pathological vanity, and led him to picture himself glittering in armour at the head of a united Israel, gathered from Dan to Beersheba, to sweep the king away (12 f.). It was subtle counsel, and psychologically sound, but somehow Hushai's role seems an ignoble one. His trickery of Absalom involved lying deceit. It involved taking the name of God in vain (16.18). At the same time it involved no little courage. The deep and difficult question is how far a good and salutary end can justify the means, and to what extent any follower of any cause can be sure that the end in view is, in God's eyes, good and salutary.

Hushai, having played his dangerous and difficult part, disappears from the page of history. Absalom appears to have had some inkling of a plot and almost apprehended the two priests who acted as Hushai's messengers. Did he discover Hushai's part, and did the brave friend of David pay with his life for the mission he undertook in Jerusalem?

Meanwhile the days passed. Hastened by Hushai's information, the royal party pushed north-east towards the Jordan. Pss. 3 to 6 seem to reflect these days. The heading of the first of the four is old and traditional. The rest seem to follow in a morning, evening sequence.

194 : Ahithophel
Psalm 41; John 13

Part of the interest of David's story lies in the abundance of material in the psalms which flowed from his poet's pen in moments of stress, or of gladness. We can read of dire events in the historical record, and then turn to observe their sharp reflection in the one who suffered under them.

Many psalms have no traditional heading, and the identification of event and utterance must often be a matter of conjecture. Allow this, and a fruitful area of study opens. We have read Psa. 41 following the chapter on Ahithophel's betrayal because it seems clearly to reflect David's reaction to his courtier's treachery (9). David had a great capacity for friendship, and people who thus give themselves react strongly to disloyalty. Treachery is one of the most detestable vices in the catalogue of human baseness. It is compounded of deceit, self-seeking, cowardice and revenge.

222

David's reaction was shocked grief. Perhaps these words took shape in his mind during the retreat to Jordan and Mahanaim when he seems to have written Pss. 2, 3, 4, 5 and 6. David had learned one of life's greatest lessons—that anything, even the grimmest evil, committed to God can be transformed into good. The sordid act of a renegade had hurt him to the heart. A base man had played him false. David handed the whole sorry packet of wickedness and pain to God, and turned it into prayer and poetry.

The result? The experience, like the other experience of pain, whatever it was which lay behind Psa. 22, broke out of the transient into the eternal. The words became prophecy and found a place in the greater pain of Christ, the Son after the flesh of Israel's king (John 13.18 f.).

Read Psa. 41 with care, and see pain turn into praise. David is 'poor' (1), and not only in material things. In a moving passage in his commentary on Isaiah, George Adam Smith shows how, from the prophets to the Sermon on the Mount and the Epistle of James, the 'poor' in the Bible, which is an Eastern book, are the deprived, the dispossessed, the victims of injustice, the stripped of privilege. David, in this sad moment, was all of this. And so Ahithophel, already judged, though David did not know it, inspired a psalm.

Questions and themes for study and discussion on Studies 188–194

1. 'The roots of most evil go deep into the past'.

2. Backsliding—definition, incidence, and cure.

3. The prerequisites of forgiveness.

4. How should a Christian deal with abuse, insult and slander?

5. Could a Christian be a spy?

6. Are lies ever justified?

7. How do we 'commit' pain to God?

195 : David and His Foes

Psalm 2; Ephesians 6.10–20

Psa. 2 breaks out of time into the eternal, and the New Testament is witness to the manner in which David's agony is caught up into the Passion story and the exaltation of the Messiah (Acts 4.25–28).

David, when the reality of Absalom's revolt and the horror of it broke with force upon his mind, turned naturally to the wider and the national implications of the perilous situation. Perhaps it is more likely to imagine his making swift and effective arrangements, first to meet the tactical situation, and then, on the march or at Mahanaim, turning to the strategic situation.

David had devoted much activity, recorded and unrecorded. to the establishment of the safety of the borders. From then till today, the frontiers of Israel were intricate, beleaguered, and difficult to defend. In pacifying the borderlands the king had made many enemies. Consider Ammon, and the hostilities between that border-tribe and Israel. This was one only of those who surrounded a damaged realm with menace.

Damaged, the realm certainly was. Swift messengers would convey the news to Damascus, and the rest of the enemy capitals, that rebellion was afoot. Absalom was base enough to solicit aid. By what devices David secured the peace, which, in the end, gave him time to defeat the rebellion without invasion from abroad, is not recorded in the story, but may be guessed from the psalm.

Two matters are certain. One is that the situation was dangerous in the extreme. The nations were conspiring and the peoples plotting. That the plotting was 'in vain' (1, RSV), at this point, was only a reality in David's new-born faith. The second matter is that somehow David's quick diplomacy kept the foreigners quiet. His line of retreat lay in the direction of the eastern frontier. This was, to be sure, a guerrilla tactic. David fell back on the friendly wilderness. He also moved in the direction of the foe.

There is a hint here for times of trouble. Put on God's armour, move in the direction of the available resources. Move also towards, not away from, the foe. Be firm. Probably such courageous language as that of vs. 10–12 daunted the enemy, and won the battle before it really began.

196 : Dawn
Psalm 3; 2 Timothy 2.1–13

A map should at this point be consulted if the perils of the royal fugitive, and his reactions to them, are to be understood. His retreat had as its goal the ancient town of Mahanaim, to the north-east and far across the Jordan Valley. The direct route would be down the Jericho road, across the river there, and then north to the desired point. David would surely avoid the open road, and strike north-east in as direct a route as possible. It was a rough march from the highlands of Jerusalem to the deep Jordan Rift far below sea-level, a wilderness journey, dropping 4,000 feet, and then up the Jabbok gorge to the plateau.

Psa. 3 is a morning prayer, probably uttered on the first dawn of the retreat. The word 'many' appears three times in the Hebrew of vs. 1 to 6, four times if we include the verb of similar root in v. 6 'God, how *many* are those who oppress me, *many* are in revolt against me, *many* are saying of my soul: "No help for him in God." ' Snatching an image from the shield under which he has lain all night, David picks up the speech of the old promise to Abraham (Gen. 15.1). Shimei's words were still echoing in his mind. The memory of old sin which they had roused was gnawing. It was with an effort of faith that David called God 'his glory'. Earthly glory was gone. His reputation was in ruins. It was a challenge to courage and to faith to believe that God had forgiven, had restored and lifted the fallen. And yet that is what the sinner who has truly repented is called upon to do. We must forgive ourselves for those sins which God has forgiven us. To grovel in them is morbid.

With the sixth verse we see confidence flowing back. The first mood, when the harassed man woke under the paling stars, had been to think of all the land raised in revolt against him. Prayer, however, was healing his hurt. Faith was returning. Around him on the hillside faithful men were also stirring. And Absalom had not attacked, though scarce a score of miles lay behind and between them. Nor was there any indication of pursuit. And so, with the next verse, faith lays hold of the reality yet to be. It was a fact that, by not winning with a swift decisive stroke that day, as Ahithophel had advised, Absalom had lost the war. But only faith could see it thus at the moment. Faith did.

225

197 : Evening

Psalms 4 and 7

There is a very clear link between Psa. 4 and its predecessor. The writer had been haunted by his own words, as the little band of refugees struggled all day down the rough slopes towards the Jordan valley. 'My glory' ('honour', RSV, translates the same Hebrew word), 'there are many who say', 'In peace I will both lie down and sleep', are obvious echoes. Add the fact that this is an evening prayer. Twelve hours lie between the two psalms.

It is also a prayer of thankfulness. The worst has not happened. The rebel prince had again missed the opportunity for pursuit. He was again the victim of his own shallow and volatile personality, enjoying the plaudits of Jerusalem, riding the tide of transient popularity, defiling the palace . . .

The future lay in the hands of the dusty train of fugitives, every hour a rough mile or two nearer to safety in the wild country their leader knew so well. And hour by hour, to David's jubilant relief, the scouts came in to report no sign of pursuit.

The key sentence in the opening verse runs: 'In narrow places you have made space for me.' Moffatt turns it well: 'O God, my champion . . . When I was hemmed in, thou hast freed me often.' David was looking for space. He had often known such escape from Saul's cordon and desert siege. The city had filled him with claustrophobia. He was himself now that he was out of it.

Life feels like that at times. Circumstances hem us in, and fill us with that 'quiet desperation' which Thoreau regarded as the commonest mood of man. There are times when troubles throng around, and there is no clear horizon. At such times there is one course only possible—move straight along the path which faith and deepest instinct have dictated as right, not doubting in the dark what God has shown to be our duty in the light. Men had turned David's royal glory into shame (2), as they turn God's glory into shame, defiling all beauty, spoiling with soiled hands all lovely and fragile things, corrupting the glory of music, speech, the landscape, love . . . all else; 'because,' as Chesterton said, 'it is only Christian men keep even heathen things.' Why? Because as the same verse (2) says, 'they seek after sham

226

('lies', RSV). 'You men,' the Jerusalem Bible puts it, 'why shut your hearts so long, loving delusions, chasing after lies?'

198 : Night

Psalms 4 and 8

We must spend some more time on Psa. **4**. This group of psalms, all of which appear to have been born of the Absalom rebellion, gives deep insights into David's character and his spiritual experience. Psa. 4 is clearly an evening prayer (8). The party is well down the rough hillsides which lead to the Jordan and safety. The sun has disappeared behind the western ridge where Jerusalem stands. The mountains of Moab have turned purple and dark. Evening moves to night.

In the last study we followed David to v. 3. He now touches with precision and insight on the reason for man's tinkering and spoiling of God's good. We shall follow here the AV(KJV). 'Stand in awe, and sin not', is the correct translation. The word is rendered 'tremble' in Psa. 99.1. In a word, the psalmist has reached a deep conclusion: 'Bow in reverential wonder before the Almighty, and the spirit of rebellion and human pride will wither.' The wilderness is teaching its old, clear lessons to its wandering son, who had been driven home again.

It is true that the Christian does not 'tremble' before God (see 1 John 2.28 in Phillips' translation). 'Bold I approach the eternal throne,' runs Wesley's hymn (Heb. 10.19–24). At the same time a proper appreciation of the Eternal God inspires awe (Psa. 8). David saw that in the deadening atmosphere of the city he had lost something of his reverence for the One who had seemed so near, so great, so wondrous under the turning constellation of the desert night. Verse 4 is the central thought of the whole psalm. Such is the theme, it concludes, for night-time meditation. And that is why Psa. 8 is prescribed as a reading. 'Commune with your own hearts . . . and be silent.' Prayer needs no special

227

language. 'Be silent' . . . In such surrender it is possible to listen, too.

Psa. **4**.5 then calls for simple faith. David had already named 'a humble and a contrite heart'—'a broken spirit; a broken and contrite heart' (**51**.17 RSV), as God's requirements. He makes such sacrifice in the very act of speech. He then can face the murmuring of the weary band. He had heard the soldiers' grumble during the weary day (6). But he can now pull his cloak around him, and sleep in confidence, sure that He who has led so far will, on the morrow, lead on.

199 : Morning Again

Psalms 5 and 11

Verse 3 shows Psa. **5** to be a morning prayer, and adds force to the contention that these early psalms are a series consequent on the third. It is the second morning of the retreat, and the river, with its surrounding jungle, was at no great distance. There was still harsh journeying, but up the Jabbok gorge and the pasture-lands beyond lay safety.

Verse 3 speaks twice of the morning, and v. 12 resumes the image of the shield. All these facts show that an ordered sequence of thought and experience runs through the words. But David is calmer now, and thinks of prayer in quieter fashion. Moffatt renders the opening clauses: '. . . listen to my words, and hear the murmur of my soul . . . give ear to my appeal.' There are 'sighs too deep for words' (Rom. **8**.26, RSV) which are none the less true prayer, for prayer is 'the heart's sincere desire, uttered or unexpressed.' Quiet prayer, coherent prayer, incoherent longing, and agonized petition, are all included here. David felt them all, as, from the lower slopes of the bare Judean hills, he looked across the green broad ribbon of the Jordan plain and the tortuous river to the blue and mauve transjordanian ranges.

This is a carefully ordered prayer, as if the writer had slightly more time for composition. Four verses (4–7) speak

228

of the confession with which true prayer must begin. David prepares his soul for the Royal Presence, and thinks of folly, falsehood, and harm to others—perhaps the sins which, at that moment of contrite review, lay most heavily upon his conscience. Nothing so distorts prayer as insincerity, posing or falsehood of any sort. 'Lying,' said the old French essayist Montaigue, 'is a hateful and accursed thing. We should pursue it with fire and sword.' 'Sin,' said Oliver Wendell Holmes, 'has many tools, but a lie is the handle which fits them all.' Remembering Bathsheba and Uriah, David knew this truth full well. He faced it and purged the memory away. His mind was back again at the opening verses of the psalm of the previous morning, and his humble acceptance of the foul words of Shimei.

Passing from meditation to petition David begs for safety and guidance (8). He begged for a straight path, literally, for there was rough land and doubtful loyalty ahead, and spiritually, for he needed desperately the counsel God alone could give. Verses 9 and 10 are a sudden outburst, the 'cry' of v. 2. Caught in a burst of agony, David cries out in a fashion a New Testament Christian can hardly follow, but rapidly calms into the final two verses. The shield is God's peace and it comes to submission. 'Peace,' said Fénélon, 'does not dwell in outward things but in the soul. We may preserve it in the midst of bitterest pain, if our will remains firm and submissive. Peace in this life springs from acquiescence, not in exemption from suffering.' The king of Israel was learning this old lesson anew.

200 : Valley of Shadow

Psalms 6 and 10

In the morning prayer of Psa. 5, David fought his way through to peace of mind, and quiet confidence in God. Now comes Psa. 6, a prayer, if our guess be true, of that same day's night. It is a sombre psalm, and the physical exhaustion of the day which preceded it must be taken into account if the mood of gloom and groping which fills the psalm is to be understood. Perils from the enemy had receded, but it must be remembered that David and his followers were short of food and water, and had now struggled through shockingly difficult terrain for three days. The narrow flood plain of the Zor, through which the Jordan cuts its serpentine path, was most difficult to break through. The fugitives must have found it peculiarly exhausting, and sheer weariness can daunt the soul, and, in the sensitive, precipitate a mood of pessimism. We should understand this natural reaction.

Then, if it is correctly assumed that the line of march was north-east to the point where the Jabbok joins the Jordan, another grim journey awaited. The route would run up the sinister Jabbok gorge, scene of Jacob's old wrestling, to the uplands and the hoped-for safety of Mahanaim. It was a long haul up the bed of the stream. The cliffs press in and overwhelm the traveller. From the night's sojourn there, and the depressing landscape, David was to draw the imagery of the Valley of the Shadow of Death, a word-picture which he wove into the best known of all his psalms. But that was not until next day.

Anxiety, too, marched with him, for no one, at this stage could tell whether they might find disaffection or loyalty at Mahanaim. But it was David's way to put all he felt and feared into prayer. Hence the opening words of Psa. 6, short sharp cries for help. God does not mistake the voice of fear for the voice of impiety. It is all very well for preachers to comment with prim disapproval on 'the sin of anxiety'. God does not regard fear, depression, deep worry or solicitude as sin, provided they are brought in frankness to His feet and placed in His creative hands.

Themes for study and discussion on Studies 195–200

1. 'Great David's greater Son' in Psa. 2.
2. How faith returns after failure.
3. The place of awe in true religion.
4. The need to pray when the day is in prospect and when it is in retrospect.
5. 'Trouble produces better poems than ease.'

201 : Barzillai

2 Samuel 17.27–29; John 6.67–71; Matthew 16.13–20

David's instinct was sound. It was safe to retire to the old sources of his help and loyalty among the shepherd-folk of the hills. All through the Bible runs a thread to be traced from Abraham abiding in the hills when Lot chose the plain, on to the shepherd-men of Bethlehem round whom God's glory shone. Here was the old core of the land's worth and faithfulness, abiding sure when corruption ate up the souls of men in the cities, and religion withered in urban corruption.

Little is said in the record of the bitter march which we have tried to trace behind the utterances of a series of psalms. And one psalm remains, the most famous of all. But before we turn to its well-known words we shall look at the man who provided the glad occasion, Barzillai, the sheep-rancher of Mahanaim and Gilead.

When David's little band struggled up out of the Jabbok gorge and the Jordan jungle, some anxieties fell to rest. Shobi (27) was the son of Hanun, who so scurrilously insulted David's envoys and occasioned the Ammon war (2 Sam. 10). David had set him on Hanun's throne and his loyalty held. Machir was a local sheik. He had been a supporter of Saul and had given political asylum to Mephibosheth. David's generous treatment of Jonathan's lame son had won his allegiance. The perilous border-lands were not aflame.

The third benefactor was a rich man of Gilead, and the subsequent story singles him out as leader in this demonstration of loyalty. He was an old man, in fact eighty years old, 'a great and good man,' said Josephus, 'who made plentiful provision at Mahanaim.' It was loyalty which refreshed David more than all the provender set before him. Loyalty which awaits no demonstration of advantage, but stakes its all in a doubtful day, is precious to the soul. And such a man was Barzillai, like Milton's Abdiel:

> *faithful found*
> *Among the faithless, faithful only he,*
> *Among innumerable false, unmoved,*
> *Unshaken, unseduced, unterrified,*
> *His loyalty he kept, his love, his zeal.*

The Lord seeks such men. And in days of stress He some-

231

times refreshes the harassed soul of His hard-pressed servants by the revelation of such presences. 'A bold spirit in a loyal breast' is a prime offering to Him and to those we love. Granted that reinforcement, a man can often face the world which might otherwise destroy him.

202 : Royal Guest

Psalm 23; John 10.1–18

Mahanaim, as we have seen, brought no betrayal, only friendship, and the glorious hospitality of the shepherd, 'Barzillai. It was delightful country, after the horrors of the Jordan jungle and the Jabbok ravine. Fears were laid to rest, and prayer, which at times had slipped into the language of desperation, was obviously answered.

Perhaps it was when the sun was sloping towards the far blue horizon where Jerusalem was, and rebel Absalom, that the feast was spread 'in the presence of David's enemies'. And when the feast was over, then it was perhaps that the royal guest rose to his feet to say thanks to his shepherd host. How better could he express his gratitude than to liken the gracious care of the great ranch-owner, and the host of that same afternoon, to God Himself, who had so obviously guided, so clearly spread the table of His grace? This is perhaps what the psalmist guest did. Was this the inspiration of the Shepherd Psalm?

The simplicity of the words is the mark and sign of David's return to the faith of his boyhood. Here is the high peak of his restoration. Here he stands at his best, brought back to the faith and purity which had once made him the 'man after God's own heart'. We should observe him well, for the years were soon to take their grim toll, and the royal psalmist was to become the sad wreck which we see in the final chapters of his life.

Read this psalm several times. No translation should tamper with the fragile cadences of the AV (KJV). It is correctly rendered there, and whoever translated it was a master of English, and a man of sensitive feeling for language. The shepherd image should be followed through Scripture. It

232

occurs five times in Psa. **74** to **80**. It runs from Moses to Christ. The Eastern shepherd went before, with crook to restrain and cudgel to defend. He was there along the lighted path, and in the dark shades of the valley. And beyond the valley lies the 'house of the Lord', where the redeemed shall live for ever. The psalm thus concludes with words not uncommon in the Old Testament, which almost break through to that confidence in another life which was not to become clear till Christ defeated death (2 Tim. **1**.10). Read the psalm yet again and understand the beauty of the writer's mind.

203 : 'Absalom, my Son'
2 Samuel 18.1–19.8

The rebellion was over. Absalom's attempt to destroy David with conventional forces in a conventional attack failed, as it was bound to do, when David fell back on the tactics of guerrilla war. Conscious of David's pathological weakness for his rebel son, the commanders had persuaded the king to remain behind in the town. The battle in the Gilead oak woods closed with Absalom's ludicrous death, caught by the hair in a tree. Joab was determined, with his rough notions of justice, that the prince should not survive his deluded followers, who lay in their thousands on the scrub-covered hillsides.

Joab defied his royal master, as he consistently did. He had held an ascendancy over David since the king made him an accomplice in Uriah's murder. And indeed, at this moment, Joab knew what was better for the country than his uncle did. Yearning and sorrow over a perverted young criminal had no doubt their pathos, but showed small concern for the devoted loyalists who had fought and fallen on that same day. No psalm, no salutary word, flowed from that last grief. It was not committed to God. It was an incongruity which Joab rightly rebuked, a shameful selfishness.

The psalms of the great rebellion were, in fact, over. They were in the last brilliant uprising of David's devotion and his song. They were the rich fruit of his last suffering. David had nothing more to give. In a later chapter (22) the chronicler records a song of deliverance, but the words are those of Psa. 18, written long years before.

Perhaps Absalom killed his father. The last flame of his energy and his poetic genius flared high during the retreat, but left only ashes behind. The shock of Absalom's death was deadly. Perhaps, and the word must be used again as we grope for truth behind the too brief record, perhaps David had hoped in his folly that Absalom would succeed him. His judgement was certainly corrupt and weak in these sad closing days. To put Amasa in Joab's place (19.13) was an act of crass folly, and certain to result in misery. David could not have been much over sixty years of age, but the rest of his life, perhaps ten years, is full of the marks of senility. It is sad to see the blight that had fallen on his life run its sad course.

204 : David Comes Home
2 Samuel 19.15–30, 41–43; 20.1–3

Here was a sorry homecoming. The returning exiles crossed the Jordan by an easier ford than that which they had used along the jungle route. Shimei, the harsh-tongued critic of the retreat, was there on the river bank to grovel before the man whom he had insulted, and won a generous pardon, later treacherously repudiated. Mephibosheth also appeared, and convinced the king that Ziba, his servant, had played him false, and in the same act had as basely deceived David. He received less than justice. Ziba was allowed to retain half of the reward of his crime (29). The suspicion lurks that David was saving face after his deception by Ziba, and was not ready to admit his fault and put right a hasty decision, which had gravely wronged a son of Jonathan.

The whole impression he gives at this time is that of a physically and mentally exhausted man, making hasty decisions often patently unwise. He was probably in no state to deal basically with the rift between his own men of Judah and the rest of the land. The appointment of Amasa to the high command was, perhaps, a fumbling attempt at conciliation, but it was without success, and nothing appears to have been done to damp the too obvious enthusiasm of the men of David's own tribe.

It was Judah which had facilitated David's crossing of the Jordan, and very rapidly an open breach appeared (19.41–43). David's old gifts of leadership seem to have gone. Perhaps Joab knew how to give the impression that the king was old, the king was a figurehead, the king had lost his dash and initiative. The story is a sad one, and Israel's response rapidly deteriorated into open revolt.

Back in Jerusalem David sequestered the harem girls who had been the victims of Absalom, by no fault other than David's own. The establishment was shameful for one as enlightened as David, as we have already remarked, set a base example for Solomon, and led to a life of unhappiness for ten helpless women. They received no protection from the king when he evacuated Jerusalem. They had small consideration now. It is so difficult to isolate vice. With shocking exactitude every breach of the moral law exacts its sanctions.

205 : Joab the Murderous
2 Samuel 19.9–14; 20.4–13

Joab was a rough and powerful man. He knew how to bide his time. David appointed Amasa, Absalom's commander, to lead his army, either to convince the rebel soldiers that no reprisals awaited them, or to punish Joab for the death of the infamous Absalom. Whatever the motive, it was a lamentable piece of foolishness. Whatever comfort it might have brought to the survivors of Absalom's unfortunate host, what sort of spirit was such an act likely to arouse in the minds of those who had followed David in an evil day, and suffered with him?

Joab, furthermore, was the sort of leader that simple fighting men admire, brave, determined and downright. Joab did not lose his confidence. Sheba led his brief revolt. The land was again in an uproar, and Amasa was sent out with a royal mandate to mobilize a task force in three days. It proved impossible, and indeed Amasa's record as a soldier was not one which suggested notable competence in such matters. Amasa's levy failed to appear.

Impatiently the king sent Abishai after Sheba, and with Abishai went Joab, who seems to have retained control of David's two bands of crack mercenary troops (20.7, cf. 15.18). Joab, when aroused, was capable of any crime, and he had long brooded over his supersession by Amasa. His brother Abishai, under whom at this moment he was nominally serving, had been his partner in an earlier assassination (3.27–30), and could do little to restrain Joab in an exactly similar set of circumstances. David had used him to murder Uriah. It was a situation David might have foreseen. He was helpless.

Joab now took command, with or without Abishai's compliance. The pursuit of Sheba continued, and in the far north of the land the rebel was brought to bay. He was a Benjaminite, probably of the house of Saul, and in his rebellion was canalized the jealousy against Judah, which Judah had done nothing to allay (19.15). It was a portent of what was to be after Solomon's oppressive reign. The tribal divisions, which had wrecked the land in the days of the judges, were not healed.

So Joab handed over command of the household troops on which he had cynically and bloodily ridden to renewed power, and resumed control of the armies of Israel in David's despite.

206 : Chimham

2 Samuel 19.31–40; 1 Kings 2.7; Jeremiah 41.17; Luke 2.8–16

With gracious courtesy old Barzillai accompanied his king to the limits of his native trans-Jordan territory. With fine common sense he refused honours which no longer attracted him. With admirable unselfishness he sought not to make his aged presence a burden to others (35). With quiet dignity he sought the king's favour for his son Chimham.

It would appear from the brief reference in 1 Kings, that David gave the son of Barzillai the task for which he was fitted—the care of the sheep on the ancestral pasturelands

236

of Jesse's family at Bethlehem. Like his father, Chimham knew what he could do, what would give him joy and fulfilment, and sought to do it. A portion of the estate seems to have passed to his possession.

At the risk of building too large a structure on slender foundations, shall we speculate a little further? Chimham brought two traditions from his father's home, shepherding and hospitality. Did he make the Bethlehem estate a centre for shepherds, and a refuge for the good men of the land? Did the hostelry which Chimham established remain in the family, after the stable fashion of the east, and become the 'geruth', or caravanserai, of the Jeremiah passage, where Johanan found shelter along with the little band of refugees after Nebuchadnezzar had destroyed Jerusalem?

That was four centuries later. Dare we move on six centuries more and ask why the shepherds thought immediately of Bethlehem when they heard of the Nativity? Was the inn at Bethlehem the same establishment, and was the innkeeper's name Chimham? Hospitality on that notable occasion had not failed as lamentably as some believe. 'Kataluma' (Luke 2.7) should not, in fact, be translated 'inn'. It means 'guest-chamber' and on the night of the census would be occupied by those of David's line who arrived first, Hillel and Simeon, perhaps, the leading Pharisees. Mary was given the next best accommodation, with no slight or rejection implied in it, probably a cavern, as tradition states, with a raised platform where visitors could watch over their beasts and baggage. So the old tradition of hospitality did not falter. A thread runs from Barzillai's banquet to the Holy Family, if we speculate aright, and to the Lord Himself. It matters much what traditions we establish in our families. They can be amazingly persistent.

Questions and themes for study and discussion on Studies 201–206

1. What is the test of true loyalty?

2. In Psa. 23.1 we usually stress the possessive pronoun. Where is the emphasis likely to have fallen in David's mind?

3. Ending well.

4. The wisdom of delaying important decisions, where possible, until rest of body and mind aids clear-sightedness.

5. The place of the shepherd and of pastoral imagery in the spiritual message of the Bible.

207 : David and the Gibeonites

2 Samuel 21

This is a difficult chapter, and might be omitted were it not part of the purpose before us to see the character of David in its entirety. Briefly, the chapter tells of the cruel and bloody avenging of old wrongs upon the innocent, the ghastly murder of Saul's decendants, and an exhibition of cruelty relieved only by the heroism and reverence of Rizpah, whose act seems to have touched David to pity.

The difficulty of the narrative lies in v. 14, where it appears to be stated that God, after the fashion of some pagan deity, a Moloch or some offended demon from the Greek pantheon, was appeased by human sacrifice. It has been clearly enough laid down in Scripture, from Abraham on through the Law, that Yahweh countenanced no human sacrifice. His law cannot have been varied on this occasion. Verse 14 need imply no more than that, after these panic-stricken deeds of blood, the pleas of a broken people were heard, and the famine passed. Certainly no sanguinary sacrifice released God's hand.

In point of fact, Israel and the eastern lands of the Mediterranean were passing through a century of climatological crises, the course of which can be traced in the archaeology of the middle Mediterranean and the Aegean world. God's purposes are intertwined with history, and there was a wrong to Gibeon which demanded righting. David was called to do this, and the urge was of God. The alien tribe was perhaps overlooked in the famine-relief operations which must have been in train, and justice could have been done here.

Where David was at fault was in listening to the voice of savagery. The Gibeonites were aliens outside the old tradition, and the opportunity before David was to enlighten them in the ways of mercy which he knew well enough. Instead he listened to their barbarism. Again we seem to see a

238

damaged spirit. We view the aged David correctly when we see a man worn by the toils of an arduous life, surrounded by lesser and by vicious men, a man of deep spiritual insight struggling with the drag and tug of an age which did not understand his higher aspirations, and now, at last, with capacities failing, and burdens of his own making lying heavily on his heart, succumbing to pride, cruelty and lamentable error.

208 : David's Memories

2 Samuel 22

The closing chapters of 2 Samuel are unconnected. It is as though the author realized that David's life was virtually over, and all that remained was to pick a significant incident, or a revealing set of circumstances, here or there. In the first book of the Chronicles other such incidents are found.

Why the sudden intrusion of this psalm? It is virtually Psa. 18, and was probably written some time before this closing period of the psalmist's life. Perhaps it was an old song of praise with which David lived a great deal in these last shadowed days. It certainly contains the deepest and the brightest lessons which life had taught him.

The first was that God could be trusted. He was rock, fortress, deliverer (2), shield, tower, refuge, salvation (3). In the light of this, all the storms of evil which had encompassed David fell into perspective and place (4-7). There follows (8-16) a splendid passage of poetry, which pictures some violent electrical storm in the mountains of the Judean wilderness—

His chariots of wrath the dark thunder-clouds form,
And dark is His path on the wings of the storm . . .

Such had been life. Like the torrents in the wadis, fed by a wild, mad cloudburst in the hills, violent events had crashed around him, the blows of hostile men and hostile circumstance had been like the stabbing lightning. In the midst of it God had kept His promises (17-22). Only God makes life meaningful and worthwhile. God alone gives it significance (32-49).

So did David survey the past. Life can be best understood in retrospect, and it is good sometimes thus to pause and survey the reality of the plan which has outworked, weaving its perfection out of darkness and light, repaired where wilfulness has tangled the threads, unexpected in its patterns, wondrous in its complexity, and demonstrating a hand that guides and a heart that plans.

Claims to righteousness (23–25) must be seen in the context of the times. There were moral inadequacies, as we have seen, to which David was woefully blind. He was also, however, conscious of the adequacy and finality of the forgiveness which greets true repentance. David's was a character marred by manifold faults, but faults which, until the weakening grip of declining years and wasted mental powers, he was ready to confess—and to one God, the true God, worshipped without taint of heathendom, and understood in clearer perception than many of his contemporaries could show.

209 : Araunah

2 Samuel 24.16–25; 1 Chronicles 21.18–30; Psalm 68

Araunah and Ornan were the same man. One name was probably Jebusite, the other Hebrew, or a Hebraized form of his name. An ancient gloss suggests that he may have been the last of the royal line of the tribe which had held Jerusalem, until David captured it to be his royal capital.

A threshing floor was always in an exposed and windy place, and that of the Jebusite farmer was on the high ledge of the Jerusalem plateau where the temple was later to stand.

Araunah was no doubt a convert to Yahweh. From the ill-fated Uriah (and earlier) to the honest soldier, centurion Cornelius of Caesarea, the Gentile proselytes of the Bible form a fine company, in a real sense foreshadowing the global Church. Josephus remarks that Araunah was a friend of David, and the fellowship may have dated from the days of David's vigour, when he showed mercy to a defeated opponent.

Look at David's noble word in v. 24. He has met generosity and understanding from an alien, and he responds with like spirit. David is about to pass from the page of history. He has just sinned in pride, for the judgement which fell upon his census-taking activities seems to have been a castigation of pride and arrogance. He has repented of whatever spiritual sin was involved, and now speaks with the authentic utterance of his old devotion. His voice is soon to be charged with words which do not sound like the speech of Psa. 23. It is good that he put this last abiding word of good into Scripture.

It was curiously fitting that the temple-site should have belonged to an alien. Psa. 68 could possibly have been written at this time, the last poetic utterance of the ageing king. See v. 29 with its suggestion of a wider fellowship than that of Israel. And thus the psalm continues. It is curious how many of the major movements of biblical history find some member of another race associated with the unfolding events. We have met Jethro and Rahab. We shall meet Cornelius and Luke. The message of Col. 3.11 was apparent for all who could see, from the promise to Abraham on to Isaiah and Jonah. It was difficult to make the Jew see what is meant to be chosen of God. It is difficult to make some people see it today. Araunah was a pioneer. He showed the way.

210 : Adonijah
1 Kings 1.5–10; 1 Chronicles 3.1–3; 22.17–23.1

Adonijah was David's fourth son (2 Sam. 3.4; 1 Chron. 3.1 f.), and, being it seems the eldest living son in the days of David's senility, had some right to expect the succession. Amnon, Absalom, and presumably Chileab, were dead (1 Kings 2.22). David did not discourage his implied claim to the throne, his assumption of a certain pomp, a bodyguard, and such trappings of royalty. Absalom had indulged in similar self-assertion.

Adonijah must have entertained a certain anxiety over Solomon, because Solomon was the only royal prince not invited to the feast which Adonijah gave presumptuously to his adherents, to whom the nomination of Solomon came as a shock (1 Kings 1.10). According to Adonijah himself all Israel expected him to succeed to the throne.

Two very different men also considered the prince's claims just and lawful. They were Abiathar the high-priest who had followed David faithfully since the days of Saul, when he was the only survivor of Saul's massacre of the priests of Nob (1 Sam. 23.6). He was David's priest in the days of his exile (1 Sam. 23.8–12; 30.7 f.), and a guardian of the ark in the days of Absalom's revolt (2 Sam. 15.24–36). As the last representative of Eli's priestly line, Abiathar may have been an aid to David in reconciling the loosely attached northern tribes to his rule. He may have been the chronicler of the first book of Samuel. That one so experienced supported Adonijah says something for the ability and personality of that prince.

Joab, the army commander, was as experienced a man. His allegiance was deeply significant. Adonijah's failure was due to his haste. David was not dead. He fell a victim to a coup d'etat initiated by the clever Bathsheba and Nathan, whose aid may reflect some religious tension between prophet and priest.

Judged guilty of treason, Adonijah was spared by Solomon, who feared an act of sacrilege (1 Kings 1.51–53), but killed when he asked for the hand of David's nurse, Abishag. Of that more in Study 61. It was a fragile ambition, and the whole sorry scene of grasping haste and unworthy intrigue could have been prevented had David been sufficiently in possession of his wits to organize the succession to the throne on a just and equitable basis.

211 : Bathsheba, Nathan and David

1 Kings 1.9–53; 2 Timothy 4.1–8

The subtle widow of Uriah, David's old love, has not appeared in the story for a score of years. She is now middle-aged, but is the same clever woman one suspects she must have been when the king was ensnared by her young beauty. She was determined that Solomon should succeed to the throne. It was in tune with David's aged apathy that nothing had been done to secure the succession.

It is possible to sense the hot-house atmosphere of the oriental court into which David's household had degenerated, and thereby to catch some sense of the deterioration the king's own character had suffered. Amid the wreckage of life which surrounded his premature old age, was the ruin of old love. For all the guilt in which that sad liaison began, David had loved Bathsheba, and it is sad to see her enter the royal presence with prostrations (16), like Esther coming before Ahasuerus. She presents her plea with none of the frankness of an honoured wife, but with the subtle and humbly convoluted arguments of the courtier.

An infection surrounded the king. Even Nathan, an old man now, has none of the forthright bravery with which on that earlier occasion he had confronted another David and rebuked his sin. He is part of the palace plot, a figure in Bathsheba's devious intrigue. Nathan, too, found it necessary to use the courtier's arts, and to approach the capricious despot, which David had become, with circumspection. The succession of Solomon was perhaps all along in David's mind. The words of 1 Chron. 22.17–19 suggest at least that he was commissioned to build the temple, a task surely designed for the royal successor. If so, it was not necessary to come to the king with subtlety and subterfuge. Nor was Abiathar free from reprehensible presumptuousness. A frank report would have been more worthy of Nathan—or perhaps the normal processes of intercourse were no longer possible with the man the moribund David had become.

The scene is a sad one. A man lives too long when he survives his simple manliness, his human dignity, and the sweetness of frank fellowship and unsimulated love. Power had corrupted the shepherd-boy who became Israel's poet king. In mercy, God allowed trouble, and David blossomed briefly afresh. Then the torpidity of the corrupt court wound round him again—and this was the ending. Such an ending it should be our prayer at all costs to be spared. We become that which we entertain at the heart's depths.

Read 2 Tim. 4.1–8 again and think of another man's ending.

212 : David's Death
1 Kings 1.1–4; 2.1–10

There was small dignity in David's end. He was about seventy
years of age, and might have expected something better than
the decrepitude which fell upon him. He had lived a hard
life. The years in the wilderness, living in caves and sleeping
under the open sky, may have left some physical damage. So
too the traumatic experiences of Absalom's revolt, and the
arduous struggle to Mahanaim.

He had also known much stress of soul, and suffering had
taken its toll of body and of mind. He was a broken man.
Winter was on him, chilling his body, in spite of the repulsive
measures taken to restore his physical warmth, and chilling
his spirit. He was the antithesis of the hale old friend whom
O. W. Holmes put into his poem:

> *Call him not old, whose visionary brain*
> *Holds o'er the past its undivided reign.*
> *For him in vain the envious seasons roll,*
> *Who bears eternal summer in his soul . . .*

There was no summer in David's soul. He scarcely controlled the present, let alone the past. Out of the past arose
ghosts to torment him. He had uttered old words of praise
not long before, when Psa. **18**, with its summary of life's
experience, had become again his song. But the last slope of
life had been a swift descent. In the midst of an exhortation
to Solomon to be true, he remembered, to be sure, the beneficence of Barzillai, but he also remembered two rankling
hates.

Joab was David's nephew, and had served his uncle well.
Unable to deal with a soldier so powerful in his own strength,
David leaves Solomon a charge to kill him. Even more base
was the sentence on mad, old Shimei, a piece of arrant
treachery. 'An old man's past's a strange thing,' wrote John
Masefield, 'for it never leaves his mind.' That has elements of
truth, but if an old man honours God, he seeks to remember
Barzillai and forget Shimei, to keep good alive, and banish
evil, lest it be buried with his bones (Job **20.11**). Revenge is a
low passion, the pleasure of an abject mind. Curiously
enough, as Bacon points out in his essay on revenge, Solomon

was to say: 'It is the glory of a man to overlook an offence' (Prov. **19.**11). But here was poor example in Solomon's last memories of his father. To Solomon's credit he tried to spare Shimei, but that is another story.

So the tale ends. We should look to our ending, for in the days when body and brain grow weary, the dark things which, if we allow them, haunt the soul's decaying rooms, creep forth and gain control. To die in honour, love and uprightness, we must allow those things of light and sunshine to flood the soul in the days of our strength.

Questions and themes for study and discussion on Studies 207–212

1. The Law and human sacrifice.

2. The many-sided trustworthiness of God.

3. Old Testament anticipations of the universality of the Church.

4. The folly of presumption.

5. The corrupting effects of power.

6. What does the Bible say about revenge?

213 : Solomon the Great
Matthew 12.41, 42; Luke 12.27–29

Let us pause before turning in greater detail to the life of Solomon, to look at the story of his person and his reign as a whole. He is a contrast with his father David. He began where David ended. He lived a life of security and peace, not of war and conflict. He had the vast experience of a royal father to guide him. He never knew persecution, injustice and rejection.

Solomon had vast advantages. He had wisdom and an intelligence derived perhaps from his mother. He had, at first, the gift of humility, the fruit perhaps of Nathan's training. He had such wealth that the Queen of Sheba was reduced to speechless amazement by his glory. As men measure earthly monarchy, in terms of frontiers, the land's adornment, and imperial pomp, he was Solomon the Great.

What, we must now ask, did Solomon do with all these immense privileges, privileges each one of which was a responsibility? First, he lived a life of self-indulgence. His sin was genteel and respectable, even within the ambit of law and custom which allowed an eastern monarch lamentable scope. It was sin, none the less, unrecognized and unconfessed. It begat no repentance. It was vain parade and flaunted sensuality.

Secondly, his wisdom turned sour in disillusionment, if Ecclesiastes reflects his later attitude to life. And contrast that cynical and disillusioned piece of worldly pessimism with the heart-revealing psalms of David, and even with the plain wisdom of the Proverbs, so many of which came from his ready mind and pen.

Thirdly, Solomon had no notion of what the New Testament was to call 'separation' (2 Cor. 6.14–18). The Old Testament had also been clear enough about the entanglements of fellowship with heathendom. His palace was filled with heathen women, collected in the pursuit both of carnality and dynastic advantage. His trade with Tyre was to open a sequence of events which led straight to Ahab, and disaster to another generation. Solomon's policies, indeed, were a major contribution to the division of the kingdom, and the sufferings of Israel in the captivities.

214 : King Solomon

1 Kings 2.10–46

How old Solomon was when he came to the throne is not known. Eumolpus, who allowed him only twelve years, is certainly wrong. So is Josephus, who gave him fifteen. He was possibly nearer twenty. David had yearned for peace. He had called one ill-fated son Absalom, which means 'father of peace'. Solomon's name means 'peaceful'. Nathan, who took an interest in Solomon, called him Jedediah ('beloved of God'), a play on David's own name. Perhaps Nathan brought him up, thus accounting for the old prophet's interest in the succession.

It was 'a close-run thing', but with Benaiah, commander of the household troops, standing by, Joab, the only real danger, was neutralized. There is no doubt that Solomon's own personal ability played a part, for the first recorded events of the reign show him in firm control. It must have been a surprise for Bathsheba when Solomon's deference and courtesy vanished in a flame of anger when she approached him with Adonijah's plea.

Solomon had spared Adonijah, and the request for Abishag in marriage seems hardly sufficient reason for such an outburst, and the deed of blood which followed. Perhaps the move was part of a policy on Adonijah's part which does not appear in the story. If so Bathsheba was unusually obtuse and she was not a foolish woman. Or was Abishag the Shulammite of the Song of Solomon, and did the request fire a blaze of jealousy?

It is revolting to see the new reign begin in deeds of blood and harshness. Abiathar had been forty years a priest, and had served the royal house well. He was dishonoured. Shimei was put under house-arrest, no doubt because he commanded the sympathy of elements hostile to the throne and loyal to the line of Saul. When it was politic to strike him down, Solomon took the chance. Joab had often enough taken the sword. He perished by the sword, and indeed had earned the capital punishment that David felt incompetent to exact. Grim politics, none the less.

So the tale of the kings begins. Samuel long since had predicted as much (1 Sam. 8). Said Plutarch, eighteen centuries ago: 'There is no stronger test of a man's real character than power and authority, exciting as they do every passion, and discovering every latent vice'. We shall see illustration in plenty, and the thought that presents itself is that it behoves us all to watch with care how we exercise any authority which falls into our fallible hands.

215 : Solomon the Wise

1 Kings 3; 2 Chronicles 1

Solomon was a curious mixture. His marriage of convenience with the princess of Egypt was no more than a piece of worldly wisdom designed to bolster his southern frontier while he turned his attention more closely to the more exposed and vulnerable borderlands of his east and north. It grates a little, none the less, to observe the obvious mistakes with which the most materially prosperous age of Israel's monarchy opened.

The worship 'in high places', mentioned by the chronicler with a touch of disapproval, was a feature of the days before the building of the temple, and the Hebrew historian is clearly preoccupied with setting the stage for the great religious project of the reign. The 'high place' was not in itself wrong, but it was a practice of surrounding heathendom, and therefore perilous to religious purity.

Two hereditary forces strove for mastery in Solomon. The dynastic alliance, with the power all the prophets were to preach against, was a piece of carnal shrewdness which one might imagine was a heritage of the cool and calculating Bathsheba. It was not the statecraft of a man of God. The prayer for wisdom, on the other hand, looks more like David seeking a plan from God in his life. With all his gross faults David desired God's will.

The prayer of Solomon is worth careful reading. There is, to be sure, a due measure of humility and desire for right. Something, nevertheless, is lacking, and perhaps it is a longing for purity and godliness. Solomon looks uncommonly like the rich young ruler who came to Christ. The treasures of heaven lie ready to our hand. Any one of us can take of them according to our choice. We get what we desire. Solomon could have had more than wisdom, good though that desire was, for as Phillips Brooks once said, it is difficult to think of any prayer which God, in giving the answer, might not have wished that we had made larger.

The story which closes 1 Kings 3 shows Solomon at his best. He is wise, indeed, full of human insight, and altogether lovable (27). Here was a man who, had he kept this human touch, might have been one of the great monarchs of all time.

216 : Solomon the Wealthy
1 Kings 4

Here, indeed, is a spectacle of affluence. Solomon's kingdom was rich and secure. Israel basked in her golden age. The royal figure who presided gloriously over the wealthy nation had nothing to fear from arms upon his settled borderlands. The world respected him, and men came from afar to tap the deep springs of his wisdom. Here was 'Solomon in all his glory'.

But perhaps in his very situation are seen the seeds of decay. A certain temptation lies in ease and in prosperity. Adversity hardens men and nations, purges their minds of many small, mean things. But, as the parable in Deuteronomy had it long since, 'Jeshurun waxes fat and kicks', forgetting the pit from which he was lifted, growing proud and hard.

Thankfulness for the toil of men and the blessing of God, which made the wealth and greatness lying too easily in the hands of men, grows faint. Pride and arrogance take its place. The Greeks used to link three words, which, with some loss of content, may be translated: 'surfeit', 'arrogant behaviour', 'disaster'. The first suggests that demoralization which comes with ease and prosperity and too great success, and the relaxing of the moral fibre which comes to the favoured of fortune. The second word speaks of a loss of moral balance resulting in outrageous confidence, and the conduct which reflects it. The third speaks of the catastrophic result which history shows to be inevitable.

The sequence is too obvious in the history of many lands to be much for our comfort today. We can see its predestined outworking. The moral law, which is interwoven with history, is inevitable in its retributions. This chapter contains no account of sin or calculated wrongdoing. Indeed the king is at the moment contemplating a great building for his God. Nevertheless here is the stage. Here is the framework of ease and security in which Solomon is to feel himself slipping, perhaps slipping without consciousness of what is growing faint in his life. He was a busy man, devoted to the administration of justice, and turning to the pursuits of botany and biology (33) and writing of many things.

Questions and themes for study and discussion on Studies 213–216

1. A select number of monarchs have become known to posterity by the description 'the Great'. Should we in-include Solomon? What is greatness?

2. The need to keep close to God when we have authority.

3. Wisdom is greater than knowledge, and holiness than both. Can we be *really* wise without being holy?

4. How substantial was the glory of Solomon?

217 : Solomon the Temple Builder

1 Kings 5; Acts 7.47-53

Men's hearts in the quiet cities of Israel were at ease. The land lived in comfort. As yet there was no wide threat of pagan cultic infiltration. The monarch himself was too intellectual a man to be tempted to base and degrading superstitions. Any incursions into idolatry which were to deface his conduct and his reign were indulgences to his wives, the strongest mainspring of his spiritual decay (11.1).

Yahweh, indeed, was honoured with pomp and ceremony, but such obeisance is by no means a guarantee of spiritual commitment or deep truth of worship. The temple was projected in this spirit. Yahweh was an honoured guest, the giver of good things, the architect of all material prosperity. So it seems, if we follow aright in the record the movements of Solomon's mind, that concept of a shrine of beauty took shape. Great building programmes have, through all history, been a feature of 'golden ages', when peace and affluence make available both a work-force and finance. Finance was a matter which fell within Solomon's natural ability. We shall look later at his great trading partnership with the Phoenicians. As expenses mounted, Solomon was not above bartering Israelite territory for northern aid. And the provision of labour led Solomon into tyrannical organization of the working-class of the land. Solomon's weaknesses show here.

The temple itself was Solomon's work, although it found place first in David's mind. It was not specifically ordered of God. It was a laudable project, like the cathedral building of the Middle Ages, and was permitted by God rather than ordained. The tabernacle of Moses' day was in quite another category, and it was full of symbolic instruction. The temple sought to honour God, and that is a worthy desire. The testimony of the Church is not aided by the mean and shabby places of worship tolerated too often by Christian congregations. On the other hand, lavish building can become a hollow symbol. It is what is within the shrine that matters, and gorgeous cathedrals, from Saint Sophia until today, have arisen in ages and in places where evangelism, the prime and indispensable task, have not weighed heavily on the conscience of men. Solomon, in pursuing his dream, neglected much which lay nearer home, as the next generation was to find. Consider, in closing, that other temple, its outward form, and what is within (2 Cor. 6.16).

218 : Solomon and Hiram

1 Kings 5 and 7

Solomon inherited his father's friendship with Hiram, the Phoenician king of Tyre. The partnership which evolved between them suited both parties admirably, but, although Solomon secured the expensive materials and the equally expensive expertise which his building projects demanded, the Phoenician ruler secured economic advantages of the first order, and it is perhaps no tribute to Solomon's patriotism that he impoverished and denuded his land in the contract.

The Phoenicians, most able of all the Canaanitish tribes, were caught between the Lebanon Ranges and the sea, blocked, in early years, by both Philistine and Egyptian from further penetration south, and unable even to overflow into Galilee and the fertile Esdraelon plain. It was the sea in front, and the magnificent cedar forests behind, which led the Phoenicians to their eminence as ship-builders and traders. What they lacked in their narrow coastal plain was primary produce. They needed the produce of the fertile hinterlands.

Hence the bartering of their timber and craftmanship for wine and oil (5.11). Ezek. 27 gives some idea, from four centuries later, of the diversity and magnitude of the Tyrian and Sidonian trade. In the days of Ahab it was a valuable process of exchange sealed by the dynastic marriage of the young king and Jezebel, to Israel's ruin.

Solomon was the one who initiated this unequal partner-

251

ship, probably sealing it in similar fashion by a marriage connection. Solomon seems to have patronized deities of Sidon, for his wives' sake (11.4), and women of Sidon were among his wives (11.5). This gives some substance to Josephus' statement that a daughter of Hiram was in the king's harem. If so it set a sinister example.

Apart from what must have been a valuable payment in primary produce, Solomon also bartered frontier areas of his northern province, twenty Galilean villages (9.11–13). There is little doubt that Hiram, genial, diplomatic, brotherly, in fact, got the best of the bargain. His frontier in the south, as Lebanon could wish today, benefited greatly by a buffer zone in Galilee. But Solomon was less than wise to give it.

219 : Solomon the Trader

1 Kings 9.10–28; 2 Chronicles 8.1–18

We have suggested that in terms of barter and frontier adjustment Hiram had the best of the bargain in the deal with Solomon. But the Hebrews had other wares to offer their northern partner besides farm produce and ceded territory. Solomon commanded access to the Gulf of Aqaba, and the Phoenicians were eager for a sea-route to the rich commerce of the East. It had long been a hemisphere of sea-borne commerce. In the Mohenjo-Daro ruins of the Indus Valley, pottery as old as Sumerian is found. And China traded as far as the African coast. The sea-lanes converged at Taprobane or Ceylon.

It is significant that Solomon must have been aware of this activity and saw the commercial importance of the Gulf of Aqaba. Here he had the better of Hiram. The ships that traded to Ophir, which was Southern Arabia (9.28), and which rode the monsoons to India (10.22)—if we may guess their destination from the cargoes—were big seagoing traders called 'ships of Tarshish', from Tartessos in Spain, whither the Phoenicians sent for tin. 'China clippers' of the last century, and 'East Indiamen', of the century before, did not necessarily trade to China or India.

Solomon controlled the ships and paid the Tyrian skippers,

Hence the apparent discrepancy between 1 Kings 9.28 and 2 Chron. 8.18. Solomon hired expert shipmen from the north. Doubtless he paid them liberally. (See again 1 Kings 5 for the careful arrangements he is likely to have made in his maritime venture also.) The difference between 420 and 450 is $6\frac{2}{3}\%$. It seems likely, then, that the discrepancy between the two accounts gives us the amount of the total salary bill of Solomon's Tyrian officers. One writer apparently records the value of the specie shipped at Ophir. The other gives the figure for the net amount paid into the Jerusalem treasury.

As we probe the accounts for Solomon's character, we encounter an able intellectual. His roving mind had a grip on foreign policy, and the international scene. He saw Israel as one of a company of nations, with a part to play, with peace to keep, with wealth to garner. Perhaps his concept of the nation was not unlike that of modern Israel. The mystic vision has faded. It was to be born again, not in affluence but in adversity. And the seeds of that adversity were sown by the clever, worldly-wise man who was born of Bathsheba.

220 : Solomon's Temple
1 Kings 6; Jeremiah 7.1–11

Solomon's temple revealed something of the man. What a man builds often shows the nature of the builder, and the temple was a notable expression of a tremendous and consuming personal ambition. It was not a large building by some standards, but it was mightily founded, and rich beyond any other building in the world at that time.

The tabernacle of Moses' day was a light impermanent structure of exquisite craftsmanship. God asked for beauty and wealth to adorn His desert shrine. The temple of Solomon was a burden to the land. It was perhaps from his Egyptian father-in-law, Dean Farrar suggested, that Solomon learned the employment of forced labour, which the temple demanded. The free people of the land provided a work-force in the forests of the Lebanon to an extent which must have disrupted family-life and distorted the economy. In their Egyptian bondage the people of Israel had known what it was to toil for the taskmaster. Now they learned to endure the burden in their own land (5.13–17). The remnants of Canaan, the 'strangers within the gates', bore an inhuman load (9.20 f.). The smoke stains are visible on the walls and roofs of the quarries whence these serfs hewed the cyclopean stones which the temple demanded—and all the rest of Solomon's building projects. As has been pointed out, for all the elaborate nature of its symbolism, the temple was not a sumptuous building. Solomon had much on his programme besides, and the labour and wealth of Israel were turned to this end. Like Pericles, like Augustus, he immortalized himself in stone. And the land must have groaned under the burden.

Three times a year, we are told (9.25), Solomon officiated at sacrifice, apparently in person, the breach of ritual which was accounted sin in the case of Uzziah (2 Chron. 26). This act was in itself an indication of what the shrine meant to Solomon, a framework within which his very formalities of worship were accounted an exhibition of his royal pomp and estate.

Solomon was permitted to build his temple. Like any act of man it could have been a sign of devotion and true worship, God owned it to that extent, and Solomon was given every encouragement to make his temple a symbol of his allegiance to his God. But the temple, apart from what it stood for, counted for nothing. The display of human wealth means nought to God. Neither Solomon's shrine, nor the two which followed it on the same site, were ever more than material symbols, of value and meaning only in so far as they measured a spiritual reality. From Jeremiah to Stephen this truth is made clear.

221 : Solomon's Prayer

1 Kings 8 and 9

It has been said that two natures seem to strive in Solomon. In his prayer and sermon at the dedication of the temple, he echoes his psalmist father, and in the closing movement of his prayer joins the prophets. He gives voice to the ancient vision of Abraham, of a world brought to worship the One true God because of His doings in the national life of one people.

A wondrous ideal possessed Solomon's brilliant mind that day (8.54–61), a land blessed and tranquil in the lap of God's peace. There are few scenes of such rest and quietness in the Old Testament. War and rumour of war, menace, bitter strife and harsh captivity, fill its pages. The message of the book was often wrought out behind frontiers of fear. The quiet and happy land of Solomon's blessed vision depended upon faithfulness, gratitude and pure devotion. But Jeshurun, as we quoted before, 'waxed fat, and kicked . . . forsook God who made him and scoffed at the Rock of his salvation' (Deut. 32.15)—and there came to pass the fears of Solomon's prayer, and redemptive disaster.

Here was the acme of Solomon's glory. The dedication of the shrine he had built, for all the toil and sweat and blood and tears which went into its building, seems to have been a time of deep spiritual experience for him. He spoke words of resounding truth, and touched the edge of prophecy. God took his words (9.1–9) and pressed them home upon his spirit. The great king, at this moment, could have been the great priest and prophet of his people.

It is clear that Solomon fell short of this ideal, and lost this appealing opportunity. What went awry? He ended in philosophic pessimism and under the chronicler's rebuke. The latter half of ch. 9 perhaps provides the key. Others had laboured, and Solomon entered into their labours. He lived in affluence. There was little soldiering for him to undertake (2 Chron. 8.3), for the frontiers were secure. The good things of life began to hold and to preoccupy a man of taste, culture, education and strong carnality.

Solomon became an eastern monarch. The people accepted him in such a role, for he had, after all, brought them peace. They lay in willing servitude, like the people of Rome when Augustus gave them ease. This is not health. It is an Indian Summer of a nation's life and the winter is soon to follow. As Milton says in *Samson Agonistes*:

> *But what more oft in nations grown corrupt*
> *And by their vices brought to servitude,*
> *Than to love bondage more than liberty,*
> *Bondage with ease than strenuous liberty.*

255

222 : Solomon's Guest

1 Kings 10; Revelation 3.14–19

Solomon's fragile glory meant nothing to Christ. He set it lower than the adornment of the flowers of the field. It meant much to the nations which the king sought to influence. His reputation travelled with his trade, and that seems to have reached the Malabar coast. Sanskrit roots lie behind the words for 'ivory and apes and peacocks', which came back with his cargoes, and they seem to be Tamil words which speak of South India.

Both by sea and along the desert camel-ways, his fame also went down to Shabwa in the Yemen, where the extensive remains of an ancient culture await the caprice of a government which forbids exploration. The Queen of Sheba, Balkis by name, according to tradition, heard of the glory of Solomon and travelled up the caravan-routes to Jerusalem to visit him, and set a hundred stories of wonder and romance circulating in the legends of Arabia, Ethiopia and Israel.

She saw the material prosperity of the Hebrew court, the wealth of its services and adornments, the pomp and circumstance of the king, and she was overwhelmed by it. She blessed God (9) for the beneficence which had heaped such wealth at the feet of one astute young man, and if Sheba's queen gained anything of worth from her visit, it was not the loads on her returning camels of Solomon's rich gifts, but this faint insight into the Hebrew faith. It might have been a deeper and more salutary conception had Solomon rather impressed her with his worth and righteousness and the depth of his devotion to God. The irony was that all the wealth which the queen admired was to feed the spoiler. Israel had really more to offer.

Did some conception of the land's destiny travel back down the desert roads in the minds and hearts of more sensitive members of the royal train? Did it find root there, and, over nine centuries later, send some watchers of the skies up the same long highways, following a star to Bethlehem?

Solomon is a pathetic figure in this chapter, robed in his glory and posing before the Sabaean queen. He looks like Haroun al Raschid of the *Arabian Nights,* or like some Charlemagne or Montezuma. Dean Stanley put it well: 'That stately and melancholy figure—in some respects the grandest and the saddest in the Sacred Volume—is in detail little more than a mighty shadow. Of all the characters in the Bible he is the most purely secular; and merely secular magnificence was an excrescence, not a native growth of the chosen people.'

223 : Solomon the Philosopher

Ecclesiastes 1, 2, 11 and 12

The writer of Ecclesiastes calls himself 'the Preacher'. He remarks that he was a king of Jerusalem, but nowhere actually says that he was Solomon. Old tradition, however, maintains that Ecclesiastes was Solomon, and if, indeed, the language is such that it precludes so early a date, the fact may be that the book was modernized, as we today modernize its translation, without losing its significance or context. If another was 'the Preacher', the book could be built round remarks of Solomon such as 'vanity, all is vanity' and many others which could not now be disentangled from the text.

Solomon fits the context. He was a prolific writer, on botany and biology, as well as on ethics. Two hundred of his three thousand proverbs survive, even if the whole collection of the Proverbs of the Old Testament is not his. The ancient world spoke of psalms attributed to him, but none survives.

But turn to Ecclesiastes as a possible final distillation of what Solomon drew from life. What is its possible significance for us? It is manifestly not a text book of biblical ethics or philosophy. 'Be not righteous overmuch' (Eccl. 7.16) is in tune neither with the Old Testament nor the New. Gloom and pessimism, mixed with a fatalistic theism, reign in the Preacher's pages. He writes like Euripides and Lucretius rather than like Isaiah. Should the book then appear in the Scripture canon? By all means. It is a record of man's mind. It is the famous wisdom of Solomon the Wise in its utmost human reach, and full of its own inadequacy. It shows us what the brilliant king was in the days of the disillusionment which followed his overdrinking of the cup of his rich life.

257

Faith and holiness are not ingredients in his sad philosophy. Set his book over against his father's psalms. Solomon's page is bitter with much thought. In David's verse there are heartbeats and the spirit's striving. In the completeness of the Old Testament both records are relevant. 'Fear God,' concludes the Preacher. David feared, but loved as well. The sum of things is vanity indeed, but faith can find another world.

224 : Solomon the Moralist

Proverbs 1 and 8

It is impossible to say how many of the proverbs in the book that goes by that name were products of Solomon's own wisdom, for 1.1 does not provide a heading for the entire book. The author in each case does not matter. Bearing in mind that it is the men and women of the Bible, their character and personality, which we are here seeking, let us ask what manner of man it was who gave such stimulus to the collection of wise sayings and crystalized wisdom.

A preoccupation with such literature dates to earliest times. Jotham's fable (Judg. 9.8 ff.), Samson's riddle (Judg, 14.14 and look at Prov. 1.6), Nathan's parable (2 Sam. 12.1 ff.), are examples of this style of speech and this preoccupation with ethics in a practical form. Such thought, and its associated literature, were an offshoot of religion, a movement of the mind born of Israel's passion for justice.

It was natural that an intellectual like Solomon should find a deep interest in the polished and sharpened conclusions of religious thought. The danger in such personalities is that a concentration on these matters, and the codes of conduct which so readily take shape from them, will form a substitute for that love of God, that committal of heart and mind to His will, and that spiritual devotion, which is true godliness.

Wisdom, as man sees it, can be alien from 'the fear of the Lord' which is the true beginning of wisdom (9.10. See Gen. 3.6). On the other hand, in Deuteronomy we read (4.6) of the Law as being Israel's 'wisdom and understanding in the sight of the nations'. Solomon demonstrates both situations.

Perhaps wisdom turned dry and sour as the years went by, and became the pessimistic philosophy of Ecclesiastes. In earlier years he perhaps saw deeper into spiritual truth, and we catch another glimpse of what the clever monarch might have been. Observe some of his penetrating insights—his understanding of what the Lord was to call the 'unpardonable sin' (29.1), his conception of the prophets' office in the same chapter (29.18), and his preview of 'the Word' of John's Prologue in the fine chapters on Wisdom (8 and 9).

Dr. Billy Graham is said to read a chapter of the Proverbs each day. Whoever does so, whatever the diversity of authorship may be, has notable contact with Solomon's mind. To gain an impression of that mind's worth and power, the exercise might be worth while.

225 : Solomon the Poet

Song of Solomon 1, 2, 7 and 8

The Song of Solomon is probably an utterance of the royal poet's young manhood. It would be difficult to believe that the ardour of love which it expresses could have survived the blighting presence of a harem, and Solomon's band of casual 'wives'.

The song may be fairly and simply regarded as a lyric of love. Sub-Christian asceticism, loath to believe that God's benediction could rest so frankly on physical love, allegorized the poem. One rabbinical school took it to be a representation of God and His loved Israel. Catching up this thread of thought, Christian interpreters have declared the song to be an allegory of Christ and His bride the Church. For most sensitive Christians this creates difficulties. The rich and ardent language, replete with the facts and symbols of physical love, repel when applied to the mystic union of the Lord and His Church.

It is best to look upon this wild poetry as the sanctification of the love of man and woman. It holds that place in the Old Testament which the story of Cana and its wedding holds in the New. The intensity and wealth of the language speak of a Solomon not yet sated with life, but meeting a beloved bride and receiving in return the uninhibited response of a devoted love.

The details of interpretation, the nature of the dialogue, whether some drama is interwoven with the poetry, the identity of the bride, these and other facets of meaning need not here detain us. What we seek is the poet rather than his poetry. We meet a mind rich in its imagination. The imagery, prior to the psychological extravagances of modern poetry, might have seemed remote and alien to Western poetic tradition, formed by the reserve of classicism and lacking the ardour of the East.

Therein lies the interest. Solomon, the cool intellectual, was also a romantic, pouring unrestrained feeling into coloured and exotic speech which reflected the free, unreasoning passion of a youthful love. There was no shame in such encounter, for there was no call for shame. The pity is that it was too probably a fire which died of its own heat, or stifled in the hot-house atmosphere of the Eastern court in which the best of Solomon was lost.

226 : Solomon's End

1 Kings 11.1–25, 41–43; 1 Samuel 8.10–18; Deuteronomy 17.14–20

Solomon knew what a good king should be, and should do. He had revealed that knowledge in the great Dedication Prayer. It was also set down twice in Scripture what abuses might follow a base interpretation of royalty. And if Deuteronomy had been lost, not to be discovered until Josiah's day, Samuel's warning must have been among the priestly records of the land. Solomon with his pomp and selfish wealth fulfilled all the dire warnings of the last of Israel's judges.

All, indeed, was vanity, as Solomon drew near his end. Polygamy always carries a curse, and despotism has a rottenness at its core. Solomon set the example, which Ahab was to follow, of importing paganism along with his pagan women. His wisdom, as well as his carnality, played him false. It was dynastically expedient, he reasoned shrewdly, to link foreign thrones with his by marriage. Spiritually it was disastrous.

The first sign of falling shadows came in the latter years of his reign. Hiram seems to have drawn away from his old friend. He had a goodly bargain in the frontier adjustments in Galilee, but for some unexplained reason was angry about the ceded territory (1 Kings 9.11–13). Probably Solomon withdrew the Hebrew population, and stripped the surrendered districts of their amenities. Economically Israel was in a bad way. Hence the meaning of the cryptic remark about Hiram's talents of gold (9.14). It was probably a well-secured loan. Solomon had offended against the Law by alienating such tracts of land as the abandoned sector of Galilee (Lev. 25.23 f.).

It had been a time of peace, thanks to David's vigorous ordering of the frontiers. Now came the shadow of war, as the frontier peoples began to realize that the golden age was paling to its end. We catch in the last chapter of Solomon's record the miasma of Ecclesiastes. Life had become a magnificent monotony. 'Solomon in all his glory' was to become a legend. Like Midas, in whose hand all things turned to gold, Solomon had won all that life could give him in pleasure, in material things. He was now in his middle fifties, and life was virtually done. There is a moral law whose sanctions cannot be avoided. Solomon was wise enough to know that fact. His backsliding was no fault of ignorance. But he was a lonely man. No bold Nathan rebuked him. The insincerities and servile flattery of an artificial court ringed him round and walled him from the truth. He moves out of the page of history leaving troubles behind him. He had, like Demas, loved this present world, and loved it too much . . .

> *That luxurious king, whose heart, though large,*
> *Beguiled by fair idolatresses, fell*
> *To idols foul . . .*

(Milton)

Solomon was about fifty-eight when he died.

Questions and themes for study and discussion on Studies 217-226

1. Church building—its purpose, its goal, its abuse.

2. The temple in the New Testament.

3. How far can the Church employ the skills of the world?

4. The perils of affluence.

5. Why was Solomon allowed to build the temple when David was not?

6. Why does philosophy so often end in pessimism?

7. Which of Solomon's proverbs seem most relevant today?

8. Religion and the intellectual.

9. Marriage and backsliding.

227 : Jeroboam

1 Kings 11.26–40; 12.16–33

When Solomon was hard at work building the huge walls and the causeway in the valley between Zion and Moriah, afterwards known as the Valley of the Cheesemongers, an unknown young man distinguished himself by his vigour and gifts of leadership. Solomon noticed him, and advanced him rapidly to rank and influence. He placed him in charge of the levies of labour and monetary contribution from the tribe of Joseph (11.28), that is, of the powerful peoples of Ephraim and Manasseh, for Jeroboam was himself an Ephraimite. Hence this perilous appointment.

Ambition was stirred in the young man's heart, and it was no doubt as he worked among his fellow tribesmen, who, outside of Judah and Benjamin, represented the major strength of Israel, that the able Jeroboam became aware of the deep unrest which seethed beneath the golden surface of Solomon's reign. The old tides of tribal jealousy were beginning to flow in strength. Absalom's rebellion had shown that they were still running. Solomon had done nothing, with his programmes of forced labour and heavy taxation, to check their course. There was pride, too, in the tribes which had once known Joseph's pre-eminence. Joshua, too, had sprung from Ephraim, and his tomb was among his tribesmen at Timnath-serah (Josh. 24.30). Gideon had sprung from them, and Shiloh was in their domain. It was not difficult to stir such feelings to fever-pitch.

It is the art of the demagogue to sense the movement of the crowd and to run ahead. It is easy to cloak a personal ambition in the guise of care for the dignity and welfare of the mass. From ancient times till today, that phenomenon has bedevilled politics. Jeroboam was not a good man, as his subsequent career amply shows, but it was easy in such a day to persuade himself of righteousness. There were undoubted abuses in the land, which united various sections of the community against the régimes. The times called for a leader, and Jeroboam had obvious qualities of leadership. The passion could not be hidden. Shishak of Egypt who, like many others, watched for the end of Solomon's Golden Age, must have heard of Jeroboam, and gave him refuge when Solomon also noted the pernicious strength of his young officer's ambitions. The situation, when Solomon died, was full of menace.

228 : Ahijah
2 Chronicles 9.29; 1 Kings 11.29–33

In the latter half of Solomon's autocratic reign, the voice of prophecy was silent. Under the shadow of the brilliant king's famous wisdom there were few who were brave enough to speak. Nathan, the old mentor of Solomon's early years, was dead. Then came a notable moment when one man dared to raise his voice. He was chronicler of Solomon's reign, a court scribe recruited from some priestly family of Shiloh, who uttered symbolic prophecy to Jeroboam.

There was bitter abuse in the land. Not only was the kingdom seething with resentment at the heavy burdens laid on men by the vast building projects of the king, and the tensions caused by his apparent favouring of Benjamin and Judah, but Solomon's compromise with paganism was producing its inevitable results. Part of the heritage of the Golden Age was a clutter of paganism (1 Kings 11.33) introduced from the surrounding nations.

The strength of Israel, as Moses and Joshua had warned, was secure only while it was built round the firm centre of their ancient faith. In Solomon's day it was built round the remarkable personality of a clever man. When that central pillar was removed by man's inevitable end, all that had depended upon it fell. The faults and fissures in the nation's structure were plastered over, but by no means closed, and Ahijah saw with clarity the deepest rift of all, when, in his symbolic demonstration of what was to be, he showed the ten northern tribes rent away, and Benjamin and Judah alone remaining true to David's reign. The adherence of Benjamin to the deprived Judah was a geographical accident, due to the fact that the border ran through Jerusalem (Josh. 15.8; 18.16; Jer. 20.2). There was little oneness of mind, for in David's reign we saw a man of Benjamin, one Sheba the son of Bichri, head a revolt against the royal house (2 Sam. 20.1). So 1 Kings 11.32 is literally true.

So, with one of those parables of action so dear to the Eastern mind, Jeroboam, on some road through the country-side out of Jerusalem, was made aware that his vast ambitions were to be realized. It is not clear whether divine authority for such a prophecy was granted Ahijah, or whether he assumed it. But it was a brave act, a sincere one, and arose from a sure prescience of events.

229 : Rehoboam

1 Kings 12.1–5; 2 Chronicles 10

Rehoboam, Solomon's only son, succeeded easily to the throne in 937 B.C. His name ironically means 'enlarger of the people'. David had won and held the northern tribes by the charm of his personality. Solomon had held them by the brilliance with which he had invested the kingdom, and dazzled them by the magnificence of his royalty. It would have required quite extraordinary personal qualities, and a gift for diplomacy of the first order, had the son of an Ammonite woman and a worshipper of Chemosh been able to hold and bind that fragile allegiance.

Significantly the tribes met at Shechem, not Jerusalem. Any perceptive mind would have recognized the storm signals. In this ancient sanctuary, between Mount Ebal and Mount Gerizim, the assembled tribes, as 'men of Israel', determined to bring their very real grievances before the king. Equally significantly, Jeroboam appeared. He had been awaiting the moment.

The offer they made was fair enough. They would accept Rehoboam as king, and maintain the unity of Israel's federation, if he would lighten the burdens that Solomon had laid so oppressively upon them. They wanted only justice, and that was an old instinct of Israel. It is sad to find that a demand so reasonable seems to have taken the young king by surprise. It is obvious that Solomon had done nothing to train his son for leadership, or if he had, he had trained him badly.

Rehoboam took counsel of the old senators and received good advice. To be sure, the words of the old men are not as frank as one might wish them to be. A certain ambiguity, some measure of Solomon's subtlety, infects them, but Rehoboam might have pacified discontent, and gained time for painless change, had he answered them as the old counsellors bade. But 'who knows,' as Solomon asks in Proverbs, 'whether his son will be a wise man or a fool?' A pagan mother and the hothouse atmosphere of the harem were almost a guarantee that he would be a fool.

The court was filled with aristocratic idlers afraid of a diminution in their standards of living. Rehoboam, after long obscurity, was in unaccustomed power. He gave, on the advice of the young men to whom he turned, a fool's answer. Ruin was quite inevitable. Thus David's grandson found his sovereignty shrink to that of a tribe. It was the beginning of endless disaster.

265

1. Ambition—is it right or wrong?

2. Folly's legacy to posterity.

3. 'He that lacks wisdom asks advice. When advisers conflict, he needs wisdom still more.'

230 : Jeroboam

1 Kings 13.1–10; 14.1–18; Hosea 8.5

Jeroboam was given a tremendous mandate by Ahijah. It was made abundantly clear to him why the kingdom was rent like his rich garment. Indeed, part of the solemn symbolism involved was the tragic loss of a fine cloak, perverted to a use far from its purpose and intention. It is a mystery why God, who knows what lies in the heart of man, should appear to act as though He did not know what use man would make of some fair gift of grace. And yet does not that puzzle go back to the very fall? God 'set man in a garden', as Chesterton put it, 'and sent him forth a free knight, who could betray his lord.'

Ahijah did not know what Jeroboam would do with his call and the glittering opportunity which was laid in his hands. He made it clear to the ambitious young man that his task was to clear away the heathen abuses of Solomon's dying reign, and return the people to their old allegiance and the loyalties of David's house. Had he been true to this commission and trust, perhaps a new unity for Israel would have cohered around his name.

Instead, Jeroboam could not trust his God. He set up his own divisive altar and his own rival priesthood. He violated the ancient prohibition against idols, and repeated the old sin of the golden calf. He earned himself a name of scorn, 'Jeroboam, the son of Nebat, who made Israel to sin.' It lies within the hands of any man to take, and bend, and twist the brightest promise. Jeroboam found his highest ambitions fulfilled. He did not recognize that it was all of God's

266

giving, and that enormous privilege and vast responsibility went together.

Ahijah watched and must have grieved for the man he had so dramatically called to high office and responsibility. It is a strange story of Ahijah's age that we read in 14.1–18. If it is true that Shishak so highly esteemed Jeroboam in the days of his Egyptian exile that he gave him his daughter Ano as his wife, the story is stranger still. The princess of Egypt comes to the blind prophet's cell, and hears terrible words of doom. The son of Nebat sinned against the light. God gave him all he sought, and Jeroboam used it ill. There is no sin more damning than when a man turns a gift of God into a thing of shame.

231 : Rehoboam

1 Kings 14.21–31; 2 Chronicles 12

The kingdom of Judah was sadly stripped and denuded. The new northern kingdom held almost all the agricultural wealth of the land. The magnificent plain of Jezreel, the fine olive and vine-clad uplands of Galilee, the rich lake of Galilee, and the upper Jordan valley, belonged to the break-away kingdom of Jeroboam. So did the lowlands of Sharon, and that portion of Israel which impinged on the cedar-laden hills of Lebanon.

Judah, in fact, was reduced to poverty. She held the hungry wilderness, the sheeplands, and little beside. The very austerity of the land, one might think, would be a challenge. They had lost much, but not their souls. In the face of the rapid apostasy which fell on the northern tribes under Jeroboam, it might have been thought that an urge to hold the ancient spiritual heritage of the land would have fallen on Rehoboam. He was middle-aged, and should have known better than to follow every opportunity to corrupt the old faith of his people.

He appears to have encouraged all the sexual abomina-tions of fertility worship, those 'mystery cults' of the Asherim and high places, with their carnalities and human sacrifice, which defiled Canaan before the salutary cleansing of the Hebrew invasion. The 'sodomites' also found lodgement in

267

the land, and for all the psychological investigations and organized permissiveness of the age we live in, homosexual practice has always been a sign of decadence in a people. Homosexual conditions and predispositions may be a deep congenital misfortune difficult for its victim to bear. The expression of such conditions in mutual carnality is a curse upon a people. Self-control belongs to the duty of all men, whatever their particular constitution and temperament.

Rehoboam's Judah, then, reflecting its half-pagan king, was a place of relaxed standards. It held many of the sacred and historic sites of Israel. A deep challenge to hold and to keep was wound with its history and geography. It was haunted by the past, and it was double sin, in the face of chastisement and in the presence of history, to turn to the gods of lust and uncleanness for solace. Rehoboam showed his worthlessness in his leadership, but how far was the more brilliant Solomon responsible for it all?

232 : The 'Man of God'

1 Kings 13

It is strange that the reign of Jeroboam, which lasted for twenty-two years, should have left so small a deposit of events in the historical records. The chapter before us tells of one or two odd happenings which were considered of sufficient spiritual significance to merit preservation.

The intruding prophet from the southern kingdom was a sort of predecessor of Amos, breaking with fiery violence into the apostate north. He was a brave man and full of scorn for the corrupted house of the northern kings. Like Abraham turning in contempt from the tainted gifts of the lord of Sodom, the Judean prophet refused to eat at Jeroboam's table.

Then, strangely, he was tempted by the lying old prophet of Bethel. His punishment was heavy. He lost his life, and he lost it by incontinently breaking out of a clear plan of God, set down for his obedience and his consequent safety. Perhaps there are vital webs of circumstances which cannot be disrupted save at our peril, and which we tear irreparably by wanton disobedience.

The withdrawing prophet was resting under some famous terebinth tree when the invitation came from the old prophet of Bethel. Perhaps his first fault, the source of further vulnerability, was in making any break at all in his journey. The surest way out of all temptation is often to fly from it, as Joseph did. He might also have been a little more suspicious of a prophet who had remained silent and unknown through the shame of his country's apostasy. When Jeroboam set up his schismatic altar, and the two calves which, after all, were a base imitation of the Egyptian worship of Apis, what was the man of Bethel doing?

This might have engendered a measure of suspicion in the victim of audacious lies. It is not everyone who professes to speak the truth of God who necessarily does so. The name of the Lord has been used to cover and conceal many earthy, human, and carnal falsehoods. Besides, the southern prophet had his clear directions. They had not been revoked, and it is a good principle, as we have remarked before, not to disbelieve in the dark what God has clearly taught in the light. The invitation to Bethel coincided with a weary man's own desires, and it is easy to see the guidance of God in some outside urge or invitation which conforms to what we want. The tempting opportunity did but meet, as it always will, the susceptible disposition. The lying old man, condemned to pronounce a doom he had engendered, never forgot his lamentable crime till his life's end. We should spare our memories.

233 : Asa

1 Kings 15; 2 Chronicles 14 and 15

The account from Kings makes terse reading, save that the picture of a good man emerges. He began with disadvantages. His mother was a scion of Absalom's tainted line. She was an heir of Geshur, the heathen kingdom from which Absalom's fiery mother had sprung long years before, and a source of pagan cults.

They were war-ridden days, and Asa stood direly in need of spiritual sustenance and help. The chronicler realizes this, and in the passage from 2 Chronicles tells the story with the spiritual principles interwoven, and the background clear. A prophet arose who bravely told the truth. God is with those who seek to do His will (15.2). The religious standards of the nation had crumbled (15.3), but God is always there for the returning apostate and repentant backslider:

> Who comes to God an inch through doubtings dim
> In blazing light God will rush a mile to him.

All this is pointed into a splendid precept (15.7). Azariah knew how to preach. The king was a prompt convert. It took courage to defy the old dowager-queen (1 Kings 15.13), but he did, and rid the land of the filth of its idolatry. Maacah's 'image' was probably a vast and horrifying phallic emblem. God can begin to act in the life of nation and individual when the scene is cleansed of its idolatries and the altar set up (2 Chron. 15.8).

Others follow those with whom they see God goes (15.9). There was something like a national revival (15.10). One man had inspired a multitude with his faith (15.11 f.). Almost anything can happen in a nation which gives itself to God, as Judah did on that inspiring day.

Here is the way to man's elusive goal of peace (15.15, 19). How passionately and hopelessly man has sought for peace. And man cannot have peace within the body of the State while he lacks peace in his own heart. The rifts which divide society find their deep fault-lines in the divided souls of men. That is why one man in authority can, by his own deep dedication, send the shock-waves of his testimony salutarily through a multitude. Such a man was Asa. He succeeded a contemptible apostate and swung his nation back to God.

234 : Asa Again

2 Chronicles 16

Asa raised Syria against Baasha of Israel, and, looked upon merely as a piece of military diplomacy, the policy was an expensive but a resounding success. The sacred and royal treasures of Judah were, after all, a small price to pay for

270

Judean lives, provided the policy did not provide a precedent for further inroads into the nation's material wealth. Said Kipling:

We've proved it again and again,
When once you have given the Danegeld,
You never get rid of the Dane . . .

So, at any rate, it appealed to the prophet Hanani, who was bold enough to rebuke the king for faithlessness, and in so doing put a lovely word into the anthology of faith (16.9). The judgement of the prophet was shrewd. He saw the truth which Kipling embedded in his little verse. It is not to be supposed that Hanani laid down thus a principle of universal application, though it is undoubted fact that an 'unequal yoke' with 'unbelievers' carries no New Testament blessing and must be shunned.

We are prompted to wonder a little, when we read the story, whether the Asa of this chapter, flying into a rage against the good and brave man who told him what he at least believed to be the truth, is quite the same bright spirit which listened to the prophet Azariah with attention, and by listening swung his nation back to God and righteousness. Life sometimes erodes the goodness of men, and the stress of events brings decay. Asa had grown autocratic and impatient, and it is sad to see deterioration in any character. There is a 'destruction that wastes at noonday', and Asa was probably in his fifties.

He was also ill. Perhaps the trouble in his feet was dropsy. Perhaps it was that creeping sclerosis which narrows the arteries of the legs, and produces claudication and sometimes gangrenous conditions. There is no mandate in 16.12 for dispensing with the expert aid of physician or surgeon in the quite different context of the modern world. The medicine of Palestine, three millennia ago, was primitive, and surgery non-existent. Asa's only hope was, indeed, trust in God, and avoidance of the various inexpert attentions of medicine without science or basis of exact observation.

So Asa died with much good to his credit and much error. Such is the epitaph which might fit many men.

271

1. Is ambition always reprehensible? How is it distinguished from aspiration?
2. What might Jeroboam have done with his opportunity?
3. Why is Jeroboam blamed more strongly than Rehoboam for similar apostasies?
4. Compare 1 Kings 13 and 1 John 4.1.
5. How confidently may we claim God's guidance?
6. What are the conditions for national revival?
7. What spiritual conditions determine a nation's strength?
8. Backsliding and middle-age.

235 : Jehoshaphat

1 Kings 22.41–50; 2 Chronicles 17, 18, 19.1–3

Jehoshaphat is the last king of Judah to be mentioned in the first book of Kings, the theme of which now turns to the story of Ahab's house and Elijah. But Jehoshaphat, to whom the chronicler devotes four full chapters, was an able and a good man, more faithful to his God than any of his immediate predecessors. In the estimation of posterity he was judged worthy to stand alongside the great kings, Hezekiah and Josiah. The passage in the Book of Kings compresses his worthy reign into ten verses, which nevertheless provide some vital information.

Jehoshaphat was thirty-five years of age when he began to reign, and seems to have been the only son of Asa and his wife Azubah—his only wife, it appears. He had watched and honoured his father, and carried on his father's religious policy. The chronicler seems to contradict the earlier account about the removal of the altars. The reconciliation of the two statements will lie in some trivial omission. Perhaps all the pagan altars were extirpated, and some dedicated to Yahweh left; or perhaps a firm and universal policy had not seen completion by the time of the king's death. Such matters are of small moment. The brevity of Scripture must always be borne in mind.

272

The big mistake of Jehoshaphat's reign was his compromising alliance with Ahab of Israel. He had made peace with Israel after the long years of tension with the powerful northern kingdom, and it was a natural enough consequence to follow up with the dynastic marriage of convenience between young Jehoram and Athaliah, the ill-starred daughter of Jezebel, princess of the Phoenicians and notorious queen of Israel. The New Testament is clear about the impiety and error of such 'unequal yokes', but it is a mistake to read back into the policy and practice of Old Testament personalities the knowledge and insight which flow from the revelation of the New Testament. They did not always see as clearly, and Deuteronomy, with its warnings, may have been lost.

Perhaps the harsh lessons of battle and military defeat brought home to Jehoshaphat the sombre fact that no blessing lay in an alliance with Israel's apostate house. See 1 Kings 22.49, which must be taken with the apparently contradictory account of 2 Chron. 20.35–37. Again there is no doubt a reconciling factor. Jehoshaphat probably opened the path to Elath by his victory over Edom, and sought to revive the profitable trade with the East which Solomon, in partnership with Hiram, had initiated. Disaster fell on Jewish maritime inexperience, and Jehoshaphat was disinclined to renew the attempt when Ahaziah offered expert help. Financial help he may have already had, but he wanted no northern traffic in personnel across Judean territory.

236 : Jehoshaphat the Good

2 Chronicles 19.4–20.37

The king's directions to the judges of Israel stand among the great utterances of Scripture. No virtue is safe unless it be rooted in reverence for God. 'Stand in awe, and sin not' (Psa. 4.4, AV) is a universal principle. It is to be doubted whether the moral bases of any society can stand if there is a complete breakdown in belief in ultimate and absolute authority. It is a significant historical fact that in lands where religion, in the true sense of the word, has been suppressed and proscribed, stability has been achieved only by the setting up of some horrifying form of man-worship, or the imposition of a binding tyranny to enforce a code of law.

The nation which has achieved justice has achieved strength, and that is what Jehoshaphat knew, and must have illustrated in his own person. Justice, in fact, is the clue to success in all good government, and Jehoshaphat's reign gives us the impression of a happy people, confident in God, and in the worthy monarch who had made Him known to them. King and people were healthily one.

From a knowledge of duty done, and obligations thus met, the king derived the confidence which breathed through his prayer when menace threatened the land from a powerful confederation of transjordanian tribes. Jehoshaphat was granted the request he sought, and Jahaziel's forecast came true. The alliance of the invaders disintegrated as they marched upon their objective, and in murderous internecine strife they fell upon one another disastrously. Judah was unscathed, enriched, triumphant.

This was an age of 'prophets'. The great Elijah was at this time functioning in the much less congenial atmosphere of the northern kingdom, and in the south we have noted several references to the ministry of these men. They were not necessarily prophets in the sense of foretellers, but, as the New Testament makes clear, interpreters of spiritual truth, men of authority and deep insight, guardians of the moral situation, and advisers of wise kings. It says something, however, for the character of the man who promoted and tolerated the intervention of such persons. The land was blessed in their presence. The message from Elijah (21.12–15) showed that such ministries transcended frontiers.

237 : Omri

1 Kings 16.1–32

This is a grim chapter, reminiscent of some of the darker passages in the story of the Judges. One by one, like phantoms through a smoke of evil, scoundrels in authority move before our eyes, their villainy the deeper because of the enlightenment they might have known in a land where a lofty religion had been held and preached.

The base Baasha died, and his equally base son Elah reigned briefly in his stead. He died disgustingly in the midst of a drunken orgy in the house of some servile courtier who, as likely as not, was party to the assassination. His killer, Zimri, himself a disgusting criminal, held the throne for seven murderous days. He died in his burning palace, and Omri, a tough soldier and shrewd politician, reigned in Israel, after a brief period in which the northern kingdom was likely to be divided into two.

Omri has no great part in the records, but that merely disguises the fact that he was a monarch of some consequence. Three important events, or sets of events, only one of which is set down in Scripture, give some indication of the man's person and his character.

First, marking the vulnerability of the royal palace and city, Tirzah, by Zimri's defeat and death (17 ff.), Omri set out to provide his successors with a fortress. He chose Samaria, a flat-topped eminence, which was one of the best natural fortress-sites in Palestine. The choice shows the shrewd soldier, for Samaria was to become one of the important cities of Palestine.

Secondly, unmentioned in Scripture, was Omri's campaign against Moab. We happen to know about it because of the Moabite Stone. In 2 Kings 3.4, it is said that Mesha of Moab paid tribute to Israel, but it was not known who subdued him until, in 1868, an English missionary became aware of a large block of basalt, bearing fourteen lines of inscription, at Dibon in Moab. The ignorant local Arabs defaced the stone, but not before a copy of the script was taken. It told how Mesha had at last thrown off Israel's yoke, and that it was Omri who imposed it, and Ahab continued it. So 'the might that he showed' (27) was not an idle word.

Thirdly, it seems likely that Omri revived the alliance with the Phoenicians on the Lebanese coast. The marriage of convenience between Ahab and Jezebel of Sidon (31) was no doubt a seal upon a trade agreement, which was to have dire consequences for the land, and, through Ahab's final doing, a continuation of Omri's policy.

275

The Assyrian records also give evidence that Omri was a figure of international importance. Palestine seems to be known in the records of that emerging empire as Bit-Humria, or 'the House of Omri'.

238 : Ahab

1 Kings 16.33-17.24

Ahab, son of Omri, was overshadowed throughout his disastrous reign by two persons, remarkable in diametrically opposite ways: Jezebel, his wife, and the formidable prophet, Elijah the Tishbite. Ahab should be watched carefully in the story of his doings, which run through the six remaining chapters of the first book of the Kings, for he appears to have been a man who might have been a better man but for a strong and evil influence in his life. At times, the perceptive reader almost feels sorry for him.

Omri's policy was carried on by Ahab, and a marriage with the fanatical pagan, Jezebel, daughter of Ethbaal of Sidon, was carried through. Perhaps some of the explanation of Ahab's character lies in a situation of strong parental dominance. How wrong it is for parents not to respect the personality of their children, nor to promote their individual responsibility! After an imperious father, Ahab found an imperious wife, and we find him converted to the worship of the Phoenician sun-god.

It was deep betrayal. Baal was worshipped with lascivious and sanguinary rites. His cult had no deep moral values, and demanded nothing of those who devoted themselves to it save the hysteria of worship which ever haunts the fringes of religion, and the material sacrifice which has been the stock-in-trade of sacerdotalism from all time.

However deeply and perniciously Ahab may have been influenced by a dominant wife and her horde of priests, he remained, as the record makes clear, personally responsible for his defection. Men have their wills, and anyone can say no. Nor was Ahab's sin without its own influence on others. Contemptuous of history and Joshua's prohibition, Hiel, who came from Bethel of all places, rebuilt Jericho with the foul accompaniment of human sacrifice.

It was into this hopeless situation that Elijah broke. The copula 'and', which opens ch. 17 ('Now' in RSV), shows how God suddenly intervenes. It was an age of affluence. Israel had found a comfortable alternative to the austere Yahweh —'and Elijah the Tishbite' appeared to show quite simply that there was a Lord above the sun and the rain. God had, without preamble, intervened (Isa. 47.11).

Events have a way of demonstrating man's folly. 'The Lord whom you seek will suddenly come to his temple' (Mal. 3.1). It is easy for man to forget who owns the world, and how fragile it is. When Israel bartered her farm produce for Phoenician luxury goods, the fact that it all depended on water was forgotten. The rain stopped.

239 : Elijah

Malachi 4.5; Matthew 11.14; 16.14; 17.3; John 1.19–27; James 5.17

Elijah is one of the great figures of the Old Testament. He haunts the New Testament. The priestly investigators were eager to test the rumour that, in John the Baptist, the old oracle of Malachi stood fulfilled. Some said Christ fulfilled it. So other-worldly in drive and power did Elijah seem that James was prompted to remind his readers that Elijah was a man like any other man, tempted and tested as the flesh is tried. The curious fact is that his story left no doubt of that at all. Those who exalted his memory beyond the human merely failed to read perceptively . . . Elijah appeared on the Mount of Transfiguration. A word, half-comprehended, from the lips of the dying Christ, was thought to signify an appeal to Elijah (Matt. 27.46–49). There are over a score of references in the New Testament to Elijah. So deeply did the rugged Tishbite mark the land's history . . .

Such reputation rose from Elijah's sudden appearance in the story. He came like the lightning, ruthless, powerful, attributes the Jews imagined appropriate in their Messiah. His message delivered he disappeared. The divine action fitted a climatic pattern of events. Professor Rhys Carpenter has gone to great pains to demonstrate that certain movements of migration in the second millennium before Christ were determined by the shifting, north and south, of the rain belts, themselves determined by the heat of deserts of Africa. He has sought to trace certain rhythms of prolonged drought and renewed rainfall. The three-year drought of Elijah's famous story fits exactly into the common shape of climatic events, when a long period of aridity is breaking up and a normal climate reasserting itself. Rhys Carpenter's theories related mostly to the Central Mediterranean, but the eastern end saw the edges of the disturbance in climate thus occasioned.

Elijah disappeared, as indeed he had to disappear, when disaster fell. He went first to the safe wilderness of his own origin, and then to the very threshold of his major enemy's ancestral home. Zarephath, the modern Sarapend, is a few miles only from Sidon, Jezebel's father's royal seat. Under such shadow, the humble widow was kept, and while freed from the task of disciplining a nation, Elijah was employed to comfort one tiny home. In God's eyes, one task was as important as the other.

240 : Obadiah

1 Kings 18.1-16; Ezekiel 2.6; 3.9; Philippians 1.27, 28

Obadiah was a good man, but lacked dauntless courage. Or perhaps he was over-prudent, and would have destroyed himself and all possibility of essential usefulness had he been a man of dashing and downright valour. It is part of the grace of God that he uses a man within the limits of his capabilities, and there are certain physical limitations upon a person's qualities, though that fact should never be allowed to become an excuse for holding back from our full potential in the service of the Lord. The power of God must not be underestimated.

It was essential that there should be someone in Samaria in the day of Jezebel's evil ascendancy who could intervene successfully to save the life of some group of young men in training, for, as we see from the later story of Elisha, that is what the hundred prophets hidden in the cave by the good

278

Obadiah probably were. For a man constitutionally timid, or perhaps bound by the need to protect a vulnerable family from a devilish woman, the act of concealment was probably one of extreme courage.

It is easier to talk about courage than to display it. Nor is it possible to measure courage by absolute standards. Many a decoration has been won for valour by men constitutionally unable to feel afraid. Some people have no imagination. They cannot see with blinding and paralysing vividness the perils of a situation. Courage must be a matter of cold calculation and deliberate choice, to merit fully the name. In the Garden of Gethsemane the Lord faced with perfect understanding, and with complete and awful knowledge, all that the morrow was certain to bring. The agony of His choice was marked on His blood-smeared brow. That is courage.

Measured against his inborn timidity, his congenital capacity for fear, for dreading the worst, for calculating terrible risks, the action of Ahab's capable vizier may have been courageous indeed. But before the rugged and raw bravery of Elijah, he was ashamed. He did not know, only God knew, and only the outcome was to reveal, what Elijah's own stand cost the man who seemed so utterly fearless.

241 : The Common Man
1 Kings 18.25–46

No Israelite left an account of what he saw and chose on Carmel. The people who watched the lonely prophet had more than theology at stake. A century before, Solomon had become the richest of kings by his alliance with Phoenician Tyre. Skippered by Tyrians, as we have seen, his ships went from Ezion-geber to India and Ophir (Southern Arabia). Judah was rich and prosperous, and such a Judah could never have mothered the prophets. When the kingdom was divided, Israel was in a position, as a glance at the map will show, to seize the rich trade of Tyre, and win the lucrative Phoenician friendship. She did. It is significant that Samaria became a rich city. Ahab had an 'ivory palace', the foundations of which still exist. And Israel decayed. Came Elijah, and the contest was set between Yahweh's prophet and Jezebel, princess of Sidon, sister-city of Tyre. Read Ezek. **27**, and see that Israel's trade was but a fraction of the commerce of Tyre. But Tyre was Israel's all. Merchants, who were asked to choose that day between Yahweh and the Tyrian Baal, had to take the hostility of the Phoenicians into account. Their choice could have involved commercial ruin. The rain that roared on the roofs that day, brought back bread and oil, but many a man who had found God again may have lost the wealth of his Phoenician trading in the finding. Few great resolves can be made without sacrifice.

In such situations the spotlight is on the central figures of the great drama, Ahab in his tent on the high hill-side with the great Esdraelon Plain spread beneath, Elijah by the altar and the spring which still gushes under the thorn-bushes, the rich robes and head-dresses of the priests of the sun-god . . . In the last analysis it is the people who matter, and we have thought in this note to turn the attention of the reader to these too easily taken for granted, 'the scorned, the rejected, the men hemmed in by the spears', on whose decisions the issues of a nation's life ultimately depend. Their choice was collective, or so it seemed as the shout of acclaim rolled round the great amphitheatre of the hills. How far did each man make it? A further look at Elijah may enable us to guess a little more closely.

Questions and themes for study and discussion on Studies 235–241

1. Compromising partnerships in business. What is an 'unequal yoke'?
2. 'Justice is the insurance we have on our lives and property, and obedience is the premium we pay for it' (Penn).
3. How is royal might rightly measured?
4. The word 'suddenly' in Scripture.
5. Can prudence become cowardice?

242 : Baal
Jeremiah 19.1–13; Hosea 4.12–19

There was an evil presence in the land. Baal was not a person, but all that the cult stood for lived so vividly in the hearts of men that the Phoenician god assumed a certain personality in Israel, spawned foul deeds like a living creature, and corrupted the minds of men.

Baal took various forms. In the Tyrian version, imported in the train of Jezebel of Tyre, he was the sun-god or, some say, the god of storm, but like most of the deities of the Eastern Mediterranean he had gathered into his person the various features of local deities. It is clear from the horrible scene on Mount Carmel that he was worshipped with the wild and sanguinary rites which gathered round the worship of Cybele in Asia Minor, with the wild beating of drums and clanging cymbals, alluded to by Paul at the beginning of his great chapter on Christian love.

The fertility rituals of the ancient world, a dark substratum in many religions, rose to the surface and found activity in many cults. Artemis of the Ephesians, Aphrodite of Corinth, Isis and a dozen other idolatrous deities, had the lascivious features of 'sacred prostitution' which were an eternal temptation in the ancient world. It was by such worship that the mercenary prophet Balaam, 'made Israel to sin' (cf. Num. 31.16; 25.1–9). It is quite certain that Jezebel, with the connivance of Ahab, introduced these rites of debased and perverted sexuality into Israel.

It is also clear from Jeremiah that child-sacrifice was part of the Phoenician Baal-cult. One consequence was the rebuilding of the city of Jericho with the accompaniment of foundation sacrifices (1 Kings 16.34). Hiel's vile act, the sacrifice of two of his sons, was a dark reflection of the breakdown of the old faith. The presence of Baal was a power in the land. His strength was no more than the embodied evil in a multitude of hearts, but that is how evil operates. The chronicler remarks that Ahab 'did more to provoke the Lord, the God of Israel, to anger than all the kings of Israel who were before him' (1 Kings 16.33, cf. 21.25), and the words seem reserved when set against the sin which introduced into the land, which had known the strong austerities of the

281

worship of the true God, the corrupting foulness of the cult from Tyre. Baal made Jezebel what Jezebel was.

243 : Elijah Triumphant

1 Kings 18; Malachi 3.14, 15

We must read this vital eighteenth chapter again from another angle. The study of Elijah is of great importance. We have seen his sudden irruption into history, and God's care for him in his three years of waiting. During that time, in bitter irony, the fierce rays of the sun-god Baal were burning the pasture-lands to dry dust, and shrivelling the crops with which, after all, Israel paid for the luxury-goods of Phoenician trade. Israel was receiving such a demonstration of the fragility of man, his hopes and his prosperity, as the whole menaced world is receiving today. The false gods have again begun to wither up the world. God was doing, as He sometimes seems to do with special purpose, 'sifting out the souls of men before His judgment seat'.

The twenty-mile-long hump of the Carmel Range looks over a great stage of Israelitish history. Below lay the scene of Gideon's victory. In the far distance could be seen the place where Saul had fallen. All the traditions involved in such history were in peril. The old stern moralities were bartered for 'a standard of living'. Yahweh, be it noted, had not ceased to be a god. He had merely ceased to be their Lord. What advantage, they grumbled, had they from His service? But 'the season of questions was over, the time for an answer had come'.

The people stood in the place of indecision and weakness. They were, said Elijah, 'stumbling along between two faiths'. There is no real religion without firm committal, and Elijah's greatness as a leader lay in the clarity with which he drove that question home. He makes a splendid figure as he taunts the cavorting priests with their day-long hysterical chant: 'Habaal, 'anenu, Habaal, 'anenu.' No one saw what it cost the man, no one saw the strength of the grip by which he clung at that vital moment to God.

The fire fell, and the time for the fulfilment of all Elijah had implied fell due. The place of sacrifice is some hundreds of feet below the crest of Carmel. From the summit the view west is over the Mediterranean. In an agony of prayer Elijah sat and waited. Again and again he sent his attendant lad up to look. At last it came, the uprising cumulus of a cold front, 'according to the hand of a man', as the Hebrew says—great fingers of upward-thrusting cloud out of a nimbus of rain, such as may still be seen. And of all the shouting crowd, of all the court in the king's tent, including Obadiah, no one, no one, came to pray with the distracted prophet.

244 : Elijah Defeated

1 Kings 19.1–10; Matthew 26.36–46

It was loneliness which broke Elijah. No one prayed with him. He was convinced that, after all he had done, suffered, and accomplished, there was no one with him. He was alone (10), abandoned, and for all his triumph, beaten. The great, strong man's wild run before Ahab's racing chariot across Esdraelon in the pelting rain was an indication of the terrible tension which sought relief in action. It also honoured Ahab, but when they reached Jezreel there was no honour for Elijah, such as he richly deserved. Ahab fell promptly under the evil influence which dominated his life. Elijah was left outside the gate, it seems, and Jezebel was free to send her fiendish message to him.

Elijah broke and fled. It was a typical case of such nervous breakdown. It came after a climax of fierce endeavour, dashed with shocking disappointment. He could not see events in clear perspective. Faith itself staggered. But instinct told him what to do. He sought the old centre of Yahweh's might—Mount Sinai or Horeb.

God was with him. The Rev. George Duncan, in a sermon with which he opened the Keswick Convention in 1958, spoke of 'the dark hours of the soul', and the way out of them. He recommended, among other steps of escape, to look for 'small tokens of God's love'. It is a useful direction, and one to be borne in mind by the distressed.

Mr. Duncan suggested that the angel of the story was not a celestial visitant, but a mere peasant woman of the arid country-side, where Elijah rested. An 'angel', after all, is merely a messenger of God, and the suggestion is reasonable and consistent with the wider meaning of the word. God uses the help which lies nearest to His hand, and someone could easily have seen the broken man, and given such help as humble hands can give.

Ordinary people should always remember that those whom they look to as their leaders, and picture as far above them in the scheme of things, stand often in need of encouragement and the simple ministrations of kindliness and love. Who, after all, is our pastor's pastor?

Such was the beginning of Elijah's healing.

245 : Jezebel of Phoenicia
1 Kings 19.1, 2; Revelation 2.18–29

We shall pause, at this point, to look at the darkest character in the story. Jezebel of Sidon, one of the two southern cities of the coastal kingdom of Phoenicia, has left a name for evil in history. She was the daughter of Ethbaal (16.31), who bore the name of the Phoenician sun-god, and gave it also to his daughter, for the last syllable of Jezebel's name is probably a Hebrew distortion of Baal's name.

Ethbaal was the seventh successor of the throne of Tyre and Sidon in the half-century which had elapsed since the death of Hiram, friend of Solomon. He had won his throne through the murder of his brother, and he reigned for thirty-two years. He was a vigorous monarch, determined to build a system of alliances against the emerging strength of Assyria, and also eager to use the land of Israel to feed his people, as we have seen.

There is some indication that the Phoenician treaty with Israel went back to Jeroboam's day, and freedom for Baal-worship in Israel went back perhaps to that time. It only required the dash and passion of the princess Jezebel to exploit the situation. The family was an evil one. The Phoenicians themselves were able, enterprising, ruthless and cruel. They invented ocean-going trade, circumnavigated Africa, held a trading-empire which extended to Ghana, founded Carthage, whose Queen Dido was Jezebel's niece, and in-

284

vented crucifixion. Their name was known in Spain and Cornwall.

Jezebel had all the cruelty, wickedness, determination and fanaticism of her family and her people. She forced the worship of her foul god to the limits, persecuting the followers of Yahweh. By sheer drive and force of character she dominated her husband, strong man and warrior though Ahab undoubtedly was. Ahab, without specifically repudiating the God of his fathers, gave service to Baal, and the court was filled with the orgiastic priests, dining in hundreds 'at Jezebel's table' (18.19), and the cities were noisy with the ravings of the Phoenician worship. Such evil flowed from one dedicated and wicked woman. Such was the woman whose wrath Elijah faced. She became a type of heathen pollution and base compromise with sin.

246 : Elijah's Healing

1 Kings 19.11–21; John 21; Psalm 4

Failure is never final for one who trusts God. Elijah had sought the old scenes of his nation's birth and early vigour. Slowly his spirit healed, and one day he saw scenes of majesty and awe. The heave and shudder of an earthquake shook the hills. The roar of a tearing wind filled valley and scree. The crackle of fire, and the billow of spark-ridden smoke, filled the forests of scrub-oak. And after the tumult came silence, utter silence—and the faintest whisper of a sound. 'Still, small voice' has, to be sure, become a phrase in the English language, but the Hebrew says quite literally: 'the voice of a faint whisper.' Elijah had to listen in order to hear it, and hearing it, he heard what God had to say. He had lived in the roar of conflict, and had lost the quiet voice of God.

He was healed, but had learned in the healing the lesson his malady of mind had to teach. God speaks in the stillness, and, immersed in the earthquake, wind, and fire of battle, men fail to hear that which they should at all costs hear. Hence the precept of Psa. 4.4. 'Be still, be silent', and in that quiet hour God can make Himself plain. Awake under the desert stars (as we saw earlier in Study 198) as the retreat wound down to the banks of the Jordan, David also had learned anew Elijah's forgotten lesson. In an age of noise and tumult, with the multitude pressing ever more closely, it is more and more imperative to bear the same lesson in mind. The body can wear, and its strength erode, and in fatigue and the mind's exhaustion, strange and damaging phantasies can invade the soul. We must take time to draw from the source of all our strength the fortitude we need.

Elijah was healed. He had finished, in fact, the major duty of his life. He was called to commission a successor, who had quite a different task to perform in the great prophetic movement which was beginning in Israel. Elijah was to live for many years, and there was to be another major confrontation with Ahab. He retired, perhaps, after the events of this chapter, to his old haunts on Mount Carmel, a strong, silent influence in the background of events. How the seven thousand fared, and whether others joined them, we do not know.

247 : Ahab and Naboth

1 Kings 21

Jezreel was the Windsor, or the Summer Palace, of Samaria, with wide and lovely views from Carmel to the hills of far Galilee, and the green of the upper Jordan valley. Naboth's vineyard spoiled the prospect for the proud and self-willed Ahab. His was a classic case of temptation—'the lust of the eyes and the pride of life', or as Phillips renders the phrase: 'greedy ambitions and the glamour of all that they think splendid.'

There is nothing wrong in loving and desiring the beautiful and the pleasant. Sin is desiring such good things selfishly, with no thought for another, at the wrong time, at the wrong place, and in defiance of God's law. No good can come from other hands other than God's.

Some eternal principles had not made an impact on Ahab's spoiled and childish mind. First: There are things which we want which we cannot have. God's law forbade the sale of Naboth's property (look at Lev. 25.23 and Num. 36.7). Also, whatever the royal whim, Naboth had his rights.

All desire should be examined before God, and in utter unselfishness. (Under such scrutiny how the nonsensical phrase: 'charity is more than chastity', withers.)

Ahab got what he desired, at a price—his happiness and his future. Jehu rode behind Ahab, when he went to inspect his new property. He was to remember that day, and Jezebel's part in the crime—'Throw her down' (2 Kings 9.25 f., 33). In the same evil situation Ahab made his break with Elijah complete, and Elijah's counsel might have steered the monarch away from the evil complex of events which led to Ramoth-Gilead and death on the battle-field (1 Kings 22). He gained a vineyard and lost his life.

The second principle therefore, is: We can have what we want at a price. Peace and joy are the first instalment in such retribution. 'The joy of the godless is but for a moment,' said Job (20.5). Ahab had his wish but it brought bitterness. Why do men pay such a price? They think God's law of cause and effect can be broken. They reverse their values. Elijah was a friend, Jezebel the enemy (20). Ahab 'sold himself' (20 f.). Ahab repented (27), and his contrition met the grace contrition meets. Jezebel, dedicated to evil, was past such benediction. There is hardly a more shocking verse in the Old Testament than v. 25.

248 : Naboth

1 Kings 21; Galatians 5.13–24

Read again the story of Naboth and his vineyard from another angle. The confrontation between the small land-owner and the king of Israel was a vital incident, and left a tremendous impression on the man who was to prove the avenger of wrongs on the house of Ahab—Jehu, the son of Nimshi. When Ahab interviewed Naboth about his coveted property, and when Elijah met the murderer in the vineyard, as we have seen Jehu rode in his train. The whole incident was deeply imprinted on Jehu's memory (2 Kings 9.25 f.).

Naboth was obviously one of the seven thousand of the message to the distraught Elijah, 'who had not bowed the knee to Baal'. The confrontation between the simple man of the soil and the apostate monarch was typical of what was happening in the land. It was the same, as Amos revealed and as the New Testament shows, through all the history of the land. In the deep country-side, in the old yeomanry of Israel, faith and uprightness still stood. It was in the cities, among the affluent, in high places, that corruption and unfaithfulness found their foothold.

Was Naboth churlish or unreasonable in refusing his royal master the gratification of a simple wish? Was it all due to a deep horror of Ahab's sins that Naboth flatly rejected what seemed a reasonable offer of purchase or compensation? This was not the case. Firm laws, as we have seen, governed the alienation of ancestral property. Naboth may have been one of those who, on Mount Carmel, meant what he said when he proclaimed with the crowd that Yahweh was God. It meant obedience.

Naboth had that salutary love for ancestral land which marks the true countryman. The view across the plain to the blue Carmel range, made more sacred, perhaps, by a rediscovery of God, was dear to him. He felt the king's demand was a test of his loyalty, and from his faith drew the courage to face it with refusal. Horace, the Roman poet, counts that man blessed who can outface 'the baleful stare of the threatening tyrant'. No miracle occurred to save Naboth. Perhaps his sons died too under the cynical perversion of the law of blasphemy (10), surely the hardest charge to face for a man of worth and piety. He died under false charges, as Christ was to die, but his name lives among those of the martyrs of Israel.

249 : Ahab's Ending

1 Kings 22.1–40

We seek in these notes characters, not events, and so need not in this place explore the policies which led to the clash with Syria and the ill-starred alliance with Judah. It was the middle decade of the ninth century before Christ. The Aegean world was struggling back to life after a dark age. Homer was putting his epics together, and preserving in song the memory of the stark, grim days which brought breakdown to the middle Mediterranean. The hills by the Tiber, where Rome was one day to stand, were not yet fortified by the plainsmen against the raiding tribes from the highlands.

Israel and Jordan, too, had seen their Golden Age. As the First Book of the Kings ends, the decline to eclipse and captivity is in full view. The war with Syria was a significant event. Ahab, unable to control his fiendish wife and rule his own house, was none the less a brave and vigorous soldier. He went out to war with a sense of doom. Naboth's death, like Uriah's death in the story of David, was a millstone round his neck. He must have felt a lonely man, and no Easterner would forget, day and night, the words of such a doom as that which Elijah had uttered.

Elijah had disappeared in his own strange way, and the doomed man rode out doubtfully to war. His urging Jehosha-phat to wear his royal apparel was no attempt on Ahab's part to draw hostile attention rather to his ally than to himself. It was the custom of kings to fight thus caparisoned. He himself, daunted by Micaiah's prophecy, and loaded with a sense of doom, declared that he would ride out disguised.

Benhadad deserved well of Ahab, but it is the nature of some vicious souls to hate those who have put themselves under an obligation, and the Syrian ruler had given orders to his thirty-two captains to take the king of Israel. As it happened it was a chance arrow that killed Ahab. Jewish legend says that it was Naaman, the Syrian, who drew the bow without particular aim. The shaft tore into the king's body below his corselet and inflicted a fierce and agonizing abdominal wound. In spite of the savage pain, Ahab remained standing in his chariot to avoid discouraging his men. It was purest, unselfish bravery, and nothing in all his sordid life so became Ahab as his leaving of it. The man had qualities, lost, ruined, smothered by an evil wife, a ruthless father, and a corrupt court.

250 : Elisha's Call

1 Kings 19.15–21

Before we leave the first of the two books of the Kings, we must look at one incident in the life of a man who more properly belongs to the second volume of the record—Elisha,

289

the successor of Elijah. One of the three highly significant tasks which Elijah was called to undertake after his flight and his spiritual and mental healing on Horeb, was the anointing of Elisha to take his place.

It is not every man who can bring himself to appoint the one who is to take over his work. The task goes against human pride. It is nevertheless a responsibility of all who hold high and important office in the Church to recognize the fact of their own mortality, and the even more unpalatable fact of their inevitable decline in strength of mind and body, and their increasing alienation from a changing world.

It is imperative that older men should see to it, as far as lies in them, that men of another generation should lay firm hold of their tasks without hindrance and that the transfer of power should be smooth. God trusted Elijah to do precisely this. He was not dismissed from service. He was to issue forth again, as we have seen, decisively, against the evil of Ahab.

Elisha's call was as dramatic as that of Saul and David. He was a young farmer, another of 'the seven thousand in Israel', and significantly again, a man of the good earth, the same stock as that from which the Lord's disciples came. Elisha recognized the call. He followed with determination, and although he does not appear frequently in the remaining story of Elijah, he no doubt accompanied that rugged character, drank of his sturdy faith, and absorbed his view of duty and the task. The village farewell, alluded to briefly in the closing verse of the chapter, is a rather charming picture. It symbolized the ending of an old life, in a pictorial fashion of the sort beloved by the prophets of the Hebrews, but it also suggested that the community was with the newly-appointed prophet. Apostasy and evil had not yet eaten up the clean countryside.

Questions and themes for study and discussion on Studies 242–250

1. The duty of sharing others' prayer.
2. How should 'nervous breakdown' be dealt with?
3. Silence in our lives. How do we achieve it?
4. The sin of making another sin.

5. 'Baal' in modern life.

6. The significance of Jezebel in the New Testament.

7. Apply to Ahab, Edith Cavell's statement: 'Patriotism is not enough.'

8. What is covetousness? Why is it a sin?

9. 'Handing over to younger men.' Apply this to the modern world.

251 : Ahaziah

1 Kings 22.51–53; 2 Kings 1

The brief and inglorious reign of Ahab's son lasted less than two years. He is the most shadowy figure in all the list of kings. Israel lay in a small patch of peace after the battle in which Ahab died, but the land was exhausted. That is why Moab, which had been held in subjection since the conquest of David, took occasion to rebel, and assert its independence. The famous Moabite Stone, discovered in 1868, records the successful revolt from the point of view of Mesha of Moab, who dutifully ascribes his victory to Chemosh, his god. It was deep humiliation for Ahaziah. The story resumes and concludes in 2 Kings 3.

There is a certain pathos about Ahaziah. Ahab must have retained enough faith in Israel's God to put the divine name into the name of his heir, but Ahaziah, which means 'the Lord takes hold', belied the appellation. He followed rather the idolatry of his bad and powerful mother Jezebel, as the event which forms the chief theme of the chapter shows.

Ahaziah had a shocking accident. Descending from some rooftop chamber of his palace at Samaria, he fell through a balustrade or an open window and was critically injured. His superstitious reaction was to send a deputation to consult Baalzebub, the god of flies, whom the Philistines absurdly worshipped at Ekron. Tormented, no doubt, in the heat of the Middle Eastern summer by the flies which added misery to the pain of a broken back, Ahaziah turned to superstitions inherited from the princess of Tyre.

The messengers met a fearsome presence. Ahab's experience of the prophet was repeated. Grim and terrible as he was four years before in Naboth's vineyard, Elijah appeared from some haunt on Carmel or by Jabbok in Gilead, and told of coming doom. It was the last message the stern forerunner of the Baptist had to give to a ruler of Israel. It was the last message the broken weakling on the bed in Samaria was to receive. Jezebel had done her work well upon her son. Nor was Ahab without blame, from whom Ahaziah could well have inherited his strain of weakness. To honour God in the giving of a propitious name is not enough. The task demands toil, precept, above all example, if our children are to walk the way of faith.

252 : Bethel's Hooligans

2 Kings 2

Across Jordan, where Elijah had sought loneliness and privacy for the last solemn event of life, strange things had taken place, so strange that, with the utmost courtesy towards Elisha who reported them, the young men of the prophets' school insisted quietly on a search of the wild haunts across the river. They obviously found it difficult to believe the report, although Elisha, ordained some ten years before, was by now an established leader.

The serious investigation served to confirm the story, but the rumour must have been widely abroad in the land that Elijah's successor may have had some hand in the old prophet's disappearance. Elisha was somewhat tense and defensive, as the incident on the road up to Bethel seems to show. That incident was much more menacing than at first sight appears.

The Old Testament is sometimes forced by its translators to tell a grimmer story than it actually does. This is surely the case with the so-called 'little children', or 'small boys' of the RSV, who jeered at Elisha. The word translated, 'children' is not infrequently used of mature men. For example, David uses it, tenderly no doubt, of Absalom, when he bids his army commanders to take care not to harm the rebel prince. Absalom can hardly have been under thirty years of

292

age at the time (2 Sam. 18.5, 12). It is also used in Psa. 119.9: 'How can a young man keep his way pure?'

The adjective 'little' is also capable of social interpretation. It is often used for 'small' as opposed to 'great' in rank, standing, or position. An example is in Jonah 3.5. It emerges that the phrase may refer to 'youths of the lower sort', the recognizable type of hooligan with which many an urban community is plagued. It is a group character which is found in the New Testament, for example, the 'lewd fellows of the baser sort', who set the city of Thessalonica in 'an uproar' (as Acts 17.5, AV [KJV] quaintly translates).

Elisha had shaved his head in mourning for Elijah's passing, so the taunt was a most unpleasant and vulgar one. 'Go up', must have been a satirical reference to what Elisha told of his master's translation. It indicated ribald unbelief: 'Bald expert in levitation—show us how!' Add the fact that the bears wounded their victims only, and such rough intervention on a scene of vulgar and perhaps violent (the Septuagint adds 'stoning') abuse seems salutary!

253 : Elisha and the Kings

2 Kings 3

Quite sharply, the picture of Elisha emerges as that of a stern, vehement and independent man, caring nothing for the great ones of the world, and held by them in some awe and reverence. After all, he carried 'a double portion' of Elijah's spirit (2.9), and the reputation of the Tishbite was still great in the land.

Unobtrusively, and doubtless to watch over the good Jehoshaphat, he had joined the expedition which set out to bring rebellious Moab to heel. It was a compromising alliance, in which the king of Judah found himself linked with Ahab's son, and Ahaziah's brother, Jehoram of Israel. Just as incongruous was the attachment of Edom's king, Judah's vassal, to the enterprise. The strategy was to sweep round through Judah and turn north through Edom, thus taking Moab by surprise, with an assault from the vulnerable south.

The march circled the Dead Sea, and they counted on finding water in the Wadi-el-Ahsa but it was dry. The position was precarious, but it brought out the natural piety of Jehoshaphat. Elisha was found to be with the column, and the three kings went to his bivouac. (Observe this attitude. Naaman was to reproduce it.) Elisha burst into scorn so violent that he required the music of a minstrel (15) before he could compose himself to prayer.

When he did, perhaps remembering the famous story of a full decade before about Carmel, Elijah, and the rain, he gained the deep assurance from the Lord of some distant cloudburst in the hills which would bring the freshet down the arid wadi floor. He commanded containing trenches to be dug, and in the morning the water filled them. But by this time Moab's scouts had discovered the attack that was forming, and Mesha was waiting at the valley head. The red dawn brought a weird sight. The flash flood in the valley had caught the colour of the early sky. Perhaps, too, the rushing water was crimson with Edom's red soil. The delusion that the ill-assorted alliance had fallen apart in sanguinary strife fell upon them, and they went down in a disorderly and ruinous attack.

The rest of the story, the Moabite king's ghastly sacrifice, and the obscure statement in the last verse about Israel's withdrawal, need not be looked at here. Elisha may have been behind it, and the indignation against Israel may be that of Judah, aghast at last at the horrible war and the compromising alliance into which their king had been unwisely led.

254 : Woman of Shunem

2 Kings 4

Shunem was the abode of Solomon's 'Shunammite', possibly Abishag, last nurse of David. It lies three miles north of Jezreel. Here lived a family of wealth and consequence, and the lady of the house was a person of kindliness and hospitality. Hence an example set for all time of 'a prophet's chamber', an institution which has brought blessing on countless families, and above all on the children. A small room was built on the roof with private access by an outside stairway, where Elisha could enjoy rest and privacy. Both can be a prize to guests.

The charming story of the chapter teaches the reader much. It is another of those episodes, like the little idyll of Ruth, which shows another stratum of life while the main stream of recorded history runs on through urban wickedness, war and strife. Indeed 'idyll' is the word, for it derives from the Greek for 'a small picture'. Here is the cameo of a household, its quiet hospitality, its joys and its sorrows. Observe the old farmer's quiet trust in the wisdom of his wife. Note how the good woman's faith held in the midst of her dire affliction. Without wasting time she made straight for help.

See, too, another side to Elisha. Carmel, where he moved amid the old haunts of Elijah, lay west across the whole width of the Esdraelon Plain, a score of miles from Shunem. Elisha was alert to hear his kind hostess' message, and flung himself into the act of help and healing with energy. He journeyed back along the road by which Ahab had driven in the tumbling rain, with Elijah running before his chariot. He did to the child what Elijah had done once, long before, at the house of his hostess in Zarephath. The significance of his actions is not explained, but some have seen here a reference to mouth to mouth resuscitation. However, the extended period of time involving an overall journey in excess of 40 miles would make the incident very different from the 'kiss of life' as we know it today, and therefore seems to militate against this view. This much is clear. God heard Elisha's prayer (33), and the dead boy was handed back to his mother alive. The prophet's life and conduct are a symbol of what a good man's presence can do to the children of a home. 'Do not forget to show hospitality to strangers,' said the writer of the Epistle to the Hebrews, 'for thereby some have entertained angels unawares.' And 'angels' are 'messengers of God', and they can take many forms.

255 : Slave-girl

2 Kings 5.1–5; Genesis 39.20–23; Matthew 5.43–48

Raiding on the borderlands was part of the lawlessness of the times, and much misery and human wretchedness lie hidden in the past. At times a sudden and lurid flash of light throws into relief some incident of pain or sorrow which opens a long vista of understanding. A Syrian raid into Israel had torn from home and family a little girl. No one has told of the anguish of the child's soul, or of the grief of her wronged parents. She was part of the long story of man's evil which is not yet over. The curse of slavery was to endure for many more centuries. It is not yet over in some vicious and obscure corners of the world.

Perhaps this unnamed child had read or heard an ancient story of her race, how a lad named Joseph was also sold into slavery in a foreign land, and how, in quiet faith, he set to work, even in the midst of servitude and injustice, to do the task which lay most ready to his hand and to do it well. Thus it was that he remained faithful to his God, and by faith attained the reward that attends on faithfulness.

The child flashes into the story and out again, seen only for an instant as she carries an ewer of water into the room of the wife of the great Naaman, or braids her mistress' hair. Only a few words are recorded from her, but they tell much. Somehow Naaman had won the child's regard and pity. He was an alien. He was her captor. He was, in complete injustice, her master. In quiet simplicity, she illustrates the most difficult of the Lord's precepts. She 'loved her enemy and did good . . .' Her young heart was not poisoned with the hatred which might have made her see with satisfaction the ravages of deadly disease in her master's body. Or perhaps it was some humanity in Naaman's wife which had won the small child's loyalty and regard.

And so an unknown child slips into the ancient tale of stress and pain, and slips out again as she might have done in life, as she entered and left the room of Naaman's wife. We are left to wonder. Did she win her freedom as reward? Was she accepted as a loved daughter into that aristocratic family? We cannot know, but the little Hebrew maid leaves a sweet savour behind her.

256 : Naaman of Syria

2 Kings 5.1–9

'Now Naaman, captain of the host of the king of Syria, was a great man with his master, and honourable . . . but he was a leper' (1, AV [KJV]). Some such adversative clause caps all eulogy of man. Nor is the glum ending confined to the statements of theology. It is as apparent in history. The Greeks invented democracy, but their history illustrates and documents democracy's decay and fall. Rome was given to rule the world, but was unable to save her empire. The Jews gave us the Old Testament, but crucified Christ. The twentieth century was heralded with guns and bells as the coming golden age of progress and of plenty but . . . The First World War was fought 'to make the world safe for democracy.' but . . . Rutherford unlocked the secret of the atom, but . . . man bears the moral image of his Creator, but . . .

> *They have much wisdom, yet they are not wise,*
> *They have much goodness, yet they do not well,*
>
> .   .   .   .
>
> *Much valour, yet life mocks it with some spell . . .*

The root of Naaman's name means 'charm' or 'loveliness', and, although this name was given at birth, the man's character may have formed under its influence. Perhaps here is the secret of the little slave-girl's devotion. He seems also to have been held in some esteem by Benhadad the Second of Syria, though it is not possible to be sure of the identity of either monarch in the story.

One of the more pleasant features of the ancient world was a species of international hospitality in medicine. There is a record of medical help offered by Rameses the Second of Egypt to a princess of the Hittites, and Babylon sent a physician to the Hittite king Hattushil. The exasperated reply of the king of Israel is very realistic. The suggestion that this angry statement implies a belief in the divinity of kings in ancient Israel is typical of the nonsense which sometimes passes for scholarship in Biblical studies. In point of fact, both kings, brief though their appearance is, are quite sharply characterized, the Syrian, business-like, concerned for his officer, and a trifle naïve; the Israelite, fearful and on edge. Naaman, preoccupied with his own sombre situation, set out down the road up which Paul of Tarsus was one day to travel to his destiny.

257 : Naaman and Elisha
Mark 2.1–12; 2 Kings 5.9–19

At Capernaum, as Mark relates, followed by both Matthew and Luke, the Lord linked the healing of the spirit with the healing of the body. Perhaps Naaman, for all the charm he held, needed a deep lesson in humility. Elisha, therefore, who cared nothing for the eminence of men and the favour of the great, merely sent a message to the party of notables standing at his door, and the message contained a strange direction.

Naaman was right. The Jordan is not one of the majestic rivers of the world. Its tortuous course runs through a plain built of its own silt-laden waters. The lucent streams of Damascus were certainly a more inviting bathing-place. It was also a long way, as a map will show, to the river from Samaria, and a downhill, rough, and heat-ridden road from the high eminence of the city to the deep trench, far below sea-level, where the Jordan wound sinuously to the Dead Sea.

Naaman's servants are a reflection of their master's quality. They were no tight-lipped attendants, accustomed to curt orders and instant obedience. They cared for their master, felt free to remonstrate politely with him, and were able to convince him. The whole little scene of discussion round the chariot (12–14) is most pleasantly human. A man loses nothing by natural friendliness with those who serve him.

So Naaman did as he was bidden, and, unlike some who take the blessings of the Lord as if they were of right and not of grace, he returned all the arduous uphill way to high Samaria to render thanks for the blessing he had received. Elisha, anxious for the spiritual benefit of his noble suppliant, refused any recompense. He was dealing with Naaman with wise and loving care. How primitive were the Syrian's religious notions is shown by his request for some Samaritan earth. In Damascus there was to be 'a corner of a foreign land' on which, as though it was embassy territory, Yahweh could be worshipped. Hence Elisha's slightly ironical acceptance of Naaman's plea to be allowed an outward conformity with the worship of Rimmon (18 f.). Life might have been impossible for Benhadad's right-hand man without this leave. It is difficult for gentle, friendly characters to stand out and be different, and Naaman no doubt was at odds with his outgoing personality as well as with his official duty.

Questions and themes for study and discussion on Studies 251-257

1. 'The evil that men do lives after them.' Illustrate from Ahab's successors.

2. What constitutes 'weakness of character'? Can it be overcome?

3. Jehoshaphat's compromise and alliance with Israel—what should his policy have been?

4. Collect six sayings and stories from the New Testament illustrating Christian hospitality.

5. 'A little child shall lead them.'

6. 'Bowing in the house of Rimmon.'

7. The Christian and his subordinates.

258 : Gehazi

2 Kings 5.20-27; Genesis 14.21-24; Job 31.24-28

A bright and honourable future lay ahead of Gehazi. He was the natural successor of Elisha, as Elisha had been of Elijah. He wrecked all possibility of such usefulness by one act of greed. To compass that end he lied to Naaman, and ruined in the process the testimony of his master in the foreigner's mind, and lied to Elisha to cover up his earlier falsehood. Evil is mightily productive and can never be contained within the hour and the occasion.

We are not told Gehazi's motives. Nor do we know what self-deceptions filled the mind of Judas. Such wrongdoing always involves deceit, and the judgement on deceit is that the deceiver first deceives himself. It is clear from 2 Kings 6 that the activities of the 'schools of the prophets' were expanding, and in need of money. Or so Gehazi could easily persuade himself. He probably thought of his master as an impractical dreamer, somewhat out of touch with contemporary life. Elisha had the Lord's attitude to money, and Gehazi may have deplored the fact enough to take in hand some counter measures.

Perhaps, considering the scorn of Abraham for Sodom's gifts, in a quite different situation, Gehazi thought that his master was unwisely imitating Abraham's example. Reflecting that Abraham himself, canny businessman that he was, had at least brought himself to accept a refund of actual expenses, Gehazi had perhaps found 'scriptural' justification for his act of covetousness in the story of the patriarch. It is astounding how people can justify, on the most sacred grounds, that which they desire to do. Man is given to such delusions. Note Gehazi's rather shocking repetition of a phrase used by both Elisha and Elijah (16, 20).

Thus, through an unsurrendered corner of a life, the invader broke in to destroy and to corrupt. Thus can men destroy their usefulness, ruin the plan of God for their lives, and construct the habitation of their own unhappiness. 'Love of money,' says Paul, 'lies at the root of every sort of evil.' It can inspire, in other words, every other kind of wrong-doing, being a basic sin like pride. Hence the insistence of the pastoral epistles on emancipation from this sin in all those presuming to lead the Church (1 Tim. 3.2 f.; Tit. 1.7). We do well to watch our use of money.

259 : Jehoram

2 Kings 6.8–8.6

This long passage tells some grim stories. It is set down for reading because some clear-cut facets of human character spring from the record, and have their lessons to teach. In reading, it is to be constantly remembered that the account is compressed, and difficulties of interpretation can consequently arise. There is, for example, no contradiction between 6.23 and 24. There is only a time-lapse. Elisha's act of clemency was for a time appreciated in Damascus, and then, after the too common fashion of human ingratitude, forgotten.

The king of Israel stands out with some clarity. He was respectful towards the prophet, at this time a man of tremendous prestige, but note the stern test to which his faith in Elisha was subjected. He had followed mercy in allowing the Syrian task-force, which had been led into his fortifications, to go home unharmed. He had thus followed Elisha's advice. And then Benhadad II had invaded again. The very fact is suggestive of the anxiety under which Jehoram continually lived. Samaria itself was a hilltop town, a fortress of impregnable solidity, but Israel's manpower was insufficient to keep the frontiers intact. Samaria was besieged by an exasperated Benhadad, who, for all the impunity with which he could intrude into Israel's territory, looting and raiding for slaves, had been too weak to enforce vassalage or an effective conquest. It was a condition of stressful stalemate.

Samaria was hard-pressed. The people were forced to eat the bulbs of Chiryonim (Dove's Dung, or Ornithogalum umbellatum) whose flowers (Star of Bethlehem) are seen in profusion in the Palestinian spring. Dried and pounded into flour, the bulbs are still eaten in parts of Italy.

Observe the harassed king with the sympathy he deserves. He was Ahab's son and Jezebel's, and ill-grounded in the worship of Yahweh. It was natural enough that his faith should stagger under the fearful strain of the siege. He wore sackcloth against his skin, as the people saw with horror (6.30) when he rent his clothes in agony of mind for his people's degradation. His flash of anger against Elisha was like Henry Plantagenet's outburst against Thomas Becket, but with a less disastrous outcome.

The siege broke dramatically. On several occasions in the historical books, gusts of panic among ill-assorted hosts have been noted—Midianites, Philistines, Moabites—and it was some such sudden God-given fear which sent the Syrians streaming for the Jordan. Jehoram handled the situation well. He was not a vicious man, and the opening of ch. 8 reveals

him not only acting like a just judge but also eagerly seeking
information about the prophet who had moved in and out of
the story of his troubled life. There is something wistful
about him.

260 : Hazael

2 Kings 8.7–29

With strange ease Elisha seems to have crossed the embattled
frontiers at will. He appears in Damascus and is immediately
the object of a deputation from Benhadad, lying sick and old
in his palace. Ostentatiously, a present, distributed on forty
camels, was sent to persuade the prophet to speak. It was
led by the army commander, Hazael.

The story of the interview must be read carefully. It can
be argued that Elisha told no lie (10), he merely set out the
facts. Benhadad was not sick to death, but he was about to
be assassinated. Look carefully at the next verse. Elisha
could read the cruel, ambitious man before him. Hazael
was Syria's Macbeth. He was already planning to murder
his king, and the prophet knew it. Hence the fixed and
penetrating glance, and then the gush of tears. Hazael's
reply is ambiguous. Was the 'great thing' the ravaging of
unfortunate Israel, or the plotted killing of the sick and
helpless king? It is not clear.

The knowledge that he was to be ruler of Syria was already
in Hazael's mind. Like Macbeth, hailed by the weird witches
on the moor as Scotland's coming king, Hazael found the
ambitions which he had long held sharpen to determination.
Elisha was in no way responsible for his evil deed. The Lord
said to Judas, who had already yielded irrevocably to evil:
'What you are going to do, do quickly.' And Hazael's mind
was already made up.

It is still the fashion of the desert Bedouin to alleviate
fever by wrapping the whole body in a wet sheet. Under
guise of this therapy Hazael suffocated his master. So
Hazael came to Syria's stormy throne. He seems to have held
it for forty-six years. Was he haunted by his crime? He
finally bequeathed the monarchy to his son whom he named,
significantly, Benhadad.

For the murdered Benhadad few tears were shed. He was a drunken creature, whose reckless and unsuccessful military adventures had weakened the land. Hence the absence of anyone to defend him, and the people's acquiescence in Hazael. His dynamic presence is felt through many coming chapters of the story.

261 : Mad-driving King

2 Kings 9 and 10

It is curious that the best known of Hebrew kings after Solomon should have become a symbol of wild driving. To 'drive like Jehu' is common parlance still. It is also odd that the only portrait of a Hebrew monarch so far discovered should be this same Jehu rubbing his nose on the ground before the king of Assyria.

Any visitor to the British Museum may contemplate the royal humiliation. He appears in the second line of reliefs on a tall sculptured stone known as the Black Obelisk of Shalmaneser. He cannot be missed, for generations of biblical scholars, conducting their friends round the Museum, have pointed out the abject Jehu, and left a black smudge of fingermarks upon the stone. It is even visible in photographs, a dark patch on the line of cuneiform script just under the king's face. There he crouches before the Assyrian conqueror, Jehu, who 'drove furiously'.

The driving was a reflection of a personality, as driving generally is. Secrecy, rapidity of action, and fierce cruelty, were the marks of Jehu's personality, and it stands full-length in the vivid account of his reign. Jehu was Jehoram's general, a tough and competent soldier, who was left in command of the siege operations at Ramoth-gilead, when his royal master retired to Jezreel to be healed of a combat injury. Ambition comes easily to ruthless commanders with troops at their disposal, some measure of dissatisfaction to exploit, and popularity to work upon. It was in 845 B.C. that Jehu staged his revolution against the house of Omri. In the camp the soldiers proclaimed him king, and Jehu moved into action with the dash, vigour and single-minded drive which marked his personality.

It is a grisly chapter. Before it ends, Jehoram is dead with an arrow between his shoulders from Jehu's bow. Ahaziah, Jehoram's royal guest and nephew, king of neighbouring Judah, was likewise shot down as he fled, and the notorious Jezebel, flung from an upper window, was eaten by pariah dogs in the alleys of Jezreel, while mad-driving Jehu dined. The next chapter is almost as grim. Jehu was a scourge to a corrupt royal house, and though it was villain against villain, the military revolution cleansed the land of the house of Omri, and broke a sinister alliance between Judah and Israel which might have caused disastrous betrayal of tradition.

The inscription on the Black Obelisk calls Jehu mistakenly 'the Son of Omri', the violent change of dynasty not being understood. The occasion was five years later, when Jehu allied himself with Hazael, and knew defeat with him at the savage Shalmaneser's hands. 'The tribute of Jehu,' runs the text, 'son of Omri: Silver, gold, lead, sceptres for the hand of the king, javelins I received from him.' It is like a fine for bad driving. It was certainly a fine for folly.

262 : Ahaziah of Judah

2 Chronicles 21 and 22

It was a deplorable mistake of the good king of Judah, Jehoshaphat, to ally his son Jehoram with the dynamic daughter of Jezebel. Of this fierce princess, more will be said in the next study. Jehoram succeeded to the throne of the southern kingdom on his father's death, and held it for eight deplorable years. He was, like Ahab, completely dominated by his wife and her aged mother Jezebel, with predictable results. The fundamental weakness of his character is exposed by the fact. The chronicler (21.11) tells of the Tyrian obscenities which the feeble king introduced into Jerusalem at the bidding of the two bad women who dominated his life. Fratricide (21.4) and paganism marked his dark eight years.

Ahaziah his son, whose death at Jehu's hands has already been anticipated, succeeded to the throne at the age of twenty-two, and survived for one ill-fated year. Athaliah, his mother, was supreme. She 'was his counsellor in doing wickedly' (22.3), the most shocking word which can be said about any mother. It was well for Judah that the reign was short. The southern kingdom reproduced so exactly over the next few years the events which happened in Samaria.

We should pause at this point to consider the clutter of evil which mars the record of Scripture. Where have all the good men gone? It is well to remember that the great age of the literary prophets was already begun. The first great movement of the prophetic spirit, developing through Samuel to Elijah and Elisha, was closing. It was time for the Old Testament to take its final shape. Recording scribes, like those who put the Chronicles together, were watching the flow of the nation's history and drawing the spiritual lessons from it which later ages were to note. There were good priests like the man whom we shall meet in the story of Joash.

Events, too, centre in the city, and the city, as David found, was no nursing ground of true religion. Jerusalem killed the Lord, and it was not the first of Jerusalem's crimes, as the Lord Himself was to remark with grief. In the country, old reservoir of Israel's faith, were men like Amos. We shall meet them in later studies. Meanwhile, as the lurid film of court and city unreels, it is important to remember them. And is the situation vitally different today?

263 : Athaliah

2 Kings 11; 2 Chronicles 22.10–23.21

Here are the final consequences of the fateful marriage between Ahab and the princess of Tyre, which brought pain and bloodshed to the northern kingdom, and then, like some noisome plague, infected the land of Judah. Athaliah was Jezebel's true daughter. Here is the same pagan fanaticism, the same savagery of temperament, cruelty, and dauntless resolution.

She had been Jehoram's queen, the dominant mother of Ahaziah. With her son dead, she saw the path to her ambition open. Jehoram, instigated no doubt by his evil wife, had murdered his six younger brothers. An Arab and Philistine raiding party had stripped the palace of all heirs save

Jehoahaz (that is Ahaziah). Ahaziah left young children. They must have been mere babes and infants, seeing that the king died at Jehu's hand when barely twenty-three years of age. Athaliah, determined to have no claimant to the throne in later years, rose and killed them all—all save Joash, who, thanks to a woman's daring, was overlooked. His nurse, and Ahaziah's half-sister Jehosheba, the wife of Jehoiada the priest, hid the child, according to Josephus, in the store-room where spare beds and mattresses were kept. He was moved from there to the Temple complex. This was appropriate retribution for Athaliah, for in her Baal-ridden reign the Temple was neglected and despised.

Mattan, high priest of the Tyrian sun-god, became the considerable cleric of Jerusalem, and Jehoiada, coldly passed by, but not yet persecuted by the cunning Athaliah, nursed Joash to young boyhood. 'There is always a thing forgotten' by evildoers, and the surviving prince grew, over Athaliah's six wicked years of reign, to the age of seven, when a Jewish boy was regarded as something more than a child. Jehoiada, one of 'the Seven Thousand' of Elijah's phrase, one of 'the Remnant', had trained the child well. He had a fund of loyalty and sullen discontent among the population on which to draw. The plot was laid with care, and the little lad was anointed king with all the sound and ceremony of a royal consecration. The French dramatist Racine makes a tremendous scene out of this historic incident in his biblical drama, 'Athalie'. With all the undaunted courage of her mother Jezebel, Athaliah hurried to the Temple. She saw her little grandson robed and throned. Her quick mind read the realities of the situation—too late. So died the last of Jezebel's line. She thought that might was greater than right, and fear more powerful than love.

264 : Joash

2 Kings 12; 2 Chronicles 24

The training Joash received under Jehoiada was like that of the boy Samuel, who spent the formative years of early childhood in the quiet precincts of the Temple, absorbing the meaning of its sacred rituals.

Joash set out to restore the ancient shrine and found himself frustrated by the torpor of the priests, content to pursue the formal exercises of their religion, and resistant to toil and change. Such is the endemic fault of those engaged in the service of God—to become content with the situation, and to conform with the fashions of the day in lethargy or timidity.

Joash intervened with vigour. Jehoiada was growing old. It is not unlikely that he was grooming his son, Zechariah, for the sacred succession, and that Zechariah was a lesser man, unfitted for the task. The account, both in the Second Book of the Kings and in the Chronicles, is too brief for the reader to unravel motives, and explain some puzzling action, but it is not impossible that Joash earned the resentment of the hierarchy by his firm take-over of the finances for the repair of the Temple.

If this assumption is correct, it might explain the vigorous reaction of Zechariah when a compromise of the monarch in later years gave occasion for strong rebuke (24.17 ff.). The reader cannot but sense a deep cleft between court and priesthood. This does not excuse the violence done to Zechariah, and Joash deserves the bitter reproach of the chronicler. On the other hand, Joash, who had served Judah well, did not merit the evil which befell him at the hands of a dissident group.

It is sad to see a reign, which had begun so well, end in such failure. Brought up in seclusion, Joash was no man of war. Hence his compromise with the ever-present bandit of Damascus, Hazael, who was bought off by sacred treasure. Perhaps his compromise with paganism, promoted by the apostate princes in spite of warning (24.19), was made in consciousness of growing hostility from Jehoiada's successors in the hierarchy. We cannot tell. The impression remains of a good man, sorely tried, who broke under testing.

265 : Joash and Elisha

2 Kings 13

There followed a time of weakness in Israel with the perennial curse of the strong dynasty in Damascus keeping the frontier ablaze, and the people the victims of raid and deprivation. The weakness of the nation was a reflection of the weakness of the leadership. The vices and virtues of authority often seep downwards and permeate the mass. This is the significance of the strange story of Elisha's deathbed. The blessing of the people was limited by the faith of its king. Joash by his act showed the streak of weakness which marred his leadership. It was a day of shadow. Joash faced the chariots of Syria with a handful of men, with infantry against armoured hosts. And now Elisha, himself worth an army (14), was dying. In the death-chamber, the prophet sought to bring faith to birth in the king's heart by a symbolic prayer. The shot arrow was a declaration of war, an established ritual in the ancient world. The king should have seized the quiver, and in a symbolism which would have been natural in that Eastern setting, he should have sped shaft on shaft eastward, winged with hallelujahs. Like the English longbowmen he should have flung his body into the arc of the bow. Elisha's hands on the king's hands were a demonstration of aid outside himself. 'Eastward' was in the direction of Syria. The meaning of the offer was plain. Instead he took the arrows and did nothing. 'Stamp upon the ground,' said Elisha, giving the bewildered man a second chance to lay hold on the meaning. He stamped thrice. 'Then the man of God was angry.' Why? Because Joash had reacted weakly to a strong symbolic challenge. The reaction showed the man. His character limited his usefulness. His puzzled response to the dying prophet showed his lack of vision. The arrows, which should have demonstrated his victorious faith, lay weakly in his hand. Elisha could do nothing for him. God, like His Son at Nazareth, 'could do no mighty work because of unbelief'. It is part of our humanity, a facet of our gift of free will, that God's grace is mediated through our faith. Where faith, like the faith of Joash, is weak, grace is restricted.

Questions and themes for study and discussion on Studies 258–265

1. The Christian and money.
2. Christ and money—collect references.
3. Money and avarice in Proverbs.

4. The worth and weakness of Jehoram.
5. The Christian and driving.
6. The Remnant in the Old Testament and in the institutional Church.
7. Plotting for righteousness?
8. Consider the hymn: 'O Love, that wilt not let me go', in the light of the closing remark of Study 265.

266 : Amaziah

2 Kings 14.1–22; 2 Chronicles 25

Like his father, Amaziah began well, but concluded a comparatively long reign in sorrow, degradation, and domestic conspiracy. He must not be condemned for bringing the assassins of his father to justice, and he deserves commendation, within the context of his brutal times, for the mercy which spared the innocent. Amaziah was ahead of his times.

Amaziah did right up to a point (3), 'yet not with a blameless heart' (2 Chron. 25.2). Pagan cults seem to have been too deeply entrenched in the land for him to extirpate them and to destroy the places where they were practised.

Whereas Joash of Judah was something of a weakling, the victim, perhaps, of his concealed and priestly upbringing, Amaziah, born to be king, had a visible restlessness, and turned his energy to the subjugation of the old foe of the eastern frontier, Edom. The Edomites had been a peril on that frontier since the days of Amaziah's great-grandfather, Jehoram (Amos 1.11). Amaziah won a signal victory in a difficult campaign. He even took Petra (Sela, 2 Kings 14.7), an almost impregnable fortress.

Then, foolishly, as though superstitiously to propitiate the deities of the conquered, he set up Edomite idols as objects of worship, and earned the stern rebuke of an unnamed prophet. Victory and success had obviously elated Amaziah, and turned his mind to pride and arrogance. On some personalities victory can have this effect. In a balanced life, as Kipling once put it, a man must learn 'to deal with triumph and disaster, and treat those two imposters just the same'. Amaziah could not deal humbly with success.

Hence the foolish challenge issued to Joash of Israel, son of Jehoahaz, the grandson of the passionate Jehu. Shameful defeat, and the shattering of Jerusalem's very walls, was the dire result, and though Amaziah was to survive his conqueror for fifteen years (2 Chron. 25.25), it was a poor and shadowed life, with the walls of the capital symbolically torn down for a long stretch near the Damascus Gate.

Dissatisfaction rose like a fog round a broken life, and the wretched man, his authority in ruins, fled to the stronghold of Lachish, where he was assassinated, flung into a dray, and brought home for ironical burial in the sepulchre of the royal house. It was the burial of a presumptuous fool.

But note that Joash, whom Elisha had found wanting, is here evident in a new and more creditable role. He had won a measure of freedom from Syria (2 Kings 13.25), and sought by a pungent parable to save Judah's king from folly. Perhaps the northern kingdom saw more clearly than the southern the cloud on the horizon called Assyria.

267 : Jeroboam the Second

2 Kings 14.23–29; Hosea 6 and 14

Little is said of the second Jeroboam. Hosea shows the land's deep departure from its ancient faith, and this thought is prominent in the mind of the historian. However, measured by the common standards of man, Jeroboam was a strong and vigorous monarch. Indeed, he was the ablest of the kings of Israel, and a map will reveal that he restored the borders of the land almost to where they lay in the imperial days of David long before.

It was what Toynbee was to call an 'Indian summer', one of those times of sunset glory, when the bright colours are the hues of autumn, and destined to disappear with the first blasts of the looming winter. Jonah, the son of Amittai, had promised as much, though Amos and Hosea saw that the greatness of a land does not rest upon transient military success but upon the quality of life lived by the men and women who form its population.

Had Jeroboam been perceptive, and we know little of

310

what went on in his mind, he would have seen that much
of the success which attended his wide-ranging military endeavour was due, in actual fact, to the pressure of the
rising power of Assyria on the old rivals. Hosea warned that
no nation could safely rely upon the chance swing of a
balance of power for ultimate salvation (12.1; 14.1), or upon
entangling alliances, certain to be transitory, with pagan
powers such as Assyria and Egypt.

What played deceptively into Jeroboam's hands was the
eclipse of Syria under the blows of the rising imperialism of
Nineveh. Syria, old persecutor of Israel, acted for a generation as a buffer against the cruel aggressor of the north.
Hence the freedom with which Jeroboam thrust his conquests up the Beqaa between the Lebanon ranges, and overran most of the territory constituting modern Lebanon.

It was a time of false peace, a lull before storm, a breathing space in which a whole-hearted return to God might
have wrought salvation. Amos was abroad and Hosea. Of
Jonah we know no more than what is recorded in his
remarkable little book. Jeroboam was a man well enough
endowed with ability and drive to lead his people to Baalbek.
He was not equipped to lead them back to God.

At this point we must pause to examine the three prophets
mentioned.

268 : Jonah Escaping

Jonah 1; John 7.40–52

Jonah means a 'dove', and the son of Amittai, who was
known by this not very appropriate name, came from the
Zebulunite town of Gath-hepher, not far from Nazareth.
The rabbis who challenged Nicodemus about the absence of
prophets from Galilee (John 7.52) were deliberately denying
the title to Jonah, no doubt because he preached to the
heathen Assyrians of Nineveh.

Jonah preached in the reign of Jeroboam II in the eighth
century before Christ, and predicted the Israelite expansion
into Syria (2 Kings 14.25). Assyria lay beyond, and prior
to the accession of Tiglath-Pileser III in 745 B.C., the future

bandit kingdom was not the peril she became, and could have been ready to respond to the passionate preaching of a Hebrew. The language was not remote, and we have already had occasion to see that frontiers were no barrier to such intercourse.

Jonah might have agreed with the narrow-minded men of the Sanhedrin who would not accept him as a prophet. He was a bigoted man who failed to recognize that, as early as the covenant with Abraham, the blessing of Israel was not meant for one favoured people, but for all the world of men (Gen. 12.3). Israel was chosen for service, and Jonah was called to serve in a fashion which he did not enjoy.

In a mad burst of folly he imagined he could put distance between himself and God. The merchantmen of the Phoenicians traded out of Joppa, and their ships went to the mining port of Tartessos, or Tarshish, in Spain, and on to Cornwall for tin. It was a wild plan of retreat from duty, for no Hebrew loved the sea. A nomad people found the ocean strange and alien.

There is no escape from God, as Francis Thompson sought to show in the *Hound of Heaven* :

> *I fled Him, down the nights and down the days;*
> *I fled Him, down the arches of the years;*
> *I fled Him, down the labyrinthine ways*
> *Of my own mind; and in the mist of tears*
> *I hid from Him, and under running laughter*
> > *Up vistaed hopes I sped;*
> > *And shot, precipitated,*
> *Adown Titanic glooms of chasmed fears*
> *From those strong Feet which followed,*
> > *followed after . . . .*

It was down the 'glooms of chasmed fears' that Jonah fled, and found that the God of the land was also the God of the sea. God's hand was upon him and those on whom His hand is laid can find no rest or peace until they find their rest in Him.

269 : Jonah Arrested

Jonah 2; Psalm 142

'Out of the depths I cry to thee . . .' (Psa. **130.**1). There are eight quotations from the Psalms in this prayer of agony, and this may suggest the part the psalter already held in the religion of Israel, though, of course, the date of the book's composition is quite unknown.

Buried away and overwhelmed in his distress Jonah cried to God. Some of the most poignant of men's prayers have come out of the depth of darkness and despair. In pain and anguish men often learn the lessons which prosperity and peace never can teach them. Jonah at last saw that the pride and deception of his own heart (7) had built a barrier between himself and the mercy of God of which he, and all men, stood and stand in need.

The way to mercy is to put away those things which stand in its way, crass folly and rebellion, for these had been Jonah's choice. Nor, unwilling that the people of a pagan land should have the mercy of God, could he hope for that mercy in his own life. The first step to restoration is the recognition and confession of sin and folly. In the depths, Jonah had not lost God. He is still, for all that men can do to thrust Him aside, within the reach of prayer.

Jonah prayed. That is why, like Peter, he had his second chance. God had not given up the pursuit. In the last note we quoted the poem of Francis Thompson, which pictures the rebel fleeing through the varied avenues of life, and the mind from the swift following Feet. And all life and circumstance conspire with the pursuing Christ to hem in the soul which He pursues . . .

> And past those nois'ed Feet
> 'A voice comes yet more fleet—
> Lo! naught contents thee, who content'st not Me . . .

. . . .

> That Voice is round me like a bursting sea:
> 'And is thy earth so marred,
> Shattered in shard on shard?
> Lo, all things fly thee for thou fliest Me!'

313

The poet found that all betrayed the one who betrayed Christ, that to drive Christ from him was to drive away Love and Mercy too. At last the footfall stopped beside him, and in last surrender he found his peace. So Jonah found and was restored.

And straight ahead of him lay the road to Nineveh. The old command still stood. It is better to obey immediately, for Perfect Love is Perfect Understanding, and Perfect Wisdom knows best.

270 : Jonah Preaching and Restored

Jonah 3 and 4; John 21.15-19

Jonah obeyed, but, as the outcome was to show, without love, and with little personal involvement in God's plan of mercy. God uses what little man will give Him, and He used Jonah, intending that obedience itself should be the path to deeper knowledge. He is content sometimes, in His mercy, with the merest bridgehead into the rebel soul of man. Given that, He can invade the rest.

By Nineveh in this chapter's story is, of course, meant the vast sixty-mile complex of irrigation canals, villages, and agricultural territory which surrounded the great central group of palaces and aristocratic mansions of which Layard found the first astonishing traces in 1840, when Mesopotamian archaeology began.

Telling how he marched through the same river plain almost four centuries later, with a retreating army of Greek mercenaries, Xenophon, the Athenian, describes just such a complex of huge canals and embankments further down the river. He passed the mounds which covered Nineveh without knowing the name. The desert had reclaimed its own, as Nahum foretold.

Jonah penetrated the area and began to preach. None can predict the effect of faithful preaching, and a gale of repentance swept the land, from the huts in the scattered villages to the great palace of the king himself. But here was a strange result. The preacher had not given up his bigotry and was displeased with his success. He had hoped to prove

God wrong, or to be a mere voice of warning, after which he hoped to delight in the spectacle of judgement.

God had not given Jonah up. He had called for mercy and he had obeyed. God meets man where man will meet Him, if he meets Him at God's call. He took Jonah, and in an object lesson He taught him tenderness and the worth in God's eyes of all the fragile life of His Creation. So the hard man learned his lesson, and passed from the page of history. It is better to learn quickly when the Lord God takes us in hand to teach.

As Coleridge ended his *Ancient Mariner*:

> *He prayeth best, who loveth best*
> *All things both great and small;*
> *For the dear God who loveth us,*
> *He made and loveth all.*

Jonah lacked love, and so had no pity.

Questions and themes for study and discussion on Studies 266–270

1. The 'two imposters'. Why the name?
2. What is arrogance?
3. What was amiss with Jeroboam's leadership?
4. Escaping from God. How did Paul try to do this?
5. What is pity?

271 : Amos Called

Amos 1, 2 and 3

Also active in the Israel of Jeroboam II was a man of Judah, a farmer from Tekoa, ten miles south of Jerusalem. He gathered the fruit of the sycamore trees, a type of fig. God chooses His men without regard for the institutions of religion. To be sure He laid hands on the superbly educated Paul, but He set Peter, fisherman of Galilee, beside him. He chose the aristocratic Isaiah, and the peasant John the Baptist . . .

What a man needs, and must have, for such a calling is

315

what Bunyan called 'the root of the matter' in him. There were, since Elijah's and Elisha's day, 'schools of the prophets' (2 Kings 2.3, 5; 6.1–7; 9.1–3). Amos had been taught in none of these. The call came to him when he was shepherding, for Tekoa was sheep-country like Bethlehem, southward along the same central ridge (7.15). He was not even a citizen of the land to which he was called to minister. The call and the task seemed to bear no relation to the vocation in which he found himself. Beyond this we know nothing. Was his ministry in alien Israel long or short? How soon was he expelled? There is no clear answer.

News of Israel's condition must have filtered south to an infinitely poorer Judah. Jeroboam II, profiting by the weakening of the old Syrian enemy under the blows and menace of Assyria, had extended her borders in a deceptive show of imperial expansion. Wealth accumulated and men decayed. As in Elijah's day, there was a time of urban affluence. The old strength of the land, the faithful farmer stock, were oppressed and impoverished. Here perhaps was the link between the moral and social problems of the northern kingdom and the convictions of the prophet from the south. He may, of course, have preached first in Judah and then perceived that his local problem was shared, in even greater urgency, by the north.

Affluence and ease dislike disturbance, and Amos was a mighty disturber of false peace. All looked well under Jeroboam's worldly leadership. The state of things seemed permanent. Our own age, in nation after nation the world over, has shown what fifty years can do. In half a century Samaria had fallen under the flood from the Tigris. Assyria had shaken Syria. She was to eat up Samaria. With a God-given political wisdom like that of the Galileans who became the apostles of the New Testament, Amos saw the international scene and called loud warning.

272 : Amos Rejected

Amos 7 and 8

Nazareth drove out its greatest Son. Florence rejected Savonarola. Vanity Fair killed Faithful. It is the old way of man to quench the protesting or the challenging voice. Thus

316

was Amos driven from prosperous Samaria. There is some significance in the fact that the northerners did not lay hands on the offender.

The nature of his preaching reflects the man. He had long pondered the stories of the 'Old Testament, the grim fate of Sodom and Gomorrah (4.11), the lessons of the exodus from Egypt and the wanderings in Sinai (3.1; 5.25), the enmity of Jacob and Esau (1.11) . . . A mind steeped in the Bible, as Amos knew it, was part of his equipment.

He knew the Law and echoed the ethics of the Pentateuch. As he watched the pattern of the seasons on the Tekoa hills, he saw the hand of a creative God (4.13), who was also the sustainer of His world, the controller of light and darkness and the mighty sea (5.8; 9.6). When he looked upon such things around him, Amos found his mind touched with poetry like some ancient James Hogg.

Such a God, holding land and ocean in His controlling hand, was not likely, in Amos' view, to lose control of history. He restrains one people (1.5), and raises up another (6.14), or puts another down (2.9). He is their Judge (1.3–2.3), and justice was the expression of His will. He saw deeply into the spiritual truths of religion, proclaiming like Isaiah that a law flouted in unrighteousness could not find mending in any form of ritual or offering without adjustment of the life and the attitude which had occasioned the breach. Ritual was itself an abomination to God without the ethical standards and the morality which His Law lays down.

Here, then, was 'an Israelite indeed, in whom is no guile', one of 'the Remnant which had not bowed the knee to Baal', a member of the old stock of the faithful who appear all through the Bible, often half-hidden behind the screen of urban and aristocratic, royal or priestly betrayal, the group from which Joseph and Mary, the apostles and the choice men and women of all the pages we are reading so often came.

273 : Hosea's Marriage

Hosea 1 and 2

Hosea may have preached a little later than Amos, but it was still in the days round the middle of the eighth century before Christ, in the bright Indian Summer of Israel's greatness, and just before the dark shadow of the imperialism of Assyria fell across the land.

Some have suggested, on the strength of 7.4, that Hosea was a baker. It is far more likely that he came from a farming family of some standing, for he knew the countryside, he was aware of political issues, and he was acquainted with the history of his people. For all that, unlike the humbler Amos, he hardly refers to alien nations.

The book, the only writing of a northern prophet to survive, is couched in the language of Hebrew poetry, and all poetry is allusive. Hence the difficulty which attends the interpretation of the book, and the unravelling, from the lessons it teaches, of the story of the prophet's broken marriage.

In view of the poetic brevity of the story, it is possible to state that Hosea did not, deliberately and under divine command, take to wife a woman of abandoned morals. The years are telescoped. No doubt, like any earnest young man, Hosea chose his bride in the days of her purity, and, he believed, under the benediction of his God. The deep significance which he was to find in his life's tragedy was an indication of this earlier happiness. His wife played him false, as Israel had played her divine spouse false. He, too, had known a bride in the days of her love and chastity, when she belonged to Him. Seduced by the gods of the land, she had abandoned her love, her 'first love' (Rev. 2.4), and betrayed her husband.

So Hosea put an image into Scripture, an image, as we shall see in the next study, which he had snatched from a pagan context and purified. It was to be picked up by Paul, who, in speaking of the marriage of man and woman, touches on the union of Christ and the Church. The Apocalypse pictures the marriage of the Bride and the Lamb as the climax of world-history. If the picture is less relevant today, in Hosea's day it touched the realities of experience.

And in the same movement of heart and mind Hosea turned his shattering sorrow into blessing. Any experience committed to God, as we have more than once seen, can be transformed. That is the message of the Cross. The 'most evangelical of the prophets', as someone has called Hosea, anticipated the truth in the sanctification of his own pain.

318

274 : Gomer—Hosea's Wife

Hosea 3 and 4

Israel came in from the wilderness austerely devoted to one God. She found entrenched in the land the worship of the Baalim, the petty deities of the fields, the 'husbands' of farm, orchard and meadow, who fertilized the land. They were forces of fertility, and a ritual of magic grew up around their worship. The obscene cults which attached themselves to the Baalim, and later to such major developments as the worship of Diana of the Ephesians and Aphrodite of Corinth, included lascivious dancing, sexual perversion, and ritual prostitution. They soiled the land.

The moral decadence, the temptation to youth, the open call to communal vice, which polluted the country-side may well be imagined. But here, in foulness and perversion, was the base origin of the symbolism of marriage, of divine 'husband' and earthly 'wife', which Hosea took and cleansed, sanctified and adapted to the case of Israel and her neglected and abandoned God.

Gomer, Hosea's wife, was a victim of a corrupt society; She may have been a gay and thoughtless girl, loved dearly by her prophet husband but perhaps not sharing the deep convictions which filled his life. Perhaps he was an older man, and under the pressure of the wild revels of the Baalim worship, the song, and dance and sensuality, she followed the droves of corrupted youth, and lost her chastity. There was no way back.

Such paths run steeply down, and, if the third chapter of the story be rightly read, poor Gomer touched the depths. She ended sold and betrayed, and exposed for purchase in the slave-market. Here Hosea bought her for the price of a slave (Exod. 21.32). She was now doubly his, as we are Christ's, the work of His creative hands, and bought back from slavery at the price of His blood. How 'evangelical' the prophet is!

Gomer passes from the story, but her husband's love, his redemptive mercy, and the ennobling of his pain left a mark on Scripture. She probably now remained true, for the prophet finds much to hope for, much prospect of reunion and renewal, in his remaining pages, and the book ends on such a note:

319

O Love, that wilt not let me go ; ; ;

Run through the well-known hymn. It might be Gomer's story, and strangely enough, Hosea's too. Pause and linger over the last verse.

Questions and themes for study and discussion on Studies 271–274

1. How does God 'call' men? What are the qualifications?
2. Willingness to face the truth.
3. Pick six 'evangelical' verses from Hosea.
4. Gomer's temptations and the modern world.

275 : Uzziah
2 Kings 15.1–7; 2 Chronicles 26

The greatest king of Judah since Solomon and David was known by two names. The meanings are not remotely different —Azariah means 'Yahweh-his-helper', and Uzziah, 'Yahweh-his-strength'. Uzziah may have changed his name, or it may have been changed on his accession.

He was a mere boy when he became king, but he set to work with all the drive and energy of youth to establish his borders. A modern Israeli, conscious of the strategic necessities of his country, would understand and applaud the measures of this energetic young ruler. He cleared the way to Israel's old southern outlet, the Gulf of Aqaba and the port of Elath. He subdued the Gaza strip, and the coastal plain where the Philistines still held a measure of their old strength. He penetrated the arid but strategically significant Negev, the desert of the Sinai Peninsula. He acquired power on his eastern borderlands, where the old Ammonite enemy threatened his rear. The situation is curiously prophetic of 1967.

Uzziah then made Jerusalem strong, built an arsenal of sophisticated weaponry, and trained an élite corps of soldiers. In this last act is a pointer to the thought and the ideal which dominated the young man's life. David had his band of 600 heroes, men of warlike valour who formed his bodyguard. Uzziah increased this regiment to 2,600. He quite clearly had

David in mind. He wanted to be like his great predecessor. Hence his measures for his land's security, and his devotion.

A fine example, a model of excellence, can be a beneficent force in a life. The Christian does not want for one in his Lord, but such glory apart, he can often find one in a fellow Christian. We shall see this theme continue for a full half-century. 'Example,' said Burke, 'is the school of mankind. They will learn at no other.' Example is the first great gift we can bestow upon the world. 'Alexander,' Sir Philip Sidney once remarked, 'received more bravery of mind by the pattern of Achilles than by hearing the definition of fortitude.' It was Goldsmith's parson who 'allured to better worlds and led the way'.

Such a force in Uzziah's life was David. He enjoyed half a century of distinguished royalty, and then through presumption contracted leprosy. Such tragedies occur. But Uzziah's influence, his salutary example, lived on. 'Of all commentaries on Scripture,' said John Donne, 'examples are the best and liveliest.'

276 : The Prophet

Isaiah 6; 32.1–8

Uzziah found an example, and in the process became one. There was a young man in his kingdom who was marked for greatness. 'In the year that King Uzziah died' the young nobleman had a vision of God which changed his life. There is surely no other interpretation of the phrase. The monarch, so royal, so able, so good, and in his end so tragic, had been a tremendous example, a shining influence, in another life. The shock of his sad ending was used of God to claim Isaiah for His own.

Isaiah probably had his hero in mind when he wrote his thirty-second chapter with its image of the rock in the wilderness. 'Where the desert touches an oasis,' wrote Sir George Adam Smith, Palestine's great geographer, 'life is continually under attack from the wind-driven sand. The rains come, and a carpet of green struggles to life on the desert's edge and there is promise of fertility. But it is doomed, for the thirsting sand creeps in, and stunts and chokes the aspirations of the green. But set a rock in the sand. After brief rains, life springs up on the leeward side and in time becomes a garden. The boulder has stayed the drift.'

So a man can stand in the wind's way, endure the harsh sand-laden blast of the hot khamsin, and protect from withering death the weaker life that finds refuge behind its protecting body. It is a noble function for any man thus to face the death-bearing wind and the beating of the storm. That is what our Lord did on Calvary. We do not know the details, but such could have been the role Uzziah played in the young Isaiah's life. According to Jewish tradition, Isaiah was of royal blood, and it may be inferred from his own writings that he was of high social station. Such situations have their peculiar temptations, and one like the king could have been a 'shelter in a weary land' to a beleaguered and bewildered boy, hard-pressed in his court and entourage.

To stand like a rock and preserve feebler life is an exacting task. If Uzziah saw his young relative grow to vigour under his shade, it was rich reward. And such worth propagates itself. Isaiah became such a defence to Hezekiah. God is creative and goes on.

277 : Ahaz

2 Kings 16; Isaiah 1

Jotham's undistinguished reign probably overlapped with that of Uzziah. It is not clear for how long the good king, whom Isaiah so admired, was incapacitated by his dread disease, and unable to perform the duties of royalty. It may be guessed that some years of Jotham's reign were devoted to a regency. And he died at the age of forty-one.

No lineaments of his character emerge from the narrative which seems to grow condensed and hurried as it moves on to final catastrophe. Then came Ahaz, at the age of twenty, to the throne. Isaiah exercised his ministry from Uzziah on to Hezekiah, and the beginnings of his major activity must have taken place in the reigns of Jotham and Ahaz.

Over neither king had Isaiah the influence which he held in his maturer years, and to such effect, over Hezekiah. Ahaz went his way, and in the record of the Book of Kings the military disaster which accompanied his activities is apparent. Israel's southern outlet at Elath on the Gulf of Aqaba was lost to a Syrian counter-attack. Uzziah's work in establishing the borders was undone.

Then in his crass folly the baffled king sought to call in the aid of the sinister power of Assyria against the old Syrian foe. He successfully bribed Tiglath-pileser with the sacred treasures of the land, who needed small inducement to move murderously south. It was a grim development.

The action showed the folly of Ahaz' mind and the poverty of his spirit. The people had, as peoples so often do have, the ruler they deserved. The first five chapters of Isaiah are probably chronologically previous to the sixth, and the indictment of a corrupt and backslidden community contained in the opening chapters of that most eloquent book of prophecy reveal the declension of Judah. It was a state of affairs against which Isaiah bravely and passionately protested. In him Uzziah's heritage continued. Ahaz stumbled on with his pagan altar (16.10) to an early death at the age of thirty-six. Wisely, Isaiah had concentrated on his son. A generation is sometimes to be written off. It need not be an older group. Ahaz' folly lay between the years of twenty and thirty-six. Find time to read the opening chapters of Isaiah.

278 : The Prophet Again

Isaiah 7; 9.1–7

In the pattern of human life God requires no more than a man's surrender to His will. Anything abandoned to His use can win significance untold, meaning and creative influence beyond and above surrounding circumstance, and worth unimagined by the one who surrenders the poor scrap of human raw material to God's hand.

There was a fool on the throne of Judah, a man whom the strongest and bravest voice in his kingdom was unable to influence. Isaiah might have accounted his work vain and his efforts wasted with the weakling Ahaz. He was probably not aware that, in looking beyond him, and yearning in eloquent poetry for a ruler of God's anointing, he was catching a vision of the King of kings.

323

Isaiah's rich writing is not always easy reading, but the mind of a great poet, a leader of surpassing worth and courage, and a man of God of deepest insight, comes through to the reader. We feel that we know Isaiah and see him in his visions.

In chapters 7 and 9 he did not know that he was writing words which a future century was to invest with shining truth. He was merely committed and surrendered to the Eternal One, ready to do the task before him, and in such fellowship spoke beyond his time and place. 'The Messianic prophecies of the Old Testament,' wrote Sir George Adam Smith, ' are tidal rivers. They not only run to the sea, which is Christ; they feel His reflex influence. It is not enough for the Christian to have followed the historical direction of the prophecies, or to have proved their connection with the New Testament as parts of one Divine Harmony. Forced back by the fullness of meaning to which he has found their courses open, he returns to find the savour of the New Testament upon them, and that where he descended shallow and tortuous channels, with all the difficulties of historical exploration, he is borne back on full tides of worship . . . "the Lord is with him there, a place of broad rivers and streams" (Isa. 33.21).' What a man was the vehicle of such unveiling!

Questions and themes for study and discussion on Studies 275–278

1. Example cuts both ways.
2. Consider the image of the Rock in Scripture.
3. Compare and contrast the characters of Uzziah and Ahaz.
4. How do we justify reading the Old Testament in the light of the New?

279 : Hezekiah the Reformer

2 Chronicles 29; 2 Kings 18.1–12

King Hezekiah was twenty-five years of age when he came to Judah's throne, and his reign of almost thirty years was one of the finest of all Jerusalem's kings. Under Ahaz the land had gone astray. The old strong, stern religion which had ennobled Jewish life had decayed before those exotic cults which demanded less in clean and upright living, and made rituals of carnality and vice. It is part of an evil bent in man to welcome release from discipline. There is always welcome in contaminated corners of society for leave to relax a moral bond.

So, in the ancient story, it came to pass that Jerusalem's Temple stood abandoned. Rubbish and dirt filled the holy place. The shrine which Solomon had built was no grand, imposing edifice, but it was a beautiful little place, lavishly adorned. The holy vessels were gone, turned into cash by the dead king, but the building itself remained, dishonoured and neglected, the sign and symbol of the state of old tradition and the nation's soul.

The young king lost no time in parley or diplomacy. Youthful, ardent, loyal, he saw no impediments, and scorned delay in doing what he knew was right. In the first month of his reign he cleansed the Temple. He called upon the Levites to begin the task by a cleansing of their own lives (2 Chron. 29.5), and having met this prime condition for all of God's work, to turn their hands to the task before them. The young man, prompted perhaps by Isaiah, showed deep spiritual insight. Youth often does.

It took the Levites a full week to remove the uncleanness from a building no larger than the average city church. No one had seen the rubble and the rubbish carried in. Evil accumulates unseen in the temple of the life (2 Cor. 6.16). The small surrenders, the petty sins, the casual indulgences, the little disloyalties, accumulate unnoticed, until the holy place within becomes a house of shame. Said Masefield:

My soul has many an old decaying room
Hung with the ragged arras of the past . . .

We must rend such things apart and let God's sunshine in.

Here, then, was a young man giving to God the rich enthusiasm of his young manhood. God can use such gifts. Hezekiah breaks into the pages of Scripture like a refreshing breeze. He had grown up in 'the shadow of a Rock'. The cleansing of the Temple was a symbolic act which Jerusalem well understood. Under the young king's dynamic leadership the people returned to their ancient ways and pure religion.

Isaiah 8 and 10

As though to mock such wholehearted reformation, the new king of Assyria moved south. The bandit kings of that brutal empire have left a name of horror. Says one of them: 'To the city of Tela I approached. The inhabitants would not come down and embrace my feet. With battle and slaughter I captured the city. Three thousand of their fighting men I slew. Many I burned. I cut off the hands and feet of some. I built a pyramid of living captives and a pyramid of heads. Their young men and their maidens I burned with fire'. The imagination reels at the monster's cruelty. And he gloried in the deed and carved it on his palace wall.

Such vile words could be paralleled again and again.

But mark the faith which dared to throw defiance at such a force. Isaiah pictures the gloating of the grim invader, and brands him for an arrogant fool who boasts of evil and fails to see that he is no more than God's axe, a tool in His hand, permitted for a season to wreak ill (10.5, 15).

They were tense and evil days. The vivid passage of dramatic poetry which closes ch. 10 pictures the invasion rolling south. They were days which this century knows too well. The smoke of burning villages shows darker in the north. The panting messengers come in, and name after name appears on the war-maps (28–32). At Michmash, where Jonathan with one brave helper had once done wonders, the Assyrian might perhaps have been held. He swept resistance out of the pass (28, 29).

Jerusalem went frantically to work. There was no water in the city, and Hezekiah's engineers took up the task of bringing the waters of the Virgin's Spring into the Pool of Siloam.

In 1880, two Arab schoolboys playing in the tunnel, found an ancient inscription. The moss was cleaned away, and scholars read: 'This is how the sap was cut. When the workers were lifting up their picks each towards his fellow (the tunnel was cut from both ends), and when there were yet three cubits to be cut, heard was the voice of each calling to his fellow. And they struck each to meet his fellow pick against pick.' There is something appropriate in the fact that the only inscription from Jerusalem which we can set against Sennacherib's proud boasts is the simple story of a band of navvies carved on a culvert wall. On the valour of simple men dictators break.

281 : Sennacherib (2)

2 Chronicles 32

Meanwhile Sennacherib was storming Lachish, a day's journey away. And here Hezekiah's heart failed him and he sent tribute. Appeasement will not work with ravening wolves. Sennacherib took the tribute and demanded surrender. Isaiah encouraged the king, and he returned a defiant answer. The die was cast, and these were the days when the city hung on the prophet's words. The king left a division to watch Jerusalem, and swung south to finish Egypt.

At Pelusium one of the strangest disasters in history happened. There was nothing strange in it, however, to the Hebrew historians. 'The angel of the Lord,' said they in boldness of faith, 'went forth and slew a hundred and eighty-five thousand in the camp of the Assyrians' (2 Kings **19**.35). There is a magnificent piece of poetry in Isaiah which probably dates from this day. 'Ah, the booming of many peoples which boom like the booming of the seas, and the rushing of nations that make a rushing like the rushing of many waters. The nations shall rush like the rushing of many waters, but He checketh it, and they shall flee afar off, and shall be chased as the chaff of the mountains before the wind, and like the whirling dust before the storm. At eventide behold terror, and before the morning they are not' (George Adam Smith's translation of **17**.12–14).

Herodotus, the Greek historian, tells a story of the same event. He heard it in Egypt. The statue which the Egyptians set up to commemorate their deliverance held a mouse, the symbol of pestilence, in its hand. Mice and rats communicate bubonic plague, and pour into the homes of men when smitten with the disease. Was it bubonic plague which 'breathed on the face of the host as it passed'?

The broken remnant struggled home to Assyria, and Sennacherib never came again, although it was twenty years before he died on the swords of his sons.

Byron wrote of the Assyrian disaster:

> The Assyrian came down like a wolf on the
> fold,
> And his cohorts were gleaming in purple and
> gold;
> And the sheen of his spears was like stars
> on the sea,
> Where the blue wave rolls nightly on deep
> Galilee.
> Like the leaves of the forest when summer
> was green,
> That host with its banners at sunset was
> seen.
> Like the leaves of the forest when autumn
> is blown,
> That host on the morrow lay withered and
> strown.

Like some ancient Churchill, in a day of stress, Isaiah had
held his people's strength against all odds.

282 : Isaiah's Secret

Isaiah 30.1–15; 32.1–17

Someone once built a verse out of words and phrases from
Isaiah:

> In quietness and confidence
> Shall be my strength each day,
> The Lord will go before me to straighten all the way.
> So I'll walk with an assurance,
> Nor fear the darkest hour,
> For God will there reveal to me His glory and His power.

Over the last few studies we have looked at the tumultuous
days of the great Assyrian attack. Isaiah can be understood
only in the dark context of such times. They were tense and
testing days of the sort which bring out the best and the
worst in the spirit of man. Set the calm confident man of God
over against the panic-stricken populace, as the peril rolled
south.

We see Isaiah move with fearless dignity through the chaos of his day, firm in his quiet faith, sure in his God. The two last verses in the passages prescribed above give the reason, Isaiah's open secret of success. Strength flows from quiet trust, and both quietness and trust are the fruits of righteousness. It is obvious enough. There can be no peace if the heart is divided, housing the disloyalty of sin. Every man needs some island of peace within his person, some place of salutary tranquillity and withdrawal. God alone can provide such a retreat, as Isaiah most steadfastly maintains (4.6; 16.4; 17.10; 25.4). All else will betray us in the pressure of disaster (28.15–17).

To this safe abiding place we must constantly retreat, to refresh and strengthen the spirit. It was Elijah's lack that, in the earthquake, the gale and the fire of his passionate life he had somewhere neglected this, and God's therapy was precisely in this area of his life. In 'returning and rest' is our daily salvation from stress, tension, the wear and tear of living, and all else that scars the mind and daunts the soul. 'Thou wilt keep him in peace, *peace*, whose mind is stayed on thee," runs 26.3. The repetition is Hebrew's device of emphasis—and how happy!

283 : The Servant

Isaiah 52.13–53.12

We must turn, before leaving Isaiah, to a figure which dominates the second part of his book—from ch. 40 onwards. These chapters could be the work of the prophet's later years. There is no reason at all to suppose that they are the work of another man, or a second prophet of the same name. A theory first propounded by Bernhard Duhm, in 1892, maintained that there were no fewer than three Isaiahs, conflated and fused in the first century. The notion is typical of the wild conjectures which, in biblical studies, so often pass for serious and reasoned literary criticism. This is not the place to argue the case, but one monumental fact may be appropriately mentioned. In the Shrine of the Scrolls in Jerusalem is a magnificent copy of Isaiah, dated from the second century before Christ. There is no division between chapters

39 and **40**. The rabbis of over 2,000 years ago obviously knew nothing of the guess of Bernhard Duhm. It is for the reader to decide whether the modern critic is correct, or whether the scholars who lived four centuries after Isaiah were in possession of the true tradition. Tradition, in all criticism, is not to be lightly disregarded.

These chapters should be read with reverence. A Suffering Servant moves through their pages. Isaiah may have woven into his poetry the pain of personal experience, his own grief at rejection, his own vindication. He may, as the rabbis have maintained, have had suffering Israel in mind. But whatever be the occasion of composition, it is clear that the prophet, overwhelmed and overshadowed of God, was describing a Person beyond and above any sort of earthly model. The New Testament applies the so-called 'Servant-Songs' (**42**.1 ff.; **49**.1 ff.; **50**.4 ff.; **52**.13—**53**.12, and probably **61**.1 ff.) to the Lord, and it is clear, as the prophecy moves on, that a single figure has emerged, clearly visible down a vista of time, who is none other than Christ. It is a clear preview of the New Testament which Isaiah was granted. To these chapters the reader should return, reverently, questingly. He is, like Isaiah, whom we now leave with his visions of glory, in the presence of his Saviour and his Lord. And consider the privilege granted a man who lived close to God to see with God's eyes, to be lifted from time, and share in the eternal.

Questions and themes for study and discussion on Studies 279–283

1. Trace the chain of Messianic prophecy previous to Isaiah.
2. Why must righteousness underlie peace?
3. Quote Christ and Paul on peace.
4. There are twenty references in the New Testament to the Servant Songs. List a dozen.

284 : Micah

Micah 6 and 7

Moresheth (**1.1**) was a settlement in the sheep hills which run like a spine down the length of Palestine, and this country village was the place of Micah's birth. We are looking for a man, not studying a book, so there is no great necessity to decide whether Micah's ministry ended with the reign of Hezekiah, or extended into the bad days which followed. It seems best to suppose that Micah did, indeed, live a long life, and uttered his last oracles under the evil rule of Manasseh. Hence chapters 6 and 7 for today's reading.

Moresheth is seventeen miles from Tekoa where Amos lived, and looks in the opposite direction. It is a thousand feet above the coastal plain, and fertile with the moisture of the Mediterranean winds. It bred no brooding children of the wilderness, but hard-working yeomen, aware of the surges of war on the plains beneath, but somewhat hidden by their hills and upland pastures, and simple in their rural detachment from the corruptions of the city. Famous scenes of Israel's history were in view . . . Lachish, Ekron, Ashdod and Gaza. Behind lay the hills of David's exile, the field of the fight with Goliath, the Adullam cave. It was a place to beget and to shape 'an Israelite indeed'. Catch the echoes in the text of Micah.

The prophecies of Amos and Hosea had been fulfilled upon the Northern Kingdom, and now, feeling the growing corruption of Jerusalem, and sensing the new perils of invasion, Micah uttered his prophecies. Whether these preceded Sennacherib, or whether they looked to ultimate destruction, need not detain us. The man's religion shows the man, and he stands in full portraiture in his small book, simple, ardent, devout.

He loathed social wrong and felt with passion for the poor (7.2 f.). He detested the hireling prophets whom Amos and Hosea had denounced (3.5ff). From such pain and involvement there arises in Micah's devoted mind the vision of hope, of a Zion yet to be, of a King yet to come. 'The Blessed Hope' is never more needed than in such days, and it was Micah's honour to focus Israel's hope, perhaps with Isaiah's clarity, on the Great Redeemer (7.7). To this the theme passes to the climax, the warning, the prayer and the doxology, which close the book. Meditate in closing on 4.1, 2; 5.2; 7.8, 18. Here was a great and good man, who, in a few words, opened vistas of eternity.

285 : Manasseh's Evil

2 Kings 21.1–16

Manasseh reigned fifty-five years, longer than any other king of Judah, and it was a grim and sanguinary reign. Judah was helpless before the power of Assyria, and was tolerated while she kept the peace. As the New Testament shows, times of subjection and even occupation can know religious revival. John led his great wilderness ministry, and the Church was founded, during the Roman domination of Palestine. At the same time Christ was crucified, and the priestly castes turned the religion of the land into a barren ritual and a persecuting force.

In Manasseh's reign, the voice of prophecy, as the account shows, was not silent, but evil, centred in the court, and grounded in the character of the king, was paramount. Coming after the days of Hezekiah's revival, it was such a time as England saw when Charles II's court unwound the ways of Puritanism. Macaulay writes: 'Then came days never to be recalled without a blush, the days of servitude without loyalty, of sensuality without love, of dwarfish talents and gigantic vices, the paradise of cold hearts and narrow minds, the golden age of the coward, the bigot, and the slave.'

A weight of evil influence surrounded the boy king during the period of his regency. Isaiah, in spite of legends regarding his martyrdom under Manasseh, was probably dead, and Isaiah's closing visions of a prince of peace, and an age of God's benediction, were misunderstood, no doubt, and made the theme of disillusionment. Judah was little more than a vassal state. Obsequious courtiers, all through Israel's history, were notoriously evil counsellors. The gods and cults of the conqueror were measured by the conqueror's strength, and all through the Middle East, at this time, Assyria was the conqueror. If Israel stood discredited, and Micah was at the end of his ministry, and the sensual cults of Assyria and other pagan lands were pulling hard on youthful society, as carnal cults have always pulled, the corruption of the young Manasseh can be explained. Of Hephzibah, the queen mother, we know nothing. She may have been a bad influence.

So the horrors of Moloch worship, and the carnality of fertility rituals came back along the path which Solomon had first trodden, and filled the land with their decadence. The

332

fact that Manasseh indulged in uninhibited persecution may indicate that there was a loyal opposition which he sought angrily to crush. Micah 7.1–6 may be the echo of this reign of terror. According to the account in Kings, Manasseh was a being of uninhibited evil. The Chronicler mentions a late repentance, as we shall see.

286 : Manasseh Repentant

2 Chronicles 33

The historian of the second book of the Kings passes by the story of the exile and repentance of Manasseh without comment. The Chronicler takes some notice of it. The former writer may have regarded the bad king's reformation as too tardily, too insincerely, made to merit comment. The fact that one historian omitted, and one included, the kindlier facet of Manasseh's reign seems to have sparked off much discussion among the Jews. Hence a crop of legends of deliverance surrounding Manasseh's exile, and also that small classic of penitential devotion, the 'Prayer of Manasseh', prompted by 2 Chron. 33.13, and included in the Old Testament Apocrypha.

Perhaps the facts are that, careful vassal of Assyria though he contrived to be, Manasseh was involved in the revolt of the viceroy of Babylon, Shamash-sham-ukin, against King Ashurbanipal. It was grimly difficult in such dynastic strife to determine which side to back, and a four-year uprising (652–648 B.C.) by Babylon's royal governor (he was the brother of Ashurbanipal) must have presented problems to Manasseh, which could account for a period of detention for an investigation of loyalty in Assyria, or Babylon, which became Ashurbanipal's headquarters.

It is quite within the bounds of possibility that Manasseh, in the stress and anxiety of such an incarceration, was led to reassess his life, and his repudiation of his father's faith. Such repudiations of evil are known in the dark hours of the soul. It was too late, however, to reverse a trend of evil now almost two generations long. It was too late, also, to save Amon, Manasseh's son, who bore the name of the Egyptian ram-god, and in his two-year reign carried on his father's programme of evil, rather than his brief epilogue of penitence.

Repentance can come too late to cover the wickedness of an ill-spent life, and too late to save the next generation. Forgiveness does not blot out all the consequences of sin. The distance, too, is great between a man's being frightened about his sins and humbled over them. 'Repentance,' said Joseph Addison, 'is the relinquishment of any practice from the conviction that it has offended God. Sorrow, fear, and anxiety are properly not parts, but adjuncts, of repentance.'

287 : Young Josiah
2 Kings 22.1–7; 2 Chronicles 34.1–7; Ecclesiastes 12.1–7

Josiah owed his succession to the throne to the people (2 Kings 21.24). Perhaps the land was weary of the evil of the two preceding reigns. The dates and years are worth watching in Josiah's life. He was placed on the throne as a small child, but must have been under devoted care, for, as soon as he reached an age of discretion and decision, eight years after, he showed his true allegiance to God. Perhaps the hand of Jedidah, his mother, may be seen in this open act of testimony. At the age of twenty he turned with vigour to the cleansing of the land. Zephaniah and Jeremiah, speaking at this time, reveal how necessary this purging of Judah was, and how superficial, incidentally, was the tardy reformation of Manasseh, a decade before.

Perhaps it has some significance that the last of Assyria's great imperial monarchs died about this time—it was 632 B.C. —and this freed the young king of Judah from the fear of foreign reprisals if he took firm action against the Assyrian pagan cults which were rife in the land. It was also in the thirteenth year of Josiah's reign—626 B.C.—that Jeremiah commenced his prophetic ministry.

Josiah was to die unnecessarily and tragically in his middle thirties, but he accomplished much for God as a young man and as a youth. His life is worth studying by young men. He is marked by conviction, and strong, swift action on the drive of conviction. Perhaps it was this swift decisiveness which, in the end, took him to a needless battlefield and to death, but at the ages of sixteen and twenty we see the character of the young king shining like a light in Judah's darkness.

334

'Youth,' wrote Ruskin once, 'is the period of building up in habits and hopes and faith—not an hour but is trembling with destinies; not a moment once passed, of which the appointed work can ever be done again . . .' It was as though young Josiah recognized this fact, had some foreboding of the brevity of his remaining years, and struck doughtily and well for God.

The Bible is a vast encouragement to all ages. It shows boys in action, girls, and aged men. Youth is the opportunity to become somebody. Josiah was to leave his indelible mark on Judah's memory. One can imagine the shaking of more, aged and more prudent heads when the boy king announced his intentions—or simply revealed them. But how true are George Macdonald's words: 'When we are out of sympathy with the young, then I think our work in this world is over.'

288 : Josiah and the Law

Deuteronomy 28; 2 Kings 22.14-20

The ancient roll of Deuteronomy had lain hidden in the rubble that had again, since Hezekiah's cleansing, collected in the holy place. Thus it is that man amid the clutter of his worldliness loses the Word of God. Its provisions none the less abide, and, as Scofield's headline has it, 'by the Law is the Knowledge of Sin.'

Josiah was young, earnest, and impressionable. The dire impact of what he read fell upon him with its full weight, and there is no doubt that the closing chapters of Deuteronomy make stern reading. 'The word of God is living and active, sharper than any two-edged sword,' said the writer of the letter to the Hebrews, and he had such incidents as this in mind.

It was a test of the young king's devotion and faith that he heard with such open and ready ears the solemn warnings and denunciations of the newly discovered Law; it was a test of his insight that he recognized the present condition of his people; and it was a test of his live intelligence that he grasped the truth, which has engaged the minds of great historical philosophers from Deuteronomy to Herodotus, and on to Spengler and Toynbee—that the rise and fall of nations is according to a normal law.

Such a story cannot be read today without the same reaction, indeed, without the same deep misgivings. The Law is lost again, amid the rubbish of an epoch, beneath the din of modern living, amid the noisy and the exhibitionist infidelities of those whose task it is to preach the truth, lost again amid the trash of broken-down standards, derided traditions, and the restlessness of materialism.

Youth found the Law that age had lost. If the book had vanished, discredited, neglected, no longer read, dishonoured in the defilement of the holy place, the principal cause, if one man is to be blamed, is the old man Manasseh, for all his vain seeking, after a misspent half-century, to restore a broken religion. It might well be the prayer of older men and women today, tardily aware of the accelerating rush of a Gadarene society, that youth should recover 'the Law', the discipline of faith, the old moralities, the forgotten Saviour. Josiah stands magnificently, his royal robes rent, before Shaphan the scribe.

289 : Huldah

2 Chronicles 34.20–33

Hilkiah, as the next chapter shows (and it should be read in the franker and clearer language of the RSV), was hardly in fit state to comment on the grim truths discovered in the book. He belonged too intimately to the generation whose craven fears, contemptible compromise, or culpable neglect had allowed the pollution to fill the holy shrine and to cover the saving truth. He was a passive instrument in the hands of whoever ruled, a Vicar of Bray, who could not be expected in a time of sharp crisis to tell the truth.

Huldah was a humble woman, merely the wife of the keeper of the priests' wardrobe, but she was now called upon to join Miriam and Deborah, the two other women in the Old Testament who were called 'prophetesses' in their own right. God always has His faithful, fearless voices, whatever the age of apostasy and concealment of the uncomfortable truth.

Huldah was not unfaithful. She spoke no soft and lulling word. She knew that the Law was absolute, that the provisions could not be revoked. She knew also that God was merciful, and would hear any cry for aid. Indeed, the very chapters of

336

Deuteronomy which had crashed so disturbingly into the peace of the moment contained such promises of grace. She knew, however, that the apostasy of the land at large had gone too deep and too far for any permanent reformation to emerge. The evil which had receded in Isaiah's day was a mounting tide again, and nothing, this time, would stay its flow. The nation was ripe for purging, and in exile it was to find the Word indeed, and be stripped and cleansed of its idolatries.

So Huldah told the truth. She appears from her humble dwelling in the page of Scripture and, her message given, disappears again. The Bible can be its own spokesman, its own unaided interpreter, as Josiah found, but the expositor has his place—or her place, as in this story—and that place is hedged by fidelity. Let preaching be within the circle of the Word. (Some have discounted the worth of Huldah's prophecy [28] by pointing out the fact of Josiah's early death. Huldah promised no length of years, and that premature passing may have spared him the misery he was urgent to escape).

290 : Josiah's Reformation

2 Kings 23

Josiah's assault on the bestial cults which had invaded Jerusalem seems to have been almost a single-handed effort. Hilkiah was no help. He had tolerated too much. An 'asherah', or phallic emblem, sign of a disgusting fertility-cult, stood in the Temple. So did the homosexual brothels—not 'by the temple', as in the AV (7). Up and down the land the young royal zealot went, rooting out the signs and symbols of a well-nigh overwhelming paganism. We who live in a similarly sex-ridden age, cannot but admire Josiah's zeal, but at the same time observe the limitations upon his effort. The doom of the ancient oracle, according to Huldah, was only postponed, and this can only mean that Josiah cleansed the land rather by his authority than by the co-operation of a changed and repentant people. Judah and Jerusalem had been too radically corrupted by the apostate son of Hezekiah for the grandson to do anything but stamp out the visible flaunting of evil. It went, no doubt, underground.

Jeremiah, who lived through this reformation, and saw the

solemn ceremony of the covenant in the cleansed Temple, was dissatisfied with the results. His eleventh and twelfth chapters probably express his concern. Jeremiah may, indeed, as this passage shows, have exercised an itinerant ministry in the towns of Judah in aid of the new covenant, and he saw perhaps the sullen resistance of dissidents at close quarters (Jer. 17.1–11), Jeremiah is permeated with the language and teaching of Deuteronomy, and he saw with painful clarity that it was not reformation, imposed from above, which Judah needed, but regeneration which found beginning in the heart of each individual man. This was why the Lord called upon Nicodemus to face rebirth himself when he came doubtless to ask about the rebirth of the nation. Josiah's movement failed because he did not carry Judah with him. The people obeyed because it was expedient to conform.

> Then to side with Truth is noble, when we share her
> wretched crust,
> Ere her cause bring fame and profit, and 'tis prosperous
> to be just.
> Then it is the brave man chooses, and the coward
> stands aside
> Doubting in his abject spirit till his Lord is
> crucified,
> And the multitude make virtue of the faith they
> have denied.

Questions and themes for study and discussion on Studies 284–290

1. Consider Micah 7.8 and how to deal with failure.
2. 'Wherever you see persecution, there is more than a probability that truth is on the persecuted side' (Latimer). What basis is there for this assertion?
3. 'Late repentance is seldom true, but true repentance is never too late' (R. Venning).
4. 'The strength and safety of a community consist in the virtue and intelligence of its youth.'
5. Can there be any genuine movement of revival without a recovered Bible?
6. 'Preach the word . . .' See 2 Tim. 4.1–5.
7. Jeremiah's acquaintance, especially in his early chapters, with the text of Deuteronomy.
8. God's permissive will in history.

291 : Prophet Nahum

Nahum 1, 2, 3

Somewhere in Josiah's day, the poet and prophet Nahum finds a place. We may, in fact, envisage something of a revival among the youth of Josiah's own young generation. Nahum, Zephaniah and Jeremiah may have been among the ardent spirits, mere boys and youths, who both caught and fed the flame for renewed uprightness and pure religion in Josiah's early reign. Perhaps there is vast encouragement in the fact for today.

Nahum wrote when the yoke of Assyria was still unbroken (1.13). This would place him before the death of the powerful Ashurbanipal, who died, after a reign of forty-two years, probably 627 B.C. No one could foresee at this time that Assyria was doomed, and that fifteen years later, in August 612 B.C., the city of Nineveh would fall, and that within two or three more years after that fateful date, the bully of the north would lie low—only to be replaced by resurgent Babylon. And that is the theme of Habakkuk's sorrow.

Probably the invaders were already closing in on the great complex of associated villages which Jonah visited, breaking down the irrigation dykes, and terrorizing the land, when Nahum wrote his 'taunt-song', as the Hebrews called such poetry of denunciation. And poetry it is. It is full of flaming language. The very noise of siege, street-fighting and destruction rings through Nahum's vivid poems. Quick, short lines are in harmony with the violence they foretell. The imagery is strikingly colourful.

But we seek the man behind the words. What was the young poet like, who could so cry in exultation over the fall of a mighty city? Consider such language in the light of the Assyrian inscriptions, which boast of genocide, the torture, enslavement and massacre of vast multitudes. No race in antiquity matched the Assyrians for sadistic cruelty. Her wolfish kings were demons of death.

Here was a man who knew the ardour of the group which had discovered the Law afresh. In faith he laid hold of the theme of God's deliverance. Perhaps he marked the growing threat to the wide borders of the gangster kings, and saw, in triumphant confidence, the certainty of imminent divine judgement. The two poems on the fall of the evil city (2, 3) are significantly appended to the opening chapter on the greatness of God. They best will understand Nahum today who have lived long, wearing, terror-stricken years under the power of tyranny. It is not wrong to rejoice in the overthrow of hideous evil and foul tyranny.

292 : Young Zephaniah

Zephaniah 1 and 2

If the Hizkiah (as it is literally) of the opening verse is Hezekiah the king, Zephaniah is the great-great-grandson of one of the great reforming monarchs of Judah. A little arithmetic will show that, if Hezekiah died in 695 B.C. and the eldest son of Hezekiah was twelve years of age at that time, Zephaniah can hardly have been much past twenty years of age at the time of Josiah's great religious reforms. Have we then another young poet to set with Nahum, another who like the king, and some other youthful members of the royal circle, laid hold of the words of Deuteronomy, and cried out against the oppressor, Nineveh (2.13–15)?

Youth seems to have called strongly to youth in Josiah's day, but not without the heritage of age (Jer. 1.5). Zephaniah's forbears are given for four generations, and with one exception 'Yahweh' ends their names. These were the days when names were bestowed because of their moral and spiritual significance. Zephaniah's own name means 'Yahweh has hidden', and suggests that his birth may have taken place in Manasseh's Reign of Terror when he filled Jerusalem with blood (2 Kings 21.16). The young prophet, then, belonged to a true family, whose tradition kept the name of God alive in an age of shocking backsliding.

Jerusalem, the corruption of its city life, the cynical apostasy of its inhabitants, horrified Zephaniah as it had horrified another aristocratic prophet, the great Isaiah. In the opening verses of Zephaniah we see almost as much of Jerusalem as we see in the whole of Isaiah and Jeremiah. His indignation, like the indignation of the young, is ardent, unsparing, uncompromising, frank.

His style also shows the man. He is a city-man, and there is

340

no flash of the country-side in all the imagery of his book. George Adam Smith writes: 'There is no hotter book in all the Old Testament. Neither dew, nor grass, nor tree, nor any blossom lives in it, but it is everywhere fire, smoke and darkness, drifting chaff, ruins, nettles, salt-pits, owls and ravens looking on desolate palaces . . . There is no prospect of a redeemed and fruitful land, but only a group of battered and hardly saved characters. A few meek and righteous are hidden from the fire and creep forth when it is over.'

Perhaps Zephaniah died young. Perhaps indignation and zeal for truth burned his frame away—a youthful Savonarola.

293 : Josiah's End

2 Chronicles 35.20–27; Lamentations 4

'Nothing is more rare in any man than an act of his own,' said Emerson cryptically. He meant that few men act independently on the strength of a conviction. That is what Josiah did, and he drove much evil from the land. But although he does not seem to have carried the bulk of the population with him, he does appear to have gathered a small group of intelligent and devoted men about his person. We have met two. We shall meet another.

Josiah appears to have enjoyed thirteen years of prosperity and peace after his own great reforms. No doubt the land knew beneficent and righteous rule. Then came disaster by an unexpected series of events. With the death of Ashurbanipal in 627 B.C., the decline of Assyria, as we have seen, began. The evil empire passed into weaker hands, and Nineveh, its vital heartland, fell in 612 B.C.

It was soon after this date that Pharaoh Necho the Second, under whom Egypt was moving into one of her periodic cycles of prosperity and expansion, decided to give the final blow to the rival empire of the north. He marched on Assyria, and appears to have used Egypt's new naval power to bypass Palestine. He could not leave unheld the great marching-route of armies, the pass of Megiddo and the Esdraelon Plain, so he landed his army at Dor. A map will show that Josiah could intervene on Assyria's part only at Megiddo. The Pharaoh appealed to him, in God's name (35.21 f.), to stand aside and

341

give him right of way. Josiah stood firm and tragically died.

Why? Assyria could no longer command him. His own friends, Nahum and Zephaniah, had pronounced her doom. Perhaps he misread such promises as Deut. 31.1–8, and rashly expected to prevent the power of Egypt replacing that of Assyria. Whatever happened, he acted impetuously, without God's clear guidance, when he should have done nothing, but allowed God to act.

Disaster befell, and new subjection. Necho occupied Jerusalem and set up a puppet government. Jeremiah pronounced a dirge over the young king he had loved. And the cynics and the pagans, who had never believed Deuteronomy, had grist for their mills of blasphemy. How essential it is to know when to do nothing! Necho's triumph was destined for the briefest life.

Questions and themes for study and discussion on Studies 291–293

1. Nahum's quotations from Exodus (Nah. 1.2, 5) and Isaiah (Nah. 1.15).
2. Indignation against sin. What are its limits?
3. Can you suggest other Bible characters, beside Josiah and Peter, who acted impetuously?

294 : Jeremiah's Call

Jeremiah 1.1–10; 2.1–13

Josiah was dead, and Jeremiah, who was to be the greatest and the most tragic of the young men who turned to preaching in the surge of Josiah's day of reformation, lamented him in haunting verse. At this point, we must turn to the life of this great man and seek to know him, for Jeremiah was one of the most Christ-like of the characters of the Old Testament, a man who suffered cruelly for his faithfulness, and whose name undeservedly became a byword for despair.

We must look at his beginnings. Anathoth, called Anata today, is a tiny village just north of Jerusalem, on the first of those rocky shelves by which the central highlands of Palestine fall away into the great cleft of the Jordan. The deep rift makes an awesome landscape backed by the purple rampart

342

of the mountains of Moab, above which each day's sun rises out of the far deserts of Arabia.

Jerusalem tops the ridge, 3,000 feet above the valley floor which lies a bare 20 miles away, and Anathoth was not remote from the restless life of that ancient city. The brilliant son of the village priest of Anathoth, a man named Jeremiah, was conscious of his people's joys and aspirations, which gathered round Yahweh's shrine in the sacred city. He was conscious, too, that a few miles west of his native village lay the main road north from Jerusalem, the old invasion-route and marching-track of armies, the land's link with the northern empires, their pride, their ruthlessness, and their domination.

And grim days were dawning. It was 627 B.C. and the life of the man who was to exercise his sombre ministry in Jerusalem was lived under the shadow of the imperial tyranny of great Babylon. It was a bitter time for a man called upon to preach, especially when the deep conviction which charged his whole message was that Israel's only hope lay, at the moment, in bending before the storm, and abjuring a futile and helpless resistance. Jeremiah's unpopular advice was rejected, and the Babylonian conqueror, Nebuchadnezzar, beat Jerusalem flat in the prophet's lifetime, burned and looted the Temple, and deported her people.

295 : Jeremiah's Message

Jeremiah 1.11–19; 5.1–31

The message Jeremiah was called upon to give was almost intolerably sad. It was not, however, without ultimate hope. A future lay beyond the desert of suffering, and this is the meaning of the prophet's first vision.

When Jeremiah was called to preach, two symbols, Eastern fashion, filled his mind. One was a symbol of horror, the other of wondrous hope, and the mingling of the two make, in fact, the prophet's message.

In a dialogue with God which makes the poetry of the opening chapter of his book, Jeremiah answers a question: 'What do you see?' And I said: 'I see the branch of an almond tree.' And God said: 'Well have you seen, for I am awake over My Word to perform it.' The English translation cannot produce the Hebrew word-play, and the punning symbolism which makes the point of the passage. The Hebrew for almond tree is *shakedh,* which means 'awake' or 'watchful'. 'I see a branch of the wakeful tree,' says the prophet. 'I am awake,' comes the reply, and the word differs only in a vowel. It is *shokedh*: 'I am awake to fulfil my will.' The almond won its poetic Hebrew name by early blossoming. First of the flowering trees, it sensed the touch of spring, and burst into bloom, to become a sign of hope.

Jeremiah needed the assurance, for the second symbol in his vision was an awful one. 'What are you seeing?' 'A cauldron boiling, and its face is from the north.' This was Jeremiah's image for the fearful menace which overhung the little land. It was the immediate threat. The almond branch was ultimate hope, ultimate, indeed, for Jeremiah's own life was ended before the scalding brew from the tilted pot of Babylon ceased spilling over the land which he loved, and sought, by unpopular advice, to save. The bitter flood consumed his people and sent him into exile. But what his faith had learned, in the twin visions of the almond tree and the seething pot, was that history is not out of control.

But is there not pathos in the picture which forms in the mind as we seek to reach back through the centuries and understand? Fascinated by the spring's beauty, the boy of Anathoth watches the wonder of life renewed in the almond bloom, and yearns over a dying age.

296 : Jehoahaz

2 Kings 23.31–34; Ezekiel 19.1–14; Jeremiah 22.10–12

The last chapters of the royal records hurry over tragic events and short unhappy reigns as though the narrative had become too painful to write. To comb the brief verses for personalities is to encounter the agony of men, doubt, stress of soul, betrayal, heroism and death.

Shallum, third son of Josiah, succeeded his father by popular acclaim and the enthusiasm of the priesthood, doubtless at this time in the hands of Josiah's reforming party (23.30). Hence the 'anointing', a ceremonial not always observed for the kings of Judah. At this time Shallum must have changed his name to Jehoahaz, which means 'Yahweh takes hold', a testimony to his faith. He was twenty-three years old.

Shallum, or Jehoahaz, as we may now call him, must have been a young man of great promise and charm, for his cruel fate won the dirges of both Jeremiah and Ezekiel. Hence the difficulty in the remark that 'he did evil in the sight of God.' No particular offence is mentioned, and the unfortunate young man had small opportunity to manifest the unexpected flaw in his personality. In some momentous way, he must have shocked and disappointed those who had preferred and promoted him over two older brothers. Ezekiel's lament seems to suggest, in the language of poetry, that Jehoahaz was a young man of vigour, the son of a determined mother. But Josephus, who preserved some old rabbinical traditions, said that the young king proved 'impious and impure in his character.'

The years might have brought improvement or deterioration, but poor Jehoahaz had little time to reveal whatever it was that lay in his heart. Pharaoh was on the march, and after nine centuries, at the end of his drive to the north, Egyptian soldiers saw 'the other river', the far Euphrates. Necho consolidated his Syrian conquest as best he could, and in the course of his activity heard that Jehoahaz had been appointed king in Jerusalem. Perhaps it was the leonine traits in the young man's character, those lauded by Ezekiel, that Pharaoh disliked. At any rate, he took him a prisoner to Egypt. Whether Ezekiel's 'hooks' were literally the hooks in the nose by which prisoners, in the cruel fashion of the day, were led, cannot be said, but Jehoahaz died in Egypt.

No king of Judah before him had died in prison. A veil is drawn over the young man's despair, his pain of body and of mind, the torture of his doubts, his memories of his good father, his agonized prayer . . . Necho's expansionist policies were short-lived. Nebuchadnezzar was a huge shadow on the horizon. Perhaps Jehoahaz died when Babylon threatened Egypt's borders, for Jehoahaz' deposition could have been for anti-Egyptian daring.

297 : Jehoiakim

2 Kings 23.34–24.7; Jeremiah 26.20–23

Eliakim, second son of Josiah, was renamed Jehoiakim by Pharaoh Necho according to a custom of the day. The meaning was the same (' God will establish '). ' Yahweh ', in the name, was merely changed to 'El.' The significance of the change is therefore not clear, but the new name meant as little as the old. The king was twenty-five years of age.

Jehoiakim's sorry story can be pieced together from Jeremiah, who could do nothing with the foolish man. He was looked upon as a puppet of Egypt, and a collector of taxes for the alien, a reputation which he might have countered by a demonstration of care for his impoverished people. Instead, he was a self-indulgent and self-opinionated man, flaunting affluence amid the land's misery. Perhaps Nehushta, daughter of Elnathan, an obedient servant of Egypt, was to blame for his folly.

Pretentious building has often been a sign of royal estate. The Emperor of Babylon, the Nebuchadnezzar of the story, was to rebuild the mighty Euphrates city to express his pride. Solomon had done no less in Jerusalem. But Jehoiakim's Jerusalem, and Jehoiakim's times, were not such that self-glorifying expense was appropriate, or a mark of worthiness. Habakkuk, whom we are soon to meet, expressed the mood of the day in words directed against Nebuchadnezzar, but finding imagery nearer home (Hab. 2.9–11).

Crime was added to folly when Uriah was extradited from Egypt at the hands of Elnathan, and murdered for speaking out.

In Jehoiakim's fourth year Nebuchadnezzar, in the strife of the two empires, Babylon and Egypt, tore Judah out of Egypt's hands, and Jehoiakim acknowledged his dominion. But Nebuchadnezzar, preoccupied with his own establishment in Babylon, was out of range of Judah for three whole years, and, gaining rash confidence, and persuaded by Egypt, Jehoiakim rebelled. It was against the most solemn advice of Jeremiah (Jer. 36.29). It was Judah's perennial fault in those days to be seduced by Egyptian promises.

Hence doom and disaster; Jehoiakim was carried off to death, and the Chronicler makes a strange remark about some sign of evil on his person (2 Chron. 36.8, AV[KJV]). Was it a heathen tattoo-mark? Few rulers of Judah have passed from the pages of history loaded so heavily with scorn. The times called for humility and hearkening to God. Jehoiakim was vain, and deaf.

346

298 : Foolish Jehoiakim

2 Chronicles 36.1–8; Jeremiah 22.13–19

We have seen the vast problem in foreign relationships which Jehoiakim faced. There was the powerful prince of Babylon, absent but aware of events to the south of him. There was Egypt, beaten back from her ambitions of a decade's renascent militarism and expansion. Which was he to follow? For Judah's helplessness there was Jeremiah's third course.

Between the imperial millstones Judah's hope was only in non-alignment. No moral issues were involved, as they sometimes are in international affairs. Non-alignment in Jeremiah's day was sense, because among the warring nations Judah's contribution to human culture was the vital element in history. The giants were sterile. The little land had something to preserve.

And at such a time, with the control of Palestine see-sawing between the two imperial powers, a young fool on the throne chose to oppress his subjects and parade his wealth. Light has recently been thrown on the sordid reign and the royal ostentation.

An archaeologist of the Hebrew University at Jerusalem has uncovered a palace of Jehoiakim, which makes him look like a Jewish Nero who fiddled while the fires swept down on Palestine.

Jehoiakim appears to have died on the way to captivity, as we have seen, at the age of thirty-six. He reigned over the menaced land from 609 to 598 B.C. and left a name of contempt behind him. The ruins of his great palace stand in the fields of a kibbutz on the old Israel-Jordan frontier to illustrate the statement. The archaeologists found that, to make room for the king's ostentatious dwelling, a peasant village had been obliterated, after the fashion of the Norman kings' burning of Saxon settlements in England to make the New Forest.

Hence Jeremiah's denunciation in 22.13–19. He refers here to the untimely building projects of the young king.

The excavations support the description. The great outer walls, nine to twelve feet wide, enclose a five-acre compound. Its fine squared stonework is only equalled in Palestine by the masonry of Ahab's palace in Samaria. The windows to which Jeremiah refers were of unusual magnificence. Architectural fragments in the debris suggest that they were enclosed by decorated columns. A most powerful impression of strength and magnificence must have been created. And all this under the black shadow of war.

Jeremiah's moral indignation at the sight was aroused by something more than the forced labour which the arrogant young king must have used. To strut thus, and flaunt wealth and tyranny, was sin in such a twilight.

299 : Jehoiakim's Folly

Jeremiah 36

For a last vivid glance at Jehoiakim we can find our way to a room in the palace which the young king had built. It was winter, possibly the winter of 605 B.C. In such a season ancient war found pause, but policy was made. Jehoiakim was considering the problem of Babylon and Egypt, a dilemma beyond the power of his mind.

For all that, had he been a man of God, able and ready to recognize the leading of God, there was the course which Jeremiah recommended, unheroic in the eyes of some of the royal counsellors, but sane. Sitting safely amid his wealth, Jehoiakim, vain and self-assured, was counting up the cost. Nebuchadnezzar appeared silent and remote. Pressure was applied by Egypt, whose Pharaoh after all had put him on the throne. Policy was veering to the south. Jeremiah was loud in warning, and the young king hated him for it. The story is in the vivid thirty-sixth chapter of Jeremiah's book . . .

Jehudi, the scribe, read out to the king the prophet's menacing words. The king sat in his private room, and it was, as we have said, winter, with a small brazier burning by his chair. It took place, no doubt, in the fine new palace. Not liking the words, the king petulantly seized the roll from the reader, drew his dagger, and slashed it. He dropped it contemptuously in the blazing brazier beside him.

Truth is not destroyed by burning the written or printed words which give it body and voice, or even by persecuting and killing those who hold to it, as Jehoiakim had murdered

Uriah, the other faithful counsellor. The chapter ends with sinister words:

> 'Jeremiah took another scroll and gave it to Baruch the scribe . . . who wrote on it at the dictation of Jeremiah all the words of the scroll which Jehoiakim king of Judah had burned in the fire; and many similar words were added to them.'

Jehoiakim, against sane advice, rebelled, challenging the ruthless king of Babylon. It was a simple matter for the royal armies of such an imperial power to overrun the little state, and Jehoiakim went away in chains, leaving his red cedar ceilings and his great windows. Nebuchadnezzar had him killed, and his body was flung outside the wall, 'the burial of an ass' (22.19), as the hated prophet had foretold, 'cast out to the heat by day and the frost by night' (36.30).

The stone walls of Jehoiakim's ostentatious palace south of Jerusalem are a sad memorial to folly and arrogance.

Questions and themes for study and discussion on Studies 294–299

1. Jeremiah was called to preach submission, or at least non-alignment. Isaiah was called to preach resistance. Why the difference?
2. Can truth be suppressed?
3. Ostentatious living and Christianity.
4. How is advice to be tested?
5. Josiah's sons. Why does a younger generation sometimes abandon its religious tradition? Is it the fault of defective transmission?

300 : Jehoiachin

2 Kings 24.6–16; 2 Chronicles 36.8–10; Jeremiah 22.24–30

The king of Babylon set Jehoiakim's eighteen-year-old son on the throne. (The Chronicler's 'eight' for 'eighteen' is a copyist's mistake). He ruled one hundred days, and had little time for evil or for plotting. He was a boy, like the young emperor Nero, dominated by a powerful mother, and it is a fair guess that the queen, Nehushta, was the author of much evil in the land.

There must have been rebellion of some sort. Perhaps Egypt, safe across the intervening desert, and immune from invasion by distance, was plotting behind the scenes again. Egyptian policy has always been to dominate Palestine as a buffer against the north. But Nebuchadnezzar was a decisive man, and was now free from the dynastic preoccupations which had been a temptation earlier to Judah. He knew the ambitions of Egypt, and was now quite determined to destroy any bridgehead that the rival power of the Nile might find in Judah. Hence his decision against Judah.

Jerusalem knew that resistance was useless. The boy-king, along with the queen-mother Nehushta, went out to the enemy camp in pathetic surrender, and the great deportation of the land's strength, talent and wealth followed. Jehoiachin was the Coniah of Jeremiah's words (**22**.24–30) to Zedekiah, and he lay in Babylon, said the prophet, as a sign of judgement on the land. Another puppet ruled over a looted, de-populated, crushed Jerusalem.

The account is too brief to tell us a great deal, and it is difficult to learn much of these hundred days from the two prophets, but tradition suggests that there was something to remember in the hapless youth. One of the gates of Jerusalem, probably that by which he left the city for his thirty-seven-year captivity, was always called Jehoiachin's Gate. Josephus preserves a tradition of kindliness and gentleness. These may have been the qualities which led him to surrender personally to the Babylonian army, to spare Jerusalem. Josephus says that his captivity was annually commemorated. The apocry-phal Book of Baruch shows the captive living in Babylon, with a measure of freedom and prosperity, but weeping for lost Jerusalem. We know no more, and much of this is speculation. It is all sad reading, and the stream of divine purpose in Judah seems reduced to a sorry rill—until one remembers Jeremiah and Ezekiel.

301 : Zedekiah

2 Kings 24.18–25.21; Ezekiel 17.11–24

Only a sombre eleven years are left for the monarchy in Judah, and Judah's last king did nothing to adorn them. Mattaniah ('Yahweh's Gift') was the third son of Josiah, and

Nebuchadnezzar gave the land one more chance in him. To cement the oath by which he bound him, the Babylonian king changed the young man's name to Zedekiah ('Yahweh's Righteousness').

Zedekiah had little left to rule over, but he had one asset in the prophet Jeremiah. Nebuchadnezzar, no doubt to Jeremiah's sorrow and embarrassment, regarded him as an ally, and a force for peace in Jerusalem. He was—but not in the interests of Babylon's power.

Zedekiah was a weakling. He permitted the reoccupation of the Temple by the abominations which his good father had expelled. Ezekiel, like the exiles generally, seems to have been well informed of affairs back in their lost homeland, and, in his eighth chapter, he describes the heathen horrors being enacted in the holy place. Perhaps many, falling to the bitter disillusionment which we shall see Habakkuk resisting, had lost their faith, and turned for comfort to abominable cults.

If Zedekiah was helpless in the hands of the apostate group who defiled the Temple, he was also unable to resist the princes of the court, who rashly worked against Babylon. Edom, Ammon, Moab and the Phoenicians were plotting against Nebuchadnezzar. Young Hophrah was now Pharaoh of Egypt, and Egypt was busy, after Egypt's fashion, in the background. Such promises bolstered the court rebels. Jeremiah fought bitterly against the folly of their plotting. A false prophet, Hananiah, clothed the conspiracy with lies, and it is the way of all peoples to applaud and hearken to what is pleasant to hear. Hananiah died (Jer. **28**.10–17), and two like-minded 'prophets' in Babylon were burned to death (**29**.21–23), but, persuaded and seduced by others (Ezek. **13**), Zedekiah took up hopeless arms.

In Jeremiah's and Ezekiel's eyes, the burden of Zedekiah's sin was not his inability to see the truth amid the wild babble of conflicting advice and exhortation, nor even a failure to hearken to the true voice of prophecy, but rather the breaking of a solemn oath to the king of Babylon, embedded in his very name (Ezek. **17**.15).

So ended five centuries of Judah's kings. It was 587 B.C. Egypt, as usual, withdrew. The grim story is told, along with that of Jeremiah's shocking ordeal, in chapters **37**, **38** and **39** of his prophecy. We may imagine the agony of his mind when he found he could not pray for the doomed land.

351

302 : Jeremiah's Agony

Jeremiah 37.1–38.4

To the 'hawks' of Jehoiakim's misguided court, Jeremiah's pacifist policy seemed, as was remarked, unheroic and passive. Controversy raged, and Jeremiah suffered all the pain, the traumatic pressure and misunderstanding which brave men suffer when they hold to truth and conviction amid tense and perilous doings. Curiously enough, some potsherds from the guardhouse of Lachish, a fortress thirty-seven miles from Jerusalem, throw light on the scene and on Jeremiah's ordeal. The inscribed shards were the last find of J. L. Starkey, before he was killed by an Arab bandit over forty years ago.

There was an officer named Jaush in charge of Lachish, a bull-dog type who no doubt scorned Jeremiah for 'defeatism', and who seems to have communicated his contempt to a junior commander who held a lonely outpost in the hills. This man was called Hoshaiah.

Hoshaiah saw the force of Jeremiah's timely pacifism, and dared, in the politest terms, to argue with his commanding officer. He had no papyrus. However, there were broken pots enough in any eastern town. He picked up a few pieces on the sidewalk, and wrote to Jaush. Let us quote from Letter Six on the file:

'Who am I, thy slave, a dog, that thou hast sent me a letter of the king to the princes saying "Read, and see that the words of the prophet are not good, liable, indeed, to weaken the hands, to make sink the hands of the men in the city and the country".'

A professor of the Hebrew University of Jerusalem unravelled the text of this ancient court circular. It is strangely relevant, for Jeremiah 38.4 runs: 'Then the princes said to the king, "Let this man be put to death, for he is weakening the hands of the soldiers . . . and the hands of all the people . . . . For this man is not seeking the welfare of this people, but their harm".'

Hoshaiah begs Jaush to intercede with the princes. 'My lord, wilt thou not write to them saying, "Why should ye do this? . . .".' The letter then breaks off. Hoshaiah probably imagined his senior officer a much more important man than he was.

352

The earthenware letters came to Lachish, and there was no doubt strong comment from Jaush for his subaltern's insolence in championing the doleful preacher in Jerusalem. But the letters were still in the guard house when Nebuchadnezzar swept down on Palestine.

Nebuchadnezzar beat a breach in the fortress walls by burning all the district's olive trees against the wall. The hole is full of powdered lime and olive-stones. Jaush doubtless swung his sword like a man, and either went down fighting, or went prisoner to Babylon.

His little office fell in ruin.

Great rains seem to have followed, and washed a silt of broken mud-brick through the ruins of the town. Thanks to this, many objects have survived—among them the pottery letters. Two thousand five hundred years go by, and they speak to another age, and throw light on Jeremiah's agony.

303 : Jeremiah's Imprisonment

Psalm 69; Jeremiah 38

Psalm 69 is set down by the rabbis as a psalm of David. Perhaps a careful examination of the language might reveal rather that it was a prayer of Jeremiah, when the enemies of his ministry put him in the disused cistern. It was such a fate as we saw Joseph suffer (Gen. 37.20–29) but in Jeremiah's case the 'broken cistern' (Jer. 2.13) was full of deep mud. In such a cruel 'prison' at Gezer a dozen skeletons were found.

There was something furtive about the action of the princes, as though they feared a popular uprising, for Nebuchadnezzar's siege was pressing hard. It seems, too, that Zedekiah was uneasy, and when the brave negro servant, Ebedmelech, hurried to tell him the facts, he immediately authorized a rescue. Zedekiah sent for Jeremiah when the good Ethiopian brought him out, and among the words of comfort, few enough, which Jeremiah sought to give, were words which are almost an echo of Psa. 69. 'They have let your feet sink in the mud, and have turned away and left you there' (38.22). It is a metaphor derived from the shocking experience through which the prophet had just passed, and a strong argument for those who believe that he wrote Psa. 69. It is a vivid recalling of the awful moment when the sneering faces disappeared from the circle of light above and the stone was replaced—not a tight fit, in order not to check the pouring down of the collected rain-water into the cistern, and to give substance, if Jeremiah did write the psalm, to his reference to flood and overwhelming water, his misery of body and soul.

In the sad narrative of distracted and beleaguered characters, which has been our main reading, we close with two vignettes. Observe that when Ebedmelech went in hot indignation to find the king, he found him at his post where a soldier ought to be—at Benjamin's gate. Zedekiah may have been a fool or a moral weakling. He was no coward in the face of physical danger. Nor was he slow to respond to the brave negro's call for mercy and aid.

And linger a moment over Ebedmelech himself, and his thoughtful collection of used garments from the royal wardrobe to take the cut and abrasion of the ropes as they pulled Jeremiah up—and probably to clothe him as they tossed aside his mire-sodden robes. Said Addison once: 'Half the misery of human life might be extinguished if men would alleviate the general curse they lie under by mutual offices of compassion, benevolence and humanity.'

Questions and themes for study and discussion on Studies 300–303

1. The role of youth and age in the country's affairs.
2. The leadership of youth in matters of religion.
3. Kindness. What is it? How does it differ from mercy?
4. Is taking sides always good?

304 : Habakkuk's Doubts

Habakkuk 1.1–2.3; Romans 8.28–39

Before we take a last look at the anguished Jeremiah, and pass on to find other characters of the Old Testament in Babylon, we must meet a troubled man named Habakkuk who wrote and spoke in Judah at the time, it seems, when Babylon was descending on the land. We must try to find the person of the prophet behind the brief pages of his book, a less difficult task than it sometimes is, as we peer behind the words of the later books of the Old Testament.

We cannot be certain of his dates, and the time when he put his agonizing doubts and his triumphant return to faith into Scripture. Some, indeed, have suggested that it was the Assyrian, and not the Babylonian, who was threatening the land, and filling Habakkuk with despair. We can only guess, and hazard a reconstruction of his life, and the framework of experience in which he wrote. We can feel the stir of pity and of understanding for the man who left the little book of meditation and devotion, which goes under his name.

Perhaps Habakkuk was born about 630 B.C., saw the days of Josiah's restoration of worship, and took to heart, along with zealous young men whose names have crossed our pages, the promises of the newly discovered Deuteronomy. They saw hated Nineveh fall, and felt that they lived in such a dawn as Wordsworth described, when it was 'bliss to be alive, but to be young was very heaven'. Habakkuk's dawn, like Wordsworth's own, faded . . .

Habakkuk, if the dates are correct, lived to see Josiah fall under the Egyptian arrow, to see Pharaoh march into Jerusalem and, in the end, see Nebuchadnezzar, the new aggressor, lay hold on the land after defeating Egypt at Carchemish in 605 B.C. Nations were falling before the young imperialist of Babylon. Cities were left desolate as he swept whole populations away to provide labour for his vast building schemes. Jerusalem surrendered her last spark of life in 597 B.C. A year later Solomon's Temple was destroyed.

Where Habakkuk fits in we do not know, but somewhere in this dark chapter of disaster he faced despair. Where, where, was God, the God of Deuteronomy, the God who saved? True, Huldah had spoken, but Huldah was forgotten. Was the king of Babylon mightier than God? Was God helpless in the midst of triumphant paganism? Habakkuk knew the old agony of the good—the biting, searing doubt about the reality of God's promises. Why, O God, why?

305 : Habakkuk's Faith

Habakkuk 2.4–3.19

Habakkuk, in agony over human pain (1.13–15), had seemed to get no light on the problem which obsessed him. He goes to his place of prayer (2.1) and pleads with God. Words come to him which he is constrained to write down. A phrase is put into history (4), which was picked up by Paul (Rom. 1.17), and again by Luther. The vital word is not quite the same as 'faith'. It is the Hebrew 'emunah', the word with which 'amen' is connected, and means faithfulness, steadiness, firmness, all of which qualities, of course, are based upon what is understood in the New Testament by 'faith'. The word is used of Moses' hands, 'steady' in the potent act of prayer (Exod. 17.12). It occurs in Prov. 12.22 and Isa. 11.5. Significantly, the Septuagint renders 'emunah' by the word 'pistis', the common New Testament word for faith.

But we seek the man Habakkuk in his message. It was a great soul which, in the hour of his people's twilight and terror, grasped the thought that it is a quality within the heart, a principle of endurance, based on trust in God, which keeps a nation alive, and keeps men and women human when catastrophe falls on a land and on a person. How far was Habakkuk's message known? Did David know his words, and Nehemiah? Read 1 John 2.16 f., as Phillips renders it, for John puts into a verse what Habakkuk grasped as Babylon fell fiercely on Palestine: 'The whole world-system, based as it is on men's primitive desires, their greedy ambitions and the glamour of all they think splendid . . . will one day disappear. But the man who is following God's will is part of the permanent and cannot die.'

On the strength of the revelation, Habakkuk was able to tell what the fate would be of the arrogant and victorious pagan. Five 'woes' will befall, and the moral law will prevail. It is like a preview of the Book of the Revelation. The mills of God grind slowly . . . The harvest, which man has sown, inevitably ripens. Evil battles with the laws of Creation. Habakkuk was the sort of man who is needed today. Such triumphantly certain proclamation is the message for our times. Christians should get to their watch-towers and wait until they know what God will say.

306 : Jeremiah's Choice

2 Kings 25.22–26; Jeremiah 40.1–41.3

Surely no one suffered so hard a lot as Jeremiah. With the departure of the caravan of the exiles, the best and choicest of the land, for Babylon, the prophet faced a choice. He stood high in the estimation of the Chaldeans, and might have lived in comfort in the land of exile. He had been called a traitor, and a destroyer of the morale of his people, and now was faced with a choice and an opportunity to restore his reputation.

Without hesitation he elected to remain with the broken remnant of his people in a depopulated defenceless land, amid poverty, hunger and anxiety. No one, surely, could misunderstand him now! And yet he had abundant motive to justify a retreat to Babylon. Ezekiel was there, ministering to the exiles, and they were the men and women on whom the future of the land depended. Was not this a more demanding call?

Jeremiah made his noble choice, and it was on his recommendation that the upright Gedaliah was made governor of the land and guardian of the daughters of the deposed king. It was probably Babylon's intention to allow him, when the girls grew up, to marry one of them, and continue the line of David. Gedaliah had a difficult rule. He set up his headquarters at Mizpah, north of Jerusalem, a sombre indication of the desolation and ruin in which the capital lay.

The historian of the Kings can hardly bring himself to write of the shocking events which followed. Jeremiah, in a flat, despairing narrative, tells a fuller story. Refugee Jews were pouring back into the land, itself a testimony to the high reputation of Gedaliah. There was a prospect of restoration in the land, a situation, indeed, which the king of Babylon may have overlooked. Whether the prospect of a stronger Israel was a motive for interference from across the Jordan, it is impossible to say, but the villain Ishmael, of sinister name, was sent by Ammon's king to assassinate Gedaliah.

The open-hearted governor was warned, but gallantly refused to credit the warning. He died at the murderer's hands. The bright page of reconstruction in Judah was finished. The dark last chapter of her history resumed its

357

theme. Perhaps Jer. 15.10–21 reflects the prophet's cry of agony over this period. We cannot say, but the darkness was unrelieved. It was to press yet harder on his hopes and aspirations.

307 : Jeremiah's Exile
Jeremiah 41.4–43.7

Ishmael's iniquity continued at Mizpah. He brutally murdered a small band of refugees who had confidently come to the little town expecting to find the good Gedaliah and, with him, some hope and comfort. And when retribution at last came with Johanan, the scoundrel made good his escape to his master, the Ammonite king, architect of the plot.

Johanan was in a dilemma. He feared the ruler of Babylon, and with his small band decided that flight was the only resort. They moved south from Mizpah, through the ghastly ruins of Jerusalem to the caravan-centre at Bethlehem, a few miles further south, where the name of Chimham, son of Barzillai, David's benefactor, still was heard, and where the Gileadites' tradition of hospitality to exiles still held. So Geruth Chimham became an assembly-point (41.17).

Here it was proposed that retreat should be made to Egypt, there to find, at least, some rest from toil, blood and anguish. Egypt had till recently dominated the land, and some hope may have been held that the southern empire might welcome refugees from its hated northern rival. The fugitives were desperate.

Jeremiah now faced another ordeal. He knew that all Judah's hope lay in rebuilding the land, and that every fugitive from Judea was a fugitive from God's task and the nation's destiny. The demoralized Jews professed their willingness to follow God's will. As too often happens to the loyalties of men, there was a hidden condition—God's will was to be followed if it chimed with their desires.

Jeremiah agonized over the problem, and finally found himself convinced that the retreat, even a temporary retreat to Egypt, was wrong. The fugitives turned on him with unworthy charges and recriminations, and Jeremiah's long

358

tragedy of suffering and misunderstanding passed into yet another act. It was hard for such a man to be called a hireling prophet, Baruch's mouthpiece.

Even worse, Johanan gathered up the exiles and refugees who had crept back to the land, following the deportation to Babylon, and a second 'going down into Egypt' was led by him. Jeremiah was forced to accompany them. Could any man have had greater stress of mind thrust upon him? Here we leave him—one of the most tragic figures of history—a veritable foreshadowing of Christ.

308 : Prophet's Call

Ezekiel 1 and 2

Ezekiel's book, like that of his contemporary and elder prophet Jeremiah, begins with a vision set in the language of vivid poetry. In the account he gives of it we see his gift of poetry and catch the ardour of his faith.

'By the rivers of Babylon,' as Psa. 137 reveals, lesser men 'sat down and wept', remembering their far homeland. Ezekiel, by the great irrigation canal of Chebar, saw a vision of God.

The thought of the East is pictorial. Our methods of thought are more at home with the abstract. As a language, Hebrew uses concrete terms in a manner quite unknown in European speech. 'Wall' means 'defence', 'rock' means 'strength', and 'horn' means 'power'. It was therefore easy to render truth pictorially. Hence the language of apocalyptic vision. We cannot enter into a detailed interpretation of the vision of Ezekiel, but it all adds up to a warning that out of the north is coming a destructive invasion—the whirlwind and the blaze of fire. The imagery was found in some mighty desert storm, with billowing sand intershot with lightning. Thus, Ezekiel envisaged, had disaster come out of the north on Palestine.

The rabbis listed man, eagle, ox, and lion as the lords of their respective divisions of creation. 'And yet,' their saying went, 'they are stationed below the chariot of the Holy One.' This is the key. Thus, to those who understood, Ezekiel showed that Babylon's hurricane of evil was permitted by God. If the storm was His chariot, He also controlled it. And so Ezekiel, like Jeremiah, was assured at the beginning of a grim ministry that God was not dethroned, though 'dark is His path on the wings of the storm'.

Human words almost break under the task of showing forth the majesty, the power, the glory of God. It is the vivid and awesome imagery of speed, mobility, purity, mighty utterance and consuming judgement. What were the tawdry idols of Babylon beside this regal Being who filled the sky? From the midst of the flashing symbols of His power came a voice, and it bade Ezekiel stand upright and fearlessly receive a message. The prophet felt strangely empowered to obey. Almighty God needed a man to bear His word, and to speak in His Name to a people. Even in this strange context, the requirements were the same as they ever are—obedience and understanding. Ezekiel was warned against sharing the sin of those to whom he ministered; he was commanded to make the Word of the Lord part of his very being. These demands still stand.

309 : Prophet's Lesson

Ezekiel 3

Ezekiel was promised no triumphant career. He was to preach to an embittered people, and not to flinch before their cynicism and spite. Like Jeremiah, he was called to a forbidding task; and both prophets trod the path the Lord Jesus was to tread. Under the Spirit's strong urging, Ezekiel set out for Telabib. The captivity involved no strict confinement. Babylon's policy was to enfeeble conquered lands and populate the Euphrates river-plain with the best elements of subject peoples; no doubt the deported Jews lived in many communities with some freedom of movement. One such centre Ezekiel sought for the beginning of his ministry. He went in 'bitterness in the heat of his spirit', but that was not the mood in which to preach God's Word, however stern the message. He sat among them 'overwhelmed' (Moffatt) for seven days. He sat, indeed, 'where they sat' (15), and no man can preach effectively unless he comprehends the pain and the problems of those to whom he speaks. Hence the restraint under which the angry, passionate prophet fell. After seven days of deepening understanding, the preacher was at last in a condition to preach. He was at last effective.

The prophet was set as a watchman and a voice of warning, and the moral responsibility which this task involved was set forth in detail. In spite of it, and with some suddenness, the scene changes at v. 22, and the prophet's ministry is withdrawn at some threat of violence. There may be some lapses of time between vs. 21 and 22; Scripture does frequently make such rapid transitions. It is none the less true enough to experience. The word of warning is disregarded and scorned, and the warning voice is stilled. The Lord had no word to say to Herod, who had long since ceased to hear the voice of conscience; He was silent before Pilate, who had sold his conscience to the priests. So with Ezekiel. The brevity of the narrative conceals labour and rejection, and the consequent withdrawal of the warning voice. It is dangerous not to listen when the Spirit of God speaks to the heart. He speaks only for good and blessing, but presses conviction on no self-willed and obdurate rebel.

310 : Prophet's Hope
Ezekiel 36.22–37.14; John 3.1–8

Ezekiel's great task as he ministered to the exiles was to convince them that their murdered nation could come to rebirth. He had a promise to preach about. It is put vividly in 36.26, 27.

With these words of renewal and rebirth in mind, Ezekiel dreamed a strange and significant dream. He found himself in a valley, or, to be exact, a valley-plain (37.1, RSV mg.). Some modern translations, with what appears a perverse zeal to be different, say 'plain'. The word is 'beqaa'. The Beqaa with the capital B runs up between the two Lebanon Ranges. Baalbek stands at its northern end. Such 'beqaas' are a feature of the land. They are invasion routes, and places of battles.

Ezekiel stood, perhaps, in such a place. The Babylonian armour and their cavalry had overrun some rearguard, and the bones of the fallen lay white and arid among the scrub and wild weed. Here was a picture of Israel, dry, dead, past hope.

The word came: 'Man, can these bones live?' 'Lord God,' replied Ezekiel, 'You alone know'. 'Tell them,' came the Voice, 'that they will indeed live.' Ezekiel did as he was bidden. There was a grisly stirring in the heaps of dead. Skeletons articulated. Flesh and sinews appeared, as the film of time ran backward . . . But they were still dead. Ezekiel is then commanded to call in God's name on the wind. And it must be remembered, if this strange word picture is to be understood, that in Hebrew and in Greek, the tongues of the two Testaments, the same word means 'breath', 'wind' and 'spirit'.

The wind often plays a metaphorical role. The wind in the Sinai gorge spoke to Elijah of the godless surge of life. Job was conscious of the desert winds. It was an east wind that Jeremiah likened to the scattering of Israel. It was by the same wind, rushing out of the burning Arabian desert, as the nor'wester presses down on Capetown out of the Kalahari, that Ezekiel saw the ships of Tyre shattered, and the psalmist the merchantmen of Tarshish. Other winds bring life, and Ezekiel, standing in the Beqaa of Death, must have had in mind the renewing breezes, that, in the north, bring life to the afternoon, or the winds that come out of the west, as they came for Elijah, rain-laden.

Dreams are built of the stuff of life's experience, and in this weird vision to which the Lord obliquely referred in His famous talk with Nicodemus, we catch sight of Ezekiel, his desperate hope, his passionate faith in God's power to transform personalities, history, disaster, and his understanding of what the New Testament was to call 'being born again'.

Questions and themes for study and discussion on Studies 304–310

1. Why do good people suffer?
2. 'Doubt is an experience, but cannot be a way, of life.'
3. Should Jeremiah have gone to Babylon?
4. Is retreat ever justified?
5. Youth and ambition. Can compromise be avoided?
6. 'Sec/et' discipleship.
7. Personal experience and preaching.

362

311 : Valiant Youth

Daniel 1; 1 Corinthians 10.23–33

It was a traumatic experience to be dragged into captivity at the beginning of manhood, and it must have seemed to them unbelievable good fortune when some of the young men were set aside to be used as leaders in the cosmopolitan empire which the king was seeking to build. The shrewd Nebuchadnezzar was looking for able civil servants, and the pressure on those chosen for such training to conform to the pagan world into which they were introduced must have been overwhelming.

The names of the boys all contained the name of their God, 'iah' and 'el'. 'Daniel' means 'God is my judge'; Hananiah means 'God is gracious'; Mishael means 'Who is as God'; Azariah means 'God has helped'. The meaning of Belteshazzar is doubtful, but it probably means 'Protect his life'. According to the lexicon Shadrach is also of doubtful meaning, while Meshach may simply mean 'Who is this?' and Abednego may mean 'Servant of Nabu' with the 'b' changed to 'g' to slur the offensive name of the pagan deity.

Thus it often goes with the world. Pagan society is content, as a preliminary step, if it can get the divine syllable out of the Christian's 'name'. It does not at first concentrate on substituting the gods of heathendom. Daniel, in his strong maturity, was aware of this. What others called him did not matter. What he did in person to aid the process of absorption was what concerned him. There he could stand firm.

The law had said much of food. It was a symbol in the Hebrew code, and Daniel saw the food of Babylon as a sign of pagan living, and its acceptance an act of surrender. In the practice of contemporary society there are features which, perhaps harmless in themselves, have assumed the nature of a test, like the 'meat sacrificed to idols' in Corinth. To participate, accept, or to partake becomes, for the Christian, an act of compromise, and a demonstration of conformity.

Daniel and his friends decided to be separate, an act of valour under the circumstances. They no doubt received much contrary advice, much warning of perilous imprudence, much angry protest among those afraid to be involved in the minority's intransigence. They stood firm, left career and

363

safety in God's hands, refused to accept the symbols of paganism, and were richly vindicated.

312 : Nebuchadnezzar

Daniel 2

The king of Babylon has haunted the background of many of our studies, a peril from the north, a sinister visitant, a harbinger of death. Now we meet him in person, a cruel, unreasonable, capricious tyrant. 'Uneasy lies the head that wears a crown,' said Shakespeare, and how truly! Nebuchadnezzar was drunk with power. Such minds are not at ease. Fear of assassination haunts them, and their suppressed suspicions and hatreds, rampant during day, emerge at night to murder sleep.

Savagely the king commanded his soothsayers to recall the dream, which had left only a dark dread behind, and to tell the meaning. None of them dared say that the problem which he sought to solve was the evil in his own heart. Fierce punishment, extravagant reward, injustice, caprice are the manifestations of tyranny. Observe now the quiet, brave manhood which was to confront the raving tyrant. Daniel's youthful self-discipline made the courageous man.

He sought the wisdom of God, and was granted his prayer. In two ways he showed himself worthy of such grace. He must have despised the wizardry and fortune-telling of the 'wise men' of Babylon, but he sought, in humanity, to save them from the punishment of the king. His first reaction to answered prayer was gratitude, and a beautiful prayer of worship followed (20–23). Too often we are ready enough with our prayers of petition, but slow to utter the prayer of gratitude and praise. In the presence of the king, Daniel claimed no special wisdom. He gave God all the glory, and sought occasion, in the service he rendered, to commend the God he worshipped. The portraiture of Daniel never varies, for there was no variety in the front he presented to the world. Two great qualities stand out: his deep reverence for God, and his fearless demeanour before men. Before God he bowed the knee; before men he stood erect and unafraid. And in his eyes Nebuchadnezzar was no more than man, to be treated with the respect his rank demanded, but with no trace of servility or flattery.

The imagery of the king's dream was probably allowed to arise from his own fears, apprehensions, and experience. Such great statues, wrought in all manner of material, stood in his courts. It was easy for him to imagine himself the exalted head, priceless and uplifted. And such was the meaning borne by the head of gold. The vast and ill-knit empire provided the rest of his dream material. It sprawled across the Middle East, its many parts cast together by conquest and with small coherence. To fit the subsequent details to any known patterns of history is a precarious process and need not detain us. It is the insight into the royal mind which makes the interest of the dream—this self-image of a colossus, most precariously standing.

313 : Royal Rage

Daniel 3

'You will be like God' was part of the first temptation, and it has always been the last folly and corruption of man to set himself in the place of God. The Pharaohs of Egypt and the Emperors of Rome indulged this blasphemy, either in the arrogance of self-delusion or in the harshness of tyranny and its cynical statecraft. The virus of such absurd but perilous evil has not been purged from the spirit of man, as the exaltation of political leaders in our own age has grimly demonstrated. Pride is a basic ingredient in all sin, and Nebuchadnezzar in this story shows sinful pride in its ultimate folly.

There are few spurs to anger sharper than wounded pride. In perpetual fear of all independence, and more and more in need of proof of men's servility and obedience, the king was wild with rage at the report of the Jews' refusal to worship. The sight was absurd, but fraught with danger. Human life meant nothing to the tyrant of Babylon. Perhaps hostile elements in Babylon saw with jealousy the rise to influence, and perhaps affluence of groups of intelligent Jews, and sought to stir the royal wrath against them. This was to happen in Esther's day. It happened in Rome in A.D. 64 when Nero rose to kill the Christians.

That violence and ungovernable excess which were the mark of the king's corrupted character are evident in this story. His very face was ravaged and distorted by rage as he cast his former favourites down and condemned them to a horrible death. God intervened and they were preserved. On many other occasions He has not intervened and evil has had its way. There is inexplicable sovereignty in such intervention.

Observe now the wild excesses to which the proud arrogance of the man was prone. He decreed horrible punishment for all who should refuse worship to the God of Daniel. God requires no such worship, nor seeks such champions as the passionate king. Those who bring others to His feet must do so with persuasion of word and deed. Those who come must come with understanding, with willingness, with humility and surrender. Man's patronage of God must be ultimate irony.

314 : Messenger of Truth

Daniel 4.1–27; Ezekiel 2.3–10

The dream again reveals the man, and shows the unseen stresses and strains which led to his mental catastrophe. The king of Babylon was haunted by many fears. His will was supreme, but he lived in daily apprehension of a challenge to it. Hence his wild wrath when any man thwarted him. Hence, too, his need to reassure himself by the visible worship of the multitudes. No man violates divine law without producing tension in the mind, and it is not the will of God that one man should hold millions in his power, and deal out capriciously life and death, reward and disaster. Such might usurps the power of God, feeds ruinous pride, and perverts the personality. The king, too, was not without some knowledge of God. His accession prayer is extant. It shows understanding of spiritual things. Hence the tangle in his soul, and the deep, hidden layer of self-distrust in his mind, a fear of a fall which he strove desperately to hide. It was of such concealed terrors that his dream was made. It was built out of the stuff of life. Nor is this to say that it was not implanted of God. God was to send judgement on the despot, but chose to warn him, for it was not His purpose at this time to destroy the kingdom.

Daniel was aghast at what he saw to be the meaning of the king's dream. He knew the wild passions of the man with whom he had to deal, and might very naturally have felt daunted at the duty of speaking the truth which he saw before him. And yet he also saw reason in the warning. All power was to pass from the king for full seven years, long enough to bring ruin on Babylon, and on the people of Daniel, who lay under the shadow of 'the great tree'. Giving warning, it might be possible so to dispose of the essentials of power and government that order might survive the loss of the absolute authority which ruled the land. Daniel therefore spoke up, and spoke the truth. It was said of Samuel that he delivered faithfully the message of God. Whatever the consequences, however sinister the peril, the man who is entrusted with the truth of God dare do no less than boldly proclaim it. Only thus, as was said to Ezekiel, is the truth faithfully proclaimed and the herald vindicated.

315 : Mad King

Daniel 4.28–37

Few men have held wider power than Nebuchadnezzar of Babylon. It was no idle boast he made one evening on his palace roof when he looked across the greatest city of the ancient world and cried: 'Is not this great Babylon, which I have built by my mighty power . . . ?' It is a fact that half the bricks in the mighty ruins by the Euphrates are stamped with his name. He had the building mania of all such despotic characters. And from the summit of his pride and self-exaltation he tumbled and touched the very bedrock of despair. He rushed to the palace lawns and tore grass with his teeth, imagining himself to be an ox.

This great conqueror and megalomaniac, demanding divine honours, was also a man prone to piety. It is, psychologically, a very likely personality which we thus can see. Further, such types are subject to the mental malady of melancholia. The sufferers plunge from self-exaltation to despair, are vague about their identity, humiliate and torture themselves, and often, strangely enough, recover suddenly with complete memory of their mental sufferings. It is a disease of high places. Richelieu, mighty minister of Louis XIII of France, imagined on occasion that he was a horse. It is also a disease of the basically pious. Richelieu, for all the corruption of his religion, was a cardinal of the Church. Nebuchadnezzar set high store by divine things. Often, too, religion clears such clouded minds. It saved the king of Babylon.

Authorities on mental disorder say that this is a commonly observed phenomenon. One says: 'The king's remembrance of the circumstances of his degradation is not remarkable. Patients are often able to tell what was their mental state prior to their madness and some are able to describe the whole course of their delusions.' Nebuchadnezzar knew that wild self-exaltation had dethroned his reason and thereafter was a better man. His madness had been purgatorial. Again, madness was looked upon as a visitation from God. The throne would be waiting for the restored king, protected during his lunacy by the awe which in those times always attached itself to the mentally deranged. The exact picture impresses with a sense of its historical reality.

316 : Belshazzar

Daniel 5

This superbly written chapter tells the tale of a dissolute royal feast and a scene of uncanny judgement. It was October, 539 B.C. Whose fingers did they see writing on the plaster of the wall those cryptic words which Daniel interpreted? Did each carnal banqueter see his own hand-writing, that characteristic crook of thumb and forefinger, that intimate trick of the stilus which each man and woman knew? Men do write their own doom, and Babylon was dying of no obscure disease that night. It was passing because the sin of men, as the Hebrew prophets saw, had sapped its life. It was passing with the evil of its king. Belshazzar had seen Nebuchadnezzar judged for his mad pride and had seen insanity fall upon him. He had seen the wisdom of Daniel applied in the councils of state, but now Daniel was forgotten, and blasphemy reigned in the palace halls. He was beyond excuse . . .

' To the vast mound of Babylon,' wrote Layard, one of the first modern travellers to visit the site, 'succeed long undulating heaps of bricks and pottery. Other shapeless heaps of rubbish cover for many an acre the face of the land. On all sides fragments of glass, marble and inscribed brick are mingled with that peculiar nitrous and blanched soil, which, bred from the remains of ancient habitations, destroys vegetation and renders the site of Babylon a naked and hideous waste. Owls start from the scanty thickets, and the foul jackal skulks through the furrows.'

'And Babylon,' wrote Isaiah, almost two centuries earlier, 'the glory of kingdoms, the splendour and pride of the Chaldeans, will be like Sodom and Gomorrah when God overthrew them. It will never be inhabited, or dwelt in for all generations; no Arab will pitch his tent there . . . But wild beasts will lie down there, and its houses will be full of howling creatures . . . hyenas will cry in its towers, and jackals in the pleasant palaces . . .' (Isa. 13.19–22). How aptly the descriptions tally!

Daniel, the magnificent figure of that night of doom, survived. As his nation, set amid the clashing empires, survived them all, so the Hebrew prisoner of Babylon bridged the eras of Babylon. No compromise preserved his life. There were lesser Jews, like Esther and Mordecai of a later year, who came to terms with the pagan environment, and bought life at too dear a cost. Daniel was of the ancestry of Nehemiah and Ezra, in whose hands the future of all history lay. The future lay not even with the Medes and Persians, who at that moment were turning aside the river, and making a road through the walls of Babylon.

317 : Man of God

Daniel 6

Verse 5 is the most magnificent tribute a man can win. If a hostile, jealous, watching world can discover nothing against a man save his devotion to his God, that man is truly Christlike. The Lord Himself, alone of men, could look with steady eyes at His foes and ask, 'Which of you convicts me of sin?' No mortal being can put such a challenge into words; but if life can be so nobly lived that the world has to admit that it cannot point its scornful finger at conduct and character, then

369

something of Christ's glory has found reflection in the testimony. Every sphere of life—business, sport, social intercourse, political activity—is related to our witness for the Lord. In all these places the Christian is watched critically and appraisingly, his deeds measured against his profession, his words weighed. To pass a scrutiny so searching, sometimes so unjust, often malign, is a task for care, diligence, forbearance, patience, self-control, complete humility, and, above all, 'watching unto prayer' . . .

No nation, no man, has a monopoly of folly. The human race is one in its acquaintance with sin. In the experience of all centuries and all nations, we are brothers under the skin. We have seen the megalomania and the insane pride of Nebuchadnezzar. We shall meet the vicious Ahasuerus. Darius was the victim of the same corruption. 'Power corrupts,' in Lord Acton's well-known saying, 'and absolute power corrupts absolutely.' We have had illustrations enough in this century. As we read this story we are made aware of two miracles. Daniel survived his awful ordeal by the mercy of One who 'stopped the mouths of lions,' as another Jew of the Dispersion wrote six centuries later (Heb. 11.33). But the favour and standing he held in the eyes of the capricious, cruel monarch was a miracle as great. God sometimes provides His children with such aid, and causes the pagan world to serve Him. There is no pattern by which such mercy may be measured. Too often hatred and the lions have had their way, and death has been permitted by One who must view death with other eyes than ours. At other times His hand thrusts evil back, and that may most justly be our prayer.

318 : Daniel the Prophet

Daniel 9.1–19; 10.1–14

There is nothing more natural than that the fall of the Babylonian Empire should turn Daniel to the searching of the Scriptures for the significance of historical events. The Book of the Revelation has come into its own again in many lands in these apocalyptic days. And note that the study of Scripture inevitably turns the devout mind to prayer. Daniel's prayer holds a solemn place in the collection of the great prayers of the Bible. It is alive and aglow with the fire of genuine repentance, assured faith, and intense petition. Like Jeremiah, Daniel, as we have seen, reveals Christlike features. He was not blameworthy in the backslidings of Israel. He had kept the faith in all perils, and at all costs. And yet, vicariously, he took the sins of his people upon himself, and suffered for them. The prayer is full of Scripture, as are always the prayers of those who have lived much with the Word of God. To pray in the words of God is to move close to prevailing prayer. It should be compared, as a devotional exercise, with the prayers of Ezra and Nehemiah. Ezra confesses the sins of his people without asking for forgiveness (Ezra 9.6–15). Nehemiah praises God, but does not cry for pardon (Neh. 1.4–11). Daniel stresses the petition which both of the others omit.

Since it was the third year of Cyrus (10.1) when Daniel had his mystic experience, it is clear that he did not return to Jerusalem with Zerubbabel. There was a ministry to be exercised among the less valiant Jews who had elected to stay in foreign parts. It is well for most people that God does not abandon those of His children who fail to follow as closely as they should. Were there such limits on His care—'how helpless and hopeless we sinners had been!'" Perhaps the theme of Daniel's deep exercise of soul was this very problem. Should he remain in Babylon, doubtless to be misunderstood and criticized by the more zealous? Or should he go, as his heart probably dictated, to aid in the rebuilding of the land and witness? He had remained for a period at his post but, perhaps, as the third year opened a crisis of doubt came to him and, as a devout soul does at such a time, he sought God's will. For three weeks he found no clarity or peace. And then God revealed Himself. Like Moses, Job, Isaiah, and Peter, Daniel's first reaction was to confess to his own unworthiness.

Questions and themes for study and discussion on Studies 311–318

1. Arrogance, pride and mental stability.
2. Christians and high office. Is it to be sought?
3. Faith and healing of the mind.
4. With whom does the future of history lie today?

5. Is there any 'writing on the wall' today?
6. 'Dare to be a Daniel.'
7. How are we 'weighed in the balances'? Against what?
8. How does the world try to change our names?
9. What basic elements of prayer can you distinguish in Daniel's prayer?

319 : Vashti

Esther 1

In Daniel's story of Belshazzar's feast, we met the dignified queen of Babylon, intruding on the scene of debauchery and fear with sane words designed to save her son. Here is the queen of the empire which succeeded Babylon, and a first glimpse of another tyrant on the throne, and new corruption taking Babylon's old path.

If Ahasuerus was Xerxes, we know the madman well. He was the despot who launched the mighty attack on Greece in 480 B.C., and had the Dardanelles branded because its current broke his bridge of boats. This was the invasion which put into European history the brave tale of Thermopylae, with its three hundred Spartans holding the narrow pass, and the battle of Salamis, one of the decisive fights in history, in which Athens and her allies smashed the Persian fleet, and sent the mad king scuttling for home along the death-strewn roads.

His mighty empire lay across the world from the Aegean to the Indus and the Nile. Ahasuerus lived in pomp and glory, fed with flattery by his vicious court, and honoured like a god. This glimpse into that court's evil life shows the corrupted king feasting his base lords, like Belshazzar before him. The eastern world lay in his hands, with vast problems of defence and organization, but here was the most powerful ruler of the day boasting of his wife's beauty, and bidding her make a public display of her person before the revelling men.

Why did Vashti refuse to do so? It was mortally dangerous to defy the order of the brutal king. It seems that she was a noble woman who prized her modesty and self-respect above her royal estate. Moral courage is a rare virtue in this cowardly world, and it requires courage of the first order to set in the balances those qualities of uprightness, integrity and loyalty to the highest against the advantages which men prize—position, status, comfort, wealth and the adulation of the world.

On the other hand, Vashti, entertaining the women in another banqueting hall, may have defied her royal lord in an act of drunken bravado, stimulated by the revelling crowd of women who enjoyed vicariously the taste of female revolt.

But in all history there seems no example of a virtuous court where monarchy is absolute. Power always plays its ancient and corrupting part. Evil cannot be confined, and tyrants corrupt their environment.

320 : Myrtle and Mordecai

Esther 2

Here indeed is a sight for sorrow. The purpose of this vivid book is to show a picture of one section of the Jewish Dispersion. We do not meet them again until the Acts of the Apostles. Nehemiah, Ezra, and Daniel show us another group. Myrtle, the Jewish girl ('Hadassah' [7] has this meaning), was brought up by her shrewd cousin Mordecai. He had provided himself with a pagan name based apparently on that of the god Marduk. It is true that all Jews of the Dispersion took Gentile names; Saul, for example, became Paul, but Jews seldom compromised thus with paganism. Esther's Gentile name appears to exalt the goddess Ishtar. Hence the comment at the beginning of this paragraph. Mordecai succeeded in his ambitions. His cousin was a notable social triumph. Contrary to all Jewish law, she married the heathen king, and Mordecai had his ally in the palace.

Esther is commonly lauded as a heroine of Scripture, and there is no doubting the courage of the Jewish girl, so lamentably married to the megalomaniac who decimated his own empire, and wasted its resources in the mass attack on Europe. A woman so strong was hardly the passive tool of her designing guardian. She should have been able, in the tight community of the Jews, to escape the notice of the king's girl-hunters. The entry of Esther into this disgraceful beauty contest was deliberate. She must have known that union with a pagan was contrary to the code of her people, but here were Jews who sought an accommodation with their environment. Without comment, this vivid book tells the story. Significantly, it avoids all mention of the name of God. The Jews noted this, and Jews of Alexandria, not unlike those who were happy in Susa, invented additions to the story, which include the divine name. The passages may be read in the Septuagint, the Greek version of the Scriptures which the Jews of Alexandria prepared, to astonish their pagan hosts.

The date, contrary to Ussher's guess, could have been 479 B.C. Note 1.3 and 2.16. There is a gap of four years. Could this have been the time during which the Shah was pre-occupied with the preparations for his vast assault on Greece, his march, disaster and retreat? It is not unlikely. So it was a badly shaken, as well as a viciously pagan, husband that Esther found, having successfully, on Mordecai's advice, concealed the facts of her nationality (2.10).

321 : Haman

Esther 3

Haman took his cue from his base royal master. He found Mordecai insolent, and in revenge sought to destroy all the people of Mordecai—genocide for offended dignity. Ahasuerus with a wave of the hand gave him permission to commit this immense crime, and to confiscate a people's goods (11). The king, as Herodotus, the Greek historian, described him, was half-insane in his cocoon of absolute sovereignty, and perhaps at the time was mentally exhausted after his retreat from Greece. He was the king of whom Byron wrote:

> *A king sate on the rocky brow*
> *Which looks o'er sea-born Salamis;*
> *And ships, by thousands, lay below,*
>
> *And men in nations; all were his!*
> *He counted them at break of day—*
> *And when the sun set, where were they?*

The poet referred to the hill west of Athens where the Persian king sat enthroned to watch his fleet in the strait below destroy the Athenians. He saw instead irremediable disaster. His eyes, after that campaign, had ceased to count the toll of dead. What was the massacre of a scattered nation?

But look at the Jew in the royal court. He is a strange sight. There was an element of independence in Mordecai, or perhaps he merely presumed upon his connection with the new queen. His motive for his dangerous act of defiance is difficult to understand on any supposition. It imperilled the Jews unnecessarily, and having gone so far as to seek small service in the palace, and to introduce his ward to the royal harem, it might be supposed that Mordecai had accepted all subservience. But, from whatever motive it was, Mordecai clung to this shred of dignity or obstinacy. He could hardly have calculated the sequence of events which fill the rest of his story.

Haman, at the moment, had the despot's ear, and perhaps he had more motives than resentment against the surly Mordecai. The Jews were obviously rich, and loot was a temptation. This is the first indication in literature of the Jew in that role of moneyman into which Gentile persecution has so often forced an agricultural and pastoral people. Confiscation and pogrom against that shrewd and able people have often resulted, and medieval England was as guilty as ancient Persia in this regard. Haman had many successors.

322 : Mordecai

Esther 4

Mordecai was directly responsible for the grim catastrophe which was about to fall on the Jews of Persia. It is a fact of life that our ill deeds cannot be isolated and contained Mordecai should not have been in the exposed position into which his scheming life had led him. He should not have been in confrontation with the vizier Haman. Finding himself in that position, he could at least have conducted himself with discretion. But the whole lamentable situation arose from materialism, the base quest for gain, and activities unworthy of a man of God. His informer's deed (2.21–23) may or may not have done good. Bigthan and Teresh might well have had good reason to strike down the beastly creature who ruled Persia, but to Mordecai they were, for good or ill, two expendable pawns in a game of self-seeking. In the outcome, whether Mordecai did right or wrong in exposing the details of the plot to the king, the service was forgotten, probably during the preoccupations of the war with distant Greece. In the providence of God, whatever Mordecai's immediate motives may have been, the service he rendered became the event God used to save His errant people. The fact that it was thus, in mercy, fitted into a divine overruling, in no way adds sanctity to the life or conduct of Mordecai.

In the face of ugly peril, Mordecai was shrill in his lamentations, and turned to Esther with the nearest expression of a living faith he ever manifested. Esther, he opined, putting a common saying into the world's stock, might have attained to royalty precisely for this purpose. One can imagine with what a rich voice of faith in God, and reverence for His name, Daniel, or Joseph, or Nehemiah, those other Jewish denizens of pagan courts, might have more worthily expressed the same truth. And note with what words Mordecai feels compelled to bracket his appeal. He had no evidence that his ward would be anything other than the brave woman he must have known her to be, but he reminds her that the royal harem is no refuge. Esther made no reproach. She should not have been queen, but, being queen, she acted like a queen. It was not in God's purposes that unbridled wickedness should destroy a remnant of His people, comfortable in a pagan environment though they had become. Esther had courage, and that courage He used.

323 : Esther, the King, and the Vizier

Esther 5 and 6

Under the base despotism of Persia, to enter the royal presence unbidden was contrary to law. In Athens, still moving on joyously in the enthusiasm of the Greek victory over Persia, liberty was taking shape in this century among men.

In Ahasuerus' court the evils of tyranny still sat enthroned, and it was peril for the queen herself to enter the audience chamber without a summons. The abominable man upon the dais held his sceptre towards her to signify that her life was spared. Esther was a courageous woman, the forerunner of multitudes who have faced peril in the ghetto for their people. She had also learned some other lessons well. She controlled features and voice, and hid with consummate art her ultimate purpose against Haman. The favourite was quite deceived. He merits little pity, as the sequel shows. His whole spirit was eaten up with his hatred for Mordecai. His wife, too, shared his vices. Hers was the cruel suggestion that now was the hour to glut his vengeance. The Greeks feared a vice which they called *hybris,* that overweening arrogance and self-esteem which go before a fall. Haman was a notable illustration. Pride corrupts the judgement. His mind bent by his own self-esteem, the vizier was in no condition to answer wisely. The twin vices of jealousy and arrogance perverted reason, and with poetic justice brought the wretched man to humiliation. Thought can move in a straight, clean line only when the heart is pure. Vice deflects true judgement from its path, distorts the vision of the goal, and betrays the one who tolerates it. 'You seek honour from one another', said the Lord in a penetrating word, 'therefore you *cannot* believe' (John 5.44). Faith, He meant, is inhibited by pride. The first requirement of those who seek God is self-abandonment and humility. Lacking these, a man lacks all. Pride is a jealous and consuming demon which eats up the whole personality, drags into its orbit of control all activity, all thought, leaving no room for cleaner, nobler, living.

Haman is a pitiable spectacle of human ruin. The king is no better. Awake at night, he feeds his pride on the records of his reign, and so finds out about Mordecai.

324 : Esther Triumphant

Esther 7 and 8

The terrible drama in the vicious court is running inexorably to its conclusion. With consummate self-control Esther held her peace throughout the first day's feasting. Then, on the second day, at the so-called 'banquet of wine', Ahasuerus, like Herod on a similar occasion five centuries later (Mark 6.22 f.), made his customary offer of beneficence.

Esther, who had betrayed no sign of excitement or emotion to this point of time, chose the precise, deadly moment to speak. It is terrible to think what must have been the childhood and youth of a young woman who could have learned such stern self-mastery. Esther was brought up in a school of suffering. Her teachers were the cruel circumstances of a harsh and pitiless pagan environment which had taught her to maintain silence against all provocation, to read the mind of an enemy, to bide her time, and betray her motives and purpose to none, to understand vicious men and use them. Such powers served her and her people well, but a better environment could have been found for the education of a girl in the toil and poverty of far Jerusalem. Haman fell into the snare which he had prepared for others. Judgement sometimes works that way.

Mordecai had won notable success. And yet he is surely a sight for sorrow in the rich livery of the vicious king, 'with a great golden crown' (15) on his head. There are some honours which are not worth winning, and commendation which is base reproach. 'What have I done wrong,' Socrates once remarked, 'that this wicked man should speak well of me?' It is even more sad to see the brave Esther point her appeal with reference to her place in the king's regard—'If I have found favour in your sight, O King . . .' The reversal of the savage royal decree was as irresponsible as its original proclamation had been. Just as the Jews were to be pitilessly massacred, so now were they free to wreak pitiless vengeance on the Persian and other subjects of the tyrant. Human life counted for nothing in his eyes. This is where the sinful human heart ends. All love dies, all mercy. All pity withers in the godless life. All love, all mercy, all pity, wherever they are found, are of God, When God is banished these qualities fade, as our own times can witness equally with Esther's century.

325 : Esther and Mordecai Triumphant

Esther 9

This is a chapter which any student of the men and women of the Bible would gladly pass over. Esther, in the passion of her revenge, is a hideous spectacle. Haman's ten sons die with their father, and in a second day of massacre the berserk Jews soaked the land in the blood of their enemies. The embittered and the persecuted, who lose touch with God, can fall victim to strange evils of the mind.

If Esther was the Amestris of secular history, the curious can see her similarly at work in another situation of savage revenge. The context is uncannily the same, an offence given, a royal banquet, a mad Herod-like promise to give the gift required, and sadistic vengeance. The hideous tale of how Amestris gained control of her sister-in-law, and horribly mutilated her, causing in the process, the death of the king's brother Masistes, is told boldly in Book 9 of Herodotus, 109–113 (Sir Henry Rawlinson's translation, Everyman's *Herodotus*, pp. 323-325). The human mind is safe only when it lies in the blessed control of the One in whose image it was first made. Shake off that control, and the beast takes over.

But turn the picture round. Forget for a moment the un-edifying picture of Esther presiding at a banquet of mass murder, and the contemptible Mordecai, with his dearly bought eminence, faithfully serving one of the most evil men of his day, and see where Haman's mad lust for power had led him. The eighty-three foot high gallows stood as a symbol of judgement upon him. We have noted before, the situation which the Greek, Aristotle, regarded as the very stuff of tragic drama, and which he called *'peripeteia'*. It is sometimes Anglicized into 'peripety', and means that reversal of fortune which comes when those measures men take for their own advantage, or to gain some evil end, produce the exact opposite to their intentions, and recoil upon their own heads. It seems part of the operation of the moral law which God has woven into the processes of life. It is another aspect of the truth of Gal. **6**, that 'whatever a man sows, that he will also reap'. What the end of Esther and Mordecai was we do not know, but may be sure that they, too, were not exempt from God's law—in this world and the next.

1. Vashti and the queen of Babylon. Name three other royal women of Scripture to set with them, and two governors' wives. (Clue: Exodus, Kings, Matthew, Mark, Acts.)
2. The mental and moral damages of power.
3. Revenge. Why does hate destroy the personality? What is the safeguard against it?
4. What is 'worldly wisdom'? Has it any place in Christian service?
5. Is the moral law always visible in life? Is justice always done in this life? What is the significance of the Last Judgement?

326 : The Damaged Exiles

Psalm 137; Romans 12.14

It is possible that the strange problem of at least one of the Imprecatory Psalms finds its explanation here. Was Psa. 137 included, under God's overruling, in the Psalter for the same reasons as the Book of Esther—to reveal the mind and fate of those who were crushed, broken and embittered under persecution? Perhaps among the characters of the Bible we should number the group 'by the waters of Babylon'.

The little poem begins gently, showing the exiles meeting, as the exiles did, by the willow-hung river (cf. Acts 16.13). A crowd gathered menacingly around, saw their musical instruments, and called for a song. The tiny band was in no mood for singing to entertain those who had caused their pain. They had no defence save that of 'commination'. There is a Form of Commination, seldom if ever used, in the Anglican Prayer Book, and in an Eastern context such a ritual curse could be the only weapon available in a menacing situation. The psalm is a drama. The first verses show a picture of Jewish worshippers meeting in peace, the gathering of threat and peril, and then, without intervening preamble, the fierce words of denunciation by which they sought to protect their lives from the savage mob, invoking on the

Chaldaean crowd the very horrors which they, or their soldiers, had inflicted in the streets of Jerusalem.

When the distinguished Arabic scholar, Professor E. H. Palmer, was murdered by Arab bandits in Sinai in 1882, he sought to save his life by this very means. He had a deep knowledge of the wild Bedouin, and his friends were shocked to hear that he had solemnly cursed them before he died. In his hands, though finally unavailing, the curse was a formidable weapon of defence. A curse to an Oriental is a solemn and an awful thing. It is loaded with foreboding, lies like lead on a guilty mind, and goes with a criminal like a demon to haunt the silence, fill the night, and sometimes to madden and to kill.

Palmer failed. The pathetic exiles under the willows may, by the same dire means, have saved their lives. But here is light on Esther. She carried into action, thanks to her royal position, the comminations of the exiles of Psa. **137**. Nor was the pogrom of the Jews against the Gentiles an unexampled phenomenon. Such vengeance precipitated minor civil war more than once in the early Roman Empire.

327 : The Anthologist
Psalm 119.1–56

If we carefully comb the later psalms, it seems possible to see some of the Jews of the Exile. Book 5 of the psalms is different from all the rest. One can almost see the working of the mind of the man who put the collection together. He had several small collections to hand, the Egyptian Hallel, as it was called (Pss. **113–118**) and the Great Hallel (Pss. **120–136**). Within these collections lay 'the Songs of Ascent' (Pss. **120–134**). Book 5 of the psalms was by way of being the hymn-book of the second Temple, built after the Exile.

The man who put this collection together, adding to the smaller collections some psalms of David which had not been included in the first four books, but which had meant much to him personally, decided, perhaps, that he would divide the book neatly into two by a collection of his own. Hence the

381

longest of all the psalms—Psa. **119**. At some time in his life, the word of God had meant all to him, and could this have been at any more likely time than during the Exile, when the devout among the troubled Jews, cut off from all the worship and ritual of the Temple, turned with fervour to the Word? If our interpretation is correct, our anthologist collected from all quarters sayings about the Word of God. Some of the mass of sayings he no doubt wrote himself. He arranged them in groups of eight, under all the twenty-two letters of the Hebrew alphabet, to make it simpler to memorize them. He arranged them round certain central thoughts, or developing processes of thought, and it is a study of some delicacy to read Psa. **119** until the patterns of its thought become real and meaningful.

In the same process we get to know the anthologist. It is fairly clear that he was the author of Psa. **1**, and so must have been the senior rabbi in charge of the collection and ordering of the Psalter. The putting together, in reverence, of the ancient Scriptures which had meant so much to them in the days of exile must have been an immediate and absorbing task, when the nation began its new struggle to rebuild in the shattered homeland. Their work has not been studied closely enough to discover the reasons for their groupings, the patterns of thought, the relation of that thought to possible experience. Here at any rate we have one of the men involved. We shall spend another day in trying to see him.

328 : The Anthologist Again

Psalm 119.57–96

Taking parts, portions, verses of the collector's mass of sayings about the Word, we may make some guesses about him and the experiences he had endured. Imagination, to be sure, but imagination under some rigour of discipline can be a pathway to better understanding!

Look closely at this long psalm. The collector of the choice sayings had known persecution (22, 23); he had suffered under the heavy or the ruthless hand of authority (61, 69). Was this in Babylon, or in Babylon's successor in despotism, that of Persia? Under the burden of it all his faith had staggered (6, 22, 31), and there was such pressure to give in and conform, such pressure as Daniel and his friends must have known (36, 37). As Mordecai has revealed to us, in material things, the great empire and its affluent cities offered tempting advantages to the covetous. The Jews were a clever people, and it is obvious that the ruins of Jerusalem and their downtrodden land were not attractive to the worldly-minded. But our anthologist, busy collecting his book of sayings, was a true man, and he was grieved that he should be so tempted. His own wavering concerned him.

His long psalm is a fascinating study. He was very preoccupied with happiness, and he made this his theme in Psa. 1 if the assumption that he wrote it is correct. Observe his first eight verses. Verses 1 and 2 speak of true happiness; vs. 3 and 4 attach happiness to steadfastness; but such is life, that they only can be steadfast who are healthily aware of the danger of falling (5, 6). And that danger is diminished by remembering the life's once-for-all committal (7, 8), and one's vows to the Most High.

The third section (gimel) seems curiously autobiographical. The anthologist had known deprivation and fear for his life (17), the dryness of soul which finds no beauty in the Word (18), loneliness and rejection (19), stress and tension ('My soul yearns all the time for thee to intervene'—Moffatt, 20). He sees hope glimmer in answer to his prayer (21), and claims the rewards of steadfastness—he has 'kept the faith' (22), even in the face of powerful contempt (23), for where else is guidance (24)?

329 : Man of Obedience

Psalm 119.97–152

The 'whole heart' is a preoccupation with the Jew we seek to know (e.g. 34, 58, 69, 145). We know that all good lightly held can slip out of the hands. He was aware that halfhearted virtue is soon no virtue at all. He was conscious that what God called for was the dedication of the whole personality. Truth must be held 'in the inward being' (Psa. 51.6) to be held at all, and all thought, speech, conduct was ultimately determined by that which dwells in the core of the personality.

He knew, too, that the fundamental virtue was obedience— the obverse of the fundamental sin, pride, which involves disobedience, the assertion of the self, the human will, against God. How basic is the lesson the anthologist had learned as he studied the Word 'by the waters of Babylon'! Obedience is the theme of the whole Bible, and a determinant factor in personality after personality of the scores we have studied during these two years. Look at Matt. 7.21, Rom. 5.21—6.2. And consider the very opening scene of the Bible in Eden.

'The first law that ever God gave to man', said the French essayist, Michel Montaigne, four centuries ago, 'was the law of obedience. It was a commandment pure and simple, wherein man had nothing to enquire after or dispute, for-asmuch as to obey is the proper office of a rational soul acknowledging a heavenly superior and benefactor.' And it was another Frenchman, a century later, the great preacher, Jacques Bossuet, who remarked simply: 'Thirty years of our Lord's life are hidden in those words of the Gospel— "He was subject to them".'

Pick verses from the psalm supporting this. The anthologist had learned a deep and basic truth, that, contrary to common opinion, command is anxiety, and obedience is peace, and that obedience to truth revealed to us is the royal and certain path to the understanding of wider truth which lies beyond the horizon of the mind. After all, if God be the end and object of our obedience, is obedience anything more than submission of the helpless soul to Love, Wisdom and Strength? That is why the anthologist came back to Jerusalem when Ezra and Nehemiah showed the way. That great move-ment will soon be our theme.

330 : The Happy Man

Psalm 1; 119.153–176

Psa. 1 is probably the last psalm to be written in the whole Psalter. It is designed to introduce the whole book, which begins, like the ministry of Christ, with defining the truly happy man. This is a preoccupation of the writer, but it is the ideal and abstract character who will be in our thoughts in this study, and we have little to do but reconstruct, in more modern language, the picture.

But take a last look at the author. He revered the Word, and knew that the task he now undertook was to introduce a book of that Word, a song-book of God's people. Hebrew poetry was based on parallelism of ideas and the writer was a poet. But how he now extended himself and poured his best gifts into the psalm! The whole psalm is a contrast of good and evil in man, but in the first verse he develops a word pattern of three times three: walks, counsel, wicked; stands, way, sinners; sits, seat, scoffers. And more, not only is the ninefold word-structure ornamental, it is also true to spiritual truth, and reveals the process of backsliding which he had combated in his own experience.

Who is the happy man? Listen to him: 'He is a happy man who never allows his course of life to be dictated by what those think who take no thought of God.' And is it not a fact that true servants of God must resist public opinion, and reject many social trends and thought patterns of their day?

And 'he is a happy man who does not find his chief pleasure in the company of those who care nothing for God's laws.' Finally, 'he is a happy man who does not adopt the way of life of those who hold God in contempt'—but 'who, in his whole manner of life, seeks to do God's will, who finds pleasure in the company of God's people, and who seeks to live as those live who honour Him.'

Such people hold eroding society together, like the trees whose clinging roots hold the crumbling soil of a denuded hill when the freshets of man's greedy devising tear the fertile soil away. Observe the point which Jeremiah adds (17.8)—'reaching its roots to the water.' To be such a child of God calls for a conscious reaching for Him, a constant feeding on His nourishment and strength.

Questions and themes for study and discussion on Studies 326–330

1. What should be the place of the Word in our devotional life?
2. Memorizing Scripture.

3. The nature of true happiness.
4. How well did the writer of Psa. **119** know the rest of the Psalter? Can you discover echoes?
5. Why is obedience important? See Rom. **12.**1 f.
6. Describe 'the heart'.
7. 'To be happy is not the purpose of our lives, but to deserve happiness' (Fichte).

331 : Cyrus the King

Ezra 1.1–2.2, 61–70

Cyrus is a name only in Scripture, but he is known in secular history especially among the Greeks. The dramatist Aeschylus speaks of him with reverence, Herodotus tells of his contacts with the West in his Third Book, and Xenophon uses him as an idealized figure in a treatise on education. In Ezra, Cyrus appears as the author of the decree of liberation which restored the Jews to their native land and permitted the restoration of the Temple worship. This was in 538 B.C., one year after Cyrus captured Babylon.

Cyrus was a founder of empire, the Persian Augustus. He was a genius, and a humane man. It is only characters remarkable in their own right who are idealized, and made a theme of anecdote and legend, as Cyrus was by both Jew and Greek. It was part of Cyrus' wisdom to dismantle the megalomaniac schemes of Nebuchadnezzar's Babylon. He saw both the folly of retaining against their will in the heartland of empire restless minorities, who could only form pabulum and raw material for disaffection, and the parallel advantage of re-establishing on the frontiers of his empire loyal communities indebted to him for their restoration and revival.

These sound political reasons formed sufficient motive for Cyrus, quite apart from any sympathy with the Jews' monotheism, which no doubt appealed to the Persians' view of God more immediately than the complicated paganism of the Babylonians. Whatever the motive, the faith of Jeremiah was finding justification. History was not out of control. God was working out His purposes. Jeremiah's vision of the seventy years (**25.**12) was finding accomplishment, and no knowledge by the Persian ruler of those oracles was needed for the wheels of destiny to move.

Cyrus' character is shown in his decree. It is marked by generosity, adequate provision for the very considerable expense involved in reconstituting a centre of worship and nationhood, and by a liberal spirit. No Jew was compelled to return to the shattered homeland. Many did not. A third generation was growing up in a world to which the Jew had become accustomed. The call had to be real, and obedience sacrificial, when Cyrus' decree was promulgated, to stir ancient longings in the hearts of good men (5).

332 : Zerubbabel

Ezra 3 and 4; Psalm 126

The leader of the second Exodus is a figure almost as shadowy as his companion, appropriately enough a second Joshua. It is often our task in these studies to seek a character, a personality, rather in the events with which their lives were twined than in any word-picture of the historian. Indeed, it is probably the matter-of-fact writer of Chronicles who writes much of the Book of Ezra. Observe how the end of one book forms the beginning of the other.

Zerubbabel must have been a noble man. He faced deprivation and sacrifice, for he was of royal blood, son of Shealtiel, grandson of Jehoiachin (Matt. 1.12), and as such likely to be of standing, even in the land of the alien. A considerable caravan went with Zerubbabel, and their number must have included, like Gideon's remnant, the truest of the land.

The Jews sensed some awkwardness over the division between those who stayed behind and those who faced the sacrifice, and, like the Pilgrim Fathers, and more than one group of colonists, returned to toil, sweat, and tears. The Talmud crudely suggests, in one place, that it was the chaff which returned to Jerusalem, while the wheat remained, and it is possible that the pilgrims and their leader faced some opposition from those who stayed by the fleshpots. They may have marched with much misgiving, and much stress of soul. And, as we have seen the Book of Esther teach, God's

387

provident care did not desert those who chose the easier road. After all, the families of Ezra and Nehemiah were among their number, for eighty years slipped by after Zerubbabel before those two patriots marched south.

Picture Zerubbabel, then, as another man who knew how to stand alone. It is one of life's most vital lessons. J. R. Lowell, the nineteenth-century American poet, was right:

> Count me o'er earth's chosen heroes—they were
> souls that stood alone,
> While the men they agonized for hurled the
> contumelious stone;
> Stood serene and down the future saw the golden
> beam incline
> To the side of perfect justice . . . and to God's supreme
> design.

333 : Haggai the Prophet

Ezra 5.1–5; Haggai 1.1–2.9

Haggai, like the other prophet of his day, Zechariah, seems to have been active about 520 B.C. It is a fair guess that both men came back to Judea as children along with Zerubbabel's caravan. There is the ardour of young manhood in Haggai's preaching, for his small book seems no more than excerpts from notable sermons preached to a community whose hands had wearied under the hardships of the restoration. Those early days must have been difficult.

Perhaps an ecstatic memory of early childhood was the sound of mingled joy and weeping (Ezra 3.12, 13), when the first stones and timber of the new Temple were visible. But the building lagged. The people, who had endured much of the rain and the cold in the early days of their return to the devastated land, had now their soundly roofed houses (1.4) and it would be difficult to grudge those settlers and pioneers this small alleviation of the arduous conditions under which they had begun their Judean sojourn. Timber, however, was in short supply, and it was a long, demanding haul to obtain cedar from the Lebanon range (1.8). Haggai was impatient at such reluctance, and seems by the passion of his persuasion to have initiated a new round of Temple-building.

Still he is not satisfied. If any man still lived who could remember the earlier building he must have been a veteran indeed (2.3), but Haggai had a vision in his mind and he left the rulers and his people no rest until they caught the flash of its glory. For the new Temple, in his view, could be the one which the Messiah might see. Perhaps there was a strain of weakness in Zerubbabel, perhaps diplomatically he sought not to stir opposition (Ezra 5.4). They needed Haggai with his future look (2.9), with his exhortation to consider motives (1.5, 7) and look at the heart's faults and hesitations. Perhaps they grew old and needed youth, and, too weary, needed the salutary dash of younger energy. We would gladly know more of Haggai. What we know of him is like a refreshing breeze.

334 : Zechariah the Prophet

Zechariah 3 and 4

Along with Haggai, Zechariah must have come to Jerusalem as a child, together with Zerubbabel's pioneers. How long he prophesied it is impossible to say, but a hint of long life and two separate periods of ministry are indicated by the difference of tone between the first eight chapters and the last six.

The difference has given rise to theories of dual authorship when the perfectly natural explanation may simply be that we have in the prophet's book utterances of his young manhood and of his old age. The first eight chapters emphasize Haggai's theme. Let the people work with a will to secure a glorious destiny. In ch. 2 Zechariah has an Isaian vision of a Jerusalem which not only serves its restored people, but forms a city for the world. Here is ardent youth, dreaming its dreams and laying hold of God. Man does not stand alone. All the synthetic power of the human arm is nothing beside the enablement of God. In this faith, Zechariah puts a word of faith into the language of the Bible (4.6).

Suppose those visions and these utterances are to be dated between 520 and 518 B.C. Then consider world events. The Ionian Greek communities in Asia Minor, in Ephesus, Smyrna,

Sardis and other Greek foundations, were a restless element in the western marches of the sprawling Persian Empire, and in 500 B.C a great revolt of the Ionian cities took place. Athens, just emerging to a foremost place in Greek leadership, intervened, and it was an Athenian expeditionary force which burnt Sardis in 499 B.C. Darius swore revenge, and it was his expedition of 490 B.C. which was broken by the Athenians at Marathon. Then in 480 B.C. the great expedition of Xerxes marched to its disaster at Salamis (Study No. 321).

Zechariah, now almost seventy years old, might have watched these events with absorbing interest. He mentions Greece in 9.13. He might have looked with wondering at the new movement of history. Indeed, he was witnessing the beginning of the historical process which brought Alexander to the East five or six generations later, broke down the partition between East and West, and made a Greek New Testament possible and inevitable . . .

Zechariah, in person, eludes us, but here is a picture of a man's activity for God in the spring and autumn of his life, a visionary who saw the need of the day for witness and activity, and who saw vast mysterious horizons widen as his sun went down.

335 : Ezra the Scribe

Ezra 7

Some sixty years had passed since the events of the last chapter. It is simply 'after these things' that the events of Ezra's remarkable ministry took place. Some of the personalities of this period, as we have seen, are difficult to know. They are names, men hidden in their message, or passed over by the hasty chronicler; passing shadows on the stage.

Not so Ezra. It may be assumed that he was in some sort of official position in the Persian state organization. Daniel is an example of the high office an alien could occupy in that system, and Ezra may have been a commissioner for Jewish affairs in an empire accustomed to the government of subject peoples. Nehemiah's appointment was a further illustration. To read the letter of commission given by Artaxerxes to Ezra is to gain some insight into his standing with the Shah. The document was fairly obviously prepared and written by Ezra himself, and presented to the monarch for scrutiny and signature. The whole situation presupposes a man of worth and ability of no common order.

Ezra was a member of a family which had remained in Persia, but he represents a Jew of a far different order from the self-seeking Mordecai. He is clearly a man who had resisted integration. And more than that: realizing, like the writer we have imagined for Psa. 119, that the one strong bond of nationhood for Jewry was the corpus of their sacred Scriptures, Ezra made himself responsible for the promotion, the promulgation and the preservation of the Law. He was for this reason known as Ezra the Scribe. Ezra had 'set his heart' (10) to this task. The phrase implies an involvement of his whole personality, a complete recognition of the priority of the project. The anthologist of Psa. 119 was fond of the phrase 'with the whole heart'—could he have learned it of Ezra?

Note the two final verses of the chapter with the beautiful prayer and the final testimony. Strength, as Zechariah pointed out, comes not from man's devising, but from the enablement of God's Spirit. This was the source from which Ezra, faced with a daunting responsibility, drew the calm and poise which gave him courage. It is a blessed experience to feel the touch of 'the hand of the Lord'. Ezra was fond of the phrase (7.9; 8.18, 22).

336 : Ezra's Courage

Ezra 8

Verse 22 is one of the great verses of Scripture. Note the engaging frankness of Ezra. He valued his testimony, and had spoken bravely of his God before the Persian king. Now came the test. Hundreds of miles of bandit-ridden desert lay between the royal capital and far Jerusalem. The caravan was immensely rich with the treasures it carried. It was heavily encumbered with goods and non-combatants. Ezra was 'ashamed' to ask for an escort of armed men.

Courage is not bravado. It consists, not in blindly over-looking danger, but in seeing it and conquering it. True courage is cool and calm, and the bravest act when courage is challenged is to act as if courage is unruffled. Conscience is the root of all true courage, and conscience was rooted deep in Ezra. It lay at the foundation of his firm resolve. To feel no fear can be stupid. It may be irrational also. To dare the danger from which the mind shrinks is true nobility and the test of true worth.

And of true faith . . . There was no presuming upon God in Ezra's faith. Fasting in the ancient Jewish worship was a demonstration of earnestness and purpose. Ezra and his band gave themselves to fasting and to urgent prayer, and God heard them. Dr. Walter Adeney, in his century-old com-mentary on this chapter, concludes with these telling words: 'In an age of rushing activity it is hard to find the hidden springs of strength in their calm retreats. The glare of pub-licity starts us on the wrong track by tempting us to advertise our own excellence instead of abasing ourselves before God. Yet it is as true as ever that no boasted might of man can be comparable to the divine strength which takes possession of those who completely surrender their wills to God.'

Finally, observe in Ezra's lists family names which occurred in the earlier list of those who marched with Zerubbabel. Some of those who refused to go on the first expedition, went on the second—like Bunyan's Christiana and her chil-dren, who set out at last in Pilgrim's footsteps. Example, it is always salutary to remember, can spread its shadow, both for good and ill, over much more than one generation.

337 : Ezra's Zeal

Ezra 9.1–10.17

Ezra's deep emotion and distress over the wide incidence of interracial marriage among the Jews, was no narrow-minded reaction against natural human affection and proper regard for those of another race. There was nothing more important happening in human history at this mid-fifth century than the re-establishment of the Jewish race in its old homeland. There was no greater menace to its role in the coming centuries than the undermining and dilution of its separate witness to God.

Balaam had once taught the foes of Israel that the surest way to break their national strength was to dilute their stock with pagan inter-marriage. Ezra knew his history. He knew the lurking peril which the sex-ridden religions of Canaan held for the people (9.11). Hence his great concern over the developing menace. True, such attitudes can lead to narrow nationalism and corrupting doctrines of racial pride, but in Ezra's hands there was no intention of arrogance. He was simply urgent to keep the revived nation untainted by those influences which had brought spiritual ruin in the past.

Whether it was God's will that the harsh proposal of Shecaniah should be followed, and the alien wives and their children also should be put away, cannot be known. Ezra seems to have assented, and the act was certainly contrary to that prescribed for such mixed marriages in Corinth by Paul five centuries later (1 Cor. 7.12–16). It is sometimes the way of the reformer to drive his zeal too hard. Nor, in the brevity of the chronicler's narrative, and the chronicler seems to have concluded the book, is provision for the proper maintenance of wives and families thus put away, recorded. It is possible that material help and settlement mitigated the apparent inhumanity of the decree of banishment.

There is mention, too, of a time of cold and rain calculated to depress and daunt the spirit of the people. It is a sad sight on which the book closes, and Ezra the Scribe moves out of the page of history. He was a great and good man. Was he also a disappointed man? And did he, in the stress of his zeal, drive a correct policy beyond the frontiers of mercy? Said Addison once: 'Whether zeal or moderation be the point we aim at, let us keep fire out of the one, and frost out of the other.'

Questions and themes for study and discussion on Studies 331–337

1. Is it ever possible to see the hand of God at work in contemporary history? What of our personal lives? Is it only in retrospect that we see God's guiding hand?

393

2. Is it ever pleasant to stand alone?
3. Was the rebuilding of the Temple in Jerusalem significant?
4. What does Zech. **4**.6 mean? What is the place of human toil in God's work?
5. What is meant by the phrase 'the hand of God'? Consult a concordance.
6. Define courage.
7. 'All true zeal for God is a zeal also for love, mercy and goodness.' (Robert E. Thompson, the American economist).

338 : The Cupbearer

Nehemiah 1; Matthew 6.8–13

Nehemiah was a trusted senior servant of Artaxerxes. Hanani, from whom he heard of the lamentable state of Jerusalem, was his brother (**7**.2). It was some thirteen years since Ezra's mission to the city, and local troubles, undisclosed in the record, had sabotaged much of the work of restoration. The ruin described could not date back to the violence of Jeremiah's day. It was local violence, of the sort which haunts the background of this book, which had so triumphed over the work of the brave band who sought to re-establish the state of Judah.

Nehemiah was a man of prayer. His grief drove him to his knees. He addresses 'the God of heaven', a Persian rather than a Hebrew form of address. It was a favourite expression of his (**2**.4, 20). But then he turns for general confession and supplication to the words of Deuteronomy, which were woven with the whole texture of his thought. Catch the spirit of the man in the words of his prayer. He might, in far Susa, conscious of the zeal and sincerity with which he pursued his Jewish faith, have turned from the thought of Jerusalem's woes, with timely texts to prove that all such suffering was judgement on the sins of those who had failed to make the work of restoration good.

Nehemiah adopted no such pious pose. He identified himself with his perplexed and harassed people. If judgement lay upon their sins, it was the sin of all, for all had sinned and 'come short of the glory of God'. How true it is that, in any service where the English Prayer Book is used, it is the words of the General Confession which unite all present in a common bond before God. It was a trait of folly to which Shakespeare made allusion when he coined his phrase, 'one touch of nature makes the whole world kin' (*Troilus and Cressida*, Act 3, Scene 3).

It is interesting to set Nehemiah's moving prayer side by side with the Lord's Prayer. It begins with the exaltation of God, it proceeds to confession, and only then passes in significant order to human need. Nehemiah prepared himself for confrontation with man, realizing his weakness, and resting entirely on enabling grace. It is a model we might well follow in our own prayers—to commit the significant event to God's guiding hand, to prepare our hearts before Him, to clear all impediments from the path of an answer, and to keep our clamant requests until they can assume the right perspective of worship and contrition.

339 : Royal Governor

Nehemiah 2

As he prayed before God, the Shah had been only 'this man' (1.11), but in the formidable presence of the ruler of the greatest empire in the world, Nehemiah was terrified (2.2). He nevertheless told the truth, although the devastation of Jerusalem might have been occasioned by the careless decree which misrepresentation had secured from the king ten years before (Ezra 4.11–23). Note Ezra 4.21, for the saving clause was now invoked.

All seemed well, and Nehemiah received a direct request. He shot a speedy prayer to God (4). It was four months since Nehemiah had first given himself to supplication on this theme. Now was the decisive moment. A man who can thus find God, and pray aright in a flash of time, is a man who has learned well where God may be found. The practice of ejaculatory or wordless prayer is one which should be cultivated. How often are we conscious only of a sense of desperate need, without being able to put words and sentences to the intercession! 'We do not know how to pray worthily as sons of God, but His Spirit within us is actually praying for us in those agonizing longings which never find words' (Rom. **8**.26, Phillips).

Nehemiah, curiously, mentions the queen. Perhaps she had a kindly part in the granting of Nehemiah's large request, and he thus acknowledges her beneficence. 'The good hand of my God was upon me,' he says (8), repeating, like a good disciple, Ezra's phrase (Ezra **7**.28). He set off in royal state, with a military escort (9), unlike Ezra's slow caravan. He came to Jerusalem, and, like the trained courtier that he was, said nothing to those in authority. Sanballat (10) no doubt had his spies in the city, and in the Persian Court a man learned to be wary. Nehemiah needed to know whom he could trust, and as yet he was not sure of many (16).

He was a practical man, nonetheless, and needed a clear idea of the task before him. Hence the night ride round the ruined walls. It must have been a brightly moonlit night, and the tumble of fallen masonry in the white light, and the dark shadows, must have been terrible to see. Only when in full possession of the facts did Nehemiah choose the moment, and tell the city authorities of the power that lay in his hands. Sanballat, the satrap of rival Samaria, was annoyed.

340 : Sanballat Annoyed

Nehemiah 4

Many have been the services of Egypt's sun and its rainless climate. Papyri, filled with records of the past, can lie unspoiled for ever in the dry sand and sunbaked ruins, and archaeologists have recovered them in tens of thousands. Among the most interesting papyrus records recovered are the Aramaic scrolls of Elephantine.

In the days of Persian supremacy over Palestine and Egypt a band of Jewish mercenaries in the Shah's pay garrisoned the south of Egypt at Elephantine, where the great new dam now holds the Nile. They developed a communal life, lived together with their families in a little frontier village, elected a priesthood, and built a temple, where, mixed with crude superstition, and debased by polytheistic ideas, a semblance of the worship of God was maintained. Preserved in the ruins of the high priest's house are records of sacrifices and contributions, and formulae of oath and contract, which show how the isolated community had lost much of the pure worship of Jerusalem. Strained relations with the Egyptian neighbours, due probably to the Jewish practice of animal sacrifice, led to a riot and the destruction of the temple, and some of the papyri contain the correspondence of the priest with the government at Susa in an attempt to secure permission to rebuild. The Jews knew that the royal policy was to favour the Jewish religion, for Nehemiah had already returned; but red tape was plentiful, and bribery and graft were the order of the day. The Jews of Elephantine may have trusted God, but they also, like the wary Nehemiah, believed in 'keeping their powder dry', and the letters show that they left no influential string unpulled. One man, who apparently had the ear of the chiefs in Susa, was one Sinuballit, Governor of Samaria—evidently Sanballat of Nehemiah, and now a very old man. The priest addresses two or three letters to him craving for support. He piously promises that, when the temple is rebuilt, Sinuballit shall be the subject of prayer three times a day, and, much more to the point, he adds: 'The bearer has full instructions regarding the money.'

We thus know why Sanballat hated the neighbouring Governor of Jerusalem. He could not now openly attack, or the king would have speedily removed him. A new decree had armed Nehemiah. He could, however, pin-prick and intrigue, and did so, because he was used to subservience from neighbours, flattering letters and bearers with 'full instructions regarding the money'. Nehemiah was not the sort of man to buy Sanballat's friendship, and Sanballat was annoyed. Archaeology has thrown a vivid gleam of light.

341 : Nehemiah at Work

Nehemiah 5

Chapters 4 and 5 form something of a parable. Building God's walls in this world has always been a task like this. There is always opposition to the work of God. Its commonest form is ridicule (4.1–3) which ranges from the polished sneer of the intellectual to the crude joke of the ignorant. We cannot invoke evil upon such opposition as the beleagured Jews were able to do (4.4, 5). (Read again the remarks on commination in Study No. 326.) We can, however, restore the spirit by prayer. Ridicule hurts, and we should not be human if we were not conscious of its impact.

Besides, there is a task to be done. There is no time to shrink into immobility before petty criticism. Nehemiah's people were filled with a will to work (4.6). The Church needs such folk, but it was the brave example of the leader which set them at their task.

Secondly came opposition by anger, the base resource of those whose ridicule is scorned. There was conspiracy (4.8) from Samaria in the north, Ammon in the east and Ashdod in the south-west. Nevertheless the builders prayed (4.9). Not, however, without discouragement. The sheer daunting mass of the rubbish (4.10) overwhelmed the ancient builders of the new Jerusalem, as it is likely, in a different sense, to discourage the builders of a New Jerusalem today!

Observe Nehemiah's remedy. He called to courage, and to the source of all courage, the active consciousness of the presence and the benediction of the Lord (4.14). He had practised this, found it to operate with blessing in his own life, and passed on to others the secret he had discovered.

With one hand on their swords (4.17) the builders toiled, ready to spring to arms, like the Boston minutemen of two centuries ago, at the clear call (4.18). Trust in the Lord does not preclude proper precautions and sensible care (4.22).

But neither ridicule, nor anger, nor violence is so hard to endure for a leader who bears the burden of a people as sabotage from within (5.8 f.). Note the good man's plea (5.11) for those who weakened the common effort by their inconsistency, to set matters right with God and man, and to dedicate themselves to the task . . . Nehemiah is recognizable to all who have sought with sacrifice and toil to 'build God's walls'.

342 : Nehemiah Wins

Nehemiah 6

Open opposition and the contemptible measures of hate and jealousy had failed to check the building of the walls. Nehemiah had fulfilled the role of a true leader of men—he had infused a sense of purpose into a disappointed and demoralized multitude. He had made them see that the stones which they built into the walls were more than stones, for they were symbols of renascent nationhood. It is the secret of good leadership to infuse meaning into action.

Watchfulness and alertness had won the day over the evil which had mobilized against the small band of Jews. Hence a change from threat of force to fraud, an open confession of defeat. The plot was too obvious. It was an attempt to kidnap the leader. It is not always wise to parley with the opposition. When orders are clear there can be no reason for any process of modification, and Nehemiah had his orders both from God and man.

Sanballat and his petty allies were no match for the courtier trained in the royal court. Failing in the first attempt, the Jews' foes tried threat of slander. Despotic governments are suspicious of separatist movements and personality cults. It was the sort of threat which broke Pontius Pilate. Nehemiah's conscience was clear, and he allowed no such blackmail to undermine his efforts.

The next movement of treachery came nearer to success. The man Shemaiah was a hired spy of Sanballat and Tobiah. His approach was more perilous and more subtle. He magnified the peril of assassination and counselled flight into the walled and defensible precincts of the temple. The retreat would have been a disastrous blow against the morale of the nervous population. Everything depended on the visible presence of the bold leader on the city walls. There is a self-respect which is not of pride but of faith and confidence. Nehemiah had it, and put another immortal word into Scripture (11). With this word we leave him. His story fused with Ezra's in the closing chapters of the book. His first battle for the restoration was won and it was won by faith and strength of character.

343 : The Messenger

Malachi 1 and 2

Among Nehemiah's helpers in the lax conditions which followed the completion of the major fortifications of Jerusalem was Malachi. This little book, which contains some of the most quoted passages in the Old Testament, links with the closing chapter of Nehemiah. The word Malachi means 'my messenger', and it is possible that it is not a proper name at all, but a title, under which an anonymous servant of God hides his identity.

His personality is by no means concealed. The small book is a revealing record of a ministry. It follows dialogue form and may indicate such activity as Socrates carried on in Athens just before this very date, and Paul too when, in imitation of Socratic method, he discussed the faith 'in the market-place daily with them that met him' (Acts 17.17).

'The messenger' points vigorously to the nation's coldness, questioning of God's love, unfaithfulness, and social sin. 'The market-place', or 'the man in the street' is made to answer, protesting innocence, expressing popular scepticism, and questioning the lofty standards set before them. The nation was burdened with ungrateful critics of God's providence, by unfaithful priests, by a loss of the sense of God's holiness, by lip-worship and social sin. In a sort of wide-eyed innocence, shot through with insincerity, the people at large professed inability to see how they fell short of God's claims on their lives (1.7).

Malachi takes them up point by point in strong plain prose, in that firm direct style which marked the post-exilic writers. It is a curious development. In Zephaniah prophetic literature passes into the poetry of apocalypse, of the sort which was to close the New Testament. In Habakkuk we saw the emergence of philosophic wisdom, and in Malachi we see the coming of ordered argument which was known among the Greeks, and which was to form the style of Paul, in the letter to the Roman church.

God's message can clothe itself in many forms, and the everlasting love of God, His fatherhood and holiness, emerge from the pages of Malachi as visibly as they do in Isaiah and Jeremiah. We observe, too, a growing awareness of a non-

Jewish world. Among the heathen, said Malachi, God was at times held in higher honour than among the Jews (1.11). It was the first note of a chord to be struck by Paul. Malachi not only foresaw the coming of Christ, he saw the beginning of the road to a global gospel. True, Isaiah had known some such faith, but it was the Exile which promoted it.

344 : The Remnant

Malachi 3 and 4

Sometimes in these studies we have found it profitable to look at character in the mass and in the abstract. We looked at the sad exiles, their harps on the Euphrates willow-trees, and now we must turn again, in the last chapters of the Old Testament, to the Remnant, the 'seven thousand' of Elijah's day, who did not 'bow the knee to Baal', the 'happy few' who again and again have saved a nation.

Discouragement is infectious, and a disillusioned multitude, talking like those whom Malachi quotes in 3.14, 15, can spread the contagion of their collapsed morale. It is familiar enough talk: 'It is useless to serve God. What gain is it to do His bidding and to walk in penitent garb before the Lord of Hosts? It is the worldly, we find, who are well-off; evildoers prosper. They dare God, and nothing happens to them' (mostly Moffatt).

Such words daunt the timid. In anxious times, under physical stress, in days of danger and adversity, it is easy for the lonely person, or the small harassed group, to feel beaten, and to be silenced by the loud voices of the renegade, the sceptical or the disloyal. Circumstances seem sometimes chillingly to support the faithless, and his loud unbelief.

The remedy is to close the ranks. Perspective is thereby gained and faith and wisdom beneficently pooled. 'What profit is it that we have kept His ordinances?' None, assuredly, if profit is measured by the scales and standards of evil. It is profit beyond measure if we prize our soul's salvation, our fellowship with Christ, and all that our religion means. So those who feared God more than they feared man and the menace of the world around them, came together, and God made a roll of remembrance of those who thought on His name.

A 'name' was a word of wide significance in ancient thought. It implied all that a person was; '. . . who received him, who believed in his name' (John 1.12) simply means, 'those who accepted Him for what He was'. To 'think on His name' means to fix the mind upon what God is, and that is the remedy for shaken confidence and fear. So did Malachi's Remnant, and the chapter ends with two beautiful words about them—they are God's jewels, God's beloved children (3.17). And their stand will in the coming day be vindicated (3.18)—and in the closing verses the book reaches out across four hundred years to the coming of the Lord.

Questions and themes for study and discussion on Studies 338–344

1. The use of the Lord's Prayer in private devotions.
2. Modern Sanballats and our 'building of the walls'.
3. Sabotage within in the building of the Church.
4. Prayer as a resource in mental persecution.
5. Self-confidence, good and bad.
6. Easy-going religion—is it stable, worthy, acceptable?
7. Disillusionment, disloyalty and the Remnant today.

345 : The Simpleton

Proverbs 1 and 7

Proverbs is the inspired record of the distilled wisdom of the Hebrews, their observations on society, the common world of men, and human character. In this collection of sayings, expressions of epigrammatic thought, and precepts based upon them, several clear abstract pictures of typical individuals emerge. They are worth looking at as we conclude the characters of the Old Testament, for men and women do not alter fundamentally over the centuries and from race to race.

The simple person is seen in clearest detail in ch. 7, aimless, drifting into gross temptation in sheer folly, indeed a prime target for evil. A vivid warning picture is given of an almost inevitable encounter in the career of the 'simple' young man.

Enter the designing temptress—and although the Hebrew word-picture sets forth rather the enticement of the male victim by the female designer, the reverse situation is as common and as deadly.

Proverbs makes no excuses for culpable simplicity. There is a man who chooses not to learn. In the first chapter of the book he meets, not a designing woman, but a band of violent and lawless men. It is a vivid picture of an urban situation, a group of delinquents out to rob, and likely to draw into their vicious fellowship some newcomer without moral fortitude who finds himself compromised and led into trouble almost before he is aware of his peril (1.10–16).

Awareness of sin is the safeguard against sin (17), for even a bird does not fall into a trap which it sees being set. The trouble with the simple is a species of mental laziness. They like their thinking to be uncomplicated and unrestricted by principles and the hard rules of a moral code (22). To be upright, the writer urges, a man must think. There is an intellectual element in virtue (14.15 and 22.3 strike this note). A simpleton is wayward out of ignorant rebellion (1.32). Proverbs has no regard for the empty-headed (12.11, 15.21).

Temptation also contains an intellectual element. The victim is outwitted by the agent of sin. Man is a thinking creature and, under God, is expected to use his mental powers, to assess and to take to heart the consequences of wrongdoing, and to avoid the dangerous and the compromising situation. Solomon can be clearly seen behind many of these precepts.

346 : The Fool

Proverbs 2 and 9

The fool is worse than the simpleton. In Proverbs the fool is not a man without high gifts of intelligence, but one who has chosen folly as his way of life. He has no care for wisdom or for truth (14.8). He is a menace in society (17.12; 18.7). He harms others (10.1; 13.20; 17.21, 25; 19.13). He has no sense of proportion (27.3; 29.9). He is impatient of all advice (1.7; 10.8; 12.15; 15.5). Above all, he 'makes a mock of sin' (14.9 AV [KJV]). His kind still live. In this 'permissive' age they multiply. As though the lesson of all history were not the necessity for moral foundations in society, the fool spurns basic standards and the experience of all the ages. He is still a mortal danger, for he is noisy (10.8), expressing opinions on all subjects. He cannot be silenced (11.12). He is deliberately provocative (18.6), and an inveterate talker (29.11 AV [KJV]).

As a social document Proverbs takes us behind the crowded world of politics and religion, which dominate the forefront of the stage in the story of the Old Testament. The characters of Proverbs are the people of the farming community, the village lane, the back street of the city, as well as of the court and the Temple.

The fool and the wise dominate Proverbs, and bring the ancient world very close to us. The terse descriptions and penetrating aphorisms about both make the whole world one. Consider the Arabian proverb: 'A fool may be known by six things: anger without cause; speech without profit; change without progress; inquiry without object; putting trust in a stranger, and mistaking foes for friends.'

Hence the relevance of Proverbs in the conduct of everyday life. A brief phrase of concentrated wisdom can arm the mind with a quick and ready weapon for the sudden and unexpected encounter, and against fools it is well to be armed. 'I am always afraid of a fool,' said Hazlitt, 'one cannot be sure that he is not a knave.' And no man is so wise that he does not need some such arming against himself, for as Aristotle said, 'There is a foolish corner even in the mind of the wise man.' Men of all ages have the same inclinations over which the reason exercises small control. Wherever men are found, there are follies and the same follies, and the greatest of fools is he who imposes upon himself, imagines he knows that of which he is ignorant, and claims authority where he has no right to speak. The most certain mark of the fool, from Solomon's day to ours, is to think that he is always right.

347 : The Sluggard

Proverbs 6 and 26

The scorn for the sluggard, hinged to his bed (26.14), and making the most fantastic excuses to stay there (22.13; 26.13), is a sharp light on the native diligence of the Hebrew people. No one can nail the lazy fellow down to a fixed time. He hates a schedule. He is never punctual (6.9 f.). If it is difficult to get him to begin a project, it is equally difficult to make him continue to the end (12.27). Even his food grows cold (26.15). He avoids all inconvenience. Even a cold day will make him avoid his task of ploughing (20.4). Hence his restless discontent (13.4), his tangled affairs (15.19), and his uselessness in any employment (10.26; 18.9).

The famous passage about the ant (6. 6–8) shows that the lazy fellow is running counter to the whole course of nature. Battle with the adverse forces of the world is part of the human lot, which is shared by the brute creation. A vital difference between the lazy and improvident man and the diligent ant is that the ant needs no prodding (6.7), and by some inner awareness knows the needs of time and season (8). To the sluggard it is 'always afternoon.' No menace looms. Hence sudden disaster. The sharp and irremediable arrival of poverty takes him by surprise. It comes to his door like an unexpected guest, or like some villain springing, weapon in hand, out of an ambush by the roadside (6.11).

In a word, the sluggard serves as a shocking warning to the sensible. Look at 24.30–34. The wise man looks at the weed-ridden field of the fellow who was too warm in bed to get out to the spring ploughing, and observes the lesson of the weeds and tangled growth. He knows that the sluggard is a man just as he is, but a man who has enjoyed his comforts too much and too long, has filled his weakling's mouth with empty excuses, and little by little has slid down to moral and social disaster.

Sloth, no doubt, smothers virtue, lives on deepening mental torpidity and ruins life. Life, in the word's truest sense, is the mark of the Christian, and life carries in its very meaning, the notion of alertness, the energy of the mind, swiftness of action and diligence in business. Nations die of sloth, and sluggards, the slugs of the wider garden, have brought peoples to decay. Man is a worker. If he is not that, he is nothing. Work is the condition of our being, from Eden to Paul (Gen. 3.17 ff.; 2 Thess. 3.11 f.). Proverbs was right. The sluggard is a figure of scorn.

348 : The Scoffer

Proverbs 21 and 22

D. Kidner, in his splendid commentary (Tyndale O.T. Commentaries), points out that the scoffer or scorner makes seventeen appearances in Proverbs, and is most commonly associated with the fool. Again, it is 'mental attitude rather than mental capacity' which classifies the man.

The scoffer, like the fool, abhors correction (9.7 f.; 13.1; 15.12). He is a peril in society, and a source of damage, but it is deeper and more sinister damage than that of the fool. He is the deliberate destroyer of good things (21.24; 22.10). He is dangerous enough to lead whole communities astray (19.25), but good men are usually sufficiently alert to him (24.9). He falls under the direct judgement of God (3.34).

How well we know him! Ridicule, in this artificially sophisticated world, is a common weapon against the Christian, but it is 'the way the Master went'. 'They laughed Him to scorn ... and those that passed by mocked Him and said, He saved others, Himself He cannot save' (cf. Mark 15.29–31; Luke 23.35). Mockery is always 'the fume of little minds', and the scoffer contemptible, whether he be the crude coward who laughs at youth's desire to be upright, or the polished worldling raising the scornful eyebrow at the Christian who refuses to pay the price of joining what C. S. Lewis called 'the inner ring'.

Ridicule through all the ages has become almost a test of truth. There is pain, to be sure, in being laughed at, but the ridiculed of all the centuries are a most distinguished and honourable company. Therefore let it cause no shock, no disappointment, no disillusionment if a clear testimony brings damage to popularity, or brings rejection or loss of this worldly advantage or that.

The scoffer steps out of the pages of Proverbs, a small and familiar figure. He changes his garb with age, status and society. His face remains the same, with the lines of Satan upon it. Watch him march on, and pity him for his folly, for his cowardice, for his jealousy and for all the other acid-laden vices which eat away his mind and heart. He is at odds with himself, playing a petty part. He fears the things which he attempts to scorn. Watch him march on, for he marches to

406

the Judgement Seat, and it will be difficult when 'the books are opened' to find extenuation or excuse for one of the lowest and most loathsome of human sins . . . or, if one can, love him, as Goldsmith's good vicar did. In his church there were 'fools, who came to scoff, who stayed to pray'.

349 : The Friend

Proverbs 17 and 18

In an earlier study (See Study Number 158) we looked at the friendship of David and Jonathan. The picture painted by Proverbs, a line here and a line there, of the real friend, might have been taken from the story of that famous partnership.

Constancy is the prime quality of the friend, for constancy is the complement of all the other virtues. Joseph Addison had that thought in mind when he said: 'Without constancy, there is neither love, friendship nor virtue in the world.' See 17.17 and 18.24. Candour, Proverbs says, is another necessary quality (27.6), but let it be candour with love. One touch of malice, and all friendship is belied. Consider Job's friends. 'If we be honest with ourselves,' said George MacDonald, 'we shall be honest with each other.' At the same time, Paul said: 'Love covers up.' Let a balance be struck.

There are two magnificent sayings about friendship and fruitful fellowship in ch. 27 (9 RSV mg. and 17). Counsel, and the willingness and ability to give wise advice, are the marks of the good and worthy friend. To have a kindred spirit to whom to turn in perplexity and doubt is a rare privilege. And then, as iron sharpens iron, there is the rub and polishing of like with like. This situation presupposes mutual goodness. Set David and Jonathan against Rehoboam and his designing friends. 'Counsel and conversation,' said Clarendon, 'are a second education, which improve all the virtue and correct all the vice of the first, and of nature itself'.

Is it not a fact that a wise man is apt to be diffident about himself and on that account is willing to listen to counsel? The foolish man is full of himself, despises advice and amputates friendship in the same act, seeking counsel only in his fallible self.

407

Tact is the fourth and final mark of a friend. A friend does not outstay his welcome (25.17), display a repugnant heartiness at the wrong time (27.14), or act with unwitting cruelty (25.20). Tact is a fragile and delicate virtue. It comes from goodness of heart and delicacy of taste. The good friend knows the untimely and inappropriate joke (26.18 f.). Tact is everything. It is not a sixth sense, but is the life of all the other five.

Friendship needs guarding. Malice seeks to estrange (16.28). In other words there is a spiritual element which binds and seals and fructifies. We can bless God for the friend of Proverbs if he come our way.

350 : Women

Proverbs 5 and 31

The latter portion of the last chapter of Proverbs is an acrostic, which D. Kidner calls 'an alphabet of wifely excellence'. It is a separate portion in the Septuagint, adding weight to the suggestion that it is a piece by an unknown author, rather than a continuation of the words of Lemuel's mother.

It is a portrait of a lady of means with servants under her and money to invest (16. f.). She is the financial partner of her husband, with duties in the estate and in the city (11–18, 24). She is a tireless person, ready with her charity, and shrewd in her preparations for the future (15, 18, 19, 20, 21, 27). She is nonetheless a kindly, human person, not rendered hard by her business and financial preoccupations (20), a happy, loving mother, and a good wife. She owes her strength to her faith (25, 30), and her dedicated intelligence (28–31).

The portrait of the good woman is a special one. It implies a certain status in society and, as Kidner puts it: '. . . it shows the fullest flowering of domesticity, which is revealed in no petty nor restricted sphere, and its mistress as no cipher. Here is scope for formidable powers and great achievements—the latter partly in the realm of the housewife's own nurture and produce (31) and partly in her unseen contribution to her husband's good name (23).'

The portrait of the bad woman in ch. 5 is much more down to earth, and reflects Proverbs' lofty view of the sanctity of marriage and its opinion of the disrupter of such fidelity. Chapter 7 also speaks of her. The loose woman sells a parody of love. She erodes honour (**5**.9; **6**.33), liberty (**23**.27 f.), possessions (**6**.26; **29**.3), and breathes physical danger (**6**.26–35). To seek life in such a context is to flirt with death (**2**.18 f.). It is to take the smooth path to the grave.

It is refreshing to find this book of Hebrew wisdom so clear and sharp in its understanding of the social and psychological ruin which sexual laxity contains. A nation is measured by the standards of its women. When women such as the blatant and thrusting bad women of this book are active in society, to the corruption of fools and simpletons, disaster is near.

Questions and themes for study and discussion on Studies 345–350

1. How far does intelligence enter into goodness?
2. The right attitude when men scoff at our deepest convictions.
3. The sluggard in modern society.
4. The ideal friend.
5. The ideal woman.

351 : Righteous Job

Job 1.1–5; Psalm 37

The book of Job, with its magnificent poetry and drama, deals with the age-old problem of human pain and unmerited suffering. Its hero is a man outside the Covenant, who was not a Hebrew. Job of Uz was an Arab, and he breaks into Scripture with the suddenness of the good king of Salem, Melchisedek. Like Abraham's friend, Job shows a knowledge of God which is outside the main stream of the Old Testament revelation. The story is told by a great poet of superb dramatic power, and the characters live before us with compelling vividness.

Job was a man of wealth, and since, in his social context, wealth and prosperity suggested the favour of heaven, Job was regarded with veneration. He was the emir of his district, the judge at the city gate. Friendliness and idyllic joy marked his household, and in fine solicitude the good man watched over his family joy, and yearned for their virtue and godliness. Job's children were dear to him, and he wanted his loved ones to know the peace in God that was his.

Job feared the Most High God, and brought offerings of humility to Him. No trace of idolatry or superstition lurks in his simple and reverent faith. He makes no mention of the Hebrew Covenant, and the promises to Moses. Presumably his was a trust born of an earlier revelation, a more ancient tradition. And from such high belief flowed character as noble and as good. Four qualities distinguish him (1.1), and together they form a picture of worth and piety without flaw or blemish. Towards man, Job was upright and beyond reproach, towards God Almighty, reverent, obedient, grateful and of unsullied virtue. An honoured chief, he ruled in wisdom and in righteousness, and was known by reputation to a wider circle than his own immediate tribal environment.

Job lived in a sort of dream world, in which the knowledge of God, for which the writer of Psa. 37 bids the puzzled child of God wait in patient trust, had seemed to come in automatic simplicity. All was well with Job's tranquil heart, and all was well around him. True, the faith of Psa. 37 was the faith of Job, but it had never been tested by disaster. It had appeared that all good came his way without his waiting. Naturally enough in a species of quiet innocence, Job thought that God thus gave when, in justice, mercy, love and peace, a man played his part in truth.

352 : Satan

Job 1.6–2.7; Matthew 4.1–11

The reality of a personal power of evil is taken for granted in the strange drama of this passage. The significance of the story is God's permissive will. He is never the author of evil, but for some inscrutable reason He permits it. Satan, flitting cynically through these verses, is not Dante's misshapen monster, nor Milton's royal and arrogant rebel. Goethe's

Mephistopheles is nearer the truth—the corrupter who seeks to persuade that evil is good, and virtue is folly. Above all he is the Accuser, the creature ready to see a challenge in all good, a spur to malevolence in all virtue, a target in all righteousness. As such he finds daily and universal reflection in the multitude of those who are 'of their father the devil, and the lusts of their father they will do' (John 8.44). Moral evil is the basis of Satan's character (Matt. 13.19, 39). He naturally twists and perverts, lives in hate, and opposes all desire and ambition for good. The lie of Eden sets the tone. He never departs from it. Hence his Accuser's role in Job. It never ceases.

> *'I sinned. Then straightway, post haste,*
> *Satan flew*
> *Before the presence of the most high God*
> *And made a railing accusation there.*
> *He said: "This soul, this thing of clay*
> *and sod,*
> *Has sinned. 'Tis true that he has named*
> *Thy name;*
> *But I demand his death, for Thou hast said:*
> *"The soul that sinneth it shall die."*
> *Shall not*
> *Thy sentence be fulfilled? Is Justice dead?*
> *Send now this wretched sinner to his doom;*
> *What other thing can righteous ruler do?"'*

For this reason, said John (1 John 3.8), was the Son of God made manifest—to destroy the Accuser and his works. And not only Accuser but Tempter. As such Satan laid hold upon the Lord Himself, taking natural desires, normal ambitions, and seeking to bend and pervert them into processes of rebellion.

Job's prologue, then, sets certain truths down as axioms. The first is that Satan initiates evil. A personality and a plotting mind are behind sin. Surely activity lacks explanation, but in experience is real enough. The second is that God permits evil, but turns evil into good.

411

353 : Job's Wife

Job 2; Romans 12.9–16

Troubles common to that time and place fell belatedly on Job,
but fell in fury, and to crown all came the horror of some
tropical disease which befouled his body and took away all
dignity and comeliness. With it, and 'most unkindest cut of
all', came the broken faith of Job's wife. It cannot be said
whether it was in pity or in disloyalty that she gave her
afflicted husband her dreadful advice. Clearly enough, she
thought that his quiet faith of earlier years had betrayed him,
and that some malevolent spirit was his God, ready, in a last
gush of anger, to precipitate an end which could only be glad
release.

Job's answer to her is one of the fine touches of the book.
'You speak,' he quietly replied, 'like a foolish woman.' He
implies by the last two words that her advice was out of
character. It was not like her to utter such words of desperation. The same words had nonetheless cut deep. Both
AV (KJV) and RSV use the word 'integrity' in v. 9. The
Hebrew noun means rather 'innocence' or 'simplicity', and
that is how Jerome rendered it in his Vulgate version. Knox,
who follows Jerome's Latin, thus renders it 'innocence'. Job's
faith had indeed been simple and uncomplicated. He had
held the tranquil innocence and simple view of God and the
world at which his wife now flings a sophisticated sneer.
It is hard to be hit thus where the heart is vulnerable.

And it is as hard to be thus met with disloyalty and contempt, where loyalty and love might properly have been
expected. A man can endure much at the callous hands of
the hostile world, so long as home and home's guardian
remains a solid refuge. With home a base on which a
battered man can retire to rearm and go emboldened forth
again, society can do its worst and a man can laugh and
bear it unmoved. Horatius, in the Roman story, as Macaulay
told it, 'saw on Palatinus the white porch of his home', and,
strengthened by the sight of it and what he knew was there,
turned and faced the Etruscan army, while Rome's defenders
hacked down the Tiber bridge behind him.

Job 'lay in dust, life's glory dead', and now there was no
one to make home the ultimate earthly refuge, with loyalty

on guard there and understanding. Home was gone, for a familiar voice had turned bitter. At that moment Job's control was supremely tested. He prevailed, and no word of evil passed his lips. Hence the deep significance of the last sentence of v. 10. It was one of Job's triumphant hours.

354 : Job's Despair

Job 3

Job was horribly alone. Then came his three- friends. They have gone down in history and the languages of man as worthless comforters, and people of small understanding. This is hardly fair. There was worth and reality in their friendship, helpless though they proved to be in the face of crushing calamity. They wept and took their place by Job's side, and sat for seven days in silent sympathy, struggling with their thoughts. Here, surely, was fellowship more real than some friends give. Like Ezekiel with the exiles by the Chebar canal, they 'sat where he sat', and might have lifted a little of the burden of Job's pain. It was far from being a heartless undertaking.

And yet it provoked somehow Job's outburst of tragic despair. Perhaps his agony called for words, any words, and perhaps he misconstrued their patent helplessness as lack of understanding. Or perhaps he misread the six puzzled eyes turned upon him from beneath the dusty burnous, and read disapproval, where there was only bewilderment too great to permit speech.

In the desolate horror of his disease Job was no sight for contemplation. There was shame in his physical torment. Hence his first complete loss of self-command, his vehemence and descent into unreason. Job is magnificently free from all taint of superstition, and yet, in his quite elaborate cursing of the day of his birth, he seems to succumb to some pagan notion that present and future can be swept of ill if the noisome pile of evil things can be thrust back on to some dark, infelicitous day of doom. His words seem too detailed to be a mere expression of present pain.

The closing verses speak of almost unbearable agony. Job finds no end or purpose in staying alive. 'There is energy enough,' writes R. A. Watson, 'to feel life a terror and no more—not enough for any mastery, even of stoical resolve.' Moffatt's rendering makes good sense of the closing two verses. It was the RV, followed by the RSV, which saw the advantage of the present tenses. The words become then a cry of ultimate pessimism, born of black despair. Job touches the depths. 'Whate'er I fear befalls me, and what I dread draws on me. I get no peace, I get no rest. I get no ease, only attacks of agony.'

355 : Eliphaz

Job 4 and 5

Job's outbursts of dark despair seem to have provoked Eliphaz to speech, and to harsh judgement. Sympathy, if such there had been while Eliphaz sat with his friend, was now dashed with horror. Eliphaz' simple view of sin and suffering was no doubt that which Job himself had held in the days before his calamity. Eliphaz is a man of eloquence, of poetry and of Oriental politeness—and of obtuseness.

In his first eleven verses Eliphaz speaks in sorrow. Job himself, he says, has professed to know the answers. Now he must endure them. Where, he asks, more in sorrow than in reproach, is his trust in God of other days? Eliphaz knows that life works on a plain, clear law—as a man sows he inevitably reaps, and the crop of sin's sowing is disaster, sickness and pain. Job must therefore humble himself and confess his sin.

And who more than Eliphaz had the right thus to expostulate? He had once had a remarkable experience of spiritual things. In some moving and unforgettable vision of the night he had been made aware of another world, and a voice emerged from it (17). The fact that the words were a truism, and had often been said by humble men before a holy God, was nothing to Eliphaz. He had been singled out for divine instruction. A 'charisma', if the overworked term may be used, lay now upon him, and made his utterances words of uncommon worth.

Eliphaz has nothing new to say. He has seen before such

catastrophes as those that have lain Job low (5.1–7). without self-criticism, analysis or comprehension. A quirk of the mind had been laid hold of by him as a manifestation of God's special favour, a compliment from the Most High. The visitation of the Holy Spirit should abash, humble, and recreate. It should not, and cannot, minister to pride.

Eliphaz has nothing new to say. He has seen before such catastrophes as those that have lain Job low (5.1–7). Indeed, they are the common lot of man. But cannot Job turn to God, the great restorer (8 f.), who is plenteous in mercy? All this is said on the assumption that, through the long and weary nights of his calamity, Job had not been doing exactly that. His despair was precisely because no clear answer seemed to come. He implies that Job has been a devious and crafty man (12 f.), and was reaping the visible fruit of secret sowing. He pours out obvious truths, dogmas of common knowledge, the religious sentiments of the comfortable, the untried, the prosperous. He gets nowhere near the seat and fountain of Job's pain. He knows all the answers —and knows none.

356 : Job Attacks

Job 6 and 7

Eliphaz has roused the sufferer to some resentment. Job's mind seems to be released from torpor, and, from the mood of dark hopelessness of his first speech, his strong mind springs to life. He stands obviously above Eliphaz in power of understanding and coherent utterance. True, he says, he has spoken rashly. Eliphaz hit home here. But let that fault be set side by side with the load and magnitude of his immense suffering (6.1–7). The very animals complain only when their need is not met. Man lives by more than bread, and Job starves for the food and sustenance of true understanding.

The overwhelming desire to have done with it all and find the peace of the grave sweeps over him again (8–13), and the sombre mood seems to have been stirred by the shock of his disappointment. When his friends came from so far to comfort him, Job had looked for the words of counsel or of

415

love which faithful friends can give. He wanted nothing more. Such gifts outweigh all material bounty (22 f.), and for help in the restoration of his earthly fortunes he was in no mood to ask.

Like the thirsty caravan struggling on through the arid wilderness to the place of waters, and finding the valley dry (14–21), so had Job himself been. He saw his friends' coming as the hope of sustenance, and like the drought-stricken river-bed, they were dry of all that which his wildly thirsting soul might have drunk.

Failing this, then let them at least convincingly instruct him. Let them not be hard, but let them show him wherein he had erred . . . In the next chapter Job seems to turn from his helpless friends to God. He complains of the misery of his nights and days, and then in bold, frank words expostulates with the Lord. Why should One so high and mighty be concerned to hem round with troubles the puny life of one insignificant man? Almost inverting the language of Psa. **8**, Job boldly asks why the God of all the high heavens should concern Himself with afflicting man so small, so ephemeral, so doomed. They are powerful and daring words for one so pious. Job reaches for something unknown, unrevealed. It was to come in Christ, clothed in whose right-eousness man can approach the eternal throne, '. . . little children remember to live continually in him. So that if he were suddenly to reveal himself we should still know exactly where we stand, and should not have to shrink away from his presence' (1 John 2.28, Phillips).

357 : Bildad

Job 8; 1 Corinthians 13

Bildad of Shuach now intrudes. He lacks the polish of Eliphaz. He is not perhaps as brutal as Zophar, but he is a man without pity. All the answers are in his creed. Job's children would not have died had they not earned death by their sin. He is the man who has a text for all eventualities, prefabricated solutions for all the problems and all the perplexities of life.

In fact, wisdom of old time had codified it all. Today Bildad would use the Bible as a bludgeon rather than a balm. His memorized texts, along with his own dogmatic interpretation of them, would be brought to bear upon the situation, and no other comment would be possible. H. L. Ellison aptly contrasts him with John Robinson, the good pastor of the Pilgrim Fathers: 'I charge you before God and His blessed angels that you follow me no farther than you have seen me follow Jesus Christ. If God reveals anything to you by any other instruments of His, be as ready to receive it as you were to receive any truth by my ministry, for I am verily persuaded that the Lord hath more truth yet to break forth out of His holy Word.'

Not so with Bildad. All truth was of old revealed—and to Bildad. Job sat in misery. Heavy affliction marred and wasted him. Pain and distress were the reward of sin. Therefore Job had sinned. Can the river-reed, the lush papyrus grow, unless there be water round its roots? With such smoke there is surely fire. 'The tent of the wicked will be no more' (22). It was all as simple as that. Job was judged of God.

Such purveyors of simple and orthodox solutions have their place in the affairs of men. It must be admitted that their comments are often correct, but such vindication of traditional and proverbial wisdom serves only to harden them in their preconceived patterns of thought. They betray little love, and are prone to blurt out the damaging word with no thought of pain inflicted.

Bildad has been provoked to speak by Job's protestations of innocence. He, too, shows that the relations between the participants in the dialogue are deteriorating.

358 : Bold Thinker

Job 9 and 10

Job answers wearily. He is infinitely sad. He could have foretold all the words of Bildad. Of course God is just. Of course man cannot vindicate himself before Him. But that assertion does not touch his bitter problem. God has condemned him, and he knows not why. And how can he know why? God is the Earth-Shaker, the Lord of the Pleiades; how can little man contend with Him? He can decide as He wills. He can toss aside human protestations of justice, pleas for pity, claims of right—and who can deny Him the freedom to do so?

It is bold, despairing poetry. Job paints the picture of a God who is an elemental force, a tyrant, beyond man's questioning, a God, in short, to make the weak and heavy-laden lose hope—and yet a God who has sometimes taken shape from the preaching of much later centuries when stress upon God's sovereignty has lost sight of His love, and the everlasting fact that Christ revealed Him.

Job's bitter hopelessness touches on impiety. It is the product of a mind distraught. Verse 23 touches the limit of sharp bitterness. Such a deity has too often haunted the sick imagination of man. Such were the gods of the Epicureans, described well by Tennyson in the *Lotus Eaters*:

> *. . . they lie beside their nectar, and the bolts are hurl'd*
> *Far below them in the valleys, and the clouds are lightly curl'd*
> *Round their golden houses, girdled with the gleaming world:*
> *Where they smile in secret, looking over wasted lands,*
> *Blight and famine, plague and earthquake, roaring deeps and fiery sands,*
> *Clanging fights, and flaming towns, and sinking ships, and praying hands.*
> *But they smile, they find a music centred in a doleful song*
> *Streaming up, a lamentation and an ancient tale of wrong . . .*

And then, most movingly, the complaints turn more directly into prayer. It is as though the last verses of the chapter (9.33–35) open the thought of a Mediator, and in the light of an unconscious prophecy Job's spirit grows calmer. He still speaks bitterly (10.1–8) but the wild words become more gentle.

A great dramatist of Greece, Aeschylus, the Shakespeare of Athens, once framed such a prayer to Zeus:

> *Zeus, whosoe'er indeed he be,—*
> *In that name, so it please him, hear.*
> *Zeus, for my help is none but he;—*
> *Conjecture through creation free*

I cast, and cannot find his peer,
With this strange load upon my mind
So burdening, only Zeus I find
To lift and fling it sheer.

Catch the accent of man's ancient longing, which Abraham Lincoln put in simpler prose: 'I have been driven many times to my knees by the overwhelming conviction that I had nowhere else to go. My own wisdom, and that cf all about me, seemed insufficient for the day.'

359 : Zophar

Job 11; John 8.1-11

Presumably Zophar was the youngest of the three. He has waited properly till now to speak, and, screwing his courage to the point of utterance, has not caught the pathos and the pain of what Job has just said to God. Hence his immoderate and harsh attack. Lies, mockery, words, words, words—when all was plain to Zophar's mind! Job simply did not understand what it meant to be clean in God's eyes. He was wilfully blind to truth.

Consider the self-righteousness of it all. Job must have sinned, or Job would not have lost all that which he had quite manifestly lost! Zophar himself was prosperous, and untouched by such evil. It followed that Zophar had fulfilled all righteousness. Eliphaz has the makings of a prophet. Bildad can claim to be something of a sage, for all the ready-made pattern of his solutions. Zophar is neither saint nor philosopher, but a simple fellow held in the grip of his own dogmatism. Such people are sorry counsellors for those confronting some real problem or some overwhelming trouble. They set forth some simple dogmas which drive the afflicted to despair—'all doubt has some sin as its cause', 'anxiety is lack of faith', 'depression is lack of trust'. Prescribed texts prove it all.

Such people, the Zophars of this world, are extroverts, people without imagination, unsympathetic, not from a cultivated cruelty, but from sheer inability to understand more complicated characters. They are suspicious of all subtlety, their religion is a plain system of punishment and material reward, they have no difficulties, and no perplexities because they are unable to grasp the issues which occasion them. They are invincibly self-righteous, usually of sound constitution and good health, always comfortably situated, not infrequently affluent—and useless in the dark hours of the soul, a peril in the sick room, and a menace in the pulpit. In the mercy of God their naïve faith seems seldom to be drastically tested.

360 : Job's Loneliness

Job 12, 13 and 14

Zophar's hurtful words rouse Job to a sharp reply, ironical (12.2), bitter (13.4 f.). He has been called a fool (11.12). He had held, he knew, an elder's reputation for wisdom, but now he was despised by lesser men who were convinced by his visible misfortune that all his past was sham.

As for Zophar's simple doctrine, let them look around. Out in the desert stood the tents of evil men, the very Bedouin who have looted Job's own goods, whose god was their sword ('who bring their god in their hand', 12.6). What a living refutation of automatic judgement, he seems to say, was the very existence of such unjudged wickedness. Evil *can* prosper, and there is no simple explanation.

There is great mystery. What of nature's self? Drought and flood come mysteriously as the wind, and in the ebb and flux of power in the world of men, no rules of right or wrong, justice or injustice, seem to be discernible. Nor are laws obvious in the vicissitudes of empire and of human right. Neither the Old Testament chroniclers nor the prophets would agree with Job in this, but Job was in a mood of dark disillusionment, and the world was chaos to him. Perhaps this was a reaction too violent to the neat solutions offered by his three friends.

He was disposed to insist that God should make it plain (13.3). Why not? Was it not, he asks (13.4–13), rather they than he who blasphemed God by their smooth and ordered doctrine? God *must* be just, He *must* listen (13.14 f.), perilous though it might be to demand such explanation. Suffering alone gave leave for such presumptuousness. 'Man's body is so small,' said Tagore once, 'his capacity for suffering so very great.'

And his time so brief. Chapter **14** is one of the great sombre passages of the book. Job had no grasp of immortality. Euripides, son of brilliant Athens, struck a note as sad in the chorus of a play:

> *If any far-off state there be*
> *Dearer to life than mortality,*
> *The hand of death hath hold thereof,*
> *And mists are under and mists above,*
> *The other life is a fountain sealed,*
> *The depths below us are unrevealed,*
> *And we float on legends for ever.*

The hope for which Job did not dare to reach came with Christ and His victory over death, but Job's passion in prayer and poetry was stirred and spurred by the looming victory of the grave.

Questions and themes for study and discussion on Studies 351–360

1. Trouble and God's will.
2. What was 'the lie of Eden'?
3. What is the significance of the home in life's experience?
4. The Christian and despair. Can moods of darkness always be condemned?
5. Slick solutions of life's problems—are they still to be heard?
6. Piety in prayer. The language of prayer.
7. Proof-texts in Christian evangelism—their use and misuse.
8. Why is John 1.18 so important a verse for the understanding of God?
9. What qualities are required in a Christian counsellor for youth, the sick, the mentally ill, the highly intelligent—and other types of people, in your experience?

421

361 : Eliphaz Again

Job 15, 16 and 17

In this chapter we see a little more of the weighty and dignified Eliphaz, although he is more on the edge of his temper here. His personality is well maintained in his discourse. 'I have seen . . .' (**15**.17) still records his appeal to his own unique experience. He is mightily suspicious of reasoned argument—the word 'crafty' appears in both of his speeches. He has his set quotations or favourite sayings (**15**.15 repeats **4**.18) and they substitute for discussion.

Eliphaz first expostulates with Job (**15**.1–13), whom in irony he calls 'wise'. He thinks Job guilty of plain profanity, or with an obtuse and quite inadequate consciousness of sin. He bends his efforts now to persuade Job to confess his sin (14–17). Could he but make Job realize the surpassing holiness of God, Job, he is sure, will see sin as he, Eliphaz, sees it, and acknowledge his shortcomings. All that is lacking in the argument is any consciousness of shortcoming on Eliphaz' own part! He is calmly and exasperatingly righteous.

Job's reply shows the futility of all his senior friend has to say. He is weary of their unfeeling arguments, and he reproaches the three of them for their failure to give him any grain of comfort (**16**.1–6). After all, he continues, and seems with the dull, despairing words to descend deeper into bitterness, after all, what can he expect of men when God Himself has set him up as a target (12), a fortress wall to batter down (14), and left him without pity to be a spectacle of grief and desolation. Nor can he see hope. He has 'sewn himself in sackcloth' (15), as though to demonstrate the permanence of his situation. He has faced the ultimate, and come to terms with death, and death's sting is that it is without meaning, flung upon him with contumely by a God who does not care. It is terrible language, this speech of the soul's midnight. Job, like those of his day, saw no clear hope beyond death, and so it became of agonizing, desperate importance that he should be vindicated before the horror of last dissolution laid hold of him. And now all hope of this seemed vain.

362 : Job's Faith

Job 18 and 19

The art of the writer of this book is tremendous. He makes
his hard and mistaken characters say the most outrageous
things plausibly and effectively. Bildad, the narrow-minded
exponent of traditional reason, is on the attack again. With
cruel and unfeeling rigour, and in a tone of bitterness, Bildad
attacks Job once more. He simply cannot understand how
anyone can reject the established findings of ancient wisdom.
The case of Job must necessarily have its explanation. It
must be according to simple ancient rules. Job is wilfully
misunderstanding the situation. He is being punished for sin,
and he is adding to the sin by denying the patent fact.
Eliphaz, of course, said as much, but Eliphaz had the
attitude of a cultured man. Bildad is a crude and simple soul,
a hopeless failure in any situation of stress. He knows all
the rules! And stress is obvious, deepening and deadly.
Job speaks of the utter rejection in which he finds himself.
Wife, children, friends, have alike cast him aside. Then
comes one of the most remarkable passages in the book.
Job has to this point betrayed no hope of vindication in
another life, of which he has no clear knowledge, but now,
in a gush of faith, some conception of a life beyond the
grave emerges. It can hardly be interpreted in any other way.
Ellison gives a bold translation of 19.25–27, which is a fair
rendering. Translation must not, as it too often is, be
determined by pre-conceived theology, and fixed opinions
of what the writer knew, and did not know. In Psa. 22 and
Isa. 53 the sufferer on a surge of passionate perception is
enabled to pierce through to new truth, and that is what Job
does here: 'I know that my Vindicator lives and will yet
stand upon the earth; and after my skin has been thus
destroyed, then without my flesh I shall see God, whom
I shall see on my side, and my eyes shall see to be un-
estranged.' Then, nearly overwhelmed by what has formed
on his lips, Job ends: 'My heart fails with longing within me.'
Job's darkest hour has become his finest.

363 : Job Exaggerates

Job 20 and 21

Job's closing words, which appeared to counter-attack and threaten his hard friends with judgement, infuriate Zophar. In some indignation he paints a portrait of the wicked man to match Eliphaz' effort in ch. 15. The only notable lines added are his insistence on the brevity of the evil person's enjoyment of the pleasures of sin. He is obviously in some difficulty over the lack of real and specific charges to level against Job, so he makes a thrust in the dark. The exploitation of the peasantry was a common sin among the rich in the old world of these events, so he boldly suggests that Job has heartlessly downtrodden the poor. He has done it slyly, but God has seen and punished. Job attacks boldly in his reply. Zophar has too rashly alleged that the evil man soon perishes. In fact, he says, this is demonstrably not the case. Job undoubtedly exaggerates. Perhaps this is for an unexpected reason. At his greatest point of tension and of faith, he has, as we have seen, broken through to a conception of divine justice and judgement which takes into account a vindication and a reckoning beyond this life. He will, he knows, in a sudden burst of confidence, be shown ultimate and perfect justice. Does it not equally follow that evil can only meet its final retribution in another dimension of being? Zophar has claimed that all happens according to a fixed and immutable law. The doer suffers. Sin reaps its own reward and always reaps its own reward.

Job knows that this is not so, and, in the stress of debate, he over-corrects. He sets against his opponent's too simple picture of majestic and automatic retribution, a rather shocking picture of sin's immunity. Measuring merely by the yardstick of superficial retribution, and leaving out of account the wealth of the mind and heart that evil is denied, it is obvious to any observer that the sinners of this world often get what they seek and die in their beds, old in evil, as frequently, perhaps, as they meet with visible judgement. Judgement is many-sided, and not always to be seen. But observe the humanity of it all. Zophar was part right, part wrong. Job, in reply, shares his error. But he is now more quiet, more collected. He has his vision.

364 : Job's Desolation
Job 22, 23 and 24

Eliphaz, best of Job's friends though he is, returns to the attack under the power of his dominant obsession—that truth which had come to him in the strange vision of the night. He will not have this firm rock in any way questioned. It makes him wildly angry when anyone seems to question in any way the validity of what had happened to him, the experience which had become his boast. Quite cruelly, he picks up what Job himself says of wicked men and deliberately aims it back at him (21.14, f.; 22.12–17). And having said his harsh say, hardly realizing its hardness, Eliphaz returns to his appeal.

Faced with such crass misunderstanding, Job touches the depths of despair again. Job's longing for a way to God (23.3) forms one of the most poignant verses in Scripture. It is life's most terrible experience to feel that God is remote, withdrawn and difficult to find, removed from comprehension, approach, hearing.

> *Gladly I'd march though the way were drear,*
> *If I could but see the oasis near,*
> *Or out in the wilderness only hear*
> *Crying the Voice of One . . .*

Job could see nothing but the mirage, hear no sound of comfort in his howling wilderness. He felt alone, abandoned, helpless. Perhaps the awesome cry of desolation on the Cross (Matt. 27.46) shows that Christ in His humanity plumbed these depths, and tasted this bitter cup. Nor, as Job contends, is it always the tyranny which brings such pain. Hope deferred, stress of mind, the bitterness of loss, even prayer inexplicably unanswered, can bring such testing. God, in His wisdom, but always for the sufferer's ultimate blessing, sometimes allows the Adversary to have his way. The Christian has so much more than Job had to make such Gethsemanes more plain. Christ trod this path, right to the Cross, and the Cross became the most creative event in the history of man. Christ for ever shows that pain has meaning. But what a picture is Job who knew not where he might find Him! We know. John 1.18 is the secret, and in Christ we can always find Almighty God. Read Heb. 10.19–22 in Phillips or the NEB.

365 : Job Stands Fast

Job 28, 29 and 30

Job is still passionately groping for God, and in a burst of poetry he pictures questing man probing the depths of earth to wrest its treasures of precious metal, seeking, discovering with toil and effort—but not finding God. Some of the more modern versions make his description of ancient mining more vivid, the digging, driving of deep shafts, the crushing of the ore. In a passage which reads like Prov. 8, Job tells where true wisdom is to be found, culminating in the fine words of **28**.28. Job has laid hold of supreme truth; that life's problems begin to find solution only when God is set first, made supreme, and trusted.

In the next chapter the mood changes. In the midst of affliction and distress the memory of past happiness is a sharp and painful memory. In a surge of new misery, Job remembers the peace and plenty which once were his when he lay in the light of God's love. Keenest of his regrets is the memory of the esteem and good will in which men held him. In beautiful words he tells how he had, in times past, used his wealth as a good man would use it in a world of poverty, to lift the burden of the heavy-laden, to uphold justice, and sweeten the community in which he lived.

It is a beautiful chapter, this bright flashback to the days of rest and joy. But, such is the manner of man, that those whom he had helped, and those who had paid him the rightful measure of reverence and regard, now turned to dishonour him in the contemptible manner of men. Ingratitude is hard to bear, and naturally enough, for, as Jonathan Swift once said, that noisome vice 'sums up all the evil of man'. And perhaps the best known quotation from Shakespeare is on the same theme—and touches Job's sombre mood:

> *Blow, blow, thou winter wind,*
> *thou art not so unkind*
> *as man's ingratitude . . .*
> *Freeze, freeze, thou bitter sky,*
> *thou dost not bite so nigh*
> *as benefits forgot.*

It is a sad picture with which we leave Job—an ageing man who expected to die in peace and who cannot understand his catastrophe. God's word to him is outside our theme. We have sought a man—and how human!.

366 : Elihu

Job 32 and 33

All this time a young man has been listening, deferential before his elders. The three older men, and Job himself, have fallen silent. There is no more to say. The discourses have, however, left Elihu angry. He worships a greater God than they, and the discovery of the fact infuriates him. Elihu had expected understanding, instruction, final wisdom, from men so much more experienced than himself, and now he realizes that it is not the lapse of years or the accumulation of experience which makes for wisdom. God instructs, God makes wise, God enlightens, and it therefore follows that a young man has something worth while to say if he has the inspiration of God's Spirit.

It is excellent characterization. Elihu has an assurance, and a certainty of rectitude which jars a little; but who, remembering youth, and the stark simplicities of first conviction, cannot see a dash of self in the portrait? It is also worth observing that God rebukes the others, as the book moves to its climax, but spares Elihu actual rebuke—He merely dismisses his counsel as inconclusive. Youth has a right to speak. Youth can proclaim truth. Youth can be enlightened by God. 'Let no man despise your youth,' said Paul to Timothy. Moreover young Elihu has meticulously observed the proprieties. He has not rushed in, nor said a word until the rest ended in frustration.

His whole speech should be read. It is eloquent and cogent. Elihu, unlike the older men with their prefabricated solutions, does not accuse Job of gross misdemeanour. Nevertheless, having laid down his premise of God's surpassing holiness, he cannot but maintain that the whole explanation of the problem must somewhere lie in the guilt, the fault, of the afflicted. He suggests that this fault is spiritual pride, a conclusion prompted by Job's survey of his standing and acceptance in his happier years. Indeed, does not the reading of that eloquent and moving passage suggest a certain naïve satis-

427

faction on Job's part against which there may be put a tiny question mark? All of us can echo every word. This is how we all think in times of stress when we look back on days of tranquillity. But most of us refrain from exposing pain so frankly to the ever-present Elihu. Elihu saw the opening and shot his bolt through this innocent joint in the armour. Alas, as the old Moody hymn has it, in this world, ungrateful, insensitive, we must often 'go, bury our sorrow'.

Questions and themes for study and discussion on Studies 361–366

1. On what is the Christian belief in another life most securely based?
2. What has the New Testament to say about a vindicator?
3. What are the essential qualities of a comforter?
4. Is justice done in this life, ever? never? sometimes? visibly? invisibly?
5. Compare Job's experience with Elijah's.
6. Can a fundamentally ungrateful person be a Christian?

367 : Between the Testaments

Psalm 119.161–176; Hebrews 11.32–40

Four centuries lie between the ministry of Malachi and the birth of Jesus, the Messiah whose coming Malachi saw afar. Over those long momentous years history did not stand still. Brave men lived, trusted, died for their faith, and Israel regained her freedom only to lose it again. Alexander, at the head of a Greece which he had united by the sword, struck a death blow at the sprawling Persian Empire and broke it up. Alexander might have built a united world had he not died in Babylon, at the age of thirty-three, in the year 332 B.C.

His Empire fell into four parts, and Palestine was part of Syria, save when Egypt under its Greek kings of Alexandria, disputed the claim. As ever, Palestine lay, a buffer and a battleground, between the powers to the north and the power to the south. As Syria weakened, areas to the west, south, and east of her empire, which originally stretched from the Aegean

428

to the Persian Gulf, and from the Caucasus to Sinai, asserted their independence, and the Jews had their century of freedom.

Some of the story of the years between the Testaments is found in the Apocrypha, often printed between the testaments of the NEB and RSV. Many of the great men and women of those days, though not 'characters of the Bible' in the strict sense of the word, are worth meeting—the family of the Maccabees, for example, Mattathias the dynamic and saintly priest who raised the Jewish standard of revolt against the tyranny of Syrian Antiochus; John, Simon, Judas, Eleazer and Jonathan, his sons, who bravely fought the battle through, amid toil, peril, tragedy and triumph; and the valiant Jews who fought beside them.

In other books of the Apocrypha we meet personalities who have had a place in Scripture. The Books of Esdras, for example, tell stories about characters of the Restoration. Susanna, and Bel and the Dragon, those ancestors of the detective story, reveal facets of Jewish life in which Daniel was a known and familiar figure. We meet again Baruch, the companion and secretary of Jeremiah, and we meet for the first time Joshua, the son of Sirach, who left a 'book of wisdom'. There are fictional characters like Judith, another Joel of the days of the Assyrian invasion, and the pious Tobit of the same period.

It is all fascinating reading, and helps the reader of the New Testament to understand what formed and shaped the character of the people whom he meets, restless under the domination of Rome in the time of Christ and the early Church.

368 : The Ancestors

Matthew 1.1–17; Luke 3.23–38; Numbers 27.1–11; 36.1–13

The prescribed readings may seem uninteresting. In fact, they are of some importance. The genealogies in the two Gospels will manifestly not be contradictory. They are as obviously different. Why? Numbers 27.1–11 and 36.1–13 are probably the key to the difficulty. Moses doubtless delivered thousands of judgements (Exod. 18.12–27). Why among them all is this one mentioned? At first sight it merely determines that daughters who are heirs to their father's property shall marry within their tribe in order that the distribution of tribal possessions shall not be disturbed. But the law means more than this. It enabled the Lord as 'son of Mary' to be 'King of the Jews'. Mary, in order that her son (who would be legally considered Joseph's son) might inherit Judah's throne, had to marry within the tribe. It thus becomes of some importance to prove that Joseph was one of the tribe of Judah. This Matthew undertakes to do, quite in accordance with the preoccupation with kingship which characterizes his Gospel. In Luke, Joseph is called the 'son of Heli'. Heli must have been Mary's father, and Joseph is called his son because he was Mary's husband and his legal heir in the absence of any brothers of Mary. The word 'begat' or 'father of' is not used in Luke. Jesus on Mary's side sprang from Judah (Luke 3.33) and His inheritance was effective because Mary married a true descendant of Judah.

Look closely at the lists. We have met many of these people before, observed their blemishes, their sins, their follies. Judah is in the list, David, Solomon, Rehoboam, even Manasseh. Of such fallible human beings, after the flesh, came the Lord. God works out His purpose, as the whole of the Old Testament shows, by means of men and women, sometimes in spite of them, sometimes with their active cooperation, seldom with their complete and whole-hearted committal. It stirs our faith to know that so He worked through the long years of history during which He prepared the way for the coming of His Son. We shall see such divine working through the men and women of the New Testament . . . As we stumble on, and see around us, and indeed within us, failure, obtuseness, and lack of understanding, as we are confronted with disaffection, backsliding and apostasy, it is good to know that God's plan was always outworked amid the same frustrations. He will not fail today.

369 : Mary, Mother of Christ
Matthew 1.18–25; Luke 1.26–38; John 1.1–18

In the first chapter of the New Testament we meet the greatest woman of all time. Mary was no less. Reacting against attempts to bestow divinity upon her, Christians have too often denied Mary, the girl chosen to be the mother of Jesus, the honour which is due to her. She was a human being, and never more than a human being. So she appears in Scripture. She must, for all that, have been a woman of surpassing worth.

It was Mary's quiet habit to set deep in her heart the memory of momentous events in her experience (Luke 2.51), and to ponder on their significance. That was how it came about that, at the middle of the first century, when Luke, the physician, used the years when his friend Paul was in protective custody in Caesarea, to scour Palestine for facts (Luke 1.2 f.), he found Mary a mine of information.

He may, of course have met her in Ephesus, at the home of John, but meet her he certainly did, and the freshness of the Nativity stories in his Gospel must owe much to the vivid memory of Mary's old age. The Nativity probably took place about five years before the date calculated as late as A.D. 325, and still observed as the basis of the Christian calendar. Mary, therefore, was born somewhere before the year we call 20 B.C. Perhaps she was in her early seventies when she gave Luke the information which remained 'in her heart'.

She told him of the Annunciation, and the heavy burden of pain, misunderstanding and responsibility her girlhood was called upon to bear. The Virgin Birth, an essential teaching of Scripture, and vital for all respect for the authority of the New Testament, rests upon the word and testimony of Mary herself, and perhaps of Mary alone, for Joseph appears to have been long since dead. Those with sufficient hardihood of scepticism, may accuse the woman who has been honoured beyond all other women of falsehood, and the covering of girlhood fault or disaster by a specious tale, but Mary gives a notable impression of quiet goodness, of devotion to God, and utter purity. Luke, too, was no gullible simpleton, but a considerable historian in his own intellectual right.

Rather let us meet the Mother of Christ, a girl willingly given into God's hands, a woman of poetry and holiness, the human vehicle of God's greatest act in history.

431

370 : Mary the Psalmist

Luke 1.39–56; 1 Samuel 2.1–10

Tradition has it that Luke was an artist as well as a physician and a most notable historian. Certain it is that there is uncommon artistry in his writing. We are indebted to him for the preservation of the psalms of the early Church, which cluster in these chapters, and set the tone for Christian praise.

Mary's psalm, known from its first word in the Latin version as the Magnificat, reveals a facet of her choice character. It is a rewarding exercise to comb its ten verses through for Old Testament quotation and allusion, for it is laced with Hebrew poetry.

The poem throws light on the education of a Jewish girl, for Mary must have lived within the sound of Old Testament music, the words of ancient psalms and liturgy forming the pattern of her thought and self-expression. Observe that she had sought her cousin in her secluded dwelling in search of comfort and encouragement. Verse 39 follows significantly on its predecessor, as though to indicate that, as soon as the fulfilment of the Annunciation became conscious fact to her, Mary had sought the presence of one she had learned to trust for counsel and advice.

The task she had been called upon to perform was not one which she bore placidly and without a natural surge of fear. She had no guarantee at all against hostile comment. It was altogether natural that she should need and seek the help of love and fellow-feeling. It was given her without hesitation, and in abundance. The result was an outpouring of song.

It is as though God requires some human nucleus on which to construct His blessing. Just as the tiny gift of loaves and fishes was multiplied to feed the throng by the lake, so, on the words of a loving and perceptive woman, He brought His surge of comfort and of fortitude to the Virgin's heart. And no blessing of God thus given can remain in fruitless storage. The gift of living water always becomes an upward-welling spring (John 4.14).

The three months' stay with the good Elizabeth is a silent period. Mary said nothing of the events or conversations of that time to the listening Luke. She must have needed solitude, limited fellowship and withdrawal. There are times

432

when we all need them. Mary was preparing herself for great events. When great events come heralded and foreseen, the example of the wise young woman may well be followed.

371 : Joseph

John 6.22–59; Mark 6.1–6

Little is said of Joseph, the carpenter of Nazareth, save that he was a good man (Matt. 1.19). There could hardly be greater honour. Seeking to demean the Lord, those who thought much of status and position dismissed Him as 'the son of the carpenter', as though a father so inconsiderable brought little glory to his son.

But Joseph was an upright man, one of Israel's remnant. He moves humbly through a few brief pages of Scripture, overshadowed even by his noble wife. No word of ill is said of him. Almost equally with Mary, he was called to share the burden of the world's slander and gross misunderstanding. Called of God to do so, he carried the load without complaining. Given a command, he unquestioningly obeyed, and had the blessed task of protecting the Virgin and sheltering the Child.

There are multitudes of Christians like Joseph. They are called to a simple task in an obscure environment. They hearken and obey. They do well and faithfully that which they are bidden to do: no one calls in praise; their thanks are the thanks that Joseph won, a loved one's smile, the love of a child. They are the salt of the earth.

Thousands of poems, hymns and carols cluster round Christmas. All the other characters of the story move in and out of verse and music. The shepherds crowd the inn. With the glitter of gifts the Wise Men come, adore, and go their way. Perhaps the place of Joseph in the story is emphasized in some poem, some forgotten fragment of verse. If that is so, long search this winter afternoon, at the world's end where this note on Joseph is written, has failed to find the reference.

Hence a touch of joy to write a word of praise for one who trod a hidden path, unseen, unregarded. He was merely the carpenter of Nazareth, whose good work and honest craftsmanship men took for granted, who took his fair and just reward for his careful work, spent it on his loved ones, and turned to the next day's task. The world would be a sweeter place were there more like Joseph. A good society is built of such good men, contented men who do the work they are fitted to do, men who house Christ in their homes, men who do their best, love their families, and leave no mark of evil on the world's marred face.

372 : The Innkeeper

2 Samuel 19.31–40; Jeremiah 41; Luke 2.1–7.

The innkeeper of Bethlehem has been misunderstood. He gave the weary family who had travelled down from Nazareth, the best he had to offer. Picture a square-cut cavern in the rock. At one end is a raised platform, where the ancient host quite naturally, and with never a thought of slighting them, disposed of his passing guests, in sight of their tethered beasts and stacked luggage. Bethlehem was full that night, for Bethlehem's absent population was home, at the command of totalitarian Rome, for the census. As a visitor of David's line, Mary might naturally have expected the best accommodation of the local hostelry. His 'kataluma' or guest room, which should not be translated 'inn', was already occupied. 'There was no room in the guest chamber.' Why? Hillel, the great Pharisee, was of the royal line, like Mary, and would perhaps be there that day. He was over a hundred years old. His son, Simeon, would also be there. So perhaps would his grandson, Gamaliel, the teacher of Paul. Did this considerable party arrive first and fill the innkeeper's accommodation? The stable sleeping place was his second best. The manger was a cosy rock-cut recess.

Is it possible to say a little more? Jeremiah (41.17) speaks of a certain 'geruth', or 'inn', which is 'near Bethlehem'. It was in the possession of one Chimham. Was this a descendant of Chimham, son of Barzillai, who, because of his father's beneficence to the exiled David (2 Sam. 19.31–38), was treated by the king as a son? Did he become thus, as the son of a great sheep-rancher, the steward of the royal sheep-lands at Bethlehem? Did he build a hostelry which remained in the family after the stable fashion of the East, to provide a

434

refuge in Jeremiah's day, and a rendezvous for shepherds (Luke 2.15) in New Testament times?

Was the innkeeper called Chimham or Barzillai, and conscious that he was keeping up a tradition almost a thousand years old when he entertained those of David's line? Do not then, imagine a harsh, preoccupied man who missed the great moment of his opportunity, but rather a harassed host who did his best on a night of labour and distress to maintain an ancient rite of hospitality.

373 : The Shepherds and the Emperor

Luke 2.1–20; Micah 5

We have already read Luke's second chapter, but this is a climax of history and we must look at others who crowded that momentous stage. As Paul told the Philippians in quite another context (3.1), it is a salutary thing sometimes to be told vital truths more than once.

Stand back like an artist looking at his picture and look again at the story covered by the brief passage of Scripture. Those who looked into the manger at Bethlehem had strange premonitions, but no clear conception of what was to be. The shepherd visitors were a despised and lowly band. The rabbis' literature has words of harsh contempt for their class. And yet it is part of the record of Israel that, when corruption and apostasy invaded high places, faith and truth found fortress and survival among the common folk of the land, the peasantry which sent Elijah and Amos to the courts of wealth and decadence, the people of the ascetic communities, such folk as those of Qumran, who hid their library, the Dead Sea Scrolls, in the wilderness caves . . . It is a pattern which history has seen recur, and in other lands than Palestine.

It was happening in Bethlehem when the hinge of history was turning there. Hillel and Simeon, the proud Pharisees, as we have seen, could actually have been asleep in the inn, with the whole Old Testament stored in their heads. History was passing them by, as it was passing Augustus by in distant Rome, brilliant, able Augustus, his plans for peace and the vital transmission of power frustrated by a restless horse, the

435

sting of an anopheles mosquito, by the invisible invaders of the torrid east, which made fevers mount and wounds inflame. Augustus' heirs fell thus one by one, by accident, wounds, sickness . . .

Augustus was a great man. He had saved his country from the chaos of a hundred years. He had brought order out of the fearsome confusion which had followed the murder of Julius Caesar. He saw hope for the world only in a strong Rome, strongly led, and for a generation now he had ruled wisely and well. He did not know that his census had caused a prophecy to be fulfilled and that a little town in a restless province, not Rome by the Tiber, was at that moment the pivot of history . . . His chosen heirs were dead—Drusus flung from his horse, Gaius and Lucius dead of battle wounds and fever . . . Christ was born.

374 : Men of Bethlehem
John 1.1–18; Luke 19.41–44

Let us stay a little longer in Bethlehem. There were those who came and went and did not know that a tremendous event had taken place. They filled the town, for Rome's bureaucracy had decreed that for census purposes, the people should assemble in the city of their family origin.

Here, for example, is a translation of a public notice, dated A.D. 104. It comes from Egypt, where rainless tracts of desert round the remains of ancient habitation, have preserved from decay masses of written documents from every sphere of human activity. The translation runs:

'Gaius Vibius, chief prefect of Egypt. Because of the approaching census it is necessary for all those residing for any cause away from their own districts to prepare to return at once to their own administrative areas, in order that they may complete the formalities of the family census, so that agricultural land may retain its proper titles. Knowing that your city has need of provisions, I desire . . .'

At this point the document becomes too tattered to read . . . But note the evidence for disrupted food supplies, strained civil amenities, crowded inns . . . And observe why the carpenter of Nazareth and his betrothed wife, both of David's line, were forced, at the command of the bureaucrats, to ride down from Nazareth's lip of hills, across the coloured Esdraelon plain, up through the high country, past Omri's and Ahab's old fortress of Samaria, where collaborator Herod's temple to Augustus was rising, simultaneously with his temple to Jehovah in Jerusalem . . . on through Jerusalem's tangled lanes, over the Mount of Olives, past Bethany, and south to where Bethlehem lay curving on its brown ridge.

'O little town of Bethlehem,' runs the carol, 'how still we see thee lie.' Bethlehem was far from quiet that night. The host who had assembled in a town as old as Genesis seethed with hate for Rome. All the beginnings of Palestine's disaster of eighty years later was there. The men of Bethlehem were Jews we shall meet again, the crowded faces of the story of the Sermon on the Mount, the Galilean seashore, the scene below Pilate's balcony, the slopes of Calvary—and along the invested walls as Titus' legions closed upon the city. They did not know the day of their visitation. They are infinitely pathetic, sheep with no shepherd, and searchers for that which is not bread. They still throng around us—our audience and responsibility.

375 : The Magi
Matthew 2

The common folk found Christ, but so did a few men of intellect, the 'wise men' of another culture, those strange visitants who studied the stars, and followed all the way to Bethlehem some message they had read in the bright constellations. Tales have gathered round them, for the 'three kings' do, in fact, illustrate properly how, over the lapse of centuries, a myth can grow. Matthew tells briefly all we really know. They came, surely, from the Yemen, Arabia Felix, the land of their gifts, 'gold and frankincense and myrrh'. They enter the story and leave with mystery behind them. It was easy enough, from Bethlehem, to connect with the caravan routes which ran through Petra, and so to avoid returning to Jerusalem, where the mad king lay in his last evil. They are symbolic of a longing world-wide, which can be sensed in page on page of ancient literature, a desire for 'a saviour'.

Misdirected, this yearning led to the worship of Rome's emperor, the cult of 'the Beast', as the last book of the Bible puts it, and the long clash with the Church.

History had prepared the path for the Magi. We do not know how many, over a full thousand years, may have shared their expectation. Solomon had established relations with the south-east a thousand years before. His ships went to Ophir, near modern Aden, and his caravans trod the desert routes through coloured Petra. Shabwa, ancient Sabota, was probably the Sheba, whose queen came to see the glory of Solomon and returned to fill Arabia and Ethiopia across the strait with legends of her beauty. And Arabia Felix watched the stars. Her wise men knew their courses. They worshipped Astarte, who hung in the sky as the Evening Star, bright as a lamp in the velvet darkness, and often visible in broad day. Is it not more than possible that with Judah's cargoes, Judah's Messianic hope went down the desert ways, and that expectant hearts read the promise aright even in Arabia Felix? Did not the eunuch of Queen Candace of Ethiopia come, years later, with his roll of the prophet Isaiah? And when the time was full, did the glowing star shine with a new message and draw the Wise Men to Palestine?

It is a restless, yearning world again, plagued by its own hates, passions, pride. A scientific age, so rich in the achievements of its reason, finds it difficult to believe what its eyes cannot see and its computers measure.

Who are the Wise Men now, when all is told?
Not men of science; not the great and strong;
Not those who wear a kingly diadem;
Not those whose eager hands pile high the gold;
But those amid the tumult and the throng
Who follow still the Star of Bethlehem.
(B. Y. Williams)

Questions and themes for study and discussion on Studies 367–375

1. What preparation was God making between the Testaments?
2. In what way did the Old Testament prescribe Christ's ancestry?

438

3. The influence of Mary in the Christian Church. How should it be recognized?
4. The spiritual blessings of solitude.
5. 'Called to a simple task in an obscure environment.' Should we be content with this?
6. Piety in the midst of poverty.
7. How historical events serve divine ends.
8. The symbolism of the gifts brought by the Magi.

376 : Herod 'The Great'

Matthew 2

When the Romans organized the east in 63 B.C., Pompey appointed a priest named Hyrcanus to rule Galilee, Samaria, Judea, and Perea. Hyrcanus had an astute premier, an Edomite named Antipater, who knew how to use his power for his family's advantage. He secured his two sons, Phasael and Herod, in key governorships, and when Antipater was murdered in 43 B.C., the two young men succeeded jointly to the premiership in Hyrcanus' court.

Phasael was a rapid victim of a Parthian raid which followed the assassination of Julius Caesar, who had intended pacifying that frontier. Herod escaped to Rome and so impressed Octavian, the future Augustus, that he received a mandate to recover Palestine, which he did between 39 and 36 B.C. He successfully carried on a pro-Roman administration for thirty-four years, marked by the building of the Roman port and base at Caesarea and a temple to Augustus at Samaria.

Simultaneously he conciliated the Jews, who hated him for his Edomite blood, by building the great temple at Jerusalem. He was a superb diplomatist, dividing the opposition by suppressing the old aristocracy and yet marrying Mariamne, one of their number, and by setting up a nobility of officials. He stimulated loyalty to his house by founding 'the Herodians', established a strong bureaucracy, secured his power by a mercenary army and a system of strongholds, of which Masada was one, and paid the price of his dangerous living by tension in his own family, murder, and ultimate paranoia.

Herod's private life was soiled by feuds, intrigue and manifold murder. The Emperor Augustus, punning on two Greek words (*hus*—a pig, and *huios*—a son) said he would rather be Herod's pig than his son. As a ruler of the Jews, presumably, he did not keep and kill pigs! He murdered his beloved Mariamne, and at various times three of his sons, one of them in 7 B.C., three years before his death. It is easy to see how the massacre of the children of Bethlehem fits the insane and sanguinary context of Herod's last madly suspicious and ruthless days.

Josephus, the Jewish priest who, as Vespasian's secretary, wrote a history of his people, paints a grim picture of the mental and physical deterioration of the ageing king, prone to delusions of persecution and uncontrollable outbursts of violence, the results of chronic hypertension and a diseased mind. Such was the creature whose evil terrors menaced the cradle of Christ. His common appellation 'the Great' means, in its ancient settings 'the Elder'.

377 : Zechariah

Luke 1.1–25, 57–80; Exodus 30.1–10; Hebrews 10.19–22

The beauty and goodness of this world have always been mingled with its evil and its tragedy. In 'the last days of Herod', when that dark and wicked life was sinking into madness and dissolution, the Remnant we have so often met was still to be found in Israel. It has always been so, from Elijah's seven thousand until today.

The members of Aaron's tribe took it in turn to make the daily sacrifice, and call a blessing on the assembled multitude. We have no information about the surviving numbers of Aaron's descendants, but it may be assumed that the privilege was a rare one and hardly repeated in a man's lifetime. A good man accepted it with awe.

When Zechariah's great day came, he went, no doubt, with deep consciousness of the holy occasion, and a heart prepared to meet his God. God met him in the place of duty, and at the hour of worship. The good man had probably planned to use the great moment at the altar to set before God the burden of his own heart, and he found his burden lifted there.

440

We are always in God's presence. Any moment is our moment of approach. Let us likewise use the privilege.

Voiceless and overwhelmed, Zechariah continued until the task was finished, and gave the people the formal blessing without the customary form of words. They sensed that some great experience had befallen him. It does not need words to show to others that God has touched and sanctified a life. It is too visible in the living presence of a man.

In the last half of the chapter, Zechariah uses his restored speech in praise to God. His hymn is magnificently in character. It is a priest's hymn, alive with references to the Old Testament in which his mind had moved. He had grasped the significance of prophecy, and knew that his son was the forerunner of Christ. He knew as little as his son, even in the climax of his ministry knew, of the true and full significance of the One who was to come, but to fulfil God's plans we do not need fullness of understanding. We need only faithfulness and readiness to act. In humility the committed Christian simply follows step by step and does immediately that which lies closest to the ready hand.

378 : Elizabeth

Luke 1.24, 25, 39–45, 57–63; Psalm 13

Luke has told us, in his opening verses, that he had taken some trouble to verify his facts. He had found aged people still living who remembered old events with all that accuracy with which age remembers the distant past. Elizabeth could have been still alive, high in her eighties. The songs of this chapter may have survived in manuscript. This was a literary age, and preserved its records.

At any rate, we owe it to 'the beloved physician' that these first hymns of the Church were preserved, and that we know a few more of God's remnant. All that was happening in 'the hill country . . . of Judea' (39), was passing the leaders of religion by. If the Pharisees saw nothing in Bethlehem, and if Augustus had not even heard the name, the Sadducees who ruled religion in the land were even further from the truth which might have made them free. The Sadducees denied a resurrection from the dead and rejected the supernatural in

441

religion. They were none the less eager for the emoluments of religion, coveted posts of dignity and the advantages of office, and accepted the profits of the temple court. They are not without posterity.

But return to Elizabeth, warm-hearted, aglow with the new experience of coming motherhood, moved by the strangeness of the events which had preceded that consciousness. How intensely human is the scene in the home of the priest and his wife—the family assembly, the tactless assumption, probably on the part of Elizabeth's parents-in-law, that the father's name would be perpetuated in the son's, and the blank astonishment when the father sided with his wife (63)! The Bible is a book about men and women, as well as about God. God moves through the small affairs of life as well as through the great movements of history. The New Testament often finds its theme where Masefield said he found his poetry. He wrote, he said,

Not of the princes and prelates with periwigged charioteers,
Riding triumphantly laurelled to lap the fat of the years,
But rather the scorned, the rejected, the men hemmed in
with spears.

The Gospels belong to the first century. If we wish to meet the proletariat, the common folk of village, farm, and countryside from that century, there is scarcely anywhere else in surviving literature where modern man may meet them.

379 : Simeon

Luke 2.25–35; Isaiah 42

Joseph, as we have seen, was a man of simple goodness, whose religion consisted in doing that which he ought to do, regardless of the cost, the toil or anything else involved. How desperately the Church, and the tormented world, need such saints.

Certain obligations of the Law (Exod. 13.12; Lev. 12.8; Num. 8.17) brought the necessary outlay within reach of the poor, and the fact that the humble sacrifices were chosen, is indication that no great wealth lay in the hands of Joseph and Mary. Jerusalem was no long journey from Bethlehem, and when Mary could travel, that was the first destination. They passed over the Mount of Olives, in through Saint Stephen's gate, or the gate which was one day to carry that name, and turned left to the Temple. It was a moving moment when the Lord first came to His shrine.

One faithful Israelite was waiting, and recognized the significance of the hour. Faith was still alive in the land, for all the clutter in the temple court, for all the absurdities of Pharisaism. God had his Few. Joseph and Mary, Zechariah and Elizabeth, whom we have already met, were of the number. Simeon was another, and Simeon was led to visit the holy place that day.

Simeon knew the Old Testament, especially Isaiah, and his canticle is a tissue of allusions which show how real to him was messianic expectation (Isa. 40.3–5; 42.6; 49.6; 52.10). Simeon blessed the parents and, doubtless with the Servant Songs of the ancient prophet in his mind, sounded the note of suffering which was to gather volume in the Messiah's story.

Simeon's blessing, called, from the first words of the Latin version, the Nunc Dimittis, has been part of the daily evening prayers of Western Christendom since the fourth century. It vibrates with gratitude for God's gift to the world, to Israel, and to him.

It was a grand moment for a good man to go. Was he an old man? T. S. Eliot in his *Song for Simeon* makes him one:

Grant us Thy peace.
I have walked many years in this city,
Kept faith and fast, provided for the poor.
Have given and taken honour and ease.
There never went any rejected from my door.
. . . .
Now at this birth season of decease,
Let the Infant, the still unspeaking and unspoken Word,
Grant Israel's consolation
To one who has eighty years and no tomorrow.

No tomorrow? We read of him today—and that is but one kind of immortality.

443

380 : Anna
Luke 2.36–38; Psalm 71

Another of God's Remnant enters the story, this time an aged woman, but with an insight as keen as that which Simeon had shown. Perhaps she had heard his words of praise and benediction. Old age, as we have more than once seen in these studies, 'hath yet its honour and its toil'. John wrote his Gospel when he was in his nineties. It is a little difficult to calculate Anna's age. Was she eighty-four, or does the phrase (36) mean that she had been a widow after only seven years of married life? If so, she was over a hundred years of age.

She could do little now save give her life to prayer. This does not mean that, at last, with nothing now to occupy her time, she began the ministry of prayer. A lesson worth learning early in life is that, save for the body's weakening, advancing years bring little fundamental change. For good or ill most people are much the same in later life as they are in their middle years and youth. If in her extreme old age, the good woman of the temple court was a person of prayer, it is a fair inference that, all through her life, she had been prayerful.

It is psychological fact that fundamental change becomes more difficult to effect as the years multiply. It is also a fact that, with the amazing triumphs of modern medicine, more people today reach old age than in any generation before. It becomes more relevant, more necessary, to prepare for old age, as the experience of old age becomes more common and more likely. We should bear the fact in mind, deal early with the faults which make old age ugly, learn to be unselfish, to rest in the Lord, not to burden others, to dispense love, to discipline the tongue, to enjoy loneliness, and to live a life of prayer. Anna shows the way. She saw the glory of God in Christ as her reward. Thomas Landels bravely wrote:

> And so in looking back at eighty-three
> My final word to you, my friends, shall be :
> Thank God for life; and when the gift's withdrawn,
> Thank God for twilight bell, and coming dawn.

Landels had Tennyson, with whose life he overlapped for thirty years, in mind:

444

Twilight and evening bell,
   And after that the dark!
And may there be no sadness of farewell,
   When I embark;
For tho' from out our bourne of time and place
   The flood may bear me far,
I hope to see my Pilot face to face
   When I have crossed the bar.

381 : Joseph Again

Matthew 2.13–15, 19–23; Hosea 11

Herod's will divided the kingdom which he had ruled so long,
so dexterously and so ruthlessly. Archelaus, son of Malthace,
a Samaritan woman, took over Judea and Idumea, by far
the choicest share. Herod Antipas, son of the same mother,
received Galilee and Perea; and Philip, son of a Jewess named
Cleopatra, took Iturea, Trachonitis, and the associated territories in the north-east. A map and a Bible atlas are tools of
study of some importance. The characters of the Bible lived
in time and place. Both time and place, circumstances and
habitation, helped to form them and are relevant to our
understanding.

Archelaus, who inherited his father's vices without his
ability, adopted the title of king, and bloodily quelled disorders which broke out in Jerusalem. The result was a wider
uprising, which required the strong intervention of Varus, the
governor of Syria. These were the troubled circumstances
which Joseph was led to avoid. He probably took the road
up through the coastal plain, over the famous Megiddo Pass,
where Josiah fell (2 Kings 23), across the Plain of Esdraelon,
and up the hills to Nazareth. Archelaus' stupid rule continued
till A.D. 6, when Jewish protest secured his banishment.

Amid these stormy events Joseph trod his careful way. No
one who saw the little party moving north with their few
poor possessions could imagine that the man with the bag
of carpenter's tools was the frail custodian of God's plan.
The Messiah was coming home, repeating, Matthew's pious
thought saw, in symbolic form, the old story of the Exodus.
The family settled in the town on the ridge of hills which

445

forms the southern rampart of Galilee, a place not mentioned in the Old Testament, but bearing a name which suggested a verse in Isaiah (11.1), where Christ is spoken of as a *netzer* (that is a *sprout* or a *shoot*) from the stem of Jesse. This is a type of mystical exegesis not familiar to our mind, but part of the Hebrew habit of thought, and valid as a sign to those who thus used their ancient Scriptures.

Joseph had no such thoughts as he plodded the weary miles up from Egypt. He had walked far for Mary's Son, and God had paid his way, for gold was one of the gifts the Magi brought. He was a good man, and in this chapter, his work done, he passes from the page of history. In the chapel of the hospital in Nazareth today, stands for an altar a carpenter's bench, the working side turned towards the congregation. Joseph was glad to set up his bench in Nazareth and prepare to provide for the Christ.

382 : The Child Jesus

Luke 2.41–52; Deuteronomy 16.1–8

The picture of the family from Nazareth, journeying faithfully to Jerusalem for the Passover feast, is a revealing one. They appear also to have remained in the city for the full length of the festival. There may have been a special reason for this visit. A Jewish boy was accounted of responsible age at twelve years, when he was said to become 'a son of the Law'. There would be some ceremony in the Temple, or in a synagogue near the Temple in which dress proper to the boy's maturity would be given, and appropriate exhortation made. It was a solemn and impressive occasion.

The caravan set out for home, in all probability by the northern hill-road, which ran up through Samaria, relatives and townsfolk travelling together to guarantee security. This is how the Child's absence remained unnoticed all through the first day's travelling. The anxious couple took a whole day to travel back, and on the third day, after visiting their late lodgings, went to the Temple and encountered a strange sight. The boy sat in the most august company.

There are several legends of Jesus' childhood and infancy, dating from the second century, and full of fantastic details.

This story, rescued from oblivion by the diligent Luke, and bearing the freshness of Mary's own telling, rings true. Jesus sat with the teachers of the Law, astonishing them by the maturity of His understanding. With His new garments, a new dignity seemed to rest on Him. Joseph and Mary must have felt, from this day on, that there was a part of Him which they were unable convincingly to penetrate.

Mary 'kept all these things in her heart'. One can almost hear her telling Luke the story. Something utterly amazed them. Joseph was too abashed to speak in such a company. Mary spoke out in her motherly concern and relief, and received a strange answer: 'Did you not know that I would be in my Father's house?'

He returned with them to Nazareth, and almost another twenty years of life are summed up in the phrase: 'he was obedient to them'. He Himself obeyed, and in the process grew up, a true man beloved of men, beloved of God (52).

Questions and themes for study and discussion on Studies 376–382

1. How many Old Testament references can be identified in the psalms of Luke?
2. How do Luke's opening chapters in other ways link the Testaments together?
3. How does Paul support the doctrine of the Virgin Birth (Rom. 5; 1 Cor. 15)?
4. Who ultimately make history—the good or the powerful?
5. Meeting in the place of service.
6. List the Remnant as they appear in the opening chapters of the Gospels.
7. Waiting for God's revelation. Is there still something to wait for?
8. The usefulness of the old.
9. Obedience as Joseph illustrates it.

383 : The Rulers

Luke 3.1, 2; Psalms 93 and 110

Like the meticulous historian that he was, Luke pinpoints the moment of John's desert ministry, and we meet a cluster of characters, only some of whom we shall meet again in the

New Testament. We shall meet the sinister Herod and the scheming priest Caiaphas.

Save for the moment when his face, stamped on a silver denarius, lay in the open hand of Christ, and save for his name called in threat and protest by the priests and their minions at the trial of the Lord, the second emperor of Rome, the dour Tiberius, will not appear again.

Tiberius was born in 42 B.C. He died in A.D. 37. He succeeded to the principate in A.D. 14, on Augustus' death, when he was fifty-six years of age. He was now over seventy. Tiberius was a deeply embittered man when he became Rome's ruler. He was Augustus' stepson, and disliked by the Emperor. Augustus did his best to find an heir to the principate more congenial to his taste, but was dogged by cruel misfortune all along the line of his endeavours. Again and again his successor-designate, or some youth groomed for that exalted position, died tragically, and in the end, anxious for the preservation of the Roman Peace of which he was the architect, Augustus reconciled himself to Tiberius.

It was too late to save a personality naturally dour, suspicious, cold and withdrawn, from the wounds and damage of such humiliation and rejection. Tiberius was an able man, and research has done much to rescue his memory from the grim reputation which the brilliance of the historian Tacitus fastened upon it. But Tiberius was the type of man on whom evil rumour seems naturally to fasten. He was now in retirement on Capri, watchful, bitterly suspicious and dangerous. That is why Pilate feared him.

But such was the background in the wide world where history, or so men thought, was made, when the Baptist lifted up his voice in the Jordan wilderness. No one imagined that the most deeply significant events of that year were made, not in Rome, nor yet in the small province where Philip, best of old Herod's three sons, exercised his authority, nor where Herod Antipater (Antipas), following his father's clever diplomatic policy with precarious deviations, managed to carry on, at least through these years, his puppet rule. It is difficult, in any year, to know where the true significance of history lies. Perhaps some hope lies there.

448

384 : John, Heir of Elijah
Malachi 3.1-6; 4.5, 6; Mark 1.1-11

In his brisk business-like way Mark speaks of a fulfilment of an ancient prophecy in the ministry of John the Baptist. The other three evangelists speak of this event at greater length and we shall look more closely at this Elijah-like character in the next two studies. Mark stresses in his brief account that John's ministry was a ministry of the wilderness, and in the fact lies a clue to the character of the man who led the great revival in Judea which prepared the way for the coming of Christ.

John's preaching-place was the wide river valley of the lower Jordan. Some touch of God on heart and mind made John aware of a divine calling, and he was haunted by the figures of Elijah, Elisha and Isaiah. The two earlier prophets were both associated with the Jordan. Elijah, as his ministry ended, felt himself drawn to that river frontier by which Israel had first entered the land, and over which he himself had come from Gilead, when he first burst upon the court of Ahab.

Here it was that Elijah, like Moses, went his way, and his spirit fell upon Elisha. It is easy to read John's mind. He knew the strange verse in Malachi which ended the canon of the Old Testament. The deep conviction was upon him that he was to begin something new. He sought the old places of bestowal and revelation. That tortuously winding stream, Israel's only river, had been marked by the giving of the Spirit, and the symbolic washing of water, for it was to the Jordan that Elisha had sent Naaman, sacramentally to bathe his leprosy away.

History can be a strong and living force. Christianity, like Judaism, is based and rooted in the historic events of a revelation. This is what John instinctively knew, and it was history which he drew from that strange landscape, the vast trench with the wide, green jungle-floor between the arid uplands of Judea where he was born and the tall ramparts of the mountains of Moab on the far side, the walls of the wilderness whence Israel had come, and the bastions of her enemies.

Hence qualities of character which made the Forerunner

449

what he was. Hence the need for Christians to know and to savour their own historic past. That is why these notes turn from character to character in the Bible. We shall meet no prophet greater than John.

385 : John the Preacher

Matthew 3.1–17; Luke 3.1–20

Down the long twisting miles from Jerusalem, high on its ridge, to the valley floor, deep below sea level, came the multitudes to hear the preaching of John. His stern, terse words again reveal the man and his training. The wild environment gave him his imagery and illustration. It was the wet shingle in the river-bed to which he pointed when he said that God could of the very stones raise up children to Abraham. And there was woodcutting in the Jordan jungle, to provide the word picture of the aimed and ready axe. Where there is woodcutting there is also the scrub-fire, such as Moses saw in Sinai. Before the flames the pests of the undergrowth, the vipers and scorpions, fled.

But it was the prophet Isaiah, as we shall see especially in John's account, that provided the Baptist with the core of his message, and perhaps there is another pointer here to a further influence upon his life. Not far from the traditional place of baptism is the Dead Sea, and round the north-eastern curve of that sea's arid shore lay Qumran, best known, thanks to recent archaeology, of the haunts of the wilderness sects.

It is a fair inference from the place of his ministry that John had spent long years of training and preparation in the desert. It is not impossible that he could have found refuge in such communities as that of Qumran although he drifted from them theologically. We know something of the library of Qumran, for when, in the Great Rebellion of A.D. 66 to 70, the Roman patrols quenched all guerrilla opposition in the Jordan valley, the folk of Qumran hid their precious scrolls in the cliff-side caves.

Perhaps their most prized book was a magnificent scroll of the prophet Isaiah. It was certainly in existence in John's day, and may have been the very book which John studied, with the six-centuries-old oracles coming to life in his mind. John preached repentance, in the sterner terms of the Old Testament, perhaps, than with the grace and persuasion proper to the New, but preaching for a verdict, for decision and committal, is as relevant today as it was when John cried aloud in the Jordan wilderness. There is no other way to prepare the way of the Lord than by repentance.

386 : John and his Visitors
Matthew 11.1–15; John 1.6–34

John was not the man to waste his time on those not there truly to listen. The interview with the delegation from the Sanhedrin is told in a manner typical of the fourth evangelist's reporting. Observe the laconic answer given to the blunt question put to him (19 f.). In the Greek text the words are even more abrupt than the translation makes them, and the Greek text no doubt reflects the Aramaic of the riverside conversation.

The delegates were, in fact, discourteous. Such questions are not directed bluntly in the East. Witness Nicodemus' courteous preamble in his interview with the Lord. Reading the question to which the priests were leading, John anticipated their words with a denial to all claims to be the Messiah. He said nothing more, for no one is under obligation to answer malign and loaded questions. In the next verse (21) crude discourtesy is apparent. 'What, then?' they say, not 'Who?'

John does not reply, so they proceed: 'Are you Elijah?' He denies it. There was a mystic sense in which John was to be regarded as Elijah, but he was replying with crushing brevity to a question intended to compromise him, and his answers are more and more sparing of words. At last (22) the officious delegation see the need for courtesy. They have come to a point at which they begin to fear for the success of their mission. After all, they have been sent by the hierarchy to make certain specific enquiries, and could be in an awkward position if it was to become clear that unauthorized rudeness of their own invention had spoiled all chance of a proper reply.

451

Given a correct approach, John replies with words of Old Testament Scripture. He rested on the Word, and such were the beliefs and preoccupations of the Pharisees that, on that ground, he was safe. It was skilful debating of the sort the Lord Himself, in similar contexts, was to demonstrate. He continued with his proclamation—that his function was simply to prepare the way.

John adapted his message to each group which approached him, as may be specially seen in Luke's account. Sin, and consequently repentance, finds first expression in the immediate environment, and the nearest confrontation with the Enemy. This was soon to be shown in the temptation of Christ.

387 : The Tempter

Matthew 4.1–11; Genesis 3.1–13; Romans 8.35–39

We have met the Tempter, the Mind behind Evil, before. Jesus had waited, it appears, until the mass movement of John's revival was past. He sought no spectacular publicity. John had known his relative as a man of God, and paid Him a splendid tribute. Then came the sign from God. John's mind had moved in the thought, language and imagery of the great Isaiah, and Isaiah had cried in stress of soul: 'O that Thou wouldst rend the heavens and come down' (64.1). So it came to pass, and a new page of history began. The Messiah stepped out on His ministry.

He was never more a human character of the Bible than at that moment when, needing no repentance, He nevertheless took His place beside sinful men at the place of baptism. And as so often seems to happen in the experience of men, the challenge was accepted by the Tempter. He had gone away to keep a lonely vigil and to face the vast issues which now confronted Him. He left the river bank, and walked back perhaps in the direction of the most ancient city in the land, the old Canaanite stronghold of Jericho.

Today Jericho lies on the green valley floor not vitally different from the Jericho of the first century, save that the mauve flowered jacaranda has joined the palms and cypress for which the town was famous. Nearby, in and under an ancient ruin-mound, lie the remnants of old fortifications which the archaeologists untangle, and which go back to the dawn of history.

A mile back from the mound stands a harsh steep mass of arid rock, a deserted wilderness of hidden tracks and caverns, where the loneliness and barrenness of a thirsty land could be felt. There went Christ. There went the Tempter. It is the way with him to await the lonely moment. Alone the Lord faced the problems of His ministry—the hungry multitude, the proud capital eager for a sign, the alien, and other nations. There was a carnal answer and a spiritual answer in each case. The Tempter suggested the former and hammered the beleagured mind for forty days. In tomorrow's reading from Luke it will be seen that the order of the three temptations is varied. The Tempter knows well how to make his thrusts repetitive, varied, infinitely subtle in their probing for the weak point in the wall, organizing the attack, ambush, storming, sabotage, switching the pressure now here, now there . . .

388 : The Tempted

Luke 4.1–13; Hebrews 2.16–18; 4.12–16; 1 Corinthians 10.12, 13

In this awesome scene we look at One who had no sin but was tempted in every way which is common to man—along the line of the body's natural needs and appetites, along the line of spectacular service, and through the imagination, firing laudable ambition. Here is Everyman but also Perfect Man, facing the storm and stress of every day.

There is, of course, no mountain in the world from which all the world's kingdoms can be overlooked together. This was a thrust at the soul's citadel through the memory. The story is using a metaphor without acknowledgement, as Eastern speech so often does. In His youth and boyhood Jesus must often have climbed to the lip of the ridge of hills above Nazareth. Beneath, running west and north to the rampart of Carmel, is the plain of Megiddo, sprawling, in Jacob's

453

phrase, 'like an ass', among the spurs of surrounding hills. This is the northern door to Palestine. All history has marched south and north this way. Here came Sisera. Yonder Gideon's commandos lay. This way, earlier still, journeyed Abraham. Assyrians and Babylonians had poured along the same road into the cockpit of the East. Alexander brought his Macedonians, Pompey the eagles of Rome, along this path. Future history was to be just as full. Vespasian, Omar, Saladin, Napoleon, Allenby, all knew the plain beneath the hills of Nazareth. It was a stage of empire. A boy's vivid mind might well have seen the vision of 'the kingdoms of the earth' below this native village. And now in the Temptation a dream of youth comes flooding back. These armies, these peoples. He could rule them. Rule them! And then He saw the Via Dolorosa and the Cross—and chose the Cross.

The character of the Tempted One, at this critical moment in time, is worth watching for its response. The Lord answered with the Word. For weeks, while the grim struggle lasted, He threw back each plausible and twisted argument with Scripture. Such is the safe reply. We must have objective standards, and they must be founded on authority. In stress of mind and body under the varied assault of evil, the Sword of the Spirit is the only trusty blade.

Questions and themes for study and discussion on Studies 383–388

1. Christianity's foundation in history. Is it important?
2. In what way did John fulfil Malachi's prophecy?
3. The role of the wilderness in Hebrew history.
4. Why is repentance vital?
5. Is John a model for the preacher?
6. Why was Christ baptized?
7. Why was Christ tempted?
8. The Bible and temptation.
9. Is loneliness a good thing?

389 : The Fishermen

Matthew 4.12–25; Mark 1.14–20

By the sixteenth verse of Mark's first chapter Jesus is on the shore of Galilee. There were ample fishing grounds at the head of the lake, and the men who fished the deep waters were among those influenced by John who had preached his fiery sermons far down the same rift-valley. From the fishermen of Galilee Christ called His first disciples.

It was a prosperous and hard-working group of men. They were not wealthy, but comfortable enough, and above all self-employed and independent, no oppressed and exploited class, servile or bitter over their lot. The choice was deliberate. It would have been easy enough in those days of fierce nationalism and class division to collect a horde of the resentful and dispossessed such as David gathered round him in the Adullam cave. But such men were not the material the Lord sought. Those men were to preach a spiritual gospel, not to spearhead a revolutionary movement—a fact to be borne in mind by groups of exotic Christians today.

'Christ,' wrote George Adam Smith, 'went to a trade which had no private wrongs, and called men, not from their dreams, but from work they were contented to do from day to day till something higher should touch them. And so it has come to pass that, not the jargon of the fanatics and brigands of the highlands of Galilee, but the speech of the fishermen of the lake, and the instruments of their simple craft, have become the language and symbolism of Christianity.'

'. . . fishers of men.' It is a vivid image. Peter and Andrew knew the silver heap which turned and tumbled in the straining net as the boats drew them heavily toward the steep beach. They also knew the empty haul, and the whole wet night's labour wasted in unrewarded toil. They knew the bream coming up one by one on the handline—the bream which carried its young in its capacious mouth, and, when they left, adjusted a temporary imbalance with a pebble— or perhaps a lost coin. They understood the figure of speech. We shall meet them again at their higher fishing.

455

390 : Men of Nazareth

Luke 4.16–30; Mark 6.1–13

The Lord appears to have visited Nazareth, His own home town, twice after the beginning of His public ministry. Luke tells of the first occasion and of the reading from Isaiah, with the significant break after the words 'the acceptable year of the Lord' (cf. Isa. 61.1 f.). The audience listened attentively and were moved by the power of His words, until someone recalled His origin. The remark: 'Is not this Joseph's son?' seems to have provoked a change of mood in the audience and a spirit of hostility which the Lord rebuked in firm terms (23–27). In a concerted demonstration of protest, the congregation arose, and thrust Him before them to the edge of the bluff which overlooks the Esdraelon Plain, perhaps the very place from which, as a boy, He had watched the historic landscape.

At this point, a strange thing happened—'passing through the midst of them he went away.' John also mentions two such incidents. In one of them (10.39) 'they sought again to take Him: and He went forth out of their hand' (RV). The escape in each case was probably due to the Lord's perfect dignity and matchless self-control. Crowds are cowardly. The steady eye, and the level voice of a brave man can often quell a multitude. It will be remembered that officers on one occasion were sent to arrest the Lord. They came back to their masters without carrying out their orders. 'Why did you not bring him?' say the irate priests. 'No man ever spoke like this man,' answer the men (John 7.45 f.). It was their only excuse! Imagine a police officer giving as a reason for not carrying out an order, the dominating personality of the man he was sent to take . . . And imagine his excuse being accepted! Yet, this is what happened. The Pharisees knew that there was a spell and a power in the words of Christ, which struck awe into those that heard them. They knew it from experience. So with the crowd. As the Lord moved through them they fell back. Their arms were powerless to strike Him. A glance, and they quailed.

So too in Mark's story, if he is describing another occasion. It was the fact that they knew Him that blocked their capacity for belief, and without their belief, the One who

456

sought to bless them was powerless to act (6.5). Poor men of Nazareth—so needy, so sceptical, and, in consequence, so deprived.

391 : Men of Capernaum

Mark 1.21–2.12; Luke 4.31–44

The people of Nazareth rejected their townsman on the absurd grounds that they knew Him. He was only the local carpenter's son. Therefore He could have no message for them. Capernaum was across the length of Galilee, near the head of the lake—no great distance as today counts distance, but far enough for those who trod the long, rough roads. Capernaum scatters its ruins today on a deserted shore, but in the Lord's day the traffic of a great east-west road passed through the town, and the industry of the lake had one of its centres there.

The people of Capernaum caught the note of authority in His voice, and the population found Him speaking to their hearts. He was never again to be so accepted. We catch glimpses of the men and women who found blessing there, and shall meet more as the story proceeds; Peter's wife's mother, the tormented and deranged, and the paralysed man who had four good friends (Mark 2.3) . . .

The story is told in the Second Gospel with peculiar vividness. Mark was Peter's pupil. Mark, counselled and healed by Peter after his wounding failure on the missionary journey with Paul, had been set to work on his real task by the great apostle who had probably led him to Christ as a boy. The story of Christ which he wrote, the earliest of the four, was at Peter's suggestion, and from Peter's information. Again and again, it almost seems that we can hear Peter's voice behind the brief chapters.

In the story of the man with the four good friends we sense strongly Peter's interest. Was Peter one of the four? Was it Peter's house, the tiling of which was removed to secure access? Were the ropes for the delicate operation secured from Peter's boat, moored, perhaps, within running distance? Was it Peter who was determined that the crowd,

457

composes it appears, of Pharisaic critics, should not stand in the way of blessing for a needy friend? We can never know, but the picture emerges of the common people of the lakeside town, recognizing the day of their visitation, and, unlike the men of Nazareth, conscious of the power, the authority and the worth of the One who came among them. Authority—how the world yearns for it in the Christian message! How helpless is the man who faces the world without it!

392 : The Pharisees

Mark 2.23–3.30

Observing the Lord's popularity among the common people who 'heard him gladly' (Mark 12.37), the Pharisees of Capernaum went to work. They invited some of the leading members of their sect down from Jerusalem to assess the situation. The pundits came, considered the case, and delivered their verdict: 'He casts out devils by the prince of devils.' In a few words the Lord demolished the absurd statement, but He continued with a statement of terrible seriousness. Here it is in Edward Vernon's little-known paraphrase of Mark's Gospel: 'But now let me tell you very solemnly: People will be forgiven all kinds of wickedness, even the vilest sins and the unholiest talk, but to call the goodness of God the work of the devil, and to call God's Spirit an evil spirit, is a sin past forgiving.'

Who were the people to whom these terribly serious words were addressed? We have seen in an earlier volume how exile turned the Hebrew captives back to their Scriptures. The Pharisees (and the name appears to mean 'the Separated'), were the leaders in this biblical revival. The Law was their incessant study. We have seen how the stress of exile divided the Jews. Some like Daniel, stood firm. Some like Esther and Mordecai conformed. From the Daniels came the Pharisees.

In ardour, faith and dedication they did fine work. And then, like so many who thus begin, they ended in pride and pettiness, 'separated' not from paganism, evil and compromise, but from the mass of Israel, the 'accursed crowd' (John 7.49). The Law became, not a means to holiness, but holiness

458

itself, a clutter of man-made regulations which they themselves could only keep by inventing, along with their detailed obligations, a parallel series of escape clauses, which poisoned their practice with hypocrisy.

They were not all corrupted in this manner. We shall meet Nicodemus. We shall meet Gamaliel. But such was the degeneration of a once noble order, that the Pharisee was capable of the sombre sin of Capernaum; the blindness, blasphemy and stark evil which could attribute the visible works of God in human lives to the power of evil. Such is sin unpardonable, for none could so calmly speak unless mind and heart were hardened and calloused beyond all possibility of repentance. We must pause in the next study to look more closely at this situation.

393 : The Doomed

Matthew 12.22–50; Luke 11.14–20; 1 Corinthians 6.9–11

No mortal man can pronounce another living person finally doomed. Christ alone of those who have walked the earth had the right to do so. He told the proud Pharisees that they had sinned beyond forgiveness. Thus came into the New Testament 'the unpardonable sin'.

Who are the doomed? Not those who have committed any of the common sins which damage, mar and ruin human life. The list of those who have thus sinned and been forgiven is evidence enough. Jacob was a liar, a cheat, deceiver of his old father, greedy, treacherous. In fierce conflict he found peace with God. In an earlier study we have lingered with David, the murderer and adulterer, who wrote Psalm 51. We shall meet Matthew and Zacchaeus, cynical collaborators for gain with those who trod down their countrymen. One of them wrote a book of the New Testament. The Prodigal Son of the famous story wasted a fortune in carnal sin. He was weak, selfish and unloving. His father received him, and killed the fattened calf. The bandit on the cross was a man of blood and violence. Christ accepted him. Peter denied his Lord and was recommissioned. Paul was the rabid persecutor of Christian men and women. He acquiesced in

459

Stephen's death. He became the great apostle to the Gentiles.

And look at the list of sinners in the letter to Corinth. They were all forgiven. What did Christ say? 'Him who comes to me, I will not cast out.' Both of the available Greek negatives are used in the verse. It is impossible to make a more emphatic negative assertion. 'If anyone, anyone at all, at any time, with any past, from any sin, comes in penitence to me, I will not under any conceivable circumstances turn that person away.' Can a promise be more absolute? Could it have been made by One more utterly true?

We have lingered a little on this theme because it can stir unhealthy fear. In the hundreds of characters of the Bible at which we have looked over these two years or more, we have met all kinds of sinners, and we have seen them again and again forgiven. Who then are the doomed? We shall look further tomorrow.

394 : The Doomed Again

Isaiah 1.1–18; Revelation 22.1–12

We have seen that all sins brought into the presence of God can find forgiveness. God remembers them no more. 'Though your sins be like scarlet,' runs a verse in the first chapter of Isaiah, 'they shall be white as snow.' And Isaiah had in mind the deep scarlet, shot with purple, which the Phoenicians made from the juice of the murex shellfish of the Palestine coast, a colour which impregnated the tissues of the garment beyond all possibility of washing away. God forgives, and will always forgive, when sin is brought to Him in confession.

What then of these men to whom Christ addressed His terrible words? Consider the subject thus: God's Spirit prompts men to face the challenge of Christ. When awareness of his passenger broke upon Peter in his fisher's boat, he cried: 'Depart from me, for I am a sinful man, O Lord.' They were wild, impulsive words, typical of Peter. Christ does not abandon those who thus respond. He draws near to save. To face Christ's challenge is overwhelming—but salvation.

But consider the contrary reaction. Dogged refusal to respond to the promptings of God's Spirit, in pride of heart or deliberately cherished hatred, diminishes the ability of heart and mind to grasp the idea of truth, goodness and beauty. Continue such determined wickedness long enough, and a spiritual paralysis envelops the personality. It is a self-willed hardness, not a statement couched in words, which constitutes 'blasphemy' of the sort Christ described.

The Pharisees in Capernaum had declared, as we have seen, in measured and deliberate terms, that Christ's work was evil work; He used Satanic power to bring peace to tormented lives. Thus to pervert truth and spurn goodness, was to demonstrate evil so determined and ingrained, a spirit so past all response to grace, a conscience so crushed and seared and a heart so wilfully hardened, that Christ (and only Christ could so diagnose) could declare that such men were already past the possibility of claiming God's forgiveness. Like the wicked friar, pictured by Dante in his *Inferno*, they were men with souls already in Hell while their bodies lived on earth. Such are the doomed—characters whom God alone can name.

And it follows that no one need fear 'the unpardonable sin'. The viciously impenitent care nothing for it. Mr. Fearing spoils life, and jettisons the joy and peace of mind which he was meant to enjoy. But he is received at last. No penitent was ever rejected for 'the unpardonable sin', for its very mark is impenitence.

395 : The Mason
Mark 3.1–12; Luke 4.38–44

The crowded weeks in and around Capernaum left a mass of stories which found their way into the accounts of all the evangelists. The man in the synagogue with the withered hand has a place in three of them, probably because of his healing evoked the bitter response of the Pharisees, and the beginnings of that campaign of hate which was to end at Calvary, and justify the Lord's denunciation of their wickedness.

But the man, like the mother of Peter's wife, restored by

461

Christ to usefulness and service, is worth looking at for his own sake. There is a legend which could be true, that the man approached Christ with the moving and simple words: 'I was a mason, winning my livelihood with my hands. I beg you, restore me to soundness, that I may not have the shame of begging for my food.'

According to the clutter of laws with which the Pharisees had loaded the observation of the Sabbath, only when life was endangered, could healing be permitted on the seventh day. The Lord brought the man forward. 'Is it lawful on the sabbath to do good or to do harm?' He asked 'to save life or to kill?' It was a skilful question, for the rabbis had decreed that if a beast had fallen into a pit on the Sabbath, the owner was to ascertain whether it was hurt. If not, he was to feed and bed it, but not extricate it until the next day. If it was hurt, he was to get it out and kill it. This was difficult and wasteful, so they had an escape regulation. The owner could get the beast out of the pit with the announced intention of killing it, and then not do so. In other words, they could twist their own laws for an animal but not for a man.

So was a man's usefulness restored. No doubt he went back to his mallet and chisel, as Peter's wife's mother rose from her bed and resumed her household tasks. Christ's presence in the life is a force which sanctifies, but also restores a man to normality and usefulness. His benediction takes away the spoiling, paralysing maladies which destroy calm and strength. To begin the life-long task of becoming like Him, is to begin moving towards the personality God intended us to be.

As with the mason of Capernaum, so with those who at His command stretch forth the hand today in another world, another century—

> But this I know, He heals the brokenhearted,
> And stays our sin, and calms our lurking fear,
> And lifts the burden from the heavy laden,
> For yet the Saviour, Saviour of the world, is here.

1. The place of natural ability and self-sacrifice in Christian service.
2. Why is it impossible for Christ to act in a climate of unbelief?
3. Signs of Peter's reporting in the narrative of Mark.
4. 'Conviction of sin'—when is it healthy and when morbid?
5. On what is God's forgiveness based?
6. What is a 'seared conscience'? What leads to it?
7. How can faith calm fear?

396 : The Tax Collectors

Matthew 11.20–30; Mark 2.13–20; Luke 5.27–32

Our readings must sometimes be repetitive because it is difficult in the tumult of events recorded in the narratives of the Galilean mission to disentangle character from character, and event from event. We have seen the Lord turning from those whom He ironically described as 'righteous', to the common people and the needy.

The conversion of one Levi, the Matthew of the First Gospel, led to a contact with a despised and hated group of men, the 'publicani' or tax-gatherers, so lamentably rendered 'publicans' in the AV (KJV). Who were these men? It was common Roman practice to farm out the taxes of a province. Financial organizations would bid a fixed sum and were free to recoup themselves. These were the men who were in direct contact with the people, and who, each in his petty sphere, reflected the rapacity, the corruption and the cruelty to which the whole vicious system lent itself.

All over the Empire men cried out in protest against the tax collectors. A grim anthology of scorn and hatred can be gathered from surviving literature against them. They were 'licensed thieves', 'wild beasts in the shape of men' . . . 'The tax-man gave a present to the merchant! After this will not wolves drop lambs from their teeth and lions let fawns go free?'

In no place was such anger so hot as in Palestine, where all tribute was looked upon as a symbol of subjection. Patriotism and religion combined in resistance to the system, and it followed that no man would undertake the task of gathering the tribute unless he was cynically prepared to set religion, patriotism and the regard of his fellows all second to gain. The tax-man was the pariah of society, loathed, scorned, rejected. He could not serve as a witness in a Jewish court. He was excluded from all religious worship.

Set as it was on a great commercial highway, Capernaum had a large group of tax collectors, who, as the victims of a common hatred, formed their own social group. Matthew was one of them. Excluded from the synagogue, he must have heard the Lord preach on shore or field, and found his heart moved to yearning for a better life. Such desire does not go unnoticed by God. Matthew left his office and followed Christ.

397 : Matthew
Hosea 6.1–6; Acts 1.1–8; Matthew 8.19–22

Look again at the thrice-told story of the call of Levi, who was to be known as Matthew. He was called directly from his place of business, and followed without hesitation. But he carried over into his new life some of the qualities which he had no doubt exercised in the corrupt businesses of the tax-office. Instinctively Matthew grasped a prime principle of witness. It begins 'at Jerusalem'. And secondly it cuts through all impediments.

The only contact with the world's need was among the outcasts of his own class. That is why, 'in his own house' (Luke 5.29), he made a banquet for the tax officials. He met them where they could be met, and found Christ with him. Mark adds the surprising detail (2.15) that there were 'many who followed him'. The imperfect tense used here might be better rendered 'they were many, and they were for following him.' That is, contrary to all popular expectation, there were many among the despised group who had felt the power of the Lord's words. The world is too often ignorant of the agony of mind and misery which lie behind some hard and

464

seemingly defiant exterior. But the Lord, as John was to remark, 'knew what was in man' (2.25).

There had no doubt been many a wild carousel in that same diningroom, and it was an appropriate place for the renegade son of Levi's tribe to bring together his old companions in sin to hear his farewell to an evil life, and to meet his new Master. There was little privacy in an ancient town. The house, as custom was, stood open, and no one had to peer through curtained windows to see the Lord at table with the hated group. It appears from Matthew (9.10), that the disciples who had already been called, also joined the company, but perhaps with some visible embarassment, or obviously less at ease than their Master.

Hence the direction of the Pharisees' attack. Perhaps they saw an opportunity to drive a wedge between Him and His followers, for it was to the disciples that they made their protest. The Lord heard them and rebuked them. It is touchingly significant that Matthew alone records the sentence from Hosea (6.6; Matt. 9.13): 'It is mercy that I desire and not sacrifice.' Mercy is what Matthew had found.

398 : Matthew the Writer

Jeremiah 33; Zechariah 9.9

We should pause at this point to consider what Matthew did for the Lord he had found, for in the historian we find the man. Old tradition has it that Matthew's first writing was a collection of the sayings of Christ. Perhaps the first impact of the Lord on Matthew's mind was in the authoritative nature of His teaching (7.29), and, being a man who knew professionally the importance of accurate records, he set out to capture on papyrus the precious words he heard.

The collection of sayings which Matthew made no longer exists in such a form, but perhaps we can see the shape of it in the Gospel which ultimately emerged and absorbed the earlier work. The book is dominated by five discourses (chs. 5–7; 10; 13; 18; 23–25), each recording an aspect of the Lord's teaching.

Here was a man captivated by the words of Christ, heard, not in the synagogue where his kind were unwelcome, but

465

from the edge of the crowd, in the street, from the report of others, and perhaps written down immediately to retain them and hold their meaning fast. So perhaps began the task which preserved for the world the Sermon on the Mount.

And then came the incredible moment of the invitation to join the band of those who walked with Him. Matthew followed, counting no cost, and the One whom he had known afar became a close and revered friend, as well as Master and Lord. And in that experience wonder grew. He saw the royalty of Christ, searching out, or perhaps already knew, the kingly oracles of the Old Testament, and found prophecy fulfilled. He chose the Davidic genealogy, and uses frequently the royal title 'the Son of David'. In the Nativity stories he chooses to tell of the august Magi, leaving Luke to tell of the shepherds. Both Matthew and Luke tell of the triumphant procession into Jerusalem but only Matthew quotes the prophecy.

Matthew, too, has more to say than others on 'the Kingdom of God'. He alone records the words about the coming Church, and leads on to the Great Commission to the disciples and the promise of Christ's continuing presence with His own. 'The style is the man', as the saying runs, and if we would know the one time tax collector, we must look rather at the truths and facts which he stressed in writing than in words which he spoke, for they are few.

399 : The Twelve

Matthew 10.1–11.1

We have looked at the fishermen of Galilee, those vigorous and industrious men whom the Lord called to follow Him. They were most probably converts of John the Baptist, their hearts prepared by the desert preacher for the call which was to come. We have met Levi, who was named Matthew, and who was called, not from the fishing-boat, but from the tax-office in the lakeside town.

At some point in the ministry in Galilee the band became complete. The Lord chose twelve, perhaps with the thought in mind of the twelve tribes of Israel. We shall meet many of them again, and have occasion to observe facets of their characters, but we should now look at them together. They were far from being the 'twelve ragamuffins' of King Frederick's letter to Voltaire.

The Twelve were called apostles, and the word implies that they were special messengers, bearing a commission, and, in fulfilling that task, wielding their Master's own authority. First, there was Simon, called Peter, whom we shall meet frequently. Peter and Andrew his brother were fishermen of Bethsaida, and met Jesus early, down at Bethany beyond Jordan. John tells us that these men were disciples of the Baptist.

Andrew had the distinction of being the first missionary of the Church, for he it was who sought Peter and brought him to Christ. Peter was a prize—'the mouth of the apostles', Chrysostom called him. To be sure, there were times when Peter spoke unwisely, but there is no denying his worth and his place in ancient history. David Smith wrote well of him: 'That impulsive man, so prone to err, so quick to repent . . . continually blundering, and in the panic of the last dread crisis guilty of a dire infidelity; nevertheless his very blunders were born of the ardour of his love for Jesus, and in the hour of his unfaithfulness, a look from that dear face broke his heart. When all was over, he could lift his eyes and say: Lord you know all things; you know that I love you.'

Next, another pair of brothers, also disciples of the Baptist, James and John. Their father Zebedee was a prosperous man, and their mother, probably a sister of the Virgin, was an ambitious woman, but brave, for she stood by the cross. It was her ardent spirit which lived in her boys whom Jesus called 'the Sons of Thunder'. James died at the hands of Herod Agrippa. John was to outlive the whole band . . . These men formed an inner circle of the Twelve.

400 : The Twelve Again
John 1.35–51; 1 Corinthians 12.12–31

There are some matters of interest which these studies necessarily bypass. The chronology of the Gospels, the order of recorded events and utterances, is not our immediate interest. We follow roughly the order of the first of the Gospels to be written, that of Mark, and draw into the list of characters studied parallel accounts in the other evangelists. Readers, however, must have observed already in the passages prescribed some divergences of order which call for explanation. Those interested would find Dr. Donald Guthrie's excellent *Shorter Life of Christ* a great help as an ancillary study. The matter is mentioned because the reading for this study raises the question of a period in Judea before the mission in Galilee.

But to continue with the Twelve. Philip was called at this time, a cautious and wary man, who liked demonstrable certainty. There is room for such men in the Church. They are a salutary check on the 'sons of thunder', and even on the 'Peters' of the community. Philip seems to have been a friend of Andrew.

Bartholomew is not mentioned again. It is said that, like Thomas, he ended as a missionary in India, no unlikely tradition, for the Italian shipmen now knew the secret of the alternating monsoons, and regularly traded with India, a fact to which many a hoard of Roman coins bears witness. There is also room in the Church for multitudes who never reach the headlines—nor want to do so. It is possible that Bartholomew was Nathanael, for just as the other evangelists do not mention Nathanael, so John, who does mention him, never mentions Bartholomew. Perhaps the full name was Nathanael Bar Tolmai (that is 'son of Tolmai'). We shall speak of him again.

Next came Thomas and Matthew. We have met Matthew and need say no more of him, but who was Thomas? The word means, like Didymus, its Greek equivalent, 'a twin'. Was he, as Eusebius said, another Judas? He was a devoted man but a confirmed pessimist.

James the son of Alphaeus, nicknamed 'the Little' (which may mean 'the younger') to distinguish him from the son of Zebedee, was, says tradition, a tax collector, converted in Matthew's house. If Alphaeus was also the father of Levi, then James was the brother of Matthew, and if Alphaeus was Clopas, then the Mary, wife of Clopas, who stood by the cross, was the mother of Matthew and James. What a household if these assumptions hold!

468

401 : The Rest of the Twelve
John 14

There must have been three among the apostles who bore the very common name of Judas. The Judas who is mentioned along with James, son of Alphaeus, is called by Matthew Thaddaeus. If this is from the Aramaic term Taddai it distinguishes him from Judas, called Thomas, the Twin, because Taddai means 'the courageous'. Mark calls him Lebbaeus, and if this is from the Aramaic Libbai, meaning 'the hearty', it distinguishes him from the cold and calculating Judas Iscariot. This faithful Judas appears again only once, in the puzzled remark of John 14.22.

And now another Simon, distinguished from Simon Peter by being called the Canaanite or the Zealot. The first term probably means that he came from Cana in Galilee, the second is much more sinister. If Simon was a Zealot, he had been a sworn member of a desperate band of terrorists, who, during the census troubles of A.D. 7, had vowed hostility to Rome. To accept such a man among the apostles, was to court the suspicion of Rome, whose agents and Jewish collaborators were very well informed on all such vital matters of security. The Zealots were diametrically opposed to the other type of Jew, such as Matthew, who took service under the occupying authorities or their Herodian associates. It is a most striking testimony to the unifying power of Christ, that Matthew and Simon could find a comon meeting place in His fellowship.

The last on the list was Judas Iscariot, the future betrayer. The surname probably means that he came from Kerioth in southern Judea. Judas Iscariot seems to have been the only member of the band who was not a native of Galilee. Why Jesus chose him, and why Judas became what he did become, is a problem we shall meet again.

But observe that the apostles were all young men. Peter alone appears to have been married. Jesus Himself seems to have been a father among them (Mark 10.24; John 13.33; 14.18). They were young men, still unfettered by custom, unbound by the prejudice which sometimes comes with years, still sensitive to wonder and unbounded hope. Except perhaps for Nathanael, they were not students, and none of them

469

had the massive learning of Paul, their future associate. This is the band which set out to subdue the world.

402 : Nathanael

John 1.43–51; Genesis 28

Nathanael was a man who required convincing. Philip knew this, and set the phrases of his announcement in careful order. Look again at John 1.45. He mentions Moses first, and the humble Joseph last. It was as Philip must have expected. Nathanael fixed immediately on Nazareth. Not only was the town without clear reference in the Old Testament, it was also the most cosmopolitan place of Galilee, and, though Galilee was not as Gentile-ridden as the Decapolis, on the other side of the lake, it was full enough of foreigners to call forth the scornful remark of the determined Israelite. A Messiah from Nazareth, indeed!

Then why was Nathanael so rapidly convinced (49)? The answer must lie in the Lord's strange remark in the previous verse (48). Nathanael obviously understood Christ's words more intimately than the rest who heard them. What if his morning meditation in some garden or orchard place of prayer (48, 50) had been the story of Jacob, who, full of guile and double-dealing though he was, saw a vision of great temple-steps leading up to God, and visible communication between God and man? Jacob of all men!

To a man so liable to fail, Nathanael may have mused, God granted a covenant, and a vision of Israel's destiny. But now, for all the prophetic fervour of John's ministry, and the breath of real revival through the land, the heavens seemed closed, and God remote. The covenant appeared forgotten, and God careless of His own. Looking at him, and hinting that He knew mysteriously the subject of Nathanael's complaint, the Lord utters the significant words of v. 47. 'No guile' refers surely to the fault of Jacob. 'Angels ascending and descending' on one who was the true path to God (John 14.6) shows the same covert reference to Genesis 28. This was the secret communication between the Lord and Nathanael.

Hence the sudden fervour of Nathanael's surrender. God

470

had met him in the place of prayer. In Christ Nathanael encountered One who understood his dreams, and satisfied the deeper longings of his heart. In a bent and twisted world, to know God is to know One, at least, who understands.

Questions and themes for study and discussion on Studies 396–402

1. How may the home be used in evangelism?
2. How do Matthew's Nativity stories differ from Luke's?
3. Could you match the apostles with twelve similar characters from your own church?
4. List the faults of the apostles already visible. Do faults preclude usefulness?
5. Why Twelve? Was there any special significance in the number?

403 : The Centurion

Luke 7.1–10; Psalm 33

There is a ring of soldierly precision about the next person who moves into the story. We do not see the centurion of Capernaum, but we hear his voice, and we have his words. It is easy to see that he was a man of rare quality. This centurion had been seconded for special duty in a sphere of Herod Antipas' administration.

We shall meet four other centurions in the New Testament, and it is a notable fact that they were all men of strength and integrity. The centurions were the backbone of the Roman army, professional soldiers, and leaders among men. Palestine was a difficult province, and there seems no doubt that the officers picked for service there were specially chosen for their ability to manage potentially critical situations. Tacitus' account of an army mutiny on the Danube, not many years before this date, shows that the centurions of the legions were not all men of the stamp we meet in the New Testament. The mutineers of the historian's account complain bitterly of their centurions' brutality.

The officer who sought the aid of Jesus was a human soldier. He was fond of his slave, and attracted to the better

471

side of Judaism. He was also a man of insight, who could see past the bitter, proud and legalistic leaders, suspicious of the new religious leader, and already excluding Him from the synagogues. He saw the Lord's worth, and came to Him with courtesy, reverence and faith. Observe, too, the centurion's exquisite tact. Knowing the tension which was rising between the Jewish leaders and Christ, he did not allow Him to enter his house, and approached Him correctly through Jewish mediators. It was for such qualities that this officer was chosen to represent the Empire in this tetrarchy. His daily habit of thought was that of a soldier, expecting unquestioning obedience, and taking discipline for granted. It was inevitable that he should see Christ in the framework of his thinking. We all do. According to our temperament—artistic, practical, philosophical—we see, interpret, and experience Christ.

Here was a Gentile, too, showing Israel the path of faith. When Luke wrote the story, twenty years after the events, the Gentiles were flooding into the Church. Luke himself was probably one of them. It pleased him to record the words of the simple soldier of the lakeside town, and the Lord's commendation.

404 : The Widow of Nain
Luke 7.11–18; 2 Kings 4.18–37

Nain, the modern Arab village of Nein, lies on the north-west slope of a hill between Gilboa and Tabor. It is two miles south-west of Endor, scene of Saul's tampering with death, and five miles south-east of Nazareth. It was twenty-five miles hard walking from Capernaum . . . We have been in this region before, because Shunem, where Elisha also gave a woman back her son, was not far away (See Study number 254).

The story of the widow of Nain is clearly one of those incidents which came to Luke's knowledge when he was wandering Palestine in quest of information, during Paul's enforced stay in Caesarea. It has no special connection with the fuller narrative. If, as some would have it, the notion was mendaciously to provide the Lord with an Elisha-like miracle, why not choose the exact place, and why a young man and not a child? Why, indeed, lie at all to no advantage?

472

There are marks of truth on the simple narrative. Look at it phrase by phrase, and observe how the poignant picture comes to life. It is told without art, in the simplest style, in all its bitter sadness. The widow need not have been out of her thirties. The girls of Palestine married early. She had long years of left-over life to live, and had now lost her last link with the days of her happiness. The world at large soon grows impatient with grief, and the sharing of sorrow is a rare virtue.

Luke writes with feeling, for all his simplicity. 'His heart went out to her,' says the NEB (13). He touched the bier, no doubt a long wicker stretcher, on which the body lay, as the pall-bearers took it to the burial place . . . And so the Lord of Life claimed the victim of death. Nothing more is known of the widow and her son. They no doubt returned to Nain, to whatever humble home and mundane task it was which the tragic visitation had invaded. But neither home nor occupation could ever be the same again after the hand of Christ had touched the thing of death. So it is always. Christ gives new life and feeds it back into the dead and dying world. Nain would be the better for its two new citizens, for they were indeed new people, both mother and son, who had known such benediction. In a sense, Christ still dwelt there, for He can dwell among men only as He dwells in the lives He has touched, and the hearts He has sanctified.

405 : John in Prison

Matthew 11.2–19; Luke 7.19–35

John lay in the dungeon of Machaerus, one of Herod's strongholds. In the murk, the heat, the squalor of his prison, doubt assailed him. The body's pain, shattered health, hope deferred, can bring darkness to the mind. Nor did all he heard suggest to John the Messiah of his valiant dreams. No conquering hero, no rider with the sword, was abroad in Israel, and doubt can thrive on self-made misconception.

The Lord in no way reproached the broken man. He sent him an answer, Eastern-fashion, in an object lesson, with the gentle suggestion that he should think more deeply and go on believing (Luke 7.22). Love, compassion, pity were abroad in the land. This was the God who was showing Himself in living flesh (John 1.18). In the synagogue sermon the Lord had broken the sentence of Isaiah before the grim phrase, 'the day of vengeance of our God' (Luke 4.19). John had his answer, and we are not told whether it brought enlightenment, calm and quietness to his harassed spirit.

And then, turning to the crowd around Him, Christ paid splendid tribute to John. He was no river reed, no tussock of the Jordan river-valley, bent like some pliant and yielding thing under the thrusting wind which poured down the great cleft from Galilee to Aqaba. He was not the princely aristocrat, clad softly and applauded at the palace gates by sycophantic crowds. He was the last and greatest of a stern prophetic line, and he saw, if he had eyes to see, the last fulfilment of all the long dream of Israel, the Coming of One . . .

At the same time John was to die before the consummation. He was not an apostle. He was never to see the Empty Tomb. He was never to know the gospel sent into a wider world, a conquest far more than his dreams. Therefore he lacked what the least of the Christians had and knew. He was never to be granted the last and deepest insight into God's plan for man. He would not live to see in Jesus either the wielder of fan or axe (Luke. 3.9, 17), or the fulfilment of Isa. 53. He demonstrated, none the less, that the saint can be tried by doubt, and what to do with doubt. . . .

> O Cross, that liftest up my head,
>   I dare not ask to fly from Thee;
> I lay in dust life's glory dead,
>   And from the ground there blossoms red
>   Life that shall endless be.
>
> George Matheson.

406 : Simon the Pharisee

Luke 7.36–50

It is difficult to know why the disdainful Simon invited the Lord to dine with him. He provided none of the common courtesies; the cool water for the guest's dusty feet, the touch of scented oil on the hair, the kiss on the head which is still given in parts of the Middle East today. The woman who broke in upon the scene of discourtesy had seen with sorrow this neglect, and, after the fashion of the emotional East, remedied the lack with her own small phial of ointment, with unbound hair and tears.

A rabbi's house was not uncommonly open, and the stranger was free to haunt the courtyard outside the dining place in order to hear the words of worth which might fall from the great man's lips. The ancient world set less store by privacy than we do, but was much concerned about a reputation for wisdom. Hence the vivid scene described by Luke. Simon was prepared to patronize the new prophet, perhaps desired to examine His doctrine, but was unable to treat Him as an equal, or even as a guest should be treated.

His outlook is clear. Here was the very test he sought. Here, perhaps, with unexpected promptitude, was the answer, and the answer he had already half-formed, to any questions he might have asked about his guest. The Lord was perfectly well aware of the movement of His host's mind, and told His simple story. Simon saw the point, and replied that gratitude in human affairs is generally proportionate to the benefit received. His own view of sin was hardly adapted to see further than this, and he no doubt judged that there was very little which God might find amiss in him.

The carnal sin of the poor woman he could well understand and shudder at. Most people are prone to paint more darkly the sins of others than their own. Pride, disdain, discourtesy, self-esteem, and lofty contempt for those marked down as inferiors, are none the less sins to set in the list with the vices of the flesh. Simon had fulfilled his day's obligations to God. He had performed the necessary ablutions and formal prayers. The process brought little sanctification to one unable to see the pathos of grief over sin and passionate gratitude for God's forgiveness.

407 : The Women

Luke 8.1–3; Proverbs 31.1–31

Any observant reader of Luke's two books will note his interest in the activities of the women of the Church. It is a fair guess that, when he was collecting the material for his narrative, he met and questioned many women, including Mary herself. This brief note seems to intrude into his text without special relevance. Perhaps he derived the story of Simon and the parable of the debtors from one of the women, and was so reminded to place these facts on record.

We are given, incidentally, a glimpse into the Lord's means of sustenance. Joanna, the wife of Chuza, a manager of Herod's estates, is mentioned once more (Luke 24.10), and Susanna does not appear again, but they have honour enough in the brief words which close the small record (3). It is a fact in which women might take deep satisfaction that, although in the four Gospels there are references enough to the ministrations and loyalty of the women, there appears no single example of a woman hostile to Christ. Traitors, cynical schemers, cowards, brutes and hypocrites among men of all ages can find their predecessors, counterparts, and old examples in Judas, Pilate, Caiaphas, the creature who plaited a crown of thorns and the wretches who could sneer at the tormented figure on the cross. Women who imitate such conduct can find no types or predecessors in the pages of the Gospels. Even Pilate's wife held Him in reverence.

Mary of Magdala is not the woman of the previous chapter. The strange reference to the seven devils means that there was a mighty battle with evil for Mary's tortured soul. The phrase also shows that Christ does not let a sinner go. Again and again, as Mary stumbled, the Lord must have healed and lifted her. He returns to reclaim as often as evil returns to the attack.

And observe how, as with the Twelve, the Lord could take people as diverse in experience and background as Mary and Joanna, and make them one in Him. 'There is nothing which the Church needs more,' writes Professor Barclay, 'than to learn how to yoke in common harness the diverse temperaments and qualities of different people. If we are failing, it is our own fault, for, in Christ, it can be done—it has been done.' If one clear lesson more than another emerges from these studies, it is this precisely.

Questions and themes for study and discussion on Studies 403–407

1. Discuss the place of discipline in a society which tends to reject authority (cf. the Centurion).

2. Remembering John the Baptist's experience, how can the Christian deal with doubts?

3. Examine Scriptures which encourage God's people to show common courtesies. What outstanding Old and New Testament examples are there?

4. Consider the lives of women who came into contact with Christ. What qualities do they exhibit which Christians could well emulate?

408 : The Galileans

Luke 8.4–15; Acts 17.22–34

The Parable of the Sower is the Lord's summary of His mission in Galilee. Some farmer on a stone-strewn hillside above the lake gave Him the illustration He sought, and all unknowingly entered the pages of the New Testament.

What does the story mean? The interpretation of parables is something of an art. The guiding rule is to seek for one simple purpose. The common faults are a perverse endeavour to force meaning into pictorial details, and to imagine secondary meanings. This story does not teach that the heart of man is foredoomed to receive or to reject the seed of God's planting. The parable of the sown seed is not an object lesson in theology or psychology. It is pure realism.

The first mission in Galilee was over. Perhaps it was less sweeping in its results than the disciples had expected. Possibly it was less dynamic in its impact than the mission of John. To meet their questions the Lord gave His parable. When the farmer sows his seed this is what always takes place. The paths through the fields absorb their quota. Nor can he always recognize the ground spoiled by the underlying rock, or invisibly corrupted by the hidden spores of useless and alien growth. So with the Word. Some folk harden the heart; some appear to respond but fail to follow out the implications; some who might have produced a rich and healthy crop are too busy with base or lesser pursuits; and some allow the deep good roots to strike down into heart and personality, and produce an abundant harvest.

Here, then, in an earthy little story, are the Galileans.

Among the hills and along the lake, life was much as life is today. All unconsciously, like the mute earth beneath, society makes much preaching vain. The Galileans had their secure, contented members, at home in their affluent surroundings, who saw no relevance, found no challenge, in Christ. They had their wishful shallow types, their weaklings and their cowards ... And they had among them men and women athirst for righteousness, who wanted of life, wanted of God, nothing but the best and noblest. It is common heresy, among those who read no history, to imagine that they live in a new world, full of new men and women, who neither think nor react as men and women once did. A. Housman put it:

> *The tree of man is never quiet :*
> *Then 'twas the Roman, now 'tis I.*

409 : Jesus' Family
Luke 8.19–21; Mark 3.31–35; John 7.1–9

The Lord was tempted 'in every respect ... as we are' (Heb. 4.15). He knew, in this process, what it meant to suffer opposition in the intimate circle of His own family. Little is told us of this painful situation, and we have no idea what Mary thought. Nor is there any background of detail at all by which the events may be set in context and perspective.

The brothers and sisters of Christ are mentioned several times (Matt. 12.46; 13.55 f.; Mark 3.32; 6.3), and He Himself is called the 'first–born' (Luke 2.7). They are obviously the children of Mary. The story that they were the children of Joseph by an earlier marriage, or even cousins of the Lord, was invented by Jerome and others, who were beginning to develop the absurd hostility towards sex and marriage which is no part of Christianity, but belongs to the obscurantism of the Middle Ages.

The Lord cannot be accused of harshness in this context, Observe the brevity of detail, and the purpose for which the story was told. There are fifty-six words in the Greek text. The visitors were not necessarily dismissed nor coldly neglected. The Lord had perhaps delayed the commence- ment of His ministry till the age of thirty, so that Mary's other children could reach maturity and be in a position to sustain her. Consider, too, the fact that this must have been one of the stories which Mary told Luke or confirmed for him. It came from Peter to Mark, and Matthew may have been present when the incident took place. Why did three of the evangelists consider this small event important enough to record? Possibly because of the saying on the spiritual brotherhood (21), a truth which was deeply significant in the early Church.

Two other thoughts emerge. James the Lord's brother, became a leader of the Church (Gal. 1.19; 2.9; Acts 12.17; 15.13–29) and the writer of an epistle (Jas. 1.1). Could there be stronger proof of the Resurrection? A man like James needed convincing. Secondly, consider the sad fact of stress in the home where one might least expect to find it. There is nothing more deeply or fiercely testing than hostility in the place where love and understanding should be supreme.

410 : The Tempest-Tossed

Luke 8.22–25; Mark 4.36–41

'And one man in his time plays many parts,' says Shakespeare. That is why we find ourselves confronting the same characters in varied moods and situations. In the story of the storm we see the men of Christ reacting to dire physical danger.

It was no less than that. The mighty trench, that scar of an ancient wound in the surface of the globe, which begins in the Beqaa between the Lebanon sierras and cuts south through the Jordan valley and the Galilee lake to the deep depression of the Dead Sea, and then climbs again to Aqaba, is a fearsome breeder of gales. Hot air rises from the furnace heat round the lower Jordan, and a funnelled stream is sucked in from the valley between the cool Lebanon snows. It swoops down to the Dead Sea and curves up to the Gulf of Aqaba. It is easy to see how Galilee, caught in its midmost descent, can become a turmoil of storm.

The disciples, tough boatmen and fishermen who knew the lake and its precarious moods well, were terrified, and had every reason to fear imminent death. Calmly, their Master slept through it all. It is moving to see the strong men of the lake turn naturally for aid to One who, in the brief months of their acquaintance, had won to this extent their trust and confidence. They had no evidence that He knew anything at all of seamanship. They did not know what they expected Him to do, or what they could ask of Him. Prayer is sometimes nothing more than a cry for His aid. And so it was that the storm-tossed band became a symbol for men and women in their desperation. So, too, we see deeply into the character of the distressed disciples. It is in such moments of crisis that men show with startling clarity what they think, that in which they place their trust, their true desires and apprehensions.

This is no myth, allegory or parable. It is a story vividly true to its environment. It is true, nevertheless, to life, real in the experience of the tempest-ridden in any sea of trouble. The Sankey hymn on the theme is well-known: 'Neither the wrath of the storm-tossed sea, nor demons, nor men or whatever it be . . .' There is a word in it for those Isaiah has in mind (54.11, 17): 'O afflicted one, storm-tossed, and not comforted . . . no weapon that is fashioned against you shall prosper . . .'

411 : The Maniac

Mark 5.1–10; Romans 7.15–25

If Gadara is the place by the lake which George Adam Smith thought he had identified, the steep declivity above the blue water may be pictured, the pleasant villas on the high slopes with a view up to Capernaum, the crowded waterfront and the high-set amphitheatre, inevitable adjunct of all Greek towns, from which the audience could look, not only at the stage, but also at a wide prospect of lake and distant farmland.

But outside the clustered houses and public buildings there were tombs, and the geographer, while in the act of examining the place, saw a local peasant, he tells us, unearth a tombstone set up as a memorial to a soldier of the Fourteenth Legion. There on the stone was the Latin word which tangled like a living, evil thing with the throning torments of the distracted inhabitant of the Gadara lakeside tombs.

It was a dark night when the Lord and His men came ashore, not a pleasant hour to be greeted with an ear-splitting yell from the gravestones among the rocks. The madman emerged with fragments of his bonds about his hands. He was held, he cried, by a legion of evil powers. He knew, as some victims of evil do not know, the immense strength of the force which possessed him. A legion, Rome's regimental unit, had become for him an awful symbol of himself. Perhaps he had once run madly from his village street, a little shrieking boy, when a Roman patrol closed in to wreak vengeance for the local murder of some drunken legionary. Perhaps the traumatic memory of his parents dead and stabbed in the reddened dust, drove him to a consuming hate which ate up his mind.

Legion! It was like that, like the rising, falling boots in Kipling's Boer War poem, tramping, tramping day and night through his hot and ravaged brain, occupying cohorts of foul presences . . . and there among the tombs he saw the hated name again on the stones: Legion, Legion, Legion, till he screamed and tore things apart. And yet, some undamaged corner of the brain called for salvation, reached out and cried to the calm face he saw before him in the band of men who climbed out of the beached fishing boat.

'What is your name?' asked the Lord. 'There are so many of me moaned the man, that I am a whole legion of people.' The edge of that experience is known to all of us. 'Dear Lord, that loose lascivious face, that leers in my own soul,' wrote Studdart Kennedy, 'wilt Thou not smash it with Thy cross and make me free and whole?' Paul spoke of 'another law in his members, warring against the law of the mind . . .'

A legion of impulses, appetites, desires, invade and obliterate the personality—and 'some such grievous passions tear that only Christ can cast them out.' Christ did at Gadara, Christ still does.

412 : The Gadarenes

Mark 5.11–20; 8.34–38

The essential fact in this story is that a herd of swine was sacrificed to save the personality of a man. View it thus, and the charge of wanton destruction falls. A curious thought is preserved in a letter of T. E. Lawrence. He saw a little girl at play on the great green lawn before the exquisite façade of Wells Cathedral. Lawrence wondered at himself when the thought took shape in his mind that, if the choice were given, he would destroy the whole lovely building to save the child. Supreme respect for the value of the human person is a gift of Christianity to the world. Where Christianity is suppressed man becomes a brute in the eyes of tyrants, to be treated like a brute, a cog in a machine to be worn and worked for the good of the machine, a number on a list in another's selfish calculations, a punched pattern of holes in a computer card, cheap, expendable. The men of Gadara so viewed life. They begged Christ to go and leave them to their pig breeding. They had the Son of God with them. They preferred swine. John Oxenham wrote:

> *Rabbi, Begone!*
> *Thy powers bring loss to us and ours.*
> *Our ways are not as Thine—*
> *Thou lovest men—we, swine!*

The Gadarenes are still about. They are not hostile necessarily to the faith, but it must not, if they are to entertain it, interfere with life. It must not disrupt. It must occasion no discomfort. He interfered with the common, base ways of daily living, and presumed to set a higher value on the souls of men than on material possessions.

> *Christ went sadly,*
> *He had wrought for them a sign*
> *Of love and tenderness divine—*
> *They wanted swine.*

His presence healed men, but that was irrelevant if swine were lost, and the Ten Towns sold their place in history for pork.

In such a harsh environment the healed man was left. A principle is involved. If one cannot witness in the circle of one's daily life, it is idle to seek remoter service. Evangelism begins in our own Jerusalem. It is easy to imagine what difficulties the man of the tombs faced in society. The boat drew away with the banished Christ. Up the hill, in his borrowed cloak, and in his right mind, into the crowded land of the Ten Towns went the man from the tombs—the first apostle to the Gentiles.

Questions and themes for study and discussion on Studies 408–412

1. What guidelines for our conduct does our Lord's attitude to His family provide? Consider the tensions and loyalties involved in one's relationships with a non-Christian family on the one hand and fellow Christians on the other.
2. The Christian and trouble—what part does Christ play in these experiences?
3. What is the significance of Christ's sending back the demoniac to his own people?
4. How should a Christian deal with opposition at home, his place of work, etc.?
5. Christ left the Gadarenes as requested. In the light of the rest of the New Testament does this say anything specific about evangelism? What should be our attitude when faced with the hostility of Communism, Islam, etc.?

413 : Jairus

Mark 5.21–43; Luke 8.41–56

Jairus' story is told more fully in Mark than in either Matthew or Luke. Mark had the facts from Peter, and Peter had seen Jairus' agony at first hand, being one of those taken into the dead child's room. Follow the ordeal of the good Jairus. Jesus had arrived unexpectedly, at what time we do not know. The party had possibly drifted across the lake in the night, and had appeared on the western shore early on the following morning.

News soon spread. The whole lake, on its Jewish west and its Greek east, was thickly populated. Jairus must have thought it an amazing answer to prayer. He came urgently to Christ and fell at His feet. His plea was heard, and the Lord accompanied him up the narrow, crowded street. The unfeeling crowd, greedy for wonder, gathered round and blocked the way. Progress was agonizingly slow. He must have seemed to the distraught and tormented Jairus not to care. And he had said that his little one lay 'at the point of death'. So often when He really plans to give more than we have asked, does God seem to wait and not to hear.

Then the worst happened. Progress had been slow enough as the little group thrust through the impeding multitude, but now it stopped altogether. And for whom? Not for a dying child, but for a woman, a woman, Jairus would think, selfishly preoccupied with her inconsiderable ill while his 'little daughter lay at the point of death'—the point of death! The words hammered his mind. And he had told Jesus as much.

And now the dreaded messenger—too late, the end had come, and all perhaps, because of that shuffling progress, that selfish crowd, that woman . . . Jairus was crushed, but the Lord turned to him and quenched his fear. 'Only believe'. How impossible a word it seemed! But the scene in the room of death revealed the full significance. It was one of those moments which burn a picture and a memory into the brain. Peter remembered the very words: 'Talitha kumi'. Jairus received 'far more abundantly' than all he asked or thought. Jairus had known crushing agony. He now knew why God had permitted him so desperately to suffer. Thus, sometimes, with life.

As when Lazarus died, the Lord was well aware of the deep distress of those He loved, but He had more to give them than the boon for which they prayed. 'Did I not tell you that if you would believe you would see the glory of God?' Jairus was to see the glory of God and to praise the Lord for His delay all the rest of his life. Men are sometimes called to endure that which appears to surpass all limits. Let it fortify the soul to know that He sees, and knows, and has not lost control. Beyond what men count catastrophe lies 'the glory of God'.

414 : The Woman in the Crowd
Luke 8.41–56; Romans 10.10–13

Look now at Luke's account. The physician leaves out the pungent phrase at the end of Mark 5.26, in which we almost hear the downright Peter's very voice as he told Mark the story. Moved by a deep and urgent hope, which proved the father of faith, she thrust through the crowd until she was near enough to insinuate a hand and touch the hem of His robe. A surge of health told her she was healed.

But with that sensitivity which was part of His uncorrupted body Jesus knew that He had given something of Himself, some of the boundless life that was His to give. Hence the question which was so baffling to the disciples, who, at that tense moment, were perhaps sharing the pain and haste of poor Jairus.

She 'fell down before him, and told him the whole truth' (Mark 5.33). It is pointless in all our relations with Christ to do anything less—or to imagine that a healing contact with Him can leave us lost and faceless in the crowd. Inevitably she was drawn out of the multitude and compelled to identify herself in public with the One who had conferred His blessing upon her.

The woman in the crowd becomes therefore an example. There are those who in diffidence, in shyness or in hesitation seek to limit contact. They desire the touch of His healing, but they are reluctant to stand out and be numbered with Him. Fear and trembling (Mark 5.33) are maladies of the mind to which many sensitive souls are subject, but they are ills which, like the damage to our soul which His touch can heal and forgive, must be brought into reach of His blessed hands.

It is *with* Christ that a man finds his peace, his standing and his usefulness. The preposition matters. To be sure other prepositions are valid and contain their truths. Blessing comes *in* Christ, *through* Christ, *by* Christ . . . but it is *with* Christ, identified, conspicuous, strong, like the house on the rock, that the committed Christian must stand. We are safe nowhere else. It is thus that we 'go in peace' and know our malady no more.

I am trusting Thee for pardon!
At Thy feet I bow,
For Thy grace and tender mercy
Trusting now.

485

I am trusting Thee, Lord Jesus;
Never let me fall;
I am trusting Thee for ever,
And for all.

—(Frances Ridley Havergal)

415 : The Townsfolk

Mark 6.1–13; John 5.33–47

We have been following Mark over some of these events, and now we meet the people of Nazareth again, among whom Christ could do no significant work of good. It is interesting to look at the Lord's townsfolk and see why this terrible impotence was manifest. God's grace is touched to effectiveness by faith. It is thrust upon none in despite of the will.

In a letter written from Pavia during his mission there, the Florentine reformer Savanarola explained to his mother why he was working in distant Lombardy: 'Seeing that He has chosen me for this sacred task, be content that I fulfil it far from my native place, for I bear better fruit than I could have borne at home. There it would be with me as it was with Christ, when His countrymen said: Is not this the son of Joseph the carpenter? But out of my own place this has never been said to me; rather, when I have to depart, men and women shed tears, and hold my words in much esteem'. It was a common bush which flamed with glory for Moses. One who sought less urgently for God's will might have seen nothing strange. This was Mrs Browning's point:

> *Earth's crammed with heaven*
> *And every common bush afire with God;*
> *But only he who sees takes off his shoes,*
> *The rest sit round it and pluck blackberries,*
> *And daub their natural faces unaware*
> *More and more from the first similitude.*

God is revealed to those who seek Him. Those whose heart and mind are set on self, who deliberately confine ambition and desire to the world and the flesh, can persuade themselves that the very words of Christ contain no wonder, that Creation can be dismissed as chance, that conscience itself is the product of chemical changes in the body. In other words, it is those who seek who find. Let but the soul cry out for relief and light, and the glory of God begins to glimmer in Nature, in the Scriptures, in Christ.

In a sense it is Gadara again, perhaps with less excuse. In the Decapolis town they were preoccupied with their pig-farming. In Nazareth, Jews not Greeks, the dull townsmen of the Lord were preoccupied each with himself, unable in sheer dullness of heart and mind to see any beauty or appeal in One whom they had seen with plane and chisel in hand at work before a local bench. And so they missed, like the Gadarenes, the glory of the Christ.

Questions and themes for study and discussion on Studies 413–415

1. The meaning of pain and God's delays in the story of Jairus.
2. What of secret discipleship in the light of Mark 5.30?
3. The people of Nazareth and Gadara and their counterparts today.

416 : The Poor

Matthew 5.1–6; Isaiah 25

We do not know just when, in the early ministry of the Lord, the words of the Sermon on the Mount were uttered. Perhaps, like most good sermons, this famous discourse was given more than once. Luke says that the same words were heard on level ground (6.17), perhaps to those unable to climb, or out of hearing. Some say that the sermon was given to the Twelve only. If so, the Sermon on the Plain, to which Luke makes reference, certainly had a larger audience. Nor does it look as if the occasion described by Matthew (5.1) was a scene of retreat.

At any rate, the Lord began with the preoccupation of Psa. 1—'Who is the happy man?' He began with the poor, and ended, as paradoxically, with the persecuted. Matthew, to be sure, renders the Lord's Aramaic by 'the poor in spirit', Luke says simply 'the poor', but it is all one. The poor were poor in spirit.

Sir George Adam Smith, in his great study of Isa. 25, writes

movingly on the theme. He points out that in the East poverty
meant more than mere physical disadvantage. The poor man
was too often, in popular religion, considered the God-for-
saken man. The poor man lay under Heaven's frown, deprived because he merited deprivation. And commonly this
is what he himself believed. It thus came about that the poor
man was deprived of justice, respect, acceptance. He was
lonely, burdened in heart, in a word 'poor in spirit'.

He hungered, therefore, for God, for justice, for love, as
well as for food. And, says the commentator, 'it was by
developing, with the aid of God's Spirit, this quick conscience
and this deep desire for God, which in the East are the very
soul of physical poverty, that the Jews advanced to the sense
of evangelical poverty of heart, blessed by Jesus in the first
of His Beatitudes, as the possession of the Kingdom of
Heaven.'

Hence, for the Remnant—the choice among them—the
worth and the lessons of the Exile when the whole nation,
the noble, the saintly, the gentle, the cultured, priest, soldier,
citizen, woman, youth and child, were torn from home and
estate, deprived of standing, liberty and all that which had
seemed the mark of God's favour, and were led to the discovery that in such degradation and bereavement God cared.
So 'the poor in spirit', no longer arrogant, purged of materialism, became the meek, and the humble, asking of God nothing
more than His righteousness. And so Christ gives dignity,
worth, meaning to suffering, and causes the poor in spirit to
see that in His sight they stand higher than the proud, the
self-sufficient and the rich of this ephemeral world.

417 : Those who Mourn
Matthew 5.4; Revelation 21.1–6; 22.1–7

The Exile taught the faithful of Israel the true meaning of
pain. We saw Job wrestle with that theme, and Habakkuk,
too. And now the Lord numbers among the happy breed
'those that mourn'. The significance of sorrow is the most
difficult of all life's lessons to learn. Sorrow can paralyse and
embitter. It can also sanctify, and the Lord meant that they
are blessed who face the opportunity to draw closer to Him
in the school of stress and grief.

These are words which it requires courage to write. The Lord Himself permits us to pray that we be not led into testing, for that is one meaning of 'temptation'. On the other hand, life being as it is, somewhere, at some time, we must face the tutelage of sorrow. Perhaps we should ask ourselves whether we can grow to full stature without it. 'As long as man remains as he is,' writes Hugh Silvester, 'a world without pain, disappointments, obstructions and frustrations might well lead to such an increase of arrogance and hardness of heart that life would become insupportable. The world as it is appears to be the only suitable home for man as he will be.'

It is a lesson which has broken through to many. Oscar Wilde in his moving book *De Profundis*, wrote over seventy years ago from his prison cell at Reading: 'I used to live entirely for pleasure. I shunned suffering and sorrow of every kind. I hated both. I resolved to ignore them as far as possible; to treat them; that is to say, as modes of imperfection. They were not part of my scheme of life. But my mother, who knew life as a whole, used to quote to me Goethe's lines . . ₃

> *Who never ate his bread in sorrow,*
> *Who never spent his midnight hours*
> *Weeping and waiting for the morrow—*
> *He knows you not, ye heavenly powers.*

Oscar Wilde read his Greek Testament in Reading Jail, but Matthew's verse never got to the centre of his being and his sorrow. But there it stands, for our challenge, and for our faith: 'Happy are those who mourn—for they shall be comforted.' And the comfort of God is comfort indeed.

418 : The Meek
Matthew 5.5; 11.28–30; 26.47–54; Isaiah 42.1–4; 53.7

It is difficult not to linger with the characters of the Sermon on the Mount. It is good to do so, and to grow to understand them, for they never walked the earth—save one. When Plato, over five centuries before Christ spoke, wrote his *Republic,* that ten-volume work on the ideal state, he ended with words tinged with sadness. It is a state, he said, 'planted in imagination, for I conceive it nowhere on earth . . . in heaven there is perhaps a pattern of it, stored up for any man who wishes to see it . . .'

So it is with the happy men and women of the Beatitudes. Only Christ fulfilled the pattern perfectly, but it is a pattern 'stored up in heaven for any man who wishes to see it . . .' That is why we must look at these 'characters of Scripture', and know them.

What is meekness? It is suffering wrong without bitterness. It is not insensitivity, unmanliness, servility. It neither cringes nor whines. It lies in the patience of Christ, in forbearance. It feels pain but not malice. It is the quality of love, which 'bears all things'. It is both active and passive, in that it not only endures, but does good. It rests on self-control, abjures self-pity, turns from petty revenge, maintains righteousness, and never harms another. It is a fountain of true life, 'for the wound which is borne in God's way brings a change of heart too salutary to regret; but the hurt that is borne in the world's way brings death' (2 Cor. 7.10, NEB).

Moses, we read, was 'a meek man', and among the characters of the Old Testament there was no man more strong, brave, and effective in his leadership. The secret lies in Psa. 37, the eleventh verse of which the Lord quoted in this saying. And that psalm was a psalm of patience and blessed quietness, of the still mind which refuses to fret and fume at the transient triumphs of the evildoers, that rests in the Lord, and meanwhile works at the ever-ready tasks of goodness, righteousness and love.

Put these qualities together into a human personality, and you have the meek man—or Jesus Christ our Lord.

419 : Those who Hunger and Thirst

Matthew 5.6; Psalm 119.105–120; Isaiah 55.1, 2

It is obvious through all the Bible that no benediction rests upon half-heartedness. Lot's wife looked back and died. The prophets burned with desire to do God's will. A single-hearted devotion breaks through the whole anthology of Psa. 119. The Lord turned away the disciples who came with reservations. No blessing awaits the uncommitted. That is what the fourth Beatitude means.

Its metaphor must be seen in its context of time and place. Few of those who read these pages really know what hunger is. The land in which Christ lived was a poverty-stricken land. The great sheet of the Galilee lake lay before Him as He spoke, with Tiberias straight ahead down its eastern shore. The fishermen of the lakeside towns enjoyed a measure of prosperity but in the little towns and villages of Galilee and Judea and in the back-streets of Tiberias itself, was destitution not to be found in Western lands today. Calcutta may show such pockets of misery. So may other towns in ill-favoured lands where multitudes lack work and bread.

There were those who heard Christ who knew what hunger was, hunger that made men desperate, obsessed with one desire. Such is the desire for good, for God, for righteousness which finds fulfilment and satisfaction. Set it beside our tepid devotion and half-hearted goodness.

And thirst . . . To know consuming thirst is perhaps a more common experience. Thirst that makes clean, cool water look the most beautiful sight on earth, thirst that is an importunate desire. This is the desire which wins its satisfaction—

> *The thirst that from the soul doth rise*
> *Doth ask a drink divine . . .*

Ben Jonson's lyric was correct in a wider sense than he intended . . . 'My soul thirsts for thee,' wrote David (Psa. 63.1), 'my flesh faints for thee, as in a dry and weary land where no water is.' Those words sprang from one who, a hunted refugee in the wadis and canyons of Judea's wilderness, knew the pain of the body's deprivation, and saw in his distress the very image of the passion with which he longed for the will of God, manifest in his life and his salvation. The world needs such men and women, needs them desperately, for we live in the age which Yeats described in his grim poem—

> *The best lack all conviction,*
> *While the worst are full of passionate intensity.*

Question : Was Yeats right in his description?

420 : The Merciful

Matthew 5.7; Proverbs 14.21, 22, 31; Colossians 3.12, 13

Few words of Shakespeare are better known than Portia's speech in *The Merchant of Venice*. The great dramatist was never closer to the New Testament than when he wrote those lines . . .

> *The quality of mercy is not strain'd,*
> *It droppeth as the gentle rain from heaven*
> *Upon the place beneath: it is twice blest;*
> *It blesseth him that gives and him that takes:*
> *'Tis mightiest in the mightiest: it becomes*
> *The throned monarch better than his crown;*
> *His sceptre shows the force of temporal power,*
> *The attribute to awe and majesty,*
> *Wherein doth sit the dread and fear of kings;*
> *But mercy is above this sceptred sway;*
> *It is enthroned in the hearts of kings,*
> *It is an attribute to God himself;*

Perhaps mercy is more easy to demonstrate than meekness, though the two are allied, for mercy, though it is equally an attitude and a quality, shows itself more sharply in specific acts of generous forgiveness.

Mercy is God's grace reflected in human conduct, just as it is God's grace in action towards man. In showing mercy, as Shakespeare said, we most closely imitate the Living God; in denying it, we most surely betray Him, for as Blake put it. 'Mercy has a human heart, Pity a human face'. He surely meant that men see both qualities and comprehend them both in merciful and pitiful actions by men and women of Christ's mould. To grant mercy or to withhold, is surely in man's power. Dryden was right:

> *Reason to rule, but mercy to forgive:*
> *The first is law, the last, prerogative.*

The thought is awesome. At the point of time when a call to show the divine quality of mercy comes, perhaps at that point a man demonstrates whether or not he knows the grace of God. Is the unmerciful man a Christian at all? Is the merciful man 'blessed', because in showing mercy, he proves his Christian standing? Does the latter half of the verse support this thought? It is not in this world that the merciful receive always in return the mercy they have shown. The merciful have died for mercy's sake. Consider Calvary . . .

We have quoted three poets. Let us quote a fourth as a final prayer. It is Alexander Pope:

> *Teach me to feel another's woe,*
> *To hide the fault I see;*
> *That mercy I to others show,*
> *That mercy show to me.*

421 : The Pure in Heart

Matthew 5.8; Psalm 51

The sixth Beatitude is a challenging word, if ever there was one. The word translated 'pure' means 'unadulterated', 'unmixed', 'uncomplicated' by admixture of alien elements. It is, as Augustine put it, a heart which is *simplex*. We have the word 'simple' from that Latin word, but the Latin word is a much wider word than its derivative. It means, according to the daunting list in the Latin dictionary, 'without dissimulation, open, frank, straightforward, direct, guileless, honest, sincere . . .'

Simplex is the opposite to *duplex* from which we derive no corresponding adjective, but a very unsavoury noun— duplicity. *Simplex* means 'having only one fold', whereas *duplex* means basically 'folded twice' as though to conceal the contents. Virtue, it implies, can be calculating, with hidden motives which, in God's eyes, destroy its worth. It can be contaminated with pride, ambition, deceit. True goodness has no other desire than to do the will of God.

Hence the qualifying phrase. It is the 'pure in heart' who meet God face to face, and know Him as a man knows his friend. 'Heart' is a common metaphor in both Testaments. It means the core of the personality, that inner man, that depth within us where the real person is, where conscience dwells, where God's Spirit finds entry or exclusion. The 'desires of our heart' (Psa. 37.4) are what the true Christian, in his moments of deepest sincerity, wants from God. The 'inward being' of David's agonized prayer (Psa. 51.6) found

493

definition in the same context (51.10). He knew where the vast tragedy began. He had allowed the citadel of his being to be penetrated long before he looked down from his roof and saw Bathsheba.

What lies at the core seeps outward into the whole. The 'inward being' contains that which finds ultimate expression in word and thought. The whole becomes ultimately what that inward part determines. The 'pure in heart' are the blessed ones who have set utter holiness in the centre of the person, and who else can take it to that all-important sanctuary save Christ? The pure in conduct will find ultimate defeat if in some decaying room lurks the impurity which cannot be contained but, like some feebly concealed and poisoned waste, escapes and corrupts the whole.

List references to 'the heart' from both Testaments.

422 : The Peacemakers

Matthew 5.9; Isaiah 55; Ephesians 2.14–17

Raymond Gram Swing, whose name was known in the middle decades of the century for his broadcast comments on international affairs, remarked of the times we live in: 'The peace we enjoy is the absence of war, rather than the presence of confidence, understanding and generous conduct'.

The peace of God is not this pale and negative state. It begins in the heart when Christ is enthroned there, and then, like the 'well of water springing up to everlasting life', it flows into the environment. The peacemakers are those whose presence and whose fellowship draw men into right relationships. There are those who, by their very nature, are promoters of strife. And they are promoters of strife because they are creatures of strife. The personality of man is no sealed container. That which lies at the heart's core seeps out and permeates the environment, be it good or evil. And that is why they only can make peace in whose heart peace reigns.

To make peace is not to impose peace, much less to destroy all opposition. 'They make a desert and they call it peace', Tacitus, the great Roman historian, makes a British chieftain say. This is not God's peace. Nor is God's peace bought at any price, for it is not acquiescence in wrong which demands resistance, it is not disregard of evil. It is the peace which comes from those who communicate peace.

'They shall be called the sons of God' . . . Semitic languages are not rich in adjectives, but inventive in a metaphor which serves the same descriptive purpose. A writer might be 'a father of ink', a merciful God 'a father of mercies'. And so the utterly godlike might be called 'a son of God'. God is the supreme peacemaker, the great reconciler. His presence fuses dissidence in love, melts hostility. 'His words', said Ben Hur, tamed at last, 'took the sword out of my hand'. And Christ cannot penetrate His rebel world save in the lives and persons of His children, His peacemakers. And that is why, as Ruskin put it, 'no peace is in store for any of us, but that which we shall win by victory over shame and sin—victory over sin which oppresses as well as over that which corrupts'.

423 : The Persecuted

Matthew 5.10–12; John 16.1–6; Revelation 7.9–17

Here is a strange saying. The persecuted are numbered among the happy. It is not simply because of ultimate reward, when the wrongs of life are at last righted. It is because, in this world, the persecuted are commonly the good. In a corrupt society and a fallen world the spectacle of moral earnestness—such is human nature—offends the morally inert, and the sight of disciplined living rebukes and angers self-indulgence. The vested interests of vice fear virtue, and corruption is uneasy in the presence of a sterner and challenging uprightness.

A familiar pattern runs through all the history of man . . . 'Crucify him, away with him, not this man but Barabbas, he has a devil, a gluttonous man and a winebibber'. 'Then said Mr. No-good, "Away with such a fellow from the earth". "Ay", said Mr. Malice, "for I hate the very looks of him". Then said Mr. Love-lust, "I could never endure him". "Nor I", said Mr. Live-loose, "for he would

495

ever be condemning my ways". "A sorry scrub", said Mr. High-mind . . . ' The smell of burning flesh, the reek of man's intolerance for man, fills history. Man will not have before his eyes the reproach of human goodness, if by stone, stick, or sword he can dash it from sight. And those sunnier generations which have imagined that such evil has at last been purged, have ended always like our own in sharp and rude awakening.

Professor Herbert Butterfield remarked in a significant passage: 'We are back for the first time in something like the earliest centuries of Christianity, and those centuries afford some relevant clues to the kind of attitude to adopt'.

No clear portrait of the persecuted emerges, as it does with the other Beatitudes. The persecuted are as varied as those who suffer for the Name. We met them in the Old Testament. We shall meet them in the New Testament. And there is persecution as subtle and as painful as that which tears body and limb. The coward's sneer, the cruel pressure of the conforming crowd, the uplifted academic eyebrow, the contempt of the corrupt 'inner ring'—all these make the way hard, lonely, sad for many good men and women, especially the young, who find ostracism more difficult to bear. Remember this in prayer and fellowship.

Questions and themes for study and discussion on Studies 416–423

1. What is 'hunger for righteousness'? Remember that those words were uttered in a hungry land.
2. Sorrow in God's plan. What did Rupert Brooke mean by the phrase: 'washed gloriously with sorrow'?
3. What is arrogance? Why does it preclude meekness?
4. Why is it impossible for the merciless to be Christian?
5. What does Paul mean by 'the peace . . . which passes all understanding' (Phil. 4.7)?
6. List forms of modern persecution.

424 : The Salt of the Earth

Matthew 5.13–16; Genesis 18.16–33

The crowd sat among the wild flowers on the hill above the lake. They listened entranced as the characters of the Kingdom rose and walked before them, stirring hunger, calling to the heart, eliciting desire . . .

In a sudden turn of speech, commencing at v. 11, Christ changed from the third person to the second, 'You', He said, 'are the salt of the earth' (13). And so we meet the Remnant again, the happy few, 'those who feared the Lord' of Mal. 3.16. Salt is a vivid figure. Salt gives savour, and Christians should provide the tang and challenge of life. Salt preserves from corruption. It is ludicrous to imagine that Christian values, and therefore the virtues which cement society, and the Christian ethics without which a nation crumbles, can survive the creed which formed and fed them, or those who held the creed.

Remove 'the salt of the earth' and corruption is inevitable. There comes the recognizable condition of Alfred's prophecy in Chesterton's poem:

> . . . thought a crawling ruin,
> . . . life a leaping mire,
> . . . a broken heart in the breast of the world,
> And the end of the world's desire.

That is why every evil force which society spawns is eager, as we saw when we looked at the persecuted of the earth, to dash Christians aside. They remind the world of better things, visible as the medieval cities which the Mediterranean world can show, set high for safety on some steep eminence, at the end of a climbing road. Or like the flame of a lamp, small perhaps, but until doused and stifled, visible from uncannily far away. We quoted Portia on mercy. She also said to Nerissa in that same play:

> How far that little candle throws its beams!
> So shines a good deed in a naughty world.

An 'evil world', Shakespeare meant. 'Naughty' is one of those words which evil has eroded.

But a last thought for those who are 'the salt of the earth', that group to which the one who writes here on this winter's night, and you who read, are called to belong. Salt, said a Chinese girl, makes one thirsty. Do we make those around us thirst for righteousness, for the water of life, for that which has obviously quenched our restless thirst? Do we?

425 : Children of the Father

Matthew 5.17–48; John 10.1–13

In Matt. 5 let us look especially at the last six verses with their cameo picture of the Christian. The Lord has spoken much of the claims, beyond the claims of the Law, which He made on the life committed to Him, and He is still on that theme.

Verse 43 touched a common Jewish heresy. 'Revenge is the Jew's right,' says old Simonides in *Ben Hur*, 'it is the Law. A camel, yes, even a dog, remembers the wrong done to it.' Many a page of history between the Testaments bears witness to that belief. And here is a curious fact. A large number of the people gathered before Him on the hillside when Christ preached His sermon were, in fact, folk who 'hungered and thirsted after righteousness'. They were 'hungry sheep who looked up and were not fed', betrayed and starved by the false shepherds.

They had gone out into the wilderness to hear the fervent preacher who was the forerunner of Christ. And like John they must have known of the desert ascetics, one of whose places of retreat was at Qumran. Among the Dead Sea Scrolls, the surviving library of the Qumran community, there is a strange allegorical document called 'The War of the Children of Light and the Children of Darkness.' It is a curious compilation, a sort of pious guerrilla manual, built out of what appears to have been a Roman military text-book, and a study of the wars of the Old Testament.

Perhaps it was knowledge of such teaching which convinced the Romans in A.D. 68 that the place was a nest of terrorists and partisans, and led to the destruction of the site. But Christ and His hearers may also have heard of the book, for the book exhorts: 'Love the Children of Light, and hate the Children of Darkness.'

The Children of the Father (45), the Salt of the Earth (13), the Light of the World (14), are not of this dark pattern. As Phillips puts it in his apt rendering of John 1.16, there is 'grace in our lives because of His grace'. The Children of the Father, as the last challenging verse puts it, move towards the likeness of their parent. It is, in the original text, more of a future statement than a command. It touches the same

498

truth as that other word which assures us that 'we shall be like Him, because we shall see Him as He is' (1 John 3.2).

426 : The Hypocrite
Matthew 6.1–4; 23.13–36

Among the characters who walked before the hearers on the hillside was a sinister person clothed to deceive. He pretended to be one of them, but merely played a part. He was an actor and the word hypocrite means precisely that.

That hypocrisy should be practised under the scorn of all the centuries is a matter of astonishment. The theme has exercised the rhetoric of all the past, for among the characters of Scripture there is none who so universally wins disapproval, even, at times, when the disapproval itself is a species of hypocrisy.

Said Francis Bacon: 'A bad man is worse when he pretends to be a saint.' 'Satan,' said Milton, 'was the first to practise falsehood under a saintly show.' 'Hypocrisy is the homage which vice pays to virtue', said the cynical Rochefoucauld. Said Pope: 'A hypocrite makes a sombre jest of God and religion.' And Johnson, echoing the Frenchman: 'The hypocrite shows the excellence of virtue by the necessity he feels himself under of seeming to be virtuous.'

In v. 2 there is an interesting word. When translating 'have' from the Lord's Aramaic into Greek, Matthew used a compound verb. The commercial meaning of this word was unknown until the discovery of masses of receipted bills among the Greek papyri from Egypt. The form of receipt was the phrase 'he is quit', and the verb used in Matthew for, 'they have their reward', is this very verb. Matthew the tax collector, the underling of the Roman tax-gathering machine, had doubtless written this word on settled tax-accounts more frequently than any other word that had ever come from his reed pen. And now, in a flash of satire, he sees the hypocrite, courting popular awe and wonderment by overdone and pompous public acts of piety. He thinks of his receipts, and as he translates the prose from the Sermon he slips a commercial reference in for vividness—'In truth they are quit, their full reward is paid.' God, as it were, no man's debtor, pays them spot cash, in the debased currency which their sinful souls covet. They get their meed of empty adulation, and Heaven is free of its obligations.

And so with Matthew we bow the hypocrite out. He will come back again, for nothing daunts him. He never learns his lesson.

427 : The Man of Prayer
Matthew 6.5–7; 1 Kings 18.25–41

The man of prayer is a sincere man. He makes no hypocritical stance. He seeks privacy with God. The 'closet' of the AV (KJV) is as colourless as the 'room' of RSV. A 'tameion' or 'tamieion' was a storeroom, some 'lean-to' on the cool side of the house, where a peasant or fisherman stored his dried fish and fruit, the only place of privacy in the homes of poor Galileans.

The man of prayer is an honest man, never more penetratingly honest with himself, never more ruthless in self-examination, never more ready to see himself as he is seen, than when he seeks God in prayer. The Lord has just spoken of the false face with which hypocrites deceive the world, but how can a man wear cover or disguise before his God? The soul is naked in His presence. At prayer's beginning a man must have done with lying, deception, excuses, posing, play-acting in all its forms.

The man of prayer is a man of faith. He does not think of God as the dervish priests of Baal thought of him, with their day-long chant and sanguinary mutilations; nor as the Ephesian mob thought of their city's patron goddess, intoning for two long hours: 'Great is Artemis of Ephesus.' A man's prayers are not only the measure of his Christianity, they reveal his understanding of God. That is why prayer is the place of testing, for prayer is itself a challenge to doubt and to all material and carnal preoccupation.

That is why prayer can at times be the place of conflict. The place of prayer bears that very name in the exquisite Blue Mosque at Istanbul. The nooks where private prayer is made are called 'the Battleground', for the Moslem, in this sphere, has glimpsed the truth that prayer is a confrontation with evil, and no man has won a deep and vital knowledge of prayer who has not been at grips with the powers of

500

darkness. 'O the pure delight of a single hour that before Thy throne I spend', runs an old hymn. Before such serenity is won, many a solitary conflict has been battled through.

Prayer is communion and communication with God. 'Oh, that I knew where I might find him,' cried Job (23.3), and effectively to pray is an art which must be learned. The things of time and place, the world and the flesh press in, and prayer tails off in incoherence and preoccupation. That is why the man of prayer is a man who has cared enough to learn to pray (Luke 11.1).

428 : Child of the Father

Matthew 6.9–7.6; Acts 17. 23–29; Luke 11.1–4

In fifty-seven words, excluding the doxology at the end, the Lord taught His disciples how to pray. The man of prayer is truly a 'son of the Father' (Matt. 5.44 f.), because the prayer begins with an acknowledgement of that relationship. The challenge stands like a sentinel at the opening. He who utters the words: 'Our Father . . .' must pause in gratitude, worship and self-examination. The fatherhood of God is an amazing concept. The Old Testament sometimes used the idea of parental love as an illustration of the love of God. Enlightened pagans, like the Stoic poet whom Paul quoted in his address to the Athenian philosophers, had deduced from the creative act of God a notion of divine fatherhood for all the race. But only in Christ is the truth seen in full fruit and power.

Who 'in Christ' may call God 'Father'? Not simply those who are conscious of their Creator. The charter of our son-ship is John 1.12. It is well, then, if we use the phrases of this prayer as the rosary of our devotions, to pause on the threshold and give thanks for the gift of grace, and the price that was paid, while in the same surge of gratitude we re-affirm the faith that laid strong hold on it.

To a loving father access is immediate and unquestioned for any child. There is no closed door between, no barriers of ritual or human mediation. If God is 'our Father', He is near, ready to hearken, eager to receive. When a Christian has uttered the opening words of the prayer, he has expressed the ultimate experience a human being can have of God.

Here is the very substance of our religion, the concept that infuses all Christian theology.

But such a Father! Let us not build Him on 'false notions of our own' (Psa. 50.21). He is no Roman *paterfamilias*, no 'Mr. Barrett of Wimpole Street', 'coming in terror like the King of kings' . . . But on the other hand He is no weakling, culpably indulgent and ready to spoil in love's name . . . But this 'character' risks becoming a description of God, not man. We are still with the Man of Prayer, and see him now in the place of adoration in which he finds refreshment, washing, sanctification. He knows the Father's presence is his right in Christ, but he does not burst into that holy place petulantly, unprepared, brashly and presumptuously. He enters and bows low.

429 : The Steadfast Petitioner
Matthew 7.7–23; Luke 11.5–13; Genesis 32.24–28

The man of prayer is a man of quiet and steadfast faith. The threefold command of Matt. 7.7 sets this forth. No frivolous asking, no wrong search, no arrogant knocking on the door, is envisaged. The picture is that of a suppliant approaching a gracious superior, an earnest seeker after truth and righteousness, a friend or member of a family coming home.

Note secondly, the rising earnestness in 'ask', 'seek' and 'knock'. The last presupposes confidence in present ability to answer. And thirdly, note that the imperatives, like the participles which parallel them in the next verse, are couched in the present tense. This tense in Greek implies continuity. It is a 'linear' tense, and it would not be wrong to translate: 'Keep on asking . . . keep on seeking . . . keep on knocking, for the one who keeps on asking receives, and the one who keeps on seeking finds, and to the one who keeps on knocking, the door shall be opened.' The notion of persistence is much sharper in the Greek text than in the English translations.

God's delays are purposeful, His plans are above our plans, and His thoughts above our thoughts, 'as the heavens are higher than the earth'; and in delay He tests our earnestness, cleanses our motives, reshapes our petition and brings it into conformity with His will. He does 'exceeding abundantly above all we ask or think', but often effects this blessing by the very process of delay.

There is no trickery or guile in His answer. Mythology has more than one tale to tell of the treachery of pagan deities. Tithonus prayed for immortality, and it was granted him. He forgot to pray for eternal youth, and so for ever grew older. Semele prayed that she might look on Zeus, and was incinerated in the answer to her prayer. Midas prayed that what he touched might turn to gold, and found his food turn metal on his tongue. God is not thus. He answers and 'adds no sorrow'.

Hence the simple words of vs. 9 and 10. There is a superficial resemblance between a stone and a loaf. In the desert, hungering after His fast, the Lord had pictured the reality of bread in the mocking stones at His feet. Hence, perhaps, this parallel. A snake and a fish have similar resemblance, and likewise an egg and the round, hard-shelled, crab-like scorpion of Palestine. God does not deal thus cynically with His children. 'Good things' are His promise, and if man seeks to give good gifts to those whom he imperfectly loves, how much more will Perfect Love and Perfect Wisdom grant blessing to His Children.

430 : The Two Builders
Matthew 7.24–27; 1 Corinthians 3.9–23

The two men who close the Sermon on the Mount might be any one of us. The word used in the Greek text for 'rock' is 'petra', which means a 'crag', some great outcrop of the earth's solidity. In the Lord's picture it probably indicates the rock walls of some river-valley, and the man who builds on it has his house high and firm, founded with the flat valley-floor of what the Arabs call a 'wadi' beneath him.

For most of the year the valley floor is dry and empty, but when some storm-born freshet in the distant watershed fills it fathoms deep with rushing water, that man's house is safe which stands on the living rock. The second man has chosen the sandy levels below on the floor of the wadi. It is far easier to build there. Furthermore, the valleys between their stony cliffs are the highways to the interior. The caravans pass that way. Trade goes with the caravans, and the faces of men are seen on the easy highway of the valley bottom. The man who seeks the day's quick advantage naturally chooses that place for his habitation. It is not lonely, not conspicuous, but popular, and certainly cheaper and better for business to site one's home where the multitude go by.

To build on the crag is frequently derided, it makes sometimes for loneliness, it is conspicuous because it is different. So it often is with the man who chooses the foundation 'other than that which no man can lay' (1 Cor. 3.11). And all seems well with the hard-headed fellow who knows where worldly advantage lies until there comes the day of stress and testing. 'The day will reveal it,' says Paul, and there is sometimes a judgement before the Judgement Day which tries the foundation on which men build the foundation of their lives.

Perhaps these men are the two best known characters of all time. They comprise, each in his own way, the two great divisions of humanity. The rock is one, the sand of varied composition. The floods are of one kind and another, but the end is the same . . .

> *We come unto our fathers' God:*
> *Their Rock is our salvation:*
> *The Eternal Arms, their dear abode,*
> *We make our habitation:*
> *Safe in the same dear dwelling-place,*
> *Rich with the same eternal grace,*
> *Bless the same boundless Giver!*
>
> (Thomas Hornblower Gill)

Questions and themes for study and discussion on Studies 424–430

1. How has Christianity created Western civilization?
2. Why must the collapse of faith in a sufficiently large group corrupt a society?
3. The Fatherhood of God as a Christian doctrine.
4. How is hypocrisy avoided?
5. How does prayer test sincerity, faith and honesty?
6. What of the place of prayer? Consider prayer in the lives of three Old Testament characters.
7. How does persistence test and deepen prayer?
8. What does the sand of the Parable of the Builders represent in modern life?

431 : Herod
Mark 6.14-29; John 3.19-36

Herod stands full length in these verses. A guilty conscience never feels safe. An evil deed had a witness in the wretched king's heart, and by his own cowardice he had produced the little hell in which he lived; for Herod had been touched by John's preaching (20). The words may be rendered: 'Herod respected John. He knew that he was a just, good man, and paid attention to him. He listened willingly to John's preaching, and John's words deeply influenced his conduct.' A surprising statement, a moving picture of what might have been. The bad blood of the old Idumaean murderer of children ran in his veins, but no one is beyond God's grace or the touch of His Holy Spirit, and a longing for purity had briefly stirred in Herod's heart. Too weak to act upon it and to do justice to his wronged wife who had fled to her father in Petra, too firmly bound by the fascination of a corrupt woman to break free, the king delayed, and found himself betrayed into deeper crime. Playing the great man in his fortress banqueting-hall, Herod joined in the cheering at Salome's lascivious dance, and made his reckless promise. The price of freedom grows with each hesitation to claim it, and Herod was faced with a dilemma. 'By and by'—this phrase in the AV (KJV) of v. 25 is incorrect. The RSV is correct with the phrase 'at once'. Salome knew her victim, and asked for John's head 'immediately', on a plate. Herod bought that one moment's prestige with years of mental torment. There is no treasure like a clean conscience. If conscience is stained, clean it by confession, and set it beneath the Cross.

Conscience, Herod's tormentor, had once been his friend. Conscience can be the point of impact of God's Spirit on the mind. Relentlessly, God pursues the soul of man, presses hard upon his sin, and stirs a restlessness which can find assuagement only in surrender. A man is only finally lost when God ceases to press upon him. The moment may sometimes be observed. Such a crisis came when the Lord looked at Judas and said in flat dull tones: 'What you are going to do, do quickly'. Judas went out, and, says John, 'It was night'. At the Machaerus party, Herod stepped into the dark.

432 : Herodias

Matthew 14.1–14; Galatians 6.7–8

It could have been somewhere before A.D. 23 that Herod
Antipas met his brother Philip's wife in Rome. This Philip
was not Herod's fellow-tetrach, but another member of the
family, who lived quietly in the capital, too quietly for his
restless dynamic wife, who had all of the Herodian love of
action and intrigue. When Herod appeared, she saw, like
Bathsheba, the chance of a royal alliance, and rescue from
her boredom. She set out to win him—no very difficult task.
Such women bend the carnal, the sensual and the weak
easily to their will. Herod no doubt knew the brief sense of
victory and exhilaration sensed by fools when they have
won cheap pleasure, and the bill in terms of pain, shame
and disillusionment is not yet presented for payment.

Herodias was determined to be queen, no mere paramour,
and the shameless couple set out for Palestine. Herod's many
foes, or her own spies, soon informed Herod's legitimate
wife, fiery daughter of the ruler of the proud Nabataeans,
the Arabian tribe whose rock-cut capital of Petra, 'the rose-
red city, half as old as time', lay in the eastern hills. The
wronged queen fled to her father, who attacked the eastern
frontier of Herod's domains. It was part of the duty of the
puppet kings of Palestine to keep this outer edge of empire
at peace, and not wantonly to provoke border hostilities.

It was as part of his anxious attempt to meet the menace
of the desert tribe that Herod was in occupation of his fortress of Machaerus, a stronghold built with others by his
father to bind the most insecure frontier in the Middle East.
It was not safe to leave the unpopular Herodias in the
royal residence at Tiberias. That is why she was present in
the officers' mess in the fortress keep.

John lay below for no other reason than that he had
greeted the royal crime with his characteristic denunciation.
He described the deed in plain frank terms, its vicious licence
for what it was. He pilloried the culprits before a land not
insensitive to moral issues. Herod, too, had his memories. He
was more easily touched than the hard woman who held
him. Perhaps he wavered. Some deep apprehension over the
security of her own vicious position may have driven
Herodias to her implacable hatred. She had won much, and

had no intention of weakening. Herodias is a spectacle of what a damned soul can become.

433 : Salome

Proverbs 28.1–18

We are still in the border banqueting hall within the Machaerus fort. The grim scene left its mark on history, and we turn the spotlight now on one of the figures on that evil stage, now on another. Salome is not actually named, but is known well enough, and named in Josephus. We have already looked at the drama's cruel end, but it is worth looking closer at the third actor in the scene. Nothing more basely vicious can well be imagined. Herodias knew the carnal lures by which she had trapped Herod. She had only one possible lower level to which it was possible to sink— to use her own daughter's voluptuous person to lead Herod to a deed of blood.

The girl may have been sixteen or seventeen years of age with all of her mother's sultry beauty. She glided in under the light of the lamps and the torches, demanding all eyes. The buzz of conversation, the drunken laughter, died. It was such an exhibition as that which Vashti scorned. Whirling, writhing, the slim girl danced some vicious dance, casting aside veils and robes to some bold, base climax of carnality.

Fired, half-maddened by the spectacle, which Herodias, with deep insight into what he was, had known so well how to arrange, Herod made his mad promise. Let her ask anything at all. Herodias had her moment and dictated the answer: 'The head of John the Baptizer'. The trap closed on a vicious coward. But there was still one way out. Physically the Herods were not cowards, but there is a distinction between physical and moral courage. Pride, as we have seen, dictated the final decision. At that point Herod virtually died. When he met Christ, He had no single word for him.

But our light was on Herodias' daughter, her mother's tool of evil, her mother's corrupted slave. She was as old, perhaps, as the Madonna. See how two lives can part. Vice in her limbs, words of blood on her young lips, Salome is a

507

pitiable sight. The word for peace (shalom) is embedded in her name, but she brought no peace, carried none within her when she moved out of the story to be the wife of her grand-uncle Philip, the tetrarch. She has the odd distinction of giving Oscar Wilde a theme for a drama, banned from the British stage in less 'permissive' days. She remains a fearful example of what a bad woman can do to her own flesh and blood.

434 : Philip and Andrew

John 6.1–59

The feeding of the five thousand made a vivid impression on those who were present, and the story found its way, with variety of emphasis, into the writings of all the four evangelists. John's story is remarkable for both introduction and sequel. He it is who reveals how the imagery of the bread was taken up in the Capernaum synagogue in a notable discourse. He also describes a brief interchange of words which preceded the event.

Andrew and Philip play a part. There was a very considerable crowd in the lakeside meadow, and Jesus turned to Philip with a practical question. John remembered Philip vividly as an able and notable man. He came from Bethsaida, and was one of the first to be called (1.43 f.); he was instrumental in bringing Nathanael to Christ (1.45–49); he was chosen by the small group of Greeks to gain an interview (12.20–23); by a plain, direct question to Christ, he occasioned a remarkable saying (14.8 f.). And it is quite in character that Philip should be the object of the question which the Lord now asked.

He was right. As He had guessed, Philip had anticipated the problem, and had the basic cost worked out. It is possible to work out an approximate modern equivalent. A denarius, lamentably rendered 'penny' in the common English version, and not better translated by the shillings and dollars of other attempted equivalents, was a day's labouring wage, the sort of labouring wage which in a ruthless economy might have justified Karl Marx' 'iron law of wages'. Viewed even thus austerely, two hundred denarii was a sum beyond the resources of the apostles' band.

Philip gave his calculated reply, and Andrew facetiously pointed out that there was, in fact, a small supply available: 'There is a lad here who has five barley loaves and two fish . . .' He pauses when Jesus turns attentively, and takes him seriously, on which he lamely continues: 'But what are they among so many?'

Observe the fresh humanity of it all. There is no by-passing the miracle in the events which followed. It is told in plain factual language by the four witnesses. There is no difficulty provided Christ was indeed Christ, and all that which He claimed to be (John 1.3). And if He was less than that, the whole fabric of Christian doctrine disintegrates. Before we leave these central chapters of the Gospel we shall look at the character of Christ, though to be sure, its presence haunts the whole story. But first a glance at a boy and a crowd.

435 : Child in the Crowd
Matthew 14.15–21; 26.26–30; Luke 9.10–17

A child played a part in the miracle of the loaves and the fishes. In a multitude of children's talks the small hero of the lakeside story has appeared as 'the little boy who gave his lunch to Jesus', but in fact five barley loaves and two fish would be a considerable picnic meal, even for a lad with a healthy appetite. It is more probable that the child was one of the many likely to haunt the outskirts of any Eastern crowd with small wares for sale. The unexpected influx of potential customers would stir more than one lonely cottage to baking and some attempt to turn the situation to profit.

So it came about, through this small link in the chain of circumstance, that the Lord obtained by gift or purchase the provision He needed. Matthew's account contains the vital phrase: 'Bring them here to me' (14.18). The small resource which was available passed into His creative hands. A divine principle of action seems apparent in the story. God seems to demand some point of entry into the world, some bridge-head of action. To bring blessing to mankind He seems to require some surrendered trifle, some shred of experience, some 'widow's mite', a small parcel of bread and fish, a sorrow, a pain, a joy. Given utterly to God the inconsiderable thing becomes active and fruitful in His hands. In Luke's account the key verse is 9.16.

The blessing was no doubt the beautiful Jewish grace: 'Blessed art Thou, O Lord, our God, King of the Universe, who bringest forth bread from the earth.' On affluent societies the poignancy of such gratitude is lost. And note, in the midst of such prodigality, the Lord's care that nothing should be lost. The Jew, on a journey, always carried a 'cophinos', or rush-woven basket, in order to avoid buying Gentile food. The Twelve were thus equipped and supplied themselves for the morrow. Our wasteful society might note the fact. Waste is unchristian.

436 : The Crowd

Matthew 9.35–38; Mark 6.30–44

We have remarked upon the human simplicity of the four accounts of the lakeside picnic-meal. The whole experience must have remained a peculiarly vivid memory. Mark's account is specially vivid. Tradition has it, as we have seen, that Peter was Mark's informant, and one can catch the colourful language of the fisherman behind the evangelist's narrative. Verses 39 f., for example, run literally: 'He commanded them to make them all sit down in dinner-parties on the green grass. And they all sat down like beds of flowers in hundreds and fifties.' John also remembered that 'there was much grass in the place'. Here, surely, is the eye-witness who remembered what the spring-green hillside looked like when the fifty or more picnic-parties splashed the turf with the bright hues of their garments. In fact, the phrase runs literally 'they sat down in flower-beds'. That was the thought that struck the watching Peter. The fare was simple enough, a relish of dried or salted fish and barley bread. Barley, as we saw in the tale of Gideon's Midianite, was the cheaper grain, despised by the eaters of the wheaten flour. Christ by-passed luxury, and limited His miracles to the provision of bare need. Economically, He ordered His own men to fill their kits for the morrow's sustenance. Waste has no part in His programme, nor would He have His own look upon God as the indulgent Provider of that which men's own efforts, toil, and enterprise can produce. Providence does not assist the idle. The crowd in the Gospels is sometimes pathetic, 'like sheep without a shepherd' (Matt. 9.36; Mark 6.34), sometimes a disturbing presence shouting royal slogans which they did not understand, sometimes a deadly and a sinister force calling for Barabbas, and death for Christ . . . Crowds move like a spectre through history, manipulated by dictators, slaughtered to promote the evil of kings—and pitied by Christ. Crowds are disloyal and self-seeking, as ready to shout 'Crucify' as to call 'Hosanna'. Crowds disappoint (John 6.26), take their morality from the lowest elements among them (Mark 15.29 f.), follow designing men (Acts 19.23–41), and are altogether unlovely. It behoves us to discipline disgust and pray the prayer of Christ (Matt. 9.38).

437 : Greater than All
Matthew 10.32–42; 11.20–30; 12.1–8

We are not attempting, as we assemble the characters of the Bible, to unravel all the chronological problems involved. To integrate all the events of John's Gospel is a task of very great difficulty, for John wrote with other ends in view than an ordered sequence of events. Nevertheless, picking our way through the four Gospels, we are taking general account of the movement of time, and over the next thirty or forty studies shall move up to the triumphant entry to Jerusalem, and then move with all four evangelists through the events of the Passion Week.

The character of the Lord Himself has not engaged our special attention, but at this point we may pause to consider the significance of some astounding statements He was beginning to make, for the words throw light not only on His person but on the character of those who heard His words and reacted to them. Christ was far from unexpected at His coming. Apart from the learned in the law the common folk awaited Him. Says the Samaritan woman at the well, 'I know that Messiah is coming.' A fisherman says to his brother: 'We have found the Messiah.' The gossiping crowd in the Jerusalem streets say, 'When Christ comes, will He do more miracles than these?' Yet His coming and His character ran contrary to all the ideals and hopes of all but those who had eyes of the soul to see with. They looked for a Messiah who would bow the knee in humility before God, but who would walk like a king before men. But He held His head high before God. 'I and my Father are one,' He calmly asserts, and, 'He who has seen me has seen the Father.' He dares to look up into the face of Perfect Holiness and say, 'I glorified thee on earth.' Yet before men He chose service. As though indifferent to the longing for freedom that burned in the nation's heart He bade them render to Caesar the things that are Caesar's, and instead of turning His power against the Roman He used it on the sick. 'I am meek,' He avers, 'and lowly of heart.' It was obvious truth. Yet they speak of the mighty Law-giver, and He says, 'If you believed Moses, you would believe me', of the Prophet to the Gentiles, and He says, 'A greater than Jonah is here', of the Great King, and He claims a greatness more real than Solomon's.

438 : The Way and the Truth

Matthew 12.38–42; John 12.44–50; 14.1–6

The character of Christ is, in fact, the great miracle of the Gospels. No Jew could possibly have invented a person who ran so strongly counter to all that they had imagined of their Messiah. John, His forerunner, had not expected a Christ like this. The writers of the Gospels wrote of what they saw, but which they could not have anticipated. They wrote in spite of themselves. He contradicted their ideas in every point. Their father Abraham had spurned the bad king's gifts at the gate of Sodom: 'I could not take a thread or a sandal-thong.' Yet the Son of Man eats with publicans and sinners. Vengeance was a vice of which they made a virtue. In Study No. 426 we quoted Simonides' conversation with Ben Hur on revenge. How true it was! No ancient Jew would have invented a Messiah who bade one love his enemy and do good to those who used him despitefully. The typical Qumran community, as we saw, taught the precise opposite. They would look with contempt upon the humility before man of this strange Being who, it would have seemed to them, knew no humility before God. Even Paul, smitten in the High

Priest's court, turned in a flame of indignation: 'God shall smite you, you whitewashed wall!' (Acts 23.3). Yet this man, smitten and spat upon and crowned with thorns, utters not a word. It is impossible that the Christ of these pages could have been either the child of His age, or the literary invention of His contemporaries.

We have mentioned His startling claims. No mere man could make them and triumphantly sustain them in His day or ours. Greater than Solomon and Jonah, Moses' prophetic theme, pre-existing Abraham, all this is claimed with calmest confidence. He asserts that He is the penitent's way to God, the end of philosophy's quest, the goal of a world's desire, 'the way, and the truth, and the life' . . . the man from Galilee, whose father and brothers they knew! As if all light, all wisdom lived in Him, He opens His arms to groaning mankind and, 'Come to me,' He cries, 'all who labour and are heavy laden, and I will give you rest', and yet of those who came He demanded an abandonment which only God has the right to claim, an allegiance which overrides all earthly affection. With no sense of incongruity, but with all the anguish of rejected love He weeps over Jerusalem, hard and priest-ridden. How often would He have gathered her penitents together, as mother bird her brood, but the city would not! Were this mere man who speaks, was there ever effrontery so preposterous?

439 : The Discoverers

Matthew 13.45, 46; John 6.60–69; Philippians 3.1–14

We have turned aside briefly in the last two studies to look more directly at the Lord Himself, and we have done so because so many of those who will move before us over the next group of studies are closely involved with Him, and show their human qualities and defects against the foil of His strange perfection.

A group of parables, those human stories so characteristic of His teaching, appear at about this point in Matthew's account, and from them we may lift one word-picture, that of a merchant who discovered a lovely treasure from the ocean, a pearl of rare beauty, lifted by some bold diver from the floor of the Red Sea or the Persian Gulf. Its worth so gripped the mind of one man, that he cast aside all his other possessions in his zeal to hold this surpassing prize.

So, said the Lord, is one who finds what God has to give. There was a time in the ministry of Christ when, in disillusionment over the nature of His Messiahship, some 'drew back and no longer went about with him'. Literally the text runs: 'They went to the things behind, and walked no longer with Him'—that is, associated publicly with Him no more. Sadly He turned to His men and said: 'You don't want to go away too, do you?' And Peter, with that sudden gush of love which so often marked him, said: 'Lord, to whom should we go? You tell us about a kind of life which is altogether different from this.' It was the pearl of great price.

Paul found it too, and tells in the third chapter of his letter to the Philippians how he sold all. Curiously enough the passage contains an echo of John in the language he uses. In John 6.66 the phrase runs literally: 'They went to the things behind . . .' The defectors were not necessarily returning to blatant sin, not necessarily to the terrorism which Simon the Zealot had abandoned, or the tax-office which Matthew had left behind—simply to the ordinary, humdrum affairs of life which they had left for the wider vision. And Paul says of such matters, in his imagery of the chariot race, that the committed Christian, 'forgetting the things behind', presses forward to a surpassing prize (Phil. 3.13). Merchant, Peter, Paul—let us stand with them, and hold in hand that which is worth all the life's devotion, 'to be found in Him', to be used of Him, to be part of the vaster purpose, to be numbered among God's Remnant.

Questions and themes for study and discussion on Studies 431–439

1. What damned Herod?
2. Do you think it is correct to say that a woman can sink lower and rise higher than a man?
3. Compare Herodias with Jezebel.
4. Philip's character: how can the Church use his type?
5. God's creative power in everyday life and our social usefulness.
6. The crowd in Scripture and in history.
7. The impact of Christ upon His contemporaries.

514

440 : Characters of John's Gospel

John 1.1–18; 20.30, 31; 21.20–25

It may be appropriate at this point to turn solely to John's Gospel and find our next dozen or so characters in its pages, carrying the story which we have more frequently followed in the synoptists, up to the last entry into Jerusalem and the Passion week.

John's stories are from life, and that fact has had abundant demonstration. For the last forty years some tattered fragments of the New Testament have lain in the John Rylands library in Manchester. They include two broken pieces of John's Gospel which lay unnoticed for fifteen years, from the date of their acquisition in 1920 until 1935, when C. H. Roberts recognized their unique importance. There were pieces of ch. **18**, vs. 31–33, and 37, 38, and the handwriting could be dated in the principate of Trajan or of his successor Hadrian. Observe the significance of this. Trajan died in A.D. 117, Hadrian in A.D. 138. Pick a point in the middle of Hadrian's principate, say A.D. 126, when his British garrison was building that astonishing symbol of empire, the wall across northern Britain. At that time John's Gospel was known, and being copied in Egypt. On those two tiny pieces of brown papyrus much fantasy was wrecked, and notably the attempt of some to thrust the fourth Gospel deep into the second century.

They were, of course, not the only piece of archaeological evidence which set John's Gospel back in its traditional place, inside the lifespan of the one who professed to write it, the last surviving apostle. His story is no 'pious' fiction. It has, indeed, been cogently argued by the historian, A. T. Olmstead, that the narrative passages in John represent the very oldest written tradition, a theory which, were this the place to do so, we might support by the story of John **8**. John wrote to refute the heresies which, in the late evening of his life, were disturbing the peace of the Church. He chose his materials to that end, but also with an eye to those facets of truth which had meant much in two generations of experience. One such truth was that of regeneration and how one already old can be 'born again'.

John had a way of tying what he taught to the incidents

515

in the Lord's life which first put the truth into words. That is how the story of the woman of Samaria was rescued from oblivion, and how we come to know of the Pharisee who came by night, and whose question put the image of rebirth into Scripture, the blind man who exasperated the Sanhedrin, the tales of Cana, Bethesda and Bethany. And so we learn of the author himself—an old man who did his life's best work in his nineties. But he must wait until we read his last letters.

441 : Wedding Guests

John 2.1–12; Exodus 20.1–12

Cana lies on the hill slopes some four miles from Nazareth if the site is correctly identified. It is on the road to Tiberias. It is said to be Nathanael's village, a place of fertility and shady fig-trees (1.48, 21.2).

It is not unlikely that the sudden and perhaps unexpected arrival of the Lord's party at the wedding was the occasion of the social disaster which befell the poor little household. Hence the anxious urgency with which Mary came to Him. In the lives of those who receive Him Christ causes no difficulty with which He is not richly able to deal.

But what of His reply to Mary? Was He harsh with His mother? The RSV, far from clearing up the AV (KJV) makes the words sound even more irritable. The Greek expression for 'What have I to do with thee?' is literally, 'What to you and to me?' Note it carefully. It means, 'What is there in common to you and to me?' Now, undoubtedly in John's story those words occur, but it is not at all improbable that John was literally translating a remark in Aramaic which ran, 'What is that to you and me?' and that He did not mean the words to be taken in the usual idiomatic sense. This version, which Nonnus accepted in the second century, and Luther at the time of the Reformation, at least clears up the story. Mary comes to Jesus. 'They have no wine,' she whispers. He replies, 'We are guests. What is that to you and me? My hour', He adds, 'is not yet come,' That is, 'When I give a feast there will be no such accident.' When He did, in the upper room, there was plenty for all.

However, as mothers do, giving no time for refusal, she says to the servants, 'Do whatever he tells you,' and hurries off. He smiles and complies. The word 'woman' had no harshness. In the tenderest scene in the *Iliad,* where Hector bids goodbye to Andromache on the walls of Troy, the hero addresses his wife as 'Woman'.

It is a vivid human little story, the Son, a trifle whimsical, the mother, bustling and certain of His unfailing help, the best man with his lame joke, perennial feature of wedding feasts . . . Phillips' 'ring of truth' is in every phrase.

442 : Nicodemus
John 3.1–16; Ezekiel 36.25–27; 37.1–10

Nicodemus came to Christ in desperate earnestness. He was a Pharisee, and for all the name of obloquy which the sect acquired through their participation in a mighty crime, the Pharisee had vowed to perform all the Law. He was a man to whom religion was everything. He came against all habit. 'Are you *the* teacher of Israel?' Christ asked him. He used the definite article, let it be noticed. Usually people came to Nicodemus. And he came by night, not in search of concealment, but of privacy. He came with a question.

The question was probably the one which tore at the Jew's mind: 'When, when, will God act, and restore the kingdom to Israel?' The Lord sensed its presence in the mind of Nicodemus, He saw it shaping on the lips of the grave man before Him, and interrupting him after his polite preamble He said: 'In solemn truth I tell you, unless a man be born again he cannot see the kingdom of God.' The emphasis lay on the last words. It is the lordship of God which matters, but the popular view of Israel's role meant little more than the pre-eminence of Israel.

The visitor was annoyed to be thus cut short, and pretended not to understand. But of course he understood the figure. He knew the Old Testament by heart. Any tag of quotations from some well-known, familiar passage sets the mind of a scholar racing along the lines of the text. A clear reference to a context of habitual meditation raises the whole associated complex of ideas to the mind. Nicodemus knew

517

that Christ was taking him in thought to passages in
Ezekiel, in what we call chapters **36** and **37** of that prophet's
book. In the quiet night it was in the context of those well-
remembered passages that Nicodemus received the answer to
the question he was not permitted to ask, and much more
truth beside . . . They spoke of life renewed but life renewed by the breath of God's Spirit in response to prayer.

The play of mind with mind continues and we need not
follow further. 'How comes this to pass?' said Nicodemus,
now alert to follow the imagery evoked. He is taken to the
tale in the Book of Numbers in which those who looked up
in faith lived. So are men reborn and enter into eternal life,
when their upreaching faith lays hold of the proffered grace.

Nicodemus went his way, and we shall meet him again.
Was he convinced? It is a fair guess that he was (cf. **19**.39).

443 : The Reborn

John 5.24; Romans 6.3–23

Read the famous sixteen verses again (John **3**.1–16). Nicodemus had his answer, and as he went away under the concealment of the night he may have heard on those uplands
of the city the sigh of the night wind that had reminded
him of Ezekiel. He had his answer. 'When will the kingdom
be restored to Israel?' 'When God reigns in the lives of individual Israelites, and they glimpse the reality of the royal
presence of God in their own deepest experience. That is
when God will move again with restoration, Nicodemus,
when the dry bones live once more in each surrendered
life'. And as he walked home he may have grasped a truth,
that God gives more abundantly than our asking, and always
answers a question more comprehensively than the ques-
tioner could even imagine. There was to be a new race,
regenerated characters, men who have 'looked' and 'lived'.

Rebirth establishes a new ancestry, a fresh pattern of
genetics for the soul. We become that which lies at the core
of the being, in 'the heart', if you will. If a principle of
falsehood lies there it cannot do other than colour thought
and emotion. It then flows into speech and action, and speech
and action constitute what others see us to be, and call our

character. Character, long enough maintained, becomes personality. The host of falsehood becomes a living lie, self-deceiving, unable to be true.

So, too, if hate is cherished in the centre of the being, or any other evil principle, it cannot be contained. It seeps abroad and eats up its host.

But so, too, with Christ. He is born again into whose life's inner depth Christ comes with power to renew. Once lodged there, He cannot be cabined or confined. He cannot be hidden. He breaks into thought, word, character, personality, until He overwhelms the whole—and yet, unlike the evil which can eat up a human being, obliterating, destructive, lethal, the indwelling Christ transforms by life's renewal. He is God's Creative Force, as the same John says in his Prologue. He makes the host who houses Him like Him, but paradoxically leaves the personality which He takes over more himself, more real, more alive than that person ever could have been when lost in the embrace of consuming death.

Such is the rebirth. Life's scattered remnants are re-articulated anew, each functioning in its appropriate place. The person is sinewed, fleshed, and equipped with sensitivity, energy, beauty. The integrated whole is made alive by the breath of God. Growth remains, as it awaits any new-born creature, but growth follows the assimilation of God's Living Bread, the Milk of His Word, the Meat of His Strength.

Questions and themes for study and discussion on Studies 440–443

1. Reality in John's narratives.
2. Christ's involvement in ordinary social life—what principles for ourselves can be gained from John 2.1–12?
3. The relationship between knowledge and spiritual perception.
4. 'Rebirth' as a figure of speech.
5. 'Perish'—what does it mean?

444 : The Woman at the Well

John 4.1–30

The well is still to be seen outside the little town, walled, padlocked and sequestered after man's common fashion. It was the heat of the day, because the woman who came down for water had no wish to face the looks of the other women of the town, nor to hear their covert sneers. Immoral, obscure, ignorant, flippant, she stood in complete contrast with the gentlemanly scholar Nicodemus. Yet both stories follow on from John's remark in 2.25. Observe how differently the Supreme Teacher deals with the two persons. In Nicodemus He spoke in the imagery of Scripture. He could not do so with the outcast alien. Meeting her at the level of her understanding and her need, the Lord asked for a drink. Proceeding no doubt to give the stranger the drink He craved, the woman is unable to resist a little sarcasm. 'You, a Jew, asking for a drink from me, a Samaritan woman!' The Lord showed no shadow of annoyance, but answered with a disarming word. 'If you knew . . .' He said, and curiosity as old as Eve was stirred. Eve's curiosity led to death; the Samaritan's to life.

Like the prodigal, the woman may have glimpsed a way out of physical distress. Her reply in v. 15 may, on the other hand, have been no more than a down-to-earth comment on Christ's strangely mystical language. The time has come to shock her into earnestness, so the Lord lays His finger on the deeper pain and shame of her disordered life (16). He does that sometimes, especially when in folly we refuse to face the reality of our sin and pathetic rebellion. So Nathan confronted David. A proper relationship is now established, but she still tries to evade the *personal* issue by provoking a *theological* debate on an issue of division and controversy between Jew and Samaritan. The reply out-distances her understanding, so the woman seeks to close the conversation on the comfortable ground that there is much mystery, but some day all will be made clear—'when Messiah comes'. Hence the sudden revelation. Humbled at last, convinced, and awake to something real, saving, new, the woman, forgetting the task of drudgery at home, hurries away to tell the town. At the well the mystified disciples wait. It is down the hill, and out of sight of the village. Over the brow of the rise the woman has disappeared.

445 : The Samaritans

2 Kings 17.24–34; John 4.31–42; 8.48

Samaria had suffered, seven centuries before, as the northern kingdom of the divided land. Devastated, depopulated, and then resettled with mixed or alien breeds, the province had met the scorn and contempt of Judah, whose divine calling was surely rather to love, and to share the knowledge of their God.

The Jews, whose national integrity had endured a century longer until they, too, went into exile, had lost their vast opportunity. Hence the division and the scorn of the Lord's day, and the pathetic situation which He sought to bridge. The woman at the well was to be His bridgehead of conquest.

He found a ready audience. Samaria, under-privileged and not possessing the full canon of the Old Testament Scriptures, was hungry for the truth of God with an eagerness not felt in hard, contentious Jerusalem. Hence the compulsion which took the Lord that way. His path ever lies near the place of man's need and aspiration. The ready response to the woman's timid testimony shows how ripe was the harvest. The Lord's conversation shows how conscious He was of the fact. The theme of 2.25 still binds the story together. By the well He prolonged the discussion with the puzzled disciples until the Samaritans came into sight round the corner of the hill. He then bade them lift their eyes and see the harvest waiting among the alien and the despised. Lands of ancient privilege, which have long known the gospel, and treated its old invitations with scant respect, should note the story. Let it also be noted that evangelism is a task for toil and dedication, a sequence of planting and reaping for which hands are all too few. Under its urgency the Lord ignored His weariness and His need for food and rest. The Church too often lacks what Jowett called 'a passion for souls', that deep and earnest desire by all means to win others to Christ by their own loyalty and love.

We hear no more of the people of the little town. We do

not know whether the woman of the wellside conversation was received as a sister among them, her integrity restored, her life remade. We do not know what happened to the man who shared her corruption. We only know that, unlike the Gadarenes who preferred their swine, the Samaritans wanted Christ to stay with them.

446 : Herod's Officer

John 4.43–54; Isaiah 55

The scene of action changes to Galilee and the succession of incidents which forms the theme of chs. 3 and 4 ends with the story of a desperate man. He was an officer of Herod's court, and far removed in social status from both Nicodemus and the unnamed Samaritan outcast. Overwhelmed by personal sorrow, he sought Christ's aid with urgency. Testing not infrequently goes with blessing, and the man from Capernaum was tried, first with apparent refusal, and then with a Divine response which went all against his expectations. Like Naaman, he was told to trust forthwith, and act upon that faith. The pattern is common enough in God's dealings with men. God's delays are God's disciplines, and He seldom answers prayers according to our small, and at times presumptuous, specifications. 'His plans are not like our plans', as Moffatt renders Isa. 55.8. They are, in fact, infinitely superior, and delightful to the soul who finds his place in them. His answers, like His tarrying, are designed to stimulate a trusting faith. Capernaum was 25 miles away, and the man went home without haste. He remembered that day, not only for a blessed boon granted, but as his life's greatest spiritual experience. Life is enriched if it is lived in the wonder of such faith. There is joy in the life which has learned to look for God's solutions, God's transformation of our pain, God's unforeseen blessings.

Revert again to the thought that the statement in 2.25 is a thread which links a series of characters and events together. He 'knew what was in man', and so could deal on varied planes with the superbly trained scholar, the rejected woman, and the incisive executive who hurried up from Capernaum to Cana to beseech His help. In each case His

522

word and His challenge were adapted to personality and training. In the rabbi He called upon that awareness of spiritual truth, and the medium which contained it, which was the very pattern of all His thought. He took the Samaritan woman, and cut away all her pathetic posing and pretence until she became conscious of the simple fact of her sin. The royal officer of Capernaum was a clear-thinking, strong, plain man. He had come to Cana with one sharply conceived purpose. Like Luke's centurion he was a man who understood authority. The Lord called him to a firm, strong step of faith. He frequently acts like this, addressing the best in us, calling for the highest response—but never beyond that to which the spirit can rise.

447 : The Man by the Pool

John 5.1–18

Many strange things have been said of the fourth Gospel. Hostile criticism has sought in vain, as we have remarked, to thrust its composition into the second century and outside the possible life-span of its aged author. If it could but be proved that the Church of the first decades of the second century, among whom were those whose parents and grand-parents remembered the apostles, had accepted as genuine the blatant falsehoods of one who pretended to be the revered and well-remembered John, and who untruthfully professed to have stood bravely by the Cross, and to have run with Peter to the Empty Tomb, what opportunity then takes shape for 'new theologies'! Anyone, in this or any other century, would be free to rewrite the story of Christ, and put upon His lips whatever sheer romance, narrow prejudice, or special pleading, he might at any time imagine that the Lord might have said in any other age than in His own.

Archaeology has frequently played a role in combating such fancies, and the story of the Bethesda well is one such case. It was Loisy, the French liberal scholar, who suggested that John, or whoever wrote under that name, had altered the traditional tale to include the five colonnades. This, of course, was to represent the five books of the Law which Jesus had come to fulfil. Of this the sick man was himself a

523

symbol. Recent excavations have revealed that, before A.D. 70, there existed a rectangular pool with a colonnade on each of the four sides, and a fifth across the middle.

The competitive miracle of v. 4 remains a difficulty. It is not consistent with the spirit of the Bible. The presence of such an anomaly in the text of Scripture would puzzle and confuse were it not for one fact. Some of the most ancient and important manuscripts do not include v. 4, hence its omission in the RSV. It is this verse which is the stumbling block. The fact that the pool was considered a place of healing is of no significance, although it is noteworthy that the Lord uttered no word of confirmation. Mind is strangely potent over matter, and healing may well have taken place there. It may even be true that at times gaseous exhalations from the pool made the waters more potent, or stimulated faith more effectively. It is the angel with his periodic visit, the apparent scramble for a gift of God, which constitutes the difficulty. Strong textual objection to v. 4, supported by the exegetical difficulty, make a very strong case for the exclusion of the verse. It is of the exact nature of a 'gloss.' A copyist writes a traditional explanation in the margin of his manuscript, and someone else, copying from him, includes the explanation mistakenly in the text. It is to be noted that the Lord did not use the pool to heal the paralytic, but gave the grace of His divine help as grace is always given—that is, in response to an act of faith.

448 : The Man in the Temple

John 5.19–29

Looking at the background of the story and the difficulty of the text we have lost sight of the despairing man who had hoped so pathetically for healing at the pool. The Lord does not argue against the common belief in a strangely competitive miracle, just as in a later healing He descends to the level of the blind man's feeble faith (9.6–12). He healed in spite of it. In effect the Lord asks: 'Do you *want* to get well?' The man's answer shows that he was eager enough for healing, but lacked strength or the help of another. The Lord's command to him to arise gave him both, and more. Straightaway he was made whole. This man, now 'found in the Temple', no doubt in grateful prayer, is bidden: 'Sin no more.' Medical science is increasingly impressed by the fact that sickness of the mind and spirit promotes the breakdown of the body, and the command seems to indicate that the sick man's paralysis was the final physical fruit of a tormented and sin-sick soul. His sin was a matter between himself and God. No public mention is made of it (6, 8, 14), but permanent cure depended upon spiritual victory. God's blessings are for those who trust and obey.

All good turns to evil in the hands of evil men. The beginnings of conflict arose from the Lord's loving kindness. The path to Calvary began in the Temple court, and by the Bethesda pool. John's method is often to attach great discourses to the incidents out of which they arose. The Jews, who were trained in symbolic language, would see the point of the Lord's words to the case of the paralysed man. The concentrated statement before us contains, firstly, a new version of the Sabbath. The institution of a day of rest was not intended to paralyse godly and beneficent action, but to energize it. Secondly, observe a clear claim to Divine worship. The Lord claimed to reproduce visibly among men the work of the Father, to bestow life, to execute judgement, and to raise the dead. And are we not still outworking the truth enunciated in 2.25? The Lord 'knew what was in the man'.

Questions and themes for study and discussion on Studies 444–448

1. Water as a symbol in Scripture.
2. The Jews and the Samaritans. Duty and failure.
3. 'Testing not infrequently goes with blessing.'
4. How did the Lord deal with the Bethesda pool? What of Lourdes and similar phenomena?

449 : The Crowd

John 7.17–44; 8.54–59; 11.54–57; 12.12–19

All through John's Gospel there is a consciousness of the crowd, the faceless multitude which was a force and a presence in Palestine in the first century. The crowd, in fact, has been a feature in all history. This day has seen it—the forest of uplifted arms under the swastikas at Nuremberg, the horde chanting war slogans before the Palazzo Venezia, thronging Red Square and the streets of Peking. The crowd can be a force, ruthless and cruel in the hands of demagogue and dictator. Wind and wave can combine to form an irresistible force. So can the gales of emotion which sweep through crowds and peoples, and change a group of human beings into a destroying mass, yelling for Barabbas, overwhelming the good around an uplifted cross, obliterating the higher scruples of individuals . . .

Jerusalem was fearfully crowded at festival times, and the occupying forces, as well as the collaborating hierarchy, were well aware of the latent power of the crowd. Well they might be! It was a crowd manifesting in its collective personality the worst features of Jewish nationalism, hate and fierce anger, that precipitated the clash in A.D. 66, and the awful rebellion which followed. It needed only the explosive injection of Galilean turbulence, or the fiery words of some demagogue to set Jerusalem in an uproar.

In John 7 we sense the presence of the Jerusalem multitude. They were unsure of the nature of the new teaching which was abroad, confused and incoherent. The 'murmuring' (12, AV [KJV]) which is a better rendering than the 'muttering' of the RSV, suggests the buzz of discussion and speculation which the rulers (26) dreaded to hear canalize into a roar of loyalty like that of the Ephesian mob (Acts 19.28). They were to hear the chanting of Palm Sunday with deep anxiety, and, had the Lord been a mob-leader, that day could have seen riot and rebellion. To this point, however, the crowd was pitiable, without leaders rather than misled, unconscious of the power which makes the mob the tool of evil, 'sheep without a shepherd'. Again and again we see the Lord refuse to use the multitude. 'He knew what was in man.' He knew that the crowd could blot out individuality, and that man's decisions were not made under the force of gregarious instinct, but by individual thought and committal (17). They were left divided (43) because this was inevitable. They had to come to Him as men and women, not a tramping horde.

450 : The Officers
John 7.45, 46; 18.1–8

Here was a strange excuse for a group of disciplined guards sent on a specific errand. They could not arrest Him 'because no man spoke as He spoke'. As strange and as significant was the fact that the excuse was virtually accepted. The Sanhedrin realized that some unnatural power surrounded the person of Christ. In their blind hostility they refused to call it a supernatural power, but it was of this that they were aware, and, in spite of angry words, they received the report of the Temple guard.

Who were these men? The Jerusalem hierarchy, in return for the quite invaluable aid and comfort which their collaboration gave to the Roman garrison and occupying forces, had certain privileges. One of them was that they were in charge of the Temple area and its national sanctity. A notice survives which threatens death to any intruder from outside Jewry, who might presume to intrude on the sacred parts of the Temple complex. In the support of this privilege the Sanhedrin had at its disposal a police or para-military force which was used to effect the arrest of Christ. With the deterioration of the political position on Palestine, and thanks to the Roman desire to avoid all provocation in the tense situation, the Sanhedrin doubtless presumed on the powers they had. The stoning of Stephen was an illustration.

Who were the components of this force? We can identify the wounded man of Gethsemane, Malchus, the servant of the high priest (John 18.10). They were all Jews, though for special tasks some officer of the Roman garrison in the fortress Antonia might perhaps have been attached to the force. They were probably young Levites, with access to the Temple, picked and paid by the ruling Sadducees, men conditioned to obey orders, and owing all they had or could hope for to the ruling caste. Hence the remarkable nature of the situation when, daunted by the words of Christ, or apprehensive of the crowd, they were paralysed in the prosecution of their duty. And catch the reflection of the tremendous personality of Christ; no despised Galilean, no desert hermit, no defenceless weakling, but a Being of elemental power in word and presence.

527

451 : Nicodemus
John 3.1–3; 7.50–53; 19.39–42

Christians who know the inside of a University common room will find something grimly familiar in the little picture of Nicodemus and the doctors of the law (7.50–53). Picking up the contemptible remark of v. 49, the learned Pharisee speaks to his colleagues of their own contempt of the Law. They silence him on an academic point. Jonah, in fact, came from Galilee. But was Jonah, with his mission to the Gentiles, to be listed as a prophet? Too cautious to argue and to commit himself in such an environment, Nicodemus lapses into silence.

Writing recently of C. S. Lewis, Mr. George Bailey remarked: 'As a popularizer of Christian dogma, Lewis was embarrassing to the academic community . . . I never heard Lewis, nor anyone else—including the college chaplain— discuss his religious works at Oxford . . . For the university, Lewis's standing as a scholar was checkmated by his unwelcome fame as an apologist of Christianity'. Many Christians of academic eminence, know how nearly impossible it is to overcome this ingrained and altogether ignorant prejudice by the worth of their instruction or by the value of their secular contributions to scholarship. The 'offence of the cross' must still be borne. The remedy for the burden is to look steadfastly at the students who watch and depend.

It is difficult to assess Nicodemus in the situation of this chapter. Says Leon Morris: 'The temper of the meeting must be borne in mind. Plain testimony to Jesus would undoubtedly have enraged the majority further. Nicodemus may have judged that Christ's cause might best be served by pointing these angry men to a legal weakness in their position'.

J. C. Ryle commends Nicodemus: 'Slow work is sometimes the surest and most enduring . . . No doubt it would be a pleasant thing if everyone who was converted came out boldly, took up the cross, and confessed Christ on the day of his conversion. But it is not always given to God's children to do so . . . Better a little grace than none. Better move slowly than stand still in sin and the world'. But how true it all is to life!

452 : The Adulteress
John 3.17–21; 8.1–11

In the RSV the story of the woman in the Temple court is
relegated to a footnote. There is a considerable number of
ancient manuscripts which omit it. It is undoubtedly part
of the Christian tradition and a genuine part of Scripture. It
may be the work of another hand and attached by John to
his manuscript. This would account for stylistic differences,
very difficult to nail down. And the wide omission of the
story could have been due to a growing deviation in the
Church, and the emergence of asceticism.

It is vividly written. We can see the surge of activity
round the bowed and silent figure. 'Here she is, Rabbi, caught
in the act. Now the Law of Moses, not our additions to the
Law, which are your constant theme of criticism, but the
Lawgiver's own solemn enactment, is clear enough. Now,
pray, your opinion?' He bent down, and with His finger
made marks in the sand on the flagstones.

They continued importunately. He looked up, and said:
'Let the one without sin among you be the first to throw
the stone'. Observe the definite article. 'Surely, in a group
so dedicated to the Law, there must be one without any sin
at all!' He continued writing, and there must be some vital
significance in what He wrote. And whatever it was He
wrote, those who watched were convicted by their conscience
and 'began to slip away one by one, beginning with the
eldest down to the last'.

The order of preference is very curious, and may be the
key to the understanding of the incident. Did He, in the
mysterious writing, communicate something shocking,
ironically following the order of seniority of which the
hierarchy was so fond? Did the eldest stone-thrower see a
name emerging?—'But she is dead, dead this twenty years'.
He drops his stone and slips away. Another sees a date, one
long banished from his mind. Another reads: 'Ephesus'. Yes,
Ephesus, does He know? The temple of Diana? That
woman? No Jew saw me, but He knows'—He drops his
stone. Something like this made them go.

But note the awful fact that such conviction was not in
any sense salutary. It stirred no desire for salvation, only
for escape. No one stepped forward, knelt by the cowering

woman, and craved pardon. All they desired in their hard and hate-filled lives was to escape the presence of the One who had hit hard on their crust of self-esteem. Like things of darkness which fear the light, they shrink back into the murk, lest the hidden corners be exposed and disinfected.

453 : The Adulterer

John 8.12–44

And so they sought to slip away into their guilty anonymity. They were not very successful. They confronted holiness, felt its light penetrate their darkened characters, and fled. Each Pharisee knew, too, that the others guessed the reason for the flight, and if no one remarked upon the fact, it was because of a tacit partnership of silence. In the whole scene there is one person alone who successfully covered his escape. We cannot even prescribe a verse in which to read about him, or on which to build some description of his person.

He is the figure missing from the vivid story, the man who found no forgiveness, as did his pathetic companion in sin. She was, according to her captors, taken 'in the very act'. There was therefore a man 'taken in adultery', who was not dragged, like the woman, into the presence of Christ. We can only guess how he was involved, and how he came to cover his cowardly escape, and to leave his associate in sin to face the consequences. Was he nimble of foot, influential, rich? Whatever the means of his escape, it could not be permanent. Guilt is a grim companion, and guilt ran off with its host. Nor is that the end. There is a judgement at the last, and no evil ultimately escapes.

No sin can be successfully confined to the place and time of its committing. Few sins can be held within the area of the person who commits them. Sin is commonly a partnership. If not that, it is an infection, too readily passed on. No person can live independently, and how often has that awesome and challenging truth emerged in these studies of the characters of Scripture. Someone persuaded the woman to sin, or even if she was the temptress we met in Proverbs, someone met her seduction with response and not rebuke, and sealed her guilt with opportunity. Someone could have said no, or helped a weakling to say no to temptation. Someone thought he had escaped, would hear no more of the doings of a shameful hour, and someone outside or behind this story made the tragic error which millions have repeated, for 'the Day shall reveal it'. It could be today.

454 : The Man Born Blind

John 9.1–12

John, as we have seen, often chooses his stories because of the significance of the events or the words consequential upon them. Sometimes a brevity of narrative results, and details require explanation. The RSV repeats the error of its predecessors in v. 3 and makes the words imply that a man was born blind in order that forty years later a miracle might be performed. It should be remembered that in ancient writing there were no punctuation marks or even divisions between words and sentences. Consequently, misunderstandings have sometimes arisen. There should be a fullstop in the middle of v. 3, and no stop at its end. The reply will then run : 'Neither did this man sin nor his parents. But that the works of God may be made manifest in him, we must work the works of Him that sent me while it is day. The night comes, when no man can work.' In other words, faced with the spectacle of human pain, the Lord first rebuts the doctrine that has found so large place in Eastern thought, that all suffering is of our own making, and then stresses the Christian fact that all need is a call to action in God's name with faith and urgency. The power that wrought the miracle was all His own. The promptitude with which He gave His help is an example we all can follow.

And in the same story why the peculiar method of the cure? Was this a concession to superstition? No, not in the sense that He Himself was the victim of a superstition. He was gloriously free from all such mental malady. But it is, perhaps, possible that the blind man may have held the popular belief that the spittle of a good man possesses healing power. It was necessary to help his faith. The Lord's miracles were a type of all salvation. The act of grace availed only when faith, however weak, met it with response. The blind beggar had little knowledge of God. The tags of popular theology which he uses in his clever duel with the Pharisees are witness enough to that. Somehow faith must awaken in his soul, if the miracle of healing is to take place. That is why the Lord steps on to his plane. He performs an act which rouses a spark of hope in the man's soul. Then He asks the man to do something with faith. The psychology is perfect. He who knew the soul of the man knew how the blind man's mind would work. With hope fanning a fire of faith in his heart, the blind man groped his way to the Pool of Siloam, 'and came back seeing'. Neither the clay nor the water of the pool had healing powers, but both were the agents which stimulated the faith which saved him.

455 : The Man Who Saw

John 9.13–41

The character of the man who received his sight emerges with some vividness from John's account of the interview with the Sanhedrin. The story bears all the marks of being an eye-witness account. John appears to have had access to the high-priest's house, and, as appears from the story of Peter by the fire, the proceedings of the Sanhedrin could be heard from the courtyard, into which those who could pass the doorkeeper could penetrate.

Observe the wary brevity with which the man tells the story (cf. vs. 11, 15). He does not betray a name to potential foes of his benefactor. He replies with studied economy of words. Like his canny parents, he has learned in the hard school of the slum and the city gate, that it is a good thing in a hostile situation to give away as little as possible. He has learned, too, not to look for help from anybody. From the two dour parents the man certainly has little help. They gave priority to the preservation of their own security.

Dorothy Sayers, in her famous broadcast radio play on the story of Christ (*The Man Born to be King,* 1943), caught the humour of the debate very well. Even in the brief Gospel story it emerges, especially when the man catches up the confident 'we know' of the priests, who had allowed themselves to be drawn into undignified argument in their frustration.

Dorothy Sayers made her Jacob say: 'Well now, that's a queer thing, ain't it? You don't know where the man comes from—and yet he knew how to open my eyes. He's a bad man, you say. All right. Does God hear the prayers of bad people? "No," says you, "of course He don't." Does He hear the prayers of good people? "Yes," you say, "He does." Well, look 'ee here. Here's a thing never heard on since the world began, that somebody should open the eyes of a man that was born blind. Nobody can't do a thing like that, only by God's help. Stands to reason.'

Read the chapter, trying to visualize the scene—the lofty theologians, the earthy ignorant man who doggedly held to the facts of his experience. The dramatist has given the flavour. One can imagine the zest with which John, who had slipped away to listen, retailed the story.

456 : The Blind Leaders
Isaiah 42.6, 7, 18–20; 44.18–20; 53.1–3; John 9.39–41

John had told the story of the blind man, not only for the relish of the Sanhedrin debate, but to set down the Lord's remark about the blindness of the soul. It is one of the commonest figures of speech in the Bible. There are those with eyes who cannot see. The rulers 'saw no beauty' in Christ. It is part of the quickening which comes with the life Christ gives that all that which the physical vision commands becomes more meaningful.

'Lord, what a lovely thing the moon is', Dorothy Sayers makes her Jacob say, 'to think I never saw it till last night'. George Wade Robinson caught up the same thought:

> *Something lives in every hue*
> *Christless eyes have never seen.*

Vision is a quality of the mind. How much do we truly see without involvement of the mind and the insights of the spirit? The animal sees but does not comprehend. Man takes the message of the eye, its report of line and hue, and relates it to another world, another dimension of understanding. Hence all poetry, all joy in beauty, all those deeper levels of awareness which make man different from the animal. Those whom Christ chided for their blindness, were unable in the grip of pride, amid the preoccupations of looking on themselves, and through the crassness of their self-willed corruption, to see the movement of the hand of God in their critical days, and above all to see in Christ the message God gave, the last and fullest revelation of Himself. He had nothing else to reveal. If men, in deliberate obstinacy, persisted in seeing in Him only the harried preacher from Galilee, the pathetic visionary, the peril to their comfort—God had no more to show. Blind to Him, they were blind to all.

Questions and themes for study and discussion on Studies 449–456

1. The cost of being a Christian.
2. How does one deal with hostility at home?
3. What would it be like personally to confront the living Christ? How, in fact, is He still confronted?
4. The academic cult of 'suspended judgement'.
5. When is conviction of sin salutary?
6. 'Sin is commonly committed in partnership'.
7. What do we learn concerning our contact with individuals from Christ's treatment of the blind man?

457 : The Shepherd

John 10; Psalm 23

The image of the Shepherd, like all the word-pictures of the Bible, must be comprehended in its ancient context of time and place. The modern shepherd presents a blurred picture. In New Zealand the sheep far outnumber the human population. They are a white dust on the rolling green of Southland, as far as the eye can see. Their hardier breeds crop the mountain grasses far up the Southern Alps. But none of them knows its shepherd, nor is known to him by name. Dogs, uncannily trained to obey a whistle, herd and gather them. Mounted men drive the great billowing massed flocks to market. Pathetically patient, they stand in two-decked railway wagons, drawn in long rakes to the killing-place. If there is a picture of humanity here, it is the proletarian multitude of some dictator-ridden land, the herded hordes of totalitarian regimes.

The Eastern shepherd 'went before' his sheep. They knew his voice. This was part of the Lord's comprehensive imagery in John 10. And such was ancient shepherding. Even in Homer's tale of the Cyclops, the blinded giant sits in the cave door and knows the sheep under which the wily Odysseus had tied his men, even by the touch of his fingers. 'The Lord is our Shepherd', and it is thus that He knows us, individually, not in harassed mass.

Sheep are foolish creatures, prone to follow a leader blindly, apt to wander, pathetically human in their carelessness. A wall-scratching in the catacombs shows the Good Shepherd, a favourite theme for those first Christian artists. The sheep are around Him. Some rest at His feet. Others graze with heads turned away, others disappear over a ridge, tails just showing. Any pastor (and the word means shepherd) could thus classify his flock.

The helpless creatures demanded continual care. Thieves preyed upon them, climbing into the fold by 'some other way' than by the door; the wild beast lurked to 'scatter the flock'; the burdened and the sick demanded the shepherd's careful strength. On the rolling hills around Bethlehem the first pastoral poet saw the pathos and significance of it all, and found the imagery and truth of the Shepherd Psalm, that veritable gem of Hebrew and English literature.

The great Moses had to learn that the shepherd of God's flock ruled by the crook, and he was sent to Midian for a span of forty years to meditate upon the desert flock, to tame impatience, and to learn to care for the helpless and lead the foolish. When the prince of Egypt burst out again long years later, as we have seen in Study number 84 and Moses beat the rock royally with his staff, he was set aside for leadership and superseded by another.

458 : The False Shepherds

John 10.1; Matthew 25.31–33; Ezekiel 34.11–19

Wherever good stands there arises the counterfeit. There are, as history, and, alas, everyday experience show, false shepherds. Milton describes them in *Lycidas*:

Anow of such as for their bellies' sake,
Creep and intrude, and climb into the fold!
Of other care they little reck'ning make,
Than how to scramble at the shearers' feast,
And shove away the worthy bidden guest;
Blind mouths!

John Ruskin comments perceptively on this passage. Creep, intrude, climb? 'Do not think,' says Ruskin, 'that Milton uses those three words to fill up his verse. . . . He needs all three, for they exhaustively comprehend the three classes of men who dishonestly seek ecclesiastical power.'

He elaborates: those who 'creep' are those 'who do not care for office, but do all things occultly and cunningly, consenting to any servility of office or conduct so only that they may intimately discern, and unawares direct, the minds of men.' Those who 'intrude', are those 'who by natural insolence of heart and stout eloquence of tongue, and perseverant self-assertion obtain hearing and authority with the common crowd.' Those who 'climb' are those 'who by labour of learning, selfishly exerted in the case of their own ambition, gain high dignities.'

Here is dual exegesis of the first order—John Milton on John 10, and John Ruskin on John Milton. Read on, for this is quotation with a purpose: 'Blind mouths.' It is not a broken metaphor. 'The two monosyllables express the contraries of character in two great offices, those of bishop and of pastor.'

A bishop, an 'episkopos' is one who 'oversees'. A pastor is literally 'one who feeds'. The most unbishoply 'overseer' is a bishop who is blind. The most unpastoral character is that of one who, instead of feeding, wishes to be fed. Or turn to Ezek. 34.17–19 and catch the reality of Eastern and Mediterranean history behind the imagery.

The passage, its ellipses supplied, runs: 'Is it a small thing to you goats to have eaten up the good pasture, but you must tread down with your feet the residue? And to have drunk of the deep waters, but you must foul the rest with your feet? A small thing that my sheep must eat what you goats have trampled, and drink what you have fouled with your feet?' The shepherd has also his goats, and separates them when he will. Hence the Lord's own word-picture of the judgement. Like the wheat and the tares the day will separate the true from the false.

536

459 : Martha and Mary

Luke 10.38–42; John 11.1–5

John has something interesting to say about the Bethany sisters in his Gospel, and we have been following John in recent studies to keep coherence of reading, rather than strict sequence of time. We must return to Luke, however, for the sake of completeness in the story. 'A woman named Martha,' the story runs, idiomatically translated, 'received him into her house. And her sister Mary sat at Jesus' feet, and was listening to his word. Martha, distracted with much serving, came and stood over them and said, "Master, do you not care that my sister has left me alone to serve? Tell her now to take a hand with me." Jesus replied, "Martha, Martha, you are troubled and upset over many things. One thing you need. And that good part Mary has chosen, and it shall not be taken away from her." ' So runs the story. The 'good part' was perhaps a reference to such banqueting customs as we find in Gen. 43.34. Martha is not blamed, but gently shown that the service which distracts and frays the temper is not to be preferred to quiet meditation. Unruffled attention to what the Master has to say leads to truest service. The rush of business, however laudable in motive, can, on the other hand, destroy the spirit's calm, and so mar our spirituality that the service itself loses its effectiveness. Mary had realized that 'man lives not by bread alone', and there is no truth more essential. Without this 'good part' the feast of life loses its spiritual vitamin. The service begins 'at the feet of Jesus'. And so the story becomes a parable of Christian usefulness.

It is interesting to turn to John and observe that it is Martha who is specifically named in v. 5. Does this suggest a preference for Martha? No. He rated differently the service of the two sisters, and Mary on one occasion won the greater share of His approval, but nowhere in the record can we find in Christ that weakness which determines all our human likes and dislikes. 'He knew what was in man,' says John. We do not. Hence our prejudices, our misunderstandings, our hero-worship and irrational affections. He knows us, knows our faults, and loves us equally. Even the phrase 'the disciple whom Jesus loved' implies no lower ranking for his fellows. John's quick apprehension and spiritual insight reached closer to Jesus' heart and won him the favour which love and faith can win, and it was on this basis that the Lord chose the inner circle of His fellowship. There are no degrees in the 'everlasting love'. There are differences in our reception of it. Consider the quiet affection of the Lord's reply to Martha, and consider a very significant phrase in the last Gospel to be written. John was an old man when he closed the canon of the New Testament with his Gospel. He had doubtless heard much misunderstanding of the incident we have considered. And so when his story came to Bethany he wrote with some deliberation the words, 'Now Jesus loved Martha, and her sister, and Lazarus.'

460 : The Bethany Family

John 11.6–46; 12.1–9

It is interesting to watch the characters in the story a little further. Note that it is Martha who is in greater command of the tragic situation (20). Mary, numb with grief, remains in the house, while her sister goes out to meet the Lord. In v. 31 it is Mary who is mentioned as the chief recipient of consolation from the circle of their acquaintance in Jerusalem. It is in such touches of detail that we find the unconscious marks of authenticity. Observe the convincing consistency of characterization.

It is curious that the chief character in the story remains elusive. It is difficult to assess a personality when no reaction in word or deed is recorded. Lazarus says nothing. The only act mentioned is the awesome movement of obedience by which, his arms and legs still wrapped round with the linen bands of death, he emerged from the tomb.

And yet there is one pointer to the sort of person Lazarus was. Jesus wept over his fate, though He knew well what He intended to do. The fact stands in sharp rebuke for those who see virtue in forced joy and cultivated stoicism in the place of death. Jesus wept and groaned in spirit (33, 35). The expression is a strong and vivid one. It is true, as the hymn puts it, that 'there is no love like the love of Jesus', but we are free to guess that it must have been a choice personality who could thus command affection.

Perhaps he was a quiet and placid man, a little overwhelmed by the dynamic Martha, and sharing more closely the contemplative ways of Mary. And his silence leaves us with the vast curiosity unresolved. What happened in those days of death? Had he a memory of any experience? Returned to life, had his values changed? Was he nostalgic for another world? Did he ever again fear death? He was to hold a rare distinction. He shared resurrection with Christ. And so shall we, else 'earth were darkness to the core, and dust and ashes all that is.'

461 : Caiaphas

John 11.47–57; Acts 4.1–22

Caiaphas, in this tiny picture of the doings among the hierarchs, is a repulsive picture. The portrait, for all the few strokes in the composition, is clear enough. This was a frightened man. He had staked all on collaboration with the Romans, and all was life itself. As a Sadducee he had no hope of another life, or for anything beyond such goods as this life might give. He was not prepared to forgo the small accumulation which his planning, intrigue and dissimulation had managed to scrape together, at the hands of a dangerous dreamer, and a reckless mob of enthusiasts.

He was like the political priest of all time, the Grey Eminence who manipulates events, the Wolsey unable to cast away ambition, the Richelieu, the plotting ecclesiastic ready to cloak crime with a crimson robe, and conceal iniquity underneath a mitre. History has no more cynical villains.

Observe the man's rough discourtesy to his peers, and imagine what mercy lesser men might be likely to expect at hands so ruthless and so rough. The Sadducees had something of a reputation for rudeness, and Caiaphas is a notable example.

And note the appeal to expediency. Expediency is the cynical resort and refuge of the hardened in sin of all the ages. Such men have murdered conscience. They have lost their fear of God and of judgement by long practice in self-seeking. They have passed the point of no returning, of which the Lord spoke when He told of a sin beyond all forgiving. Let a man die, innocent or not, said the scoundrel, to save the whole people.

Had that been a sincere word, it would still have stood as inexcusable wrong. Nations founder when principles die. Peoples are lost by abandoning righteousness, even when one life only is at stake. But Caiaphas cared nothing for the nation—'the accursed multitude that knew not the Law' (John 7.49). He was concerned rather for himself, his comfort, and his caste, and it was

539

for that reason that he was willing to murder an innocent man.

There is nothing to redeem Caiaphas. Such creatures, large and small as man measures such matters, are the curse of history, the foes of goodness, the enemies of light. Judgement dogs their steps. It is grim irony that Caiaphas' words contained a meaning beyond his intentions.

462 : The Secret Disciples

John 12.42–50; 1 John 4.2–15; Matthew 10.32, 33

Conviction which produces no action is sterile. Nicodemus is not included in this group. He had, falteringly, made a confession, ineffective though it was. Along with Joseph of Arimathea, his conviction was to force him into the open on a yet more notable occasion.

The unknown men of whom John writes so strongly, won no salvation. The alternatives were stark—the praise of men or the praise of God?—the synagogue or Christ? Visibly before us they make their fatal choice. Westcott is scathing in his comment on this passage: 'Such ineffective, intellectual faith is really the climax of unbelief.'

A heavy burden, indeed, lay upon these men because of their very enlightenment. They knew without doubt where the path of duty lay, but did not take it. They were unwilling to pay the price. The price was popularity and standing in the community, all those advantages, real or imagined, which Paul counted loss for Christ. 'Seek not the favour of the multitude,' said Kant, 'it is seldom got by honest or lawful means. Seek the testimony of the few. Number not voices but weigh them.'

There is no call to court persecution. It is perhaps possible for a devout Christian to be popular, but not likely that his popularity will be permanent. The open avowal of Christ is so frequently the occasion for the world's dislike, that a Christian should examine himself if he finds universal acceptance and approval. It is possible that he has bought the advantage by compromise.

Discipleship cannot be hid, and those who sought to do so were naïve. Discipleship, on the other hand, is not called upon to be brash, tactless, noisy, crude, or in any way to court the world's hostility. Testimony is varied, and is given in a hundred ways.

Where the word of the lips might be inappropriate or out of place, the attitude of the person, the manner of his living, the cast of his character in a thousand common and unavoidable situations, will show the committal of the life.

We cannot serve Christ and live a lie, and that is what the men who believed among the rulers sought to do. They began with foundations. They could not remain at that immobile point. They either lapsed into open sin or moved on to open discipleship.

Questions and themes for study and discussion on Studies 457–462

1. The kind of spiritual leadership represented by the shepherd image.
2. The marks of a true and of a false shepherd of God's flock.
3. Martha and proper hospitality.
4. The true balance of Christian activity and personal devotion.
5. Is expediency ever a correct guide to a proper course of action?
6. 'Secret discipleship' as a contradiction in terms.

463 : Peter

Matthew 14.22–36; Mark 6.45–56

Here is something curious. Matthew tells of Peter's characteristic over-confidence, and his failure on the water. It was typical of the rash disciple to act on a gust of emotion and to underestimate his capabilities. But why does Mark, who drew his facts from Peter, omit the incident? There is no ready explanation. Peter was not a man to suppress any matter which did not reflect well upon himself. That is more than once demonstrated in Mark's narrative. Nor had he anything of which to be ashamed. 'Beginning to sink', he cried for help to the only available source, and received it. There is nothing else to do when there is nothing solid underneath the feet. We must leave Mark's brevity unexplained. On the other hand there are some familiar marks of Peter's presence behind the words of the story. Perhaps there is an echo of the blunt words of Peter in v. 52. This, in fact, may be the point Peter stressed for Mark, and so determined the character of his narrative. It is the way of men to require repeated assurance; Gideon asked for the double sign of the dew and the fleece. And it is the fashion of the heart to forget the boon received and the mercy given, to doubt the wonder of it, and imagine that, after all, some astounding chance or unusual circumstance produced a seeming miracle. In our dealings with God there is always this margin of uncertainty, for God thrusts His presence on no man; He reveals Himself to faith and not to sight. That is why He tested His men immediately after the miracle on the hillside. On the earlier occasion of storm on the lake, He had been with them in the ship. Now He withdraws, as though to teach them to battle alone and to rely upon an aid they could not see; He sends them into the tumult and darkness without His visible presence. God often does this. It is His will that we should grow to spiritual maturity, and trust where we cannot see. Too often in such situations of testing, past lessons are forgotten, and fear banishes faith. But God is always in the shadows, keeping watch over His own. We have only to cry out and He is by our side.

464 : The Pharisees Again

Mark 7.1–23

As we resume the tenuous thread of narrative from Mark, we meet the Pharisees once more. Again one can almost hear the blunt words of Peter behind the account, and the niggling, hostile custodians of formal Judaism appear again in firm portraiture before us, eager to preserve the petty observances and sophistries of their elaborate code, but blind, as Isaiah put it, to the realities of life, and to the enormous obligations of mercy and duty.

Such is human nature that it is much easier to obey a set of rules and to call that obedience righteousness, than to live unselfishly and daily to seek the will and pleasure of the Lord. The Pharisees are a sad sight. They began as a great people, and to them, as we have seen, goes the credit for purging Israel of idolatry and establishing that reverence for the law and word of God which was Judaism's great contribution to the world. But the nature of man is such that great movements and institutions seldom escape ultimate corruption. God uses and discards—and discard He must, when that which began in purity ends in self-seeking and pride . . .

The old order changeth, yielding place to new,
And God fulfils Himself in many ways . . .

In meticulous observance of their own interpretation of the law, the Pharisees forgot mercy and loving-kindness. In jealous watching for infringements of their petty taboos, they failed to see the glory of God in Christ. Nor is such a pernicious attitude limited to the ancient Pharisee. Christianity has its ethics and observances, but it is the never-ending fault of man to reduce its grand obligations to formal codes, with their exits and their entrances; to set form above the spirit, to condition salvation beyond the Lord's intent, and, commonest fault of all, to resurrect the old Pharisaic interpretation of a Chosen People set apart from lesser men.

We shall meet the Pharisees again. Blind in their pride and folly, they were blundering on to the great crime which has darkened their memory—the alliance with the worldly Sadducees and the murder of Christ.

465 : The Woman of Tyre

Mark 7.24–37; Isaiah 23.1–12

This was the Lord's furthest journey north. It was the only occasion on which He left the proper territory of Israel. A track leads over the hills from Galilee, cut today by a hostile frontier, and to the astonishment of His men the Lord led that way, down to the ancient city of Tyre, once a seat of maritime empire. One might imagine that He knew of one in need there. In the wide ruins of Tyre a street paved in mosaic is uncovered. It is a first-century street, once a shopping mall, with geometrical designs in the paving and columns on each side. At the street's western end the Mediterranean glitters over the ruins of ancient port facilities.

Here they met the clever Phoenician and a strange conversation took place amid the circle of the disciples standing disapprovingly round. There was no harshness in the Lord's reply to the woman of Tyre. It is obvious that there must be a background not detailed in the narrative. The territory was populated by remnants of the Canaanites, and was sure to stir the racial consciousness of the disciples. The conversation all morning as they entered Gentile territory may have been in scorn of the foreigner —'these dogs'. In sad irony the Lord speaks rather to His protesting companions than to the needy woman. With quick wit she catches His meaning and replies in the same spirit, but in a humble tone which wins commendation and reward.

His healing, indeed, was for the world. Even in alien Phoenicia, as v. 24 puts it, 'He could not be hid.' Christ cannot be concealed. Secret discipleship is not discipleship at all. We have already discussed that truth. A home must be different where He truly resides. A character which owns His lordship must reveal its allegiance. A life which seeks His will, however haltingly, cannot disguise the fact. A Christian's path and the world's do not coincide. Situations arise which call for confession in word or deed, in protest or abstention. We must accept the truth that our allegiance cannot be hid, and seek to make life, speech, and attitude, a worthy testimony to our Lord—quiet, gracious, tactful, free from arrogance, from all suspicion of self-righteousness, and, above all, from inconsistency.

466 : Peter's Confession

Matthew 16.13–20; Mark 8.27–38

The strange words of Matt. 16.19 do not mean that Peter was given special authority over the destinies of men. Peter was recognized, by these words, as possessing didactic, not judicial, authority. An interpretation must be true to its context. Take the former. Peter has shown a God-given insight into truth which has delighted his Master. He has grasped a doctrine fundamental to Christian faith. It seems natural, then, that any authority he may be granted in reward should have reference to doctrine rather than to administration. Then think of the psychological context, the imagery, in other words. In English the metaphor in the word 'key' is coloured by Roman law, by feudalism, and medieval keeps. A word can suggest vastly different ideas in different lands and ages. The 'key' in the Lord's word here quoted had reference to the schools of the scribes. A proficient scribe was said to be in possession of the keys of the Law. Peter, as it were, graduates. So keen has been his apprehension of truth that he can be trusted to unlock the expressions of Heaven, to loosen the bonds of unsanctified doctrine, to confirm the constraints of Heaven's behests. This interpretation is not upset by the use of the key as a symbol of authority in Revelation. The two contexts support each other. Peter's authority was that of the school, not the court-house.

Turn then to Mark's account. Mark's brevity draws closely together in the story Peter's confession and Peter's mistake. From Matthew's account it is clear that some time lay between. Nor does Mark mention the word of splendid tribute to Peter. It is easy to see why, if Peter was Mark's chief source of information. One can imagine the brevity with which that great spirit would pass over the record of commendation, or even bid that no mention be made of it. The deep humility, born of the tragic denial in the high priest's house, would similarly prompt frankness for the record of mistakes. Out of his failure Peter was eager to pluck good. Failure, equally with success (if completely surrendered to the transforming hands of God), can be used for the blessing of men. Many a bruised, defeated man, remembering Peter, has risen from defeat and battled on. Had Peter suppressed the story of his fall, or hidden the words of the Lord's rebuke, there would have been failure unhealed in all the centuries and defeat un-remedied. Peter's faults, handed in penitence and helplessness to God, were transfigured by the Hands which can turn all things to good.

467 : On The Transfiguration Mount
Mark 9.2–13; 1 Kings 12.12–16

The pattern of worth and failure is seen throughout Peter's story. He is selected by his Master as one of the privileged group which was to see His Transfiguration; it is part of the love of God to measure us by our desires for good rather than by our achieve-ment, and Peter's intent was true. If the favour of God and the blessing He bestows depended upon our understanding of His purposes, our lot would be hopeless indeed. The meaning of the awesome scene on the mountain still eludes us. It is recorded as an amazing experience of three bewildered men, and Peter's reaction was in conformity with his character. In moments of tension or emotion he took refuge in speech, and often his hasty words were ill-advised. We have seen him earn rebuke. On the mount he makes a wild suggestion which may mean the setting up of a standard of revolt. Was this 'seeing the Kingdom of God coming with power'? Peter may well have asked himself. Peter was afraid, and speaking excitedly, when he suggested the setting up of the three tents, 'one for you and one for Moses and one for Elijah,' but, as people do under such circumstances, he was revealing his inner thoughts. 'To your tents, O Israel,' (1 Kings 12.16) was a rallying cry for Jewish rebels. Peter believed perhaps that the Lord was about to 'manifest Himself', as the conquering Messiah, and he made his suggestion in that light. His confused mind pictured Jews streaming to the wilderness, armed for final battle with the Roman, and rallying under three standards, those of Jesus, Moses and Elijah! Little wonder the apostles proved so spiritually impotent the very next day! And we may imagine the disappointment of their Lord. They quarrelled over precedence in the Kingdom on the last journey to Jerusalem. Two of them, walking to Emmaus, revealed that they had held a narrow nationalism to the end of their relations with the Lord. And now Peter fails to grasp the wonder of his Master on the Transfiguration Mount. The Lord was ever under the necessity of avoiding enthusiastic crowds, lest they 'make Him King'. Too many false Messiahs arose, too many tents were 'set up' in the desert only to be mopped up by Roman flying columns. Peter's project is passed by in silence, and with that gentle suppression with which God seems so often to quench our feverish scheming. It found no condemnation, for the motive was pure.

468 : The Disciples
Mark 9.14–32; Psalm 9

The three, with their Master, came down from Hermon. A considerable crowd awaited them, 'a great crowd', Mark says, with some intermingling of doctors-of-the-law from Caesarea Philippi. It is difficult to account for such a popular demonstration unless some unwise boasting or courting of popularity on the part of the disciples is the reason for it.

The centre of interest was a stricken man in agony of mind over his son. He had come to seek Christ's help for the afflicted lad, who was torn and tormented by an evil thing which possessed him. There is no greater pain than the helpless anguish of a parent who would gladly bear the burden of a child's woe, but can only watch and grieve.

The man came seeking Christ and found His followers. Men still come in fear and in yearning to seek the assurance and the hope He has to give and find too often the preacher without conviction, or the Christian without a message. Let all who diminish Christ, make God remote, too little, the servant of a sect, or anything less than the Lord Omnipotent get out of the way. There is more in the story than Mark's brief narrative tells. Peter, after all, was not at first present, and Peter was Mark's authority. The story is full enough from the point of his arrival. The nine disciples were riding a wave of popular interest. It is easy enough to collect a crowd. Pathetic stunting in the Church often succeeds well enough in this trivial process. But to what end?

Note, too, that the scribes were there. The doctors of the law were interested in the prophet from Galilee and His men, and the disciples were not a little proud, and anxious to turn the situation to profit. Perhaps in their innocence they were out to impress the religious leaders with a notable miracle. But as the great James Denney once remarked: 'No one can bear witness to himself and Jesus Christ at one and the same time. No man can at one and the same time show that he himself is clever and that Christ is mighty to save.' 'Here now, you rebels,' shouted Moses, 'shall we bring forth water for you out of this rock?' It was disaster in his great career.

A man-made mass-movement is harmful. The exaltation of a person or an institution in empty religious excitement is lamentable. Christ is hidden, the way barred to His healing hand, when strutting self-important men advertise their sham religious wares before the multitude. Christ can work only through the humble, the devoted, the dependent. He chooses 'the weak things of the world' to do His work. The man who said those words was one of the most powerful intellects of his age, and God chose Saul of Tarsus because he wished to use the sharp clean tool of his great mind. But that mind had to be surrendered, conscious of its need, malleable in His hand . . .

469 : The Parent
Mark 9.14–32; Luke 11.11–13

We have set down the passage from Mark for a second reading, for we now shift the emphasis from the disciples to the father.

'Bring the boy to me,' said Christ, and there in five words is the divine commission for parents and teachers. It is an awful thought that we are the child's first image of God.

'Bring the boy to me,' said Christ, and we ourselves dare not approach that Presence unworthily. How humbly must we tread when we lead a child by the hand!

And so they brought the child to Christ. There is a note of hopelessness in the distracted father's voice: 'I asked your disciples to cast him out but they could not.' It is possible to catch the dull, flat tone of a disillusioned man. The chill of impotence of those who should have aided him is on his heart even in the presence of the Lord: 'But *if you* can do anything', he says without much hope, 'have pity on us and help us.'

The Lord looked at him and said: 'If *you* can! All things are possible to one who believes.' At the words the man's heart caught fire. In days of doubt we should look steadily on His face. Turn the eyes on Him, and the world grows dim, the clutter of humanity falls away, and the heart grows strong. 'Lord,' he cried, 'I believe. Help my unbelief.' So the AV (KJV) and Moffatt. 'I do believe. Help me to believe more,' says J. B. Phillips. 'I have faith. Help me where faith falls short,' runs the New English Bible. Or translate: 'I believe, I believe, pity my faith's feebleness.'

So cried the poor man, and put a magnificent prayer into history. It is a prayer which, of all prayers, can claim an answer. The Lord demands no impossible coercion of mind or soul. He presents no list of man-made dogmas. He asks for no intellectual dishonesty, no vain words, or insincere profession. He asks us to look steadily in His eyes, and trust Him to be what He professed to be. He asks for a willingness to try, for the merest bridgehead in the soul. None can help the surge of doubt, but doubt need not be fostered and cherished, misnamed integrity of mind, and laced with pride and posturing.

A burning desire for God must lie at the core of all faith. Perhaps in the mystery of God's ways with men, that is why faith saves. Doubt too often finds its origin in a half-suppressed desire *not* to believe, to find some way out of faith's stern obligations. The father in the story wanted blessing, and with that firm invincible desire beneath its feet faith found a place to kneel and then to stand.

470 : The Child

Mark 9.25–29; Matthew 18.1–10

There is an unnamed person in the crowd which the Lord joined with His selected disciples—silent save for the cries of an afflicted child. A small figure leaves the scene quietened and healed, but he stands for the multitude of children to whom Christ has brought love, peace and manifold compassion.

The life of children was of small account in the ancient world, and it is a significant mark of those sections of society which abandon Christ today, that the tenderness which comes with Christian parenthood fails and falters. Unborn life is considered of less and less account in a sex-ridden society. It is a small step to the contempt for newly born life which marked the ancient world, and permitted the casting out of unwanted babes to die on the town's rubbish-heap.

Among the multitude of papyrus letters which have survived from the arid sands south of Cairo, is one written within a year or two of the birth of a Child in Bethlehem. A certain young man had gone north from his native village to find work in the teeming metropolis of Alexandria. His wife had written to him anxiously. She was to have a child in his absence and no doubt enquired concerning her husband's wishes. He writes back with some affection, but casually bids her throw the babe away if it is a girl. Here is the letter. (The date is the year we call 1 B.C.):

'Hilarion to his dear wife Alis, very many greetings, likewise to my lady Berous and Apollonarion. Know that we are still in Alexandria. Do not be anxious; if they really go home, I will remain in Alexandria. I beg and entreat you, take care of the little one, and as soon as we receive our pay I will send it up to you. If by chance you bear a child, if it is a boy, let it be, if it is a girl, cast it out. You have said to Aphrodisias: 'Do not forget me.' How can I forget you? I beg you then not to be anxious. The 29th year of Caesar Augustus, Month of Pauni, 23. Deliver to Alis from Hilarion.'

There is a certain significance, then, in the shaken little boy who walked off with his father to some small home in Caesarea Philippi.

Questions and themes for study and discussion on Studies 463–470

1. 'Beginning to sink' as an experience of life.
2. Pharisaism today.

3. References in the Gospels to Gentiles.
4. How could Peter's faults of too ready speech be turned to good account?
5. How can Christians obscure Christ?
6. You have read material from John and from Mark. How do their styles differ?
7. Human character. Has it changed?
8. 'Christianity is a charter for children.' Discuss this.

471 : Rich Young Man

Mark 10.17–31; Luke 18.18–30

A dramatic incident took place as the journey to Jerusalem began. Someone came running, forgetful of all dignity, and kneeled impulsively in the dust. He was young, Matthew tells us; he held high office in the Jewish religious community, says Luke. All three evangelists who tell the story leave us in no doubt that he was a rich man, and by the common standards of society a blameless character. As Harold St. John puts it: 'he seemed to have all the keys of life hanging at his girdle—wealth, youth, prestige and a blameless character, but withal an empty heart.'

The Lord answered the young man's question with another. 'Why,' He asked, *'why* do you call me good?' The emphasis is on the first word. He sought to bring leaping to the young man's lips a glad confession of His deity. So He led Peter to blessing (Matt. 16.13–19). But here no answer came. The young man failed to rise to the faith that would have solved his problem. Imagine a pause after this verse. The Lord next seeks to elicit a confession of sin. He refers him to the inexorable standard of the law, which is 'our schoolmaster to lead us to Christ'. The young man is quite unabashed. He has performed the impossible. As touching the law he is blameless. He has been perfect since boyhood. It thus became necessary, as it was with the woman at the well, to touch the weakness in the life. The young man was shown that in spite of his eagerness comfort was his supreme desire. He loved this life rather than the next. In the pain of self-revelation he left the cross upon the ground, and went away with heavy steps. Looking after him, and turning to His disciples, the Lord said: 'How difficult it is for those who have riches to enter into the Kingdom of God!'

550

The word in the Greek text is *chremata* which also means 'things'. The root is that of the verb 'use', and fundamentally *chremata* are 'useful things'. Wealth, in other words, is what we can use, and it follows that wealth is what we should use. It was the fault of the unprofitable servant in the Parable of the Talents that he hid away the money he had, and denied it useful employment. So it must have been with the young man in the story. His 'useful things' were denied their usefulness because they had taken the character of a soul that was dull and barren, and fired by no generosity or love. And yet Christ loved him, perhaps for the spark of that day's desire, perhaps with a wider pity than we, His followers, can feel.

472 : The Nobleman

Luke 19.11–27

The road ran down the east of Jordan to the fords near Jericho where the baptism had taken place. Probably from the slopes across the river, as the road descended, they could see the white mass of the Herodian palace among the green palm trees on the lush valley floor. The sight suggested a sermon, and Archelaus (Matt. 2.22 f.) enters the story again.

The will of the first Herod divided the kingdom which he had ruled so long, so dexterously and so ruthlessly. Archelaus, son of Malthace, a Samaritan woman, took over Judea and Idumea, by far the choicest share. Herod Antipas, son of the same mother, received Galilee and Perea; and Philip, son of a Jewess named Cleopatra, took Ituraea, Trachonitis and the associated territories in the north-east. Archelaus, who inherited his father's vices without his ability, adopted the title of king, and bloodily quelled disorders which broke out in Jerusalem. The result was a wider uprising, which required the strong intervention of Varus, the governor of Syria. It was at this time that the holy family returned from Egypt. 'But when Joseph heard that Archelaus was reigning as king over Judea in the place of his father Herod, he was afraid to go there . . . but withdrew into Galilee, and came to a town called Nazareth.'

It was imperative for Archelaus quickly to reach Rome, and to secure from Augustus confirmation of his position, before the situation in Palestine could be presented in too lurid a light by his many determined enemies. Archelaus' petition was opposed in person by Herod Antipas, who made much of Herod's testamentary incapacity, and also by a Jewish embassy. Somewhat surprisingly, Augustus declared in favour of Archelaus, though he cautiously denied him the royal title. The incident provided the background for the Parable of the Pounds, related by Luke. Archelaus was the 'nobleman' who went 'to receive a kingdom', and the facts were no doubt brought to mind by the sight of the palace which Archelaus had built at Jericho, where the story was told. It is a striking illustration of the fact that the incidental machinery of a parable is exempt from theological and moral significance. It remains a canon of such exegesis that the main point only must be disengaged, and no meaning attached to the pictorial and background detail. Archelaus maintained his stupid and tyrannical reign for ten years. In A.D. 6, a Jewish embassy finally secured his deposition and banishment to Gaul. (Herod I had built the palace at Jericho which suggested the parable. It was burnt down at the time of his death, but rebuilt and restored by Archelaus. The site was discovered and excavated in 1951.)

473 : Bartimaeus
Matthew 20.29–34; Mark 10.46–52; Luke 18.35–43

Mark, telling his story after the account of James and John on the Jericho to Jerusalem road, speaks of the healing of blind Bartimaeus. Matthew speaks of two blind men. If the three accounts are collated it would appear that the incidents took place as the party entered Jericho, and as they left it. Much has been made of these alleged discrepancies by those eager to find damaging 'contradictions' in Scripture. It is not careless reporting. It is the brevity of the narrative which occasions such misunderstanding.

If the three accounts are read precisely as they are set down, it will become apparent that three or four men found healing, one of whom was named Bartimaeus and whose name stuck in Peter's mind to be passed on to Mark. News spread through the town, and others sought the touch of Christ. Incidents therefore took place on both sides of the town. There is no need to suppose that the narratives have two Jerichos in mind—the old Canaanite fortress whose ruins stand outside the modern town with its jacarandas and orange trees, and Herod's city, which occupied the present site.

Bartimaeus, the 'son of Timaeus' as Mark obligingly translates for his Gentile readers, was a determined man. All good, as we have again and again had occasion to see as we have looked at the characters of Scripture, demands a certain eagerness, passion and desire. It is those who 'keep on asking . . . knocking . . . seeking' who attain their desire. Elisha was angry at the young king's half-hearted response to the symbolism of the arrows. Lot's wife looked back and shared Sodom's fate. 'If with all your hearts ye truly seek me, ye shall ever surely find me' . . . Quotation and illustration could be multiplied, from Genesis to the enduring saints of Revelation.

Bartimaeus set a fine example. He cared nothing for the crowd in his desire to find Christ and the blessing He could give. He was 'importunate' like the widow, like the neighbour, in the two familiar parables, indeed, after Zacchaeus' example. Observe the human touches in the story caught by Peter's observant eye—the word passed on to the shouting beggar: 'Cheer up! He's calling you', the garment left behind . . . Dignity hardly mattered with such salvation waiting.

474 : Zacchaeus

Luke 19.1–10

And speaking of dignity, consider Zacchaeus. The incident took place in Jericho itself, and was rescued by Luke. Zacchaeus was a fiscal officer. Much trade passed that way, for the place lay on an east–west artery of Judean trade. At such points there were dues to collect, and Jericho had always been regarded as a source of income by Herod's house. There were rich balsam groves owned by the royal house, and Jericho was looked upon as the winter capital of the kingdom.

Zacchaeus could have been a man of considerable wealth, and Christ may have been entertained in one of the finest houses in the city. The buildings, colonnaded, and constructed round cool courtyards, could have been like those of Pompeii. Zacchaeus was the chief tax-collector (2) in this important place. For a man of such position to climb a roadside sycamore tree to win a mere sight of Jesus, was a remarkable action and indicates the sharp concern for better living which drove him. He must have hated the life he lived with its temptations, corruptions, and unpopularity.

Zacchaeus, like Bartimaeus, forgot all obstacles, and cared nothing for the crowd. Nine of the ten verses in Luke's account begin with 'and'. The copula occurs twenty times. Does this style suggest that someone, gripped by the mingled humour, pathos, humanity and triumph of the occasion, wrote the story in Aramaic, and thus passed it on to Luke? If so we are grateful to an unknown chronicler.

Zacchaeus sought a glimpse of another, cleaner world, a world of peace with God and a heart at rest. He did not at first realize that such a world lies close to any one of us, and requires but a firm step of faith. The immediate delight of the rich outcast, incongruously up his tree, is evident. Christ cannot come truly as a guest into any house or life without cleansing it. It all illustrates two remarks in the earlier chapter (18.24, 27). And so the Lord passed through Jericho, the town which reeked of Herod and his house. He left it a sweeter place. Ahead lay the long winding road from the deep trench of the Jordan plain to Jerusalem and all that awaited there. The Lord was to know little peace from this day to the Cross. Zacchaeus gave Him His last quiet hour.

475 : James and John

Mark 10.32–40

Phillips has translated 10.32: 'They were on their way going up to Jerusalem, and Jesus walked on ahead. They were puzzled and bewildered at this, but went on following Him with fear in their hearts.' 'They were awestruck,' says Weymouth's rendering. 'They were filled with awe,' says the New English Bible. What is awe? It is, says the Oxford English Dictionary, 'a solemn and reverential wonder, tinged with latent fear, inspired by what is sublime and majestic.' There was a deep change in their Master, which the disciples could not miss. Luke, describing the same scene, remarks that, 'He set His face steadfastly to go to Jerusalem.' 'He made His face firm,' says the Greek text, as though to meet something formidable and unwelcome. Underline the thought 'they went on following'—in spite of fear.

The Lord knew what lay at the end of that long climb up to the city. He was desperately lonely. He had done His best to prepare

His men for what was to be by the instruction of those weeks under Hermon, round Caesarea Philippi. But for all His instruction, how little they had understood! Fired perhaps by their own interpretation of the Parable of the Talents, they were excited at the prospect of an earthly kingdom, and the vision corrupted them. Truth, misconceived, can be bent into a lie.

They were no team, no band of brothers that day, but a divided group of self-seeking men. Nothing more awesomely demonstrates the patience of Christ than His response to James and John. He had taken them apart at some hour of rest by the roadside, and quietly told them again what awaited at Jerusalem—betrayal, pain, death, and resurrection. As though the words of direct solemn import had made no impression at all, the two brothers came with a selfish and ambitious request. 'Could they sit on either side of Him in the day of His power?' Without anger, without scorn, He answered them with careful sadness, gently disposing of their untimely selfishness. But consider this also. Anyone among the disputatious band on the road up from the Jordan could have abandoned lesser company and walked out ahead with Christ. Stepping on before, He found loneliness. In the same determination the Christian finds his Lord, and shares in the fulfilment of a plan. Preoccupation with lesser purposes holds us back from that full fellowship, half-heartedness, and lack of understanding . . .

Questions and themes for study and discussion on Studies 30–34

1. Was the rich young man sincere?
2. Distinguish the five Herods of the New Testament. The article 'Herod' in the New Bible Dictionary will help you.
3. Half-heartedness in religion. Read the letter to Laodicea (Rev. 3.14–22).
4. A new life requires but one step out of the old life.
5. Why were the disciples so slow to understand their Lord's teaching?

476 : Reluctant Disciples

Luke 9.57–62; 14.25–35; Matthew 10.35–42

We have been following Mark and Luke conjointly as the story has been traced from Caesarea Philippi to the ascending climb of the Jerusalem road. At this point we must turn to Luke and collect a whole series of characters which are peculiar to his Gospel. Luke's ninth chapter might, in fact, have ended appropriately at v. 51 because at that point, and on through ten more chapters, he inserts a long tract of material not found in the other evangelists. The events seem to cover the last days in Galilee and on to those at which we have already looked in Mark's narrative, but we cannot disentangle an exact chronological sequence. We shall follow Luke to ch. 21.

In today's readings we meet some nameless men, one of them the scribe who, in a burst of emotion, promised to follow Christ. He had not counted the cost, and we are not told what he did when he was told the cost. Following Christ can often mean Winston Churchill's old price—'nothing but blood and tears and sweat'. He wants no one to follow Him under hope of material gain, under any illusion, false hope, selfish or ill-considered motive.

And He must come first. Hence the 'hard word' of Luke 14.26. The saying does not forbid filial affection. It is perfectly certain that He who bade His followers love their enemies would not have prescribed hatred for their parents. He was speaking in terms of comparative loyalty. He was speaking, too, in the colourful language of Eastern thought. Hyperbole is natural in Hebrew and Arabic. So also is vivid and concrete illustration. No eastern hearer of the precept concerning the 'second mile', and the 'cloke also', would misunderstand so far as to obey literally. They would readily understand that the figure of speech commanded only extreme long-suffering and sacrificial generosity. And all would see, with a readiness we exact and logical northerners do not find easy to understand, that the precept which speaks of hatred of one's parents means only that, when affections clash, loyalty to God must come pre-eminently first. 'Let me,' one has said, 'first bury my father'. He meant, of course, 'Let me wait until my father dies'. Abraham had done precisely this at Haran. 'An earthly affection,' said the Lord, 'must not bind us thus.'

477 : The Samaritan
Luke 10.30–37; Colossians 3.11–15

The Jericho road ran through the ancient wilderness of Judea, and was a notorious haunt of bandits and terrorists. Jerome in the fifth century, and H. V. Morton in the twentieth, confirm that the evil reputation of the road was not confined to New Testament times. The priest feared ceremonial defilement if the still figure by the path should prove to be dead. The Levite was perhaps afraid of a trap. Modern men might similarly shun involvement in some down-town situation of assault or underworld strife. There is no indication that the victim was a good man. The Samaritan did all that which the others failed to do. As a visitor from the hated north, he lacked the Jew's knowledge of the Scriptures. Samaria had only the books of Moses, and it is ironical that Lev. **19**.18, which counsels love for one's neighbour, was part of the Samaritan Bible, and was probably worn in a tiny leather case on the scribe's waist when he posed his question. The legalists, after the age-old fashion of their kind, had a way out of such obligations. They defined 'neighbour' to suit their prejudice and convenience. The splendid and challenging common sense of the Lord's reply cut through the clutter of their nonsense. We are free to deal similarly with that which darkens truth.

Thus it was that 'the Good Samaritan' became one of the best known characters of the New Testament. A good Samaritan, wherever he is found, and the commercial traveller of the Jericho Road has his vast posterity, is one who helps another even when the needy is the author of his own trouble. He helps regardless of race, caste or creed. He helps in spite of the cost. As Sydney Smith once remarked: 'You find people ready enough to do the Samaritan without the oil and twopence.' The Samaritan is a practical man in his beneficence. He acted first, regardless of consequences. We are not surprised to find that his credit was good. The innkeeper trusted him to make good his promise. He seems to have been a known character on the Jericho Road, and therefore was well-enough aware of the risk he ran, should the battered figure in the ditch prove to be a decoy. But are we treating fiction as fact? If so, what a tribute to the Lord's story-telling.

478 : The Importunate Friend

Luke 11.1–13

We have already looked at the Lord's prayer and observed that He was never more simple than when He was speaking on this theme. Some turn prayer into an exercise of meditation, into contemplation, or a species of self-therapy. Prayer, in the Lord's teaching, is speaking to God, an infinitely wise and loving Father. For some reason which eludes our human understanding He seeks fellowship with His children, and if these matters defy such explanation as human speech can give, is it at all strange that the Lord should resort to penetrating simplicities?

That is how this nameless character comes breaking into the story. It is a homely scene. The little village is silent and the small houses are dark, when the knocking comes on the barred door. The neighbour is neither thoughtful nor unselfish. He is concerned to feed his hungry, unexpected guest, and he knows that the man next door has a spare loaf. Hence the clamour in the street and the determination not to be put off. He was importunate indeed, a nuisance and a selfish nuisance.

Parables, as we have seen, are not meant for multiple interpretation. They have a point to make and must not be used to teach that which they were not intended to teach. The neighbour who awakened and besieged his sleeping friend was not like God. He was an awkward man to have next door. He may also have been a careless housekeeper. The Lord simply means that, in the common affairs of ordinary life, a man is not put off, if he wants something ardently enough, by the reluctance of another. How much the more, then, in the matter of prayer, should we pray with perseverance and invincible expectation. The importunate neighbour also had a certain confidence in his friend. Should we be less earnest with God, especially, as the last three verses stress, God is no sleeping neighbour but a father, infinitely more willing to give than His children are to receive?

And so an unknown man of Nazareth, of Cana, or some other small place in Galilee, strayed into Scripture to teach a lesson, as he may have strayed once into the experience of Christ. Perhaps he was Mary's neighbour.

479 : The Pharisees

Luke 11.37–12.15

We have met them before, these religious leaders of the nation. They watched Him when His ministry began in Capernaum, caught up His words, and denied Him the synagogue. The washing which the Lord omitted was not a simple act of cleanliness. It was a ritual performance, regulated to the last detail, with the exact amount of water specified, the movements of arms and hands legally prescribed, along with the manner in which the water was to be poured, and the way palms and knuckles were to be rubbed and rinsed. It was part of the rabbinical clutter of nonsense which deserved the Lord's contempt.

Pharisaism, which had begun nobly in the days of exile as a movement to conserve and exalt the Word of God, had degenerated into such a pernicious legalism that life under its endless regulations was almost impossible without sanctioned subterfuge, and prescribed escape. Hence two damaging results. The practice of Pharisaism, as some conceived it, promoted hypocrisy, pride and self-righteousness. It also made little of the wider obligations and positive duties of mercy and love, as it wasted effort and fervour in the prosecution of endless regulation.

To reduce religion to a set of obligations and prohibitions, a pattern of attitudes, and a pursuit of rituals, while neglecting the committal of the whole person to God, is a common enough fault of man. By-products of such misdirected zeal are censoriousness for those who reject its enslavement, and a vicious self-righteousness. All Pharisees were not thus damaged. Nicodemus and Gamaliel were not men who fell under the Lord's stern indictment. Paul, in his days of Pharisaic zeal, sinned direly in his persecution of the Church, but it is difficult to think of him as a dedicated legalist.

There were good men among them, but their sin was, like that of the professional experts, the 'scribes', to darken that which was light, and to make a beneficent system a complicated and enslaving web. It is always and everywhere true that any system of religion, or any interpretation of Scripture, which makes religion difficult to follow, irrelevant to common life, hard to understand, and impossible for ordinary men and women, is wrong. Hence the Lord's denunciation. The 'common people', we are told 'heard him gladly', and this was because He brought God near, made Heaven real, and faith relevant to life. Those who, then and now, deny men this gladness, merit the words of His rebuke. Read also Matthew 23.

480 : The Farmer
Luke 12.16–40

The man whom Christ called a fool was a successful farmer. That in itself was no mean achievement. Palestine is not good farming country, save on the coastal plain and the great triangle of Esdraelon, where the confronting highlands precipitate the rain-laden winds of the Mediterranean. The brown soil of the valley bottoms is rewarding for the cultivator, but, for the most part, arid and boulder-strewn slopes offer grudging return for the labour expended. The Parable of the Sower gives a fair enough picture of the hard toil of the average farmer.

Nevertheless, the man in the story was a successful farmer. Good fortune or good management had made him rich. He had made his money by honest toil, defrauding no one, exploiting none. At least the story has nothing to say to the contrary. He also saw that wealth was meant to use. He knew when to take a holiday and to retire, and who was there rightly to grudge him his pleasures?

He was a fool, none the less. He thought he could control the future, not realizing how fragile life was. His farm should have taught him that trifles can destroy. He thought life was secure if he had a few barns full of corn. He confused his body with his soul. Life for him was 'eat, drink and be happy'. Happiness, he thought, was something that could be cornered and confined. Too insensitive to observe the crushing poverty of Palestine, un-conscious of the needs of others, he proposed to feed his flesh and so make life happy. He lacked a whole dimension of under-standing, and he must have cultivated this insensitivity by think-ing only in material terms. He imagined that he was in complete control of circumstances, and he mistook a means for an end. It would be difficult to find in one person a fuller list of follies. That night his heart stumbled, blocked and was flung into fatal faltering by one impacted clot . . .

He is a fool who fails to find a meaning in life wider than a shed full of food. What is life, this wondrous reality compounded of our hopes and fears, pleasures and pains, love and passion, tingling awareness, years like minutes, and hours like years, strife, peace . . .? It is, said Macbeth, glutted with his cruel ambition,

. . . a walking shadow, a poor player,
That struts and frets his hour upon the stage,

560

> *And then is heard no more; it is a tale*
> *Told by an idiot, full of sound and fury,*
> *Signifying nothing.*

'A narrow vale,' cried atheist Ingersoll, 'between the lofty peaks of two eternities—we cry aloud and the only answer is the echo of our wailing.'

Life is Christ, said Paul, a gift to share, a communion with the eternal. It is 'the childhood of our immortality, a quarry from which to chisel a character', said Goethe. It is a glory Christ came to give in unimaginable measure. He is a fool who misses it.

481 : The Faceless Crowd

Luke 12.49–13.9

We have thought, in an earlier study, of the crowd whose presence in the background of the story is so apparent in John's Gospel. We sense their reality in this passage. Christ's presence divided them, awakened them to life as individuals, and presented them with challenge. Christ brings peace (John 14.27), peace that passes understanding (Phil. 4.7), but He also sets men at variance. A new, demanding loyalty challenges some old allegiance, and divides those who were less worthily bound by it. Origen reports a saying of Christ: 'He who is near me is near the fire', and fire can never be approached lightly or carelessly.

The Lord besought them to look, think and choose. They knew the signs of the weather. The west wind rolled up the rain-clouds which Elijah's servant saw from Carmel (1 Kings 18.44 f.). Out of the Arabian desert and the wilderness of Sinai, the east and the south wind brought scorching heat. And yet, wise as they were in such matters of common observation, they shut their eyes to the 'signs of the times'. Like foolish people who rush to court, they were blundering on to disaster. And that disaster was in full view, as it is all through the Gospels and Acts. The Great Rebellion was looming.

An illustration follows, its relevance obscured by the unfortunate break between the two chapters which the reading straddles. Someone in the faceless, anonymous crowd listening to these words, calls out some comment on Pilate's Galilean massacre, and someone else mentions the catastrophe of the fallen Siloam tower. They were both tragedies which make some think of

561

judgement, and others question the ways of God. Man, the Lord implies, is exposed to the vicissitudes of life, caught in some crowd on whom Pilate's indiscriminate brutality fell, harmed or maimed in the street by some sudden disaster. God does not always intervene to save the innocent. Goodness must be for goodness' own sake, not to secure some special privilege of protecting angels.

Nor has the Jew a special place. Hos. 9.10 and Joel 1.7 give the key to the imagery of vs. 6–9. The crowd would see Israel in the image of the fig tree. National enlightenment conveyed national responsibility, and failure to bear the fruit which God expected might lead to the withdrawal of privilege. It is a compacted narrative, but we seem to see the multitude, tormented, divided, ravaged by doubt, prejudice, racial hate—and denied a clear message by those who should have given it (11.52). What of the present day?

Questions and themes for study and discussion on Studies 476–481

1. The 'hard sayings' of Jesus.
2. The priest and the Levite on the Jericho road.
3. The importance of rightly interpreting the parables of Jesus.
4. The proper relation of the internal and the external in religion.
5. Do material things contribute anything to happiness? Be frank.
6. 'Sins of the times' in a modern setting.

482 : The Woman and the Rabbi

Luke 13.10–17; 14.1–6

For the last time the Lord appears in the synagogue. Luke, physician though he was, spoke in the language of the day, and the 'spirit of infirmity' was a vivid enough way of expressing that feeling of painful resistance to all efforts to straighten her bent, arthritic spine. Touched with pity, the Lord healed her. It was the Sabbath.

The leader of the synagogue, a dedicated Pharisee, saw in the act a scandalous incursion into the sanctity of the day. He did not dare to speak directly to the Lord, another testimony to the power and dignity of His presence—so remote from the base and denigrating caricatures of today's imagination—but addressed Him by way of a rebuke to the congregation. It is well, in the affairs of life, to speak with frankness, face to face, and to avoid the craven innuendo. It was a piece of typical pharisaical 'play-acting'. Hence the Lord's strong word, for, as we have seen, 'hypocrite' means literally 'actor'.

Sham and posing always evoked the Lord's scorn. It is the very beginning of all virtue to have done with them and all falsehood. The scribal regulations for the Sabbath were typical of the legalism which had played a disastrous part in the corruption of the Pharisees' character. Provisions for the care and sustenance of livestock on the Sabbath laid it down that water could be drawn for ox or ass on the sacred seventh day, but that it must not be brought to the animal's mouth. To such meticulous absurdity could religion be reduced.

And as the Lord said, men such as the chairman of the board of ten managers who directed the affairs of this place of worship, could be anxious and concerned over trifles such as this, and have no mercy or pity for a woman with a bent, contorted spine. Human affliction and human deliverance were not their prime concern. They thought more of petty taboos.

Observe that the poor woman, in spite of her pain, attended the place of worship. This was a demonstration of the faith which found reward at the hands of Christ. The phrase 'whom Satan has bound' is no concession to superstition, nor reproach to the woman. It is merely a recognition of first causes. All evil has an origin, and it is well to face the fact.

483 : More Pharisees

Luke 13.31–14.15

We have remarked that there were Pharisees of nobler character than those who murdered Christ. There were Nicodemus and Gamaliel. We may meet others of their number here. The Lord was still within the boundaries of Herod's territories, which embraced both Galilee and Peraea, and certain of the religious leaders seemed anxious for His safety (13.31). The lament over Jerusalem is placed in the narrative as a footnote to v. 33, and out of chronological sequence. The whole narrative, in fact, is sketchy, and the mere sequence, in Luke's mind, was not of prime importance. It is clear enough that these events took place as the

Lord and His men moved down the east of Jordan, to Caesarea Philippi, and then on to Jericho and Jerusalem, and in earlier studies we have already followed them further along that road. Luke was working against time as he scoured Palestine for facts, while Paul lay in Roman custody at Caesarea. He was more concerned to record than to arrange, and for this his readers are grateful.

But meet now another Pharisee (14.1), the Lord's host. Why he issued his invitation (and it may have been in the region of Caesarea Philippi) we do not know, but the occasion was one of moment, and provoked a certain scrambling for places at the dinner. Looking on a trifle whimsically, the Lord expounded some rules, simple enough, but containing a rebuke for pride, the Pharisees' fundamental, and inhibiting sin (John 5.44).

'How is it,' asks C. S. Lewis, in his chapter on The Great Sin, 'that people who are quite obviously eaten up by pride can say that they believe in God and appear to themselves to be very religious? I am afraid it means that they are worshipping an imaginary God. They theoretically admit themselves to be nothing in the presence of this phantom God, but are really all the time imagining how He approves of them . . . this does not come through our animal nature at all. It comes direct from Hell. It is purely spiritual: consequently it is far more subtle and deadly . . .' The whole chapter should be read (*Christian Behaviour*, pp. 42–47).

Another facet of the Pharisees' hospitality was its introverted form. They entertained in order to be entertained in turn. There is no reason why we should not thus share fellowship with friends, and the Lord implies no prohibition. He does, however, deplore the closed society, the building round and within religion of the social group, repelling strangers and intruders, an 'inner ring', after Lewis' imagery in another of his books. Let us be outgoing in attitude, mood and manner, and reserve some of our hospitality for such activity.

484 : The Reluctant Guests

Luke 14.16–24; Lamentations 1.12

The table talk went on. Perhaps the audience was responsive and in some way drew the Lord out. Observe those who rejected the invitation. The first man had urgent business, but his insincerity is apparent, for no one would buy land without previous inspection. He really wanted to enjoy his purchase, and there was nothing reprehensible about that. Christ's invitation denies us no legitimate joy. The man lied. His system of priorities was also wrong. Harmless interests, pursuits, pleasures become corrupted when they deprive us of Christ. The first man was a typical denizen of an affluent society, comfortable in his easy environment, satisfied with his earthly goods, and too shallow to think further.

The second man was not unlike the first. He was full of delight in his new team. He was anxious to see the brown earth of the valley bottom turning under the plough, as the beasts' muscles played in the harness, and pulled the share through the turf. A deep interest in one's profession or trade, concentration on study or work, all these enthusiasms and preoccupations are good. They are the marks, in fact, of good and worthy men. But these, too, can become too absorbing and deprive us of Christ. How common is the type among successful men!

The third man actually had the Law behind him. A Mosaic regulation freed a newly married man from military service for a year. With something like a conscious rectitude, this man answers that he 'cannot come'. Perhaps he is like the man who 'cannot' be a Christian, 'much though he would like to be', because the Church is 'reactionary', 'the tool of the establishment', 'out of date' . . . how the list could be lengthened! Or perhaps he had some substitute for faith in public service, in social activity, in political involvement. And too often the polite 'I cannot come' is, in truth, 'I will not come.'

There, then, they stand, so typical, so transparent, shirking the responsibility of committal, tenacious of respectable self-esteem and equally to blame . . . And there were those who saw the vital application to Israel. Israel had, after the Eastern fashion, received the preliminary invitation through John and Jesus Himself. The despised Gentiles, from the world's streets and lanes (21), were to take their place. Luke, travelling with Paul, had seen it happen.

565

485 : The Prodigal

Luke 15.1–24

The story of the Prodigal Son is probably direct from life. A letter from such a boy to his mother comes from the Egyptian papyri. It was written at the turn of the first century and runs thus:

'Antonius Longus to Nilous, his mother, greeting. Continually I pray for your health. I had no hope that you would come up to town. On this account I did not enter the city either. I was ashamed to come for I am going about in rags. I beseech you, mother, forgive me. I know what I have brought upon myself. I have been punished, in any case. I know that I have sinned . . .'

Where was the 'far country'? Only across the lake opposite Galilee, in the Decapolis, where a million Greeks crowded 'the Ten Towns'. Gerasa, modern Jerash, is a ruin, one of the most imposing ruins of the ancient world, an oval forum completely ringed with pillars, and a high-lifted theatre, from which the audience on the stone seats could look over the heads of the actors down the pillared porticoes of a long and lovely boulevard, tall temples, houses, shops. They stand, a solid stone memorial to the city to which the boy from Galilee could have come on foot in a couple of days. 'He went into a far country and wasted his substance in riotous living.' Miles do not matter. It was a country far enough if its common way of life was set beside the quiet dignity of the old-fashioned household in Galilee.

Some itinerant Greek sophist, no doubt, had persuaded the lad that the Hebrew Scriptures sought to put the unknowable into words, that nothing indeed *could* be known that the senses could not tell us, that obviously life is physical experience, and that Gerasa offered scope and opportunity. What he did not tell him was that the capacity of the body is limited, if its responses and reactions alone are the source of pleasure, that today's philosophy is discredited tomorrow, and that by weaving words philosophy can argue itself out of argument, and destroy by words the validity of the words in which it communicates. The same Greek doubtless aided his cynical townsmen to fleece the country boy from around the lake.

Came famine. There are more famines than one in the stricken wastes of life. The rebel ended feeding the alien swine and found no pity in the pagan land he had sought in his mad quest for liberation. Fortunately, enough sanity remained to prompt him to action. He did what man must do, can always do, and will always be called to do if he will but stop, think, listen.

486 : Father and Brother

Luke 15.25–32; Matthew 23.13

Back on the farm in Galilee the father waited. The view is wide from the Galilean uplands above the Jordan valley. The upper end of the fertile river plain is visible, tessellated brown and green and gold. The river, a blue sinuous line, winds south. The lake is a level floor to the east and north. The father often watched the road winding down the hill slope to the river. The highway passes through Bethshan, where the Philistines hung Saul's body on the wall, curves round the lake, and there enters the predominantly Gentile territory of the Decapolis. This, the waiting father knew, was the one way he could come home.

Parents, like the good man of this famous story, should seek to mirror their God. Then and now parents were not always so Christlike . . . And he saw him one day 'afar off', limping home in rags, 'and he ran and fell on his neck and kissed him'. The wait was over, but not the pain. There was an elder brother, meticulous in conduct, but merciless, jealous, and without an inkling of what went on in his father's mind, the very picture of the Pharisees whom Christ had in view. In Gerasa's oval forum they would have shuddered in their purple-bordered robes to jostle Greeks and caravaneers from the Persian Gulf. They knew all the rules of religion, every subtle detail of the Law, but knew no mercy, no care for the outcast, the underprivileged, the alien.

There are many such documents among the papyri, some of them almost savage in their expression of deep resentment against wayward children. The following, for example, is part of a deed of disownment in which a father cast off two sons and two daughters:

'Thinking to find you a comfort to my age, submissive and obedient, you in your prime have set yourselves against me like rancorous beings. Wherefore I reject and abhor you . . .'

The document runs on with legal abuse for some five hundred words. If the papyri are any indication, the father who killed the fatted calf for his lost boy's returning was gracious beyond custom of that ancient world.

567

1. Why was the Lord so vigorous in condemning sham?
2. Hospitality true and false.
3. Modern excuses.
4. The 'far country' today.
5. The prodigal's brother. Can you blame him?

487 : The Steward

Luke 16.1–13

This is another story from life told after the Lord's manner to illustrate a point. We could compile quite a list of such scamps from the Egyptian papyri. There is, for example, a whole letter file from the office of a petty official named Menches, from which it is apparent that he bribed his way to office in his village community, and used the small powers that his office conferred to extort, to manipulate and to embezzle. It is obvious that the trickster of the Lord's pungent little parable is no isolated type. The file from the Tebtunis crocodile burial-place, which exposes Menches of the early second century to modern scrutiny, is evidence that the parables were contemporary, relevant, and intimate.

But read this parable as parables should be read, disentangling the purpose from the pictorial detail. The parable in no way suggests that the steward's sharp dealing is to be admired. Look at the concluding verses more closely. The 'lord' (AV [KJV]) who commended the dishonest fellow was not the Lord Jesus. He has no capital L, just as the 'master' of the RSV has no capital M. He was the steward's own lord, his master, his employer. Rich enough to laugh at the loss of a few barrels of oil and wine, the owner dropped a word of grudging praise for the smart dealing of which he was the victim. And this was the parable's point. The rogue of the world will leave no scheme untried to win his end. The world will watch and grimly praise him as he turns the world's resources to his purpose. What of this spirit in a nobler sphere? Cannot Christians scheme as indefatigably for the Kingdom's sake? Should they not turn the world's resources into instruments of service? 'Make friends,' the Lord concluded, 'by means of the mammon of unrighteousness.' It is the legitimate use of money. And it earns its name. What crimes

568

any coin may have taken part in! Its very silver may have been part of Judas' thirty pieces. It is poor stuff. But it can be used and turned to noble ends. If scamps can use it to build themselves comforts, cannot we use it for God?

488 : Lazarus

Luke 16.19–17.6

Lazarus, the beggar, has the distinction of being the only person named in a parable of Christ. He may have been a well-known figure, devout but shockingly poor. His sores were no doubt the result of some deficiency disease, and his helplessness under the foul attentions of the dogs of the street must show that he was near his end when fellow mendicants took and placed him outside the gate of an unnamed rich man. He craved to eat the pieces of discarded bread that were used by the feasters on which to wipe their greasy fingers. And none took pity on his desperate condition.

The parable is highly symbolical, and follows the current Jewish imagery of the other world. The story is not meant to teach that bliss in an after-life is the reward of indigence in this, or that acceptance can be won by charity. The rich man's callous disregard of his neighbour's dire need revealed the hardness and alienation of his heart from God and all good. Moses, and the Old Testament at large, had stressed mercy and care for the out-cast and the unfortunate. In pride and self-esteem the rich man probably thought that his affluence was the mark of God's special blessing. The rich man died as all men die. He was rejected by God because God could do no other than say: 'Your will be done.' The poor man was not saved by misery, for want is no more a way to God than plenty. It is the grace of God, accepted or scorned, which, then as now, produced the final result. In this particular case the attitudes of two human hearts reversed earthly circumstance. And note the sad prophecy—those who failed to heed God's preached word, failed also to pay attention when One indeed came back from the dead.

Observe that the prescribed reading covers portions of two chapters. In the central portion of the Gospel there is little attempt to set the events and discussions related in chronological or geographical order. The note on Luke 17.1–10 in the Bible

Study Book series (The Daily Commentary) begins: 'These crowded chapters in which Luke presents material from the last discourses of Christ read sometimes like notes taken by hearers or disciples. Indeed that is what they may have been. Much of the teaching of the philosopher Aristotle survives in what appear to be notes taken by his students, and only roughly edited. Luke, eager to record and to preserve the precious words of the Lord, packed this portion of his book with all the sayings he could find, and the connecting thread is not always to be found. It is, however, there, more often than not. Forget the artificial intrusion of a chapter heading, and let the story run on. Woe, indeed, to such men as the merciless rich man who allowed a helpless beggar, one of God's "little ones", to lie in unrelieved and unpitied misery. Better by far had he been drowned before the years piled guilt's weight or burden on his soul.'

489 : The Grateful Samaritan

Luke 17.11–19; Romans 12.1, 2

There are three routes down from Galilee to Jerusalem. One can cross the Esdraelon plain in a roughly north-south direction, and proceed to the Holy City down the central spine of hill-country and Samaria, or else over the low pass of Megiddo, down the coastal plain, and up to Jerusalem by the steep road up from Lydda. Or alternatively one can proceed south-east across Esdraelon, pass through Bethshan south of the lake, cross the Jordan where it winds south circuitously through the wide valley floor, and seek Jerusalem up the Jericho road.

We know that this is the journey the Lord undertook, for He spent much time at Caesarea Philippi east of Jordan. Perhaps one reason why He took this route was the boorish attitude of some Samaritan villages (9.51–53), and perhaps, in a stricter chronological ordering of events, we might have expected to meet this incident earlier. We have already stressed the fact that Luke was hasting rather to record than to arrange.

At any rate, somewhere along the road which threaded the border of Samaria and Galilee, a band of lepers met Him, and found healing. Of their number, only one returned, and found in so doing a much wider blessing than the cleansing of his diseased body. And this man was one of the despised Samaritans. He alone was grateful.

570

Gratitude is a basic virtue. It reveals much of the soul's condition. It opens the personality to view. There are those who feel no gratitude for benefits received, spirits even base enough to feel some twisted form of humiliation if another confers a gift or blessing upon them. There are those perverted enough actually to sense resentment against some other person who puts them under an obligation. Such people touch the damning depths of evil self-esteem. To maintain such evil is to thrust the soul beyond all possibility of salvation.

The generous person in whom love, and all that flows from love, still lives, takes pleasure, not only in benefits received, but in rendering thanks for them both to man and God. It is better to err in the direction of too rich an expression of gratitude, than to fall under the charge of thanklessness. Gratitude, said dour old Samuel Johnson, is not to be found 'among gross people'. One in ten returned to give thanks. One in ten showed that he could humble himself thankfully to receive freely that which he himself could not obtain. One in ten could give glory to the Giver in simplicity and joy. How frequently in the talk of men, is unmerited evil discussed! How seldom is unmerited good talked about! One in ten found salvation, for one only in ten could thank his God. And he was a Samaritan.

490 : The Unjust Judge

Luke 18.1–8; Deuteronomy 24.10–18

Like the Unjust Steward of the earlier parable, the Unjust Judge is no image of God. Like the story of the neighbour who hammered on the closed door for bread, this poignant little tale aims at teaching determination in the quest for good.

There was plenty of corruption, graft and unfair dealing in the land. In his moving chapter on 'God's Poor', George Adam Smith showed how poverty was not only a state of want, but it denied a man standing, dignity, justice itself. It is wrongly said that 'prosperity is the blessing of the Old Testament'. There was, none the less, in Old Testament times, a damaging tendency on the part of many to look upon poverty, misfortune and loss, as the judgement of God, not to be countered by the mercy and the kindliness of men. We saw this thought haunt the attitudes of Job's friends.

How simple it was, in such a climate of opinion, for those with some breath of corruption in their lives to cloak natural hardness and uninhibited self-seeking with some perverted semblance of religion. Why help the indigent, if their helplessness was the will or the judgement of God? Hence widespread disregard for the rights of the poor and the outcasts of society.

The judge in this story had no theology to cover his injustice. He cared nothing for God. He was an atheist. He scorned public opinion. His like can be found in more than one ancient record. The oratory of the Greeks and Romans, their satiric literature, and the homely papyri of Egypt, alike speak of such characters. This evil man is drawn from life.

He met his match in a determined widow. She knew the law, and she knew her rights. She was vividly aware that, alone among the nations, Israel had care for the poor and fundamental justice written into the sacred Scriptures. She had faith enough to believe that such principles could prevail over human corruption, dilatoriness and procrastination. Day and night she besieged the corrupted administrator of justice to demand her simple rights, and obsessed him so that, in spite of his atheism and contempt for his fellows, he surrendered for the sake of peace.

God does not act thus in answer to prayer, but the Lord is moving on the level of popular thought. If grim determination and simple faith in the ultimate triumph of justice can produce results in a base environment, how much more can persistent prayer win its way and secure an answer when the Judge is the Judge of all the earth, certain to 'do right', as Abraham said, altogether good, eager to help . . . It is a true, vivid little story. We are left to hope that the widow won her case and lived happily ever afterwards, and that the unjust judge rode doggedly to his inevitable fall.

491 : The Pharisee and the Taxman

Luke 18.9–14; Isaiah 1.1–18

This is a finely told little story. Luke had it from someone with a vivid memory, and a gift for pungent language, which held and transmitted the spoken style of Christ. We can hear the Lord speaking in gentle satire and moving compassion.

The Pharisee is sharply drawn. He had his special place to

stand and pray, conspicuous and self-advertising. He 'took his stand' says the verse literally. He was perfectly convinced of his goodness. He was 'separated' from the common run of men. He tithed! He scorned the sins of the flesh. He looked with searing contempt upon such men as the corrupted moneyman who had chanced to visit the sacred place at the selfsame time. He prayed aloud as the men of that age commonly did, just as they read aloud (Acts 8.30). Everyone was permitted to know that this man was different, apart, good, accepted of God. And yet, says the Lord, he prayed 'with himself'. His words did not leave the Temple. God does not hear such prayers. They are noises in the air, inaudible beyond the failure of the sound-waves which carry their self-righteousness.

Not so the taxman. He heard the prayer of the hypocrite and accepted his definition. None of the versions seems to notice the definite article (not indefinite) which is in the text. 'God be merciful to me *the* sinner', he says, humbly accepting, without resentment, the self-righteous humbug's words: 'Yes, I am indeed the sinner he speaks about. He is quite correct in thus defining me.' It was salutary humility. He bowed himself under the condemnation of God, and pleaded for mercy. There seems to have been a deep and divine discontent among the petty officials of Palestine's occupation authorities. Perhaps Matthew, followed by Zacchaeus, had begun it all. The 'publican' in the Temple was another who sought some escape from a life of grim temptation, of vicious opportunity, of popular contempt and of agonizing compromise.

It was the duty of the leaders of religion to promote such a spirit of repentance, to welcome and to receive all who were disposed to abandon their chosen way of life, and to seek God and God's people. Contempt was no contribution to this salutary end. Pride is everywhere evil. In the holy place of God, and in a context of testimony, it approaches the blasphemous. But 'a broken and a contrite heart' God will not despise (Psa. 51.17) as He certainly despises all sham and all arrogance (Job 40.1–42.6; Isa. 2.12). Ritual practices and self-display weigh nothing with God. Giving, pious exercises, charity of this sort and that, are no substitute for sin unconditionally abandoned and the life committed in surrender.

Questions and themes for study and discussion on Studies 487–491

1. The Christian and financial responsibility.
2. 'The poor' in Scripture.
3. Ingratitude and what it signifies.
4. The disciplines of prayer.
5. Pride and humility in the practice of religion.

492 : The Owner of the Ass

Luke 19.29–48; Zechariah 9.9

We return to the story of the Jericho road which we followed in Mark's narrative. The long climb to Jerusalem reached its highest point where the road crossed the Mount of Olives. The modern highway skirts it, but in ancient times the approach seems to have been designed to give the incoming pilgrim a grand view of the city. It lies across the valley on its plateau, tilted like a shield, and from the summit of the Mount the magnificent pile of Herod's Temple must have been a feature of the foreground.

As the Lord looked, His mind seemed to pierce the veil of forty years and He saw the sight as Vespasian and Titus were to see it, the slopes seared and devastated, the gates closed, the walls manned, the earth littered with rubble and ballista stones, and the streets full of the dead killed by famine and internecine strife.

Jerusalem was to choose Barabbas, and this was to be the end, but it was not to come without His earnest offer of God's peace. He deliberately chose to fulfil the oracle of Zechariah, and enter the passionate, rebellious place riding on an ass, the symbol of peace. On such terms He was to offer Himself. He had said nothing to His men. Their lamentable strife down the Jericho road gave little hope that they would understand. Knowing the Old Testament, they should, like the rest of Jerusalem, have found the message plain.

Bethphage and Bethany lie just over the brow of the hill on the side of the Jordan road, and somewhere here lived a man who played a part in the story. The Lord must have had an arrangement with him to borrow an ass with which to stage His eloquent piece of Old Testament symbolism. This nameless character in the events of the King's coming is typical of many in the story of the New Testament and the Church, the men and women known

574

only to God who are vital links in a chain. There is immense encouragement in the thought for the multitude of those who have little place in the records of men, but who have been God's workmen in tasks of eternal significance.

We saw in the story of the loaves and fishes the same divine principle. God's acts seem so often to depend upon some shred of human help. He enters life and history through the bridgehead of some human surrender, the bread placed in His creative hands, the submission of some Mary, the loan of an ass . . . The nameless man of Bethphage or Bethany played his part and slipped back into the host of those who will one day find a name, a recognition and a reward.

493 : The Husbandmen

Luke 20.1–18; Isaiah 5.1–7

The Lord sought the Temple court for the next few days of teaching. He cleared the sacred place again of its clutter of evil, but the hucksters were not the only ones who defiled its sanctity. A group from the Sanhedrin 'came upon him'. Luke uses the same verb as that which he used in 10.40 of Martha's descent upon the Lord and Mary. They stood over Him, determined to discredit His authority. They were desperately fumbling for a charge against Him and found themselves frustrated to the point that their questions ceased (40).

Observe His method. He countered question with question. He carried the assault into the enemy's territory. If such a strife of words is thrust upon a Christian in debate, in television interview, or in unavoidable public controversy, it is well to apply the method. There is no need to stand backed against a wall. The offensive should alternate with defensive. Thrust must succeed parry. Be ready, by all means, to return the 'reasoned answer', as Peter enjoins (1 Pet. 3.15), but let question succeed question. The opponent of the gospel has many serious questions to answer, and should be compelled, if he chooses argument, to answer them. He also has a faith to defend, and for which he must give a reason, for he too has staked his life upon a belief—in chance as his God, in chaos for his view of life, in annihilation as the end.

The satiric picture of those who should have kept the vineyard

575

for its master was devastating comment. The image is deep in the Old Testament. The Bible Study Book (The Daily Commentary) on Luke comments: 'History was woven bitingly into the story. Those who were entrusted with the guardianship of the vineyard looked upon it as their private preserve, and neither Israel nor Israel's rulers, who were the twin objects of the parable's twofold significance, held a prerogative here. The parable passed from history to prophecy in vs. 14, 15. Verse 17 is from Psa. 118.22, a song said to have been sung at the completion of the walls of Jerusalem in 444 B.C. The Lord showed the true content of the words. The Early Church remembered this—see Acts 4.11; 1 Pet. 2.7 f.; Rom. 9.33.'

So ended Tuesday of Holy Week (Mark 11.12, 20, 27).

494 : Tiberius Caesar

Luke 20.19–26

A coin lay in the Lord's hand, probably a silver denarius of Tiberius, and that stern Roman visage, side-faced on the palm of Christ, speaks of another character of Scripture. Augustus' stepson, a competent soldier and administrator, Tiberius came to power at the age of fifty-six because Augustus could find no other. Naturally suspicious, embittered by such treatment, and unlovable by nature, Tiberius suffered much at the hands of circumstance. His trusted minister Seianus, head of the household troops, and probably the patron of Pilate, betrayed him, and was struck down by the old emperor in his last years, in one of his few popular acts.

Tiberius also found Tacitus as an historian, a writer of mordant power, who blamed him for the evils of Domitian's reign under whom he, like John and the Church, suffered. It has been difficult for modern historians to find the record of the real achievements of his rule. Tiberius handled power clumsily. Heredity and environment conspired to make him dour and unsociable. It is easy to blame and vilify such personalities, less simple to commend and grant the justice of fair appraisal.

It is difficult to bear firmly in mind while reading Tacitus' vivid narrative of Tiberius' time, that the Roman world at large was still tranquil in the peace which Augustus had established. The frontiers were adequately maintained, and the Parthians, perennial problem of the north-east, had no cause to suspect that weak hands held the weapons of Rome. History, as Rome recorded it, was, of course, centred on the Tiber, for a picture of life as men at large lived it, one must turn to the multitude of inscriptions which archaeology diligently collects and records, to papyri from Egypt, and to those small books which classical historians too commonly overlook as documents of the first two Roman principates, the four Gospels of the New Testament, and the opening chapters of the Acts of the Apostles. Christ was born under Augustus, and 'suffered under Pontius Pilatus', Tiberius' steward. The Church was founded and first organized under the same prince.

His 'graven image', stamped on the elegant bright coin, and the occasion of the Jews' hatred, heard one of the great sayings of all time: 'Give back to Caesar what Caesar owns, but give back to God that which is His . . .'

495 : The Sadducees
Luke 20.27–38; 1 Corinthians 15.12–19

The Sadducees were a worldly sect who had cornered the prestige, the possessions and the emoluments of the priesthood. They accepted only the five books of Moses, and so, among the vital doctrines they were constrained to reject, they abandoned all belief in a resurrection and an after-life (Acts 23.6–10). Belief determines conduct. With no thought of judgement to come, the Sadducee found it easy to turn the Temple court into a sordid place of merchandise. He found no impediment to murder, when an awkward Galilean disturbed, or was thought likely to disturb, the relationship of compromise and collaboration which had been worked out with the occupying forces. Life must be viewed in the light of eternity, if life is to be viewed whole. Distort, narrow or corrupt the full doctrine of the eternal hope and ultimate responsibility, and vicious twists are formed in matters of morals and daily living.

The Sadducees were ignorant as well as worldly. Learning was with the Pharisees and the scribes. The Sadducee rejected a whole culture along with his rejection of great tracts of the Old Testament. It is the way of ignorant men to be supercilious in argument, and to attack by ridicule. They sought to make the teaching

577

of Christ appear absurd, and argued with crass insincerity. Accepting Moses, they professed also to accept the existence of God, and found themselves on the horns of a dilemma concerning both Moses and the living God.

The Sadducees remain a type of worldly-minded priests. The world has had enough of them. To lose a faith is tragedy enough. To lose the keen edge of conviction, and find the message, which ardour once sought to communicate, crumble in the hands, is a bitter experience too often encountered by those who seek Christian usefulness through a gauntlet of decayed theology in those places where training is sought. Such loss falls short of sin, and sometimes finds remedy. But sin it is, and, if the Lord's words have authority, sin past forgiving, to continue to hold the status and emoluments of office when the reason for holding office is gone. And if the resurrection is folly, deceit or superstition, what gospel, as Paul said, what Church, what message or reason for preaching remains?

496 : The Widow
Luke 21.1–19

Sitting in the Temple, weary with battling the legalism, the treachery and the apostasy of those in whose hands lay the religion of Israel, the Lord 'looked up and saw' a sight which gladdened His tired eyes. A woman cast a tiny coin into the treasury chute. The *'lepton'* ran over one hundred to the denarius, but God does not measure gifts by the standards of men.

Here first of all was another member of the Remnant. Amid the vast betrayal of the 'shepherds of Israel', the common people of the land still retained their faithful. Here was one of them. A widow in that hard world had a grim life. It proved one of the first requirements of the Church, as both the story in Acts and the Pastoral Epistles show, to make merciful provision for widows. The tale of Ruth illustrated the same need. Sacrifice, therefore, there must have been in the giving of the one small coin.

But consider the implications. Without knowing it, an unknown woman had slipped into the story and out again, bringing encouragement to the wounded Christ. She also performed the function we have observed before—that of providing God with that small fragment which enables Him to invade some tract of human life. The *lepton* of the day's giving has been mightily productive. The sacrifice which it represented has stirred to action a multitude with far more to give but no greater generosity.

And, slipping back into the Jerusalem crowd the nameless woman taught another lesson. True service is not necessarily spectacular. It is *not* measured by the applause, the estimation or the regard of men. It *is* measured by the applause, the estimation and the regard of God. It is measured by devotion. The tiny coin was a symbol. It was a sign of a surrendered soul. James Russell Lowell, the American poet, invented a story to add to the Arthur Saga. It was about Sir Launfal, the knight who found that the Holy Grail was a cup which he used for a beggar's need. He concludes:

> *In many climes, without avail,*
> *Thou hast spent thy life for the Holy Grail;*
> *Behold, it is here—this cup which thou*
> *Didst fill at the streamlet for Me but now;*
> *This crust is My body broken for thee,*
> *This water His blood that died on the tree;*
> *The Holy Supper is kept, indeed,*
> *In whatso we share with another's need;*
> *Not what we give, but what we share,*
> *For the gift without the giver is bare;*
> *Who gives himself with his alms feeds three,*
> *Himself, his hungering neighbour and me.*

Read sometime *The Vision of Sir Launfal.*

497 : The Foolish Virgins
Luke 21.20–38; Matthew 25.1–13

First of all grasp the point of the parable. It is absurd to imagine that the refusal of the wise to share their resources with the foolish in an emergency sanctions selfishness. We have seen that it is always good exegesis to limit the meaning of a parable to the specific purpose for which it was constructed. In the accepted manner of the east, the Lord taught by means of vivid pictures from real life. Some of the details are designed to colour the picture. Others contribute to the didactic end in view. That end must be carefully considered. The parable of the virgins is designed to teach the need for spiritual preparedness for every soul awaiting the coming of the Lord. It is designed, too, to show that in such matters we cannot live on another's experience. The oil signifies that unction of the soul that feeds the living flame of devotion, zeal and spiritual fitness. It is the gift of God's anointing, and the fruit of willing faith. No one else can get it for us. If our religion is merely dry-souled fellowship with a social group, it will fail us in the ultimate realities. The experience others have won cannot then, at a moment's notice, be transferred effectively to us, and if we were to press the meaning of the story one step further, it would be to suggest that it speaks of judgement. A crisis finds all asleep, indistinguishable as wheat and tares. But a crisis sifts and judges the souls of men. Those who had known reality respond.

Here are some characters of Scripture too common for our comfort. It is the commonest of human faults to put off consideration of vital matters until it is too late. The voiceless, silent, uncommitted, faceless majority are everywhere and in all times. All that is required for the triumph of evil is for the good to do nothing. They only meet the demands of a compelling moment who in times past have prepared their soul for the response. Delay is deadly. The whole trend of modern life is directed to the avoidance of all consideration of ultimate questions.

> *Tomorrow, and tomorrow, and tomorrow,*
> *Creeps in this petty pace from day to day,*
> *To the last syllable of recorded time;*
> *And all our yesterdays have lighted fools*
> *The way to dusty death.*

How right was the disillusioned Macbeth.

Questions and themes for study and discussion on Studies 492–497

1. The unnamed allies of Christ.
2. The attack on the Christian today.
3. What must we 'render to Caesar' today?
4. The resurrection—fact or fantasy?—literal truth or symbol?
5. 'The gift without the giver is bare.'
6. 'Avoiding ultimate questions.'

498 : Peter
Mark 14.17-31; John 13.1-20, 36-38

John alone records the events which preceded the breaking of the bread at the supper in the Upper Room—probably a rooftop structure on the house of John Mark's mother. The quarrel which had marred the walk up from Jericho on the long dusty road had not subsided (Luke 22.24-30). The ritual of foot-washing had been disregarded. They had no servants, and the humble duty of fetching water, and thus helping each other, had gone by the board in the heat of their contention over precedence. It is difficult to imagine the pain the Lord endured as He sought to shame them from their sin by taking the duty upon Himself.

Peter's outburst of love is typical—unwise, unreasoning but surging up from a loyal, devoted heart. It shows that he, at least, was humbled and broken by what his Master had done. John omits the story of the Supper itself, but tells again of Peter's expression of loyalty and the Lord's sad reply. He knew what Judas was doing. He knew that the hour was near. He could easily plot the course of events till sunrise. And He knew what was in poor Peter.

Mark, so brief in much else, reports the Lord's prediction to Peter in fuller fashion than the rest: 'Before the cock crows twice, you will deny me three times.' Travellers in Palestine in the last century, before the modern revival of the land obliterated ancient patterns of events, are said to have noted the frequency of two periods of night-time cock-crowing. Peter's three denials were thus punctuated by the warning of the first sounding of the cock. Others say that 'cockcrow' was the first bugle call from the Roman garrison barracks. The poignant touch in the story is this: Peter, according to tradition, was Mark's authority for his account. He must have directed his friend to tell the whole truth about him, realizing that the best use he could make of his deep shame was to turn it into warning, and with it block the path of others' stumbling. Peter was no Judas. In spite of His sad prophecy, the Lord looked at the surge of love and loyalty which had prompted the confident assertion. He knew that Peter had been moved by the strange symbolism of the Supper, and stirred to concern by the reference to betrayal. Verse 31 is pathetically emphatic. It runs literally: 'He kept saying with the utmost vehemence. Even if I die by your side, I shall certainly not deny you.'

499 : Judas

Luke 22.1–6; John 12.1–8

There has been much speculation over Judas' motives. He was the one member of the band who was not a Galilean. Perhaps he had built up some notion of rejection, of unpopularity or resentment, against the closer knit society of the rest. Perhaps he had so set his heart on earthly position in some imagined concept of the coming Kingdom, that he could not endure the disillusionment when it became apparent that Christ's Kingdom was not of this world. Resentfully he began to embezzle to reimburse himself. Or did he think to put Christ to the final test, to drive Him to use His power by confronting Him with dire peril or with death? He could have perversely argued that this test would solve his own bitter problem. If the Lord did nothing, fell into captivity, died, then Judas would have proved to himself that his years of discipleship had indeed been wasted, that he was rid of an impostor or a visionary. On the other hand, if the last challenge provoked divine response, then he, Judas, had set the machinery in motion. So he may have argued.

Disloyalty was of long standing and long carefully concealed. As far back as the events of John 6.70 f. the Lord had been aware of a traitor in the midst, and had openly expressed His knowledge. It was, it seems, subsequent to this knowledge that He made him treasurer of the poor funds of the little band, as though to appeal to the covetous man by an act of confidence and trust. By the time of which we read in John 12, Judas had become an embittered man. He saw no beauty in Mary's sacrifice, no pathos in the knowledge it expressed. He saw only that which he had fitted himself to see. His bent mind could see only through the veil of its own distortions.

Truth rejected is dangerous. Judas had lived in the presence of Christ. He had hardened his heart against all appeal. Somewhere, somehow, he had been disappointed. At that point he should have examined his life, faced his own inadequacies, and opened heart and mind to a loftier call. Instead he cherished evil, and it grew like a cancer until it ate up its host. But Judas was no monster at the beginning. It is what man accepts in the heart's depth that determines what man becomes.

582

500 : Judas Again

John 13.21–35; Psalm 41.9

Judas had chosen, but the Lord did not give him up. Three separate appeals, unnoticed by the uncomprehending men round the table, are visible in this story. Sixty years later John could look back and recognize their significance. Girded with the linen towel, Christ washed Judas' feet along with those of the rest. He must have looked up into the hard determined face and read the worst there was to read. Judas was past the point of recall.

Then He must have asked Judas to sit beside Him. Otherwise the conversation recorded would have been impossible. They reclined at table, and it is a fair guess that John was on one side of his Master, Judas on the other. How else could He have conveniently spoken to him or handed him 'the sop'?

And consider the sop. It was (and is still among the Arabs) a custom to pass a choice morsel to a favoured guest. Judas was singled out for this attention . . . Three times, then, the Lord marked with special favour the one whom He knew to be a traitor. He was unable to touch him. Judas was quite determined on his sin. His play-acting must have been cynically perfect, because he knew that the Lord was aware of his betrayal. He was playing with skill a dangerous part.

He was not bidden go and do his grim deed until every possible opportunity to repent had been set before him. The fact that he was not unmasked was itself an appeal, because Judas must have known full well how precarious his safety would have been had the others of the band been plainly told about his treachery. John only had some inkling . . .

Inkling enough to feel with peculiar sharpness the significance of the moment. Judas went out, 'and it was night', wrote John, an old man now in distant Ephesus. But everyone, who had followed the story or read it in the other evangelists, knew that it was night. Why the phrase? John, deeply aware that evil was afoot, and that Judas was at the centre of it, saw the door open, and the traitor disappear. He was never, all his long life, able to forget that sudden oblong of darkness. It seemed so hideously appropriate as Judas stepped into it. Such touches mark the work of the eye-witness.

1. 'You call me Master and Lord, and so I am . . .'
2. The mind of Judas. Can any man play his part?
3. The divine pursuit of rebellious man, and this theme in Francis Thompson's poem *The Hound of Heaven*.

501 : Philip

John 14

We have observed the consistency through the New Testament in the characterization of the apostles. Philip has already appeared in the Gospel of John. He came from Bethsaida and was one of the first to be called. He was a friend of the devout and careful Nathanael, and appears to have been a man of somewhat similar character, knowing his mind, sceptical of the emotional approach, and seeking a certain basis of reason for projected action.

It is noteworthy that Philip was singled out by 'certain Greeks' who sought an introduction to Christ (12.20–23). Bethsaida, if the site is correctly identified, lay across the upper Jordan near its entry to the lake, and opposite Capernaum. It was the nearest lakeside Jewish town to the large Greek population of the Decapolis east of the lake. The Lord spent some time here, and it was here that the feeding of the five thousand took place. Perhaps here also is the key to the anxiety of Philip that the people be fed and his ready calculation of the magnitude of the task. They were his townsfolk (6.5–7).

Here too he had probably met Greek citizens from one of the Ten Towns which formed Decapolis, and may have been instrumental in stirring their interest in Christ. He is likely to have been, like his namesake in the Acts of the Apostles, more open to the ways and words of the Palestinian Greeks, than perhaps some of the other members of the group were. He was a ready evangelist as he showed at his call (John 1.43–46).

In this brief conversation Philip's longing for certainty produces one of the great words of Scripture. 'Don't carry that fear deep down in your hearts', says the Lord (1) 'believe in God and so believe in me.' 'Let us then see God,' cries Philip, with Moses' experience in mind (Exod. 33.12–23). The Lord answers with words which pick up the theme of 1.18—He, the Messiah, the Son of God, is God's demonstration of His invisible Person on earth, in terms which the human mind can understand.

Philip's reaction is not described. John is preoccupied with other matters. But here, for the mind's satisfaction, is the answer which cool minds like Philip's mind can grasp.

502 : The Branches

John 15

Chapter 14, you will note, ends with the words: 'Rise, let us go hence'. Chapter 18 begins with a reference to the departure for Gethsemane. Where, in the meantime were the actors in that night's tense drama? It is a fair guess that they were in the courtyard of Herod's Temple, in the headquarters of the foe, the last place where Judas and his band would be likely to look for them. They had left the Upper Room, to which he was likely first to come, with some abruptness. When the time was ripe they went to the Garden where he would surely next prosecute his search. In the meantime, they were safe, and the opening words of ch. 15 seem an indirect reference to the place of their concealment. He still had words to say.

Over the gateway of the Temple, carved in the white marble, was a vine. In the moonlight the gilded clusters, six feet long, would glitter gloriously. The disciples, countrymen all, were ever amazed at the mighty building on the hill, and it is easy to imagine their drawing their Master's attention to the sight, as they had earlier called to His notice the Cyclopean stones. It was ever His habit to link teaching to realities, and one can imagine the conversation. 'Master, see the great vine, see the moonlight on its carved fruit.' 'I am the true vine, you are the branches, and My Father is the vinedresser.' And pointing to the glow in the distant sky where the cuttings from the spring pruning burned in the Valley of Hinnom, He added solemn words of withered leaves and broken communion.

They, He said, were the branches. He meant that all who followed them in trusting Him, were also the branches. Here is where we become 'characters of Scripture'. The vine still has its enlivening sap. It still has its branches—those that bear richly the fruits of His Spirit, and those which lose their touch and wither.

585

503 : The Ordained

John 16

Look at ch. 15, v. 16. The word 'ordained', the verb in the AV (KJV), is an inadequate translation. In modern English it is inseparable from the notion of ecclesiastical practice. At the time of its use by the translators it was no doubt an exact translation, for in Psa. 8 they spoke of 'the moon and the stars which Thou hast ordained.' The verb, in fact, meant, in the seventeenth century, 'set precisely in place'. It contained, if Psa. 8 is witness, the notion of astronomical accuracy. The Greek text asks for nothing more. It simply says: 'I have placed you that you should go and bring forth fruit.'

That statement covers the case of every Christian who truly seeks God's will. God promises in that word the employment of His perfect wisdom in the ordering and management of our lives. We are so 'placed' that fruitfulness must follow if we are prepared to accept the blessed fact that our circumstances are of God's ordering. No promise is made as to the nature of our place. For some it is prominence; for some it is obscurity: for some it is in the midst of all the activity commonly known as 'Christian work'; for others it is in apparent uselessness or unemployment, remote from all the tasks and offices of witness: for all it is God's best.

We, then, are the 'ordained', if we 'abide in Christ'. And, said Godet: 'Abiding is that continuous act whereby we lay aside all that which we might derive from ourselves to draw all from Christ by faith.' Let us leave circumstances to Him. He is preoccupied with what we are, not with what we can perform. His gospel, though committed to our hands, does not depend upon our hands. He cares first for our characters in Christ, for our spiritual fruitfulness. While, in the daily habit of surrender, He 'goes on increasing' all else will follow—'more fruit', 'much fruit'; and in that process other problems will find solution. All activity, each and every calling, any framework of trade, profession or business, is an opening and occasion for witness. The Christian presents his faith within the context of his daily life, but assuredly presents it more effectively, coherently, persuasively when study has sharpened his understanding, when a time of withdrawal, devotion and challenge has deepened faith and comprehension, and when reading and guidance have promoted maturity.

504 : The Sleepers

Matthew 26. 36–46; Luke 22.39–46

Gethsemane, the garden of the oil-press, for that is what the name means, lay across the Kidron, the stream whose ravine lies between the city walls and the Mount of Olives. Here the party went after the late hours spent in the Temple court. The men were worn out. It had been a tense and weary day. The emotions of the Supper, sensed but little understood, lay just beneath the surface of their thoughts. The puzzling words which occupy three whole chapters of John's Gospel had bewildered and wearied them. There was something about their Master which eluded their comprehension, something in the whole situation which gripped inexplicably at heart and mind. Wearied with grief and anxiety, they fell asleep under the gnarled olive trees. He had grown accustomed to loneliness these last days. The gap between Him and His men had opened on the Jericho road. It was wider still under the moon in the garden.

They slept. There is only Christ left for us to watch, and the sight is daunting. The agony in the Garden is one of the most awesome pages of Scripture. He was 'sore amazed', says Mark's account (14.33, AV [KJV]), using an unexpected word. What amazed the Son of God in this dreadful hour? Was it the depth of human evil which surrounded Him, the devastation Satan had wrought in the hearts of men, the depth of the abyss into which He knew He must step to achieve man's salvation? Was it the very pain of loneliness which amazed Him? It overwhelms the heart to think that God the All-sufficient yet craves the fellowship of man. 'The only-begotten Son, He has explained Him,' runs John 1.18, which we have more than once had occasion to quote, and the words must be taken to mean what they say. In a laudable desire to exalt God, some have removed Him far from man in splendour, sovereign might, and everlasting calm. And yet here was Christ, and Christ was God, seeking, in the hour of fierce pain, for the love and comfort of men. The solemn truth need not be evaded. God created man for Himself, and desires man's loyalty, fellowship and devotion, however inexplicable that wish may seem. We, too, can grieve the Lord by failing to 'watch with Him one hour' in the busy preoccupation of our days.

505 : The Youth in the Garden
Mark 1.1–8; 14.1–52

We have already seen that the cameo biographies of Scripture should not be neglected. We have met Enoch in an earlier volume. We shall meet Demas. Each has only a few words. All we know of Apollos is in a dozen verses. We have hardly any more for Mark, son of Mary, a widow of Jerusalem, nephew of the wealthy Cypriot Jew, Barnabas.

John Mark was the full name. John (Johanan) means: God is gracious, and was the boy's proper name. Marcus was his Gentile name, as Paul served for Saul, Jason for Joshua, Apelles for Abel, and so on. Mary's house, as we shall later see, was the meeting place of the Christian leaders. A maidservant is mentioned (Acts 12.13), but not Mary's husband, unless he was the man to whom allusion is made in 14.14. Perhaps he died soon after making his 'upper room' available for the Last Supper.

Imagination must play around the brief allusions if we are to form a picture of young Mark. Perhaps as a youth of fifteen or sixteen years he lay awake listening to the vague noises above, as the events of John 13 and Mark 14 took place. He might have sensed the tension which held the group that night, and felt the presence of danger. Listening and alert, he hears Judas descend the outside stairway, and perhaps recognizes him in the bright moonlight. Later there is the noise of many feet, and the rest depart.

Seizing a linen sheet from the bed, he rises and follows. Perhaps, lurking in the shadows, he heard the discourse of John 14, 15 and 16, and then, still keeping out of sight against the houses, followed the party to Gethsemane. There is a flare of torches under the olives, and the betrayer is there with the guards. With the reckless loyalty of youth, the boy shouts a protest, and angry hands lay hold of him. Perhaps this was the occasion of Peter's violence on the servant of the priest.

Mark slipped out of the linen sheet and fled, perhaps with a mutilating sword-slash across his fingers, for, in the early Church, Mark was the bearer of a nickname: 'the Stumpfingered'. Conjecture, no doubt, but the mysterious reference to the young man in the garden is in the fashion of an ancient signature. It is somewhat in the manner of a modern film producer, who makes a brief anonymous appearance in any film of his making. John 21.24 demonstrates similar anonymity.

Such is the first page of Mark's story. We shall meet him again, some fifteen years later, and we know him well in the terse, vivid pages of the Gospel he wrote for the Romans at Peter's request.

Questions and themes for study and discussion on Studies 501–505

1. 'He who has seen me has seen the Father' (John 14.9).
2. The use of imagery taken from farm and garden in the Bible.
3. Ordination in its modern meaning.
4. The meaning of 'watching in prayer' for us.
5. Loyalty and youth.

506 : Annas

John 18.1–14; Psalm 22.1–13

It is not quite clear why Jesus was sent first to Annas, father-in-law of Caiaphas, the functioning high priest. The houses of the plotters of that night, Pilate and the hierarchy, were no doubt contiguous or near to each other, and Annas' family may, indeed, have occupied the same dwelling, so no great distance was involved.

Annas was a Sadducee, appointed by Quirinius in A.D. 7, and deposed by Valerius Gratus seven years later for presumptuously encroaching on a Roman area of jurisdiction. Cynically working on the Jewish assumption that a high priest was appointed for life, Annas continued to be the power behind the throne, a man of such influence and political acumen, that at various times he succeeded in securing the appointment to the high priest's office of five sons and a grandson, as well as Caiaphas, his daughter's husband.

The fact is testimony to the determination and the unscrupulous love of power which possessed the man. Edmund Burke once remarked that the possession of power, as nothing else, discovers with certainty what, at the bottom, is the true character of a man. It revealed Annas as a consummate villain. He was bitterly hated by the common people, but he would have agreed with a phrase quoted by Cicero from the lost tragedian Accius: 'Let them hate, provided they fear.' He was a man who enjoyed the reality of power, and cared little for its trappings.

On two counts Annas was determined to destroy Christ. The

more personal reason was the twin assault on the cynical occupancy of the Temple courtyard by the notorious hucksters' market. Much wealth flowed into the hands of the hierarchy from this polluted source. And then, Annas, being in office in A.D. 7, must have been directly concerned in the establishment of the agreement with the Romans, hammered out on the deposition of Archelaus the year before. He and his wanted no one about who could form a centre for a 'king movement', or become a focus for Galilean demonstrations and rebellion. In this he found himself in agreement with Pilate, anxious for a quiet Passover. That it meant the death of a good man did not enter into consideration. Tacitus was to write before the end of that century: 'Power acquired by guilt has seldom been directed to a good end or useful purpose.'

507 : Caiaphas

John 11.47-57; Exodus 23.1-8

Caiaphas, Joseph Caiaphas as Josephus his namesake calls him, bore a responsibility greater than any other person on a judge's bench has ever borne. We know little enough about this villain. He became high priest under Valerius Gratus in A.D. 14, and was deposed by the Governor of Syria, Lucius Vitellius, in A.D. 36, immediately after Pilate's recall to Rome. Perhaps both careers ended in the same context of circumstances.

Caiaphas was therefore in office when Pilate came to Palestine in A.D. 26, and held power all through the period of the procurator's term. He must have had a difficult task in view of Pilate's shocking relations with the Jews. Such matters played their part in a despicable and designing mind when the menace (or so he regarded it) of a new religious movement arose from the turbulent district of Galilee.

Caiaphas is a not uncommon phenomenon of life and history —a man of low character in a high position. In religion he found, not a way of life, but a career. All he truly believed in was himself. It was La Fontaine who remarked well three centuries ago that 'anyone entrusted with power will abuse it, if he is not also animated with love of truth and virtue, whether he be a prince or whether he be a man of the people.'

There is in fact no difference. Vice is common to all ranks of society. Evan John Simpson once put it into verse as he watched the crowd in the lounge of a Jerusalem hotel in wartime. He could see the universal types of sin:

> *Herod from Egypt with corn and with cotton*
> *Held from the children till prices increase,*
> *Young Pontius Pilate with gleaming Sam Browne,*
> *Sipping pink gin as he passes the buck:*
> *'I've washed my hands of it, turned the job down,*
> *'Tisn't my pidgin, if things come unstuck . . .'*
> *Oh, you who felt the blood, the nails, the blows,*
> *Pardon us now, as once you pardoned Rome*
> *And breathe on us who have forgotten you*
> *Your ancient peace—'They know not what they do.'*

Caiaphas, perhaps, deserved no such charity. He knew what he did, and did it all the same. And yet, perhaps, he knew a life of gall and wormwood. It is significant that Annas, deposed though he was, is called high priest in Acts 4.6. The Jews looked on the office as lifelong. Caiaphas held his position by Rome's sanction. Hence the humiliation of having his father-in-law called by his title.

508 : The False Witnesses

Matthew 26.57–68; Deuteronomy 19.16–20

Jewish law, both as laid down in the Mosaic code and in the Mishnah, the corpus of law composed by the Rabbis from their oral traditions, was extremely careful on court procedure. There were clear directions laid down regarding the testimony of witnesses. Those giving evidence were admonished before the court and then put out and heard separately one by one. Only if they were found to agree together were the judges to consider their evidence.

The criminals who bore witness against the Lord did not fulfil this condition. They disagreed among themselves and should have been dismissed for the scoundrels they were. They must have been bribed denizens of the streets, chosen rather for their unscrupulous disregard for the truth than for any other quality. Caiaphas and his associates in the night's crime touched a new low level of evil when they found it necessary to associate their cause with such allies. It is difficult to see into minds so darkened.

The solemn penalties laid down in the Mosaic ordinances against the crime of false witness, make it clear that only men who had abandoned all good could be induced to utter such falsehood—and against such a one.

Again, the type has not departed from our midst. False witness is still brought forward against Christ. His presence haunts the world and challenges conscience, and if some can diminish Him, misrepresent Him or distort Him, they undertake the task in an effort to dismiss Him. And if 'this is the way the Master went, should not the servant tread it still?'

Lies and misrepresentation are evil's favourite weapons against good. It should not astonish the Christian to find his words subtly twisted and quoted out of context, to find action and motive misconstrued. To tell the truth about the good exalts it, and if evil would be rid of good and bring it down, it must necessarily use falsehood to discredit and destroy. The forms and process of a fine judicial system were perverted to this end. It was expedient, the rulers had decided, to be rid of the disturbing presence of Christ. Caiaphas had said as much, in words to which history was to give an awesome twist (John 11.49–53). In lowest hypocrisy they employed the instruments of justice to this end.

509 : Peter

John 18.15–27

Sadly enough, there are more ways of bearing false witness to Christ than lying about Him. Somewhere into the passage prescribed from Matthew's Gospel yesterday, must be fitted John 18.19–21. It runs literally, though few of the English translations do it justice: 'Therefore the high priest asked Jesus about His disciples.' Unable to see how 'therefore' can refer to Peter's loud denial by the coal fire in the courtyard, Moffatt at this point makes one of his unjustified transpositions which so mar his translation.

The verse means what it says. From the story of the examination of the blind man in John 9, it appears that proceedings in the hall where the Sanhedrin met were visible and audible from the courtyard. John, who for some reason had access to the high priest's house, must have heard the debate from that vantage-point and so reported it. Peter's denial was audible both to

Caiaphas, who was conducting the inquisition, and to the Prisoner.

The case was going badly. The witnesses were contradicting each other. The Sadducee was becoming desperate. Then he became aware of a disturbance by the brazier in the courtyard and a distinctly Galilean voice loud in denial. Caiaphas was no fool. Here was an opportunity. '*Therefore* he asked Jesus about His disciples.' Knowing that Peter could hear Him, Jesus replied that He had made no secret of His teaching. Many had heard all He had to say. 'Ask them,' He concluded.

It could have been Peter's finest hour. He could have accepted the dual challenge, stepped forward and denied that his Master said anything blasphemous or seditious. He was silent. The company beside the coal fire had been too much for him. It is well for us to see a symbol here. To seek comfort by the world's coal fire can be harmless enough provided we are sturdy enough in character to withstand the confrontation of those who share the place. Comfort should have no priority, if compromise or breakdown is too large a temptation there.

Christ Jesus has one vulnerable point when the hostile world seeks to discredit Him. No truth prevails against Him. False witness of the baser or more blatant kind, from 'rationalist' argument to crude rock opera has no ultimate power to harm Him. His vulnerable point is His fallible disciple—I or you. Luke (**22.61**) reports a poignant phrase: 'The Lord turned and looked straight at Peter . . .' In the act of betrayal they are difficult eyes to meet.

Questions and themes for study and discussion on Studies 506–509

1. Power as a revealer of character.
2. Caiaphas and Pilate in today's world.
3. 'False witness', conscious and unconscious.
4. 'The world's fire of coals.'

510 : The Procurator
Luke 13.1–3; Acts 3.12–19

A procurator was a minor governor, responsible directly to the
emperor. The name means 'manager' or 'steward', and such
officers were used in difficult and dangerous areas, where the
emperor desired direct contact with events. Hence an element
of urgency in Pilate's position.

Pontius Pilate, procurator of Judea, is known almost as well
as any Roman of the first century. He stands full length in the
four small books which tell the story of the trial of Christ. A
baffled and frustrated man, neatly netted by the subtle priests in
the web of his past follies, arrogance and compromise, Pilate is
both victim and villain in the Easter story. He betrayed Roman
justice, and he betrayed it because he was a coward, unwilling
to pay the price of courage. He could not afford another appeal
to Caesar. Twice the clever priests had already challenged his
rule, and made him pay for an act of folly. It is not uncommonly
the experience of men that the price of moral dignity and uprightness rises with each failure to claim it as a human right.

So it was that the procurator of Judea was driven into the
crime, the gravity of which he was quite conscious of, and found a
place of scorn in history. He would have had a minor place apart
from his fatal confrontation with Christ. He appears twice in the
pages of Josephus, the Jewish priest who became the Emperor
Vespasian's secretary and used his leisure time to write a detailed
history of his people. He appears briefly in the writings of Philo,
the Jewish scholar of Alexandria. And in all these non-biblical
contexts he shows the same hard face, cruel, foolishly contemptuous of the difficult people he was called to rule. He was a bad
appointment for the enormous task of holding the peace with a
garrison of only three thousand men, in a country where the heat
of rebellion and frustrated nationalism was daily rising. Above
all, his task was to keep peace in an area of turbulence behind
a difficult and sensitive frontier. Old Tiberius, in grim and silent
retirement on Capri, was no person with whom to trifle. Pilate
could have outfaced the Jewish plotters, had past misrule not
betrayed him into their hands. Ultimately, the price of evil must
always be paid.

511 : The Judge
John 18.28–40; Luke 23.1–7

This is a revealing passage. The accusers would not enter the Gentile judgement hall for fear of ritual pollution—they who were murdering a man. Pilate came out to them and asked the formal question which opened a Roman trial (29). It was the question they might have expected, and any accuser, knowing that such a query always initiated proceedings, would have been ready with the formal indictment. These men were experienced in such procedure. Why then were they not ready with a formal reply to a formal and customary question? Their documents should have been in their hands.

They answered in blank amazement. 'We would not have brought him to you, were he not an evil-doer.' This was no reply. Pilate was a judge, not an executioner. Why did they not treat him as a judge, and make their accusation? The only explanation which fits the facts casts an ill light on the character of all the participants. They expected, not a trial, but the signing of the death warrant. They expected no legal exordium, no question at all, no waste of time.

And why could they be sure that a magistrate of the occupying power, a trained judge and servant of Tiberius, would thus dispense with the formalities of justice? They had no right to expect such informality, save under one set of circumstances. Pilate must have given an undertaking that he would not conduct a formal trial, but hand the Prisoner over, on the word of the priests, to the execution squad. There must have been a discreditable understanding.

There is a chapter missing from the story. Caiaphas and Annas, or one of them, must have been in conclave with the procurator the night before, and by some form of cajolery, menace or subtlety, secured a promise that a trial would be by-passed. And why then, when thus presented with the occasion he had been led to expect, did Pilate change his mind, and, fighting for time, slip into the lifelong habit of the bench, and open the proceedings, to their indignant amazement, with the formal expression of 'the Accusation'? Perhaps Matthew's story gives a clue, and to that we will soon turn.

512 : Pilate and Truth

John 8.31–36; 14.1–6; 18.37, 38

On this high-lifted stage words and events assume cosmic significance. John was an eye-witness of the trial, and he it was who caught up Pilate's despairing remark about the truth. 'What is truth?' he said with an angry frustrated shrug of the shoulders, and strode off to tell the Jews that he found no fault in the Prisoner. He had, in fact, confronted the truth. It even found a lodgement on his lips. All he needed for salvation was to act upon it.

Francis Bacon, in opening his famous essay on Truth, misinterpreted Pilate. 'What is truth? said jesting Pilate; and would not stay for an answer.' Pilate was in no jesting mood. He had a touch of the modern academic about him. He despaired of absolutes. In the modern world, he might have sloughed off the superstition which allowed his wife's dream to disturb him. He would have fallen easy victim to the cult of the suspended judgement, the perpetual and unsatisfied enquiry into the exact significance of words, and that habitual dismissal of all which lacks the senses' proof as 'meaningless', the habit which makes faith so difficult for those who succumb to certain types of education.

'It is heaven upon earth,' says Bacon later in his essay, 'to have a man's mind turn upon the poles of truth.' And it is no comfort to have it swerve and oscillate on doubt. 'I am the truth.' Christ said, not long before the morning of Pilate's question. By that He meant that His presence sets much in perspective, informs the moral judgement on which so much of life depends, and lays a groundwork for a plan of purposeful living.

But return to Pilate's 'moment of truth'. To the Jews waiting impatiently outside his judgement hall, he proclaimed in downright words the innocence of the One they had brought for condemnation. There is no fit search after the truth which does not begin with the truth it knows. Pilate had a pathway from that one clear realization to salvation. No further truth becomes manifest to man unless the truth he knows is accepted and fused with thought and being. 'It is not enough,' said Coleridge rightly, 'that we swallow truth. We must feed upon it as insects do on the leaf, till the whole heart be coloured by its qualities, and show its food in every fibre.' Pilate had his opportunity. The answer to his question lay down that path.

513 : Pilate's Wife
Matthew 27.11–26

Was it Pilate's wife who caused Pilate, in the midst of his plot with the Jews, to change his mind? The whole incident rings with truth. Governors of provinces were frequently accompanied by their wives. Tacitus describes an attempt made by the Roman Senate to put down the practice, which was completely unsuccessful. Pilate, too, was a man who stood in frequent need of counsel.

One tradition has it that he was a member of the College of Augurs, a contention borne out by the device on one of his coins —a *lituus*, or priest's staff. As such he would be interested in the interpretation of omens, and a dream was ominous material of the first order.

Consider, too, the psychological likelihood of the narrative. Was Pilate's wife present or within hearing when he made his disgraceful bargain with the priests? She obviously knew enough about the Lord to have formed her own most definite conclusions about Him. He was 'a good man'. She must have known that crime was afoot, and that her husband was lending himself, contrary to all Roman justice, to its consummation. She was ashamed of him, and no woman cares to be ashamed of her husband. Nor, with such a woman, would pleas of expediency avail.

She went to rest with these preoccupations gnawing at her mind. Dreams are normally made out of the stuff of the day's experience, especially of its fears and its frustrations. She dreamed some frightening and disturbing dream, woke before dawn to find her husband gone, remembered the pre-dawn meeting corruptly arranged between Pilate and the hierarchy, and in haste wrote a swift brief note to try to save her husband from his crime and folly. Conjecture, to be sure, but the story hangs together, for what that is worth.

Conjecture aside, all that which cold factual history knows about this woman is contained in one verse (19). Apocryphal literature and tradition have played with the theme, and Claudia Procula, as she is thus named, along with the man she tried to save, is honoured by the Greek and Coptic churches. It is a pity that we do not know more. Pilate's wife, on the brief evidence of the one verse, must have been a remarkable woman. What were the 'many things she suffered' in her dream? Hers is the first Roman tribute to Christ recorded in history.

514 : Herod

Luke 23.1–25

We move from narrative to narrative as the story builds itself before us. Could there be more striking evidence of all absence of collusion between the authors as we discover one detail here and another there? The interview with Herod is mentioned only in Luke. Pilate was seeking in desperation to avoid administration, and he laid hold of the slender pretext that the Prisoner was a Galilean, and therefore under the jurisdiction of the king.

Herod was in Jerusalem, where he had a residence, for the Passover. He observed such formalities as part of his precarious dual policy—safe and impeccable relations with both the Romans and the Jews. Herod was 'glad to see Jesus'. He expected perhaps some demonstration of extraordinary psychic power from Him. There is an odd phrase in the account (9). Literally it runs: 'He questioned Him with words enough.' It was evidently a determined cross-examination, with the doomed kinglet, so accustomed to the petty sycophancy of his small court, unable to extract a word from the silent person who had now nothing to say to him. It was Jesus' silence, perhaps, which prompted the other evangelists to omit the story of the visit to Herod. Luke saw its significance.

There comes a time in the experience of a determined evil-doer when the process of evil becomes irreversible. The Lord spoke of this solemn fact to the Pharisees, as we have earlier seen. There is a sin against the Holy Spirit, a sin unpardonable, and physical life can continue past the moment of spiritual death, which the final commission of this sin represents. 'My Spirit shall not always strive with man', runs an awesome saying, and God had ceased to strive with Herod. He made his choice, and it is possible to pinpoint the moment of that choice. It was in the heat of prurience and wine, when a girl had finished dancing, at a birthday-party in the grim fortress of Machaerus. It is ironical that a birthday should be a day of death.

The grace of God reaches infinitely far. Herod at that moment of damnation had only to play the man and slash the bonds which held him. He could have halted short of catastrophe. He did nothing, and now, face to face with Christ, his doom was patent. Christ had no words to say which he could have grasped or understood. Here is Hell, self-made, personal, chosen.

515 : Barabbas
Mark 15.1–15

Palestine was guerrilla country of the first order. The Zealots and the Knifemen were two only of many groups which sought to make the way of the occupying forces and their Jewish collaborators difficult. Treacherous criminals for the most part, preying equally upon their countrymen and foreigners, such men of blood haunted the hills which had sheltered David and have sheltered the assassins of all the ages. And yet, in lands where nationalism and racial hatred burn like a fire, such men attain the status of patriots. Observe the priests. They had betrayed Jesus on political pretexts. They persuaded the mob to yell for their political hero with cynical inconsistency. Pilate, desperate to find a way out of his dilemma, must have seen the blatant hypocrisy, but took the risk.

The terrorist Barabbas was the sorry choice of the Jewish world. Nothing is known of this man. Picture him as the bold and dashing rebel, the idol of the mob, catching the crowd's imagination with deeds of daring, the patriot posing as the people's champion. His was no meek voice, calling to self-abnegation and endurance of wrong; he was no advocate of rendering Caesar's rights to Caesar; he had no challenging presence. He had given words to men's hate and a hand to their resentments. The world is prone to choose such projections of its own vicious ambitions and base desires. The choice is fatal. Men become like the objects of their worship and regard. To revere the man of force is to become violent. To respect the man of hate and blood is to corrupt the soul with the passions of the murderer. Israel made its choice, and Barabbas prepared the spirit of the nation for the two great rebellions which poured out the people's blood and left the very land a depopulated wilderness. There are moments which, in Winston Churchill's vivid phrase, are like 'sharp agate points' on which destiny turns. They chose the bandit, and rejected Christ. The sequel was woven into history. So, too, it can be with the individual life, for nations are built out of men and women. When man chooses evil in deliberate self-will, God allows him to reap the harvest of events. 'Hold to Christ,' said Professor Herbert Butterfield, 'and for the rest be totally uncommitted.' It is safe so to be, for when the right choice stands firm the rest follows.

516 : Pilate's Hands

Matthew 27. 24–31; Isaiah 1.15–18

Over these studies on the Passion of the Lord, prescribed readings have sometimes been repeated. This is by design. We are turning attention now to this character, word, or action, now to that, and we cannot read too often the story of history's most notable event. It might perhaps help if several versions were used.

Pilate scourged Jesus and showed Him to the mob, perhaps seeking in some desperate way, to stir their pity. It was of no avail. He had tried wildly to avoid decision in the case, sent Him to Herod, offered Him to the Jews, only to find the case back continually on his own hands. One course only was open to an upright man, and all the mighty drive of events thrust Pilate to the point of decision. It was his vital test. He could still have paid the price and done the right. He failed, and sinned direly.

But Pilate felt dirty. He had betrayed justice, and justice was a Roman virtue. He took water, in a symbolic action which Jews, of all peoples, would have been most likely to understand, and washed his hands before the yelling multitude. Shakespeare had the scene in mind when he made the murderer Macbeth look at his bloodstained hands in a moment of sin's self-awareness, and know that they were beyond all cleansing:

> *What hands are here? Ha! They pluck out mine eyes,*
> *Will all great Neptune's ocean wash this blood*
> *Clean from my hand? No; this my hand will rather*
> *The multitudinous seas incarnadine,*
> *Making the green one red.*

Cleansing, as Isaiah once told Israel in his immortal first chapter, must go deeper than ritual. There is a way, only one way, he said, to purge the deep-dyed crimson of wrong from the texture of the soul, and that is by bringing it to God . . . 'though your sins are like scarlet, they shall be as white as snow; though they are red like crimson, they shall become like wool.'

Pilate had tried to force others to carry out that which was his responsibility. Now, in equal error, he sought to shift the burden of his guilt on to other shoulders than his own. Those others, in their cynical wickedness, were ready enough to carry that load, but it is Heaven's accounting in such matters which avails. Such was the folly of the procurator of Judea.

517 : The First Crowd

Luke 19.35–40; 23.13–25

The chanting, shouting crowd in the street outside Pilate's place of judgement was one of the two crowds distinguishable in the story of these days. In all crowds there is an 'activist' element which determines action and gives the colour of its morality to the inert mass. At times the vicious minority stands apart and acts as a spearhead. Such was the case here. No doubt some of them were the immediate attendants of the priestly households, or the bribed clients of the Sadducees, perhaps resentful traders from the Temple court or others who found their personal advantage involved. Others were those who, like Judas perhaps, found a passionate hope for insurrection, self-assertion or revenge, disappointed by a Messiah who had shown Himself no royal figure, no leader of rebellion, but 'meek and lowly of heart'.

Wind and wave can be ruthless, and like wind and wave are those gales of emotion which sweep through crowds and change a group of human beings into a destroying force. A crowd can be carried away by the consciousness of its own power, and the individuals which compose it are led to instincts which, apart and alone, each one might have held in check.

We do well in this mass age to note the phenomenon. It is another feature in which the twentieth century resembles the first, and we have drawn attention to the phenomenon which haunts the background, especially in the Gospel of John—the sense of the crowd, the nameless multitude which the priests and

601

the Romans feared. When the clash came in A.D. 66, and the awful years of the Great Rebellion began, it was all because of a crowd, swept by a gale of emotion, fanned to force and fury by its 'activist' element, which got out of control in Jerusalem.

We have seen demagogues use crowds thus in our own century. The priests knew such trickery. They knew that reason dies in such heat, that what the Germans call a 'group-personality' emerges, and this can be a demon which will do the will of its creators. It is all the negation of justice, ordered thought and democracy. As Tennyson put it, watching such social phenomena emerging in his disillusioned age:

> Tumble nature heel o'er head, and, yelling with the
>   yelling street,
> Set the feet above the brain and swear the brain is
>   in the feet.

The noisy crowd were as spurious when they shouted, 'Hosanna' as when they yelled: 'Crucify'. God speaks to individuals. How often, as the 'demonstration' moves down the street, do we catch the sound of the old evil. It is all in the Bible.

518 : Simon of Cyrene
Mark 15.21; Romans 16.13; Philippians 2.5–11

Cyrene was a long way from Jerusalem. It was a magnificent Greek city west of the Libyan desert, a trading centre mediating commerce between Egypt and the Phoenician cities of the west. There was a large Jewish minority there, strong enough to set the place in an uproar during the widespread Jewish city revolts in Trajan's principate at the beginning of the second century.

Simon, probably a well-to-do Jew of Cyrene, had travelled 1,500 arduous miles by land or sea to attend the Passover in Jerusalem. It was the ambition of every Jew of the Dispersion to sacrifice in the holy centre of his faith once in a lifetime. Caught in the crowd, and swept along with them to the place of execution, Simon was near at hand when Jesus stumbled under the heavy crossbeam of the cross, and fell.

Perhaps Simon was a sturdy man, and rough hands seized him, flung the beam across his shoulders and forced him to join the procession of death. It was shocking disaster for the pious visitor. Not only was it dire disgrace and a bitter blow to dignity, comfort, and all that which made a worthy man's pattern of life, but the whole purpose of the pilgrimage to Jerusalem was thus frustrated. Having handled the bloodstained instrument of death, Simon could no longer keep the Passover for which he had travelled so far.

But why the personal identification in Mark's Gospel? Simon was 'the father of Alexander and Rufus'. And is Rufus the Rufus of the greetings list in the letter to Rome? It is a fair guess, too, that Mark knew the Christian group in Rome. Paul had deep respect for Rufus' mother, and calls Rufus 'the chosen of the Lord'. Did Simon become a Christian, and is he 'Simon the Swarthy' (Simeon Niger) of Acts 13.1? Did carrying the cross lead Simon to Calvary in more senses than one? Did disaster to a lifelong wish bring him to Christ in a way other than that which was visible along the Via Dolorosa?

Intriguing questions, but Mark had some clear intention in identifying Simon's family, and that a Simon became a member of Mark's circle is fairly clear. . . . At any rate, here is a man of whom we could wish to know more. His story of catastrophe strangely used of God and transformed, could help many an embattled soul.

519 : The Second Crowd

Matthew 27.37–44; Psalm 22.15–18

Round the place of the crucifixion was a larger multitude. The group which yelled outside the judgement hall was there, no doubt, and some smaller groups stood out which we shall look at soon. Voices detached themselves from the general murmur which any assembled multitude makes, and Mark's account records the fragmentary remarks best.

For the rest there was a vast inertia. The mass was composed of human beings, each drawn by his own motives, fears, hates, concerns, anxieties, to the place where evil's triumph rose so high. But all alike were helpless, as the mass of men so often is. And worse, they formed a hiding-place, a stifling blanket to cover and paralyse those who should have been seen in open testimony. In the anonymous crowd there were, perhaps, ten of the Lord's own men. Somewhere Judas was wandering. Perhaps Mark was there—a youth with a bandaged hand.

And crowds like this, inert multitudes, commonly block the way to the cross, but only for the weak and the cowardly. John, bidden to take Mary home, broke through the crowd and did his last duty. If John's account is read carefully it will be seen that it contains a gap. The events which can fill that gap may be culled from the other narratives. But what does this teach us? First that John, writing at the end of his life, was determined not to set down one fact which he had not personally observed. And, secondly, note this—the story resumes, and therefore John, in pure cold heroism, with his duty to Mary done, must have returned to the cross and taken his stand once more. He battled his way to the place where he had to be.

The crowd can be pierced. Brave men find their path to Christ, in spite of the inert horde, and through them. There is a pathway to Christ's feet from any place, any moment, any sin, any failure, any condition; and commonly it lies through the crowd. The crowd could have saved Christ. They could have overwhelmed their own vicious minority. They could have frustrated the priests. They did nothing, and so allowed evil to gain its victory.

520 : Judas

Matthew 27.3–10; Acts 1.15–20

'There is a path to the feet of Christ from any sin . . .' So we said yesterday. Was there a path for Judas? Presumably there was, had the traitor been able to summon resolution to seek a pardon. But we have seen him before. He had killed little by little and piece by piece that which, in the human heart, commands such response.

'Satan entered into Judas . . .' says Luke 22.3. And this was because Judas opened the way. Someone has remarked that there is no handle on the *outside* of the door of the human heart; it must be opened from within. Consciously, we 'yield our bodies to be instruments of unrighteousness'. The only safeguard is to have Christ in full occupation. To preserve and cherish unsurrendered corners of the life is to endanger the whole structure. Judas had kept his greed and ambition in a place apart. He had not set out with any notion of great betrayal, but he loved money and looked for some place of power or advantage in the Kingdom.

This unsurrendered sin withstood the presence, the fellowship and the teaching of the Lord. He became harder with each day's resistance. Conscience spoke with accents more and more blurred. Defences crumbled. Then, at the proper time, Satan struck. The life which he had undermined became his to use, and he used Judas to commit the most horrible sin of all time; and having used him, he cast him cynically aside to writhe in agony of remorse.

It is perhaps idle to speculate whether such a sinner could at this point find repentance. He flung his silver down, and this is the first requirement of those who would seek forgiveness. This is where the murdering king stuck fast in *Hamlet*.

> *. . . but, O! What form of prayer*
> *Can serve my turn? 'Forgive me my foul murder'?*
> *That cannot be, since I am still possessed*
> *Of those effects for which I did the murder,*
> *My crown, mine own ambition, and my queen.*
> . . . .
> *My words fly up, my thoughts remain below.*
> *Words without thoughts never to heaven go.*

Judas was one step further on than this—but it is the last step which counts, so Judas died by hanging, fell shattered from his hanging place, a thing filled with remorse, but no salutary repentance. 'Remorse,' said someone, 'not only turns God against us, but turns us against ourselves, and makes the soul like the scorpion in the fire, which stings itself to death.'

521 : The Hierarchy
Mark 15.16–36

From the second crowd two groups detach themselves. There was the tiny, valiant band, John and the women, who stood by the cross. There was also a pompous group of priests and scribes, who had so far sacrificed their dignity as to stand with audible comments where Peter could hear them in the multitude. He remembered their base words and passed them on to Mark. They had triumphed. Here was the one who had parried their loaded words, and flung their subtle questions back at them. Here was the man they had feared for his hold on the proletariat—here, hung high, his life draining away. They could not resist the chance to feast their eyes. They form a hideous spectacle.

Here stands man caught in the bright beam of truth. Here is the last act of his rebellion, the natural end of sin. Could the vicious depths of the human heart be more horribly revealed? Granted that they 'knew not what they did', granted that they failed to see in the tormented victim of their sadism the Son of the living God, it still remains true that they committed a horrible crime; they took an upright and gentle being, whose life had been spent in doing good, swept him cynically from the path of their own base ambition, judged him in the travesty of a trial, spiked his wrists and feet, and left him to die in gasping agony in the sun. Pitiless, selfish, vicious, cruel, Roman and Jew were here without distinction. But here too was God. We wrote above of 'him', without the reverential capital letter 'H', for a man was all that their base minds saw. But He who died was God, revealing once for all the length to which love would go to show man his sin, and to redeem him. No man has plumbed the depths of meaning of that act, but let this thought suffice and sanctify the day. Had you or I been the only sinner, Christ would still have died, for He could not be less than Perfect Love.

Among the characters of the Bible are some sights of horror and evilly marred humanity. Look at these Sadducees well. Look steadily at the experts in Moses' great books. This is what man, without God, feeding the vice of his rebellious heart, can become.

522 : The Soldiers

John 19.23–37

The duty section from the garrison at the Antonia Fort was a brutal set of men. They were no doubt resentful of the spell of duty in a tense Jerusalem, and in Palestine the Roman legionary walked in perpetual fear of the terrorist's knife. Pilate's own harsh leadership filtered down to the ranks. Apart from the centurions, who seem to have been picked men, the Palestine garrison was probably chosen for its toughness.

They hated Jews. Hence the childish but sadistic mockery in the barrack-room, and the cruel crown of thorns. One of them drove the great four-sided spikes through the wrists of the Victim, and they all sat down under the agonized figure of the Crucified, and diced for His cloak. One of them was entrusted with the task of smashing the legs of the three crucified men to prevent the fierce lifting of the body on the nailed feet so that a lungful of air could be gasped out from the strained, uplifted chest. Thus they would die more speedily of suffocation . . . Whoever held the hammer abstained when he came to Christ and found Him already dead (and Roman soldiers, be it noted, knew a dead man when they saw one). Was this a more sensitive man who for some reason hesitated to maim a corpse? Another, less humane, drove a spear into His side, and in blood and water revealed the damage to the lungs, and the traumatic pleurisy occasioned by the scourging.

One of the band in a gust of pity drove his spear into a sponge, used no doubt to wipe blood from the hands, dipped it into the jar of ration wine which stood there, and offered it to Christ. John used a rare dialect word for spear, '*hyssos*', which some early copyist, not recognizing a genuine Greek word, saw fit to change into '*hyssopos*'. A hyssop bush cannot provide the stick which they saw from deep in the crowd (Mark 15.36). It was a spear-shaft, of course, the head covered by the sponge. But observe the accuracy of the reporting—John's use of the word he heard, Mark's or Peter's mention of the uplifted stick. Such were the soldiers—a section of a harsh world's brutal life, but graced by an odd touch of pity, one man among them perhaps. Was it the centurion himself (Mark 15.39)? He it is who would appear to have been the first of all Gentiles to accept the inner truth of the death he had just witnessed.

523 : The Thieves
Mark 15.32; Luke 23.39–49

There is, of course, no contradiction between the two evangelists. Both criminals, terrorists like Barabbas from the Jericho road or other haunting-places of the Knifemen, at first, as Mark reports, soiled the last hours of their life with abuse and blasphemy. But one must have observed the Lord's demeanour, heard His words, and remembering, perhaps, old instruction in the synagogue school, actually observed the fulfilment of prophecy. And then, in eternal demonstration of mercy and of hope, he turned, in the midst of unimaginable pain, to the Saviour.

Forgiveness was immediate and complete. The broken man bleeding and gasping to death, had no opportunity at all to do anything to remedy or to compensate for a life's misdeeds. He could only cry for pardon, and pardon he received. It is a striking demonstration of Eph. 2.8 f.—'not of works...' William Camden, who founded a famous Chair of Ancient History in Oxford University, antiquarian and historian, who wrote largely and learnedly in Latin, is remembered by the *Oxford Dictionary of Quotations* for one small piece of English verse of no great distinction. It is an epitaph on a man killed by a fall from his horse:

> *My friend, judge not me,*
> *Thou seest I judge not thee.*
> *Betwixt the stirrup and the ground*
> *Mercy I asked, mercy I found.*

Legend has been busy with the penitent on the cross, giving him names like Dimas and Demarchus, and building stories round him. Nothing is really known save what is briefly recorded in this story of his pardon. The authorities, inventive in every manner of evil and misrepresentation, crucified Jesus between the two convicted criminals, in order to associate His name and person with banned political movements. It was part of the significance of the cross that the situation of sin and devilry was turned by a cry of penitence and the love of God into an occasion of salvation.

William Cowper wrote two centuries ago:

> *The dying thief rejoiced to see*
> *That fountain in his day;*
> *And there may I, though vile as he,*
> *Wash all my sins away.*

524 : You and I

Luke 23.24–38; 1 John 2.18–28

There is a sense in which we are all participants in this scene. The events of Calvary have an eternal character about them. An ancient kauri log once lay in the bush behind the house where these words are written. We set out to cut it up for winter's fires, and drove a great scarf into the wood. It exposed the growth rings of centuries. We could count back to the discovery of these coasts by James Cook. But the log was cut at one point. The same record ran up the wood and down.

Calvary is such a cut in history. Man has always been the same. As the old negro 'spiritual' asks: 'Were you there when they crucified my Lord?' We were—you who read, I who write. We are 'characters of Scripture'. With whom were we standing? By the cross with John? With the cynical priests? Hidden in the silent crowd far off, identity lost, sympathies concealed, useless, ineffective? Were we with Judas, wandering distraught?

The crime of Calvary was the work of many hands. Who crucified Christ? Was it Caiaphas and the priests, eager to conserve their life of ease, profit and comfort, and to avoid all peril of a popular movement which might embarrass them with Rome? Was it Pilate, held in the web of his past administrative mistakes, determined at all costs to protect his career, and to avoid all danger of another appeal to Caesar? Was it Herod, tangled in his sin, refusing to lift a finger to save a man of Galilee, because he enjoyed Pilate's dilemma? Was it the mob, ready enough to shout applause when they thought advantage came with the King of Israel, and who shouted for His blood when they found that He called for sacrifice? Was it the soldiers, who obeyed their orders, and drove the nails through human flesh, and diced beneath the spectacle of pain? Was it the carpenter who shaped the cross for wages, knowing that the innocent wood was to be stained with the blood of a fellow man in agony? Was it the smith who shaped the special nails, because a man must eat, regardless of the use to which the product of his hands would be put? Or was it Adam and all Adam's sons, from Adam's day to now, who have sinned and tolerated sin? There lies the answer, and what shall we do?

525 : Pilate Writes

Matthew 27.37; Mark 15.26; Luke 23.38; John 19.19–22

In Matthew's Gospel it is stated that the inscription on the Cross read, 'This is Jesus the King of the Jews'. Mark reports only the last five words of this. Luke has it, 'This is the King of the Jews', and John, 'Jesus of Nazareth, the King of the Jews'. Is there not contradiction involved here? No. All four could be abbreviations of 'This is Jesus of Nazareth, the King of the Jews'. There is, however, another and very probable explanation. The inscription was in three languages. In a multi-lingual inscription the language which is most familiar to us always stands out most prominently. Matthew, the Roman employee, would be likely to read Latin, the language of many a document in his office, with greatest readiness. Luke, on the other hand, student of the medical writers and Hippocrates, if presented with a copy of the inscription, would read the Greek, and John, the Galilean Jew, the Aramaic. If Matthew's version is written in Latin uncials, Luke's in Greek, and John's in Aramaic, they are found to occupy roughly the same space. Neatness and symmetry, we may suppose, would be the object of Pilate's signwriter, and a modification of the language in the three lines would help to effect this. Mark's version, in accordance with Mark's style, is a drastic abbreviation of all the rest.

Pilate, frustrated, and beaten by the priests, and, hard man though he was, hating them for compelling him to do a deed of bitter wrong, took vengeance on his enemies by a last insult. It hit home, as John, always well-informed about what went on in the high priestly inner circle, tells us. The priests, in the passion of their hatred, were foolish enough to protest to Pilate. He snapped: 'What I have written stands.' He used, or John used in reporting him, two Greek perfect tenses. This tense always implies a present state arising from a past event. Hence the rendering above.

The three Greek words throw a last beam of light on Pilate. Short of an act of ultimate courage, ultimate nobility, he had, he considered, done his best for justice. His wife did not think so, but, as we have seen, ancient sections of the Church gave him much credit. What of it all in God's eyes? God demands full surrender, and Pilate held back from the last brave step of committal which might have saved him.

526 : Joseph

Matthew 25.31–46; 27.57–61

Arimathea, if the site is correctly identified, lies some ten miles north-east of Lydda, in the lower foothills of the Shephelah, the spine of Palestine. The place is named once in each of the four stories of the Lord's burial, because it was from this town that the 'counsellor', or Sanhedrist, Joseph, came to beg Pilate for the body, and to bury it in his own unused tomb in the garden.

Luke describes Joseph as 'a good and righteous man' (23.50), and John, who must have known the later years of Joseph, as 'a disciple of Jesus, but secretly, for fear of the Jews' (19.38). According to the so-called 'Gospel of Nicodemus', one of the apocryphal books, Joseph was the leading figure in the establishment of the Christian community at Lydda. According to other legends, Philip sent twelve disciples to Britain to preach the faith, and Joseph was their leader. They were said to have founded the first church at Glastonbury. It became ultimately the famous Abbey. Here Joseph was buried and his staff, planted in the ground, became the Glastonbury Thorn. So at least said William of Malmesbury, the medieval chronicler.

All that is really known of Joseph is that which the Gospel writers tell us. He did a humane deed in the midst of a clutter of inhumanity. His action shines like a light in the darkness. Secret disciple though he may have been, the visit to Pilate was an act of open testimony, and no mean deed of courage. Perhaps, hating Caiaphas and his brood of murderers, Pilate was not sorry to cultivate a gentleman of breeding and quiet decency. Such men were not common in the corrupt hierarchy.

Being 'a good and righteous man', a man of humane feelings and concern for the right, Joseph would also have been the first to make the facts known of the empty tomb of the Easter morning had there been possible any other explanation than that which the disciples believed—that Christ had risen from the dead. It would have appeared to such a man not only criminal, but desperately perilous to suppress the facts, if a mistake, a deception, a planned removal of the body, or anything else short of the truth that Christ had risen, could account for the events which John described, the race in the dawn to the garden, the grave-clothes lying, and 'the linen cloth that had been about His head, folded by itself apart . . .'

527 : Nicodemus

Matthew 21.28–32; John 19.38–42

Legends also gathered round Nicodemus' name. In the apocryphal book *The Acts of Pilate*, Nicodemus appears as the instigator of a search for the body of Jesus, in keeping with Elisha's demand for such a search following the disappearance of Elijah. No body was found but the searchers did discover Joseph of Arimathea, who, having been imprisoned by the Sanhedrin, had been released by the risen Lord Himself.

Likely though the story of such a search is, at the instance of both friends and foes, the document is quite worthless save as romance, and is dated as late as the fourth century. As unreliable historically is the story that Nicodemus was alive at the fall of Jerusalem to the besieging Romans in A.D. 70.

All we really know of Nicodemus is that he was eminent as a teacher ('*the* teacher of the Jews'—John 3.10), that he warily showed sympathy with Jesus in a meeting of the Sanhedrin, on formal rather than theological grounds (7.50–52), and that, still warily, he joined Joseph in approaching Pilate with a request that the dead Christ should receive proper burial.

The courage, as well as the significance, of this act should not be underestimated. All men do not come to Christ in a burst of sudden glory. Some come thoughtfully, less emotionally, more timidly and tentatively than others. Nicodemus may have been one of those who took the longer, slower path. The general opinion is that the visit to Pilate was an act of committal, of open testimony. David Smith, writing in Hastings' *Dictionary of the Bible*, says: 'After the crucifixion, ashamed of his cowardice, he at last avowed himself . . .' Henry Vaughan, who wrote fine religious verse three centuries ago, has two puzzling lines which carry a similar opinion:

> *Wise Nicodemus saw such light*
> *As made him know his God by night.*

And with the act of mercy and final tribute, the gentle Pharisee passes from the page of Scripture and our knowledge.

Questions and themes for study and discussion on Studies 517–527

1. 'The crowd' and its mentality today.
2. 'Disaster is not always what it seems.'
3. 'Lost in the crowd.'
4. 'There is always a path to Christ.' Is this true?
5. The central significance of the cross. How would you state it?

6. Accuracy of detail in the Gospels.
7. Deathbed repentance.
8. 'Were you there when they crucified my Lord?'
9. The gospel for the Jew, the Greek, the Roman, the modern man.
10. What is 'a good man', from the biblical standpoint?
11. Nicodemus today.

528 : Peter and John

John 20.1–10; 21.3–11

We have read from several angles the shocking story of the crucifixion as John, who stood nearest to the scene, told it.

Turn to the next chapter, remembering that, as John wrote it, the story contained no chapter divisions, no break in the continuity of the narrative. Still factual, still honest, still stamped with the mark of the eye-witness, it runs straight on. The story of the death of Christ cannot be classed as reporting and the story of the tomb in the garden as pious fiction. Evidence for truth or falsehood, as every cross-examining barrister knows, lurks in details. Ruthless dissection can always expose the plausible fabrication. Not that the broken men, who had followed Christ, were in any mood to fabricate. Theirs was no state of imaginative exaltation. They had no sense that He whom they had seen nailed, hung high and stabbed, was still with them; no reason in their menaced and perilous situation to dream suicidal fictions. They were hiding somewhere, in utter defeat and despair when Mary came with the incredible story that, not only was the tomb open but that the body was gone. It is not clear whether she told eleven or two, but the same convincing and authenticating point emerges, whether Peter and John were the two out of the whole broken band who responded with energy and action, or whether Mary, who knew them all well, chose precisely those two because she could count on such response—Peter the practical and John the sensitive, opposite temperaments, who seem to have found fellowship in their variety.

Follow them, running to the grave, the younger man outrunning his older friend. He bends down and peers in, too awe-stricken or sensitive to tread in so hallowed a spot. Peter hurries up. Uninhibited, practical, prosaic, he steps straight in, and only

613

then, when John follows, is the cloth which had swathed the dead Christ's head observed, folded up apart. Peter and John appear, true to the same form, in another story. It is in Galilee, and faint dawn is on the water. On the beach is the dull gleam of a banked fire and a dim figure is standing. There is a hail across the water, and the disciples in their heavy fishing boat are told where to cast the net. The fish swarm to the right. 'It is the Lord,' whispers John, more perceptive than the rest. Peter, practical, energetic, girds his cloak tighter, jumps over, and splashes ashore. . . These stories, so factual in their unobtrusive detail, so true to the character of those who move through them, do not look like fiction.

529 : Mary

John 20.11–18

After the visit to Peter and John, and after their dawn run through Jerusalem and their discovery of the empty tomb in the garden, Mary had evidently made her way incredulously back to the place, perhaps to satisfy herself that she had indeed seen aright. She had seen no more of Peter and John, so had not, apparently, become aware of their confirmation of the vanishing of the body.

She stood helplessly by, and then, hoping again that she might have been somehow mistaken, she peered in once more (11). Observe the naturalness of all this detail. It was then that she saw the unearthly presence in the tomb, and heard a voice behind her asking why she wept. Amid the surge and play of these bewildering events she did not recognize the One who stood beside her, and thought it was the keeper of Joseph's garden.

Distracted, she asked what he had done with the body. Let him tell her, and she would take it away. How could she? She was a woman, and it would have been quite impossible for her to move the body of a man. But could any remark be more in keeping with the situation? And then He spoke her name, and in some accentuation of His voice, she recognized Him and threw herself at His feet.

There followed the puzzling remark of v. 17. Perhaps it was simply playful. 'Don't try to hold me. I have not yet gone.' Perhaps it had some meaning which eludes us. It is certainly curious that Matthew tells us (**28.9**) that they 'held Him by the feet'. No involved and ritualistic process based on Lev. **16**, as some have prosaically imagined, is involved. Unless the remark was utterly simple, we do not understand what it meant. But this is itself evidence for factual reporting. No weaver of deception would inject into his story statements which create a puzzle. This is what Mary heard. This is what Mary reported. And Mary having reported thus, John set it down in his account.

530 : 'And Peter'

Mark 16.1–15

Mark was writing his last words in haste. There is evidence that he did not finish his last chapter, and that a few verses were added by another hand. Mark's account of the empty tomb is therefore the briefest of all in the Gospel narratives, but in spite of this he does manage to import into the story one unique phrase: 'Tell His disciples and Peter', the command ran. The other evangelists do not report the last two words. They were meant indeed for the stricken Peter alone, and treasured in his grateful memory as the foretaste of the Lord's forgiveness. Peter, as we have seen, was Mark's authority, and through Mark, his son in the faith, Peter passed on the precious phrase to the world. There is also an unrecorded interview with Peter, mentioned in an oral tradition, which Paul passes to the Corinthian church. Paul's passage was written two or three years before Mark's narrative, and is, in consequence, the first published report of the resurrection (1 Cor. **15.5**).

Was the promise to 'go before them into Galilee' partly fulfilled when the Risen Christ met the two unknown disciples who accompanied Him to Emmaus, as Luke records? The road ran that way; v. 12 briefly touches the incident. So hope came to the world; it is still the world's hope. If Christ rose from the dead, the last enemy is defeated, the man in faith can endure a world where death reigns. For death and evil are inseparable allies, and if death be conquered, sin also, its confederate, has lost its power. If such foes be discomfited, life is sweet, and, however dark the day and fierce the onslaught, beleaguered man can look beyond to the relief and final victory which are his in the conquering Christ.

615

Let us lay hold with both hands upon the fact that the Lord is risen. Dr Dale of Birmingham tells how that truth once laid hold of him. ' "Christ is alive," I said to myself, "alive"—and then I paused. "Alive? . . . living as really as I myself am?" I got up and walked about repeating, "Christ is living!". At first it seemed strange . . . but at last it came upon me as a burst of sudden glory. "Yes, Christ is living!" It was to me a new discovery. I thought that all along I had believed it . . . I then said: "My people shall know it. I shall preach about it again and again until they believe it as I do now." ' For months afterwards, in every sermon, the Living Christ was the great preacher's dominant theme. Paul speaks (Phil. 3.10) of 'the power of His resurrection'. He meant, surely, the remarkable strength and steady confidence in the life of those who are utterly and absolutely convinced that the Lord they serve is not dead but alive—real, all-knowing, all-powerful, and with them always. This is what transformed Peter.

531 : Thomas
John 20.19–31

Census documents recovered among the Egyptian papyri, identified those mentioned by scars. Here is one dated A.D. 48, a document of the fourth census after the one mentioned in the Gospel of Luke:

To Dorion chief magistrate and to Didymus town clerk, from Thermoutharion, the daughter of Thoonis, with her guardian Apollonius the son of Sotades. The inhabitants of the house belonging to me in the South Lane are: Thermoutharion a freedwoman of the aforesaid Sotades, about 65 years of age, of medium height, with honey-coloured complexion, having a long face and a scar on the right knee . . . (A line is missing here which describes a second woman). *I, the aforesaid Thermoutharion* (the document continues with an affidavit), *with my guardian the said Apollonius, swear by Tiberius Claudius Caesar Emperor, that I have truthfully presented the preceding return of those living with me, neither a stranger, Alexandrian, nor freedman, nor Roman, nor Egyptian, except the aforesaid. If I am swearing truly may it be well with me, if falsely the opposite.*

Such references abound in ancient documents, and, in fact, it was not a bad idea, for most people can find some mark of damage . . . Thomas was the last of the eleven to see the risen Christ, and he was no man to hazard life on a false report, mistake, hallucination or fabrication. Observe how conformably to his character Thomas acts. Remembering documents he had no doubt filled in, he said, 'Unless I put my finger into the print of the nails, and my hand into the spear wound in His side, I will not believe.' Such were Christ's identifying scars, and such demonstration Christ offered the doubter. 'My Lord,' cried the broken man, 'and my God.' Do you catch the 'ring of truth' in the breathless simplicity of that affirmation? 'Blessed,' said Christ, 'are those who have not seen and have believed.'

'Hath He marks to lead me to Him?' asks Stephen of Saba in the hymn which he built round Thomas' experience. He has, indeed, His marks, marks on all history, marks on countless transformed lives, and He still calls for Thomas' affirmation. No despite is done to reason in making it. Once it is made, life can never be the same again. Such committal involves all life, penetrates the whole person . . .

532 : Emmaus Walkers

Luke 24.13–35

The exquisitely told story of the walk to Emmaus is peculiar to Luke. Two Christians (they were not apostles) lived at Emmaus, possibly today's Kalonich, north-west of Jerusalem. They were walking home with the declining sun in their eyes, when a Stranger joined them. Here is a simple rendering of what followed, choosing a reading for the end of verse 17 found in the *Codex Sinaiticus*, the famous Great Bible of Sinai, and one other ancient text: 'He said to them: "What words are these which you are tossing back and forth as you walk along?" They stopped and looked sadly at him, and one of them named Cleopas replied: "Do you live alone in Jerusalem seeing that you do not know what happened there in the last few days?" He said to them: "What sort of things?" They said to him: "concerning Jesus of Nazareth, a man who spoke the words of God, a man of power in word and deed before the people, and how the high priests and our rulers handed him over to be condemned to death and crucified him. And we were hoping that it might have been he who was going to redeem Israel." . . .'

The words ring with the hopelessness of the disciples over the events which had closed the week. But set this broken spirit over against the jubilation of the days which followed. Only some cataclysmic event could have so transformed a shattered group of men. The Emmaus road saw no illusion. It was no deluded pair of enthusiasts who suddenly recognized His hands, and hurried back, forgetful of their weariness, over the seven miles to Jerusalem.

Only one of them is named. But this is singularly appropriate. Christ belongs to all mankind. A German painter shows the walk to Emmaus in a Rhineland setting. The three robed figures move among summer elms. A village church is in the distance. In the stained glass windows of a church in Fifty-Eighth Street, New York, the same scene is set in New England.

The Christ of the Emmaus road is the Christ of every road. He still walks the ways of earth with those who are eager for His company. Men are still dull and slow of heart to apprehend His plans. He is the guest of any home and any heart which offers welcome.

533 : Real People

1 Corinthians 15.1–19

Let us draw a few details to the fore as we look at the familiar figures we have followed through the narratives, as they face the tremendous facts of the resurrection. Facts they are, capable of scrutiny. E. M. B. Green aptly quotes Lord Darling, once Chief Justice of England. Speaking on the resurrection, the eminent judge said: 'We, as Christians, are asked to take a very great deal on trust—the teachings, for example, and the miracles of Jesus. If we had to take all on trust, I, for one, should be sceptical. The crux of the problem of whether Jesus was, or was not, what He claimed to be, must surely depend upon the truth or otherwise of the resurrection. On that greatest point we are not merely asked to have faith. In its favour as a living truth there exists such overwhelming evidence, positive and negative, factual and circumstantial, that no intelligent jury in the world could fail to bring in a verdict that the resurrection story is true.'

All is so intensely natural, and true to temperament and character! These people are real—Peter, ever active and practical and instinctively turning in a time of waiting and uncertainty to the therapy of deeds (John 21.3), drawing the net ashore—it had lain in the shallow water while they had gathered silent (John 21.12) and wondering round the Lord—the great fish flapping in the cords; John, following his friends, and counting the fish (He betrays more than once his interest in numbers) . . . Whether belief be accorded or withheld there is no alternative to accepting these stories as the writing of history.

Canon J. B. Phillips remarks in his remarkable little book, *The Ring of Truth*: 'I have read, in Greek and Latin, scores of myths, but I did not find the slightest flavour of myth here. There is no hysteria, no careful working for effect, and no attempt at collusion. One sensed again that understatement which we have been taught to think is more British than Oriental. There is an almost childlike candour and simplicity, and the total effect is tremendous.'

534 : Peter Again
John 21.1–19

The little church 'of Peter's secrecy' stands by the lake, its beach stony and bare, or deep under clear water when the snows of Hermon are melting and brimming Galilee high with their flood. This is where, according to ancient tradition, the Lord had His private talk with Peter, and where Peter and John walked with Him by the lake.

The conversation with Peter recorded by John is not as complicated as commentators have at times made it appear. Much has been made of the fact that in the Greek text of John's account two different words are used for 'love'. It is true that a general distinction can be drawn between the two verbs, but in John's Greek it is very difficult to define it sharply. The two verbs seem very interchangeable. Then again, the conversation was in Aramaic, and it is impossible to state whether John was translating a distinction clearly drawn in the original speech.

There is a much simpler explanation. Peter had denied his Lord three times. Each one of those separate occasions was etched on his memory. Each one cut a deeper furrow into the tissue of his brain. He remembered every stinging detail. He thought day and night of every facet of each shocking experience—what he could have said, what he should have said, where, how, why he should have retreated, resisted. . . . It all milled torturingly round in his memory, and drove him to desperation.

And now Christ was risen. Peter was beginning to see the truth of Christ's Kingdom in a new and more penetrating light. But had he, who had proved himself so weak under stress, any part in it? He did not know, and fear was added to sorrow. Christ spoke to him in the hearing of the rest, or so it seems, and three times recommissioned him and gave him a position of leadership and pastoral care. It was magnificent psychotherapy from the Great Physician. The three affirmations cancelled gloriously the three denials. Three times the words of grace and forgiveness cut their blessed channel in his consciousness. He could now never remember his fault without at the same time remembering his forgiveness, and a forgiveness charged with a task and fused with a commission.

535 : John

John 21.20–25; 1 John 2.18–28

Peter's curiosity about John is indication of the load that had been lifted from his own mind. It is a clear symptom of his vast relief, and the renewal of his interest in life. John was near them, and Peter asked after him and his future. He was gently rebuked. Let him carry on with the task delivered to him, and leave others to theirs.

The conversation was heard by the rest and remembered. The remark about John and the return of Christ became generally known in the Asian Church, in which John passed the years of his ministry. As is the way with men, the words became encrusted with what meanings others gave them, and the word went round among the Christians that the old 'bishop' would live until his Master came again. Christ, of course, had said no such thing, but it is the common way of men to make Him say what they would have Him say.

And John was inordinately old. The average life span in those days was much less than it is now. Few attained the psalmist's 'three score years and ten'. But here was John still living, thirty years after the Neronian persecution had decimated the church in Rome, almost thirty years after the death of Paul, surviving most of his fellow apostles by a full generation, outliving the persecution which had become severe in the eighties of the century under Domitian. He was in his nineties, a remarkable age even in these days of geriatric science. Hence an outbreak of superstition which set John to work again, and gave us the treasure of his last chapter.

He had finished his Gospel. He had had every reason to write that Gospel. He laid some dire heresies by the heel. And at the end of the section which we call ch. 20 he laid down his pen with something like relief. Then the rumour of his immortality reached his ears, and John took up his pen again to set the words which had occasioned such misunderstanding in their proper context. It was a weary task but reveals the wealth of confirmatory information in the possession of the disciples which did not reach the surface of papyrus. John finished his task a second time and ended with a whimsical touch which revealed that the aged man had not lost his quiet sense of humour (25). He had written well. He had woven words and teaching into a significant pattern. He had placed an affidavit in his closing section that he had written as he had seen. He had told no detail not personally known to him. He had rounded off the Bible.

536 : Five Hundred

Acts 1.1–3; 1 Corinthians 15.6; Matthew 28.16–20

Before we turn from the closing chapters of the Gospels and prepare to move on to the characters of the early years of the Christian Church, we must take note of a sea of heads—people waiting just off the stage of history. Writing to the Corinthians in A.D. 52, as we have seen, Paul set down against a report of their scepticism, the traditional evidence for the resurrection of Christ. He mentioned a group of five hundred people who had witnessed the Lord's living presence.

And, said Paul, something more than half of them were still alive at the time of his writing. Note how statistically probable this is. In any adult cross-section of the population, it might be supposed that about half would survive a subsequent twenty years. Paul must have known many of these people, and since

621

he was, in all probability, the instigator of Luke's project of writing, the third evangelist must have met many of these people. Perhaps that is how he came to rescue the beautiful story of the two who walked to the village of Emmaus, and met the risen Christ on the way.

Some have surmised that the occasion of this large anonymous gathering may have been the unnamed mountain in Galilee. Matthew makes brief mention of it, and adds frankly that 'some doubted'. In a large gathering no doubt the personal contact and verification was less easy for some than others. On the other hand hallucination can hardly command so large an audience.

The five hundred were the nucleus of the Galilean church, if this guess about locality be true. They were people of Nazareth who had seen the town turn against its Townsman. They were people who had been guests at a wedding in Cana. They were fisherfolk of Capernaum. And who shall tell whether some upright centurion, some rescued tax-gatherer, some nobleman whose son had been ill, some man who had been lowered through the tiles of a stripped roof . . . whether these and such as these, folk like those next door, from the street below, from the farm yonder, from the shop, the factory, the school . . . saw the sight of all sights—The Conqueror of Death?

Questions and themes for study and discussion on Studies 528–536

1. The value of eye-witness testimony to the Gospel facts.
2. Why Mary first of all?
3. 'Christ is alive!' The implications of this great fact.
4. Why did not Thomas accept the invitation of Jesus to put his finger into the print of the nails?
5. 'The Christ of *every* road.'
6. The marks of reality in the Gospel accounts of the resurrection.
7. Peter's forgiveness.
8. The tasks of old age.
9. The five hundred.

537 : Friend of Luke
Acts 1.1–3; Luke 1.1–4; John 15.12–16

In Luke's Gospel Theophilus is 'most excellent', but in Acts he has no honorific title. Had a friendship ripened? Had Theophilus become a Christian? No one knows, but conjectures are many. Was Theophilus a high Roman official, perhaps connected with the forthcoming trial of Paul? (See Acts 23.26; 24.2; 26.25 for the respectful mode of address.) Was Theophilus a secret name by which the Roman church knew some member of the imperial family? We know that Christianity had infiltrated such circles early in its history. Luke's formal beginning of his history suggests that he had in mind readers who knew the proprieties of contemporary literature. No one can tell. It seems quite certain that, whoever the exalted person was who became a friend of Luke, and the object of his books' dedication, he was real. Some have fancifully played with the thought that Theophilus means 'lover of God', and that Luke symbolically addressed his writings to all men anywhere who sought and worshipped God. This is hardly possible. Luke followed a universal practice of his day in addressing his book to a person.

It is the happy fate of some people to win immortality through a friend, a point we have previously remarked upon. Boswell would have been unknown but for his friend Samuel Johnson, and Atticus not even a name had not the great orator and statesman, Cicero, addressed his letters so frequently to him. And who would any of us be but for the fact that we have become the friends of Christ Jesus? Theophilus, at any rate, holds the distinction of being the only recipient of a personal dedication in the New Testament. If Luke wrote at his request he played a part indeed in the history of the Christian faith. It is a part which may well be played to prompt others to good deeds. It comes next to doing them ourselves. Luke's first dedication contains one verb which reinforces the argument that Theophilus was a real person. The rendering 'informed' of the RSV is not so accurate as 'instructed' of the AV (KJV). The word is one used by Luke and Paul of formal instruction in religion (Acts. 18.25; Rom. 2.18). It seems certain that Theophilus had heard the truth, and had been carefully taught the facts. He must surely have been a seeker whose blessing Luke sought.

538 : Luke the Historian

Acts 1.1–14; Luke 3.1–3

Luke, as we shall have occasion to note, was, in his own right, a notable historian. He professed to have carefully investigated the facts, to have tested the truth and to have been personally convinced by it himself. Every writer has his reasons and his motives, a point of view to urge upon his readers, vital information to set down and transmit. He is measured by the power of his persuasion, by the art with which he marshals and balances his facts, by the worth of what he has to say, and by the value of the history which he preserves and records. The writer's purpose can be multiple, and to compass successfully more ends than one in any piece of historical writing is a heavy demand upon intelligence and conviction. Such success is the mark of Luke's ability. More than one aim and purpose are clear in his work.

He sought first to give permanence to extraordinary events, and to record the birth of a movement which he was confident would change the course of history, and in which he himself was a privileged participant. His aim was that of the most exact of the great Greek historians, Thucydides of Athens. The Great War which determined the future shape of Greece, and ended the Golden Age of Athens, had broken out between Thucydides' Athens and the totalitarian state of Sparta. The young historian, for Thucydides was no more than thirty years of age, set to work, 'believing it would be a great war, and more worthy of relation than any which had preceded it. . .' Indeed it was, he believed, likely to be the greatest movement of events yet known in history. . . Luke might have had the very words in mind when he penned the prologue to the Gospel, of which the Acts of the Apostles is the necessary sequel. Paul was in prison. His friend set to work.

The Great Commission spoke of expanding areas of witness from Jerusalem, to Judea, to Samaria, and 'the uttermost parts of the earth', and Luke's book interprets the words. The Gospel had set out to record with historical exactitude all that Jesus 'began to do and to teach.' The word 'began' is significant. The first book was a beginning, the second records the next phase of the great spiritual movement, with Christ's power operative in the lives of His men. It was an exciting task to undertake.

539 : Luke at Work

Acts 1.15–26; Psalm 69

It is interesting to observe Luke's mind at work. In the book we are reading we shall see much of the physician friend of Paul, because a man lives in what he writes, and Luke's trained intellect is often visible to perceptive students. Observe his purpose. It was multiple, as was remarked in the last study. One aim which he kept before him, as the one Gentile writer in the New Testament, was the vindication of Paul, as the apostle to the wide world of men. Like a clever chess player, he can see many moves ahead. He stresses the work of Peter in the first half of his book, and of Paul in the second, showing how they interlock. From Peter's recorded sermons in the first chapters, Luke underlines the appeal to the Old Testament, of which Peter had in these days become most vividly aware. This was to be exactly the manner of Paul. . .

There was also another motive for stressing this incident. Peter, exactly true to the impetuous nature which found a need in times of stress and waiting to be up and doing something, proposed the filling of Judas' vacant place. He discovered Old Testament justification for this in Psa. 109.8. In point of fact, the only clear direction which the disciples had been given was 'not to depart from Jerusalem' (4) until the enlightenment of God should come to them with His Holy Spirit. God had His candidate for the vacant apostolate, a candidate possibly known to Peter.

The worthy Matthias had all the qualifications which Peter laid down. He was quite possibly one of the Seventy chosen by the Lord Himself. He does not appear again in Luke's story, which follows only the stream of witness which led to Paul and on through him. Tradition had it that he took the gospel to Africa and died a martyr in Ethiopia, but nothing certain is known. There are multitudes whose names are in the Book of Life who are in no other book.

Questions and themes for study and discussion on Studies 537–539

1. The usefulness of friendship. Consider Luke, Theophilus and Paul.
2. The ministry of writing. Should Christians do more of it?
3. 'God's man and God's time.' Can you illustrate further?

540 : The New Peter

Acts 2.1–36

It is the same clear mind which is seen at work in this vivid chapter. Luke is careful to show that the first sermon to be preached after the visitation of the Holy Spirit was delivered to a host of Jews and proselytes from all over the Eastern Mediterranean (5). The listening multitude would be versed in two languages only—Aramaic, the common language of the Levant, and the basic Greek, which had become the second tongue of the Mediterranean basin. Many might add Biblical Hebrew to their repertoire, and Roman Jews would know Latin. Jews, like Israelis today, might follow Arabic, but Jews, for example, from Parthia, would be no more likely to speak native Parthian than the average New Zealander would be likely to speak Maori. This is a 'character study' and no place to discuss 'the gift of tongues'. The writer of this note has expressed a tentative opinion elsewhere (*Tyndale New Testament Commentaries, Acts,* pp. 55, 56).

But observe the transformed Peter. Chrysostom said that Peter functioned as 'the mouth of the apostles' (cf. Matt. **16.16**; **17.24**; **18.21**; **19.27**; Luke **12.41**; John **6.67** f.; **13.6**). He was the chief of the band. In Matt. **10.2** we read in the list of the apostolate: 'The first, Simon, who is called Peter.' He similarly heads the other lists, but it is only in Acts that he seems to assume command and the post of spokesman. There is, none the less, a new facet to Peter's prominence, following the Resurrection and Pentecost. The Old Testament, dormant in his mind, had burst into life. It is part of the function of God's enlivening Spirit, to invest all knowledge and experience with new significance. The hymn is true:

> *Heaven above is softer blue,*
> *Earth around is sweeter green;*
> *Something lives in every hue*
> *Christless eyes have never seen.*

The truth of the remark extends to Scripture. Seen through a transforming experience of Christ, the Bible becomes luminous, its words live and vibrate. Peter had a strong and retentive mind. Like every Jewish boy, he had memorized great tracts of the Old Testament in the synagogue school. The old words, in his new heart, were blazing and pulsing with new significance.

541 : The Converts

Acts 2.37–47

A solid core of three thousand converts (41), with daily accretions (47), from all parts of the Mediterranean world (5) formed the heart of the early Church. There are group characters in Scripture, and, in the familiar urbanized society of the first century, we are likely to meet with many such groups with common characteristics. It is possible to gain some idea of this considerable congregation of Jewish Christians.

They are from widely different backgrounds, as various indeed as those which constitute something of a social problem in modern Israel where Russian Jew, American Jew, and Yemeni Jew rub shoulders and learn to live with one another, with little more than the bond of a common language. These converts of Pentecost and its aftermath were drawn into unity by their common faith in a resurrected Christ—a singularly strong argument, be it noted, for the historic fact of the empty tomb. This was Jerusalem, not Rome or Antioch where certain essential evidence was beyond verification.

The converts had no thought that they would be separated from the ancestral faith which had drawn them from parts so diverse and remote to the mother-city of Judaism. History is full of the unexpected, and further enlightenment was to follow events. The Temple (46) was still the centre of their worship and their fellowship.

They repudiated a corrupt world (40), they listened, learned and prayed together, seeing no division between their religious and their secular activities (46). Did their zeal go too far? How is it that the experiment in communal living extended no further than Jerusalem, and, as far as the evidence goes, was soon modified or discarded? It is, of course, a fact that all real estate possessed by any Jew in Jerusalem was doomed, but the catastrophic events of the Great Rebellion were, at this time, many years away. A possible explanation might be that, in the first flush of enthusiasm, and perhaps in the mistaken view that Christ's Second Advent was imminent, the first Christians outran the will of God in their social organization. Then, perhaps, the passage of time and the growth of conviction modified the situation. It would appear to be a fact that a pocket of penury was left among the Christians of Jerusalem, which later required the monetary relief of the Church abroad. It is, none the less, an idyllic picture.

542 : The Man at the Gate

Acts 3.2–11; John 9.8–25

In those who are truly His disciples, the experience of Christ has a way of repeating itself. The situation at the Temple gate is not unfamiliar. Above stood in costly splendour a work of human art, part of Herod's lavish gift to Jewry, and near, according to some, to the place where doves and other offerings were sold to pilgrims. The gate, where the passing crowd was confined, was a natural place for the human derelict to crouch and beg for alms. The East has still such piteous sights to show.

The steward was ashamed to beg (Luke 16.3), and beggary takes some dignity from the spirit of man, be it disguised as the common 'tip', or practised in open solicitation. It was a merciless society. Pity was the gift of Christ, and if mercy and care for men survive a society's rejection of Him who gave them, that survival is fragile, a heritage which will erode. The psychologist Jung well remarked:

'At a time when a large part of mankind is beginning to discard Christianity, it is worth while to understand why it was originally accepted. It was accepted in order to escape from the brutality of antiquity. As soon as we discard it licentiousness returns, as is impressively exemplified by life in our large cities.'

The man whose sad presence marred the Beautiful Gate, sought pity, and received it as men do from God in ampler measure than their prayer had hoped. No word of his is quoted. He is shown, joyous in his new liberty and praising God, but, like the blind man of John's story, who had much to say, the lame man identified himself with those who had brought him blessing. His person was a testimony and it is patent fact that it needs no words of exposition to make apparent to a watching world that something has happened to a personality.

The incident was no doubt one of those recounted to Luke as he scoured Palestine for facts during Paul's captivity in Caesarea. He tells it in a manner which John was to use in the Fourth Gospel—as a lead-in to an important utterance, in this case a sermon by Peter. Luke is always with us as we read his writing,

628

and it is often possible to see his careful links in the narrative. The early Christians frequented the Temple (2.46). It was on their way to the Temple (3.1) that this notable event took place.

543 : Peter the Preacher
Acts 3.12–26; John 20.2–8

Peter's new stature and new dimensions of strength, become more and more obvious as the narrative proceeds. Alert to seize the opportunity, he turned to the crowd which had gathered round the three and turned it to divine use. This was no prepared sermon, but Peter spoke from the depth of conviction and it is of small use to speak from any other prompting. In speech and writing words come when the mind knows and the heart feels, and all else is likely to be 'tinkling cymbal and sounding brass'.

Peter begins and ends with Christ. To exalt Him should be the aim of every utterance. And to exalt Him for what He is—God's Son (13), the Holy One and Just (14), the Author of Life (15), of all-prevailing Name (16). . . No diminished Christ, denied His deity, reft of His Messiahship, is potent to daunt evil and save the souls of men.

Peter was merciless with the sin which had rejected the Lord and done Him to death. He spoke with utter conviction of the resurrection. John was beside him, and both remembered the dawn race through the empty streets of Jerusalem as he spoke of their witnessing the historic facts of six weeks before. And here, in a broken man mended, was further evidence of a Living Lord.

But Peter has no harshness. Ruthless with sin, he pleads with the sinners. He points to the blindness and the vicious leadership, which had prompted the crime of Calvary (17)—a crime for which God was prepared, and for all its abysmal evil, not past the remedy of repentance, nor beyond the forgiveness of God. Here, indeed, was part of a mighty plan, the beginnings of which, as the apostles' new enlightenment was now seeing, ran back into ancient revelation and the words of prophets.

And Peter ends where all sermons must end, with a plea for decision. He preached for a verdict. But why Luke's desire to report him so carefully? Because here was the very manner of Paul. Luke desired no division, such as Paul had known at

Corinth. Peter and Paul were not men apart, with different gospels. Their message was one, based on Scripture, urgent, demanding faith and surrender.

Peter might have agreed with Richard Baxter:

> *I preached as never sure to preach again,*
> *And as a dying man to dying men.*

Is there any other mood for such a task?

544 : The Hierarchy

Acts 4.1–7; John 11.47–53

In human affairs it is often the sad fate of silent and helpless majorities to fall into the hands of vocal and dynamic minorities, who govern and manipulate them in their own interests. Such abuse of position and responsibility is not at all unknown in the institutions of religion. Entrenched groups determine policy, initiate action, and provide expression which in no way represents the wish of the mass. It was so in the citadel of Jewry. 'This crowd, who do not know the law, are accursed', they sneered cynically (John 7.49).

It is of little use blaming the supineness of the mass, saying that organizations and people get the government they deserve, or even pointing to the preoccupation of the majority with more profitable activity than politics of one sort and another. There are those, even in the Church, as Milton put it in *Lycidas*, who 'creep and intrude and climb into the fold'. . .

> *Blind mouthes! that scarce themselves know how to hold*
> *A Sheep-hook, or have learned ought else the least*
> *That to the faithfull Herdman's art belongs!*
>
> . . . . .
>
> *And when they list, their lean and flashy songs*
> *Grate on their scrannel pipes of wretched straw,*
> *The hungry Sheep look up and are not fed.*

Here is the brood of them in full assembly and full voice. Note the subjects of the hierarchical grievance. 'They taught the people.'

Their duped flock must remain docile in such false shepherds' hands. To teach the truth stirs awareness, restlessness with tyranny, discernment which heresy and dominance find awkward, and discontent with corrupt leadership.

'They preached through Jesus the resurrection from the dead.' The Sadducees, of course, like some of their successors, did not believe in the resurrection. Therefore it should not be preached. Truth did not matter, only the comfort of doctrine unchallenged. Facts needed no examination.

And yet how correct they were in matters of their own concern. Based on Jer. 21.12, they had a practice of postponing late judicial examinations until the following day. It was convenient to by-pass this law in the case of Christ, but how deep the hypocrisy of such tamperers with justice and the truth!

545 : Peter's Courage

Acts 4.8–22

Winston Churchill once declared: 'Courage is the first of human qualities, because it is the quality which guarantees all others.' That is true. To have the right words to say, to be endowed with the eloquence that can say them persuasively, both are useless in one who lacks the courage to speak.

Peter, who had once been daunted by the challenge of a servant girl, answers the most formidable concentration of civil power in the land eye to eye. 'In whose name?' they had asked. He tells them in plain and downright speech. This is a man utterly convinced by what he had seen that recent morning in a garden tomb, no less.

There is something of Christ about His servant. Note the echo of a well-remembered word (John 18.23) in v. 9, and catch the directness of the challenge in v. 10, and the resort to familiar Old Testament quotation in the very manner of the Lord in v. 11. Their priestly examiners, all perceptive and clever men, were not slow to recognize the source of this blazing courage. Here was boldness, swiftness of repartee in men without their schooling, and unity between Peter who spoke, and John, once more his fellow-witness, who stood beside him, which could have only one explanation—'They had been with Jesus' (13).

The admission is itself a witness to the impression which the

Lord had made upon those who had sought to dash His challenge aside. And observe the unnamed hero. The man who had been healed and who was the indirect occasion for this uproar, stood silently beside them. Witness does not always need words. Indeed, the silent figure of the one-time beggar-man seems to have been the final clinching argument.

But even thus refuted they could not change. The Lord had said as much. They had sinned against the Holy Spirit. The natural conclusion should have been the admission of their need. That 'a notable miracle had been done' in no way prompted repentance, in no sense suggested that men whose policy had been condemned, stood in mortal danger if they pressed their charge. They merely judged it expedient to extricate themselves from an embarrassing situation. They sought to do so with scant success, and Peter and John, correctly assessing the measure of defeat and victory, made no move of compromise, gave no undertaking. Their insight equalled their courage. The Spirit of God can quicken the mind as well as warm the heart.

546 : The Church in Jerusalem

Acts 4.23–37; 1 John 2.15–19; 3.13, 14

The opening verse of this section (Acts 4.23) is worth a sermon. The world is all round the Christian. It is seductive. It tempted Demas from Paul's side when he needed friendship most (2 Tim. 4.10). It can deaden and overwhelm. It can destroy faith and discourage zeal. The test comes when we turn our back upon it. 'We know that we have passed out of death into life,' said the aged John with most penetrating simplicity, 'because we love the brethren.'

To be sure, the brethren are not a band of blameless saints. In the group to which Peter and John, in accordance with John's as yet unwritten dictum, returned with such significant alacrity, were Ananias and Sapphira, so soon to fall into crass hypocrisy. They were none the less 'their own company' (23, AV [KJV]). The Christian should mark the onset of decay when he finds that he prefers the company, the fellowship, the functions of the world outside to the fellowship of Christians. Samson and the Philistines is Old Testament illustration.

The Church was already learning to sing: a liturgical form is apparent in these verses. This primitive hymn was built round the second Psalm. Much Christian truth was passed on and retained at this time in the form of song. It is, in fact, becoming clear as evidence multiplies, that the written records of the Church are older than was once thought. For many years now, critics with a vested interest in late-dating the Gospels, have repeatedly experienced what the late J. F. Dulles called 'an agonizing reappraisement'. At the same time, there must have been an oral tradition. More than once, explicitly or implicitly, Paul says: 'I received of the Lord that which I delivered to you' (1 Cor. 15.3).

There is, however, no better way of learning and transmitting truth than by way of song, a truth which oppressed minorities through the ages, and 'protest movements' have known. The Church, gathered perhaps in Mary's house, the place of 'the Upper Room', was aware of the fact. Perhaps the song was chanted by a leader such as James, with the group chiming in with the appropriate 'Amen'.

They were 'of one heart and soul' (32), a situation soon to pass and be riven by falsehood. The experiment in communal living is again mentioned, but observe Luke's purpose—the next story relates to sin arising from the situation, and also Barnabas appears. It is Luke's common fashion to introduce a major figure at some point before his chief appearance.

Questions and themes for study and discussion on Studies 540–546

1. The place and importance of the Old Testament (a) in the New Testament; (b) today.

2. Where and how does the New Testament refer to Christian giving?

3. Could law and order, mercy and gentleness, survive the death of Christianity?

4. What did Peter's preaching emphasize?

5. Are there still those who 'creep, intrude and climb into the fold'?

6. The sources of courage.

7. The place and purpose of hymns. What should hymns contain?

633

547 : Ananias

Acts 5.1–6; Matthew 23.23–28

The Bible is not silent on the faults of those who profess the faith. Luke has mentioned (Acts 4.36 f.) the sacrifice of the gentle Barnabas. He proceeds without pause to tell of Ananias' hypocrisy. Perhaps jealous of the reputation Barnabas may have won among the people for his notable generosity, Ananias sought the same, but sought it with lies and misrepresentation. He was free to retain his property, free to give it. He was not licensed to deceive and this is what he did.

These were days of intense devotion and, set in the context of those times, the fault was an enormous one. Judas had betrayed his Lord for money. Hypocrisy, flayed by the Lord in a well-remembered utterance, was the fault of the hierarchy which had murdered Christ. If Ananias' fault appears less considerable today, that is because apprehension of evil is blunted with the years, and the vice of deception less vividly appreciated.

These were also vital days. The Church had not yet been invaded by the less-committed men who were to dampen the fire of its witness and to dilute the strength of its pure testimony. Here was the damning, spoiling, soiling thing infiltrating the undamaged community in the person of one man. Ananias must have been crass of soul indeed not to realize the viciousness of what he set out, for his own ends, to do. The act of giving was motivated by evil. Luke picks up the last verse of the preceding chapter. First Barnabas, then Ananias. Hypocrisy is a sort of tribute which vice pays to virtue. This was a direct imitation of a good man by a bad man, and the shock of public disclosure was too much for the sinner. He died.

Giving from any personal motive is vicious. Those who promote schemes of fund-raising must bear this fact delicately in mind. People can be tempted to sin, and to promise, in God's name, material recompense for tithing, or any other form of systematic giving, is to deceive and to encourage sin.

It is a sad story. 'So familiar are we,' writes Rackham in his splendid commentary on Acts, 'with spots and wrinkles in the Church, that we can with difficulty recognize the significance of this first sin in and against the community ... It corresponds to the entrance of the Serpent into Eden ... and the first fall must have staggered the apostles and the multitude.'

548 : Sapphira
Acts 5.7–16; Romans 12.9–16; Revelation 21.27; 22.15

The Lord had warned against 'the leaven of the Pharisees', that permeating vice of false pretence, whereby the religious leaders of Jerusalem sought to gain a reputation for sanctity and piety. Here were man and wife conspiring together to deceive. A sin shared is more than a sin doubled. When man and woman agree to sin together, they sin against each other, as well as against God.

It is the duty of those allied in bonds of marriage to counsel each the other. It is a guard against sin and temptation if two people in close human fellowship are prepared in love and frankness to warn and to restrain in the presence of temptation. Ananias and Sapphira joined in sin, and without shame plotted to deceive.

Peter's apparent hardness stems from the horror which he, in common with the Church, must have felt at this unexpected invasion of evil. He saw that hypocrisy, once grounded in the Church, would destroy all true fellowship and brotherly love, for how can divisions disappear if man is suspicious of his fellow, and how can suspicion die, if deceit, posing and false pretences are rampant?

The sin of Ananias and Sapphira was many-sided, and, in the pure atmosphere of their community, and in proximity to God's visitation at Pentecost, drew perilously near to the sin against the Holy Spirit, which the Lord denounced in the Pharisees—that deliberate and calculated hardening of the heart against the manifest action and guidance of God which constitutes a final rejection of salvation.

Both man and woman in the shocking story were in the direct lineage of Judas, who had joined the apostles' band in search of his own advantage. Their sin would not have ended with the act of deceit, for it was probably part of a plan of infiltration. Invested with a false reputation, they would find other doors to exploitation among the simple and sincere open before them. The portion they gave was an investment, a deposit so placed that advantage would come their way. Giving is not infrequently haunted by this peril.

Luke omits details of the first two funerals in the Church. No doubt there were formalities concerning death and burial but in the fashion of the Old Testament, Luke omits the irrelevant. It was a painful occasion and the narrative faces the painful facts, exposes them and has done with the sad story.

549 : The Sadducees
Acts 5.17-33

The theme passes naturally enough to the corrupt hierarchy. The Sadducees, on another social plane, were using religion for the advantage it might bring them. More successful in terms of material and worldly emolument than Ananias and Sapphira, the high-priestly group had built themselves a position of comfort and conformity.

They trimmed their doctrine and belief, as men not infrequently do, to suit their desires and preoccupations. They did not believe in any retribution in another life, doubtless because they themselves would be prime subjects for castigation. They rejected belief in any form of resurrection, because they were comfortable enough on the hither side of the grave, and desired no haunting anticipation of a changed lot on the further side.

It is shocking sometimes to observe with what facility men can adjust their convictions to accommodate their lusts. In the growing corruption of a 'permissive society', illustration enough surrounds us. And frequently it is to be observed that, in practice, the propounding of convenient doctrine first appears, invested with all the claims of honesty and sincerity, to be so rapidly followed by the exposition of consequential ethics, that the suspicion lingers that the psychological priority was the reverse.

The Sadducees needed peace in the land and all tranquillity. Their comfort lay in collaboration with the occupying powers. They saw their direct danger in some hot-headed patriot stirring the multitude to rebellion, or in some movement of nationalistic fervour to which the land was prone. Such fears, indeed were real, as the Great Rebellion of A.D. 66 to 70 was tragically to demonstrate. Fearful men are cruel men. Apprehension lies at the root of much tyranny. This century has seen great nations fall into the hands of groups of men who gain their power by destroying freedom and overriding the free spirit of man. History demonstrates that it is impossible ultimately to retain control. As Kipling put it in *The Dawn Wind:*

So when the world is asleep, and there seems no hope
of her waking

636

> *Out of some long bad dream that makes her*
> *mutter and moan,*
> *Suddenly all men arise with a sound of fetters breaking,*
> *And everyone smiles at his neighbour and tells him his*
> *soul is his own.*

History lay with the persecuted. The Sadducees disappeared.

550 : Gamaliel

Acts 5.33–42; Proverbs 2.1–15

An unexpected ally steps on to the stage. Luke had some reliable source of information concerning events in the inner counsels of the Sanhedrin. It may possibly have been John, who, on more than one occasion, shows an extraordinarily detailed knowledge of intimate debates among the hierarchy, too obviously factual in the reporting to be fiction.

The baffled religious rulers are confronted by a quiet and dignified scholar, Paul's teacher, Gamaliel (Acts 22.3). This notable person was the grandson of Hillel, the liberal Pharisee, who did much to mitigate the growing severities of the law, as the extreme legalists conceived it. Carrying on the gentler tradition of his grandfather, Gamaliel now sought to quench the persecuting passion of the priests. The Pharisees were evidently still associated in the religious courts with their rivals, the worldly-minded Sadducees, and provided a check upon their more vicious activities which we shall encounter again in the story of Paul.

What lay behind Gamaliel's intervention? It may be nothing more than that which lies clearly on the surface of the story—a wise man's caution, and a good man's concern to see that no injustice is done, no flouting of the will of God take place. He asked for time, time for passions to subside, and for truth to emerge. Gamaliel had seen enough of life, and read enough of history, to know that God sometimes moves in mysterious ways. He had perhaps seen enough of Christ Himself to convince him that here were men who followed no impostor, and that it might be well to allow the new movement to find its place in an enlightened and reformed Judaism.

On the other hand his motives may have been more complex. He could see well enough that the hate of those who counselled persecution was likely to defeat its own purpose. One perilous

637

climax was the death of Stephen, and that piece of public iniquity must have brought the Sanhedrin perilously near a Roman intervention. The fact was that the power of the Sadducean priesthood was almost out of hand, and the situation held more dangers from a sharp Roman reaction than the brief tolerance of a group of enthusiasts.

However it may have been, the Christians found an ally. God sometimes provides help in strange and unexpected places. No one had looked for aid in the counsels of the great. But here it was, in the person of a wise, humane and gracious man.

Questions and themes for study and discussion on Studies 547–550

1. Hypocrisy: its source and damaging effects.
2. Wrong reasons for Christian giving.
3. The descendants of the Sadducees.
4. The sources and consequences of persecution.

551 : The Greek Jews

Acts 6.1–8; John 7.32–36

The small group of men mentioned in v. 5 are Hellenistic Jews. The Jews of the capital with that base pride which was part of their heretical and vicious thinking, hated the Jews of the Dispersion, and looked upon them with lofty contempt. In the Church the Jews from abroad found a place, but, amid the tensions and imperfections which were already beginning to plague the community of the Christians, some differentiation, real or imagined, was marring fellowship. It says much for the wisdom and generosity of the apostles that, when they set up a committee to deal with the alleged abuse, they chose solely for its membership Jews who came from abroad.

The Greek Jews were members of the multitude of communities overseas which functioned in Gentile environments. The local synagogues were the centre of their lives, and there the Laws were honoured and the prophets read. They could not, however, escape the influence of the surrounding community. The spirit of enquiry, the ingrained liberalism, which characterized the Greeks in centres, for example, like Alexandria, where Jew and Greek almost shared the city, was bound to modify a rigid legalism, and to dampen the hotter enthusiasm for Judaism.

The Jews of the Dispersion were not only bilingual, they were bi-cultural. Paul's speech in Athens (Acts 17) contains numerous allusions to Greek thought and liberalism, the first four chapters of the first letter to Corinth similarly contain a dozen references to Greek philosophy, not deliberately thrust in but as natural allusion as though they were a part of normal thinking. The Greek Jews, in short, demonstrate a better, a wider, and a more liberal education than that which the metropolitan Jews had enjoyed.

Luke introduces the group with a set purpose in mind. Stephen was of their number, and Stephen is to be prominent in the next chapter. And Stephen is to be the link, in both event and teaching, with the great man, his teacher and friend, Paul, whom Luke is preparing to be the principal figure of the latter half of his book. Without Paul there might have been no lasting Gentile Christianity, and Paul was a Jew of the Dispersion.

Their function, first, is that of social workers amid the activities of the Church. Preaching was to take over, and hold pre-eminence in at least two of the number listed here—Philip and Stephen. Opposition, as the next movement of the story shows, rose from their own number, members of two overseas synagogues, and Paul's own story was to demonstrate this stratum of hostility outside Jerusalem. In more ways than one the great writer is linking his story together.

552 : Stephen the Historian

Acts 7.1–53

Stephen's faith was grounded in history. So is ours. Hence the extreme importance of firm, strong teaching of the Bible. The faith stands or falls with the reliability of the record. The same need for historical knowledge applies to the life of nations. History, interpreted in their Old Testament, kept the Jewish nation alive through the vicissitudes of their harassed centuries. History is so vital to a people's self-consciousness that, for a nation to lose contact with its past, its struggles and its achievements, is to lose a source of its strength and its survival.

It is not without significance that the study of history is under manifold attack today, and that régimes anxious for the survival of some form of tyranny or dominance give nervous attention

639

to the slanting and distortion of history, and the suppression of truth.

Stephen, strong-minded, aware of a wider world and supremely intelligent, had grasped the vital fact that what had happened in Palestine was a climax and a consummation of a vast sweep of history, which began with the call of Abraham from Ur of the Chaldees. He tells the story in fascinating detail, stressing the relevance of events. He would agree with the contention that history is not as the Marxist views it, an interplay of economic forces, but properly biography, the work of notable men. He traces an unfolding purpose of God, but subtly stresses the spiritual ancestry of the group he had before him, ready to resist the Lord who sought to save them, and prompt to persecute even Moses who set out to deliver them.

In fact, Abraham, of whose lineage they boasted, and Moses, in whom they trusted, form Stephen's central theme. He knew how to bring history into focus and application. And all with an eloquence which breathes through the whole oration, for it was no less, brought to stinging conclusion in the last three verses. Stephen was a brave man, and his courage was used in a manner he could not have foreseen. It did not save his life, but he died like Christ, at the same hands as those which slew 'the Just One'. He was the first of the host which the Book of Common Prayer calls 'the noble army of martyrs', and if ever there was illustration that 'the blood of the martyrs is the seed of the Church' it was true that day outside Saint Stephen's Gate.

553 : Sanhedrists

Acts 7.54–60; 8.1–4; Matthew 26.57–68

The wild tempest of emotion which swept round the semicircle of seats is difficult for us to imagine. The gnashing of the teeth (54) and the shrieks of the assembly as the members of the august court clapped hands on ears and rushed on the offender make a scene of bestial behaviour hard to parallel. Was Stephen surprised? He sought to stab the audience to wakefulness, and to some awareness of their sin. He must have known in a moment that he had failed. Perhaps he was accustomed to the frank debates of Greek communities. In Athens Paul met rejection, irony, some mirth and polite indifference. The passion of this band of dignitaries, erupting into shocking violence, may have been a reaction which a polished Hellenist had not thought to encounter.

He knew at once that he was doomed, and about to suffer what his Lord had suffered three or four years before. Hence the words reminiscent of Calvary (59 f.). He tried to be like Christ in death as he had sought to be like Him in life. It is impossible to tell why the normal processes of law were so wantonly by-passed in the hot madness of the moment. The Jews had no power of life and death. The Sanhedrin, preoccupied as its collaborating members were with correct conduct towards the Romans, were either driven to such fury that they forgot a careful policy, or at the moment Roman authority was in some phase of retreat. Rome was baffled in Palestine. The Jews were their most dangerous subjects. They were trying to hold the land with half a legion, and it was common policy, save at festival periods, to avoid too obvious a military presence in Jerusalem. Perhaps Rome was holding its collaborating allies at this time with a light and unobtrusive hand. We do not know, but the crowds in the streets must have looked with wonder at the priestly aristocrats dragging one bleeding battered man to death.

The Lord had spoken sombre truth about His foes. Consciously and in the face of God, they had rejected Him. When such a sin is deliberately committed, it is difficult to tell where evil will end. Violence, hatred which inspires violence, the bodily distortions which demonstrate the possessing force of evil, the abandonment in wild words and vicious action of all semblance of gentleness and humanity, all these sights of wickedness beyond all healing demonstrate the truth of the Lord's awful condemnation. They had committed sin unpardonable.

554 : Saul

Acts 7.58; Philippians 3.4–11

At any given moment of history it is difficult for anyone to estimate the ultimate significance of the situation. It is in retrospect that the truth appears. In looking back Luke saw that the entrance on to the stage of history of one of the greatest men of all time was the fact that gave final meaning to the martyrdom of Stephen.

It would appear that Saul, as he was then called, was not swept away by the sanguinary torrent of mob violence which disgraced the assembly. To be sure, he cast his vote against the Christian (26.10) and in the midst of the scene of crime was not averse to the violence done (8.1). But he appears to have retained a shred of dignity. He threw no stone, but stood apart in such conspicuous inaction, that the Sanhedrists who flung off their garments to dash boulders on the helpless man, placed them for safe keeping at Saul's feet.

The young man Saul, as Luke describes him, may have been thirty years or more old. Josephus uses the same Greek word of Agrippa the Second when the king was forty. To be a member of the Sanhedrin, a man was required to have reached years of discretion (Deut. 1.13–16). Requirements in Rabbinical literature vary. In the Mishna it is said that, for such office, a man must not be a dicer, a usurer, a pigeon-flyer or a violator of the Sabbath. In later writers it is laid down that he must be without bodily blemish, stainless in character, learned in science, acquainted with more than one language, and with a family of his own, because a husband and a parent might be supposed less inclined to harshness and to cruelty than those without wife and children.

It is impossible to say whether Saul was at this time, or had been, a married man, though there is a strong likelihood that such was the case. A man of maturity and responsibility he certainly was, or he would not have been a voting member of the chief religious court of Jewry, and would not have been entrusted by the hierarchy with the commission which took him on his errand of persecution to Damascus.

As he stood and watched the stoning he was a tormented man. In Athens he echoed a word from Stephen's speech, and the whole scene must have shocked, impressed and deeply convicted him. He refers to it no less than eight times. That he continued passionately to ravage the Church is no argument to the contrary. A convicted man sometimes contrives to crush conviction in fierce activity.

555 : Philip the Evangelist
Acts 8.5–12, 26–29, 40; 21.1–9

Philip was one of the Seven—men chosen as 'deacons' to deal with the social work of the Church. It is of some interest to note that such activity was not intended to be a substitute for preaching the gospel, because, after the first mention of his name in ch. 6, Philip appears exclusively in the role of evangelist. Luke was entertained by him at Caesarea, as Paul was making his last journey to Jerusalem (21.8; 'we'), and it was then, no doubt, that these incidents were recounted to the historian. They met with deep interest, for Philip, a Hellenistic Jew, appeared to anticipate the office of Paul as an 'apostle to the Gentiles'.

He went to Samaria, in this context apparently the old capital of Ahab. In the days of the first Herod, a temple to Augustus had been located here, a monument to the policy of collaboration with Rome which marked the Herodian house. A centre more pagan it would have been difficult to discover. Here Philip preached with power and effectiveness, and seems to have won from a superstition-ridden population the nucleus of a strong church.

Under the urge of God, Philip then travelled half the length of Palestine, for his encounter with the Ethiopian on the desert highway through Gaza. The vivid story shows how thoroughly the quick mind of the Hellenists had grasped the recent significance of the Old Testament oracles. Luke has already repeated Stephen's historical survey at length. He now stresses, in the story of Philip, an approach to the Old Testament which was characteristic of Paul. Luke shows here one of his aims of authorship. He insists that his friend Paul had not taken a movement of the Spirit directed to the Jews, and turned it illegitimately into a world religion. He did no more than others had initiated. Note, too, how he stresses the approval of the Jerusalem church in the movement in Samaria, and involves Peter and John in the activity of Philip. Later Philip settled in the garrison town of Caesarea, where he fulfilled a settled ministry aided by his gifted daughters.

What happened to this able, energetic and faithful man is not known, but it is good to meet this member of the first diaconate, active in mass evangelism, equally concerned for the individual seeker, the hospitable head of a household, knowledgeable, gracious, a pattern in all that makes for true leadership in the community of Christ.

556 : Simon

Acts 8.9–24; Matthew 27.1–5

Simon was a sorcerer, who, like other religious charlatans, had taken to himself a high-sounding name, 'the power of God which is called Great' (8.10). Whether his conversion was genuine it is impossible to say. He has been regarded as an impostor throughout, both before and after a sham conversion, but the fact that Simon, after a fierce denunciation from Peter, repented and humbly asked for prayer, may indicate that his conversion was a real experience of Christ. If so, the total of his wickedness was that he thought the gifts of God could be bought with money. The matter caused considerable debate in the early Church and all manner of strange myths were woven around his name. A century later than the story in Acts, Justin Martyr found cause to attack Marcion as a follower and descendant of Simon. Justin, however, did not question the fundamental Christianity of Marcion's followers. The later legends about Simon need not concern us. What is sadly significant is that a defective or deviant Christianity can perpetuate itself with increasing decay, through many generations, and it is Simon's sombre reputation to have initiated evil within the Church.

He did more. He gave his name to a new vice, one of life's deepest dishonours; 'simony' came from Simon's name, just as 'sadism' came from the name of the execrable Marquis de Sade. Simony is the crime of selling ecclesiastical benefits and preferments, traffic in spiritual things, the subject of an Act of Parliament as late as 1898. Money can form a root of all manner of evil, and money is a vile thing when it intrudes into sacred places. It should be handled with care, for love of money, like pride and other vices, can insinuate itself into the careless mind, and turn the very act of giving into a transaction with God, a fact, as was remarked above (Study 547), that those who sponsor stewardship and other such campaigns in the Christian Church should bear carefully in mind. It is fatally easy to damage a soul as Simon's was damaged.

Simon is said to have emigrated to Rome in Claudius' time (A.D. 41–54) and there to have founded an heretical sect, which held him in high honour—a personality cult which was attacked by Peter. Of this there is no certainty. It is sad to see the vices of unregeneracy carried into an uncertain Christian life.

557 : The Ethiopian
Acts 8.27–39; Isaiah 53

The treasurer of the Queen of Ethiopia ('Candace' is a generic term like 'Pharaoh' and 'Caesar', and simply means 'Queen') was a proselyte to Judaism. The Ethiopia mentioned was the kingdom of Meroe on the Nile, in the modern Sudan. The Greeks who ruled Egypt after the partition of Alexander's empire, had penetrated the southern reaches of the Nile, and Greek, the second language of the eastern Mediterranean, was known there. It was the Greek Old Testament that the Ethiopian civil servant was reading, after a pilgrimage to Jerusalem. Luke tells the story vividly and well, and again with an evangelistic purpose in mind. The Ethiopians, from Homer's day, eight centuries earlier, were commonly referred to as 'the dwellers on the uttermost fringes of the world'. Luke saw one fulfilment of the Lord's last prophecy (1.8). He may also have had Psa. 68.31 and Isa. 11.11 in mind, when he heard and wrote the story.

We can see something of the man himself in the account. He was reading, as was commonly done, aloud, and in no way resented the question from someone who did not belong to his own entourage. He was quietly gracious and courteous, with no sense of his own importance. He invited Philip to join him in the chariot. He was also an obvious seeker after truth, and listened carefully to what his new acquaintance had to say on the Scripture which had puzzled him. Once convinced, he acted immediately, translating into action the faith which had been born in him. He is altogether pleasing as a person, for all his brief appearance in the story.

We should gladly know more. The man had probably bought the roll of Isaiah in Jerusalem as an inspiring souvenir of his visit. Had he heard of the activities of the Church on the same occasion? What became of him and his book? Ethiopian tradition claims him as the land's first evangelist, but nothing is really known, save that one so gracious, eager in his response, and earnest in his search for a faith by which to live, can be confidently marked as a propagator of the blessing he had won. Luke has made his point. The gospel was deep in Africa.

Questions and themes for study and discussion on Studies 551–557

1. Christianity and social work. Its purpose and perils.
2. How far is it true that Christianity is based in history and cannot abandon that heritage?
3. Why did men die for Christ?
4. Why did Saul play a passive part at Stephen's death?
5. Philip's type of evangelism.
6. How, if at all, does simony show itself today?

7. In what passage besides ch. **53** does Isaiah foreshadow Christ?

558 : Man from Tarsus

Acts 8.1–3; 9.1–9

We have noted Luke's habit of allowing a fleeting, but always significant glimpse of a character about to take a leading place, at some earlier point in the narrative. Paul was born at Tarsus in Cilicia, a fact which he himself notes with civic pride. Tarsus was an ancient city, the seat of a provincial governor when Persia ruled, and, in the days of the Greek Syrian kings, the centre of a lumbering and linen industry. During the first century before Christ the city was the home of a philosophical school, a university town, in a word, where the intellectual atmosphere would be coloured by Greek thought.

Tarsus stood, like Alexandria, at a confluence of East and West. The wisdom of the Greeks, and the world-order of Rome, mingled with the good and ill of Oriental mysticism, were deep in its consciousness. A keen-minded Jew, born and bred at Tarsus, would draw the best from more than one world. He would catch the flavour of western thought, and learn to appreciate the Graeco–Roman outlook. He was also in touch with the strong bases of his own tradition. For such a man the synagogue would be no place of refuge from an alien society. There is evidence enough of a missionary zeal among such Jews which prepared the way for Christianity. The Greek translation of the Old Testament stands as a monument to their enthusiasm in Alexandria, and we have already observed the fresh and vigorous minds which Stephen and Philip brought to Christian evangelism.

It was one of the best minds of Jewry, and indeed of the century, which burned with hatred against the Christians. Saul thought like a Greek, and felt like a Jew. He was trained at Gamaliel's feet as well as in the Greek schools of Tarsus. He also knew Rome, which, as a member of a family which had had Roman citizenship for perhaps two centuries, must have been an influence in his civic, social and international awareness. Paul drew his great knowledge of the law from Gamaliel, who was a liberally minded Pharisee. He drew the deep fanaticism, which moved him at this vital time, from the right wing of the Pharisees, which had more in common with the Sadducees. But it was a deeply tormented man who took the road to Damascus that day. The death of Stephen had done more to influence him than his passionate mind was prepared to admit.

559 : The Persecutor

Philippians 3 ; Acts 26.1–11

Someone has suggested that Saul's zeal at the time of Stephen's prosecution and death had led to his election to the Sanhedrin, or at least to the judicial part he seems now to have been chosen to play. He was appointed chief inquisitor for Damascus. The high priest in Jerusalem had no real authority over the Damascus synagogues, but the very stoning of Stephen was a demonstration that Roman rule, as we have seen, always compromised by a desire not to provoke unnecessarily the most passionate of the Eastern dependencies, was at this time passing through a weak phase. It is impossible to pinpoint the fault, for lack of exact knowledge about the date, but the Sanhedrists were acting with impudent high-handedness.

At any rate, it would appear that the Damascus synagogues still held their Christian minorities. The Christians were still dubbed the People of the Way, a reference, perhaps to John 14.6. It was the task of Saul to awaken the synagogue heads to the peril in their midst, provoke the local rabbis to action, and to bring suspects, at their instance, to Jerusalem for trial. It is often the manner of the persecutor to feel insecure in the presence of dissent, and to feel a need to stir others to his own depth of passion. The Sanhedrin did not realize how fragile their officer's conviction had become.

Two roads led to Damascus. Paul could descend to the coastal plain and join the road from Egypt, an ancient caraavn route which ran due north, past Megiddo, across Esdraelon, and then strike east across the Jordan north of the Galilee lake. The second, went up through Samaria, following the hilly spine of the land, crossed the Jordan south of the lake near Bethshan, and ran either through or near Gadara, over the Golan Heights which have featured so prominently in recent conflicts, and cut north-east, through hot and arid territory, to Damascus. This was in all likelihood the road which Saul followed, for it was the faster, and so more fitting to his mad mood. Somewhere along this road Saul met Christ, and the encounter changed not only his own life but the course of history. The story is told three times by Luke, a certain indication that his historian's mind saw the supreme importance of an event which put the Damascus Road into universal metaphor.

560 : Saul's Conversion

Acts 26.1–25

What shattered Paul's resistance? Ramsay, the great commentator on Luke, believed that Saul was so sure that the impostor was dead, that, when Stephen's dying vision was repeated in his experience, the whole ground of his hostility crumbled beneath his feet. He saw, he heard, he knew—he could only surrender. God does not usually deal thus with men. In His grace He sometimes reveals truth with special clarity, but not to complete and implacable hostility; rather to bewilderment, however despairing, and to nascent conviction, however overlaid, repressed and beaten down.

It is rather as S. H. Mellone says, that 'the moment of a conversion may seem quite sudden and unexpected; but experience shows that such a fundamental and abrupt occurrence always has a long period of unconscious "incubation" ... Let us observe again the case of that conversion which changed the history of the world. St. Paul had for long been deeply impressed by his experience of the devotion of the Christians whom he persecuted. Perhaps it would not be going too far to say that he had already been a Christian for a long time but unconsciously; and just for that reason his fanaticism against the Christians increased; for in personalities of this type, fanaticism exists as a compensation for, and in conflict with, secret doubts.'

These words ring true to the situation. Paul's furious persecution finds its explanation in a wild desire to silence conscience by zealous action. He was trying to fill life and stifle thought. Along the desolate road east of Galilee, he had time to think. He was alone with the haunting memory of Stephen's death. Stephen's survey of Hebrew history rang like an echo in his brain. Conscience pricked, and the pressure of God's Word, God's Spirit was upon him. Hence the phrase: 'It is hard for you to kick against the pricks'—a homely phrase in the very style, and in the very tone perhaps of Jesus of Nazareth. It exactly summed up what Paul was doing, thinking, feeling at that hot midday.

J. S. Stewart lists the pricks strikingly: There was first Saul's own growing sense of the failure of Judaism. His religion had not brought him peace with God. Hence the fury of his attack on the new sect. Action might relieve his brooding. Then there was the fact of the historic Jesus. The Pharisees had watched the Lord's ministry carefully. As an honest man Saul could not brush aside the evidence of something extraordinary. Third, he had to account for the lives of the Christians, and, fourth, there was the death of Stephen.

561 : Ananias of Damascus

Acts 9.10–22

The gentle man in Straight Street, who looked after the stricken persecutor, was called to a great act of faith. The Church owes much to the brotherliness of Ananias. The natural attitude of the Christians, so recently the objects of dire persecution at the hands of the powerful Pharisee, might well be, what it proved to be in Jerusalem itself years later, one of suspicion and deep distrust. What if this 'conversion' was really a trick to discover and unmask any Christians still lingering in the capital of Jewry? The sponsorship of the brave and gentle Barnabas availed him there, but Barnabas followed Ananias of Damascus, who had no evidence of a successful ministry to hostile Jews to convince him when he was first called upon to minister to the shattered Pharisee. Paul perhaps remembered both men when he wrote long years later: 'Love believes all things . . .'

Once Ananias was given his difficult commission, he took it up with zeal. He asked no searching and probing questions, undertook no inquisition. He approached his one-time enemy with open-hearted graciousness: 'Brother Saul,' he said, and in the one astonishing vocative was the forgiveness for which Saul yearned, the promise of friendship to a man who, in one blinding moment, had lost every friend he had, and acceptance in return for the rejection which he now knew would be his part. Ananias fed a hungry soul with the nourishment it needed most.

Stephen by his death was the first great formative influence in the new convert's Christian life. The martyr's valour and faith went far to break the persecutor's resistance. Ananias was the second great formative influence. His character showed the broken man what Christ can do to the life in which He comes to

649

dwell. He gives courage, for it sometimes requires bravery to forgive. He gives love, for we pardon only as we love. He brings joy, for it is correct, as someone said, that he who has never richly forgiven has lacked the greatest joy life has to give. Ananias was a 'man of Christ', before the Antiochenes gave the 'people of the Way' that descriptive name (11.26). His trust was rapidly vindicated among the Christians of Damascus, who must at first have looked upon the initiative of Ananias with some trepidation.

562 : The Fugitive

Acts 9.23–31; Galatians 1.15–24; 2 Corinthians 11.32, 33

To become a Christian does not clear life's problems away. It often increases them. Evil seldom fails to take up the challenge of a changed and converted life. Paul was immediately in danger and seems, after his hazardous and dramatic escape from Damascus over the city wall, to have spent many years as a refugee. No experience of life is, however, wasted. With a slow and splendid deliberateness God forged and tempered the splendid tool of Paul's superb mind, which He needed for the production of so much doctrine, and for the vast assault upon the pagan world which was to be this one man's tremendous responsibility.

Paul appears from Luke's account to have proceeded to Jerusalem and sought contact with the Church. This is to take no account of the manner in which Luke, when it affects his major theme, is prepared ruthlessly to abbreviate. He knew when to cut, a virtue for which both writers and preachers should most earnestly pray. We can, however, in this case fill in the gaps. Paul told the Galatians that he withdrew into Arabia, though what he did there or how he was maintained is not revealed. It would seem that he sought readjustment, and thought out under the Spirit's guidance that synthesis of the Testaments which was to be his great contribution to the Bible. When withdrawal is enforced by circumstances, the opportunity should be faced and diagnosed. We have seen it in Moses, in Abraham, in Joseph. Withdrawal is followed by return.

Paul returned to Damascus for three years' ministry. He had found acceptance there. It was his 'Jerusalem'. He then went up to the Holy City, met Barnabas, and found his way back at last to his old family haunts in his native Cilicia—the most difficult of all places in which he could appear as a Christian. If a man is a new man it is best that those who know him best should see it. The main door was not yet open. At length it would swing wide, and the events of many years, which to this point may have seemed chaotic, would assume coherence, unity and significance. So it is often in life. At last the traveller tops a rise, looks back, and sees the landscape in shape and contour. In the vision the crooked becomes straight and the rough places plain.

Questions and themes for study and discussion on Studies 558–562

1. What is fanaticism?
2. What is conversion? Need it be dated, sudden, complete?
3. What 'pricks' do men still kick against?
4. 'The People of the Way'—what does this mean and imply?
5. The virtues of brevity.

563 : Lady of Lydda

Acts 9.31–43; Luke 8.49–56

The two passages for reading are set side by side to demonstrate the unity of authorship of Luke's Gospel and Acts. Peter followed his Master's pattern in clearing the room before he turned to the act of healing. But observe, too, Luke's careful mind at work in this ordering of the whole story. Paul has now moved to the centre of the stage, and is soon to occupy it alone. Luke, however, regards it as important that all who read should realize that it was not Paul, but Peter, who opened the door to the Gentiles. The old Philistine coast was heavily Gentile in population, and Peter's move into that territory was a deliberate journey outside exclusively Jewish areas of evangelism.

Moreover, Luke was anxious to show that Peter had not made this move to a wider ministry in any hesitant change of policy, but of deliberate intent, and also in the full tide of his apostolic activity. Hence the two acts of healing, both signs that God's sanction lay upon his doings at this time. Peter was authenticated by deeds like his Lord's.

But to return to the story of the gracious Dorcas. Lydda is Lod, an outer suburb of Tel Aviv, and the location of the international airport of Israel. Joppa is a close coastal suburb of the same great Israeli city. In the first century, the two places, Lydda and Joppa, were apart and distinct. In the little town, Dorcas was loved for her good deeds. Named after the beautiful, gentle creature of the desert, the gazelle, she demonstrated the spirit of her Lord in doing what her busy hands could do.

It is a story full of circumstantial detail. Outside Jerusalem a body could remain unburied for three days and nights. In Jerusalem, as was illustrated in the case of Ananias and Sapphira, no corpse could lay overnight. The weeping women, as a subtle touch in the Greek verb seems to indicate, were wearing the garments that Dorcas had made. Note too the natural touch of the woman's gradual return to visible life.

Acts of charity were part of the witness of the early Christians. They were active in preaching, and passionate in their proclamation of the Word, as every page in the book so far has demonstrated. Attention to the needs of the unfortunate and the destitute was, none the less, considered an obligation, and in some cases, a consuming and potent mode of witness. Dorcas was one who heard such a call.

564 : The Centurion
Acts 10.1–8, 19–48

Cornelius was a senior centurion in command of an élite cohort attached to the Palestine command. Caesarea was the Roman garrison town and port of entry to the land, a fine fortress, scene of a government residence and seat of government. We have remarked before that the type of centurion who appears in the New Testament, suggests that the Romans seconded only responsible and able men to the difficult task of duty in the Palestinian area. It was a sensitive territory, excitable, and one which needed strong but tactful handling.

Perhaps men who found Judaism attractive were assigned to such a post. Such allegiance crops up in many odd corners of surviving literature. A member of the Flavian family, for example, was accused of 'going astray after the customs of the Jews', and Juvenal writes with scorn of one who accepts Jewish food taboos and circumcision,

> And, taught the Roman ritual to deride,
> Clings to the Jewish, and observes with awe
> All Moses bade in his mysterious law.

For all the contempt of Roman satirists and historians, an earnest minority of dissatisfied pagans had found in the Septuagint and the synagogue a satisfaction for the soul denied them in the state cults and mystery religions. We meet them repeatedly in the New Testament and again and again find them ripe for the message of the gospel, and free by nature from those inhibitions which made it so difficult for the Jews to see beyond a national religion.

There were many in the world of rampant paganism and corrupt religion who sought truth. Greeks came to Jesus, and a centurion of Capernaum was the first Gentile to receive the benediction of the Lord (Luke 7). A hunger was abroad, as it is today, and God's Spirit is not confined. Guided probably by what he knew of the Old Testament, Cornelius had done what lay to his hand. He had given to the needs of the unfortunate. He had sought God's mind in prayer. He had sought, apparently with success, to lead his household along the same upright path. Such aspiration was rewarded. The seeker finds. He who moves earnestly towards God finds that God moves to meet him. John 7.17 declares, and the truth is fundamental, that one who seeks the will of God for his life is led inevitably towards an understanding of truth. Cornelius is a prime illustration of the Lord's words.

565 : Peter at Joppa
Acts 10.9–19; 11.1–18

Tel Aviv lies like any great coastal city of the world, tall and glassy along its beach, part of that open coast which harbour-builders have sought to tame since Jonah found a ship at Joppa. Joppa, a sombre contrast with the Israeli city, still stands on its shore where coastal reefs once gave a minimum of protection for mariners. It is an old port of the Philistines, and the house of Simon the tanner is still shown above the sea.

The tanner was a kindly man, but in the eyes of Jews unclean because of his trade in skins. He was no doubt a little awed by Peter's visit, and spread a leather awning, hung by its four corners, on the roof where the cool wind blew in from the Mediterranean, and there, weary from his long journey down from Jerusalem, Peter lay on his couch, prayed, and like many who pray in weariness of body, fell asleep.

It was 'a trance', say the common versions. The word is

actually 'ecstasy' and means that the dreamer is in that half-waking half-sleeping state in which reality is withdrawn and the objects around assume a significance and form other than the real. Peter had no doubt reflected on the strange situation in which he found himself. We have Paul's own testimony (Gal. 2.11 f.) that his colleague found it difficult to divest himself of Jewish prejudices, and it was for Christ's sake only that Peter lodged with the tanner, with the hides of 'unclean' beasts about the place. And in his mood of 'ecstasy' the awning above may well have become the stuff of his vision, 'a sheet knit at the four corners' and let down from heaven. Out of such homely material was fashioned the imagery of the dream which was to have vast historic consequences. Luke set such store by it that he followed his practice of repetition. The story is repeated in Peter's report to the Jerusalem church.

It remained only for Peter to travel up the coast to the vastly different port of Caesarea, and to put into practice that which he had been shown in the house of Simon the tanner. Observe the precision with which Peter summarizes the story of Christ and testifies to the reality of the resurrection. And it was Peter who thus used his keys (Matt. 16.19) and opened the door to the Gentiles.

566 : The Antiochenes

Acts 11.19–30; 13.1–3

Three hundred miles north of Jerusalem lay the first 'city of refuge' of the Church, the Syrian Antioch. The great Greek city is first mentioned in the list of 'deacons' appointed to organize the charitable activities of the little community. Nicolaus, one of their number, was a 'proselyte of Antioch' (6.5). Nicolaus was a Greek, one of the many aliens who had been attracted to the worship of the synagogue. The synagogue was active in Antioch, where there was a large and ancient colony of Jews.

It was perhaps the influence of Nicolaus which led many Jerusalem Christians to migrate to Antioch before the persecution which fell upon the Church after the martyrdom of Stephen. The new arrivals confined their activities to the ghetto, but Jews from Cyprus, who came soon afterwards, in a second wave of displaced Christians, adopted more liberal policies, and preached to the Greeks (20). There was considerable interest, and a strong

Christian community emerged. The Jerusalem church, exercising its role of leadership, despatched Barnabas, himself a Cypriot, to look into the situation (21 f.).

Barnabas, an intelligent and liberal man, was quick to see the strength and promise of the movement, and by one of the great historic acts of history, he sought Saul in Tarsus, and established him in Antioch. A momentous year of ministry from two notable men rapidly consolidated the Antiochene church (23–26). Its first act of public policy was to demonstrate its unity with the Jerusalem community when the great famine of Claudius' principate fell with peculiar severity on the impoverished Christians of Judea (27–30).

It was at this time that the Christians first found their name. Previously, where they had been recognized at all as a dissident sect, they had been known as 'the People of the Way' (cf. 9.2). It could have been the well-known nicknaming and satirical propensity of the Antiochenes which coined the term. It is likely that it was the invention of some clerk of the Roman administration, who sought a classification for a new group which had come under bureaucratic notice. Thus came into language the honoured name we claim. It remains to adorn it.

The Christians of Antioch were an independent group, who retained the stamp of an early Pauline ministry. It was the church at Antioch which first initiated planned missionary enterprise (13.1 ff.). Just as significantly, it was the Antioch deputation which won from the Jerusalem leaders those vital concessions which made Gentile membership of the Church possible (15.1–21). The Antioch church must have been a good church to know, friendly, enterprising, united, zealous and out to win the world.

567 : Herod

Acts 12.1–4, 19–23; Proverbs 29.1–5

Herod Agrippa I, grandson of the scoundrel Herod 'the Great', who murdered the children of Bethlehem, had grown up in Rome where he had been the friend of Caligula, the third emperor, who had followed Tiberius, and he had done well out of his imperial connections. Claudius, the middle-aged and learned spastic who followed Caligula, had also responded to Herod's diplomatic charms, and, in fact the Jewish prince had played a small part in

655

Claudius' accession to the principate. Hence the addition of Judea and Samaria to the territory which Caligula had granted him. This was the tetrarchy of Philip (Luke 3.1), later extended by the further assignment of Galilee and Perea, the old domain of Herod Antipas. The title of 'king' accompanied Caligula's appointment. Notorious in Rome for his prodigality and extravagance, in Judea Herod posed as a champion of the Law. The attack on the Church was no doubt a policy move to gratify and conciliate the old Pharisaic and Sadducean enemies of the Church.

It therefore follows that Peter's imprisonment comes naturally after the events of the previous chapter. The hierarchy had their spies, and must have heard of a new outbreak of activity following Peter's mission at Joppa. Perhaps they had heard of the apostle's appearance in Caesarea. Just as they thought matters were settling down, here was a new outbreak of the nuisance, which they hoped was being contained and absorbed by Judaism. They took fright. Word reached the king, and a new outbreak of persecution followed. It was the time of the Passover, so trial and execution were delayed for seven days. We shall resume that story in Study 568.

Luke takes us back to Caesarea for the grisly story of Herod's end. The Phoenician coast, given to seagoing and maritime trade, depended on the hinterland, as in Ahab's day, for primary produce, and division was serious. Herod, at the instance of the bribed Blastus, met a large delegation in the theatre at Caesarea. It has been restored, and one may sit there today imagining the scene. The king, says Josephus, came in dressed in glittering silver cloth. The material may still be bought in Lebanon, and was probably a Tyrian gift. The excitement stirred by the Phoenician adulation was too much for an ill man. He was, says the Greek, 'wormeaten', a medical term describing the fearful, visible appearance of violent and agonizing peristalsis which accompanied his intestinal malady. It was a gruesome end to an evil life. He was fifty-four years of age but senile in his sin.

568 : James the Martyr

Mark 10.35–45; Revelation 3.21, 22; Acts 12.1–3

The lives of two brothers can follow widely different paths. James, son of Zebedee, was to be the first apostolic martyr, the

656

victim of an evil man's schemes to win popular support. John, his brother fisherman, was to die in Ephesus, sixty years on. James, or Jacob, to give him his Hebrew name, was the son of Salome (Matt. 27.56; Mark 15.40), and just possibly a cousin of the Lord. Hence, perhaps, the bizarre desire to share the Lord's royalty in the earthly kingdom which the brothers and their mother imagined.

James, John, Andrew and Peter seem to have formed a special group, and James was perhaps the most prominent Christian in Jerusalem at the time. James was killed, and Peter, later arrested, owed his life to the intervention of the formalities of Passover week. It was between the years A.D. 41 and 44, the span of Herod's reign. Many years, therefore lie between the martyrdom of James and his last recorded activities which are scattered through the Gospel narratives and are worth an hour's study.

James and his brother John shared a whimsical name given by the Lord (Mark 3.17)—'the sons of thunder'. This must refer to a passionate disposition and vehemence which, to be used, must be disciplined and contained. As F. W. H. Myers wrote:

> He as he wills shall solder and shall sunder,
> Slay in a day and quicken in an hour;
> Tune him a music from the Sons of Thunder,
> Forge and transform my passion into power.

Indeed all our quirks of temperament and individuality can be bent into vices or exalted into virtue. Take a concordance and observe the situations in which James appears. He had the rigidity of a sectarian, unworthy personal ambition, and yet was trusted with the Lord's intimacy, and gave his life for his Master.

And so the criminal record of the Herods continued. The first of the name murdered the babes of Bethlehem. The second murdered John the Baptist, and the third James the apostle. James withstood to the end. Herbert Lockyer suggests perceptively that the prayer of Acts 4.24–30 was the utterance of James—full of steadfastness, ringing with the triumph of the Old Testament psalm, and calling for courage. James leaves us with this page. Others continued. It is always so.

657

569 : Peter at the Door

Acts 12.4–18

The story of Peter's peril and escape is a human little piece, full of touches of reality. The breathless tiptoe progress past the guards, the desperate prayer-meeting in the house of Mark's mother Mary, the girl Rose (Rhoda) who came nervously to peep and forgot to open, the unbelief of the household before prayer so promptly answered, all make the most natural of stories.

Note Peter's business-like directions before his prompt departure for a securer hiding-place. James (17), the Lord's brother, was evidently regarded as the head of the Church now, and James, once hostile towards Jesus, was surely a living testimony to the reality of the resurrection. It was no myth or hallucination in the dawn which convinced this strong man . . .

They watched the muffled figure of the apostle slip away into the shadows down the street. No one knows where he went. What was 'another place'? He was, in fact, stepping out of the story which his personality had dominated so long. He now makes way for Paul. Did he go to Antioch? We know that he spent some time there, and probably came from Antioch to the momentous conference of Acts 15. See Gal. 2.11.

Did he go to Corinth? He seems to have had wide influence in that early Christian community, to the extent that an ill-advised group called themselves 'Cephas' party' (1 Cor. 1.12). Perhaps he lived in the isthmus town with his wife (1 Cor. 9.5) who seems to have accompanied him wherever he went. Some say he went to Rome, and an ancient tradition says that he spent twenty-five years there. There is no firm evidence, important though tradition is. Recent archaeological work under San Pietro claims to have found the apostle's grave.

Luke has made his point. The great missionary outreach of the Church began with Peter, the great leader who had held the community together by the strength of his leadership and the firmness of his testimony to the resurrection. We should be glad to know more about him, but that is not the purpose of Scripture. It is as John said: 'These things are written that you may believe'—not that curiosity may be satisfied. That is why the Acts of Peter now becomes the Acts of Paul, and the acts of both are sufficiently fused in purpose and in action for Luke to send the hurrying figure down the dark street and into a world which still had unrecorded work for him to do. He went with God's blessing and the love of all in the house where Rhoda failed in gladness to slip back the bolt.

Questions and themes for study and discussion on Studies 563–569

1. Charity. Why the name? How has the word changed?
2. What is 'a seeker after truth'?
3. 'Touch not the unclean thing.' Relate this to the story in Acts 10.
4. The significance of the word 'Christian'.
5. What of 'prophecy' today?
6. Fear and persecution.
7. '. . . bent into vices or exalted into virtues . . .'
8. Peter's contribution to the Church.

570 : Barnabas

Acts 4.36, 37; 9.26, 27; 11.22–26; 13.1–3

The scattered passages set for reading are important, for they reveal the part a good and gracious man played in the ministry of the great apostle to the Gentiles. Barnabas seems to have been a Jew from abroad who found Christ along with such men as Stephen and Philip in the first apostolic preaching in Jerusalem. Spiritually and culturally he had some kinship with Paul and was able to dispel suspicion about the converted Pharisee, and lead the Church to the recognition of his worth. There is a ministry for unselfish, large-hearted men in this sphere. They must be men prepared to play the second fiddle well, a test of magnanimity which not everyone can pass.

Barnabas was 'a good man, and full of the Holy Spirit and of faith'. No finer testimony could be accorded any Christian. The rustic population of Lystra, thinking Barnabas and Paul were divine visitants, gave the premier position to Barnabas. They called him Zeus, a testimony to his dignity, bearing and stature. John Bunyan probably built his Mr. Greatheart on the tradition of Barnabas. They show others the way . . . 'The Interpreter then called a manservant of his, one Greatheart, and bade him take sword, helmet and shield: "And take these my daughters," he said, "and conduct them to the house called Beautiful where they will rest next." So he took his weapons and went before them . . .'

They are found behind many great men, these promoters of others' good and usefulness. Philip Melancthon had the first vision of the Reformation. It was left to his friend Martin Luther to take that vision and by his drive and energy make it a fact of history. Barnabas, like Peter, is to fall out of sight—but more tragically than Peter. Barnabas, gentle in spirit as he was, may have fallen a victim to a tragic clash of loyalties, to the great man whose ministry had been partly his creation, and to his loved sister Mary and her son whom she was determined, perhaps, should be a missionary. It was a quarrel which found healing, for if Mark was restored to the friendship of Paul, so surely was the noble Barnabas. We shall not meet him again, but the characters of Acts must place Barnabas, Levite of Cyprus, in the front rank.

571 : Elymas

Acts 13.1–12

It was natural enough for the party to begin with Cyprus, the ancient seat of civilization which lies like the skin of some animal in the north-eastern corner of the Mediterranean. The deputy (or pro-consul—as usual Luke uses the correct name) was Sergius Paulus described as 'a man of understanding' (7).

Paulus, for all his reputation for wisdom, had a soothsayer in his entourage. The emperor Tiberius had set this fashion, he whom Juvenal, the satirist, described as sitting on Capri, surrounded 'by his wizard crew'. The situation must be seen in its context. The contemporary Roman was extraordinarily prone to superstition, and the 'Chaldeans and soothsayers', the casters of horoscopes and all manner of associated charlatans, mainly from the east, formed a host who battened on this failing. Tacitus describes them as '. . . a tribe faithless to the powerful, deceitful to those who hope, which will ever be banned among us—and ever tolerated.'

Who the scamp of Cyprus was we do not know. There has been much learned controversy over his name, and some have sought to identify him with a wizard who, according to Josephus, aided the procurator Felix in seducing Drusilla, wife of Aziz, prince of Emesa. Such conduct is not uncommon in those who have always been at hand to batten on the base superstitions of man. We have met Simon of Samaria, similarly silenced by Peter (8.9–24). We have met Balaam, and Paul was again to encounter the breed at Ephesus (19.13–17). It seems to be a fact that renegade Jews found openings in this disgraceful profession, and constituted a strong opposition to Christianity. Their type and fashion change with the times, and the Church must ever be on guard against perversions of things spiritual.

Sergius Paulus was certainly disillusioned by the missionaries' prompt exposure of his soothsayer. Whether he became a Christian is not clear. Certainly the same word 'believed' (12) is used again in v. 48 in the sense of committal to Christ, but nothing in the text or in tradition leads us to complete certainty. Inscriptions seem to identify both the proconsul and the connection of his family with Cyprus.

572 : Unsuccessful Missionary

Acts 12.25–13.13; 15.36–40; 2 Timothy 4.11; Philemon 24

We have met Mark before (Study number 505). Something near fifteen years have passed since the boy in the garden escaped from the temple-guard, leaving a linen sheet behind him. The next chapter of the story is brief enough, and again we are driven to conjecture.

Mark had accompanied the party, apparently at Barnabas' insistence. Perhaps Mark's mother, Mary, concurred. Mark served well enough in Cyprus, but when Paul purposed moving inland to the Roman military bastion of central Asia Minor, Antioch of Pisidia, the young man could no longer feel confidence in the enterprise.

Whatever the reason Mark advanced for his defection, it deeply angered Paul and caused a breach between him and Barnabas, which, it seems possible to show, Paul lived sincerely to regret. It may be that Mark, remembering the traumatic experience of Gethsemane, and perhaps of Calvary, was in no mood to condone the giving of the evangel to the Romans, and to leave Perga and its synagogue community for Antioch.

In the judgement of one of the greatest intellects of the ancient world, and the most effective missionary of all time, Mark had been a failure in his career as a missionary. There must have been hot words, and it was a wounded young man who went back to Jerusalem.

How then does it happen that Mark and Paul were reconciled, and that Mark was a comfort to the great man in the last harsh days of his imprisonment? We wish that an explanation had been given. Peter was no doubt the mediating influence. Peter was Mark's 'father in God,' and would certainly undertake the task of healing. Peter also grew to appreciate the intellectual power of Paul, and to see the correctness of his plan for global evangelism. He must have led Mark, in spite of his prejudice against the Empire, and perhaps his fanatical Jewish nationalism, to see the truth of this, and to accept Paul's view of the gospel. And it is a measure of the Christianity of both Paul and Mark that their differences melted in Christ, and they became one in the gospel.

The lessons? A career of service is not a subject for dictation, coercion, or any form of prejudiced, selfish or carnal persuasion. It is not everyone who is fitted for any kind of service. To discover God's will in such matters calls for care, prayer, and the delicate handling of circumstance. A parent's one duty is by all means to bring a child to Christ, to guide humbly and prayerfully advise, but for the rest to be uncommitted.

573 : Paul in Pisidia
Acts 13.14–41; Galatians 1.1–12

Luke regards this Sabbath as a great turning point. Perhaps Paul found a vision of 'the Empire for Christ' in Cyprus—an argument, if the suggestion stands, for the real conversion of Sergius Paulus. Hence the by-passing of Perga, and the rapid ninety-mile journey to the uplands of Asia Minor. It could also be that Paul was ill and sought the cooler healthier air of the hinterland. It was a malarial coast.

Pisidian Antioch (there were, in fact, some sixteen towns called Antioch—after Antiochus, son of Seleucus, who succeeded in 332 B.C. to the western and northern quarter of Alexander's empire) was a bastion of Roman power in a barely subdued plateau, and one of those key places in which we shall see the Apostle to the Gentiles eager to plant cells of Christians. From this point he clearly had a plan.

The sudden deceleration of the narrative is always a mark of Luke's conviction that he is describing significant events. Note the speech to the Sabbath congregation in the synagogue, and set its argument and its very words alongside the addresses of Peter and Stephen. Again Luke is demonstrating, not the novelty of Paul's ministry, but its continuity with that which Peter had already taught. And psychologically, the historic approach through the rapid conspectus of Old Testament history, shows how real in Paul's memory was Stephen's long address before the Jerusalem Sanhedrin. We shall see this happen again in Paul's reported words.

Coming to the close of Paul's speech the reader feels a sudden abruptness and a rapid change to a tone of warning. Had he sensed a surge of hostility through the congregation? He was not among metropolitan Jews. The synagogue of this foreign town ought, he might have imagined, to have contained many Jews like the Hellenists we have met, men open to less prejudiced argument. But, of course, he had only to remember his own hostility to understand that a wider environment was not necessarily the guarantee of a broader outlook. He would grasp in a moment the signs of rising feeling in the congregation before him, and this would account for the swift alteration in tone. And before the end of the visit the reality of the situation was seen in hostile action from the traditionalists among the Jews.

Paul's policy of beginning with the synagogue was nevertheless sound. It is clear that the Jews were an integrated part of the Antiochean community, that they had a liberal wing which accepted Paul's message, and that they had a bridgehead in Gentile Graeco–Roman society in the shape of a body of proselytes who spread the news.

574 : The Pisidians

Acts 13.42–50; Galatians 5.13–26

We have no means of estimating the size of the population, and Luke does not tell us how many of the synagogue congregation initially accepted Paul's message. It has been obvious that his first impression was a fairly wide hostility and he may have been surprised that a certain number followed him. Among the Gentile adherents, whose very presence suggests some life and activity in the synagogue, he seems to have been more generally accepted.

Adherence to the synagogue cannot have branded the proselytes unfavourably, because something of a city-wide demand arose for wider publicity, and the next Sabbath a very considerable crowd collected to hear. They not only listened but gave approval, and the leaders of the synagogue saw their place taken by the two brilliant and popular visitors. The popular response stirred not joy but envy, and revealed the shallowness of any Jewish approval manifested the week before. The purely Jewish ranks closed, and many of the Gentile adherents were swept along by the tide of Jewish disapproval. For all their accepted place in the composite society, the test revealed that the Jewish minority still secretly rejected the Gentiles. It was Paul's obvious offer of the new interpretation of their faith to the wider society of Antioch which swung a majority of the synagogue in behind a strong original band of opponents.

One verse in the sad tale of prejudice and rejection stands out. A group of good and devoted women spearheaded the opposition on the wider front. The women of Asia Minor were not a subjugated and suppressed group. They played a free part in society, and found attraction in Judaism, perhaps due to its stern moral code. In the Jewish community of the city there seems to have been an influential group of those women converts. Luke is distressed to note that they, too, were influenced to oppose the new teaching and its advocates. It is to be expected that evil will find supporters among those who are obviously bad. It is sad when, by deception and pride, it recruits adherents among the apparently good. The situation is not without its parallels in history and the modern world.

The devout women doubtless had the ear of the city rulers. Members of the leading households of Antioch may have been among those persuaded to reject Paul and Barnabas. Their expulsion was assured.

575 : The Jews of Iconium

Acts 14.1–7; Mark 3.22–30

It was ninety miles journey to Iconium, the modern Konya. It was an ancient city, and if its claim to be older than Damascus is sustained, the city of today is one of the oldest continuously inhabited places on earth. There were three strong elements in the population, Jews, Greeks and Romans. In all three, Paul, a man of three cultures, moved at ease. Luke is in one of his clipped, abbreviating moods, and though the few opening verses cover a considerable ministry, the writer obviously does not detect in the situation elements important to his main theme. It is a fact that Iconium became a major point of diffusion for the gospel, and Paul must have accounted the mission a success.

The synagogue was, however, divided. The dissident Jews, moved by that species of nationalism which so often, when their community was strong, overrode their caution in a Gentile environment, stirred up the city against the missioners. The old pattern was repeated—riot, menace, withdrawal. The Jewish community obviously had Gentile connections, and perhaps there was a good deal of integration and intermarriage in the central highlands. Timothy's family provided an example. The city magistrates condoned the disorder. Paul had not yet decided to use his Roman citizenship, no doubt because of the remoteness of the region, and another ephemeral triumph for evil was recorded.

Curiously, a second-century fiction tells of the Iconian ministry. Some grain of truth may lie within the story of the girl Thekla and her conversion, with the persecution which fell on her. The romance is interesting for the description of Paul which it contains. It could contain a memory, but might not have pleased the apostle. He was, says the account 'a man of small size, with meeting eyebrows and a rather large nose, bald, bow-legged, full of grace, for at times he looked like a man and at times he had the face of an angel'. The last part of the sentence is rather difficult to assess.

But the prominent characters of this story are the hostile Jews of the local synagogue. Were they a majority, or were they the noisy minority of which the world is weary, marked by violence, din, emotional protest and refusal to debate with decency and order? We do not know, but evil seemed to win.

576 : The Lystrans

Acts 14.6–28; Galatians 6.14–18

Lystra was a refuge. It was a Roman colony but seems to have had a large native Lycaonian element in its population. The account implies that, by crossing into Lycaonia, the refugees passed to the safety of another administrative district, and this, at one time, appeared to be contrary to fact. It was his discovery, on archaeological evidence, that Luke was accurate on this point, which first led to Sir William Ramsay's conclusion that Luke was a first-rate historian, and to the championship which marks the writing of that great classicist and historian on the theme of Luke's two books.

Ramsay discovered an inscription at Lystra dedicating a statue to Zeus and Hermes (the Jupiter and Mercury of the unfortunate AV [KJV] rendering), and some light is thrown on the Lystrans by the discovery. Legend had it that the two gods had once visited the area in disguise, and had been gruffly refused hospitality save in the cottage of an aged couple, Philemon and Baucis. These old folk were the sole survivors of a penal inundation which the offended deities let loose upon the district. They became, in fact, priest and priestess of a temple created miraculously from their small dwelling. The story may be found in the *Metamorphoses* of the Roman poet Ovid, written a century before Paul came to Lystra. Filled with fear of a second disastrous error, the priest of the temple of Zeus-before-the-Gate (13), a temple archaeologically attested, saw the second advent of the two gods in Barnabas and Paul. The former, evidently a more striking figure, was named as the chief god. Paul, the spokesman, was set down as Hermes, the gods' messenger. It was with difficulty, and loss of prestige, that the visitors persuaded the excited and superstitious crowd to abstain from sacrificing to them. Paul knew no Lycaonian, a Gallic language, and so was unaware of the brewing folly. Observe that no miracle gave him the vital comprehension.

The old enemies arrived (19) and were able to turn the mob's disillusionment into violence. Paul nearly lost his life. The whole incident is light on the character of the people. A backwash of Celts, of the same order as the Gauls who settled France in the great folk wanderings, had formed the basis of the Lycaonian population. Their volatile character, excitability and fickleness are evident in the story. This back-country area, not unlike the remoter Turkish towns today, had the thinnest veneer of European culture.

577 : Visitors from Jerusalem

Galatians 2

It is necessary at this point to turn to a story which illuminates a difficulty soon to become acute, and the occasion, as the next chapter of Luke's narrative will show, of a momentous conference. Acts **14**.28 suggests a time lapse, with the church of

Antioch enjoying peace, and that harmony between Jewish and Gentile Christians which was natural in Christ. Such unembarrassed fellowship shocked a deputation from Jerusalem, sent by James from the Jerusalem Christians, who seemed to have forgotten their former liberation in matters of the Jewish Law, when Paul had consulted them first in the capital (1–10). Paul, with characteristic vigour of speech makes this abundantly clear to the Galatians, for the bigotry had spread at the time he wrote (perhaps about A.D. 52), and was likely to split the community.

When James' deputation arrived (one ancient text states expressly that they were one-time Pharisees) Peter was abashed, and even separated himself from those with whom he had, to that time, enjoyed uninhibited fellowship. The action shows how hardly won was the battle for Christian freedom, even in men of Peter's worth and strength of character. A lifetime of indoctrination dies hard in any man. Peter, as Paul says, was to blame (11), and Paul dauntlessly stood up to him in protest. Even Barnabas joined the separatists.

It is easy to see how strong the temptation must have been in the clear and ardent mind of Paul, at this time, to wash his hands of the Jerusalem church, and to set up at Antioch a Gentile church which set no legalistic requirements upon converts to Christ. No situation could more clearly demonstrate Paul's wise statesmanship, and his unassailable claim to leadership in the global Church over the vacillating Peter. There is a lesson in such self-control. In the end the Jerusalem church died. It grew more and more exclusive, but Paul at the time of this dissension was right not to withdraw. To withdraw from a situation which causes tension and frustrates is sometimes easier than to stay and fight the matter through. God's time for secession sometimes comes, but those who separate themselves should be certain of their ground. Paul appears to have won back Peter and Barnabas, but it remained to convince the church in Jerusalem. With the weight of the second church of the empire behind them, and with some ceremony (Acts 15.3), a deputation went which sought to clear up in debate a situation rightly recognized as perilous in the extreme.

578 : The Judaizers
Acts 15.1–35

Among the Christians of the Jerusalem church, and possibly also of Antioch, were numbers whose whole life had been lived in loyalty to the tenets of Judaism. They could not realize that their new faith had superseded the teachings of the synagogue, and had no understanding of the outlook and difficulties of the Gentiles who had found Christ with no knowledge of the Old Testament. It was part of the vast wisdom of Paul that he saw the reality of Christ's emancipation. It was also part of the immense understanding of Peter that he opened the door to the Gentiles without cluttering the entrance with a mass of Jewish demands. Peter's path was more difficult than Paul's, for he had not Paul's magnificent education nor Paul's acquaintance with the Greek and Roman world.

It is the way of men to complicate the simple things of God, to find reappraisement of their whole way of life and system of belief an agonizing experience, and to halt short before that which seems to require no contribution on their part save surrender, committal and trust. The Christian gospel is still marred by those who add to its requirements fragments of the superseded law, perhaps, promises of financial support injected as conditions of church-membership, shreds of invented ritual, prescribed attitudes, and footnotes to a simple creed.

There is one way to Christ's salvation—a sincere acceptance, as personally relevant, of the sacrifice He made for sin, appropriation of His forgiveness, trust in His finished work. It may be put in many ways, but no church or institution has Scriptural right to demand more of those who come to Christ than the clear profession of that faith.

In this magnificently reported debate we catch the spirit of the Jerusalem church. Observe the rapid eagerness of the Pharisee wing to make its point; see Peter's nobility and his acceptance of primary responsibility for the welcome to the Gentiles, the patient attention to Paul, and Paul's tactful concession over things not prepared for food in the Jewish way (20). The letter was carefully framed but it would appear that, though Paul carried the wavering fringe of the mother church, he had merely silenced the Pharisaic element. The communication to the Gentile churches soon became a dead letter.

1. The men (and women) behind great men.
2. Superstition and Christianity.
3. 'Failure is not final.'
4. Racial jealousy.
5. Good people in bad roles.
6. Noisy minorities and the ethics of protest.
7. Paul's ignorance of the native speech of Lystra, and the divine economy of miracles.
8. Contrast Peter and Paul in the Antioch situation.
9. In what ways is the simplicity of the gospel still corrupted?

579 : Paul and Barnabas

Acts 15.36–40; 1 Corinthians 13.1–8

The narrative becomes terse again as Luke runs rapidly over a long series of important events. A compromise which cost the Jewish Christians more than it cost the Gentiles had been worked out, and in the pattern of Luke's narrative Peter disappears from the story, though not from life and activity. Barnabas also is about to leave the stage, and the occasion was a painful one for two great Christians. In characteristic fashion Paul introduces another personality, Silas, or Silvanus, to give the evangelist his full name. Paul's assumption of leadership is now apparent (36).

Conscientiously, Luke records a sad 'contention' (39). The word is a strong one—*paroxusmos* from which comes 'paroxysm', and AV (KJV) is correct in strengthening the noun with the adjective 'sharp', as do several of the other versions. Paul and Barnabas separated, and again a strong word is used of the rift between them. In the whole of the New Testament the verb occurs only once again, where the heavens depart in catastrophic ruin (Rev. 6.14). Paul was a vehement character, strained perhaps and still tense from the contentious weeks through which he had lived. Perhaps, also, there was a residue of reserve left between him and Barnabas after the defection of Barnabas in Antioch (Gal. 2.13). John Mark, too, had behaved very badly. At any rate, Paul, always sensitive to what he classed as disloyalty or sluggish response to his firm, bold leadership (Phil. 2.20 f.), took a strong stand. Barnabas and Mark went their separate ways.

669

It was said earlier (Study 572) that Paul not only lived to be reconciled to Mark, but perhaps also to regret his sharp quarrel. One can almost hear Paul's voice in the word *paroxusmos*, as he told the story to Luke. And it is certain that he remembered the word in A.D. 52 when he wrote his wonderful chapter on love to the Christians of Corinth. Love, he says, in the fifth verse, 'is not easily provoked', and he uses the verb *paroxunetai*, cognate with the noun which described his 'sharp contention'. He could hardly have written that verse without a touch of self-reproach over an unhappy memory. Good came of it all. The able Silas was enlisted for the work, and Cyprus, Barnabas' native island, received an unrecorded mission.

580 : Silas

Acts 15.22–27; 17.14, 15; 1 Peter 5.12

It is well to pause here in the onward flow of the narrative to look briefly at Paul's new associate, Silvanus. Whereas Luke uses the familiar abbreviation, Paul (see beginning of the two Thessalonian epistles) always employs his full Roman name. Silas appears to have been, as was Paul himself, a Roman citizen, no mean estate in the world of the first century, as the commander of the Jerusalem garrison remarked years later to Paul. Perhaps that is why Paul abides by the dignity of the full name.

Observe that Paul did not see fit to undertake his second incursion into Asia Minor (it was ultimately to lead on to Europe) alone. He had in mind to replace both Barnabas and Mark. He was obviously no lonely and austere man, hesitant, or unable to share his confidence and his task with others. We saw in an earlier study (Study number 74) the loneliness of high leadership in the case of Moses. Paul was not aloof. He had a faculty for sharing, a genius for friendship. He needed good men around him, and had a capacity for finding them and drawing them into fellowship. His friendship with Luke is apparent in the whole book, and in the pages of that book and in Paul's own writings a considerable band of men and women of all ages appear for whom Paul manifests affection, and of whom he writes with warm appreciation.

Paul seldom appears alone. In Athens he did seem, for tactical reasons, to be working without support. His companions had been left for a gleaning operation in the north, and Paul was clearly feeling their absence. He depended on others, and in one so able, and so strong, that dependence may have appeared strange. It is not an uncommon situation, and one which those fitted for the task should regard as a precious ministry. Leaders need support close at hand. They often yearn for support, and too frequently lack it, because those who might bring simple fellowship and comfort are abashed and shy in the presence of greater ability and higher station. Paul provides, then, a prime example of a great man made more useful by his friends. He had no wife, that nearest, best and most effective support for a man's life, and failing such benediction, others were called upon to supply the lack. If reward for work be given, theirs will be rich.

581 : Timothy
Acts 16.1–5; 1 Timothy 1

Timothy, son of mixed Jewish and Greek parentage, is an associate of Paul from this point onwards, a tract of some seventeen years of active life. The young man was known and esteemed in the churches of Iconium and Lystra, but to the reader of the New Testament he is an elusive character difficult to know. Paul looked upon him with love and confidence, and as his son and heir. He gave him heavy tasks and responsibilities. Two of the pastoral epistles were addressed to him, and it is from the two letters to Timothy that we learn most of the young successor of John Mark.

Timothy came from a remote country town. He had not moved, as Paul had done, through the great cities of men and met great teachers. His home was perhaps divided, for there is no evidence that his father was an adherent of the synagogue, and he did not carry in his body the sign of Judaism. In an act of curious compromise with Judaism, Paul provided it (3). From the letters written to him it might appear that Timothy was not robust in health, was somewhat shy, and constitutionally timid, and perhaps too dependent upon others.

He was a third generation Christian, so rapidly had the faith struck root, for he owed all to the faithfulness of a mother and a grandmother. In such a man one might expect the small weaknesses of character we have noted. Mothers and grandmothers must in no wise underestimate the influence they can exercise upon the life of a boy, but perhaps they must take care not to blend too much of their feminine nature with his emerging masculinity. It could be that Timothy suffered a little from the lack of a Christian father's sturdy and strengthening influence on his character.

There is no apparent 'generation gap' between Paul and his young associate. The so-called 'generation gap' is an alienation created by wanton hostility or insensitive disregard between people of different ages, and dug with equal blame from both sides. There is no need for it. Both young and old have lessons to learn from each other, and youth must ever remember that the generations ahead of them know quite as much as they do about the problems of being young, and obviously more about the successive problems of later years. It is foolish not to listen.

582 : Man from Macedonia
Acts 16.6–13; Colossians 4.14; 2 Timothy 4.11

A rapid piece of narrative follows. Some compulsion which he recognized as divine guidance thrust Paul to the south-west corner of the great peninsula, and headed him away from the north-west where a strong church was established at some later date. We have despatches to the emperor Trajan, from the governor of the province, dated A.D. 110 to 111, which make this fact clear. Paul's party found themselves at Troas, named after Troy, some eight miles away, scene of Homer's *Iliad* and the famous war of Greek legend. Troas was a Roman colony and Paul confronted the Aegean, and the road to Europe. He was in a disturbed and uncertain state of mind, and was brought to decision by a vivid dream.

It has been suggested, with some plausibility, that the 'man of Macedonia' who figured in the dream was none other than Luke, the writer of this story. 'They' in the narrative becomes 'we' at v. 10, indicating that Luke first joined the company before Paul crossed into Europe. Luke was a physician and Philippi was a seat of medical science. It is not wholly unlikely that Luke, hearing of miracles of healing, journeyed to Asia Minor under the same compulsion which had brought Paul to its western borders. An interview with Paul followed. In his sleep that night Paul, in the disturbed dreaming which often follows indecision, saw 'a

672

certain man from Macedonia' (9). The Greek pronoun suggests that he could name him if he would. The Macedonians had no distinctive dress. It was the Turk who divided Asia from Europe at the Dardanelles. To cross that famous strait in the ancient world was not a passage from East to West, and involved no great consciousness of change. It was the Adriatic Sea which divided the Greek and Roman world. The Aegean and the Hellespont merely flowed between two Greek-speaking provinces of the Empire. How did Paul recognize the visitant of his dream as a man from Macedonia, if he did not know him as an individual?

At any rate, the direct and determined journey which follows, shows that Luke, certainly now in the party, was at home in Philippi. The route should be traced on the map, an indispensable aid to these studies. They ('we') spent a night on the island of Samothrace, landed at Neapolis, the modern Kavalla, and proceeded straight to Philippi by the Via Egnatia, the great Roman road which connected the Aegean and the Adriatic.

583 : Lydia

Acts 16.14, 15; Revelation 2. 18–29; Philippians 1.3–5; 4.5, 10

Philippi must have appealed to Paul. His vision of planting the gospel in the key cities of the Roman world was emerging. Philippi was a base of empire. Philip, the father of Alexander the Great, had founded the town, and that ruthless militarist had an eye for a strategic position. So had Augustus, more than three centuries later, when he founded a colony of discharged veterans there. Europeans now move into the story.

If Luke is the first Philippian we meet, Lydia is the second. This 'seller of purple' came from Thyatira in Asia Minor. Archaeology has shown that place to be a centre of varied trade, and Lydia represented some firm engaged in marketing cloth dyed 'turkey-red', from the juice of the madder-root. The dye was a cheaper rival for the crimson expensively extracted from the murex shell.

Lydia, like many other able and upright people, was attracted to the Jewish way of life, and Philippi had a small Jewish community which, in the absence of a synagogue, met by the river (13)—a Jewish practice, as Psa. 137 may show. She listened to Paul talking to the Jews (14), 'and her heart the Lord opened so that she paid attention to Paul's words', sought baptism along with her family, and offered the party hospitality. The whole story suggests that this Thyatiran business-woman, active in her work many leagues from home, was a person of some position, strong in character and open-hearted. Luke, as we have seen, was eager to stress the role of women in the earliest movements of Christianity, and it would not be without pleasure that he would see the first preaching of the gospel in Europe win a convert of such standing. We probably see in her the founder of the Thyatiran church whose lamentable disarray provoked a stern epistle from John many years later.

She also founded a tradition of hospitality in Philippi, and open-handed generosity, which finds mention in the letter Paul later wrote to the little community. Hospitality is a form of evangelism (Rom. 12.13). 'Use hospitality towards each other,' says Peter (1 Pet. 4.9), 'and never grudge it.' There is a role for women here going back to Martha. Lydia carried on the noble practice. The tradition of 'the church that is in your home' was also founded—a tradition which could well be revived.

584 : The Magistrates

Acts 16.16–26, 35–40

The Christian faith not infrequently interferes with corrupt business. Many a person who finds Christ discovers that there are matters in his mode of living, and the practice of his trade or profession which fall under the critical scrutiny of a newly enlightened conscience. Paul was to encounter the same situation in massive proportions at Ephesus. In Philippi he restored a strangely afflicted girl to sanity and found himself in court.

The judicial authority in a Roman colony was in the hands of a bench of two magistrates who were expected to know the laws of Rome. It is obvious that in Philippi the two praetors (a title such petty magistrates often assumed) had small regard either for legality or dignity (22). They were probably under the influence of such leaders of corrupt business as the owners of the slave girl. Pilate, a much more considerable official of Rome, found himself enmeshed by the power of an authority other than that to which he owed his first allegiance. There is a guideline here for life. It is important to serve only one master, and to carry that loyalty to its honourable conclusion, scorning all that urges its modification. Paul was given no opportunity for defence, or to make known his Roman citizenship.

The magistrates, in consequence, found themselves in a most difficult situation. In a speech for the prosecution against Verres, the tyrant governor of Sicily, Cicero speaks with horror of a Roman citizen who was scourged while protesting 'in the midst of his pain and the noise of the blows, "I am a Roman citizen".' It was regarded as a most serious offence to make such a claim untruthfully, or to disregard it if truthfully made.

The situation next morning is not without a certain grim humour. It certainly shows marks of authentic reporting. Note the gruff attempt of the now frightened magistrates to preserve their dignity and get rid of their embarrassing prisoners (35); note how the jailer's rendering softens the words (36). Paul 'calls their bluff' (37). They had no right to flog a Roman, even condemned. Paul's point would be that only a plea of ignorance could excuse flogging a Roman, but that such a plea at least pre-supposed a trial.

Paul's stress on the word 'uncondemned' must have filled the self-important officials with terror. It was probably the presence of Silas which gave Paul freedom to claim his political privilege. In Asia Minor he abstained because Barnabas did not share his advantage. Silas was probably a Roman citizen too.

585 : The Jailer

Acts 16.25–34

The machinery of the miracle is vividly explained by Ramsay in his comments on this passage. Philippi, for all its strategic importance, was a back-country town and not unlike remote areas in that part of the world until today, or at least, quite recent times. Ramsay writes:

'Anyone who has seen a Turkish prison will not wonder that the doors were thrown open; each door was merely closed by a bar, and the earthquake as it passed along the ground forced the doorposts apart, so that the bar slipped from its hold, and the door swung open. The prisoners were fastened to the wall or in wooden stocks (24); the chains and stocks were detached from the wall which was shaken so that spaces gaped between the stones. In the great earthquakes of 1880 at Smyrna, and 1881 at Scio, I had the opportunity of seeing and hearing of the

675

strangely capricious action of an earthquake which behaves sometimes like a playful sprite, when it spares its full terrors.'

The jailer enters, and assumes a clear personality in Luke's rapid description. He may have been a Roman by descent as well as by his colonial citizenship, perhaps a grandson of one of the legionaries settled by Augustus seventy years before in the town. His stern devotion to duty is apparent (27), and his rapid realization of Paul's spiritual command of the situation—a feature of Paul's personality which we shall see emerge from the narrative on other occasions. Note his clear-cut decisiveness, his kindly, practical response, and his obvious command over his household. (Verses 31, 32 and 34 must be taken closely together. The household was brought to Christ by personal hearing and personal belief, both aided by personal respect for the head of the house. No doctrine of gratuitous salvation for wife or children, by virtue of a father's faith, can be built upon this story.)

We do not hear of the jailer again. He is one of many who enter the story of the Church and of its Lord, linger long enough for us to notice and appraise, and then are gone. We leave the jailer standing at the gate, a changed and softened man, watching with a certain irony as the magistrates come and beg their prisoners to leave his custody. Hostile authority and persecuting officialdom for once were thrashed. The little church in Lydia's house was happy (40).

Questions and themes for study and discussion on Studies 579–585

1. Christianity and the clash of personalities.
2. Partnership in evangelism.
3. Timothy's advantages and disadvantages.
4. Paul's guidance from Troas to Philippi, and what the Christian can learn from it.
5. Hospitality as a form of evangelism.
6. Paul's reaction to personal injustice.
7. How does faith 'save'?

676

586 : The Thessalonians

Acts 17.1–9; 1 Thessalonians 1

Look at a map. Paul and Silas followed the Via Egnatia, through Amphipolis and Apollonia and reached Thessalonica, named four centuries before after Alexander's sister. It is the modern Salonica, and in Paul's day a prosperous seaport, as a prolific coinage shows.

The Thessalonians pass before us, here and in the two letters, a varied crowd of moving faces. Paul began with the Jews of the synagogue and the Greeks they had drawn into their fellowship (4). Among them, a not unusual situation, were a considerable number of leading matrons of the town. Women were notably emancipated in Macedonia.

Trouble had its usual origin. Observe that the Jews who sought to stir up a riot found their support, not so much among the educated, as among the 'bad men from the market place' (5), the unemployed (cf. Matt. 20.3), and the proletarian associates, no doubt, of the Jewish business-houses. This is one of many pieces of evidence which refute Gibbon's once accepted opinion, that Christianity made its first appeal to the dispossessed and the ignorant.

Proceedings here were more regular than at Philippi. Voluntary prosecutors, as was the custom, set the law in motion, and a charge of treason (7) was one which 'the rulers of the city' had to treat with the utmost seriousness. Luke twice (6, 8) calls these officials 'politarchs'. Since the term was unknown elsewhere, the critics of Luke once dismissed it as a mark of ignorance. Sixteen epigraphical examples now exist in modern Salonica, and one is located in the British Museum on a stone which once formed part of an archway. It was evidently a Macedonian term. It was Luke's general practice to use the term in commonest use in educated circles.

The case seems to have concluded with a stated guarantee from poor Jason that the awkward visitors would go and not return to the city. From the second and third chapters of the first letter which Paul wrote to the little Christian community, it seems clear that pressure on the church continued (2.18, then 2.13, 14 and 3.3). But a strong church had been founded during Paul's stay—probably from December, 50 to May, 51. It was active in evangelism from the beginning (1 Thess. 1.8 f.) and reached out, north and south, with the gospel.

677

587 : The Work-shy

1 Thessalonians 2; 2 Thessalonians 3

Paul's preaching touched other levels of society than those with which he first came into contact. The fact that he made a point of working for his living while in the city, would seem to show that his influence moved into the lower levels of society where the example of labour, diligence and independence was of importance to his testimony (1 Thess. 1.9 f.; 2 Thess. 3.8 f.). There was obviously no Lydia in Thessalonica to provide hospitality, and perhaps Paul thought it necessary to protect Jason.

It requires an effort of the imagination to realize that the church at Thessalonica rested on Paul's word alone. They had no New Testament. Jews and Jewish adherents among the converts had their Old Testament in Greek, but it was impossible for them to turn to a body of authoritative doctrine for study, confirmation and guidance. The fact that the little group stood firm in faith, endured persecution, and revealed the fruit of their belief in life and character, is a testimony to the evangelism Paul has described in the first half of this chapter, to his genius as a preacher and teacher, and to the power of God which went with him.

At v. 6 in the third chapter of the second letter, as though he had overlooked some stern advice, Paul bids them exercise discipline in the community; for there were some, clinging to a false view of the Second Advent, and forgetting the example of Paul himself, who were living on their more active and energetic brethren (11). An idle and work-shy community is no commendation of the faith it professes—a fact which applies in more contexts than one. 'In the name of the Lord Jesus Christ,' says Paul, 'we appeal to such people—we command them—to quiet down, get to work, and earn their own living' (12, Living Bible).

Then, in the anxiety of love, Paul bids his Christians not to close their heart because some had been found to abuse generosity. And let even such necessary discipline be exercised by the church without rancour or bitterness (15), for redemption and peace is the aim. Rebuke loses all its moral meaning, if a taint of personal hostility invades it. An ancient rabbinical comment on Deut. 25.3 suggests that, after punishment, the offender should be expressly addressed as 'brother' or 'sister'. Paul obviously has this generous precept in mind.

It is a very clear picture of a church community—some ardent, self-sacrificing, loving; some puzzled by death which had visited their group, by prophecy, by persecution, and some finding occasion to live on the work of others, and using the society of Christ for personal advantage.

588 : The Bereans
Acts 17.10–15; John 5.36–47

Things had been hard so far in Europe, but two churches had been founded, and Paul along with Silas, refugees once more, found themselves on the highway to the south again. It was sixty miles to Berea, and, as was his dogged habit, Paul began with the synagogue. He found there a better type of Jew, 'more noble' in Luke's phrase. He probably means that they were more free than their nearest neighbours from the endemic jealousy of their contemporaries, their 'racialism', in a word. There is no nobility in prejudice, in self-esteem, in vain claims to superiority, in ignorant refusal to listen to a contrary opinion.

Paul, after long meditation during those hidden years in Arabia, had concluded that the Old Testament was laced and filled with foreshadowings of the faith and the gospel he had been given. This was the burden of his message. Instead of shrinking from a reappraisement, the Jews of the Berean synagogue studied the Scriptures in an earnest endeavour to discover the truth. It is implied that they were prepared to accept the truth they found.

Their example abides. The Scriptures are the final authority for that which we believe. Let the authority of the Scriptures be shaken, and the gospel falters. Hence the confusion of the Church today. The authority of Christ Himself is bound up with the trustworthiness of the Book. He believed that the Old Testament was the Word of God. Shake that assurance and inevitably He becomes the child of His age, sharing its mistakes, naïve in His acceptance of the false and erroneous. It follows that His Person is diminished, and a Christ in error, in a field so vital, becomes, for those who consider Him, a Christ in error concerning His own claims. So the leaven penetrates the mass, and the gospel loses edge, thrust and challenge. With authority goes effectiveness.

At what point in the Bereans' salutary search the envoys from the Thessalonian synagogue arrived, it is impossible to say. Paul must have made progress with them and found friends, because

679

there were those who cleverly extricated him from yet another situation of peril. So far, from Damascus to Greece, Paul had left six cities in flight, in haste, in danger or under the menace of judicial action. We wonder at his spirit.

589 : Paul in Athens

Acts 17.16, 17; Deuteronomy 4.14–24

The circumstances merit an effort of the imagination. Paul had come along to the great city, somewhat troubled and anxious. Northern Greece, his first encounter with Europe, had seen stormy experience, and in Athens, suffering some reaction, Paul was a prey to that sharp loneliness felt by sensitive spirits amid an alien throng, and in an environment which disturbs and repels. And it seems clear that Athens did appear to Paul for all his deep understanding of the Greeks, a hostile and uncongenial place in the summer of A.D. 51.

The reasons are not far to seek. Those who view with wonder the magnificence of Athens' ruined heart today, are without the Jew's deep loathing of idolatry. The modern visitor who climbs the steps through the Propylaea, and sees the breath-taking majesty of the shattered Parthenon, mellow in its golden marble, superbly placed, has no thought of Athene, who once stood in the dim interior, the object of man's devotion. He may trace the base of another colossal image of Athens' patron goddess in the precinct. It stood with spear upraised so high that sailors off Sunion caught the sun's glint on its point from forty miles away. When the Goths intruded at the beginning of the dark fifth century after Christ, they scattered in flight at the first sight of the image. The modern visitor standing on the flat foundation regrets the destruction of a great statue. The reverence of the Athenian, the terror of the Goth, the repugnance of the Jéw for blasphemy in bronze and stone, mean nothing to him.

Perhaps the Christian can still touch the edge of that deep sensation only in the revolting presence of the phallic image. Some fragments, vast and intricately carved on Delos, reveal the gross mingling of carnality and religion which stirred the wrath of the Hebrew prophets, and which evoke a Christian disgust. The sculptured sensualities of some Eastern temples stir the same nausea. Athens must have had examples enough of this baser use of Greek art. Athene Promachos and the Wingless

Victory were not its only creations. There were the crude herms of every common street, and if evidence is needed to prove that these rough cult images were something more than decoration, there is a famous case which their wanton desecration once provoked, a serious crisis in Athenian political and judicial history. So real was idolatry.

The remedy for loneliness and oppression of spirit is work, and adapting himself with his usual dexterity to the Athenian environment of endless talk, discussion and public argument, instead of the synagogue Paul sought the *agora*, excavated in the last generation, and went to work.

590 : The Athenians

Acts 17.18; Proverbs 17.4–7; 18.13–16

Athens, living on its past, was a loquacious, questioning, decadent University city, ready with nicknames, and academically snobbish. But Paul had small regard for such shallow culture. His sturdy faith could be pungently contemptuous of 'aimless philosophies'. (Col. 2.8 in Phillips' rendering.) His shrewd mind must have noted the speculation for speculation's sake, and the glib talk for the sake of talking, the old vice of sophistry which Aristophanes and Plato had flayed, turned then, as never before, cynically to profit. He must have observed the commercialization of knowledge and culture, the horde who lived by wits and words, in short, all the sham, the artificiality, the dishonesty, and empty pride of a city living on its past, its ghosts, and its relics. The encounter was no joyous experience to a Christian Jew ardent for truth.

It was disturbing, too, to be taken for yet another fortune-seeker, eager to sell his doctrine. 'What,' they asked, observing his Socratic activities in the *agora*, 'does this "seed-picker" want?' The word was Athenian slang. It was used by Aristophanes in his uproarious comedy *The Birds* to signify the busy winged things of the meadows, snapping up the chance fallen seed, the pert sparrows and finches of the furrows. In Athenian vernacular it came to mean the sophistic picker-up of scraps of learning, the one who lives on his words and wits, a 'babbler' only in the sense that such charlatans were compelled to talk long and persuasively to conceal the second-hand, second-rate quality of their doctrine. The word is an authentic echo of the crowded *agora*, where

Paul, conforming easily as we have seen, to Athenian tradition as old as Socrates, met the inquisitive quick-tongued populace, joined in the animated discussion which was the habit and manner of their market-place, and attracted the attention of the Stoics and Epicureans.

Hence a polite summons to appear before the Court of the Areopagus, which the philosophers of both schools seem to have controlled. They were rivals for the attention of their day, for the Greeks lacked somewhat the Roman penchant for eclecticism which enabled urbane folk like Horace, the poet, to be Stoic and Epicurean at one and the same time. Within a mile of the *agora* were the Gardens of Epicurus. The Stoa Poikile, or Painted Porch, from which the Stoics took their name, closed the end of the market-place. Paul was in the ancient centre and capital city of both philosophies, four centuries after their first foundation. At Athens both were professed with academic exclusiveness.

591 : The Epicureans
Acts 17.18; Job 12.7–25

The Epicureans, a philosophic school founded by one Epicurus who lived from 342 to 270 B.C. were materialists. Basing their world view on the atomic theories of Democritus of Abdera, they sought to explain all phenomena on physical principles. It was a philosophy born in a time of stress, which sought to banish tension and anxiety by explaining the sources of such disturbances away. The soul was, they taught, atomic in structure, and therefore died with its host. There were gods, for men saw such beings in dreams, and dreams had a material explanation in films of atoms penetrating the brain, but the gods were not involved in life. As Tennyson puts it in *The Lotus Eaters*,

> ... *they lie beside their nectar, and the bolts are hurl'd*
> *Far below them in the valleys, and the clouds are lightly*
> *   curl'd*
> *Round their golden houses, girdled with the gleaming world:*
> *Where they smile in secret, looking over wasted lands,*
> *Blight and famine, plague and earthquake, roaring deeps*
> *   and fiery sands,*
> *Clanging fights, and flaming towns, and sinking ships,*
> *   and praying hands ...*

Behind such doctrine lay Epicurus' passionate quest for peace of mind. He saw religion, the hope or fear of survival, the expectation of judgement, a power which punished, cared or interfered, as disturbance for the soul, and a poison of its peace. Let man seek only happiness, and happiness could only be pleasure.

The true sage, Epicurus taught, curbed passion, scorned excess lust, ambition, for all have aftermath of pain. He narrowed desire, so that disappointment, anxiety, apprehension, desire's by-products, might not ruffle his calm; he sought health, quietness, simplicity, for all are part of the unseen unenvied way; pursued, in short, a species of quietism, without much doctrine save the view of physics on which so much depended, and without mystery. Virile souls may have turned more readily to Stoicism. The timid of a disillusioned age found more obvious escape in Epicureanism.

There is no means of knowing the colour of the Epicureanism held by the philosophers of Paul's audience. They were academic types, sound, no doubt, in doctrine, virtual atheists, contemptuous of all belief in divine care for human virtue, human sin, or human life. Josephus, who described the Epicureans as the Sadducees of the Athenian philosophic world, probably touched the truth. The worldly Jewish sect, holding doctrine lightly, and denying another life, resurrection and judgement, were not dissimilar. Significantly, Paul disregarded both groups in two notable addresses. It is idle to speak to those with whom there is no point of contact, no overlap of experience. Paul chose to speak rather to the Pharisees in Jerusalem, and to the Stoics of his Athenian audience. Those committed to Epicurus, or to what carnal men had made of Epicurus, were not open to his argument.

592 : The Stoics

Acts 17.18; Romans 8.28; Ephesians 1.10; Philippians 4.8–14

Paul must have known much of Stoicism. Zeno, the founder of the school, came from Paul's corner of the Mediterranean, Citium in Cyprus. A second Zeno, who was head of the school in 204 B.C., actually came from Tarsus. He it was who gave Stoicism the practical turn which so attracted the intelligent Roman. Aratus, scientist and poet, who is quoted by Paul in the speech before the Areopagus (Acts 17.28), was a Stoic of the first vintage, born at Soli in Cilicia, and converted to Stoicism a few yards from where Paul spoke. Cleanthes, whose hymn to Zeus also uses the words of Paul's quotation, was a man of Assos in Asia Minor. As second head of the school, he infused a deeply religious element into Stoicism.

Zeno, first founder of the Stoic school, and it appears, a Semite, came to Athens about the year 320 B.C., at the very time when Epicurus was finding delight and relief in the atomic theory of Democritus in Colophon across the Aegean. Two questions confronted Zeno, as they confront all seekers after truth—what to believe, and how to live.

Nothing but goodness is good, he averred. Rank, riches, health, race, pleasure are incidentals. Epicurus might argue that pleasure is good, and find the bulk of the world to support him. But does history ever praise a man because he was happy, healthy, long-lived, or rich? No. What lives in memory is a man's goodness, virtue, heroism. The verdict of history is obviously groping after some form of ultimate justice. A man, therefore, possesses all good in his person. What matters is what he is, not what he has or what happens to him. No earthly power can make a man bad outside his will. It can rob him of freedom, possessions, health, but not goodness.

God, they conceived as a mighty life force surging through all things, and thrusting towards perfection. It was a near pantheism not unlike the 'Ultimate Reality' or 'the ground of being' of some philosophic theologians. Hence a way of life, toilsome, enduring, defiant of an evil world.

It is easy to see why Paul addressed himself to the Stoics of his audience. He, too, believed in a purpose working to a vast consummation, and the need for man to co-operate with it. He, too, believed that what a man was mattered supremely, and not what he possessed. He, too, sought superiority to circumstances. His God, too, was, in Paul's view, transcendent, and beyond the patronage of man. There were points of sympathy and contact, a bridgehead of persuasion. It is always wise thus to begin. This is why Paul usually began with the synagogue.

593 : Paul the Preacher
Acts 17.19–31; 7.47–50

The address itself must now be considered. The approach was conciliatory and courteous, but perhaps just touched with that irony which was the common fashion of Athenian speech.

'Athenians,' said Paul, 'I observe that in every way you are uncommonly religious.' Here was Athenian *parrhesia*, 'freedom of speech', of the first order, tactful yet challenging, polite yet without sacrifice of the speaker's position. 'As I have moved about your city looking at the objects of your worship,' Paul continued, 'I came upon an altar inscribed TO THE UN-KNOWN GOD.' Thus it must be translated. He was not deceived about its meaning, but like any perceptive preacher sought an illustration and a point of contact in a known environment. The device captured attention and anchored the theme in experience.

It was convenient to Paul's approach, and simple, to slide from the altar's dedication, to the Stoic God who needed nothing from any man. Or was it quite the Stoic God? Not perhaps in the more austere significance of their belief. Paul's Creator was still his own personal God, the great I AM. Indeed, he snatches a remembered phrase from a speech which had burned its memory on his brain. It was Stephen, on trial before the Sanhedrin, who had protested in Paul's hearing, that 'God does not dwell in temples made with hands'.

Stephen spoke of Solomon's shrine. Paul quoted the words under the great stone altar of Greece, the Acropolis. Whether he spoke on the traditional site, the lower outcrop of stone below the greater, called the Areopagus or the Hill of Ares, or whether the hearing took place in the Royal Porch in the *agora*, as others contend, the magnificence of the temples on the height was in full view, the glorious Parthenon, the Erechtheum, and the fairy-light shrine of the Wingless Victory on its promontory beside the entrance portal. And wherever he deprecated the thought that deity could be set forth in 'gold, silver or stone, carved work of man's devising', the commanding statue of Athene Promachus lifted its bright-tipped spear above him, and the gold and ivory figure of the same Athene listened from the religious light of her sanctuary in the great temple. Paul was a bold man, and his listeners amazingly tolerant.

He proceeded to quote two Stoic poets, dexterously applied. Indeed in this report of masterly brevity several allusions to Greek literature are discernible. Paul's educated allusiveness is impressive. Then, having spoken in the language of his hearers, within the context of their thought, and with amazing adaptation, Paul thrust home with his point and his appeal.

594 : Departing Audience

Acts 17.32–34

Paul sought no compromise with the two philosophies. He met his audience where he could, sought by all means to graft his teaching on to accepted ideas, and to express it in acceptable and comprehensible terms. But he knew that a point of challenge had to come. It came with his introduction of Christ, and the divine authentication of His Person. In the act he lost the bulk of his audience. The Epicureans had listened impatiently throughout. They would have been those who scoffed. The Stoics dismissed him with more polite formality. The true Stoic, the Wise Man of their famous concept, needed no repentance, feared no Day of Judgement, looked for no resurrection or reward.

The psychology of such rejection is not far to seek. C. S. Lewis, in his trenchant fashion, hits it off well. 'We who defend Christianity,' he writes, 'find ourselves constantly opposed, not by the irreligion of our hearers, but by their real religion. Speak about beauty, truth and goodness, or about a God who is simply the indwelling principle of these three, speak about a great spiritual force pervading all things, a common mind of which we are all parts, a pool of generalized spirituality to which we can all flow, and you will command friendly interest. But the temperature drops as soon as you mention a God who has purposes and performs particular actions, who does one thing and not another, a concrete, choosing, commanding, prohibiting God with a determinate character.'

It was precisely such a concept which formed the climax of Paul's address, indeed inevitably formed that climax, for he was preaching Christianity as a final revelation, and Christ as God's full exegesis, a fact forgotten by some proponents of a dechristianized Christianity today.

The audience dispersed. If the function of the Areopagus was the informal or formal investigation of new teachings, they no doubt regarded their function as fulfilled. The newcomer had nothing pernicious to disseminate, only the stock-in-trade of the religious enthusiast the world over, and Athens could absorb such trivialities and survive. One member only of the court crossed the Rubicon, and some of the bystanders, for there was no doubt a listening circle. Round the Acropolis in modern

Athens runs the Street of Dionysius the Areopagite. Paul's convert would have been amazed.

The whole address remains a model for those who seek in such circles to present the Christian faith, and warning to those who, in misguided moments, have seen a virtue in crudity, and a loyalty to truth in a disrespect for the views, the habits of thought, and the attitudes of intelligent people who fail in all points to follow them. Confrontation there must be, if the popular word may be used again, but with preamble of courtesy, with the tolerance which is not incompatible with earnestness, and with the sincerest of efforts to see good where good has found a place.

Questions and themes for study and discussion on Studies 586–594

1. What does resort to violence always reveal?
2. 'He will find me picking cotton when He comes.'
3. What did the Bereans study?
4. Idolatry, ancient and modern.
5. Discussion, its use and abuse.
6. Epicureanism in its modern forms.
7. What grains of truth would Paul see in Stoicism?
8. Adapting the gospel to the audience.
9. Estimate Paul's success at Athens.

595 : Paul's Friends

Acts 18.1–6; 1 Corinthians 2

Paul passed on to Corinth, possibly a prey to one of his periodic bouts of illness—if Ramsay is right in diagnosing the 'thorn in the flesh' as the debilitating malaria of coastal Asia Minor (1 Cor. 2.3; 1 Thess. 3.7). Paul was comforted by meeting two friends. Some disturbance in the Roman ghetto had led Claudius to expel the Jews from the capital. It was probably trouble connected with the first preaching of the gospel in the city. Hence the presence of Prisca (or Priscilla) and Aquila in Corinth. They were a much travelled pair. We find that they accompanied Paul to Ephesus where they instructed the preacher from Alexandria, Apollos (18.18, 24–26). Theirs was an open house. They returned to Rome when Claudius' decree was revoked, or became a dead letter (Rom. 16.3 f.). Again their home is a meeting-place for Christians.

Aquila, observe (2), had been born in Pontus on the Black Sea. The couple played a noble part in the founding of European Christianity.

There is still a church of Saint Prisca on Rome's Aventine Hill, and there is a cemetery which bears her more affectionate and familiar name, Priscilla. This cemetery, William Barclay points out, was the burial ground of the ancient family of the Acilii, which gave Rome a consul, Acilius Glabrio, in A.D. 91, who seems to have died a martyr's death as a Christian five years later. If the Priscilla of the catacomb cemetery is the Priscilla of Acts, Aquila may have been a freedman of the family of the Acilii, an ex-slave, perhaps a Jew. Speculation, no more, but intriguing. And since Prisca is a common name of the Acilii, there could be in their partnership a moving illustration of the faith breaking through the barriers of caste and station, and uniting a Roman lady with a freedman of her house. It is a curious fact that in four of the six passages in which the pair are named, Prisca, contrary to custom, is named before her husband.

Paul needed friends. He was in another great Greek city, one of the most iniquitous places on earth. It was to be his triumph to plant the faith in its cosmopolitan streets. The home which the worthy couple provided was to be his refuge, his bridgehead and his shelter. Prisca and her husband played a vital part.

596 : The Corinthians

1 Corinthians 1

Paul recalled four years later that he had approached Corinth with some misgivings. He had spoken to the philosophers of Athens with deep understanding of their doctrine. This was, as we have seen, notably true of the Stoics. There were also aspects of Greek philosophy which he despised or actively repudiated and in Corinth Paul sensed a shallow intellectualism which made him determined not to preach the gospel in philosophic terms (1 Cor. 2.5), lest the truth which he desired above all else to stress should lose its impact and meaning. This is what the determination to 'know nothing else' (1 Cor. 2.2) but the simplicities of his message means. It is not a repudiation of the approach of the recent Areopagus address, but a demonstration of the writer's acute awareness of the peril of pandering to the pretentions of the Corinthian audience.

Corinth was not Athens—not Philippi, nor Tarsus. It was the

most cosmopolitan of the cities of the Mediterranean, with the possible exception of Rome itself. Vicious, prosperous, without deep roots in tradition, the people of Corinth were too ready, with the facility of immigrant communities, to adopt the vices rather than the virtues of the land of their adoption, and to conform to Greek ways with little of deeper understanding. The letter deals with no fewer than five major problems—faction, morality, secularism, worship, and death. Philosophy, or what Corinth understood by that much tormented term, underlay all these problems. No common habit of thought gave the Christian group stability, coherence, and a form of unity, as it no doubt did in churches formed from synagogue communities. The Jews were probably a minority. There was no background of Scripture. The New Testament was hardly begun. The Old Testament had not the accepted authority which it had at Berea. Speculation, debate, conjecture were rife ... It was, in short, a situation which has much to teach the modern world. For the first time since the first century, the world we live in is again a world of cities, with a mass of problems similar to those which confronted the Corinthians. Corinth might be London, New York, Sydney, wherever this note is read. It is a sombre yet exciting thought.

597 : The Converts

Acts 18. 7–10

Paul's eighteen months of Christian preaching began in the synagogue but encountered again the fierce pride and nationalism of the Jewish minority, and the evangelist moved next door to the house of an adherent, one Justus. The rabbi of the synagogue came with him, a notable convert. The imperfect tenses of vs. 4 and 8 give an insight into Paul's patient teaching: 'He used to debate in the synagogue every Sabbath, and press his message on Jews and Greeks ... and many of the Corinthians who heard him would believe and be baptized.'

Paul felt deeply the vital nature of his task. Corinth was a crossroad of trade. From that point the faith could be disseminated down the sea-lanes of the world. He felt the urgency of the gospel on his heart. The brevity of time, the magnitude of the task, a sense of weakness, and withal of responsibility, all these, together with a consciousness of God's indwelling power, led to a change of method. Instead of reasoning (4) Paul now testified (5).

689

Exactly what this means is difficult to say. Personal experience is certainly the keynote of the later speeches in the book of Acts. Perhaps 1 Cor. 2.1–4 refers to this simplification of his message.

The Corinthian Christians were a varied mixture. A few of the converts, some indeed 'wise men after the flesh' and 'noble' (1 Cor. 1.26), are known to us by name—Crispus, the ruler of the synagogue, Erastus, the city treasurer (Rom. 16.23; and perhaps Acts 19.22 and 2 Tim. 4.20), Stephanas and Gaius, who seem to have been in a position to exercise generous hospitality, and the lady Chloe, who had a large household. Also mentioned are Fortunatus, Achaicus, Quartus, and Tertius who acted as amanuensis for the Epistle to the Romans. A strong Latin element appears likely.

It was to prove a difficult congregation as the two letters to Corinth show. A Christian community tends to reflect the qualities and defects of the community in which it is located. The turbulence and spirit of faction, the fundamental scepticism, the deplorable relapses, the undue tolerance towards sins of impurity, the intellectual arrogance and philosophical posing, and the very abuse of the gifts of the Spirit for self-display, which seem to have marred the Christian community, were reflections of the life of the restless Greek city itself.

Paul, for all that, loved them and said some of his richest words to them. If the Corinthians could be welded into a Christian community, no congregation need despair.

598 : The Proconsul
Acts 18.12–17

Junius Annaeus Gallio was the brother of the Roman philosopher and tutor of Nero, Lucius Annaeus Seneca. They were a Spanish family, two of many men, writers, senators, emperors, whom the great Romanized Iberian peninsula sent to Rome to be leaders in politics and culture. An inscription discovered at Delphi in 1905 indicates that Gallio was proconsul of Achaia in A.D. 52, thus providing a useful dating point for Paul's activities in Greece.

Gallio, according to the Roman poet Statius and also his brother Seneca, was a gentle and amiable person, and the Jews obviously misread both the magistrate and the situation. He was not the man to yield to noisy demonstrations and violence, a characteristic of such characters which not infrequently surprises those who seek to take advantage of what they imagine to be weakness. The Jews also thought to profit by the new magistrate's inexperience, and phrased their charge to look like one of treason. Perhaps, too, they forgot the fact that, with Claudius' expulsion of the Roman Jewish colony, the nation was somewhat under a judicial cloud, and not likely to obtain from the most impartial Roman court anything more than their bare due. Gallio proved quite capable of distinguishing, in spite of the ambiguous phraseology, between matters of serious political significance and matters relating to minutiae of Jewish law.

It is possible in Corinth to picture the scene. The old agora has been excavated with its row of shops overlooked by the remaining eight pillars of the temple of Apollo. The vast bulk of the acropolis, the Acrocorinthus, topped by the temple of Aphrodite, whose host of priestess-courtesans did much to give Corinth its rank flavour of moral corruption, stood high above the town. At the end of the market-place still stands the massive stone platform (the *bema*) on which Gallio sat, and in front the wide pavement on which the angry leaders of the synagogue crowded round their victim. There are few places where it is so easy to imagine the drama of the ancient scene. Paul must have met the magistrate's brusque intervention with some amazement. He had not even found it necessary to appeal to his Roman citizenship. As for the Jews, and Crispus' successor Sosthenes, their judicial unpopularity prompted the turbulent Corinthian mob to assault them. This was deplorable, but Gallio, annoyed at the presumptuous and arrogant attitude of the synagogue, took no action.

599 : Paul's Vow

Acts 18.18–23; 2 Corinthians 3.7–14; Galatians 3.23–28

The popular Scofield Bible, first published sixty-five years ago, heads this section of Luke's story sadly: 'The author of Rom. 6.14; 2 Cor. 3.7–14; and Gal. 3.23–28 takes a Jewish vow.' It is, in fact, a minor inconsistency difficult to reconcile in one so clear in his doctrine and so decisive in his way of life.

Cenchreae, the modern Kichries, lay some seven miles from Corinth on the Saronic Gulf. It was the great city's outlet to the Aegean Sea. Phoebe, who is commended to the Roman church, first of all the list in Paul's letter (**16**.1), came from Cenchreae, where a church functioned in her home. It was probably here that Paul found shelter during the period of his vow.

It was a Jewish ritual of gratitude to take a Nazirite vow. The whole proceeding is set out in Num. **6**.1–21. Paul may have wished to thank God for the blessing and preservation he had known in Corinth. It may also have been prudent, after the ironical outcome of the prosecution in the proconsul's court, to withdraw from sight for a period of time, and Cenchreae was a convenient place of retirement. Nor, indeed, was a man with a shaven head without some salutary semblance of disguise. The normal proceeding was to withdraw from the common pursuits of life for thirty days, while hair and beard grew again, to abstain from meat and wine, and in the end make certain offerings in the Temple.

The full story of what Paul had in mind eludes us. The convenience of the Nazirite withdrawal has been noted, and there is no doubt that, after his arduous time in Corinth, earning his own living and founding and instructing a church, the weary man needed rest and time for prayer and meditation. It may, on the other hand, have been a proceeding not without its peril. The sequel is perhaps found in a later chapter (**21**.18–26), where Paul is persuaded by the Pharisaic wing of the Church to demonstrate his continuing loyalty to Judaism by meeting the charges of four men who had undertaken precisely such a vow. The Jerusalem Christians, unsure of their Christian liberty, must have heard of Paul's act of compromise at Cenchreae, or observed its continuing evidence on his head, and seized upon it as a concession to them. It led to deep and serious trouble.

600 : Apollos

Acts 18. 24–19.7; 1 Corinthians 3.1–6

The world's largest colony of expatriate Jews was in the great Egyptian city of Alexandria. Two-fifths of its million-strong population were Jews, rich, cultured, turbulent and powerful. A papyrus letter from the emperor Claudius, dated A.D. 42, rebukes both Jews and Gentiles for riotous behaviour, and seems to suggest that the trouble in the city was due to 'immigrants from Syria'—perhaps Christian missionaries.

The Jews of Alexandria, proud of their cultural and literary heritage, had given the world the Septuagint, the Greek version of the Old Testament. The Alexandrian synagogues were also the proponents of varied allegorical interpretations of the Old Testament, not unlike exaggerated forms of typology sometimes found in Christian contexts.

Apollos (the name is probably an abbreviation of Apollonius) was brought up in this tradition. He was accurately informed about Jesus, either by the 'visitors from Syria' mentioned in the memorandum of Claudius, or from some early written account—and the whole drift of papyrological study suggests that written information of this sort was of earlier date than was once thought possible. Apollos was a man of natural gifts and received the message with enthusiasm. He set out, in true Christian fervour, to propagate the truth he had discovered, and humbly received the deeper teaching given him by the devoted Priscilla and Aquila.

He moved from Ephesus to Corinth, where he showed a truly Pauline ability in dealing with the informed Jews of the synagogue. There must have been in his teaching some characteristic features of Alexandrian scriptural interpretation for a group to gather round him, and exaggerate his distinctiveness, as the reference in the first Corinthian letter implies. Paul saw it as a genuine contribution to understanding—'Apollos watered'. Perhaps on the other hand the Corinthian faction had no centre in teaching but was merely a 'personality cult'. Apollos was eloquent, perhaps fervent in spirit, attractive . . .

Perhaps Apollos' desire to dampen such unnecessary controversy lay behind his reluctance to return to Corinth, as Paul had requested (1 Cor. 16.12). He was still active years later, and in Paul's confidence (Tit. 3.13). The suggestion that he was the author of the epistle to the Hebrews is based on the allegorical exposition common in that book. It is a suggestion as old as Luther's days, but has no certain evidence to back it.

Questions and themes for study and discussion on Studies 595–600

1. The value of friendship in the Church.
2. Urban, suburban and rural Christianity.
3. The reflection of a community in the Church.
4. The law and evangelism in the modern world.
5. Paul and his vow.
6. Variety in evangelism.

601 : The Ephesians

Acts 19.23–41

The story of the riot in Ephesus is most interesting. It is a picture of a great ancient city in the days of its decline, difficult to match in surviving literature. Sir William Ramsay regarded it as a most revealing chapter, 'the most instructive picture of society in an ancient city which has come down to us . . . We are taken direct into the artisan life of Ephesus, and all is so true to common life and so unlike what would occur to anyone writing at a distance, that the conclusion is inevitable: we have here a picture drawn from nature.' The terse account reads, says Charles Seltman the classical scholar, who had no sympathy for Paul's 'puritanical' and Christian invasion of the Asian city, 'like a modern press report'.

The facets of life and history in the plain and well-told story are worth a closer look. The chief characters stand out—the two Macedonians, recognized as friends of Paul, and hustled down the street, whose marble paving still proclaims its elegance, on the wave of the moving horde; Paul, cool as ever in a crisis; the provincial custodians of the Caesar-cult, not sorry to see some damage to the religion of Artemis; Alexander, probably a Hellenistic Jew who was anxious not to be exposed to unnecessary unpopularity or pogrom because of the conduct of a splinter-sect . . . Observe too, the germs of coming conflict with the proletariat, which Tacitus and Pliny note in their first secular accounts of Christianity. The metrical chant is almost audible, as it takes the place of reason in the collective mind of an eastern mob, which Luke describes with a phrase of classic irony (32).

Observe too, the sure touch of Luke's plural, which slips into his report of the city-official's politic speech. 'There are pro-consuls' (38), he reminds the promoters of the tumult. Read this in the context of the speaker's anxiety over the privileged standing of his city, and another convincing mark of historicity appears. The plural conveys a touch of obsequious respect for the two imperial stewards, who, having murdered the proconsul of Asia, M. Julius Silanus, the great-grandson of Augustus, must have been left with the administration of the province on their hands pending the appointment of a successor. The crime was of Agrippina's devising, shortly after her son Nero's accession in the autumn of A.D. 54. Tacitus takes occasion to make a bald account

694

of it the preamble to his vivid narrative of Nero's principate. The
tactful plural in the official's speech could then be evidence in one
letter of the aftermath of political assassination. The Ephesian
official is a clear-cut picture.

602 : Sceva

Acts 19.8–22; Deuteronomy 13.1–5

Ephesus was a den of superstition. The worship of Diana, or
Artemis of Ephesus to give the ancient Anatolian goddess her
Greek name, was the occasion of a great pilgrim trade. It was a
corrupt worship, that ultimate degradation of a nature-cult, with
prostitute-priestesses in attendance for ritual obscenity. Amid the
hordes who visited Ephesus were the superstitious, the seekers of
sensation, and the motley host who, the world over and through
all time, have been the provender of the charlatan, or the scamps
who have battened on the vices and the folly of their fellows.
Such villainy is not confined to ancient history. The holocaust of
books on magic and allied superstition, which marked a genuine
movement towards Christianity in the great pagan city (19),
reveals the extent of the market which the writers of horoscopes,
spells and charms could command among the cosmopolitan
crowd. The city no doubt lived on such parasitic commerce,
and this too is a situation not altogether unfamiliar in another
city-ridden century. Pandering to vice and foolishness can prove
rich gain. Sceva and his family were Jews who had seen the possibility of drawing financial advantage from the Christian movement. They were exorcists, who practised a base 'psychiatry' amid
the unbalanced and the idly rich of the population. Observing the
attraction which Paul's gospel was obviously manifesting, they
thought to turn the name of Jesus to profit—with startling results.

As Jews their sin was doubly heinous. They knew well enough
the denunciations of the Old Testament against the blasphemy of
false prophecy. Sceva was a priest, and therefore of better than
ordinary education in matters of Jewish religious concern. Not
only was he prepared to deny and debase his own sacred calling,
but he was careless of the spiritual well-being of his sons. A
parent has touched the nether depths of sin when he deliberately
communicates his wickedness to his offspring and initiates them
into the practice of iniquity. Vice which seeks to propagate itself
deliberately is a shocking spectacle, and no less horrifying is the

evil which invades the holy place, and seeks, like Sceva's family, to enlist God in the quest of unclean gain.

603 : Demetrius

Acts 19.23–32; Isaiah 40.12–26

Demetrius was a scamp of another sort. He too lived on a corruption of religion. The man stands out with some clarity in the terse account Luke writes of his rabble-rousing speech in the guildhall of the silversmiths. If an addition in the text of Acts in Codex Bezae is to be accepted, the place of meeting stood in the marble-paved street which sweeps up to the great theatre. Here is the speech as Luke gives it; it tells its own story:

'One Demetrius, a silversmith who made souvenir shrines of Artemis, provided plenty of work for his craftsmen. He gathered them together along with workmen in associated trades, and, addressing them, said: "Men, you are aware that our prosperity depends upon this business, and you see and hear that, not only in Ephesus but through almost all of the province, this Paul, by his preaching, has turned away a great host of people, telling them, as he does, that you cannot manufacture gods. Not only is our trade in danger of falling into contempt, but the temple of the great goddess Artemis will cease to be respected, and her majesty, whom all Asia and the civilized world worships, will be heading for destruction." When they heard these words they were filled with rage, and shouted: "Great is Artemis of the Ephesians." And the whole city was a scene of confusion. They surged with one accord to the theatre' (E.M.B.).

Note the familiar drift of the man's speech. He had a likeminded audience, and it is easy to produce, by inflamed rhetoric, a yell of approval from a crowd whose pockets have been similarly touched. The guild-master does not even trouble to put priorities in other than the obvious order. Trade is in danger from this new cult. Their livelihood depended on the silver souvenir trade. Furthermore respect for Artemis will decline, and the respect is world-wide! The mob took the cue and began shouting for Artemis.

The object of this misguided and hypocritical loyalty was the Diopet—'the Thing Which Fell from Zeus'. It was probably a piece of meteoric iron or stone, perhaps bearing some semblance to a human figure and housed in the mighty temple. But here, in a

696

vividly described incident of riot, demonstration and contrived disorder, is the full-length picture of a scoundrel who spearheaded a proletarian protest against the Church. It was to happen again in Bithynia in A.D. 111.

604 : The Asiarchs

Acts 19.31; Ezra 1

The State is not always hostile to God's people. Ezra 1 reveals the favour shown by the Persians, who saw an ally for their comparatively lofty view of God in the Jews' religion. Something of the same preoccupation moved the 'rulers of Asia', or 'the chief men of Asia' to some show of friendship for Paul.

This honorary assembly was a body of substantial citizens who were called upon to finance public spectacles and games in the province of Asia. Perhaps such a festival was at the moment in train in Ephesus, with a vast influx of pilgrims and tourists providing more ample fuel for Demetrius' fiery speech. In such a case the presiding Asiarchs would be most reluctant to have their great occasion spoiled by a riot in the city. The Roman government, by whose grace and favour they held the honour, was most sensitive to any disturbance of the peace, and Ephesus, as a so-called free city, was notably anxious to avoid all cause of offence to the imperial authorities.

Asiarchs were elected for a term (it is not certain whether it was four years or less) and when the term expired, the incumbent of office retained the honorary title permanently. It might be that several such men lived at Ephesus, and that, seeing they were, among other duties, the presiding priests of the imperial cult, the formal worship of the spirit of Rome and the Empire which was later to occasion the disastrous clash between State and Church, they were not sorry to see the rise of any religion which weakened the influence of the prevailing cult of the Ephesian Artemis.

It may therefore be guessed that the Asiarchs passed a word of warning to Paul, not so much out of acceptance or regard for his message, as because they approved of the social consequences of his activities. The Christian sometimes finds friends in unexpected places. It may be also true that they added a word of advice to leave the city, and not risk further mob action on the part of the silversmiths. Paul seems to make a fairly prompt withdrawal across the Aegean. A strong church had been founded, and of that church we are to hear more in the later pages of the New Testament. Paul was becoming accustomed to such retreat.

605 : Eutychus

Acts 20.1–16

We select one obscure and unknown character from several crowded months of evangelistic activity. Even a plot against Paul's life is passed over in a verse (3). We get a brief picture of the church at Troas, its communion service, and the evening sermon. Paul was no half-hour preacher, in spite of the fact that his congregation gathered after working hours in a crowded upper room of the house.

The poor lad Eutychus tried hard to keep awake. He found a window, open to the night air, high in a wall, and sat there in an attempt to breathe the stimulating air. His calculations miscarried, for the smell of the burning oil-lamps and the heavy air rose, and increased the boy's malaise. He dozed and fell into the street from the window alcove. Curiously enough, a second century papyrus from the days of Marcus Aurelius, contains the report of just such an accident. A little slave-boy, named Epaphroditos, eight years old, leaned out of a high window to see some dancers in the street of Oxyrhynchos, and fell to his death.

Luke was a physician, and perhaps that is why he picks this one incident from a crowded period. (The pronoun 'we' [7] shows that he was in Paul's company again.) The story is told with the reserve which might mark swift action to restore life in an emergency in a hospital or some scene of accident. Luke appears to vouch for the lad's death, though Paul retains hope of restoration. There is no contradiction, apart from miraculous intervention. Paul's prompt command of the situation is again apparent. In a surge of agonized concern, Paul's faith and action rose to the tragic occasion and the lad's life was restored.

The meeting continued, sustained by the passionate interest of Christians who had no New Testament. It went on till dawn was breaking over Mount Ida. Paul did not sail with them when they left. He wanted to walk alone across the headland by the old Roman road to Assos in Mysia. Did he dislike the thought of a stormy voyage round Cape Lectum? Did he stay behind to see how Eutychus fared? Had he heavy preoccupations or problems, and wanted to be alone to think? We do not know.

698

606 : Ephesian Elders

Acts 20.17–38; Ezekiel 3.15–21

Luke reports in this moving passage the only speech of Paul in his book which it is certain he actually heard. Usually he reports in outline, probably from Paul's description or Paul's notes. Here he is setting down words which he actually heard, and it is interesting to note how he uses Pauline expressions found in the letters. In consequence the speech authenticates the epistles and the epistles the speech. R. B. Rackham, in his fine commentary on Acts develops this theme, but those who find such authentication interesting could look in sequence at the following list of echoes in the text: Rom. **1.1**; Phil. **1.1**; Tit. **1.1**; 2 Cor. **2.4**; 1 Cor. **10.33**; 2 Tim. **4.7**; 1 Tim. **1.12**; 1 Cor. **11.23**; 2 Cor. **7.2**; Col. **4.17**; 1 Tim. **4.16**; Eph. **1.14**; 2 Tim. **4.5**; Col. **1.12, 28**.

The words are vivid. Verse 19 is Paul's picture of himself. 'The narrative in Acts,' writes A. W. F. Blunt, 'has told us nothing of "tears"; it pictures Paul as the man who is always equal to a public emergency; Paul himself knows more of the private depressions and discouragements which he had to live through.'

There is also a clear picture of the three years in Ephesus. Paul sought no cheap popularity. Set like Ezekiel to the task of a watchman, he did his duty with zeal and consistent testimony. Note his tireless evangelism. Publicly and from house to house he had preached the gospel and founded Christian communities, not only in Ephesus but in the inland valley towns of Thyatira, Pergamum, Laodicea, Sardis, Philadelphia, Colossae and Hierapolis, as well as in the port of Smyrna. He lived in sturdy independence, earning his own bread. And with clear foresight he saw the shape of the troubles which John's letters to the seven churches (Rev. 2 and 3) show truly came. He left the church efficiently organized and, as far as human organization could guard against trouble, he left constituted leaders, duly warned and strengthened against subversion, to meet and solve problems yet to be.

It seems clear from the fact that Paul met the elders of Ephesus on the Miletus beach that he no longer had access to the city. The sailing programme of the ship may of course have precluded a visit but it is as likely that the Asiarchs had suggested that abstention from future intrusion might add to his safety and minimize their own problems.

1. Does Christianity still embarrass commerce?
2. Commercializing religion.
3. The art of rabble-rousing, the 'demonstration', and the Christian attitude.
4. Courage and prudence in the face of danger.
5. Luke's brevity and expansiveness.
6. Paul's warning to the Ephesians.

607 : Philip's Daughters

Acts 21.1–9; 1 Corinthians 13.8–13

It is interesting to follow the course of the ship on a map. It was a frequented sea-lane, which was determined by the direction of day-time winds, a meteorological pattern itself dictated by the contours of the great land mass of Asia Minor and the contiguous sea. It was a route mentioned by two first-century Roman writers, and was probably full of ships. It took seven days to unload the galley at Tyre, where Paul may have seen the mosaic-paved shopping street, where Jesus could have walked on His one journey to the north. It is visible today.

Indefatigably Paul sought out the church, and was warned not to go to Jerusalem. It seems difficult to avoid the conclusion that Paul was moving against the revealed will of God in his determination to carry the monetary evidence of the Gentile Christians' goodwill to the Jerusalem church. Great and good men, in the grip of a fixed idea, can err.

The great galley unloaded, and moved on to Akko (Ptolemais), and the large Herodian port of Caesarea, where Philip had long been in residence. It must have been on this occasion that Luke talked with the evangelist, and heard the story of Candace's officer, which he recorded in Acts 8. Always interested in the part women played in the Church, he noted the fact that Philip had three unmarried daughters active in the Christian ministry.

To 'prophesy' is to preach. Jeremy Taylor's work on 'The Liberty of Prophesying' was written, not to uphold the liberty of prediction, but freedom to preach and proclaim the message of the gospel. Such was the wider Elizabethan use of the word. In the New Testament the 'prophet', as distinct from the teacher, seems to have been a person of insight into spiritual truth. The teacher worked within the borders of established and approved doctrine. Hence the meaning of Paul's remark to the Corinthian church about the end of prophecy, as the ancient world knew it. He was pointing out that, when the full corpus of Christian doctrine was complete, there would no longer be an office for the person whose prime duty was to show new facets of truth. To be sure, in a lesser sense, the prophet has always been active. There are infinite varieties of presentation of the faith and its significance. It may no longer be basically expanded or diminished. It may be no longer reshaped, only infinitely applied.

608 : Agabus

Acts 21.10–17; Jeremiah 13.1–11

Into the quiet household at Caesarea where Paul found refuge, came the strange person about whom we first read in chapter 11. He was shaped on the model of an Old Testament prophet. The three greatest Old Testament writing prophets used symbolism and object-lesson to drive home some spiritual truth, and Agabus carried a warning which must have had a strong impact on a man of Paul's training.

It convinced the congregation at Caesarea (12), who were loud in their entreaties. After all, apart from the alarming character of Agabus' warning, he knew Jerusalem and its tense atmosphere, for the passions which, a few years later, broke into the conflagration of the great rebellion of Jewry, were already hot in the air. Paul was known as a declared Roman citizen. His work among the Gentiles was considered by some a betrayal. A plot against his life had already been foiled. Luke himself added his plea ('we' in v. 14 shows that he supported the general warning).

Paul's determination to persist in the course of danger is puzzling. Perhaps he sought to follow the steps of Christ's passion and His 'setting His face steadfastly to go to Jerusalem' (Luke 9.51). Some deep inner compulsion moved him, and it is not for anyone to question the validity of such conviction in the case of another. At the same time, it is certainly a fact that a good man, unable to face objectively the nature of his motives, can be lamentably wrong. On the face of it, Paul seems to have moved on against unanimous, wise, loving and sincere advice, and commonly such counsel can be regarded as a major factor in the guidance of God. Scripture never hesitates to record a failing or a weakness in a noble man, and it is difficult to believe that Luke did not deplore his friend's determination. It is quite certain that a mighty ministry was to be tragically abbreviated by the events which the visit to Jerusalem precipitated. On the other hand, the custody of Paul produced the work of Luke, even if it did silence for vital years the potent preaching of Paul. Good can be drawn from error, if error be committed to God, and Paul's voice rings in the writings of his friend.

609 : Jerusalem Church
Acts 21.15–26; 1 Corinthians 9.19–23

Luke remarks that the Jerusalem church received Paul and his party with warmth (17), and they no doubt took over, at some official reception, the considerable sum of money which Paul brought from the Gentile congregations. Luke says no more and it is a fair guess that the meeting proved to Paul a bitter disappointment. On the other hand, Luke is in one of his abbreviating phases, and the narrative, moving swiftly on to more vital events may disguise a time lapse which absolves James, the undisputed leader of the Jerusalem church, of any charge of a suspicious and unworthy attitude towards Paul.

The Jerusalem leaders could have been in a difficult position. In the Jerusalem Conference (Acts 15) they had gone as far as they could to conciliate the Gentile congregations. Ten years had passed. Such liberalizing influence which men like Peter, Barnabas and others might have exercised was weakening, as missionary activities abroad withdrew such leadership from the mother church. The Gentile church was growing more and more powerful, and the Jewish church in Jerusalem, a continual scene of Pharisaic and Judaizing activity, was probably growing narrower and narrower amid a resurgent Jewish nationalism. The atmosphere of the capital was becoming heavier each year with the menace of coming rebellion against Rome, and it is difficult for any congregation to escape the influence of its time and place. The Jewish tide was rising. Hence the suggestion, almost an order, from James. The Gentiles, he hints, had won a great concession. Why should Paul not yield a little, and demonstrate publicly that his now famous ministry among the Gentiles had not destroyed his old Jewish loyalties. It was a little thing, and had they not heard that he himself had made such a vow in Cenchreae, and had he not written of his willingness to be 'all things to all men if by any means he might win some'?

Paul, agonizingly anxious to win his old associates, conceded the point. It was a magnanimous second mile, but, as it turned out, a disastrous mistake. He was not to know that within a decade the stiff-necked Jerusalem church would cease to exist. He was weary of conflict. He sought to love and understand—and failed.

610 : The Crowd

Acts 21.26–40

The riot in the temple court, entirely the fault of the unwise advice given to Paul, is told in fine terse prose, obviously the narrative of an eyewitness. Paul's old enemies from Asia had been overlooked in the apostle's eagerness to meet the wishes of the Christian Pharisees. Ephesus had already demonstrated the possibilities of mob violence, and the peculiarities of crowd-psychology. It appeared again.

There is cruelty in all primitive forces. Wind and wave and fire can be ruthless. So can the gales of emotion which sweep through crowds and peoples, turning groups of human beings into destroying hordes. Crowds tend to reflect the morality of their basest elements. They act in mass ignorance, as Luke remarked of the Ephesian mob (19.32). As Gustave Le Bon said at the beginning of the century: 'The individual forming part of a crowd acquires, solely from numerical considerations, a sentiment of invincible power, which allows him to yield to instincts, which, had he been alone, he would perforce have kept in check.'

Crowds, in consequence, lack self-consciousness and any sense of responsibility. They are prone to be carried away by a feeling of power, in which the individual, losing name and identity, lends himself to deeds of evil. The Romans feared the Jerusalem mob, and had good reason to do so. It was to be just such a mad riot which, in A.D. 66, would spark off the terrible four years of the great Jewish rebellion.

Crying havoc against Paul, the Ephesian group stirred such a tumult that the garrison, stationed in the Tower of Antonia overlooking the area, was alerted and driven to intervention. A strong patrol descended one of the two stairways which led to the area, and drove violently through the crowd to the rescue. The impression was that a Jew from Egypt, a member probably of the notoriously riotous Alexandrian ghetto, was at his rabble-rousing again.

Holding the crowd at bay, the tough soldiers carried Paul off with the old familiar cry of the Lord's passion ringing: 'Away with him . . .'

611 : Lysias and Paul

Acts 22

The tribune in charge of the garrison, Claudius Lysias, appears to have been one of the career men frequently met in the days of Claudius' two notorious freedmen ministers, Pallas and Narcissus. He was a Greek, as his second name indicates, and his first name was acquired when, at the price of a considerable bribe, a piece of corruption common enough in that venal group, he was granted the still coveted Roman citizenship. On the other hand Lysias seems to have been a vigorous and capable soldier, with good relations with his staff (26). The centurion is at ease with his commander.

Obviously Paul made a strong impression on the Roman officer. He did not reveal his Roman citizenship until after the second outburst of mob rage, and it says something for the commanding personality of the prisoner that a senior officer paused in the midst of a tense and perilous operation, and allowed an un-identified prisoner, just snatched by force from the hands of a wildly excited mob, to stand on the stairs which led to the security of the tower, and, over the narrow barricade of the soldiers' spears, address the seething crowd below. We have remarked that Paul was the first European, the first character of whom history has clear record, who bore in his own person the integrated heritage of the three cultures from which European civilization has sprung. It was his speaking Greek which first caught the attention of the Roman tribune. He addressed the crowd in their Hebrew dialect. He was soon to claim his Roman rights and win them.

It was also on Paul's part a remarkable exhibition of cool courage and superb self-control. He had just been saved from lynching by the intervention of a rough detachment of soldiery, men who probably took little care to be gentle with the person at the centre of the disturbance. Most people would be too shaken

704

by their grim experience to be able to stand and speak coherently, as Paul quite obviously did. He seized the opportunity to testify, and, in spite of the violence of which he had just been the victim, did all he could to conciliate the crowd. He postponed as far as possible any reference to Gentiles, even at one point (15), modifying Christ's words to do so. The spirit of the mob is revealed by the explosive power of this one word (22).

612 : The Sanhedrists and Paul

Acts 23.1–11; Matthew 26.57–66

Snatched into the safety of the fort, Paul, no doubt, faced trouble with Lysias, who probably knew no Aramaic, and may have regarded the new outbreak of protest as a poor return for the concession he had granted his remarkable prisoner. Hence the threat of scourging and the centurion's wise word of caution. Paul was now in the hands of the Romans. He was to remain there for five years.

Now for the fifth time the supreme court of Jewry was to adjudicate on the claims of the Christian Church. Lysias obviously had full briefing on how to deal with the Jewish leaders. Rome was handling the situation of deepening menace in her most turbulent province with care. Eager to fulfil all the requirements of justice, and in pursuance of an enlightened policy towards the Jews which Pilate's heavy-handed attitude towards that difficult people had more than ever shown to be necessary, Lysias set Paul before the senior tribunal of his own people, and found it necessary in the outcome (10) to rescue the prisoner a second time.

Paul's dexterous conduct must have astonished him. The atrocious action of the high priest, in such contrast to the disciplined attitude of the Romans, enraged Paul. How it was that he failed to recognize the high priest is a matter of conjecture. He had, of course, been long absent from Jerusalem, and if his swift reaction contrasted with that of Christ on a like occasion, it conformed to common norms of human conduct which most people will too readily recognize.

Paul could see that constructive argument would be fruitless, and appealed to his own class, the Pharisees, with whom he at least had a point of contact. The worldly, venal, heretical Sadducees were in any case beyond all argument of piety or reason.

F. W. Farrar, one of Paul's early great biographers, condemns Paul for thus dividing the assembly, but Ramsay has a convincing reply. 'His defence was always the same,' says Ramsay, 'and therefore carefully planned: that his life had been consistently directed towards one end, the glorification of the God of Israel by admitting the Nations to be His servants, and that this was true Judaism and true Pharisaism.' Hence the relevance of the defence before the Sanhedrin. 'If one party,' Ramsay continues, 'was more capable of being brought to a favourable view of his claims than the other he would naturally and justifiably aim at affecting the minds of the more hopeful party.' That is exactly what Paul did at Athens, when he addressed himself almost exclusively to the Stoic element in his audience. He was claiming, moreover, 'to represent the true line of development in which Judaism ought to advance'.

613 : Paul and the Plotters
Acts 23.11–15; 2 Corinthians 11.16–33

We might pause a moment to try to imagine Paul's state of mind. He had just passed through days of terrible mental and spiritual stress. He had escaped a plot against his life, and was about to hear of another. He had been twice rescued by force from the insane violence of his own people. He must have been deeply hurt by the narrow-minded group of his own fellow Christians who had demanded a demonstration of formal agreement with their erroneous prejudices, and in so doing had opened the path to catastrophe.

He must also have been overwhelmed by misgivings, for he had battled his way to Jerusalem and disastrous suffering against road-block after road-block of advice to retreat. Like Abraham, who had flung his hastily armed shepherds against an invading force from the Euphrates Valley, and had faced, in the outcome, and with time to weigh the consequences, a painful collapse of confidence (Gen. 14), Paul needed a word from God (11). The great Abraham was his hero. He had pondered deeply over the life and adventures of the patriarch. It seems not by accident that, in his moment of crisis, in those sombre hours of the night when the darkness of heaven seems to penetrate the soul, he received a word from the Lord which is almost an echo of the word which came to Abraham (Gen. 15.1).

The encouragement sets no seal of divine approval on Paul's journey to Jerusalem. The wisdom of that enterprise still stands open to question. But it is like God in such dark hours of the soul to show some token of His love. And there came in confirmation the revelation of the plot by the forty Jews. It was a climax of hate. There is, unfortunately, no evidence that the plotters, frustrated of their purpose, starved to death by the terms of their vow. The scribes and lawyers had sophistic devices by which they could circumvent any of the inconveniences with which they had loaded the Mosaic law, and it is quite certain that there were hypocritical escape clauses whereby the plotters could extricate themselves from the ultimate consequences of the hunger and thirst they had undertaken to face. It is a not uncommon situation in life that a revelation of God's care should stand in juxtaposition to a demonstration of human viciousness.

614 : Paul's Nephew

Acts 23.16–35

The plot, quite unexpectedly, throws a ray of light on Paul's family, the only scrap of information we possess. If the secret plotting of the fanatics became known to Paul's sister, the family must have had the highest connections in the city. It was, moreover, an act of no small courage thus to lay information. The deference with which Lysias treats the boy is also notable.

Loyalty is a pleasant sight, and after his night of darkness, Paul must have seen in his sister's and his nephew's love yet another token of God's continuing care for him. And it would come with greater sweetness to him if such loyalty was seen against the background of family repudiation. John Pollock, commenting on Paul's home circumstances, remarks: 'My personal reading of the scanty extant evidence is that Paul was . . . a widower, or, more probably, had been repudiated by his wife when he returned to Tarsus a Christian—he suffered the loss of all things for Christ.'

However this may be, Paul's sister and her son saved Paul's life. The efficient Lysias set arrangements in train. It is a deeply significant fact that it required a detachment of 470 troops to ensure the safety of one political prisoner travelling down the descending highway to Caesarea—probably the high road down to the coastal plain where the shattered trucks and jeeps lie in the scrub as a memorial of another guerrilla-haunted day. The situation in Palestine must have been grave indeed, and it seems clear that firm Roman control was practically confined to the cities.

The chapter closes with a last glance at the tribune. He takes a small liberty with truth when he advances the hour of his regard for Paul's status as a Roman. It was a neater story, set Lysias in a somewhat more favourable light, and is quite in character. He was a good type of officer, and reinforces the suggestion already made that the imperial government set some store by the type of man chosen for service in Palestine.

Paul was now safe. The garrison port of Caesarea, Rome's bridgehead and stronghold, was completely secure. There was a church community there. Paul was free to write, Luke to pursue his researches through the land. The extensive ruins visible today are of immense Christian significance.

Questions and themes for study and discussion on Studies 607–614

1. Paul and Philip's daughters.
2. Give examples from the Old Testament of symbolic teaching.
3. Is compromise ever justified?
4. Are crowds dangerous? Why and when?
5. The nature of true courage.
6. Pharisaism, good and bad.
7. The nature of hatred.
8. How did Paul spend his time at Caesarea?

615 : Felix

Acts 23.26; 24.1–10, 22–27

Felix, like Pilate, was a lamentable mistake. All sorts of ir-regularities disgraced his governorship. He was the brother of Pallas, the notorious freedman and senior minister of Claudius, an upstart of whom Tacitus, the mordant Roman historian, speaks with blistering scorn. He is no less contemptuous of Felix who, he said, 'thought he could commit every sort of iniquity and escape the consequences.' He felt secure under his powerful brother's shadow. Nothing could be more untrue than the opening gambit of Tertullus' artificial oratory. We have seen what state the country was in from the fact that Lysias detached the major part of a cohort to secure the safe arrival of Paul in Caesarea.

Such was the man before whom Paul preached of 'righteousness, self-control, and judgement' and who put off consideration of such things until a 'more convenient season'. Tacitus mentions him again in describing the events which led up to the rebellion. He describes him as 'a master of cruelty and lust who exercised the powers of a king in the spirit of a slave'. Nero recalled him in A.D. 56 or 57, and he passes from the scene.

The scene in court is dramatic, a striking illustration of the lines of James Russell Lowell:

Truth forever on the scaffold, Wrong forever on the throne,
Yet that scaffold sways the future, and, behind the dim unknown,
Standeth God within the shadow, keeping watch above His own.

For a brief moment Felix seemed to have been touched with fear, and faced himself. He is visibly confronted with a crisis and makes a decision. His greed was the last factor which turned the scales. There is no 'more convenient season' than the passing moment when the vital choices of life are to be made. As Lowell's same poem puts it:

Once to every man and nation comes the moment to decide,
In the strife of Truth with Falsehood, for the good or evil side . . .

Felix was tangled, like his predecessor Pilate, in a web of his own weaving. As with Pilate, it would have taken a mighty act of the will to rise and cut himself free. He was unable to make that painful reappraisement and died as he lived.

616 : Drusilla

Acts 24.24

Drusa (Drusilla is a pet-name as Priscilla is of Prisca) was one of the daughters of Agrippa I. She married, probably about A.D. 53, Azis of Emesa, a principality in the north of Syria. In the following year, still only about sixteen years of age, she was seduced by Felix, and became that scoundrel's third wife, a situation which provoked contempt even in Rome. It was probably the influence of Drusilla's sister, Bernice, and Agrippa II, after Claudius' death and the consequent passing of Felix' protection, that secured the recall of Felix from his mismanaged governorship.

According to Josephus, who, as Vespasian's secretary, and a Jewish historian, is likely to have been in possession of factual knowledge, Drusilla bore Felix a son, whom she named Agrippa, after her father. She survived her husband's recall, and subsequent death, and lived in the Campanian town of Pompeii until August A.D. 79. On the 24th of that month, Vesuvius exploded in the famous eruption which Pliny describes vividly in two letters to his friend the historian Tacitus. Drusilla and her son appear to have perished under the ash which sealed Pompeii for the discoveries of the modern world. Some Jewish slave wrote 'Sodoma Gomora' on a wall, possibly when doom descended. Could it have been Drusilla's house? She was 39 or 40 years of age.

Drusilla must have had some knowledge of her father's unfortunate relations with the Christians. She had the immense privilege of hearing a direct appeal from the most famous Christian of her day. She heard Paul preach of 'righteousness, self-control and judgement to come.' It is intriguing to imagine what she may have remembered of words in that distant courtroom, when the great mushroom cloud 'like a pine tree', said Pliny, referring to the umbrella pines of his land, rose above the shaking land on that hot August day, and the mephitic vapours began to roll, under dense darkness, on the little city.

Like Felix, whose importunity had seemed to open such vast possibilities of romance, excitement, social standing, and travel overseas, she too came to the end of the road. It is the end which counts in the affairs of life. She chose disastrously, had the chance to choose aright, and lost her opportunity.

617 : Tertullus

Acts 24.1–9; James 3.1–10

Before leaving the scene in the Caesarea court, it may be interesting to look briefly at the orator Tertullus. He was possibly a Roman trained in the principles of rhetoric fashionable in the capital. Roman oratory, deprived of its political themes with the establishment of the imperial autocracy, flourished in the schools and the courts. Soon after Paul's death, Quintilian returned from Spain to Rome, and his work on rhetoric is one of the few surviving pieces of Latin literature from that century.

The study of the principles of speech and of persuasion can be mentally and morally damaging. Debate for the sake of debate can weaken regard for truth, and it is the duty of any speaker and any hearer to consider content and truth before the manner and method of its presentation. Aristophanes, the great Athenian writer of satirical comedy, attacking the New Education in his play *The Clouds*, quips that the object of sophistic instruction in his day was 'to make the worse appear the better reason'. Tertullus was of such a class.

Tertullus, in fact, was no great orator. Felix, scoundrel though he was, seems to have been quite unimpressed by the suggestion that a case of treason was on his hands. The prosecution made a serious mistake in directing a side-blow against the capable commander of the Jerusalem garrison. Felix knew that his covertly corrupt rule depended on the efficiency of such officers. Nor, in fact, was the plausible fellow well-trained in his corrupt art. In oratory the greatest art is to conceal art, and Luke seems to take a subtle pleasure in reporting the prosecutor's too obviously elaborate flatteries, an obsequious approach no doubt somewhat dimmed by the sour presence of the high priest in the court.

Commenting on such rhetoric, the cynical Lord Chesterfield said: 'Elegance of style and the turn of the periods, make the chief impression upon the hearers. Most people have ears, but few have judgement. Tickle those ears, and, depend upon it, you will catch their judgement, such as it is.' Misreading Felix, the Sanhedrists thought to apply such advice. They failed, probably because of Felix' regard for Lysias, whose further advice he thought it prudent to await. It is fairly obvious that, when the tribune came to Caesarea, he counselled prudence. It is to be hoped that Tertullus was not paid his fee. The world has had enough of those who use words to hide the truth.

618 : Festus

Acts 25.1–27; 26.24, 25

Porcius Festus succeeded to the mismanaged procuratorship in A.D. 57 or 58, and the brief episode of his examination of Paul and the consultation with Agrippa II is another interesting glimpse of a Roman governor at work in a difficult situation. Festus had inherited from Felix a lamentable load of trouble. There was lawlessness in the countryside, and armed rivalry between the factions of the hierarchy. Events were in full flow for the disaster of eight years later. Festus could not afford to alienate collaborating elements, and the determination of the priests to make away with an obviously innocent man was a problem which required most careful handling. It was the situation of thirty years before, repeated with other actors and on another stage. Festus, however, was a luckier man than Pilate. He found a way of escape through the prisoner's own action. He had offered Paul an acquittal on the charge of sedition, and added the proposal, not unreasonable from his point of view, that the ex-Pharisee should face a religious investigation before his peers.

For Paul it was a crisis. He knew the perils of Jerusalem. Perhaps he grasped the realities of the political situation, the growing tension, and the deepening anarchy, better than the procurator himself. If Festus found himself inhibited by official policy from refusing and frustrating the Jerusalem hierarchy, Paul proposed to cut the knot, to save himself and free the governor from all embarrassment by exercising a Roman citizen's right. He appealed to Caesar.

The process to which Paul had recourse was the act by which a litigant disputes a judgement, with the consequence that the case is referred to a higher court, normally that of the authority who had originally appointed the magistrate of the court from which the appeal originated. Caesar had appointed Festus. Festus was obliged to accept the appeal, and refer it on, accompanied by relevant documents and a personal report, which must have presented some difficulty. He saw no fault in Paul by any standards of law and justice familiar to him. He was newly arrived in Palestine, and Jewish law and Jewish religion were both unfamiliar to him. In his difficult office he was not free to sweep such matters aside with a Gallio's contempt. Festus had his career to make. His difficult province was a hard testing-ground, and the lucidity and correct terminology of a document over his signature in a court so exalted as that of Caesar himself must have been a matter of anxious concern. Hence the alacrity with which he availed himself of the help of Agrippa II.

The Jews had no complaints to level against Festus. He was possibly the best of the procurators. It is a pity that he died two years or thereabouts later.

712

619 : Agrippa II
Acts 25.13–27; 26.1–3, 25–32

Agrippa was a man of ability, of wide knowledge of Judaism, and of more than a nodding acquaintance with Christianity. He must have known the policy of his house. Paul's attitude and careful apologia show that he valued the opportunity, doubtless for the sake of the Church and its freedom, equally with his own. It was of prime importance to the prisoner, as well as to the procurator, that the report to Rome should be accurately phrased and properly supplied with detail. It is an interesting situation. The careful governor, obviously anxious not to make a false step amid the growing perils of the province; the care of Rome's representative to honour the client-king, so true to official policy as old as Augustus; Paul's battle for justice, so often to be repeated; the background of menace outside the safety of the garrison town—where else in ancient literature is so authentic a document of the Empire in action to be found?

There is little more to say of Herod's house. Agrippa makes one or two brief appearances in later history. Josephus shows him actively and despairingly at work in an endeavour to preserve the peace in Palestine, when the great rebellion was looming. With the sure diplomatic instinct of his family, he was active in support of Vespasian, the successful survivor of the troubled year of civil war which followed Nero's death. He was actually in Rome, whither Vespasian had sent him, to salute Galba, the first of that year's ill-fated emperors. In Tacitus' brief phrases it is possible to catch a glimpse of the old decision and sure choice characteristic of others of his house: 'Soon after, Agrippa, informed by private message from the East, left Rome before Vitellius received the news, and hurried back on a fast ship. With equal spirit Queen Berenice espoused Vespasian's cause. She was in the bloom of her youth and beauty, and had made herself agreeable to Vespasian, old though he was, by the magnificence of her gifts.' It was not the first bold voyage of a Herod across the sea between Italy and Palestine. Agrippa took an active part in the war in Palestine, was wounded at Gamala, and was with Titus at the siege of Jerusalem. From the safety of Caesarea he saw the final ruin of the country he had sought to save. With Agrippa II ended the Herods, an astonishingly able family, whose pro-Roman policy went far to postpone the clash between Rome and the Jews, and played in consequence an

713

unwitting but significant part in holding the peace during the formative years of the Christian Church in Palestine.

Josephus, who, as archaeology proceeds, proves a more and more reliable guide, is the supplier of most of the information on the king.

620 : Bernice (Berenice)

Acts 25.13–27

We have looked at this passage before in connection with Agrippa the Second, but the remarkable woman who accompanied the king is also worth consideration. She was a daughter of Agrippa the First, sister to Agrippa the Second and Drusilla, and was born in A.D. 28. Her first husband was one Marcus, a Jewish official of Alexandria who soon died. Herod Agrippa the First then betrothed her to her uncle, also a Herod by name, the ruler, under Claudius, of the kingdom of Calchis. Of this marriage there were two sons. Herod of Calchis died in A.D. 48.

As a widow Bernice lived in close friendship with her brother, and there seems to have been a strong bond between them—with the inevitable result that rumours of an incestuous relationship were rife. Even in distant Rome, half a century later, the rumour was still remembered, and Juvenal wrote in his Sixth Satire, sometimes called 'The Legend of Bad Women' of

> *That far-famed gem which Berenice wore,*
> *The hire of incest and thence valued more,*
> *A brother's present, in that barbarous state*
> *Where kings the sabbath barefoot celebrate,*
> *And old indulgence grants a length of life*
> *To hogs that fatten fearless of the knife.*

Of this allegation there is no concrete evidence whatsoever, nor of the actual marriage of brother and sister—an arrangement not uncommon in the East.

Bernice was present in Jerusalem when the procurator Florus pillaged the Temple in those last tragic acts of Roman folly which preceded the outbreak of revolt. She risked her life in begging him to show sense and desist, and was almost killed by Florus' undisciplined troops. She wrote to the proconsul Cestius in Syria to complain of Florus, and stood, in superb courage, by her

714

brother's side, when he appealed to the Jerusalem crowd to abstain from violence. The mob burned the palaces of both brother and sister when rebellion broke out. The couple took refuge in Caesarea.

For all this information, which sets the brother and sister in a rather fine light, we are indebted to Josephus. Tacitus, the Roman historian, picks up the story at this point, and he tells how Agrippa and Bernice swore allegiance to Vespasian. According to Suetonius, Bernice and Titus, Vespasian's son and short lived successor, were lovers, and only such prejudice as still lived in Juvenal who was quoted above, prevented Titus from marrying her. Hers was a strange and lurid career. At Caesarea she too had her hour of opportunity.

Questions and themes for study and discussion on Studies 615–620

1. Paul's text before Felix. What times are 'convenient' for decision?
2. Drusilla's fault and folly.
3. The use and abuse of oratory.
4. Appealing to Caesar.
5. 'Almost you persuade me . . .'
6. 'The hour of opportunity.'

621 : All Aboard
Acts 27.1–15

Luke's vivid writing in this chapter gives us one of the best-told stories of shipwreck in all literature. It is useful to follow a map and imagine the talk, the argument, the apprehensions of this strangely assorted party as the ship's master, under orders no doubt from some Roman shipping firm, risked a late voyage with his cargo of Egyptian wheat for the capital.

The Roman centurion, a man of quiet and effective command, shipped his party in a vessel from Adramyttium, the likeliest craft to put the company into the stream of east-west trade, for Adramyttium lies on the Aegean opposite Lesbos. The vessel had beaten north along the low Palestinian coast, cut between Cyprus and the mainland, as the seasonal winds demanded, and then worked west along the coast of Asia Minor to Myra, at the extreme southern point of the blunt peninsula. Here the party transferred to an Alexandrian cornship, which had perhaps chosen this northern route because of the lateness of the season.

The map at this point reveals the hazards of ancient navigation. The shipmaster made for Cnidus, a port on the south-west extremity of Asia Minor. He was unable to make the harbour, for a wind off shore drove the heavy galley south, and the shipmaster took refuge from the insistent blast under the lee of the 140-mile long island of Crete. Halfway along lies Fair Havens, the port where Paul, one of the most experienced travellers of his age, besought them to stay for the winter—the common practice of ancient mariners. The shipmaster rashly decided to try for another anchorage.

The eastern half of Crete is low, the western quite different. In great heaped terraces, it rises into a group of lofty snow-capped mountains. The old enemy, the north-east wind, funnelled down through the clefts of these highlands, now found them again and drove them off shore round the island of Clauda. The passengers were called in to aid the crew in managing the lurching ship, for Luke remembered vividly the fierce struggle under the brief protection of Clauda to haul on board the boat which was towing water-logged behind.

Danger unites men of diverse character. There were the rugged soldiers, picked men of the centurion's special corps. The centurion himself was a chosen officer in a brigade set aside for special service. Pulling on the same ropes was one of the greatest scholars of his age, the citizen from Tarsus, and Luke the cultured historian and physician.

622 : Paul the Leader

Acts 27.16–44

The nor'easter now had the lumbering corn ship in charge. Far to the south, off the African coast, lay the Syrtes, the graveyard of many ships, as underwater archaeology has vividly revealed. Hence the battle to hold a westerly course, aided, it appears by a veering of the wind to the east, as the cyclonic disturbance shifted.

The tremendous gifts of leadership of Paul emerged at the crisis. His advice at Fair Havens had been rejected, and he was human enough to mention the fact, but in Luke's vivid account it is clear that the apostle, not the Roman centurion, nor the captain, was the one who held and stiffened the morale of the

716

company. They were indeed at the end of human resources. They had looped tautened cables precariously round the hull to bind the straining timbers against the stress of the violent seas, and the strong leverage of the mast; they had cut loose and jettisoned all dispensable tackle and gear. And it was all under a murky heaven, with the spray and driving cloud blotting out the stars, and the galley lurching west at nearly 40 miles a day.

The end came. Hearing the sound of distant surf, the sailors suspected land or shoals ahead. The lead showed a shelving seabed, so the hulk was hove to for the night with anchors out astern. This arrangement kept the ship heading in the right direction before the pressure of the still thrusting wind. It was on the fairly transparent pretext of similarly anchoring the bow, that the crew proposed to launch the boat and escape, a plot frustrated by the alert Paul, and a few quick sword-cuts on the ropes at the centurion's prompt orders.

At this point the centurion Julius, or the captain seems to have numbered the ship's complement, a sensible measure before the abandonment of the vessel. They spent the night heaving overboard the cargo of Egyptian wheat, and with the dawn saw an unknown coast, a beach, and a practicable bay. A bar, due to a cross-current, frustrated the attempt to beach the ship which probably drew 18 feet of water, and it was at this point that the escort, who were responsible for their charges, proposed to kill the prisoners. The centurion's admiration for Paul is apparent in the refusal. There was a struggle through the breakers and the whole ship's company reached the beach. It was a triumph for Paul's faith and no small tribute to his dynamic personality.

623 : The Centurion

Acts 27.1–6, 31, 43; 28.16; Matthew 8.5–13

The centurion's regard for Paul appears again at Puteoli. We have glanced at this man in passing, but he is worth a closer look. One characteristic of the Roman imperial system, initiated by Augustus himself, was a notable ability to pick men. Even Nero was aided and supported by able ministers like Burrus and Seneca. The army, in important tracts of its history, seemed to produce the most able officers. Lysias was a man of firmness, swift decision and tact, as we have seen, and Paul's centurion maintains the reputation of that class of soldier as they appear in the

717

Eastern command. The Augustan Cohort was itself an *élite* corps, a body of guards, to whom courier and escort duties were committed, and to be a commanding officer in such a regiment was proof enough of fine quality.

He is one of the two centurions whose names we know. He preserved Paul when his men were all for killing the prisoners, as the galley ran ashore. The men, after all, were responsible for the secure delivery of the persons in their charge. In Puteoli, the modern Pozzuoli, the same centurion allowed Paul to lodge with the Christians. It is remarkable that the Christians were so promptly to be found, or that communication between the Christian groups in the Empire was such that the Christians of the busy port were aware of the coming of Paul on such and such a ship.

Paul must have been supremely trusted. This, for Julius, was a much more chancy situation than that off the small island of Malta. The port was big and cosmopolitan. It was full of hiding-places. The Christians were obviously in touch with their brethren in Rome. Rome with its population of a million people was a great warren into which any man could disappear as Onesimus was soon to do. Paul could have been spirited away up the Via Appia with the greatest of ease. It shows courage, acute judgement, and even friendly regard on the part of the senior soldier, to allow freedom.

To be trustworthy as a citizen and a man was a lesson Paul taught. Writing soon afterwards to Philippi, he besought the Church to 'live as citizens worthily of the gospel of Christ' (Phil. 1.27). He was himself a prime example. He had appealed to Rome. He was ready to go there. The centurion duly delivered him to the prefect of the praetorian guards. This was the competent Burrus, who had only two years to live.

624 : The Maltese

Acts 28.1–11; 14.8–18

The 'barbarous people', as the AV [KJV] so curiously translates the phrase in v. 2 were the native Maltese, who had watched the galley lurching through the surf. The Greek *barbaros*, of course, simply means those who speak another language than Greek— whose speech, in short, sounds to Greek ears as intelligible as a lamb's bleating (bar-bar). The Greeks called their Persian foes *barbaroi*, while most freely admitting the material superiority of Persian civilization.

Malta had been colonized by Phoenicians ten centuries before Christ. Six centuries before Christ, the island came under the control of the great North African Phoenician city of Carthage which, over the space of a century, disputed the possession of the Eastern Mediterranean with Rome. Hannibal, one of the greatest military commanders of history, was born there. In 218 B.C. Rome took Malta and never lost it. The position, as all history has shown, is strategically vital.

The peasantry of Malta continued to speak their native Phoenician, a Semitic tongue, as closely allied to Hebrew and Aramaic as Arabic is to modern Hebrew. It is not impossible that Paul could make some sense of what they said. Hence the knowledge of what the bystanders thought when Paul, ready as ever to lend a hand at humble work, shook the torpid snake into the fire. This, observe, is Paul's second contact with 'barbarians', or 'foreigners', 'non-Greek speaking people', however it may be translated. He had made a similar impression at Lystra on a Lycaonian community.

The party made itself useful on the island. There is always work for those who look for work to do. The Maltese responded, from the Phoenician proletariat to the 'first man', Publius (Luke again uses the correct term for the chief Roman administrator—it has been epigraphically attested). It is significant, however, in his missionary endeavour, that Paul worked out from a periphery of common culture. The retreat to Lystra was forced on him. Shipwreck landed him on Malta. He planted his Christian cells in points from which diffusion, he hoped, would be spontaneous. He fostered the home base. If semantics made the word for villager (*paganus*) a word for a non-Christian, that was the fault of those who failed to penetrate their country hinterlands.

625 : Paul Comes to Rome

Acts 28.11–16; Revelation 17.1–6; 18.9–20

Caught in a web of provincial maladministration, Paul, as we have seen, had appealed to Caesar, and on the chill February day, with the mists from the sea haunting the Campagna, Paul neared the end of his journey. Rome was in sight.

He had long looked forward to that visit. Some ten years before the Christian Church had struck root in the teeming capital, and Paul had written the most difficult and closely argued of his letters to the Roman church. It met no doubt in the house of Hermes, whose frescoed rooms were excavated in 1932. Paul was fascinated by the imperial spectacle of Rome. The great empire straddled the world, netted and tied its parts together with the amazing system of its military roads, policed the far frontiers and held all the strategic points with a firm ironclad hand.

Paul had long since seen that the way to conquest was to meet the might of Rome and the world where it was strongest and most deeply entrenched.

It must have been with eyes of excitement that Paul saw the crumbling monuments and tombs thicken beside the cobbled Appian Way. The smoke and noise of the capital lay ahead, and the traveller had no reason to anticipate anything but justice there. Many more years were to pass before John wrote into the visions of the last book of the Bible a picture of Rome far different from that which occupied the mind of Paul on the cold February morning. The writer of the Apocalypse had seen the great empire turn to persecution, and he pictured her as a woman 'arrayed in purple and scarlet and decked with gold . . . drunken with the blood of the martyrs'.

In February 59 or 60, Rome had not turned on the innocent, and Paul saw that morning the beckoning of opportunity. True, he came a prisoner, when he had hoped to come in freedom, but he may have reflected ironically that he also came at Rome's expense. A million strong, Rome awaited him, and Rome's need was great. The world-weariness of the age was written into the inscriptions he could read on the tombs by the wayside. 'What I ate and drank I have with me,' ran one, 'the rest is lost.' 'Come and have a spot with me,' said another.

South of Rome today there are bits and pieces of the landscape which must be much as they were nineteen centuries ago. The umbrella pines stood then as they do today. So too the pointing candles of the dark cypresses, the dry stone walls, the crumbling, pumicy soil. There are bits of the city rampart which Paul may have seen, grey-green olives, hill-slopes of hungry soil. . .

Paul must have found the challenge daunting and a burden on his heart. Hence the lift of spirits when a band of Christians, alerted by their friends at Puteoli, appeared at the village of Three Shops with welcome.

720

626 : The Praetorians

Acts 28.16; Philippians 1.1–13

Rome's praetorians provided the guard for Paul in his house confinement, and gave him a sphere of evangelism of which we get one glimpse only. It is in the letter to the Philippians, written from Rome. Correctly translated Phil. 1.13 runs: 'It has become clear, through the whole Praetorian Barracks, that it is because I am a Christian that I am in confinement.' The words indicate some wide interest among Rome's household troops.

Augustus had established this special corps in 27 B.C. and half a century later, Tiberius' powerful prefect of the Praetorian Guard, Seianus, concentrated their nine cohorts, till then scattered, into a single camp just outside the city walls. It was from this dangerous action that the political importance of the Guard and its commanders dated. They proclaimed Claudius and Nero as emperors, and sealed Nero's doom by deserting him. They killed Galba, first of the four emperors to be proclaimed in the fearsome civil strife of A.D. 68, 69.

Having murdered Galba, the praetorians supported Otho, second of the four emperors which that year of blood was to see. They supported Vitellius, who defeated and succeeded Otho, and were destroyed by a running fight in the streets of Rome and the final storming of their camp, by the vanguard of the legions which raised Vespasian to power. Thus was 'the Beast', wounded almost to death, 'healed of his deadly wound, and all the world wondered' (Rev. 13. 3).

These scenes of violence, death, treachery and manifold disaster took place eight or nine years after the final events of Luke's story. If Paul succeeded in bringing some of the troops to Christ, they could have been among those involved in the street-fighting and the battle for the barracks, which were only some of the incidents of blood and carnage which cursed the whole land of Italy in the horrible year before Vespasian seized and held power.

With the changing of the guard at each watch, it could be that, over the space of two years, half of the 4500 troops in the guard had some contact with the notable prisoner. It was their day of opportunity, had they but known it. But that remark passes for any day. It is quite certain that Paul recognized it and used the hours to advantage.

627 : The Roman Church

Philippians 1.14–30

This passage gives a picture of the church in Rome during Paul's confinement there. The congregation had been established at least ten or twelve years before, if the riots in the ghetto at the end of the forties are to be interpreted as hostility to the Christians. The nucleus of the church could go back to those who found Christ at Pentecost. There were Roman Jews among them.

Who then were the group who were proclaiming Christ 'out of party-spirit, insincerely', thinking to make Paul's imprisonment even more burdensome than it was? He does not seem to disapprove of the general content of their preaching in Rome, so there can hardly have been too much of the Galatian heresy (which laid undue stress on the Law) involved. Magnanimously, though he deplores the spirit of the Roman partisans, he sees a certain propaganda value in their efforts. Perhaps they were the old leaders of the Roman Christians. Corinth is evidence for embryonic sects based on diversity of leadership and teaching. Apollos is evidence for some variety of doctrinal emphasis. So is the first Ephesian church. It is possible that some feared for the future of their teaching, and human nature is tragically prone to treasure a system of thought, and to shun the agony of reappraisement. Pride, too, most pervasive of the mind's faults, enters in, and corrupts even sacred things. Good men took courage from Paul's brightened prospects, and preached Christ from purity of motive. With purpose less pure, others took occasion to establish their own version of the faith, in the absence of the dynamic personality who was confined at Caesar's pleasure. Many a pet doctrine may have been menaced by Paul's authoritative elucidation of the truth. Pet doctrines are difficult to give up, and Paul, a man of conspicuous intellect and learned in three cultures, may not have suffered pretentious error gladly.

It is a little saddening to find the human faults the world knows too well showing themselves so early in the life of the Church, but we have met defective characters already in Acts. It is always well to remember that the Church is not composed of people who are better than the rest, but of people who are seeking by God's grace to be better than they are; not of people who are perfect, but of people who are dissatisfied with their imperfection.

628 : The Roman Synagogue

Acts 28.17–31; Romans 3.1–26

Paul's theme in his discussion with the Roman Jews would undoubtedly follow the argument of the letter to the Roman Christians written two or three years before while he was in Corinth. That famous document, to be sure, was for the church, but its very nature reveals the strength of the Jewish section of the community, and the synagogue would be familiar with it, because it would have been the inevitable subject of debate among Jews, Christian and orthodox.

The Jews, according to Paul's consistent policy, had the first chance. They were back in Rome, and obviously Claudius' decree of banishment (18.2) must have been rescinded. Claudius was a learned man, and it could have been his whim to apply what the Athenians called 'ostracism' whereby, without criminal charge against him, a person was asked, for the good of the city, to leave for a period of ten years.

In consequence, if some attempt is made to see matters from the point of view of the Roman rabbis, it is fair to concede that they had their difficulties. Nero had succeeded Claudius, and during the first five years of his principate, that pleasure-loving youth left affairs largely in the hands of the competent Burrus and the wise Seneca. If one or both of these men was instrumental in allowing the Jews to return, it would have been on condition that they keep the peace. A phrase in Suetonius suggests that the earlier banishment had been because 'of Christ', or 'Chrestos' as the historian's garbled information had it some seventy years later.

And now a notoriously controversial figure had arrived, one whose path through the eastern and central lands of the Mediterranean had been strewn with riot and disorder. Or so, at least, the career of Paul could be represented by the timid and the cautious, not to mention the openly hostile. No Jew cared to have his hard-pressed community wantonly disrupted. Reception, in consequence, was mixed (24), and Paul set before them the honoured words of the great Isaiah. We are allowed to be present at the last interview when, with some severity, the apostle announces again his 'turning to the Gentiles'.

Colossians 3

Glance back at the host of people we have met in Luke's book. The Christians of its thirty years of story would make a typical congregation for any church. They range from the servant girl Rhoda to the brilliant intellectual Paul. They include the physician Luke, the business-woman Lydia, the jailer of Philippi, two synagogue heads, a member of Athens' most sophisticated judicial body, an Ethiopian cabinet-minister, a country-boy from Lystra, two tent-makers from Rome, a lame beggar from Jerusalem, a Cyprian landowner and a strong-headed young man who quarrelled with an elder.

They came from a dozen cities Jewish, Greek, Roman in race. They were far from perfect, for on their periphery were sly deceitful folk like Ananias and Sapphira, scamps like Simon, and charlatans like the sons of Sceva. Their enemies ranged from Herod the king to the Sadducees and Pharisees of the Sanhedrin, the head of a trade-guild and the rabble of the market-place. Their message was received with yells of rage and the throwing of stones, with the polite deferment of Stoics, the mirth of Epicureans, the fear and self-seeking of one Roman governor and the impatience of another, and the irony of a well-informed king. (In spite of a once well-known hymn, Agrippa really said: 'In short, you think to make me a Christian?' Paul's reply was a play on words: 'In short or at length, no matter, but I could wish one and all here stood where I stand—save, of course [ruefully said] these bonds.')

There is a fine picture of the Empire at work—the magistrates, men of cool integrity like Gallio, anxious like Festus, calculating, and taking risks with peace, like Felix. One can sense the atmosphere of Palestine, moving forwards to the great explosion. There were the lesser levels of authority, functioning smoothly, the Asiarchs of Ephesus, the Areopagus of Athens, Lysias and the Jerusalem garrison ... It is almost 'a conducted tour' of major cities of the Graeco-Roman world, as a leading modern historian has recently remarked. We see the crowds, the minorities, the majorities, the sects, the denizens of the streets. It is the same world today, the same men and women, the same Church— fortunately it is the same Christ.

1. Luke as a reporter.
2. Paul's leadership. On what did it rest?
3. The centurions of Scripture.
4. Equality on the beach.
5. Rome in Paul's strategy.
6. Paul's concept of opportunity.
7. The old congregation and the newcomer.
8. Absorbing controversial figures.
9. What have you learned in Acts?

630 : Paul's Humility

Romans 1.1–17

This beautifully written introduction reveals much of Paul. Rome was one of the goals he sought, for the strategy of his evangelism, as we have seen, was world-wide. He had planted churches in key towns of the eastern Mediterranean. He now looked to Italy and Spain, and Rome was his essential base of operation. It was the heart of empire, and if ever there was a place in which Paul's theory of radiation applied it was in the great city on the Tiber. There had been a church in Rome for over ten years, and Paul had no thought of by-passing its witness or dispensing with its aid, although he must have known how much such beginners in Christ, with no New Testament to guide them, needed his help and instruction. We have guessed some of the pain certain members of that community were to cause him.

Humility is the teacher's best gown. Read again vs. 9 to 12 to see how Paul wears it. 'I long to see you,' he says. 'I want to bring you some spiritual gift to make you strong; or rather, I want to be among you to receive encouragement myself through the influence of your faith on me as of mine on you' (11 f., NEB). He owed a debt, he said, to people of all nations, for 'Greek' must be understood to contain the notion of Roman and of Jew, and 'barbarian' was simply 'foreigner', as we saw in the case of the Maltese islanders. It is the common way of man to imagine that life and the world at large owe a debt to him. The Christian, bought by grace to serve, should have no such misconceptions. Paul never did. He is writing to a young church which he had no hand in founding. He is writing with the immense prestige of established and proven leadership. He was

725

accepted as 'the apostle to the Gentiles'. And yet no arrogance, no unnecessary assumption of authority, mars the graciousness of his approach.

Said John Ruskin: 'I believe the first test of a truly great man is humility.' And Sir Thomas More: 'To be humble to superiors, is duty; to equals, it is courtesy; to inferiors, is nobleness; it being a virtue that, for all its lowliness, commands those it stoops to.' Such was Paul's leadership. He was a great soul.

631 : The Romans

Romans 1.18–32

Paul's picture of a godless society can be illustrated from a century of Roman poets, satirists and historians. Paul was writing during the principate of the young profligate, Nero, when Roman society was sunk in hideous vice. It has been left to the present day to produce again on the stage the nude and open sexuality which scandalized the more sober writers of Nero's day. Petronius, so ably portrayed in Henryk Sienkiewicz' historical novel *Quo Vadis*, was writing, at about the same time as Paul, a piece of fiction which has partly survived. It concerns the base doings of three Greek scamps in the sea-ports of Campania, and is dark confirmation of all Paul here writes. Anyone who seeks evidence in support of the apostle's grim description can read Petronius' *Satiricon*, Seneca's *Letters*, Juvenal's *Satires*, Tacitus' historical works, and Suetonius' *Lives of the Caesars*. Paul was writing to dwellers in Rome, some of them 'of Caesar's household' (Phil. 4.22), who had all this before their eyes.

Paul was, in fact, describing a doomed society, and much of what he writes hits too shrewdly home for comfort in the 'permissive society' of today. No nation was ever destroyed from without which had not already destroyed itself from within.

In a little-known speech of January, 1838, Abraham Lincoln put the thought well. 'At what point,' he asked, 'shall we expect the approach of danger? By what means shall we fortify against it? Shall we expect some transatlantic giant to step the ocean, and crush us at a blow? All the armies of Europe, Asia and Africa combined could not by force take a drink from the Ohio, or make a track on the Blue Ridge, in a trial of 1,000 years . . .

'If destruction be our lot, we ourselves must be its author and finisher. As a nation of free men, we must live through all times, or die by suicide.'

The words retain notable relevance in Lincoln's own land—and in many other lands—almost a century and a half later.

And what is society but the sum-total of its members? It is evil men and women who build an evil society, and no community can be organized and legislated into good. A society, a people, a land, are what individuals make them by faith, their virtue, and their justice, or by their base surrenders, their lack of reverence for God or good, and by the evil choices of their secret thoughts.

632 : Paul's Learning

Romans 2

The personality and character of a man, as we have had more than one occasion to remark emerge from what he writes, especially when he writes to persuade, with a cause hot in his heart. We meet Paul, the rabbi and the Jewish scholar, in this chapter, and then pass on to encounter Paul, the Hellenist, skilled in Greek debate, and appreciative of the best in Greek philosophic thought.

Verse 11 is a key verse, the thought of which Paul characteristically expands. The possession of the Law, he maintained, here and always, carried a heavy responsibility. The incredible sophistries of the scribes angered Paul. Some of them actually quoted: 'If you will diligently hearken ...' as a proof that doing took second place to hearing. With Paul, as with James, it was no true faith which did not demonstrate its reality in conduct. The Pharisees, to whose school Paul belonged, were clear enough on this point. They regarded doing, not merely learning, as 'the Leader', that is, the guiding precept in any division of their code. It is interesting to see, in the easy flow of his argument, how familiar Paul was with the fashion of such theological debate.

But not every Pharisee could have passed with Paul's versatility to the continuing discussion, which any Greek would have recognized. Anyone with a sensitive ear for that irony which is so characteristic of cultured Attic writers, will recognize it in the last dozen verses of this chapter, as they will in the first four chapters of Paul's letter to the Corinthians. Paul's knowledge of the Stoics, the noblest school of philosophy active in the world of his day, was obvious, as we saw, in his address to the Athenian court.

It is also visible in the central verses of this chapter of close and urgent argument. The Stoics had a doctrine of a law written on the heart. They were the first Greeks to use the word 'conscience' in a Christian sense. Aristotle, too, before the Stoic school was founded, had written: 'The truly educated man will behave as if he had a law within himself.' Sophocles, in his noblest play, five centuries before Paul, had made Antigone tell the tyrant that there were 'unwritten, irrefragable laws of heaven' which could not be broken. Paul moves with graceful ease through these tracts of thought.

633 : Paul and the Law

Romans 3

The Stoics, who invented preaching and the sermon, often taught by setting up an imaginary objector. Paul follows their method in this chapter. Indeed, he could have had a real objector in mind when he speaks of those who took and twisted his doctrine of grace to make him say that the more we sin, the more God has to forgive, and the more wondrous the benison of His grace—a fiendish perversion in Paul's estimation (8).

But the agony of his soul lies behind much of what follows. He was a Pharisee. He had revered the Law. Could the Law then do nothing? Was it a vast and sterile failure? In long brooding in Arabia, after he came to Christ, Paul had come to see the truth, that the Law set standards which, in his human strength, man could not keep. The Law, therefore, convicted of sin, and stressed the need of a Saviour and salvation by grace.

In the whole chapter, Greek though the shape of the dialectical argument may be, Paul speaks as a Jew, using, as Christ used, the accepted and honoured words of the Old Testament, to prove that, for all who had eyes to see, this truth had always been clear. There is a rapid-fire quotation, which was called a 'catena' or 'chain', in which verse follows and reinforces verse, to one irrefutable end. It was characteristically rabbinical, and in such debate the context of a quotation was not always of prime importance.

But return to the blasphemy, as Paul would describe it, of the argument advanced, sometimes libellously (8), in the opening verses. It is not so remote from later heresies as might at first sight appear, and Paul gives us an inkling with what sort of rapier logic he would deal with much of our modern decayed theology.

728

I have written elsewhere: 'By one means or another, by diminishing man's responsibility or by misrepresenting God, man, the sinner, seeks to avoid the admission, in all heinousness, of his sin. The modern theologian, compromising with "permissiveness", murmuring excuses about "situation ethics", speculating on God's "involvement" in the world, and avoiding the Bible's downright condemnation of sin, has no cause to be impatient with his ancient counterpart.' (*The Daily Commentary* [*Bible Study Books*]—*Romans*).

634 : Paul's Peace

Romans 5

At the beginning of ch. 6 Paul is to return briefly to the distortion of his gospel which had so shocked him (3.8), but meanwhile he breaks into a fine passage on the fruit of faith in the life. Like so many parts of this intense letter, it is obviously biographical, and an expression of what had been given to him in the stress of experience.

His conversion had ended one conflict. He gave in, and kicked no longer, like a maddened ox, against the goad. Then came the mental conflict of discovering the meaning of the Old Testament and the Law. But underneath the intensity of his thought and the labour of his daily living, was the peace beyond all understanding. It was the peace which came to his troubled soul when he realized that he was justified by faith, that the battle was over, and the calm which he could by no means win through obedience to the impossible standards of the Law, was his by the grace of God. The rebellion was finished. The soul which was at odds with God was accepted by God's action. Peace once made, the reconciled sets out, as Paul set out, to become the sort of person God intended him to be.

God is available (2). Nothing bars the way or alienates, and faith becomes, not only the act of appropriating salvation, but a daily pattern of life. Hence victory over anything life can do. Paul never said, and no one ever should say, that Christianity is easy. No one had a more trouble-strewn path than he. But trial and tribulation, he had found, committed in faith to the wise, transforming hand of the Almighty, produced rare qualities of character. The endurance, of which Paul speaks, must be seen in the context of his whole life. It is no crouching under the shield of

729

faith while adversity hurls clanging down every missile in its armoury. The shield could be a weapon of offence, and Paul's endurance was active. Hence character (4). No sturdiness forms in a hothouse. The English archer made his most trusty arrows out of the wood which grew on the side of the tree exposed to the north. Hope grows from this, and no man lives joyously without hope. God is real to the surrendered life—a theme Paul is to resume in ch. 12. And hope is real, because faith makes God real. This is what his faith had taught Paul.

635 : The New Paul

Romans 6; 7.15–25

Paul was acutely conscious that he was a new man in Christ. He was utterly convinced about the resurrection of the Lord. He makes that clear enough to the Corinthian church which contained a faction prepared to regard the doctrine of the risen Christ as a species of symbolism, a myth, if the oddly abused modern term is to be used. To Paul it was historic, proven fact.

At the same time, he thought of the death and resurrection of the Lord as a mystical experience in his own life. He had died with Christ at baptism, and risen from the water as though coming back from burial to a new life altogether in which old ways withered, and new vigour surged.

And yet, such is the daily experience of Paul and of any one of us, that such a condition demanded the unbroken nurturing of faith. The 'old man', a brilliantly imaginative conception of Paul, was alive, and struggling for dominance against the 'new man', brought to birth by faith. It requires daily exercise of faith to 'reckon' old urges dead (11), and to promote and further every thrust and aspiration of the soul towards good and God, by the continual infusion of trust and ready belief. It is a reorientation of all thinking and desire.

Such was the pattern of his living. Plato, in a famous dialogue, had taught something similar under the myth of the two horses of the charioteer we call the soul. The dark horse dragged downwards, the white horse strove gallantly upwards, and it was the task of him who held the reins to make them pull together. Both Plato and Paul were psychologically sound. Paul never strikes a more universally audible note than when he talks of this strange strife within the personality.

Paul knew that life was conflict, and that the nature of man slips easily towards evil. Those who teach otherwise deceive themselves and those whom they teach. The Bible sets no limits to the Christian's victory over his baser self, but it can lead to nothing but frustration and despair to suggest to those who come to Christ that all sinlessness lies effortlessly within the reach, and to give the impression that there is no strife, no temptation, no chance of defeat save in unbelief. Paul never taught this, for he knew better. His words at the end of ch. 7 are no mere recollection of unregenerate days. They arose from his daily experience.

636 : Paul's Testimony

Romans 8.31–39; 2 Timothy 1.12

We have not read all of ch. 8. This letter is commonly read for the doctrine it contains and that is set forth for Scripture Union readers in *The Daily Commentary* (*Bible Study Books*) on the epistle, and in many conservative commentaries. We need not here look again at the often misused doctrine of predestination and its reconciliation with free will. We seek the man behind his words. We are looking for Paul, and how can he be better revealed than by allowing him to utter his ringing testimony in his own words. He is about to begin a detailed exposition which occupies three chapters. It is a characteristic address to the synagogue. He concludes ch. 8 with a moving paragraph. Paul had a gesture. He 'stretched forth his hand' (Acts 13.16) and began to speak. The RSV does not do justice to the passage. The NEB and Phillips are better. But let him speak in a completely new translation:

'In view of these things, what then shall we say? If God is on our side, who is against us? Since He did not spare His own Son, but gave Him up for all of us, how shall He do other than in grace, along with Him, give us everything? Who shall lay a charge against those whom God has chosen? God, who counts them righteous? Who condemns? Christ?—He who died, more, rose again, who is also at God's right hand, who also pleads on our behalf?

'Who shall part us from the love Christ bears us? Shall trouble, the pressure of life, persecution, deprivation of food or clothes to wear, danger, violent death? (The word says: 'For your sake we face death all the time. We are considered sheep to be killed'). But in all these things we win more than victory through the One

731

who loved us; for I am utterly convinced that neither death nor life, neither beings of another world nor powers or authorities in this, neither what is here present, nor what yet is to be, neither what is above nor what is below, nor anything else created shall be able to part us from the love of God shown us in Christ Jesus our Lord.'

These words are no idle words. They are the words of a great soul and proven in the fires of life. He suffered under every head. They killed him, and, were he here, might kill him again, so fragile is good, freedom, the rule of law. The words are true, and in them we meet the man. Let us hearken.

637 : The Committed Christian

Romans 12

In these character studies we have looked at characters that are, and characters that ought to be. Romans 12 tells us what the Christian should look like. Let us read the first two verses, translating the first verb in the sense in which a modern Greek would take it. He uses 'I beseech' (*parakaleo*) as 'Please'. Probably it meant that in Paul's day. And so; 'Please, brothers, in the name of God's mercies, dedicate your bodies as a living sacrifice, consecrated to God, well-pleasing to Him, which is the worship proper to your nature.

'And cease trying to adapt yourselves to the society you live in, but continue your transformation by the renewal of your mind, to the end that you may test out for yourselves the will of God, that namely, which is good, well-pleasing to Him and perfect.'

This crowded chapter which so reveals the writer's yearning soul and is to cover every phase of Christian living with detailed precept and exhortation, begins with an appeal to the most compelling of motives. God's compassionate dealings with man never failed to stir the wonder of the one-time rebel and persecutor of the Church. It appeared to Paul, and it has appeared to every true follower of Christ from then till now, that it was an obvious duty to respond to God's love with all the poor means in man's power. Forgiven much, Paul gave much.

Man has a body, the instrument and vehicle of his spirit. Let him take it, and all that goes with it, and 'place it by the altar'. In one of his passages of grand eloquence, which we have recently read, Paul has already said something like this: 'So sin must no longer reign in your mortal body, exacting obedience to the body's desires. You must no longer put its several parts at sin's disposal, as implements for doing wrong. No: put yourselves at the disposal of God, as dead men raised to life; yield your bodies to him as implements for doing right . . .' (Rom. 6.12 f.).

A Christianity which did not penetrate and interfuse the activities of the body, daily living, business, social life, the human person, in all its actions, reactions and common tasks, was not, in Paul's view, Christianity at all. He returns thus, from the loftiest flights of theological instruction to the human situation as it confronts every man. With a new outlook, a cleansed purpose to guide and determine action, members which might easily become the tools and weapons of evil can 'glorify God' in a new service. That service finds its first occasion and expression in ordinary life. Christian citizenship is the Christian's first duty, and Christian citizenship begins in complete surrender of the person to God.

Read this 'character study' in several translations, and set it beside performance.

Questions and themes for study and discussion on Studies 630–637

1. The importance of city-based Christianity. What of the future?
2. 'No nation was ever destroyed from without, which had not already destroyed itself from within.'
3. Unwritten laws. Have you any?
4. The importance of authoritative Scripture. Can evangelism function without it?
5. Faith, committal and character. How are they linked?
6. How is 'the old man' weakened?
7. Can we make Paul's testimony ours?
8. 'Adapting ourselves to the society we live in.' What are the limits?

638 : Paul the Citizen

Romans 13.1–10; 1 Peter 2.13–17

The chapter contains several echoes of the words of Christ. Paul must have been very much aware of matters yet to find their

733

written form. Paul was to tell the Philippians, themselves, many of them, Roman citizens to 'live as citizens worthy of the gospel' (Phil. 1.27). He now speaks as one who sought to do so, and in so doing reveals much of himself.

It is important to see Christian society in the first century in proper perspective. The Empire, running to the Rhine, the Danube and the Black Sea, and bounded to the west by the Atlantic, and to the south and east by the great deserts, had given the Mediterranean world a stable peace. The Roman Peace was the social and political framework within which the Christian Church attained its first international form.

Roman history, written from the standpoint of the aristocratic writers of the capital, inevitably concentrated on Rome itself, on the vices and doings of the court and the prince, ignoring the proletariat and the provinces. It is historic fact that, during the principate of the youthful Nero, whose vice and profligacy became legendary, the provinces enjoyed such quietness and stability that 'Nero's Five Years', the quinquennium during which government was largely controlled by the wise Seneca, and the soldierly Burrus, became a legend of just administration throughout the Roman world.

Paul had learned in Gallio's court, and he was to learn again in riotous Jerusalem, that Roman discipline and justice, rough though it sometimes was, and corrupt though it could be in such vicious hands as those of Felix, was a protection and a shield. Moreover, the Jews were restive throughout the world. The mood of the Empire's most difficult people was heading towards the tragic explosion of A.D. 66, and that event had world-wide repercussions. As Paul found when seeking a passage from Corinth to Jerusalem, and again in Jerusalem itself, a collaborating Jew such as he was, with his assumption of Roman citizenship, was in acute danger.

He was also, perhaps, hopeful that the fabric of the Empire could be christianized, and he did not wish the Church to become branded as a dissident, rebellious group. A decade later Rome drove the Church into this position, but hope of partnership still lived when Paul was writing. The Empire, too, was sensitive about organizations within its body.

639 : Paul in Uniform
Romans 13.8–14; Ephesians 4.22–24

Let this touch of Paul's poetry (in vs. 12 to 14) mingle with the testimony of a great Paulinist, Augustine of Hippo. In spite of the word picture of v. 12, the concluding verse of the chapter would seem to speak of clothes. J. B. Phillips translates: 'Let us be Christ's men from head to foot . . .' and Conybeare: 'Clothe yourself with Jesus Christ . . .'

This was Augustine's famous text. Augustine and his friend Alypius were in Milan where, under the counsel of the great Ambrose, they had turned to the study of the Epistle to the Romans. One afternoon the pair were sitting together in a garden in a suburb of Milan. The roll of the apostle's letter lay on the seat between them. Augustine was in his thirty-second year, deeply concerned over a wasted life, and obviously in a state of serious tension. Something in the letter moved him to tears and wild lamentations. He rushed from Alypius and fell weeping under a fig tree in a far corner of the garden.

Now let him tell the story: 'So I was speaking and weeping in the bitterest contrition of my heart. And look! I hear a voice from our neighbour's house, a boy's or girl's I know not, chanting repeatedly: "Pick it up and read, pick it up and read." Suddenly with changed countenance I began with the most concentrated thought to consider whether children were accustomed in any sort of game to chant anything like this, nor could I at all remember having anywhere heard the like. Checking my rush of tears, I rose with no other thought in mind than that here was God's command to open the book and read the first chapter I should come upon . . . So I hurried back to the place where Alypius was sitting, for there I had put the book of the apostle when I got up. I seized it, opened it, and read silently the first section on which my eyes fell: "Not in revelry and drunkenness, in debauchery or vice, nor in quarrelling and jealousy, but put on the Lord Jesus Christ and take no thought for the flesh and its appetites." I did not want to read on. I had no need to do so' (trans. E.M.B.).

The figure is a vivid one. Clothes cover, protect, envelop, preserve, like the 'grace which covers all my sin.' But more than this. Is it not a fact that the clothing of man or woman is the first impression their presence makes upon us? Before any word has revealed a personality, the outward appearance has confronted

735

our sight. Face and features vie with the clothing of the body to make an impact on the mind.

When Paul repeated his figure of speech in the letter to the Ephesians (4.22–24) he sharpened this point. Phillips has caught up his meaning well; 'No, what you learned was to fling off the dirty clothes of the old way of living, which were rotted through and through with lust's illusions and ... to put on the clean fresh clothes of the new life which was made by God's design for righteousness and the holiness which is no illusion.' So Paul hoped to do.

640 : Paul's Plans

Romans 15

Observe the graciousness with which Paul writes. He now takes the Roman Christians into his confidence about the future. He has travelled arduously and long. Christian churches were strewn along his path. He tells us here of journeys about which we know nothing—the journey into Illyricum, for example. Whether he ever reached Spain, the western province of the Empire, we do not know. It was an important project. Only a few remains of Latin literature are in our hands from the fifties and the sixties of that century, and most of it is the work of Spanish Romans. Seneca, Nero's tutor and prime minister, his nephew Lucan, the epic poet, and several others prominent in Rome's contemporary cultural life, came from Spain. Spain was also to provide three emperors, including Trajan and Hadrian.

It was a brilliant piece of strategy, to set his eyes on the great Iberian peninsula, and if Paul failed in that well-planned objective, it was because of the visit to Jerusalem, and the arrest which followed the unwise advice of the church domiciled there, so timidly anxious to reconcile its narrow-minded Pharisaic wing (Acts 21).

At the same time, such is the creative power of God, out of that tragic misadventure came the 'prison epistles' and perhaps the two books of Luke. Paul was no man to see other than a second opportunity in the thwarting of his plans. Denied one alternative, Paul took another, and found himself flung into the midst of a pattern of Gentile evangelism which he had not envisaged.

He went opened-eyed into the danger which he knew lurked in

736

the capital of Judaism. Read closely for the poignancy of their autobiography the four closing verses of the chapter. He asks them to pray for his deliverance from the most vicious anti-Christian group in the world, and that his demonstration of Gentile goodwill might find acceptance with the reluctant Christians of the Jerusalem church. Neither prayer received the answer he sought, but out of the denial God brought unmeasured good. Such is the lesson of Paul's fate. And another lesson: consider the scope of his evangelistic plan along with the meagre resources with which he undertook it. And ask whether we, with distance annihilated, and a world of science and technology at our disposal, can proportionately match it.

641 : Paul and the Women

Romans 16.1–8; Galatians 3.28; 1 Corinthians 11.12

The passages above are a clear enough indication that Paul was no misogynist. In the word to the Corinthian church listed in the readings, there is a touch of poetry, for does he not mean that, though Gen. 2.23 speaks of woman taken from man, since then, without woman, man could not be born?

In the greetings to the Roman church, of whose personnel Paul seems to have had the most detailed information, out of the twenty-five people in the full list about one third are women. Of the eight mentioned specifically by name, only two lack comment. The other six all have some word of warm and appreciative regard. Priscilla, now back in Rome from Corinth and Ephesus, along with her husband, 'risked their lives' for Paul. Mary 'worked hard' for the Christians. So did Tryphaena and Tryphosa, who seem to have been twins. William Barclay points out the whimsicality of Paul's commendation. The meaning of their names was 'Dainty' and 'Delicate'. The verb for working hard was *kopian*, a participle of which is used of the Lord sitting wearied on the kerb of the Sychar well (John 4.6). It suggests that the sisters' toil belied ironically their tender names.

We meet again Phoebe of Cenchreae, a woman of substance, who seems to have journeyed to Rome to deliver the letter. She is honoured with the title of 'deaconess'. Junias, as the RSV puts it, appears in versions which follow another textual tradition, as Junia, and the name was probably feminine. She is, to be sure,

737

called an apostle, and this was accepted as early as John Chrysostom in the fourth century.

The list is therefore eloquent of Paul's regard for the women connected with the Church. He also believed, and most people would agree with his conviction as biological and psychological fact, that the sexes differ, that there are, in general, tasks for which women are better fitted than men, and other tasks for which men are commonly better fitted than women. In a smoothly functioning Christian community, such division of labour falls into proper place without tension or rivalry. Paul has been misunderstood, mainly by the defensively belligerent, over women and their place in life. His regulations should be read and examined only in the context of his life.

642 : The Rest

Romans 16.9–27; Mark 15.21

Many of the names listed here appear in contemporary documents. Some of them are of special interest. Narcissus was one of the two freedmen (Pallas, Felix' brother was the other) who acquired a corrupt and dangerous influence over the emperor Claudius. Narcissus amassed a fortune, and had great political power. After Claudius was feloniously poisoned in A.D. 54, he was arrested and driven to suicide. His household, however, servants, professional staff, and the hundreds of skilled men such a minister would gather round him would continue, though absorbed into the vast imperial family, to function as a coherent whole.

So too with the household of Aristobulus. It seems likely that Aristobulus was the grandson of Herod the Great. Claudius, a conscious imitator of Augustus in his foreign policy, had fostered the Herodian house, and it is known that Aristobulus was educated at Rome, and given a 'household', that is a staff, by Claudius. At Aristobulus' death, this body would be absorbed also by the imperial *familia*, but, in the interests of administrative efficiency, would be preserved as a separate unit. Apelles (Abel), and Herodion, mentioned before and after the group, were probably members of it.

It is quite clear that Christianity was penetrating high circles in Rome. Whether Nereus is another indication is a matter of conjecture. Nereus certainly, a generation later, was a high official in the household of Domitilla, grand-daughter of Vespasian, who married Titus Flavius Clemens of the same imperial family. She became a Christian as did also, it seems, her husband. Clemens was executed by the base Domitian, last emperor of the Flavian house, and Domitilla banished. The cemetery of Domitilla, on the Via Ardeatina outside Rome, was used for Christian burial in the first century, and the name of one Nereus was connected with it. There is no evidence to prove that the Nereus of this list is the same person, caught in the apostolic reference at an earlier period in his life, but it is intriguing to think that he, freedman or slave, could have been the entry-point for the faith into a household so exalted.

And is Rufus possibly the son of Simon who bore the cross for Christ? Conjecture, to be sure, but these 'characters of the Bible' were living men and women, serving the Lord a few years before the grim date in July A.D. 64 when Rome went up in flames, and Nero, seeking a scapegoat for what was probably his own crime, fell upon the Christians.

643 : Caesar's Household

Philippians 4

While we are meeting the Christians of Rome, so soon to be the harried victims of Nero's hate and panic fears, we might turn to a greeting Paul sent from Rome two or three years later, when he was in house-confinement there awaiting the hearing of his appeal to Caesar.

He underlines a greeting from Caesar's household. It would seem likely that he found much help and alleviation of his lot by the contact he obviously had with Christian and Jewish members of the staffs of Narcissus and Aristobulus, who, on the decease of their household heads, had become a part of the imperial 'family'. It seems likely that the 'household of Caesar' (Phil. 4.22) was, at least in some part, composed of these two earlier groups into which the Christian faith had penetrated early in its Roman history. They probably formed the strength and nucleus of the church in Rome when Claudius banished the Jews from the capital in A.D. 49, and, as the emigration of Aquila and Priscilla to Corinth shows, swept a Christian minority along with them.

This infiltration appears to have been maintained. Tertullian and Dionysius of Alexandria both speak of considerable groups of Christians in the imperial household, and it has recently been pointed out by Professor G. Clarke of Melbourne that certain surviving Latin inscriptions, which mention 'the one God', and 'brethren', common Christian expressions, could be epitaphs of the church. One inscription mentions a school on the Caelian Hill which was staffed and equipped to train administrative officers for the imperial civil service.

'Caesar's household' means precisely the imperial civil service, not the palace slaves, so here is evidence that, early in the history of the Church, the faith had formed a bridgehead in the most influential levels of the Empire. We know nothing more, but it is obvious that Christians so entrenched were in a position to exercise incalculable influence.

Scripture tells us nothing more. We should be glad to know these pioneers of the gospel, and it is possible that archaeology may yet have fragments of information to add to the little we know. But why did Paul say that it was principally those who were of Caesar's household who sent their salutations to Philippi? It was easier to answer the question when it was thought that the members of Caesar's household were poor and deprived slaves, who had shared Paul's gifts from Philippi. This appears to be far from the truth.

Questions and themes for study and discussion on Studies 638–643

1. How should a Christian exercise his citizenship today?
2. 'Putting on' Jesus Christ. The word picture of clothing.
3. The second opportunity of thwarted plans. Failure as a path to success.
4. Women in the tasks of the Church.
5. The social spread of Christianity today. Does it affect all classes?
6. The strategy of Christian infiltration. Is it available still?

644 : The Corinthians

Acts 18.1–11; 1 Corinthians 1.1–16

Paul's foundation of the church at Corinth was one of the signal triumphs of his career. 'The church of God which is at Corinth', is a striking phrase, for Corinth was the most notoriously vicious of the cities of the ancient world. And yet the grace of God found lodging there (4), and with divine incongruity there were those found in the evil cosmopolitan port on the isthmus who were called 'saints', and 'sanctified in Christ Jesus' (2).

Along with Rome, Corinth was more like a cosmopolitan modern city than any other of the score or more of towns and cities which find mention in the New Testament. We also know more about its church, its people and its problems, than we know of any other church in the New Testament. In a world which is becoming increasingly urbanized, Corinth is a significant and vital study.

The society in which it operates colours a church for good and ill. The strength and weakness of a city find reflection in the problems, the qualities, and the defects of the church which is drawn from its multitude, and Corinth clearly illustrates this fact. That pseudo-intellectual, sex-ridden, argumentative, yet enterprising society, produced a church prone to faction, division, controversy, and which sometimes is quite horrifying. The early Church is sometimes idealized. Corinth is evidence enough that most of the problems which afflict the twentieth-century congregation were known in Corinth, from denominationalism to scepticism over the physical resurrection of Christ.

The lessons are many. God can redeem in the most corrupt environment; God can redeem the worst sinners; God redeems progressively. Paul saw the potentialities. He looked to the end. He never lost hope. That is why he begins his letter with words of gracious confidence. He sets forth the remedy as he writes. Christ is mentioned eight times in these eight verses. He is preparing the way for the great evangelical statements which close the chapter and come to a climax in the testimony of 2.2. An exalted Christ, uplifted and undiminished, is the one solution to the problems of the Church.

Paul turns rapidly to the first major problem of Corinth, that of division. The city was a melting-pot, a tangle and mixture of races. The languages of all the Mediterranean were heard in the streets. The church, which, like the net (Matt. 13.47), drew all manner of fish ashore, had gathered its congregation from people of different races, of different social background, of different orders of society. There were Jews and Greeks, Italian traders, Phoenician sailors, girls emancipated from the temple-service of Aphrodite . . . It was natural enough that tastes would differ and variant loyalties emerge. Perhaps there is no church in the New

741

Testament whose members, as men and women, emerge more clearly from the words of the great man who sought in wisdom to meet their needs.

645 : The Corinthians Again

1 Corinthians 1.17–25; 2.1–10

Three groups of Corinthians emerge from this passage, representing three attitudes towards Paul's preaching, and perhaps continuing to reflect attitudes within the church. Verse 18 might be rendered: 'The message of the cross is, to those who are destroying themselves, foolishness, but to those who are being saved it is the power of God.' The present tenses should be stressed. 'In the language of the New Testament,' says Lightfoot, 'salvation is a thing of the past, a thing of the present, and a thing of the future ... The divorce of morality and religion is fostered by failing to note this, and so laying the whole stress on either the past or the future—on the first call or on the final change.'

Such was its simplicity. Christianity is a faith, and faith implies the staking of the life on a conviction, a conviction that God revealed Himself in Christ. The Corinthians, prone to philosophic speculation, baulked at such simplicity. Most modern error had its ancient counterpart, and that was always so. Paul quotes Isa. 29.14 in illustration.

The Jews wanted 'a sign'. It was an endemic malady. Theudas, in A.D. 45, led multitudes into the wilderness and disaster with the promise that he would divide the Jordan like another Joshua or Elisha (Acts 5.36). Almost twenty years later, a certain 'Egyptian' led 30,000 dupes out on to the Mount of Olives with the promise that he would destroy the walls of Jerusalem (Acts 21.38). Their misconception of the Messiah gave rise to this quirk. A humble Christ, who offered no vast demonstrations, and who called for self-abandonment, 'stumbled' them.

The Greeks sought philosophy and found the cult of the crucified absurd. The 'wondrous cross' is a phrase which baffles their successors. The Greeks could not see how the love of God, and the depth of human sin, could not be shown in a less shattering way than both were shown on Calvary. Pride and intellectual arrogance is the crippling fault of the 'Greeks'. And yet the Greeks for whom Paul wrote had no substitute. 'How can I say more unless I have the word of some God?' the great Socrates

742

had asked four and a half centuries before, after he had spent his last day piling reason on reason for believing in immortality. The Word came, was made flesh (John 1.14), died and rose again. This was the gospel (2.2) which Paul preached. There is no other Christ, no Christianity without a cross. The Corinthians stood challenged and confronted.

When Paul came to Corinth he was determined not to pander to the Corinthian love of words. The itinerant teachers, who earned a living by rhetorical display and dexterity of speech, had a happy hunting ground in the city of the isthmus. Having been taken for such a person in Athens, Paul was now resolved to abandon the arts of persuasion so carefully taught by the Greeks, skilled though he was in such oratory (e.g. Acts 17.22–29; 24.10–21). Nor would he rephrase his message in the terms of an ephemeral philosophy. Christ, Paul knew, would remain. The sophists would pass. 'Their poor displays of wisdom,' said Cicero of them, 'only prick like pins ... they do not change the heart, and the listeners go away just as they came.'

646 : The Leaders

1 Corinthians 3

Corinthian controversy did not involve the leaders round whose names the unwelcome loyalties grew. Peter has a charming word to say of Paul (2 Pet. 3.15f.). There is no sign of division between Paul and Apollos. Christian workers are partners in God's enterprise. The reaper cannot claim the crop, as the Lord told His men at the well of Sychar (John 4.36–38). Paul recognized that his eighteen months in Corinth had been but a scattering of the good seed. He is tacitly referring to a Galilean parable of Christ. Apollos had stayed on to foster and bring to maturity the seed which had found fertile ground. Christ would reap the crop. This surely is ideal evangelism. It is a blessed partnership of faithful proclamation, devoted pastoral care, and God's Spirit active in the church.

There is a touch of Paul's experience in the pictures of the strong foundation and the temple. Paul had come to Corinth from Athens. He wrote from Ephesus. In Athens, Corinth, and Ephesus, great temples rested on vast blocks of hewn stone. The Greeks knew well that it was what lay beneath which gave steadiness, permanence, and grace to what stood above. The beauty of the Parthenon, Athena's great Doric shrine, still astonishes the

743

world. Its foundations, firm and unshaken after twenty-four centuries, rest on the great rock of the Acropolis. The picture of it was surely in Paul's mind, as also a saying of Christ, (Matt. 16.18) when he wrote to Corinth of 'no other foundation'.

Above the ruined market-place of Corinth, there still stands on a low ridge with a far view down the Corinthian Gulf, a few columns of Apollo's temple. The Romans left the building standing, alone amid the desolation, when they sacked Corinth in 146 B.C. A century later, when Julius Caesar rebuilt the city, the ancient Doric shrine still stood, dominating the city centre, as its remnants do today. 'You,' Paul tells the church, 'are God's temple in the place.' The Greek temple was kept scrupulously clean. The Greek temple was simple, and housed only one deity. It stood high for all to see, Athena at Athens, Poseidon on the high promontory of Sounion, Apollo above Corinth's agora ... No Corinthian would miss the point. Let them build on the one foundation. There was no other. Let them build grandly and conspicuously, a clean dwelling-place for God, unshared, elegant, enduring.

It is fine strong writing, with words and imagery relevant to the experience of the one who wrote, and of those who read. A man writes well when he writes from conviction, and with a burning passion to persuade. And such a man, deeply versed in the interwoven cultures of his day, caught in a great historic movement, and fervent for a cause, frequently writes prose of purpose and power beyond the need and call of its immediate occasion.

647 : Paul's Courtesy

1 Corinthians 4

Paul has dealt kindly with the philosophical pretensions of some in the Corinthian church. Any close student of Plato and the Stoics can recognize in Paul's first four chapters allusions, and easy half-references to the writings of both, which make it clear enough that he knew far more of philosophic thought than the small group in the isthmus church which despised the simple presentation of the message.

And yet observe in this chapter how gently and humbly he deals with them. Paul was, as we have again and again had occasion to note, superbly educated. He was willing, none the less, to be called a fool for Christ's sake—in such contrast to those in the small church who imagined they had outgrown his teaching. Verses 11 to 13 form a moving picture of what it meant to be a Christian—indeed, what it still means for some. There is a persecution which seeks to inflict pain on the body. There is a more cruel and subtle persecution which seeks to hurt the mind— the high contempt of the academic for one committed to a faith, the covert sneer against the man who holds fast to his uprightness in a bent and crooked world . . . Paul knew it all.

There is no hot scorn for those who added pain to what the world at large had already inflicted. There is no sharper tooth than that of ingratitude, but Paul merely seeks, forgetting his deep hurt, to turn them to self-examination and to thankfulness. They had been blessed by many who had sought to teach them—Peter himself, and the brilliant Apollos among the rest. Paul was their father in Christ, and there could only be one.

Hence the sending of the well-loved Timothy, instructed to tell them again of those simplicities of Christ which were all they needed to know. There is some evidence, if references in the second letter are read aright, that Timothy came, but was not well-received. C. G. Findlay remarks that Timothy was Paul's complement, as Melancthon was of Luther. Such a reception for his beloved ambassador would grieve Paul deeply, and some wonder is due that one so strong in his views and his loyalties, no less than in the firm insistence on the absolute integrity of his gospel, should deal with a disordered and falsely proud congregation with courtesy, restraint, and reserve so notable.

Paul was a personality of manifold facets. Such characters are too commonly and too shallowly judged on the evidence of one controverted opinion, or one incident such as the clash with Barnabas. Paul had schooled his vehemence to gentleness, his immense intelligence to patience with the foolish, and his swift decisiveness to humility.

648 : The Weaker Brothers

1 Corinthians 8

The theme of v.7 continues to its climax in the fine closing words of the chapter. The dangerous minority in Corinth which claimed 'knowledge', and turned Christian liberty into an excuse for licence, lacked love and care for others. The intellectual is commonly impatient with the emotional, and both types were present in Corinth. In the former the head outran the heart. The latter reversed the process. It takes both to make a church. It is also true that in the balanced personality both head and heart, the intellect and the emotions, have their place, part and partnership.

Love is the answer, and the reader catches the first notes of the theme which is to reach its climax in ch. **13**. Pride is the vice which dogs the intellectual, and there was pride, as well as lack of feeling, in the Christian who confidently and contemptuously 'sat at meat in the idol's temple', taking part in a pagan ceremony because it was meaningless. Another, following his example, as the emotionally bent are prone to do, is damaged in the act, trapped into a weakening compromise with conscience, and marred in his Christian integrity.

Paul's comment is still valid. In modern society the problem may have shifted its ground, but day by day brings situations which are similar in import and solution. Hughes, author of *Tom Brown's Schooldays*, wrote of his hero, Arnold of Rugby: 'He taught us that in this wonderful world no one can tell which of his actions is indifferent and which is not. He taught us that, by a thoughtless word or look we may lead astray a brother for whom Christ died.' This is Paul's meaning. 'All things are lawful', but through all and over all such liberty stands the constraining power of Christian love.

Why, it might be asked in conclusion, did not Paul quote the Jerusalem Decree which had ruled in the matter of 'idol meat'? (Acts **15**.29). It is probable that the Judaizing party had so disregarded it that Paul himself treated it as a dead letter. Or else he regarded the decree as inoperable in Europe and in a fully Greek community.

But observe again the tender care for 'the weaker'. We are learning to know Paul. Learn by heart the last verse. It has much to say.

649 : Paul's Testimony

1 Corinthians 9

Paul has made it clear that he cared enough for others to be willing not to claim a freedom if that claim could cause misunderstanding or lead some other person into difficulty or wrongdoing. He proceeds to illustrate his attitude by some remarks which are a light upon his character and manner of life. The theme becomes vividly autobiographical.

He claims that, as a witness of the resurrected Christ, he was an apostle, and therefore entitled to such privileges as befell an apostle—to be a charge, for example, on the churches for maintenance. To avoid all jealousy, to by-pass all criticism by lesser folk in the Christian community, he had foregone such privileges, and earned his own living in humble employment. The Judaistic party in the church were, no doubt, denying Paul's genuine apostleship. But note the tact with which Paul, having vindicated firmly his own rights, does not make his deliberate waiving of them an embarrassment to his fellow-workers.

He acted thus because he had a consuming passion—to win men for Christ. He has renounced much in order that, untrammelled by obligations, he might meet all classes on conditions of equality. Hence the oft-quoted (and not infrequently misapplied) words of vs. 19–22. The words mean that he sought to approach the various classes and conditions of people he met with understanding of their outlook, sympathy for their difficulties, mercy for their prejudices, patience with their preoccupations. He 'spoke their language' in more senses than one. He sought to share their interests, discover points of contact, make them sense his concern. Perhaps it was an over-emphasis in this delicate task which led him into the error we have noted, and be too ready to conform to a Jewish preoccupation—with the consequent misadventure in Jerusalem. But it is a noble ideal, and we have seen it illustrated again and again.

It required the discipline of the athlete, a matter with which Paul closes the chapter. He often refers to the Greek games with the demands for asceticism, training, perseverance, and dedicated energy for which they necessarily called. God's athlete could do no less than those who strove for the crown of wild olive.

Questions and themes for study and discussion on Studies 644–649

1. A church and its environment.
2. Salvation as past, present and future.
3. Philosophy cannot produce a theology but sound theology can produce a philosophy.
4. 'The grace of God is in courtesy'—Belloc.
5. The weaker brother today—for example, in relation to alcohol.
6. 'All things to all men'—how does this principle apply today?

650 : Paul's Appeal

1 Corinthians 12.12–13.3

Patiently and wisely Paul sought to guide, to teach and to advise. With care and precision he went over all the problems and difficulties which had come to his notice, and had made his ruling. It was always his manner to turn from such detail to the deeper truths of Christ, and to the great eternal principles which underlie all true godly living. On such occasions his style takes wings. Observe the sweep of eloquence with which Rom. **8** ends (31–39). Then see ch. **12** of the same epistle conclude a section of close argument with a call to consecration and the practice of life's simplicities in a manner reminiscent of the moving chapter before us. 'Look,' says Paul, 'I will show you a higher path' (**12.**31), a 'way of sovereign excellence.'

His tone has been lofty, almost vehement, and we are hardly prepared for the lyric beauty of the chapter which now opens. Passion, strength and simplicity were the deeper qualities of Paul. They infuse the poem on love. Uneasy about the Corinthian preoccupation with 'tongues' and spectacular 'gifts', he offers now, like a good psychologist, a path of sublimation. Tongues? 'Though my language be heaven's own,' he answers, 'without a Christlike character, I am so much senseless noise, no better than the noisy priests of Cybele or some other Asiatic mystery cult, worshipping strange gods with tom-toms, clashing brass, and mad din. I am a heathen without love.'

'And though I have the gift of interpretation, and am able to elucidate the deeper truths of the Christian faith, though I am an expert in theology (Eph. **3.**4), though I profess and appear to exercise a faith which baulks at no difficulty or challenge, and lack the gentle spirit of Christ, I am nothing.' There is no substitute. Giving of one's substance can be mere show without love, martyrdom itself mere exhibitionism, as indeed it has been known to be. Motive only counts in all sacrifice. The motive can be only one. Illustrate this truth from the Gospels. Consider the motives of Judas, John, James. What purified and exalted them in the case of the last two? Only love brings real advantage and all other advantage is worthless.

748

651 : The Christian

1 Corinthians 13.4–7; James 2.1–9

Read the Corinthian passage again and again in more than one of the 30 or so available English translations. This is the picture of a man of God as he ought to be—and of Christ as He was. We shall translate as we go . . . 'Love is long-tempered and kind.' An enduring spirit is difficult to cultivate in this exasperating world of stress and tension. It is more difficult for some than others, and the first line of defence is what Homer called 'the barrier of the teeth'. It is a mark of Christ (Rom. 2.4 uses the same word) and if we would be like Him this trait should be woven with our character. Also 2 Pet. 3.9 uses the word: 'The Lord is long-tempered, not willing that any should perish.' The second part of the verse adds an active quality to the passive virtue. A cognate of the same word is used of the Lord in 1 Pet. 2.3, and of Christ's yoke in Matt. 11.30. Kindness is full of active well-doing (see Psa. 37.3) and finds no time to nurse wounded feelings.

'Love is not envious, is no braggart, is not swelled with conceit, is not unmannerly.' Envy, boasting, conceit, and discourtesy are not the marks of a Christian. Contemptible vices. Envy destroys all magnanimity as boasting precludes dignity. 'Conceit,' said Ruskin, 'may puff a man up, but cannot prop him up.' One might imagine that Ruskin had read this verse in Greek, for the verb Paul uses (for 'swelled' with conceit) is literally 'puffed up', like the frog in the fable of Aesop which sought to emulate the cow. Paul uses it several times in this letter (4.6, 19; 5.2; 8.1). It was a Corinthian vice to overestimate personal attainment.

Nor is the Christian a boor. Christians belie their name when they are brusque, unapproachable, vulgar, rude, tactless, indelicate, overbearing. Courtesy sweetens life. It opens doors to influence and Christ. The Christian makes no difference between high and low. He does not need the injunction James found it necessary to give. He is gracious to every man whatever his status, his class, his wealth.

J. H. Newman touched on that point in his fine definition of a gentleman. He wrote: 'The true gentleman carefully avoids whatever may cause a jar or a jolt in the minds of those with whom he is cast; all clashing of opinion, or collision of feeling, all restraint, or suspicion, or gloom, or resentment; his great concern being to make everyone at their ease and at home. He has his eyes on all his company; he is tender towards the bashful, gentle towards the distant, and merciful towards the absurd; he can recollect to whom he is speaking; he guards against unseasonable allusions, or topics which may irritate; he is seldom prominent in conversation, and never wearisome.' It all adds up to courtesy.

652 : The Christian Again

1 Corinthians 13.5–12; Philippians 2.5–8

The searching description of the true Christian—the man of Christlike love—continues ... 'Love is no stickler for her rights, is not sharp-tempered.' These qualities again add up to absence of self-assertive pride. The first phrase literally runs: 'Love does not seek her own things.' Two major ancient manuscripts insert a negative making the phrase mean: 'Love does not seek that which it is not entitled to.' That is common morality—or used to be. Paul used no negative. In ch. 9 he had illustrated from his own forbearance. And if the first phrase is biographical so is the second. Paul speaks of sharp-temper with a word related to the noun used of the quarrel with Barnabas (Acts 15.39)—a noun which Paul probably used in telling Luke the painful story. This is his word of self-reproach—and perhaps reconciliation? Was Barnabas dead?

'Love is not mindful of evil, does not rejoice because of wrongdoing, and shares in the joy of the truth.' The first metaphor is from accounting. It is the word used in Rom. 4.6, 8 for the 'imputation' of righteousness. Love does not keep a record of evil, noting down every deed done. It forgets, throws such rubbish of memory away. Nor is it glad when others go wrong. It has nothing of the evil quality which the Germans call 'schadenfreude' —a malicious joy in another's misfortune. The absence of an English equivalent is no indication that the vicious thing is confined to the German people.

'Love is always tolerant, always trustful, always hopeful, always patient.' This is not a prescription for making money. It is four co-ordinated blows arranged in a pattern of a,b,b,a, against cynicism and disillusionment, four heavy demands calculated to call for the ultimate of a Christian. The whole passage points an unwavering finger against comfortable adaptations of Christianity. Here is the character of the Christian—and of Christ, his Lord. It might be a salutary exercise to read this chapter every day for a month, to learn its words by heart . . . It shows us ourselves, not, alas, in a mirror such as those Corinth made exquisitely in bronze, but in a portrait, a portrait of what we might be, should be, perhaps one day shall be.

653 : Paul's Conviction

1 Corinthians 15.1–32

There were those in Corinth who anticipated the speculations of certain modern 'theologies', and explained the historic truth of the rising of Christ from the dead on poetic or symbolic principles. Paul was utterly convinced of its literal truth. Watch his mind at work in this chapter, for it contains much of his character.

First, it is obvious that he had examined witnesses, and knew what contemporary Jerusalem and Galilee said of the risen Christ. In the first nine verses we have what is probably the first written record of the resurrection—unless it should finally be established from the Marcan fragment recently recovered from a Qumran cave that the first narrative of Christ's ministry narrowly antedated this epistle.

Then note the close and firmly pressed argument. We can do no better than translate vs. 12–19 quite simply: 'If then the proclamation is that Christ has risen from the dead, how do some of you say that there is no resurrection from the dead? If there is no resurrection from the dead, neither is Christ risen. If Christ be not risen, our gospel is without content, and your faith as empty. And we are proved false witnesses of God, because our testimony was that He did raise up Christ, and, if indeed the dead are not raised up, He did not raise Christ. For if the dead are not raised, I repeat, neither is Christ risen. And if Christ be not risen, your faith is useless, and you are still the sinners that you were. Those, too, who fell asleep in Christ are dead and gone. If only in this life we have faith in Christ, we are of all men most to be pitied.'

These are the words of one of the most powerfully intellectual men in the ancient world; and in the modern world, as in ancient Corinth, any who continue to profess or preach a version of the Christian faith which disregards the repeated insistence of the apostle concerning the very heart and substance of the message, can do so only on the basis of a complete rejection of the authority of the New Testament and of Paul's contribution to it. And they reject that contribution in the face of a clear and logical argument advanced by a man of first-class mind, whose whole plan and purpose of living was transformed by an over-powering conviction that a certain fact was true.

654 : Paul's Mind at Work

1 Corinthians 15.33–58; John 12.20–24

We have come to know Paul well as we have read what he did and what he said over the busy years of his ministry. He is actively remembering, as he writes, the events of his first visit to Corinth. Heard in Athens, or heard in Corinth, an apt quotation from the writer of comic drama, Menander, slips into his mind: 'Evil communications corrupt good manners.' It is one of two such quotations. 'No mean city,' applied by Paul to Tarsus, was a phrase of the dramatist Euripides applied to Athens.

But Paul remembered something else. If he went from Athens to Corinth on foot, he passed along the coast of the lovely Saronic Gulf, and on the way saw Eleusis, once the seat of a great, and not ignoble mystic cult, but now an industrial suburb of Athens. The cult of Eleusis must have interested Paul, because it is a fact that he took religious vocabulary from the 'mystery religions', and appropriated it for his exposition of the faith, while the substance of that faith remained Hebraic and Christian.

Demeter, the Earth-Mother, said the Eleusis myth, had come to Eleusis in search of her daughter Persephone, whom Pluto, god of the underworld, had kidnapped. She was kindly entertained, and on her departure gave a corn of wheat to the small son of the king, telling him that if it was put into the ground to die it would bring much fruit. The cult grew round this myth, and those who were annually initiated into the Eleusinian Mysteries were said to be 'born again' when, after secret rituals of cleansing and preparation, an ear of corn was uplifted. Paul may have seen the sculpture, now in the Archaeological Museum in Athens, which depicts the gift of the corn of wheat. He may have seen the plinth, which still lies in the ruined precinct of the temple, carved with an ear of corn.

He may also have reflected on the known, but as yet unwritten story of the Lord, who met the Greeks, and hinted to them that in the ritual of the Athenian cult, they had an inkling of vaster truth. As he writes to Corinth, these well-remembered associations flit through his mind. It is fascinating to watch that swift and comprehensive intellect at work linking circumstance and observed scenes to the complex of his faith. It is clear that he had combed Greek thought, pondered the words of Christ . . . 'To the Greeks he became as a Greek that he might win some . . .'

655 : Paul the Administrator

1 Corinthians 16

It is interesting to see Paul turn from the high poetry and deep doctrine of the great chapter which has ended, to the mundane arrangements of the closing page of his epistle. 'Now about the collection . . .' he begins, and the theme is back on the solid earth of every day. The collection for the poor of Jerusalem was a project near to his heart. Jews all over the world were in the habit of sending contributions to their motherland, and it was Paul's deep desire to make sure that the Christian communities in no way fell short of their fellow Jews in such ministration. We have already seen how sadly the project failed. It was, none the less, nobly conceived.

We are more concerned here to see the swift decisiveness with which he goes to work. He sets no absurd standards. He makes no measure of duty, generosity or obligation in percentages, or in regulations borrowed from the Law or Judaistic practice. He makes no pressing and formal appeal. He would be the last man on earth to add to God's conditions for church membership, or to make it difficult for anyone to become an active Christian. His bases of giving are simple. Let it be an act of gratitude. The amount and the method are determined by the conscience of each, viewing his own resources and prosperity, in the light of God's grace.

He asks also for an escort to be provided to carry what was probably a considerable sum of hard currency to Jerusalem. We gain the first glimpse of the able administrator who appears again in the pastoral letters, busy with the framework of discipline, order and leadership in a Church soon to be menaced by the grim power of a persecuting state.

The programme next preoccupies him. Think of his rapidly formed plans in terms of lumbering galleys, mule-back, or the hard road trodden mile on weary mile with sandalled feet. Timothy was, it would seem, sent in Paul's place. Apollos had

753

plans of his own. Some from Corinth stood firm, clear-minded, faithful. Of such was Stephanas who had committed himself to the ministry of the Word. Such too were Aquila and Priscilla, late of Corinth, now of Ephesus, whose home was invariably a church ... The faces flit and pass and we wish we could know more.

Questions and themes for study and discussion on Studies 650–655
1. Define love.
2. Are there limits to tolerance?
3. Is anger ever free from taint of sin?
4. The defence of the doctrine of Christ's resurrection today.
5. Have concepts in non-Christian religions any value?
6. What guidance on Christian giving may be truly found in the New Testament?

656 : Paul's Pain

2 Corinthians 1 and 2

No document in the New Testament is so full of tantalizing questions as the second letter to the Corinthians. We are left to conjecture so much. A large tract of events has escaped our knowledge and scrutiny, and we can do no more than guess at the strained relations between Paul and Corinth, and wonder whether an unrecorded visit was behind some of his pain, and what, at last, was the outcome.

Another visit, in the existing state of tension, was evidently ruled out (2.1), but Titus was sent, and so anxious was Paul over the unsatisfactory conditions in Corinth that he went as far as Macedonia to hear more quickly his personal report. The whole letter is full of Paul's personality, his character breathes in every line, and although we must resign ourselves to ignorance on much of the Corinthian story which we should be glad to know, it is worth reading the letter through with care in order to understand better the loving, anxious, yearning man who wrote it in much agony of mind.

Paul was worried. That was no blemish on his faith. 'Some people,' wrote C. S. Lewis, 'feel guilty about their anxieties and regard them as a defect of faith. I don't agree at all. They are afflictions, not sins. Like all afflictions, they are, if we can so take them, our share in the Passion of Christ.' This is what Paul said (1.5).

Apart from the anxiety and stress which the isthmus church had inflicted on him, Paul had recently faced some dire danger. No one knows what it was. Perhaps it was a bout of the malady which periodically afflicted him (12.7-9). It could have been some form of persecution. Whatever it was, it remains a mystery as obscure as the act of indiscipline on the part of some member of the difficult Corinthian congregation, and it was a wound salted and chafed by the attack upon his reputation which seems to have taken place.

What is notable in these two chapters is the very matter of our quest—the character of the writer, tender with those who had deliberately or thoughtlessly hurt him, concerned even with the chief offender, lest he suffer unduly for his sin, anxious not to say a word too much in condemnation, but exalting Christ in all his sufferings. Joy flashes through his pain, for Paul lived in the conviction that he walked no untrodden path, even in the valley of the shadow. One had gone before—to Gethsemane and the Cross.

657 : Titus

2 Corinthians 2.12-17; 8.1-6; Galatians 2.1-3

Titus is not mentioned in Acts, but was obviously a trusted helper and messenger of Paul. He went with Paul and Barnabas to the Jerusalem conference mentioned in Galatians (2.1). He was a Gentile, but was not compelled to undergo the Jewish rite. He had a large responsibility in the troubled period in Corinth, and came to report progress to Paul with major parts of the task unfinished, for Paul wanted him to return. Titus must have been a man of great diplomatic gifts and notable tact to undertake this difficult and delicate task. One might therefore imagine that he was Timothy's senior, and nearer middle age than youth. He might also have been the stronger personality of the two aides.

A comparison of references in chapters 2 and 7 of this letter, suggests that Titus carried to Corinth a communication which has not survived (called 'a severe letter'). In 7.6 we read that he was able to tell Paul in Macedonia some good news about the troubled congregation. They probably met in Philippi. It was in consequence of this Corinthian assurance, that the letter before us was written and carried off to Corinth (8.16,17) with some eagerness. This fact would suggest that he was deeply involved with the Corinthian congregation, and glad to carry a token of reconciliation. In 8.23 Paul speaks warmly of Titus as his 'partner and fellow helper'.

The remaining information is to be surmised and culled from the pastoral letter addressed to him by Paul. Titus must have accompanied Paul to Crete, in the period following the apostle's release from his first confinement in Rome. A church was founded among the islanders, and Titus was left there to organize it and consolidate it—another position of considerable trust and responsibility.

Titus was then asked to join Paul in Nicopolis, when either Artemas or Tychicus arrived in Crete to take over from him, and it is conjectured that he was despatched from Nicopolis to evangelize the towns of Dalmatia (2 Tim. 4.10). Later tradition speaks of his returning to Crete and living out his long life as the leader of the Christians there. It is also surmised that he might have been Luke's brother, which would, at least, account for his omission from the story in Acts. We follow the movements of a good man, but fail to see his face or to know him. He was most obviously faithful and true.

658 : Paul's Courage

2 Corinthians 4

This is a valiant chapter. Paul knew the body's weakness. He knew the power of anxiety. He was no stranger to the assaults which evil presses home upon the mind. He knew the weight of the Enemy's attack. Often he felt like Alfred in Chesterton's poem, which we have quoted before—

> *With foemen leaning on his shield*
> *And roaring on him when he reeled . . .*

His shield was faith, and he crouched behind it, though the arrows and the slingstones clanged.

He preached, he says, a plain gospel with no subtle devices of persuasion, no concealing of all that faith involved. 'I use no crafty tricks, no dishonest distortions of the Word of God,' he says (2), 'I state the truth with clarity, setting myself before the honest judgement of the world at large.' He was no sophist, no popularity-hunting charlatan, no sly deceiver. And if the gospel was obscure to any who heard, it was obscure because of the self-inflicted blindness which is known in the modern world as well as it was in the world of Paul. There is still the 'academic mind' of the Epicurean, unable to listen to a statement which cannot be tested by a narrow range of rigid criteria. There is still the bigot, religious or irreligious, incapable of challenge or rebuke, committed in such fashion to wrong or to evil, that no thrust of truth or goodness can pierce the defence.

Verse 7 tells of weariness. Treasure was stored in pots of earthenware. In 1947 a Bedu boy threw a stone into a cliffside cave, heard the clatter of shattered earthenware, and so discovered the Dead Sea Scrolls. Paul felt a little like a fragile jar, containing such treasure—'This treasure, the glory of God in Jesus Christ, is lodged in a vessel of fragile clay.' With which the old soldier rises to fight again, 'hard pressed but not beaten down, puzzled at times but never without hope' (8), 'hounded but never abandoned, struck down but never beaten' (9) ... Read the chapter carefully. Paul has had a brush with death, and realizes afresh his frail mortality. It fills him with awe to think how weak a container it is which carries the ardour of his mind, the power of his faith, the reality of Christ's indwelling. But he carries on—'to seek, to strive, to toil and not to yield' ...

659 : The Ambassador
2 Corinthians 5.14–6.10

The Epicureans believed that the gods took no thought of man, they were remote from sound or sense of human sin or sorrow. Paul served a gospel whose whole meaning was that God was intimately involved with man to the point that He revealed in Christ His character, His presence, His love, all, indeed, that the mind of man could comprehend of Him.

All that which is committed to God is transformed by His Spirit. Paul wrote much of this letter under stress, and with the 'severe' communication which has disappeared in the forefront of his mind. He sought to exalt Christ, and in the ardour of that endeavour put into inspired words the whole Christology of the New Testament: 'God was in Christ reconciling the world to Himself.' God Himself, such is the overwhelming and amazing truth, suffered in the Crucified. He was no aloof and demanding

Judge, insistent on some quantum of punishment exacted from a loving Lord who stood between errant and sinful man and a wrathful Yahweh. He was Himself the Loving Lord. In the Son the Father bled. He truly bore our sins. It was the only way God could show how He was involved. Christ and He were one, in sacrifice, in agony, in love.

Searching for an image Paul saw himself as an ambassador. The ambassador, in Paul's world as in ours, was the envoy of an authority, royal or political. The envoy was sacrosanct, and his standing was generally accepted. He bore his master's message, his terms of agreement, his invitation or appeal. He spoke, not from his own authority, but from that of the one who sent him. With all the fervour of his soul, Paul begs his hearers to accept the terms of peace he carries.

As Lightfoot put it in his perceptive commentary: 'The ambassador acts, not only as an agent, but as the representative of his sovereign . . . His duty is not only to deliver a definite message, but he is obliged to watch opportunities, to study characters, to cast about for expedients, so that he may place it before his hearers in the most attractive form.'

Paul's consuming passion was to be such a man, to hide himself, to speak Christ's words, in humility to witness for another, to be not his own, but Christ's.

660 : The Christian in Society

2 Corinthians 6.11–7.1; 1 John 2.15–18

The characters of Scripture, as we have often seen, were men and women of flesh and blood, caught in the net of life's circumstances. Or they were beings of the imagination, built of ideals and aspirations, like Plato's Ideal State, 'a pattern laid up in heaven'. It was a familiar thought in Paul's world. The Stoics, with whom he had much sympathy, had their Wise Man, the ideal being who always acted according to the dictates of reason.

The Book of Proverbs had several such characters. So has Paul. Here he shows the Corinthians the sort of Christians he would have desired them to be; clean, uncontaminated, separate from the godless society in which they lived. It was asking much. In the close-knit city of the ancient world, paganism was pervasive. It is becoming the same again, and the Christian boycott of evil and contaminated features of society is becoming more and more an obligation—a challenge which increasingly demands decision to cut clear from the marks of character and practice which distinguish godlessness. To hold fast to Christian values and standards, to act as a Christian in business and society, in work and in play, to converse as a Christian in the community of men, daily calls for more abstention, daily reveals a stronger distinction between those who follow Christ and honour Him, and those who own no such loyalty, or upon whom the faith sits lightly.

Verse 16 refers to the temple image which Paul used before (1 Cor. 3.17; 6.19) with the Doric temple of Apollo in mind, on the ridge above Corinth's agora. He also remembers how Manasseh brought an image into the temple of God (2 Kings 21.1-9), and how Josiah, in the glad ardour of religious revival utterly destroyed such abominations (2 Kings 23.3f.). Ezekiel 8.13-18 may also be in his thoughts. Such a demand called for much in Corinth. Could a Corinthian Christian mason decorate Aphrodite's temple? Could a Corinthian Christian butcher sell the sacrificial meat? Could a Corinthian Christian artisan attend the banquet of his trade-guild in the patron deity's temple, where worship was offered as part of the proceedings? Parallels can be found today. Do we wish to be 'characters of Scripture'? Here, at any rate, is the prefiguring of what we should be—and what Paul was.

661 : Paul's Forbearance

2 Corinthians 10

There is no part of this intensely autobiographical epistle which we should be more glad to understand than this chapter. Clearly enough, some cruel and cutting words had been said about Paul in Corinth. He was bold enough when writing to them, some said, but did not dare to speak so frankly in their presence. No one could properly charge Paul with lack of courage in his public utterances. Acts is proof enough of that. They had mistaken his humility for hesitancy, his restraint for cowardice. To place an evil interpretation upon what is good was a Pharisaic sin which earned one of the Lord's most awesome words of condemnation.

They had also misinterpreted his motives. He was, they said, exalting himself. He had personal reasons for chiding them. He can only say in reply that he sought only the honour of Christ. He gently tells them that he could, if he would, assail them with all the carnal arguments they seemed to value. He preferred simplicity and the dominance of Christ. This was his theme in the gently ironical first four chapters of the first letter he wrote to them.

And then, most contemptible criticism of all, some, it would appear, had made fun of Paul's undistinguished personal appearance. The nether depths of discourtesy, dishonour and cruelty are touched by any man who taunts another with any defect, blemish or uncomeliness of person. Amid the vices which multiply in the world, there is one which seems, strangely enough, to have diminished. Even the compassionate Charles Dickens could find matter for fun in bodily peculiarities. Charles Lamb, as gentle as Dickens, describes without burning protest, the marred skin, and doomed, bloodshot eyes of a small victim of the Victorian chimney-sweep, who laughed at Lamb's misadventure in the street. Perhaps the world today is more aware of the pathology of ugliness. Perhaps Corinth, too, lacked conscience here.

Finally, some said, he claimed an authority to which he had no right. Paul was a rabbi, had probably been a Sanhedrist and was a brilliant intellectual. That such criticism was made of him, revealed the smallness of the critic. The theme to follow in this sad record of slander and malice on the part, surely, of a Corinthian minority, is the meekness, gentleness, and forbearance of the victim. Here is one example. It was a man of surpassing faith, love and humility who could so withhold his hand.

662 : Paul's Path

2 Corinthians 11

Here is another page of biography, much of which eludes us. Some of Paul's sufferings are known to us and can be aligned with details in this chapter—the stoning, for example at Lystra (Acts 14.19). The earliest date which can be assigned to the second letter to Corinth is A.D. 57 or 58, so some of the events in later chapters of Luke's narrative are to be added to this daunting list. The wreck on Malta was Paul's fourth shipwreck. We are faced with unrecorded pages of history.

Like Valiant-for-Truth in Bunyan's story, Paul had 'fought till my sword did cleave to my hand, and when they were joined together, as if a sword grew out of my arm, and when the blood ran through my fingers, then I fought with most courage.' And it was after this, says Bunyan 'that Mr. Valiant-for-Truth was taken with a summons, and had this for a token that the summons was true, that his pitcher was broken at the fountain . . . Then said he: "I am going to my Father's; and though with great difficulty I am got hither, yet now I do not repent me of all the troubles I have been at to arrive where I am. My sword I give to him that shall succeed me in my pilgrimage; and my courage and skill to him that can get it. My marks and scars I carry with me, to be a witness for me that I have fought His battles who now will be my Rewarder.''

Paul might have been the model for Bunyan's brave picture. Linger over v. 27. It gives a picture of such travel as Paul endured, no plush speeding from place to place, but travel as travel was in a world which the Romans, the first great road-builders, were only beginning to open up with their vast network of paved military highways. It was largely unpoliced, with large hinterlands filled with still dissident tribesmen. In Asia Minor, the distances still seem vast to the visitor who speeds round the sites of ancient churches with all the rapidity and ease of modern travel. What they seemed to the weary-footed missionaries of the first century, is difficult to imagine.

And consider the fact that all the stress of limb and muscle was, in Paul's mind, secondary to the burden he bore upon his spirit— the care for the souls of men, the anxiety he felt over the unceasing pull and tug of the pagan world upon the loyalty and life of those so hardly won, the fragility of many, the sabotage within, the crass betrayal. Such loads lie heavy on the soul, but they are part of the task a man undertakes who decides to be a Christian. Paul saw in it the privilege of taking up Christ's burden, sharing, in a mystic way, His sufferings. And as he did, so must we. The load of the world's pain lies on the heart.

Questions and themes for study and discussion on Studies 656–662

1. Mental persecution, slander and personal criticism in the Church.
2. The qualities of the peacemaker. What is tact?
3. The worth and limitations of the 'academic mind'.
4. The role and qualities of an ambassador.
5. Christian abstention in modern society.
6. Cruelty and humour.
7. Our debt to Paul.

663 : The Galatians

Galatians 3

In Volume 13, we accompanied Paul on his missionary journeys to Iconium and Lystra. It is most likely that it was to these southern Galatian congregations that the apostle wrote his anguished letter. He wrote probably round the year A.D. 52, after his second visit to the area, and after the determined Judaistic party had found time to follow Paul's tracks and seek to draw Christianity into the fold of Judaism. They were an active, determined group.

Paul saw with intense clarity that justification by faith, the central doctrine of his theology, and the very heart and core of Christianity, could not be powerfully or persuasively preached if the plan of salvation was also to include certain requirements of the law. What he had preached was so simple. Those who came to subvert his work, made it obscure and complex. They came, moreover, as their varied successors have done, in the name of Christ. They were the more dangerous because they appeared as Christians, speaking in the same Name, professing loyalty to Christ, along with criticism of Paul.

And, as is so commonly the case, they secured a following, which was likely to split and divide disastrously the earnest and uninstructed congregations. It must always be firmly borne in mind, as we seek to understand the thought of the early converts, that they had no New Testament. It is possible that some of the basic material, at least of Mark's Gospel, was in their hands, but this letter itself is one of the first documents of the New Testament to be written. The wonder is that the Christian communities remained as coherent and faithful as they evidently did.

But how true to human form the 'foolish Galatians' ran! Paul could only conclude that someone had 'bewitched' them, and put them under some spell which inhibited the realization of the simple doctrine so clear to his comprehensive mind. Paul had done no more than uncover in his Galatian converts a characteristic of human nature. In one way or another, man seeks to add to the requirements of the gospel—to insist on some act of initiation, to prescribe some specific form of procedure, to demand some work of the hands, some human contribution to the 'finished work' of Calvary, to exact some promise, sometimes even in cash contribution ... It panders to human pride to feel that man may make some small addition of his own to what has been done in overwhelming completeness for his redemption. The Galatian folly has been repeated in sect and individual, in the name of institution, hierarchy, cult of leadership or heresy. 'Foolish Galatians' . . .

664 : The Ephesians

Ephesians 2

Although we know none of the Ephesian church personally in the fashion of the Corinthian and Roman Christians whose names have found their way into the records of the New Testament, we do encounter the Ephesians in many different ways. In Acts 19 there was a striking picture of religious revival in the pagan, superstition-ridden city, culminating in a highly emotional demonstration, which ended Paul's ministry in the city of the powerful Artemis cult.

The Asiarchs, not at all displeased at any undermining of the cult, had advised Paul to leave Ephesus, but had as clearly hinted that it might be unwise to return. Hence the meeting of the elders on the Miletus beach (Acts 20), and some urgent warnings of Paul about dissensions to come in the congregation. These events covered four or five years, from the beginning of Paul's ministry in the city. Chronology is not certain to within a year or two, but say that we are speaking of A.D. 56, 57 to 58, 59.

The letter to the Ephesians in the New Testament is a theological treatise as well as a pastoral. It may have been circulated round the other Asian cities as far into Asia Minor as Laodicea, so it cannot be said that we gain much knowledge of the Ephesian Christians from it. Paul seems to have been in his house imprisonment in Rome. He is 'the prisoner of Christ'. At any rate it seems possible that the letter, like the first epistle to Timothy, was a work of the early sixties.

Soon after, John wrote his Apocalypse with a letter to Ephesus which we shall look at in a later study. The date again eludes us. The second letter to Timothy was certainly written during Paul's last imprisonment, and at a time not far from his death. This, we have conjectured, may have been in the vicinity of A.D. 67.

It is, in consequence, difficult to see the Ephesian Christians with the sharp clarity with which we were able to see those of Corinth. They would be a mixed multitude. The worship of

Artemis was built upon an ancient Anatolian cult, but had been Hellenized by the Greeks who had founded most of the cities in Asia Minor, and especially the Province of Asia, during the great age of Ionian colonization. Hence, along with the Jews, a strong Greek element.

We shall gain a slightly more intimate glimpse of the baser types in the congregation when we examine some of the advice given to Timothy, who had the difficult task of managing the church, and also in the more cryptic phrases of the letter John wrote from Patmos. Paul's letter should be read right through. It is a noble utterance. He calls for faith, for a clear view of faith's all-sufficiency, for stability amid the gusts of false doctrine (4.14), for strong loyalty, for love, for ethical standards commensurate with all—but what congregation is above such exhortation? Perhaps the Ephesians were like any group in just such a pagan environment; violent, sex-ridden, torn by sect, faction, social stress—and 'standing in the need of prayer.'

665 : Strong Man Armed

Ephesians 6

Paul learned much about the Empire in his journeys through the eastern and middle Mediterranean world. He knew how precariously those far-flung frontiers were held. He had spoken long and intimately with the legionaries of Rome, men who had seen the Rhine and the Danube, had served in Britain, and who were aware, as every easterner among Rome's citizens was aware, of the great, perilous open gate through which a Parthian invasion could come.

Vast pressures from the European and Asian hinterlands bore upon the frontiers of the Empire, and the soldiers who held those borderlands had the gate of Rome in their hands in more ways than one. And Paul's evangelism was, as we have so often seen, imperial in its strategy. He knew that forces of evil pressed hard upon the Church, evil which had a planning Mind behind it, and who, amid the mounting pressures of 'spiritual wickedness' in our own place and time, can deny the logic of such belief?

Let us, then, stand fast, says Paul, equally to Ephesus, to his own century, and us. He took a metaphor as old as Abraham (Gen. 15.1), and built it into the picture of a soldier of Christ, girt about with truth. The belt of the soldier held the breastplate firm, made a place to sling the sword, and girded the loins. The breastplate, so dependent upon the belt, as righteousness is on truth, guarded the vitals of life. No true religion can subsist on lies or on unrighteousness. Integrity and utter honesty must ever be the front the warrior of Christ presents to the world.

Above all, the shield must cover the body, held high, with the helmeted head held low, that helm and targe may fend off the blows of evil. The Roman soldier could use his bossed shield offensively as well as defensively, to throw an enemy off balance as he attacked with his short Thracian sword. He could stand with his cohort, shields locked overhead in a 'tortoise', so that a roof could cover a commando on attack. To lose the shield, in Greece and Rome, was ultimate military disgrace. 'The Greeks had a word for it'—*leipsaspia*—leaving the shield behind. The helmet covered the seat of thought, the head, as the consciousness of a Saviour-God keeps thought steady, safe from shattering blows, inviolate.

The sword, two-edged, sharp, is the Word, the soldier's essential weapon. Let it be blunted, bent, made useless by the arm's weakness or inexpertise, and the soldier can expect no victory. Paul knew the praetorians well. He saw them at weapon practice, medallions glittering on their belts, breastplates shining, helmet and plumed crest down ... He saw another soldier, steadfast, disciplined, one of a legion, conquering ...

666 : Tychicus

Acts 20.4; Ephesians 6.21; Colossians 4.7; 2 Timothy 4.12; Titus 3.12

Tychicus, described by Paul as a beloved brother and fellow-servant, and as a faithful minister of the Lord, was the bearer of the letter to the Ephesians, and, in company with Onesimus the returning slave, also the bearer of the letter to Colossae. Probably the gracious note to Philemon, covering Onesimus' return, travelled in the same mailbag, for it is reasonable to assume that Philemon lived at Colossae. Paul intended to make a visit to this area in the likely event of his discharge from his Roman custody, and some identity of phraseology between the two major letters is no matter of importance. Paul also intended the message to be made known in Laodicea. Ephesus was the mother church of the cluster of Christian congregations in the Lycus valley. There was probably another congregation in Aphrodisias, a city unmentioned in any ancient text, and only recently located and excavated. Archaeology may have some surprises there, as the work proceeds.

Tychicus is mentioned by Luke, along with Trophimus, as an Asian citizen, who met Paul in Greece and accompanied him to Troas at the conclusion of the third of Paul's journeys. He is not mentioned again in Acts, but is probably contained in the pronoun 'we', used of the party who travelled on with Paul. If the references above are followed in this scattered biography, it appears that Paul gave Tychicus a task in Ephesus, a natural appointment for a native of the province of Asia. He later seems to have replaced Titus in Crete. It is also suggested that Tychicus was the unnamed 'brother' of 2 Cor. 8.22. Tradition, at this point takes over, names Tychicus as Bishop of Colophon, and mentions final martyrdom. Of this there is no certain knowledge.

We have, then, a man who is little more than a name. He moves in and out of the story, casually mentioned, but whenever he appears, busy with some useful task. To carry mail from Rome to Colossae was no mean achievement, an arduous journey of five or six weeks' travel, in three peninsulas, and over two seas. Tychicus is a type of many faithful men and women, who without fanfare or prominence, carry on the work of Christ. The Church cannot do without them. They are the strength of its being.

Questions and themes for study and discussion on Studies 663–666

1. The Galatian folly today.
2. The problems of Ephesus today.
3. 'Without truth there can be no other virtue' (Sir Walter Scott).
4. The ministry of letter-writing.

667 : The Christian Citizen

Philippians 1; Luke 20.19–26

To be a citizen of Rome in the first century was no mean advantage, as the commander of the Jerusalem garrison remarked to Paul (Acts 22.28). It was in the small Macedonian town that Paul first claimed and exercised his rights as a Roman citizen. The freemen of Philippi were no doubt conscious of their standing as citizens of the Empire. Verse 27, not well translated in the RSV, refers to this coveted status. The Greek is very clear: 'One word to you, live on as citizens worthily of Christ's gospel, in order that, whether I am to come to see you, or only hear of you from afar, the news may be that you stand in one spirit, striving like a team with one accord for the faith of the gospel, dismayed in nothing by the ordered ranks ranged against you . . .'

Let the men of Philippi, says Paul, exercise their civic privileges as Christians should, in unity, with courage and without dismay. Paul is edging a little nearer in this word to the subject which disturbed him most in the news which Epaphroditus had brought from Macedonia concerning that emergence of faction and strife, with which he is determined to deal when the way has been cleared. Faction was the old curse of Greek politics. It is a malady of democracy. Where men have free speech and un- fettered wills, it is inevitable, human nature being what it is, that differences of opinion will arise on matters vital to the state. In the little states of Greece, before Macedon's and then Rome's dominion imposed a unity from above, it was not always the fashion to argue and debate such differences to the peaceful end of compromise or persuasion. The Greeks invented democracy. No people had thought more constructively on the issues of politics. Few people have more impatiently thrust principles aside and reddened their history with violence and strife.

Responsibility cuts both ways. A Christian should be a better citizen of Philippi and Rome. A Roman citizen, a privileged member of a great society, should be a better Christian, balanced, respectful of others' rights, responsible. Rome and the Church were to clash. It was the Empire's great and most awful mistake, the most evil legacy of the execrable Nero. That disaster had not yet come. The Christian citizen could have given Rome new life. Christian citizens are the only hope for the world's community to- day. Their portrait stands clear. Would they were more numerous.

668 : Paul's Impatience
Philippians 2.1–24

Paul, as the first chapter shows, had some reason to be displeased with certain elements in the Roman church, who, in spite of some admitted soundness of Christian doctrine, were taking advantage of the restrictions on Paul to undermine his authority. The Jews generally, and many Christians had shared their fate, were only just back in the capital after Claudius' decree of exile. They no doubt saw some need to walk circumspectly and with caution, a wariness with which Paul may have felt a trifle impatient (20f.).

In ch. 2 Paul seems to question the dedication of the Roman Christians, and it is a little difficult to fathom his full meaning. The true nature of Nero's government was now in full view. Two years before this letter was written, Nero had murdered his mother, Agrippina. About this time Burrus, the competent commander of the city garrison, died. He and Seneca were restraining influences on the vicious young emperor, and on Burrus' death, and almost seventy years of age, Seneca sought to withdraw from politics. City dwellers could read the signs, and may have been a little reluctant to identify themselves too closely with a state prisoner whose case had still to be decided. In another two years, the Great Fire and the ensuing persecution, made it apparent how precarious the Christians' position was.

Perhaps, too, no one was to be found in Rome ready to undertake the three weeks' journey to Philippi. Paul, utterly dedicated himself, was prone to vehemence against lesser spirits. His stern treatment of Mark was an indication of a certain intolerance against what he deemed weakness and selfishness. Imprisonment must have been trying in the heart of a Roman summer, and Paul's outburst of feeling can be ascribed to the strain under which he lived. A man of vigour, forced to depend on others, and finding those others half-hearted by his firm standards, might very naturally express himself with emphasis. The Roman church need not, therefore, at this distance be judged harshly. Congregations too often fall short of their minister's ideals. Paul likewise merits no mark of condemnation. He is the more human in our eyes for his words, and it is the fashion of Scripture to permit frank self-revelation.

669 : Epaphroditus

Philippians 2.25–30

Let us set the story in modern language for it contains its own message.

'I consider it necessary to send to you my brother Epaphroditus, my fellow-worker, and fellow-soldier, your delegate and the minister of my need. He longed for all of you, and was in great distress because you had heard that he was ill. Ill he was indeed. He almost died. But God had pity on him, and not only on him but on me, that I might not have one grief on top of another. I send him therefore the more eagerly, so that you may see him and rejoice once more, and that I may be less distressed. Receive him, then, in the Lord, with much joy, and hold such men in honour, because for the sake of Christ's work he came near to death, gambling with his life to make up the full total of your service.'

This little chapter of biography with its splendid testimonial is quite revealing both of Paul and the brave messenger from Philippi. The church probably intended him to remain in attendance on Paul, and the apostle thought it wise to leave no doubts that it was at his express command that the good man returned home. Epaphroditus had almost died in his zeal to serve. Rome in summer was an unhealthy place. August, said the poet Horace, is the month that unseals wills. The same poet describes a journey he made almost exactly a century before from Rome to Brundisium. He was accompanying Augustus' 'minister without portfolio' on a diplomatic mission. The Pontine Marshes, not drained until Mussolini's day, lay across the path, and it was the common custom to save time by abandoning the Appian Way, and traversing the marshlands by barge. Horace describes the mosquito-ridden night.

Hence Rome's indigenous malaria, to which the man from Macedonia's healthy uplands may have been a ready victim . . . It is a delightful picture, this small sketch of a devoted man who had gambled with his life for Paul's sake, and whose chief concern was lest those at home should be concerned about him. Such men are, as Paul said, rare. The RSV correctly renders v. 30. The same word is used in 1 Cor. 16.17, which should be rendered: 'They made up for the fact that I have not you.' Epaphroditus tried to do this for the church at Philippi, and nearly broke his health.

670 : Hebrew of the Hebrews

Philippians 3.1–9

Paul opens with strong words which show how intensely he feels. 'For the rest, my brethren, rejoice in the Lord . . . To continue writing the same things to you is not irksome to me, while it is salutary for you. And so I say: "Watch the dogs, watch the evil doers, watch the Mutilation." For we are the Circumcision, we who worship God in spirit, and exult in Jesus Christ, and have no firm confidence in the flesh.'

The outburst is sudden. Perhaps a lapse of a day or two had brought some new experience with the Jewish deviants. They appear again later in the chapter. Or perhaps Epaphroditus, recovered and preparing to depart, had mentioned some new matter which disturbed Paul deeply.

A piece of passionately written biography follows. They, without doubt, trust in ordinances and a mere mark in the flesh, but had he not all and more than any Nicodemus, any 'ruler of the Jews'? No one had so utterly fulfilled the law, if that was all. He was of the 'chosen people', ancient in descent; he was a member of a loyal tribe, no separatist northerner; he bore the covenant sign, given on the correct day, not in the thirteenth year like some child of Ishmael (Gen. 17.25), or in adulthood like some proselyte of the synagogue. He belonged to the Jews' strictest sect, whose whole history and whose whole life was dedicated to the preservation and keeping, even to the minutest detail, of all the Mosaic Law. He had also, in the continually remembered way, fought against the Church, and had demonstrated in the act the most fanatic loyalty.

And then he had found Christ, and, in that surpassing experience, had realized that all else was trash. All his life since then, as the mystic verses which follow indicate, had been an identification with Christ. We have again and again noticed this line of thought. Paul sought to die to evil as Christ had died for evil, and to rise again, as Christ rose again, to a life utterly different. He passionately desired to imitate in personal experience the whole historic process, to the day of resurrection itself. He lived in the power of that thought, the power of the faith that Christ lives, lives in us and we in Him.

671 : The Charioteer

Philippians 3.10–17; John 6.66–71

Commentators seem not to have noticed that in this passage is a word-picture of a Roman chariot race. Paul often illustrates a point by a reference to the athletic festivals of the Greeks. In this one case, writing from Rome to a Roman colony, he illustrates from the fierce and perilous sport of the Roman race. Under the encouragement of a playboy emperor, Rome, at the time of Paul's custody, was race-mad. Nero himself, as the Christians died in his gardens, after the Great Fire of A.D. 64, rode round in the colours of one of the racing factions. The common talk of the soldiers would be of racing, and Paul would gain a vivid impression of the sport.

Such a race is described well in *Ben Hur*. The charioteer stood on a small platform built on strong wheels and axle. His knees would press against a curved front wall perhaps two feet high. He bent forward at the waist with thighs flexed, and the reins were wound round his body. He leaned out, holding the reins as far forward as possible. This is what the phrase 'stretching out to the things before' must mean. The body, flung back on the reins, and braced at toe and knee, made a taut spring.

In such pose charioteer and team became one, and the charioteer was utterly dependent on his equipage. In a messenger speech in one of his plays, Euripides, the Athenian dramatist, describes the awful consequences of a fall. Ovid, the Roman poet, tells of the same disaster. The driver dared not look behind. The roaring crowd, yelling praise or taunts, the other chariots, all else had to be forgotten. A mark ahead could be the only point in the charioteer's eye ... 'The things behind' occurs again in John 6.66: 'Many went to the things behind, and walked no longer with him.' What a picture the whole passage gives of Paul's intensity of living! So, says v. 15 with a touch of the impatience we have observed, 'is life ... but perhaps some of you have other views—if so God will show who is correct. Meanwhile, having made a start, keep going.' So let us pray:

> *Lord make me deaf and dumb and blind*
> *To all those things which are behind;*
> *Deaf to the voice that memory brings*
> *With praise or scorn for many things,*
> *Dumb to the things my tongue could tell*
>
> *Of stumbling or of running well,*
> *Blind to the things I still might see*
> *When they come back to trouble me.*
> *Forgetting all that lies behind,*
> *Lord make me deaf and dumb and blind.*
> *Let me forget all I have done,*
> *'Tis through THEE, Lord, the race is won.*

672 : The Intruders

Philippians 3.15–21; Romans 6.1–13

The seventeenth verse can just possibly be translated: 'Become my fellow-imitators' that is, 'let us all imitate Christ.' However the enjoinder, even in its common translation, need not, indeed should not, in the light of the rest of the chapter, be taken to indicate a tone of self-righteousness. They were called upon to imitate him in striving for the goal, in abandoning the horrors of paganism, in resting all on faith, and nothing on works their hands had done.

It would appear that there was some danger in the faithful little church from some who perverted Christian liberty. Possibly the group which was a trouble in Corinth was visible, those who coalesced into a liberal faction called by John 'the Nicolaitans.' 'Ill-informed and unbalanced people,' wrote Peter (2 Pet. 3.15f. Phillips), distorted Paul's doctrine, received the gospel as a system of liberal philosophy, a scheme of emancipation which broke the bondage of old taboos, not indeed to replace them by the higher loyalties and loftier standards of Christian love, but by a libertinism which outraged the true Church. 'The Law is dead', was the motto of these antinomians, and they proceeded to make the fact an occasion for the flesh. The context of Paul's stern words in this passage illustrates a remark of James S. Stewart: '. . . there is one factor in the apostolic gospel which, even alone by itself and unaided absolutely, rebuts the antinomian charge brought against Paul and tears every criticism of the kind to shreds. The factor is union with Christ, union in His death and resurrection.'

'We should remember,' says Paul to these members of a Roman colony, 'that our real citizenship is of a spiritual realm. It has its laws, this realm, which so far transcend the laws of earth as heaven is above the world beneath. Let our thoughts be fixed there, and freedom from the taboos and restrictions of non-Christian cults simply frees the soul for loftier loyalties and deeper obligations.'

'Then, too,' he continues, linking, as always, eschatology and ethics, 'it is from that other realm that Christ will one day come, Christ for whom we wait with eager hope. Christ who will make us like Him. Such mystery is beyond us. But He who is above all and over all, He who is omnipotent, has power to transform this thing of flesh and pain into something divine and glorious.'

We cannot believe that these intruders were prominent in Philippi. It was a Roman-minded, sensible congregation. Paul was urgent to keep it so. Hence his frank warning. Hence, too, a warning which must be our next theme.

673 : Two Women

Philippians 2.12–16; 4.1–7

It was a century before that, on the rolling plain of Philippi, Octavian, later to be the Emperor Augustus, had seen the army of Brutus and Cassius, assassins of Julius Caesar, driven in defeat. That was the beginning of the Pax Romana, the Roman Peace, which ended a century of strife. To be sure, there was another decade of tension which ended only with the Battle of Actium, which assured the continuation of one Rome, undivided into east and west. Augustus gave peace. Augustus restored unity. A grateful senate hung a 'civic crown' above Augustus' door on the Palatine. They gave him, till then Octavianus Caesar, his imperial name. And now Paul calls his beloved church his crown (4.1).

But through all the letter he has been working to one point. Paul had heard from Epaphroditus that two women were becoming a problem. In Macedonia women were emancipated and free. No doubt Epaphroditus stressed the fact that both of the offenders were good women. They were both right, both strong. Personalities clashed—always a problem.

Paul at last reveals his purpose. The purpose of writing his letter suddenly emerges. The tension between two women was actually the occasion for this splendid piece of exhortation, and in the light of the fact some hasty estimates of Paul's character must be revised. At first sight he appears a blunt and downright personality. Witness him expelling Mark, parting with Barnabas, withstanding Peter, defying the Sanhedrin. But if Paul is rightly read in this epistle, he has filled three chapters with winsome appeal for Christian unity, before turning suddenly, as if in some embarrassment, with one brief word of exhortation, to the two offenders. Observe, too, the shape of the verse in which he addresses the women. The names appear in alphabetical order; neither is singled out; the verb is used with both . . . Then before the two can regain breath, or recover from the stratagem of surprise arranged perhaps with Epaphroditus, the one who administered a swift rebuke is speaking generous praise. If necessary rebuke were always so handled, there would be less pain, fewer wounded spirits.

773

The 'true yoke-fellow' is unknown. It could have been an elder at Philippi, the originator of the complaint to Paul, whom Paul thinks it wise to restrain a little in this kindly fashion. The whole passage is not only a model of tact, but a classic pattern for managing from afar a dispute among good people.

674 : The Philippians

Philippians 4; John 14.27

The Philippian Christians, for all the threat of an intruding minority, were practical folk. We have already seen some members of the church. The burghers of the town were Roman citizens, and a colony was a favoured place, and always conscious of its responsibility in the scheme of Rome's defences. The tribal menace from the north had, indeed, retreated, and the northern frontier in the Balkans was to hold for two more centuries, but Philippi, for all that, remembered that the Roman colonies were, in the phrase of Cicero, 'bulwarks of empire'. The Roman Peace was a blessing which the world prized. Rome could police the world, and so pacify the lands which clustered round the Inland Sea that Palestine no longer feared the raiding Parthians, and those who lived behind the Rhine and Danube were secure from the fierce marauding German tribes. But the Roman Peace rested on the fallible arms of men. At about the time this letter was written, London, Colchester, and St. Albans lay in ash and ruin. Under Boudicca the wild Iceni had broken out of Norfolk and struck back at Rome.

This is why Paul spoke to them of Christ's peace 'garrisoning' the soul (7). This is why he besought them to 'live as citizens worthily of Christ' (1.27)—a remark to which we shall return. It was perhaps some Roman instinct which led the folk of Philippi twice to minister to Paul's need. They are an attractive group. Of all the congregations mentioned in the New Testament, Philippi seems to have been the church to which one might belong most gladly.

Bishop Handley Moule closed his edition of Philippians in the *Cambridge Greek Testament* with the words of J. Agar Beet, and the century-old paragraph, with its touch of Victorian romanticism, and in spite of changes on the site of Philippi, is well worth quoting: 'With this reply, a gift infinitely more precious than that he brought from Philippi, Epaphroditus starts on his homeward journey. The joy caused by his return, and the effect of this wonderful letter when first read in the church at Philippi, are hidden from us. And we may almost say that with this letter the church itself passes from our view. Today, in silent meadows quiet cattle browse among the ruins which mark the site of what was once the flourishing Roman colony of Philippi, the home of the most attractive church of the apostolic age. But the name and fame and spiritual influence of that church will never pass. To myriads of men and women in every age and nation, the letter written in a dungeon at Rome and carried along the Egnatian Way by an obscure Christian messenger, has been a light divine, and a cheerful guide along the most rugged paths of life. As I watch, and myself rejoice in, the brightness of that far shining light, and glance at those silent ruins, I see fulfilled an ancient prophecy: The grass withereth, the flower fadeth: but the word of our God shall stand forever.'

Questions and themes for study and discussion on Studies 667–674

1. The role and qualities of the Christian citizen.
2. 'Congregations too often fall short of their minister's ideals.'
3. The role and qualities of Epaphroditus.
4. What was the real worth of Pharisaism? How was it corrupted?
5. The charioteer as a picture of 'committal'.
6. The Christian and compromise.
7. How to deal with tension in the church.
8. Thoughtfulness towards Christian workers.

675 : Epaphras of Colossae

Colossians 1.1–14; 4.1–18

Epaphras, a shortened and familiar form of Epaphroditus, was a native of Colossae and the founder of the church (1.7; 4.12), probably after being converted under Paul's ministry in Ephesus. In no part of the world was Paul's strategy of radiation more successful than in Ephesus and in the surrounding cities on the trade routes and river valleys, which ran up into the high country of Asia Minor. Epaphras was also active in nearby Laodicea and Hierapolis (4.13). This energetic Christian must be distinguished from the man of the same name (Paul does not in his case, use the contraction) who carried the monetary contribution of Philippi to Rome during Paul's first imprisonment (Phil. 2.25–30).

Epaphras of Colossae was the messenger of the Colossian church who journeyed to Rome with the disturbing news of heresy in the young congregation. He seems to have lived with Paul in the hired house in which he was under confinement, and so earned Paul's description of 'my fellow-prisoner'. This is a more likely assumption than that of actual arrest for the sake of the faith. If Colossians was written at the time of the first imprisonment, it antedated the measure of imperial repression against the Church which came only after the Neronian persecution in the summer of A.D. 64. Paul also calls Epaphras his 'fellow-servant' (1.7), no small honour, and 'a servant of Jesus Christ' (4.12), a phrase which he applies only once to Timothy (Phil. 1.1).

Such is the eminence of Paul himself that it is difficult to see clearly some of the figures around him. Epaphras must have been a man worth knowing to have done such sterling work. The Lycus valley, even greener and more fertile, and certainly more populous in the first century than it is today, was the sphere of his evangelistic activities. In the wide rolling valley plain, and very close together, lay the rich and prosperous city of Laodicea; the spa, holiday-resort and market town of Hierapolis, where the silica-laden springs attracted many visitors, and Colossae. In this triangle of towns, with their varied populace, most of them in comfortable circumstances, Epaphras exercised his successful ministry. It must have been in the Pauline mould for him to be so concerned for the integrity of the gospel. His journey to Rome is eloquent of this zeal. He must have been a man of deep concern, vast energy and faithfulness.

676 : The Colossians

Colossians 1.15–2.15

There was false teaching in the church at Colossae. God was pictured as remote and aloof, ministering to men through many intermediaries; Christ was but one of these, great and effective, but not all-sufficient. Hence the superb description (1.15–23). Note the wonder of it. Thirty years before, Jesus of Nazareth, rejected and betrayed, had died on a Roman cross. And now one who had harried His early followers to death, writes of Him in terms proper to God alone. A change so glorious speaks solemnly of the reality of God's intervention in history, of Paul's own deep experience, and of the magnificence of the divine glory manifested in Jesus.

Observe Paul's method with the absurdities of the heresy which some at Colossae had accepted. What he means by saying that in Christ are stored all possible resources of wisdom and insight amounts to this: let no tamperer with the pure gospel deceive the little church into imagining that anything further is needed for salvation over and above union with Him (2.3). Let them walk worthily of that loyalty. The Christian life, commented Guy King on v.6 (where the RSV 'live' represents 'walk' in the Greek), 'is not a sedentary occupation, but a pedestrian affair'. 'Pedestrian' can be taken in two ways. It suggests a certain dogged perseverance through the common and ordinary paths of life, but it also suggests progress, a determined movement towards a goal. At any rate we must move on, not stand still. And then v. 7—rooted in Christ, let them like good trees demonstrate in the beauty of leaf, the strength of branch, and the usefulness of fruit, the deep sustenance which such roots can give (Psa. 1.3). Roots are mobile questing things. They probe and seek for sustenance, and move unerringly towards the richest supply of what they need. Let us so seek Christ.

In a tumult of metaphor, Paul seeks further to warn his flock against those who would explain away the simplicity of the gospel, render obscure that which God had made so plain, and make difficult for ordinary folk that which God had intended that a child should understand (8). Christ, he insists, is no inadequate 'go-between', but one with God Himself (9). And if that is the case, are not they who are joined to Christ by faith saved utterly, completely, triumphantly (10)? Like those who became proper Jews by the observance of the ancient rite of circumcision, so by the act of faith they became members, inalienably and eternally, of a new order (11).

It is stimulating to meet a mind so powerful, so ardent, and yet so simple.

677 : The Mind of Paul

Colossians 2.16–3.11

We may sometimes almost be grateful for heresy and bent teaching, because of the magnificence of the response which it provokes. Paul's concern distils into eloquence and wealth of mystic illustration. Patiently and vividly, he has explained (2.9–15) how the Christians of Colossae became Christ's people, sharing His death and resurrection in the symbol of baptism, alive to a new and glorious life, as different from the humdrum, fear-ridden paganism around as vibrant living is from death. The great transaction, says Paul, employing yet another picture, is done. The charge against the sinner was nailed to Christ's cross, and blotted out by His blood. They were forgiven—let them grasp the fact with both hands, and realize that no more obligations lay on them. No power could daunt them, for Christ had defeated all evil.

And then we are given a glimpse of the extra-religious duties which the sectarians were seeking to foist on to the church at Colossae. There were prohibitions of meat and drink, and observances of sacred days. These, says Paul, had their place in the teaching of the Old Testament, but were not binding on Christians. Such was the teaching of those who sought to turn Christianity into a sect of Judaism.

Those referred to in v. 18 appear to have derived some strange ideas from the pagan 'mystery religions'. The 'self-abasement' may be a reference to physical ordeals and initiation ceremonies, evidence of which is found in the shrines of Mithras. The angel-worship of the next phrase touches a false doctrine already mentioned—the idea of a descending range of angel 'go-betweens' of whom Christ was only one; eminent, no doubt, but incomplete.

No, says Paul, giving us another vivid metaphor, those who are in Christ are His very body, as closely knit to Him as the limbs which move at the impulse of the head (19), alive with His own immortal life. Again, he concludes, Christianity is not a matter of rules and regulations. Those who trust Christ live not by rule but by love. In a word, the 'man in Christ' needs no irksome book of rules, no complicated and Pharisaic table of prohibitions. His conduct and his character are determined by his daily contemplation of his Lord, his daily fellowship with the risen Christ, his constant hope of being like the One who might at any moment come again. The challenge is tremendous; it forms a motive for purity of life, unselfishness of conduct, and integrity of character which by-passes all petty regulations. And here, unconsciously, Paul paints his own portrait.

678 : Man in Christ

Colossians 1.24–29; Hebrews 13.12–14

Inevitably, in looking at the men and women of Colossae, and the false and foolish ideas which plagued them, we have looked into the mind of the great man who has dominated the theme for a hundred character studies. We cannot leave him speaking to the little congregation in the distant Lycus Valley, which he had never personally visited, without turning back to a strange saying which reveals much about him. It occurs in 1.24, where Paul speaks of 'completing that which is lacking in the sufferings of Christ.'

What can be 'lacking', and how can any man 'complete' such a total? Certain it is that Paul, like every writer in the New Testament, regarded the death of Christ as efficacious, sufficient, and once for all. No further sacrifice of saint or priest can provide a lacking element in that complete redemption, do anything to extend that 'finished work'. But in this world, all who associate themselves with Christ, and, in the great Pauline phrase, are 'in him', and seek to be faithful to Him in both conduct and testimony, must expect to become fellow-sharers in the same kind of treatment which Christ Himself received. Only so can Christ's body, the Church, be served and increased in number by ministry and evangelism, as Christ's followers are willing to share His reproach. This is what Paul means.

In speaking of completing what is still lacking of such suffering, Paul is thus referring to the sufferings which Christ foretold for him: 'I will show him how much he must suffer for the sake of my name' (Acts 9.16). Each day's pain, for the gospel's sake, brought him nearer to the end of his appointed course.

This is far removed, as H. M. Carson points out, from Stoicism's tight-lipped endurance. 'The Christian,' he rightly says, 'goes beyond mere endurance, and rejoices because he sees his sufferings as part of the divine purpose, and so gladly accepts them as a means of fulfilling his part in the eternal plan of God.' This is an ideal difficult to rise to, but why, in fact, are we engaged in these studies—encounters with men, some of which are dark with warning and some ablaze with daunting light? Is it not to nerve ourselves for like tasks, tasks in this case not unlike those which await our faithfulness in a not dissimilar world?

779

679 : The Children of Light

1 Thessalonians 5

The letters in the New Testament sometimes give us tantalizing glimpses of people in the Church. It is like looking at a building from the outside, aware that it is occupied, but sensing the activity and the nature of those within by the occasional movement past a window, or by the opening and shutting of a door.

In the story of Paul's visit to the northern Greek port, we met some of the personalities of the Christian congregation (Acts 17.1–10). In the two letters Paul wrote to them we can guess what some of the rest were like. Paul, in fact, was anxious about them on more than one count. The subject of his care in Athens was the precarious state of the little group he had left behind.

He felt that he had not had time adequately to instruct them, and one theme which had given him cause for concern was the teaching of Christ's Second Advent. It is a subject which can be easily misused. The Lord Himself was clear enough on the fact that a second intrusion into history was a future historic event. He is coming again. He was also perfectly clear that it was impossible to fix the date, and that only the spiritually perceptive would read the signs aright.

It is, none the less, of the nature of man to pry into the patterns of the future. Man wants to know the shape of coming events, and every age of the Church has seen those who have chosen to disregard the Lord's clear words, and fix a date for the Second Advent. In the process they have obscured the real truth, and turned people from a blessed expectation, and in the same act corrupted some and seduced them from the proper and Christian activities which are woven into every day.

It is obvious that Thessalonica had its quota of such people. Paul warns them against such unjustified extravagance, and in his second letter is to warn them again in stronger terms. He speaks here in kindly fashion of the advantages they have. They are 'children of the light' in a real, exciting sense. They do know that the evil of a godless world is to end. They are not without hope. They need never despair. They are alive, awake, watching. It is a pleasant picture of a clever teacher leading a mistaken group of enthusiasts back to creative sobriety by extracting the good from the very texture of their error.

680 : Man of Sin

2 Thessalonians 2

Sobered or puzzled by what Paul had to say about the Second Advent the Thessalonians had asked for further explanation. We can picture the more responsible members of the congregation seeking an authoritative word with which to bring some sense and order to an excitable and troublesome minority, who were distorting and misunderstanding what Paul had said.

In the process of his explanation, Paul introduces the darkest character of Scripture to be seen on earth—the man of sin, the lawless one. Paul is at pains to make it quite clear to the group at Thessalonica, who had so grievously misconstrued his words, that there were certain situations which would foreshadow the catastrophic end of 'the age'. There was to come a period of moral collapse and open rebellion against God. Some restraining power was to be withdrawn and there is still controversy regarding Paul's meaning here. Did he mean that God would cease to control evil—a statement unlikely from him? Or did he foreshadow the end of such legal protection as he had had from the Asiarchs of Ephesus (Acts 19.30f.), from Gallio (Acts 18.12–17), and from his privileged status as a citizen? Such a situation came after A.D. 64, when the mere profession of Christianity was written down as a crime against the state.

Above all the horrific incarnation of evil in a person, one destined in character, in policy, in practice to be the antithesis and opposite of Jesus Christ, would be visible among men. Paul may have anticipated this fearsome creature in the person of an emperor, and the characteristics appeared in more than one. Indeed, as John was to remark, there were many foreshadowings of the ultimate apparition (1 John 2.18), and the world still awaits the final consummation. Some would say that there has never been a time before today when the rising flood of conscience-less evil, the growth of technology and computer science, the spread of tyrannical wickedness, and a shrinking world, have so set the stage for the second to last 'character of Scripture'. The last will be his Conqueror—Christ Himself. For us it is well to remember the lesson which Paul brought home to his misguided converts—time is not to be wasted idly anticipating an end. There is work to do, and only we to do it.

1. The role and qualities of Epaphras.
2. The Colossian heresy today.
3. The 'man in Christ'.
4. 'The Christian goes beyond mere endurance.'
5. 'The blessed hope.' How real is it today?
6. Antichrist—the relevance of that concept today.

681 : Grace Abounding

1 Timothy 1

This is obviously the chapter from which John Bunyan took the title for his autobiography: *Grace Abounding to the Chief of Sinners.* The chapter is itself notably autobiographical. If nothing else of the New Testament had survived it would be possible from this score of verses to guess that an outstanding man had been redeemed from a career of violence and hatred against God, who, in Christ Jesus, had offered salvation to the world. In that Name, Paul under divine commission, had proclaimed the gospel, and had founded churches in two continents. And already the purity of the message was challenged by those who promulgated false doctrine, dishonouring to God, and complicating a primitive simplicity.

This is the first of the three Pastoral Epistles, a title in use for the last two centuries, and in the name there is indication of the problems of the expanding Church and the new considerations which were occupying Paul's mind. Timothy appears to be in charge at Ephesus, and Paul seems to write from Macedonia. It is a fair guess that he had been released from his first imprisonment in Rome, and had four or five years' activity of which nothing is recorded. Perhaps he went to Spain during this interval. He was certainly busy, and busy with a new urgency.

He could see, at any rate after the summer of 64, that grim days were coming, not only for Rome, increasingly restive under Nero, but also for the Church. It was no time for nonsense, with heretical teachers making difficulties for the Christian community with strange perversions, fables, genealogies, and those manifold perversions of God's truth in which the imagination of deviant theologies and pseudo-intellectualism, no less than the exponents of exotic cults of 'experience', have always been fertile.

Moreover, Paul could see that organization was a prime necessity. The old coherence of love and mutual fellowship in the Christian groups obviously needed the reinforcement of discipline. Leadership of a tried and tested sort had to be established, and Paul's letters to Timothy and Titus are full of his rapid and concise directions. Crisis was in his mind, and critics, assault and sabotage, could only be met by a proper ordering of defence. It is the same Paul, and yet a new Paul who confronts us, a man convinced that time is short, and that nothing in the world, his own life included, mattered so much as the continued functioning and endurance of the Church he had given toilsome and perilous years to found.

682 : The Elder
1 Timothy 3.1–7; Titus 1

We first see in these chapters the picture of men who are to march through the centuries—the leaders of the church. There are saints among them, the salt of the earth. There are martyrs and heroes —and there are John Masefield's 'princes and prelates with periwigged charioteers, riding triumphantly laurelled to lap the fat of the years . . .' But whatever the worth or the worthlessness of men have made of honourable office, the portrait is clear, and among the ideal characters of Scripture must stand the elder, the deacon and the minister.

It seems likely that, in the New Testament, the bishop (or overseer) and the elder are identical. Paul was eager to see, above all, good, sane, upright men in control. The senior officer must be a man of blameless reputation, a 'man of one woman', as v. 2 puts it. He must be alert, self-controlled, with open home, a good teacher. He must not mar his testimony either by drunkenness, or violence, or money-grabbing—a man, in short, of dignity and obvious integrity. No bad-tempered bully, greedy, unable to exercise a proper discipline among his own, can qualify.

The verses in the parallel passage in the letter to Titus which correspond to vs. 6 and 7 omit the corresponding directions. Paul's magnificent common sense saw that what applied to an old urban community, where the church was well-established, might not equally apply in the primitive island community of Crete. The responsible officer must not be 'a new shoot', he says. The word is used in the Septuagint, the Greek Old Testament, for newly planted trees (Psa. **144**.12). A man too immature and thrust into office, might be more easily tempted to damaging pride in a place like Ephesus, than among the simpler people of Crete.

Note that Paul expects his elder to hold a good testimony with the world outside the church. Abraham reminded Lot that 'the Canaanite and the Perizzite dwelt in the land' (Gen. **13**.7f). The non-Christian pays the Church the unwitting compliment of knowing what the Christian ought to be, and expecting it. Add these qualities together, picture the character which emerges, and you have the fair ideal. It would be hard to say that it has never been completely attained. Ideals would cease to be ideals, were they too easily in reach. Such, at any rate, is the elder—the bishop, or what you will.

683 : The Deacon

1 Timothy 3.8–16

The deacons were the lesser serving officers of the church. They must be worthy of respect, dignified. The AV(KJV) 'grave' seems to contain some of the Roman virtue of 'gravity', the Stoic 'reserve', which Paul may have admired. In a modern setting the word suggests a thoughtful avoidance of extremes in demeanour, dress and speech, a freedom from frivolity and extravagance, above all from exhibitionism, the common temptation of all office holders in any sphere of authority.

Above all the good deacon is not double-tongued. He avoids the reprehensible adaptation of one mode of address for one person, another for another. He is plainly truthful, never deceitful and insincere in what he says. This does not mean he is a man of brutal and hurtful frankness, nor devoid of the common courtesies and graceful proprieties of conversation. It merely forbids a form of falsehood and hypocrisy. The deacon also must be no addict of the bottle or the money-bag.

Then comes (9) simplicity and sincerity in belief, allied to like qualities in speech. A clear conscience forbids reservations in belief. The unsure, the uncommitted and the unconvinced are not men for office. The church can only be safely led by men who believe every word they say. The tragedy of recent years has been the easy victory won by a small band of liberal theologians over churchmen of feeble faith—the group whom someone has dubbed 'the Munich school of theologians', ready to sell the pass in the weak belief that they can hold some vague position, if only their own, somewhere in the lower foothills, and too busy listening to their enemies to say anything useful to their friends. No one should function in the Church, in any mode of leadership, save men of muscular faith, and sturdy conviction. Such men must be chosen only after long scrutiny (10). And such men depend upon good wives. All men do, for good or ill . . .

It is another fine picture of men who should be common in the Christian Church. Those who thus qualify and serve, 'have won for themselves high standing, and the right to speak openly on the Christian faith' (13). No others have.

684 : The Young Minister

1 Timothy 4

The good minister, as Paul envisages him, with Timothy and Ephesus in mind, must function in the midst of a hostile world and a church infiltrated by the enemy. He must, above all, know where he stands and speak with conviction. 'In setting these matters before the church, you will be a good minister (servant) of Jesus Christ, ever nourishing yourself on the words of the faith and the good doctrine you have followed.' Weakness in a ministry, weakness in a church, comes from weakness in the exposition and study of the Word. And such weakness stems from a decayed faith, and a diminished concept of biblical authority. 'Minister', it must be remembered, is the Latin for slave or servant. It is the opposite of 'magister' or master, the antonym which has survived only in derivatives in English. To lead, we must serve. It is a fundamental law.

'Turn away from the babbling of old women,' Paul tells Timothy with a touch of impatience, 'and exercise yourself rather for godliness.' If we had Timothy's letter to Paul we might understand this remark a little better. Perhaps some dissident women's group was making the young man's task difficult. 'Bodily exercise,' he goes on, 'has its minor place of usefulness, but godliness is of all-round value, containing as it does the promise of life here and hereafter (8), and I do want you to believe this (9). This is the whole theme of our toil and endurance . . . So pass it on' (10, 11).

Timothy's ministry emerges from the urgent and insistent

advice to be strong and not to be abashed by arrogant women, or arrogant older men. Authority can belong to a young minister, provided he sets, on all occasions, secular and sacred, a good example in speech, in manner of life and in the basic qualities of character set forth in the three nouns which conclude v. 12—love, that is compassion, mercy, tolerance and Christlikeness, faith, that is the sturdiness and steadfastness of Christian conviction, and thirdly, purity, that is personal integrity and self-control. And observe the test of self-discipline which follows. The young minister must be diligent in reading, preaching, study. Timothy was probably in his early thirties. This was Paul's portrait as Paul hoped to see him, and as he no doubt endeavoured to be.

685 : The Talkers

1 Timothy 6

There is in this chapter a group to be found at many times and at many places, not only in the church but in all the institutions of democracy—the lovers of talk for the sake of talking, the habitual controversialists, the specialists in discussion for no constructive end, the promoters of vain questionings.

It is interesting to read the various renderings of Paul's strong words about this group at Ephesus. There was many a 'pompous ignoramus' (NEB) in the church, people filled with 'a morbid appetite for discussions and arguments' (Williams), 'quibbling over the meaning of Christ's words and stirring up arguments' (Taylor), from which naturally and inevitably arose, and still arise, 'defamations, quarrellings, wrangling, ill-natured suspicions, recriminations, malicious innuendoes, abusive language, perpetual contention, constant friction, minds warped . . .' This grim list is collected from five translations of vs. 4 and 5, checked against the original. Any modern Timothy, plagued in like fashion by the wrong kind of 'discussion groups', can be assured that Paul meant no less.

Paul was no stranger to constructive and necessary controversy. He had fought a good fight against those who corrupted the simplicity of his message. He had 'withstood Peter to his face.' What he deprecated was the old vice of Greek communities with which some who share the democratic and dialectical heritage of the Greeks are not unfamiliar—the habit of exhibitionist talking.

The Athenians, said Luke, in an ironical phrase, 'spent their time in nothing else but either to tell or to hear some new thing' (Acts 17.21). In vs. 3 and 4 note the metaphor of health and sickness. These folk were sick, 'morbidly preoccupied', or as the RSV puts it 'with a morbid craving for controversy and for disputes about words'.

The fact that Paul next reverts to riches and their snare, may suggest that the questioners of sound doctrine were the affluent of the congregation, which produced the sect of the Nicolaitans, a group we shall soon be meeting. Some find it convenient to justify a self-willed position by the cover of a privately interpreted text.

686 : Two Men
2 Timothy 1.1–15

We have met Timothy before, observed his rural origin, and the formative influence in his life of a Christian mother and grandmother. It is strange to see that the Church was already housing a third generation of Christians. In this chapter, with no sense of incongruity or division, age meets youth. Paul may have been in his sixties. Timothy was probably half that age. Paul, supremely trusting, had left the somewhat nervous, dependent and not very robust young man in charge of the Christian congregation in the great Asian centre of commercialized religion, and religious vice.

He is handing on the torch, and in his words of encouragement to his young successor Paul shows the manner of men both were. Note the open-hearted affection. To be aloof, critical, gruff or impatient with youth, is not of Christ. Youth is the inevitable successor. It is inevitable that the passing of the years will make it certain that other hands will hold the helm, and other minds will plan. If the tradition is to abide intact and fruitfully developing, those other hands, those other minds must be trained and accept the training. To embitter and frustrate is not service to the cause, which must continue. The 'generation gap' can be dug from both sides. Paul was aware of no separation.

Gently, and with his habitual tact, he suggests that, for the task of leadership, Timothy required a strength of character which he had determinedly to lay hold of and develop, love which was not soft indulgence, but compassion uncompromising with sin, and a self-discipline which, in strong and balanced sanity, steadied self and others. In the exhortation there appears a picture of

787

what Paul was, and what he thought Timothy capable of becoming. Verse 12 sums up, in one of the finest testimonies of Scripture. Faith grows into knowledge. Steadfastness in belief produces the evidence of personal experience. Doubt can certainly attack any Christian, but doubt cannot be a way of life, and is a malady which should seek healing.

Paul had a load on his heart. Some in the province where he had worked so well, had turned on their old leader. There were tongues of disloyalty wagging, like those of Phygelus and Hermogenes, mere names, but set in a context of shame. Paul trusts Timothy to stand. To break a chain of witness which, with every Christian, goes back to Christ in truest 'apostolic succession', is a sin most grievous.

687 : Onesiphorus
2 Timothy 1.16–18; Matthew 25.34–40

The tiny cameo pictures of Bible characters are supremely interesting. Some, as we have seen, in the province of Asia, had turned from Paul. Not so the patron of all prison visitors, Onesiphorus. As Christ had done, long years before, the good man of Ephesus had 'sought Paul out and found him'. Paul's second imprisonment was no honourable house-arrest. It was not without its danger to be associated with him. In the teeming metropolis of a million souls by the Tiber, Onesiphorus sought diligently until he located the prison, and brought Paul refreshment of soul.

There is worth and beauty in such friendship, and honour in standing by a friend in distress. In his moving confession, *De Profundis*, Oscar Wilde tells a story of a friend. Oscar Wilde was no Paul. He fell grievously and suffered deeply, but a moment's act of courtesy brought him near to God. He tells the story thus: 'When I was brought down from my prison to the Court of Bankruptcy, between two policemen,——(Wilde omits the name) waited in the long dreary corridor that, before the whole crowd, whom an action so sweet and simple hushed into silence, he might gravely raise his hat to me, as, handcuffed and with bowed head, I passed him by. Men have gone to heaven for smaller things than that. It was in this spirit, and with this mode of love, that the saints knelt down to wash the feet of the poor, or stooped to kiss the leper on the cheek. I have never said one single word to him about what he did. I do not know to the present moment whether he is aware that I was even conscious of his action. It is not a thing for which one can render formal thanks in formal words. I store it in the treasure-house of my heart. I keep it there as a secret debt that I am glad to think I can never possibly repay. It is embalmed and kept sweet by the myrrh and cassia of many tears.'

Onesiphorous did more for Paul. What happened to him? Did Rome's climate claim his life, as it nearly did that of Epaphroditus? It is thought that he died. Did his visit cost him liberty and life? Paul prays for his family and trusts that Onesiphorus found mercy with the Lord. The phrase is hard to understand for Paul could have had no doubt of the acceptance of such a saint. It remains a mystery, but here was a man who was kind in Ephesus and kind in Rome, who was a blessing when all was secure, and no different when the air was rank with death and danger. Such souls are rare.

688 : Self-portrait

2 Timothy 2.1–13; 3.10–17

Paul inevitably wrote of himself in the three word pictures of the second chapter. Rome was full of soldiers in A.D. 67. Anyone who could read the signs could see that the Empire was moving fast towards the civil strife of 69. The city garrison had set up the last two emperors, and were determined not to be outdone by the frontier legions—which, in the end, they were. But as Paul watched Rome's best troops, he saw that to be a soldier a man did what he had done. He had handed over his whole life, was prepared to battle against any odds, to endure discipline, and to be conspicuous.

It was also, he reflected, like being an athlete. At Corinth he could have witnessed the Isthmian Games, the athletes' intensity of effort, the dedication to one end, the striving before a watching crowd. And on many a weary tramp for the gospel's sake, he had seen the peasants of the eastern provinces at work, facing the storms of winter, the mud and the murk, to sow the seed, rejoicing in the harvest, trusting the unseen powers of Nature to bring to growth and to maturity that which they strove so faithfully to plant in the cold, reluctant ground.

He saw that, common to soldier, to athlete, and to farmer, was an end, envisaged and anticipated before the reality, a harvest, a victory. He saw that it all began with a choice involving toil or strife, a continuing in spite of resistance, be it the unyielding soil or the power of the foe. It involved faith in the ultimate, and the overpowering conviction that it is the ultimate in life which counts. He saw that, while farmers and athletes faced their tasks, their tests, their toils alone, the soldier was part of a cohort, a legion, and was held by a common cause and loyalty to his fellows. There was self-discipline, training, defiance of difficulty, sustaining hope, in all three cases.

Paul made no secret of the fact that being a Christian is no easy task. He reminds Timothy that, when as a boy, he threw in his lot with him, he had seen with his own eyes what suffering and persecution had befallen in Timothy's own district—round Iconium and Lystra. There is no easy path in life to any harvest, any victory. Paul knew it. So do we—or if not, as Christians, we soon will learn. But if our society endures, it will be the Christians' doing—and 'never will so much have been owed by so many to so few'.

689 : The Last Men

2 Timothy 3.1–9; 4.1–5; 2 Peter 3.1–4

The grim forecast in the opening verses of 2 Tim. 3 looks too familiar for comfort to anyone who watches or reads the news of any day. 'I bring nought for your comfort,' says Paul, as Alfred says, in Chesterton's poem, 'save that the sky grows darker yet, and the sea rises higher.' Here is the picture of a decadent society, the characters of a corrupt age rising like a dank smoke from the prophetic page of Scripture. Watch them march, like the mob in Vanity Fair, across imagination's stage, or if you will, down the city street, the victims of moral breakdown, of the 'permissive society', of triumphant wickedness. Read the passage in several versions: 'they will be proud and contemptuous, without any regard for what their parents taught them': 'they will go to church, yes, but they won't believe a word they hear'; 'they will collect teachers who will tell them what they want to hear'; 'constant liars, thinking nothing of immorality'; 'rough and cruel, sneering at those who try to be good' . . .

Such is the picture Paul sets before his young successor. There have always been such creatures in the world, but it would be blindness indeed not to see their multitude increasing. It is time, if ever time was, to stand firm. And, says Paul, 'you have your Bible'—it 'resets the direction of life'; 'it straightens us out'. 'All Scripture is inspired by God . . .' That, be it noted, is the correct translation. No one with any feeling for Greek, no one, at any rate, who can read Greek without translating it and spelling out its meaning—not a common achievement of commentators—would think the words could be taken in any other way than the RSV and AV(KJV) take them: 'All Scripture is inspired by God and it is profitable for teaching . . .' And furthermore, anyone with any feeling for the teaching of Paul could not imagine that he would say anything else. The alternative: 'Any scripture which is inspired of God . . .' leaves the door open to as many private classifications of Scripture as there are expositors with individual heresies, obsessions, private notions, or what you will. One could imagine Paul's comment.

690 : Demas

2 Timothy 4.1–10

Demas is mentioned twice in other contexts—in Col. 4.14, where his name occurs without comment, and in Philem. 24 where he shares the title of fellow-worker. Since both letters went to the same locality, at about the same time, some significance attaches to this. Some years have slipped by, and Demas, seeking what life has to offer, has left his post at Paul's side. 'This world' is the society to which Paul bids us 'be not conformed' in Rom. 12.2, and Demas had found reason to merge with it and make for Thessalonica. There is no evidence that his home was there. Since he is mentioned both to Philemon and the people at Colossae, it might be supposed that he was an Asian, and known in the Lycus valley congregations.

Why did he defect? Life had little left for Paul. To those around him his end seemed certain, and the temptation must have been strong to live and fight another day. Demas did not necessarily abandon the faith, only what Paul thought to be the post of duty. Someone in Thessalonica, parent, friend or one who loved him, may have offered security, even service. There were many who were not in complete agreement with Paul, and with many-edged arguments would press the need for withdrawal.

Or it could have been apostasy. He 'loved the good things of life', says one free translation, and the rendering could be correct.

Life has many good things to offer, advantages, pleasures, wealth, popularity, none of which the Christian need deny himself, provided the price is not too high. And the price *is* too high when it involves integrity, testimony, loyalty to God or good, duty or anything else held or professed in the Sacred Name. Paul thought that Demas had paid far beyond his means.

Luke saw fit to stay, and so did Mark, for all the quarrel Paul had once had with him. Both men knew as well as Demas what the situation in Rome held of opportunity, of duty or of peril. They also knew that there was nothing intrinsically evil in physical withdrawal before threat or persecution. It was a case of weighing this against that, and Demas must have added to the scale his measure of disloyalty, self-seeking or regard for self-interest. It is a tiny biography, and it is sad, when history can spare no more than a sentence, to find it thus expressed. If history can grant us this much and no more, what would our sentence be?

Questions and themes for study and discussion on Studies 681–690

1. Does a local church need organization?
2. When is the approval of non-Christians desirable and when is it not?
3. 'The unsure, the uncommitted and the unconvinced are not men for office.'
4. 'Weakness in a ministry, weakness in a church, comes from weakness in the exposition and study of the Word.'
5. The distinction between harmful and necessary controversy.
6. Eliminating the 'generation gap' in the church.
7. Our identification with those in prison for Christ's sake—how can we express it?
8. Is persecution inevitable?
9. The last days—and our days.
10. The troubles of our friends as tests of *our* character.

691 : Onesimus

Philemon 1–25

There are three men in this exquisite little letter, Paul, Philemon and Philemon's runaway slave. Onesimus seems to have robbed his master, a Christian of Colossae, and made his way to Rome, which one of Rome's own writers called 'the common sewer of the world.' Onesimus sought hiding and anonymity in the multitude of Rome's slum-dwellers, was perhaps robbed in turn, and in desperation had discovered Paul. Perhaps Epaphras from Colossae had recognized him. He found Paul and found Christ, and the question of restitution arose. Paul solved it with austerity and sent Onesimus home, but sent him home with the gratitude he owed him and with a moving appeal to Philemon which forms the theme of this exquisite letter.

Apphia was, of course, Philemon's wife, and Archippus, not improbably his son. They, and the church which made its centre and meeting place in their home, were probably converts of the Ephesian ministry (Acts 19.10). Archippus appears to have been something of a figure in the community, as witness Col. 4.17. Only once elsewhere does Paul use the expression 'comrade in arms', or 'fellow-soldier'. The word occurs in Phil. 2. 25.

What happened to Onesimus? For what it is worth we may look at a phrase in a letter of Ignatius written to the church at Ephesus some half-century later. Ignatius praises the bishop of Ephesus, 'a man of inexpressible love'. The bishop's name was Onesimus, and like Paul, Ignatius puns on it. Was the bishop the one-time slave in grand and useful old age? And is this why one private letter of Paul, prized through a grateful man's lifetime, found its way into the New Testament? It is fairly certain that the final collection of Paul's letters was made at Ephesus. Speculation, but it could be true.

Perhaps we may end with a quotation from R. D. Shaw: 'It was by his affectionate personal interest that Paul undoubtedly obtained his singular hold upon men ... The sunshine of his solicitude seemed to focus itself on each single life and to make that life its peculiar care. Great as he is when panoplied in theological armour, "sheathed with logic and bristling with arguments", he is greater still as he lavishes himself in the personal ministry of love, and seeks to win his crown in the growing grace and peace of the souls whom he has brought into the kingdom of Christ.'

692 : Last Word

2 Timothy 4.11–22

We have been a long time with Paul. We leave him today. His closing words are a cry of triumph and a plea for human friendship. 'Come before winter,' he tells the young man. He is to stop at Troas and pick up some books and notes. He is also to bring the cloak he left with Carpus. Perhaps the soldiers arrested Paul in the street. He had no time to pick up proper clothes, or hesitated to involve others by revealing where he lived. Dr. C. E. Macartney had a moving sermon on this verse. 'This is Paul's only robe. It had been wet with the brine of the Mediterranean, white with the snows of Galatia, yellow with the dust of the Egnatian Way . . .'

Summer was waning in Rome. The chill winds would soon be breathing down from the Apennines, and winter would close the seas to navigation. Paul's voyage and shipwreck showed what November sailing could be like in that stormy sea. We may guess that Timothy set out at once, to Troas, past the high hump of Samothrace to Neapolis, along the Egnatian Way, with a night at Philippi, across to Brundisium, and up the long Appian Way to Rome. Did he serve Paul again? Did he see him die at Cestius' Pyramid?

'Come before winter.' Haste was necessary, and Dr. Macartney put it well. It will soon be a score of years since that great preacher passed like Paul to his crown, and he would not object to quotation. 'Come before winter . . . Before winter or never! There are some things which will never be done unless they are done "before winter". The winter will come and the winter will pass, and the flowers of the springtime will deck the breast of the earth, and the graves of some of our opportunities, perhaps the grave of our dearest friend. There are golden gates wide open on this autumn day, but next October they will be for ever shut. There are tides of opportunity running now at the flood. Next October they will be at the ebb. There are voices speaking today which a year from today will be silent. Before winter or never!'

But suppose Timothy stayed to finish affairs at Ephesus, hurried to Troas and heard the words: 'No ships till April', waited there, and reached Rome at April's ending! So Dr. Macartney's sermon imagined. 'He goes to the house of Claudia, or Pudens, or Ampliatus and asks where he can find Paul. I can hear them say: "And are you Timothy? Don't you know that Paul was beheaded last December? Every time the jailer put the key in the door of his cell, Paul thought you were coming."'

693 : The Writer of Hebrews

Hebrews 13

There is an unknown writer in the New Testament to whom the Church stands in deepest debt. He wrote the unsigned letter to the Hebrew Christians. Paul was once thought to be the author, though even the early Church thought, in some quarters, that it might be Barnabas. There are good grounds in style and language for supposing that Paul did not write the famous letter. Erasmus, Luther and Calvin disputed his authorship. Luther thought Apollos was the writer, a not impossible suggestion. Ramsay suggested that Philip wrote the letter from Caesarea to the Jerusalem church, after Paul had stayed with him, while Harnack made a case for Priscilla and Aquila. We do not know, but a man can hide himself behind his work, and sometimes it is better so. Whoever the writer was, he was deeply under the influence of Paul's teaching, and was a man with a deep knowledge of the Old Testament. He thought habitually in its imagery, and built his doctrine round it. He was a man of faith, and saw faith as the dominant note in his nation's history. He was a man of poetic mind, the creator, on page after page, of penetrating and memorable statements. His literary capacity is notable.

The recipients knew the writer (13.19). It is possible that the Jews of Rome were those to whom the letter is addressed. The synagogue was strong in the capital, and supplied a considerable section of the church there. If Rom. 9 to 11 was understood by them, they were educated Jews of the sort who might readily appreciate the kind of teaching which the letter contains. Does it somehow fit in with the visit to Paul in Rome which Paul besought Timothy to make before winter set in? And was Timothy in some way hindered by a time in prison? (13.23). Italian Jews in the writer's home town send their greetings, as though there were considerable numbers of Roman Christians who had sought safety in flight. No mention is made of the passing of Paul or Peter, though the reference to Timothy might indicate that the writer was close to Paul. The recipients were under persecution, a trial which had led to the defection of some of their number. More cannot be said. We are grateful especially for the eleventh chapter and the first verse which can be rendered: 'Faith is the title-deeds of things we hope for . . .'

694 : The Runner

Hebrews 12.1–15

The writer pictures the stadium filled with the watching multitude of all the saints who crowd the previous chapter. Greek stadia can be seen in many places—in Olympia itself, by the Alpheus river, where the old Olympic Games were held, high above the temple of the oracle and the theatre at Delphi under the coloured walls of Parnassus, where the Pythian Games were held ... Thousands crowded the long seats to watch the stripped athletes run, and this fine picture of the Christian running the straight race before a gazing multitude was one which would make any Greek recognize a familiar scene.

A race brooks no impediment. No man can run with flowing garments entangling the limbs, with 'ungirded loins'. The athlete had to throw aside all which might inhibit the fierce energy of his limbs, and the verse is quick to define the entanglement. It is sin which so readily spoils, slows the pace, defeats the end, and makes the runner finally a laughing stock to all who see his folly.

Like the charioteer in the race pictured in the letter to Philippi, the runner in the stadium could take no thought of the idle crowd, observing his pace, his style of running, his person. Of all men he had to be single-minded. What the multitude said or shouted, what they thought of his performance was irrelevant. All that mattered was the race. For this test, this moment, he had trained. In writing to Philippi, in writing his last letter to Timothy, Paul had this thought in view. The Greek race had its rules. It had its prescribed training. It was a test of all a man could do and be. It had one object—the prize. Indeed the Greek word 'athlete' means a 'prize-man'. Christ, in this bold metaphor, He the Great Runner, endured the contest and all its agony, for the prize set before Him, His reunion with God. Can the runner for Christ do any less? Christ is his prize, Christ is the mark at the end of the course on which he must set his eyes and run, run, with every muscle in the utmost play, all the strength of life concentrated to one end. It is a fine word-picture, illustrated in much ancient art—and in modern life. With what patience, with what endurance do we run?

695 : James

James 1

Who was James? James the son of Zebedee was martyred too early to have written the letter. The good Greek argues that the writer had lived some time in contact with a Greek-speaking environment. The language recalls that of James in Acts 15, and there seems no good reason for disputing the assertion that James, the brother of the Lord, was the writer.

It is down-to-earth, practical writing. James sets forth the truths which are given to him in a rapid series of pointed remarks. His epistle is almost like a set of sermon notes, and if he could have but expounded them at length, as the bearer of his letter may perhaps have done on the writer's own instructions, no hearer would have found a contradiction between statement and statement, or between James and Paul, as Luther imagined. Indeed James' opening remarks are almost a rephrasing of what Paul says in Rom. 5.1–5. James places his prime emphasis on faith, and sees as the fruit of the testing of faith the strong quality of endurance (3), the essential basis of mature character (4).

The latter half of the chapter is a splendid illustration of James' epigrammatical style. It is full of familiar quotations. Nor do the well-known words lose their flavour in a modern translation. Here are two renderings from J. B. Phillips' translation which strike home: 'Let every man be quick to listen but slow to use his tongue, and slow to lose his temper. For man's temper is never the means of achieving God's true goodness' (19, 20) . . . 'If anyone appears to be "religious" but cannot control his tongue, he deceives himself and we may be sure that his religion is useless' (26). James' sturdy common-sense has no use for words not backed by deeds, for mere profession without reality behind it, or for a so-called religion which does not transform life and build unselfish conduct.

Here was obviously a man who was weary of the sort of bent and spurious profession of faith, which had no supporting evidence in speech or action. He was a man with two feet firmly on the ground who wished to see reality visibly demonstrated. He was a preacher who believed in stirring a congregation to life. He hit hard and hit home.

696 : The Affluent

James 2.1–3.12

James had a grand impatience and magnificent contempt for class distinctions. The Church today is paying the price for some of the regard for wealth and position which too frequently marred the Christian witness of some in Victorian times. Canon Adam Fox, in his biography of Dean Inge, quotes a letter of the Rector of St. Margaret's urging his friend to consider a West End rectorship: 'The congregation,' wrote the rector, 'almost exclusively parochial is aristocratic: there are no poor save a few hangers-on (coachmen and stableboys, etc.) belonging to the well-to-do residents. Thus the parochial work is limited to what may be described as "friendly and sick visiting" ' . . . James' first-century exhortation is sufficient comment on 1904. All are 'poor and wretched and blind and naked' before God. Andrew Carnegie, on his death-bed, asked his loved ones to sing, 'Come ye sinners, poor and needy . . .'

James in fact, seems to be considerably preoccupied with the problems of class barriers and social tensions in the Christian community, and we should be glad to know the situation in which he found himself, and the city of his ministry. Laodicea, as we shall see, had just such a self-satisfied community. This is one reason why James' message has some relevance today, when racial differences present problems in some Christian groups. James would have presented the obvious Christian solution with some vigour and downrightness.

And who shall say that the vigorous passage on the ungodly use of the tongue has no relevance today? For what purpose do we use the glorious gift of speech? The tongue can communicate the truth of God or the lies of the Devil. It can bring comfort, aid and blessing; or it can ruin a reputation, spread pain, distress and misery. It reveals as nothing else the true character of a man or a woman. Its movements can demonstrate a lack of understanding which might otherwise lie hid, or a wisdom which no action could readily reveal. What should a Christian do with his tongue? He should control it, never seeking to dominate in conversation. He should train it to say less than it might. He should never use it for falsehood, half-truth, malice, innuendo, sarcasm, unclean talk, or empty chatter. He should always use it where circumstances call for testimony, confession, or the word of encouragement. If he is one of those strange folk who find it difficult to say 'Thank you', he should train his tongue to utter the words, and deal with the vicious pride which inhibits them.

697 : The Businessmen

James 4

James was a stern and vehement preacher. A sermon from him must have been a devastating experience of straight preaching and downright language. There is something of the Old Testament prophet about him. Consider v. 4, where he takes a familiar image from the Jewish Scriptures. Phillips forcefully renders: 'You are like unfaithful wives, flirting with the glamour of this world, and never realizing that to be the world's lover means becoming the enemy of God!' Loyalty is a demanding virtue. No man can be loyal to God and neutral on the moral issues of life at one and the same time. Hence James' burning insistence that faith must be demonstrated in upright living, sanctified lives and visible character.

In verses 13 to 17 we come near to picturing the congregation in which James ministered. It would not appear to have been a church purged or plagued by persecution. It was astonishingly modern, or, at least, early twentieth century, Christian but not as vigorously busy at the tasks of faith as it might be, a trifle easygoing, respectable and largely respected.

These verses, in fact, are a quite vivid picture of the successful businessmen of the Jewish Dispersion. Many of these expatriates were very wealthy men, and this is perhaps the reason that James finds it so necessary to speak of the difficulties of a mingling of poor and rich in Christian congregations. We catch a glimpse of the typically successful businessman, cosmopolitan, hurrying from city to city, carefully scheduled in his programme of buying and selling, confident, and boldly ordering the future. Such well-planned and organized living, said the apostle, could breed arrogance and a damaging self-assurance. Let such men hold lightly the things of life and the transient world.

Indeed, here is a word for those who, in this contracted, crowded, busy world, amid the many who 'rush to and fro', conduct their daily business—on crowded highway, on the narrowing seas, in the canopy of air. Life is menaced in new ways and James is right. Here are two verses to add to a well-known hymn:

O Lord, who art Thyself the Way,
The Truth, the Life—to Thee we pray—
On mountain road and freeway wide,
Where sweeps our traffic's roaring tide—
  Beneath the shadow of Thy hand,
  Guard those who travel on the land.

O God of sea and earth and sky,
Beyond the paths where eagles fly
O'er ocean vast and coloured land,
Do Thou control the pilot's hand.
  They cannot soar beyond Thy care
  Keep those who journey in the air.

698 : The Rich

James 5

The first Beatitude named the poor as blessed (Luke 6.20), and
the meaning of that paradox was that the dispossessed at least
have a straight path to God, cleared of the arrogance, the self-
confidence and the pride which inhibit all faith, all humility, all
willingness to confess a need to be blessed. How few, said the
Lord, of those who are loaded with the goods of this world's
devising, can qualify for 'the kingdom of heaven'—the Lordship
of God in their lives. They too easily develop the character of the
farmer in the parable (Luke 12.16–21) who, in a poverty-stricken
land and age, could think only of more storage space for his
wealth, and a self-indulgent ease which took no thought of other
happiness than his own—and that a happiness which conceived
no wider scope than carnal holiday and a stomach filled with food
and drink.

Rich men, said James, and they were becoming common in a
Church which must have had more than one 'Laodicea', should
sanctify their thoughts by taking account of the fragility and
ephemeral character of their possessions. How eternally true are
his words in this day of financial instability, of inflation, and those
thousand economic ills, which rise in a thousand ways from
human sin and extract all value from hoarded wealth, and destroy
all confidence in material possessions.

And then before the ultimate reality of death, who is not
penniless? Shakespeare put it well in one of those flashes of
wisdom which illumine his very comedy:

If thou art rich thou'rt poor,
For like an ass whose back with ingots bows,
Thou bear'st thy heavy riches but a journey,
And death unloads thee . . .

Like the Lord, James saw riches as a small thing, possibly something to endanger soul and character, to be held of small account, to be used in faithful stewardship. There is a burden of anxiety in getting riches, there is anxiety in keeping them; there is temptation in using them, and mortal danger in abusing them. And there is a burden of account to be given at last concerning them. They are not an end of life, but a tool of living.

Questions and themes for study and discussion on Studies 691–698

1. What can we learn about courtesy from the epistle to Philemon?
2. 'There are some things which will never be done unless they are done "before winter".'
3. When is anonymity desirable?
4. Single-mindedness in Christian life and service.
5. 'Religion and life are one thing or neither is anything.' (George Macdonald)
6. The tongue as a revelation of the man.
7. What are the ingredients of 'straight preaching'? Is any other sort of preaching relevant?
8. What did Jesus say on the subject of riches?

699 : Peter Again

1 Peter 1

It is pleasant as we draw near to the end of the New Testament, to meet Peter again, mature, experienced, and a writer of no mean power. A map should be used to show the route taken by the messenger who carried this letter through a great circle of territory in Asia Minor. He landed, perhaps at Sinope, on the Black Sea coast, and left by the port of Nicomedia. Much of this territory was outside the limits of the evangelism recorded in Acts. Paul was prevented from penetrating Bithynia (Acts 16.7), but it is known from the correspondence interchanged between the governor of the province and the emperor Trajan, which survives as the Tenth Book of Pliny's letters, that in A.D. 110 the area was so solidly Christian that the temples were deserted, and a problem created for the trades whose subsistence was dependent upon pagan worship—the situation of Acts **19**. Vast tracts of Christian activity went unrecorded. They go unrecorded still.

Peter addresses the Christian congregations as 'exiles' (1), and it must have been true, as it is increasingly true today, that the followers of Christ, Jews of the Dispersion, and Gentiles, increasingly found themselves alienated from the culture, if that overworked word may be used, in which they lived their daily lives.

Such exile was made endurable by hope, and hope, a living, vital force, was based on a risen Christ. Observe that the death of Christ is immediately linked with His resurrection (3). The writer was one who ran to the tomb in the murk of the morning, and 'saw the linen clothes lying, and the cloth which had been about His head folded up by itself apart.' (John **20**.6f.) He spoke of no myth, no delusion, but of an experience in history, which had transformed his life. Hence the paean of praise to God which opens with vs. 3 and 4, and runs on to v. 12. The writer is aware that persecution looms. Hence v. 5. The embattled Christians, which Pliny describes, needed this verse. We still need its assurance.

These converts had never seen the Lord in the flesh. They stand with us, and those on whom Christ Himself pronounced a beatitude. Link v. 8 with John **20**.29. Peter heard those words, and they never left him. It is a verse of rhythmic English in the AV(KJV), on which none of the translators has succeeded in improving.

700 : Peter the Preacher

1 Peter 2

In an earlier volume we heard Peter preach in those five cameo sermons in the first years of the Church. They were devoted to doctrine, exposition and pure evangelism. Almost thirty years have gone by. The Church has penetrated the world. Peter now, a man past middle age, has words to say to Christians.

Christianity was first called 'the Way'. It is a proclamation, but a proclamation not confined to the words of exhortation. It is also a manner of life, and half the impact of the Church upon the pagan world lies in the upright and devoted lives of those who belong to it. Consider a free translation of vs. 11 and 12: 'My dear friends, I do beg you, seeing that you are like aliens in a foreign land, to control your carnal natures which strive against your spiritual selves. Live upright lives in pagan society, so that your neighbours, slander you though they may as "evil doers", may see clearly your upright conduct and praise God, when the time comes for them to confront him.'

Peter's exhortation to godly conduct passes on to slaves. 'Household slaves, be submissive to your masters with all respect, not only if they are kind and gentle, but even if they are overbearing and unreasonable, for it is pleasing in God's sight, when, conscious that God knows all, a man bears his troubles patiently, unjust though his suffering is' (18, 19). The hideous institution of slavery lay viciously at the foundations of ancient society. The Church nowhere called the slaves to revolt, protest, demonstration, or to passionate claims to justice, and the freedom which is a human right. The apostles knew too well that violence begets its like, and that the doom of slavery, and the cruelty which it involved, lay in the slow, sure pressure of the Christian way of life. Paul sent Onesimus back to his master. 'In Christ Jesus,' he had already written, 'is neither bond nor free' (Gal. 3.28). Once man was granted freedom and equality before God, and once agreement was granted to the truth that personality, precious to the Father, was the possession of all men, slavery had no foundation on which to rest. A foul institution could not stand thus undermined. So with surviving shreds of slavery in another world. They will wither before Christian love, not before violence, arson, murder and rebellion. It is interesting to observe the wisdom which the memory of Christ, and the moulding of His Spirit, had begotten in the mind of the Galilean fisherman.

701 : Peter's Warning

1 Peter 4

The twelfth verse of this chapter begins the letter's final section of exhortation. The most reasonable dating of this letter is about the time when the fire of Rome in A.D. 64 and Nero's panic-stricken search for scapegoats initiated the first State-directed persecution of the Christians. To be sure the year A.D. 64 or its proximity cannot be conclusively set down as the time of writing. It might have been an even earlier communication. Perceptive observers could well have noticed, before the fatal climax of the fire of Rome, the growing antipathy of the proletariat and the mob's resentment against the Christians, a bitter spirit which had found expression in riot and misrepresentation in Ephesus (Acts **19**). 'A fiery trial' (12) was to fall on the Church, and Peter sadly marks it down as an emerging pattern. 'I beg you not to be unduly alarmed,' runs Phillips' rendering (12) '. . . as though this were some abnormal experience.'

Unfortunately, no century has been free of such spite and sadism. There have been more martyrs for Christ in the twentieth century than there were in the first, and probably in any century. The diabolical persecution which scientific barbarism has directed against mind and heart, as well as against the body, has written a sorrier and more sanguinary record in our own time than in Peter's. The ancient exhortation still stands. It is an honour, if courage can but rise to it, to suffer for Christ. Let but the conscience be clear, and no contribution of fault or guilt lend colour to the base allegations of the persecuting pagan (15). 'Steady then, keep cool and pray!' (7, Moffatt). 'Commit the life to a faithful Creator, and persevere in doing good' (19).

The pathos and power of Peter's words is enhanced by the fact that the writer was no cloistered preacher, uninvolved in the fate of those to whom he delivered his brave and solemn message. It is likely enough, if we date the letter aright, that Peter suffered along with those to whom he sought to give strength in the day of trial. A persistent tradition in the early Church links the deaths of both Peter and Paul with the imperial policy established in A.D. 64, and carried out with some vigour over the ensuing years, at least until Nero's own sordid death in A.D. 68. Judgement indeed fell 'on the ungodly' (18), in that young sadist's suicide, and the grim events of 'the Year of the Four Emperors', A.D. 69.

702 : Peter and Mark

2 Peter 1

This chapter speaks of a great service which Peter rendered. Verses 15 and 16 perhaps refer to his commissioning of the first Gospel to be written, the narrative put tersely together by Peter's protégé, John Mark. A strong tradition, as we saw, connects Peter with the book, and there are many marks of Peter's personality visible in it. 'But I will see to it that after I am gone you will have means of remembering these things at all times' (15, NEB). The oral tradition, with persecution threatening the eye-witnesses, was not enough. 'It was not on tales artfully spun that we relied,' he continues, with a word for the modern tribe of 'demythologizers'. The Gospels are not mythology. They are without a doubt history, and investigation must begin there or be frustrated. Since the last century's attempt to place the Gospels in the second century ended in disaster, it has been impossible to dub the narratives myths in any sense of the word. The obstinacy with which certain critics continue to use the out-moded terms of mythology in New Testament studies, is a phenomenon found only in that branch of literary research. The methods of the 'form-critics' would run the risk of ridicule if applied to any other body of ancient literature.

Peter then reverently makes mention of one of life's great experiences which assumed deeper significance in Peter's life as the years went by. Verse 19 implies that, long pondering over the event on Transfiguration Mount, and the voice of confirmation which still echoed in his memory, Peter saw Christ more and more clearly in the light of the Old Testament oracles, which were available for all to study.

This leads him to pen a solemn warning against the distortion of that precious message by heretics such as those who were in the act of disturbing the Church by their 'private interpretation' of the Word of God. Scripture is too often the playground of those who seek tag or text to support their own view of doctrine. Peter, with his apostolic insight, saw strange deviations taking shape. The main lines of interpretation, wrought out by the Holy Spirit, through the broad awareness of the Church through all time, cannot be lightly disregarded. It is well for us to note the fact. There is always new light from the Word, but let the novel and the strange, and certainly the disruptive and the contradictory, be received as both should be received. Old truth may find new forms of expression, but new language must not damage or dissipate content or meaning. So relevant is this chapter. The strong common-sense of the writer comes through to us.

703 : Peter and the Liberals

2 Peter 2.1–22; 3.13–18

It seems quite clear from Peter's stern and passionate language, especially the reference to Balaam in v. 15, that the dissident sect under attack are those whom we shall meet again in Jude and Revelation, the Nicolaitans, whose compromising activities are likened to the policy of Balaam, who sought to break the rigid segregation of Israel from surrounding pagan corruption.

They are denounced in emphatic terms, the full impact of which may be best sensed from modern translations ... Peter's old vehemence of speech, which once betrayed him, is now used to some purpose. The saboteurs of the Church were 'daring, arrogant, defiled, presumptuous, sensual, audacious, bold, scoffing, blasphemous, abusive, bestial, unreasoning, a stain and a disgrace, playing their tricks at your very dinner tables, with eyes for nothing but women'—all these are words and phrases of downright description culled from this or that version, and all justified by the uncompromising denunciation of the Greek text.

The words of the old Galilean again are tragically relevant. It is challengingly true that the rift between the Christian and the pagan world has widened. We live in a community which no longer disapproves of the abandonment of the Christian standards once observed and respected even among those who were not committed Christians. The Christian is no longer at one with the moral conscience of society.

The whimsical reference to Paul is comfort to those who find the Epistle to the Romans difficult. That letter is probably the document in view. It stresses, for example, the patience of God, which is the theme here (15, see Rom. 2.4; 3.25f.; 9.22; 11.22f.). On the other hand, it could be that Paul's letters were being gradually assembled, and read to the Church in many places. All of the great man's writings contain exhortation, passages of profound thought, and words capable of distortion. Some bent minds were busy at that mischief.

It was probably Paul's doctrine of Christian liberty which 'illinformed and unbalanced people' (16, J. B. Phillips) perverted to their undoing. Taken with Paul's repeated calls for self-discipline, integrity of conduct, and upright living, no practice of permissive morality or unregulated conduct can be sanctioned by Paul's appeal for freedom from the law ...

But that is by the way. We have said farewell to Paul. It has been pleasant to meet Peter again, feel his rugged strength and his power of leadership. And in this last page, he and Paul are once more side by side—great souls to whom the Church owes a mighty debt.

1. In what special sense is Peter evidence of the Resurrection?
2. Was the Church soft on slavery?
3. What is the psychology of persecution?
4. What marks of Peter can be discerned in the Gospel of Mark?
5. What should be the attitude of the Christian to so-called 'liberalism'?

704 : Jude's Epistle

Jude 1–25

We shall read Jude before John, because he wrote at least before John wrote his first letter. Jude's tract against emerging heresy belongs to the same order of writing as the second and third letters of John, except that Jude writes to all the community of Christ, while John, although with a whole congregation in mind, addressed primarily in his second and third letters, one person. There was a general alarm about heresy at the time, as we have seen in reading the second letter of Peter. There is also striking similarity between 2 Peter and Jude to the point of actual quotation. It would appear that Jude quoted Peter rather than the reverse, assuming again that the traditional date for the death of Peter is near the truth. The name Jude, or Judas, was made common by Judas Maccabaeus, the Jewish resistance-hero and freedom-fighter, and six of that name are mentioned in the New Testament, two of them actually in the apostles' band. Jude decribes himself as 'brother of James'. There was only one James who could be referred to without further definition after the death of the apostle James, and that was James 'the Lord's brother' (Gal. 1.19). If, then, Jude was the brother of James, he was also the brother of the Lord, perhaps the youngest (Matt. 13.55), or the next to youngest of the family (Mark 6.3). Both James and Jude were missionaries, travelling with their families (1 Cor. 9.5). We know no more.

Jude seems to have decided to write a doctrinal treatise on salvation (3) and it would have made an interesting contribution to Christian literature. And evidentially a most significant one, for James and Jude did not, in His lifetime, accept their brother's claims (John 7.5). Could there be a more striking proof of the historicity of the Resurrection, than the ascription of saviourhood and divinity to Jesus by James and Judas of His own household? Jude was turned from an original plan, which may have been carried out in a later letter lost to us, by the sudden need to write, like Peter, and later John also, in stern denunciation of theological corruption. The form taken by the heresy was no doubt the misinterpretation of Paul's salutary doctrine of Christian liberty (4) by men with 'no true acceptance of God, but who abuse his grace as an excuse for immorality'.

And so Judas, of better fame, comes briefly into view as the New Testament ends—a valiant fighter, just glimpsed in the fray.

705 : John at Work

2 John 1–13

John's second and third letters preceded the first in the earliest ordered collection. Hence the present sequence. God spoke and speaks through the simplicities of life, and this little letter is like thousands of others which have survived among the papyri of Egypt. Scholars too prone to pass by the plain meaning of a text, have also imagined that the 'elect lady' is a church. Such a disguised form of communication would be more proper in Revelation. 'Lady', in Greek is 'Kuria', and this word, as many contexts in the papyri show, can be a proper name. This letter is therefore in all probability addressed to 'Kuria, a Christian'. Since Kuria is the Greek for the Hebrew Martha, it has been suggested, but with no possibility of proof, that we have here a flash of light on the later years of Lazarus' and Mary's sister, a widow with a grown-up family. Travel was easy in the first century, and the Bethany family could easily have sought refuge in Asia. It appears that some of Kuria's children had visited cousins, children of a deceased sister (Mary?) who lived in Ephesus (13). John had found them fine Christians, and sends his and the cousins' greetings to Kuria in her home town. Here she used her home (10) as a Christian centre, as did Nympha at Colossae (Col. 4.15) and Philemon of the same city (Philem. 2). It is interesting to observe the apostle at his pastoral work, and to see the continuing role of faithful women in the early Christian communities. He takes occasion to sum up his favourite message: 'The commandment is love; love is walking according to the commandments: His commandments are summed up in a word—love'. The gracious tone of the little letter, penned, no doubt, in the midst of multitudinous duties and distractions, is an illustration of the love which John preached.

Further communication the elder left until a personal visit—always a wise proceeding. To meet and discuss a question at issue is likely to be a safer and more gracious process than the laying down of firm principles for others' interpretation, or possible mistaken emphasis. To meet face to face is the surer way to understand, and to allow the free play of the third Person, who is always present 'where two or three are gathered in his name'. The great R. W. Dale of Birmingham had reservations about Moody until he heard him speak, and was won by the grace and yearning of the evangelist's appeal. John shrinks from any diminution in Christian joy (12), and so postpones much serious discussion until a visit which was part of his pastoral plan. The whole letter is a fascinating glimpse into the activities of unrecorded years in the city where Paul had founded a church, and Timothy had organized it.

706 : John the Pastor

3 John 1–15

Gaius was a common name, and several who bear it appear in the New Testament. Gaius of Corinth (Rom. 16.23; 1 Cor. 1.14), is said to have been John's amanuensis when he wrote his Gospel, and he may be the Gaius commended in this letter. A Gaius is said to have been placed in charge of the church at Pergamum by John, and this may also be a reference to 'the well-beloved Gaius'. In v. 3 John mentions the source of his information about the good man. The verse suggests much going and coming from Ephesus of itinerant teachers and officials of the church, and the existence in Asia of a closely-knit organization. Hospitality to such ministers of Christ was a duty, and in v. 5 Gaius' faultless record is praised. A sure means of bringing blessing to a home, and of building some Christian ideals in its children, is to entertain good men and women. But let the adjective be emphasized. In both of these small letters, the existence of those who abused the hospitality of the Christian community is implied. Let hospitality, like all else, be mixed with discernment. In v. 8 the worth and place of the Christian home in such a ministry is stressed. William Carey once compared his missionary work and enterprise to the exploration of a mine. He said: 'I will go down if you will hold the ropes.' A sound core of Christian hospitality was vital to the witness of the church, but John wished to have a sharp distinction drawn between the parasites of highway and pavement and his itinerant teachers and preachers.

Trouble had arisen in Gaius' congregation, and the ringleader was one Diotrephes, probably a rich layman. The division may have been on some such doctrinal rift as that which weakened Corinth (1 Cor. 1.10–17). At all events, the offending Diotrephes was a domineering man, who objected to the hospitality which Gaius had given to visiting evangelists, who had John's approval (9f.). John saw the harsh treatment meted out to worthy men as an attack upon himself. The group had reported the incident in Ephesus, and this epistle was the result, sent by the hand of Demetrius, and promising a personal investigation. John does not threaten any form of excommunication, only a confrontation. Demetrius is set in contrast with the tongue-free slanderer Diotrephes. He was not known to Gaius, and so has this letter of commendation. There is threefold testimony to his worth, that of the Ephesian Christians, that of 'the Truth', which surely means that Demetrius' life exemplified the reality of the Christ of whom he spoke, and that of the apostle and his immediate colleagues. The letter ends as the second letter did, a fact which suggests that the two documents were written about the same time and just before a visitational circuit. The worth of the letter historically consists in the light it throws on the early Church.

707 : John the Beloved

1 John 1

We have met Peter in his epistles. We shall now meet his friend in extreme old age. We shall see John, and the Church at the end of the century. The first of these three letters, so revealing, so penetrating, was in all probability written to accompany the Fourth Gospel. The New Testament was approaching completion. The Synoptic Gospels were in circulation; the writings of Luke were generally known; the letters of Paul, Peter, Jude, and James were in common and already cherished possession of the Church. And now, with the ministry of Paul behind, with half a century of Christian experience to shape the life and reveal the problems of the Christian community, and with a life-time of pondering over those glorious three years in Palestine to enrich his memory, John felt the deep urge to write his Gospel. That

810

precious book was to close the New Testament, and was to show Christ afresh against the background of the years, and in relation to the now completed body of Christian truth. If the letter was written to accompany and to introduce the Gospel, the two must be read side by side in mutual and fruitful commentary.

The letter dealt more directly with the spiritual problems of the hour, and attacked error with a directness which would have been out of place in the Gospel. It applied to the moment's need the truths developed in the Gospel. It formed, in a manner, a sermon upon it. And the letter, together with the Gospel, cast the only light we have upon the last thirty years of the first century.

We find more than history there; we shall find the author, and to gain some notion of the mind and heart of one who walked with Christ, half a century beyond those moving years, is fascinatingly interesting. We know little of the apostle's life over those fifty years, but enough to follow its main outlines. Several references in the Book of Acts and one in Galatians, suggest that he remained in Jerusalem until about A.D. 50. It is possible that he was in Rome at the time of the Neronian persecution in the middle sixties, and very probable that, after the martyrdom of Peter and Paul, he went to Ephesus. His mature ministry was certainly exercised here, and the 'seven churches of Revelation' were no doubt his 'circuit'. Revelation itself was written during this period.

708 : The Heretics

John 1.1–18

John's Gospel, John's letters, would not have been written had it not been for the emergence of a subtle attack on the Church. It thus appears that we must treat Cerinthus and the Nicolaitans as 'characters of Scripture', but must fortify the mind before describing them by reading John's first eighteen verses in which he tells what the whole Testament is about.

Irenaeus, who knew Polycarp, the disciple of John, wrote that John set out 'to remove the error sown among men by Cerinthus, and much earlier by those who are called Nicolaitans'.

Who were these sectaries? Cerinthus appears to have been a forerunner of those, who, in the second century, were called Gnostics. Their doctrine was a species of theosophy. The 'deep things' of the gospel were for the enlightened few, for 'those who knew', for that is what the word Gnostic means. They were a sort of self-constituted spiritual *élite*, exempt from the rules of holy conduct which were observed by the simple souls who took the gospel literally. Cerinthus, clearly of their ancestry, had some special notions about the nature of Christ. He distinguished, in fact, Christ from Jesus. Jesus was the human son of Joseph and Mary into whom the Son came at the Baptism, only to withdraw before the Crucifixion. It was Jesus who died, not Christ. John clearly has this pernicious error in mind in the first chapters of the letter.

And the Nicolaitans? It is quite clear to any careful reader of the New Testament that there was a group in the early Church whose muddy trail begins in the First Epistle to Corinth and runs through Jude, Peter and John to the Apocalypse. They are called variously the followers of Balaam and Cain (Jude 11; Rev. 2.14), and both terms are illuminating. It will be readily seen, if the Old Testament background is remembered, that we have in the Nicolaitans those who saw little ethical compulsion in the faith of Christ. In Corinth they probably frequented the temple of Aphrodite, everywhere they attended the guild-feasts, conformed, no doubt, to the State Caesar-cult, and sought to keep a compromising foot in both worlds. Clement calls them 'dissolute he-goats', and no lower term can be found in the vocabulary of ancient abuse. All this is suggested by the reference to Balaam. And Cain suggests the bloodless altar, flower-decked, the mark and emblem of a religion void of moral sternness. Jude and Second Peter should be read by those who seek to understand the danger which lay in this vicious movement. Writing to Thyatira, John calls one of their leaders Jezebel (Rev. 2. 20) and that name is redolent of a ruinous alliance between Israel and Tyre, a mingling of light and darkness, of God and Belial. Such were the forms of the pagan attack on Christianity—an intellectualism which emptied the gospel of its content, and a libertinism which soiled its testimony.

Their only use in history was that they provoked the writings of John's old age.

709 : John and His Children

1 John 2.1–17

In a sudden burst of tenderness the old apostle turns from 'we' to 'I', and addresses his readers with the affectionate vocative which he is to repeat six times. No one had a better right than the last survivor of the Twelve to look upon himself as the father of the family of faith. Those who seek long and intimate study of the mind of John should note and seek in this letter the thronging echoes of the Gospel. It is often possible to seize and to enjoy the passing images in that rich store. Here he is remembering the strange, tense atmosphere in the room which Judas had just left, and hearing again the accents of a Voice which had haunted sixty years. 'Little children, yet a little while I am with you . . .' (John 13.33). How true it was now of the last remaining member of that party. And how well he was using those last rich years. The aged should study John. The Venerable Bede in the famous story, using his last breath to dictate the translation of the Fourth Gospel, was John's true disciple. He deserves more. Something of the scorn of Tennyson's Ulysses for those 'who store and hoard themselves', would bring back vigour and usefulness to many lives which have become too preoccupied with death.

This Christlike tenderness precedes a warning. He would have his people know that there must be no surrender. In the latter half of ch. 1 he has insisted on the reality and sinfulness of sin in special reference to those who were making light of evil. He writes, 'that they may not sin', for nothing in his message must be understood as conferring a licence to sin. He foresees, in fact, a twofold perversion, the base notion that sin is an abiding necessity which, like a physical defect, we 'must learn to live with', and against which strife is useless, or the equally base idea, that we may sin with licence, since we have Christ to cleanse us. No, no, John answers, the whole drift of my message is that we should not sin. In truth, we have forgiveness if we seek it in humble confession, but the whole effect of knowledge of God, God who is Light, should be to inspire a hatred of darkness and all that belongs to it.

710 : Son of Thunder

1 John 2.1–17

The reading is the same as that given for Study 709, but some poignant autobiography haunts vs. 7 and 8. Love had not always been the burden of John's message. The writer of the letter we are reading had been self-seeking (Matt. **20.** 20–28; Mark **10.**35–45), fiery and passionate (Luke **9.**51–56), and had earned a name which contained no gentleness (Mark **3.**17). The Son of Thunder, his Master called him, and for all the love which his Lord, who, seeing

813

deeper than others, saw the unborn years, gave to him, John was not then the figure whose gracious features are seen behind this epistle.

The key to the understanding of the paradox is autobiographical. The paramount necessity of love is an old commandment. It was the very essence of the gospel, 'the word which they had heard'. It was embodied in the very elements of the message 'from the beginning'. It was 'in him', part of every discourse and action of the Lord. It was 'in them', the fruit of the Spirit, and the most consistent lesson of experience. And yet, says John, it was a new commandment, and a touch of sadness haunts the phrase. The old apostle appears here to confess a life-long lack. In the evening of his ministry he had discovered the supremacy of love.

When did the change take place? The 'Son of Thunder' still lived at Ephesus. Irenaeus and Eusebius quote a story of the great Polycarp who sat at John's feet. The apostle once visited the public baths, and seeing the heretic Cerinthus there cried: 'Let us flee, lest the building fall, since Cerinthus the foe of the truth is in it.' This looks like the old John. When did the new man appear? Was it the exile on Patmos, and the vision of his Lord, which changed the character of his ministry? The day of withdrawal is sometimes the chosen time of God's Spirit, and the opportunity He makes or takes to teach a lesson long unlearned. Or was it the writing of the Gospel? Did that blessed urge, which sharpened thought and memory and moved his pen, bring back so gloriously those three years of fellowship that the aged man was sanctified anew?

Let us draw two lessons from this moving passage. The first is that it is never too late to learn. It is true that the arteries harden and the mind stiffens, but it is also true that the Holy Spirit is not restricted, and that the willing heart at any age can be delighted with fresh revelation. And note secondly that the fierce critic of Cerinthus lost none of his power by the change. In a new spirit of love he deals as faithfully with error and as uncompromisingly as he ever did in the fierce speech of an earlier ministry. With fallible tools the Great Builder builds His Church. But when for a season they lie docile in His hand, sharpened as He would have them, with what loveliness He builds. From the last years of John's ministry came the Fourth Gospel and the Epistles. The 'Son of Thunder' could not have written them. The Lord waited patiently for his death.

814

711 : The Antichrists

1 John 2.18–29

The 'antichrists', foreshadowings of a figure of evil which haunts New Testament prophecy, have marched in grisly train through the centuries, in nature, word and action the antitheses of Christ. Here they are the sectaries of whom John writes, nominal members of the Church at one time, but never really part of it.

John was not prepared to regard the purveyors of deadly heresy as the members of Christ. 'They withdrew,' he says, 'to make it plain that they were none of us.' He means that this was a deliberate demonstration on the part of those who had left the fellowship. The heretics left the Church in bitterness. They thought to build something greater, and in pursuit of a perverse design abandoned the Lord's people. Out of evil God brought good. The secessionists were seeking their own advantage. It turned out that they fulfilled a plan of God whereby the truth was protected. Falsehood declared itself and withdrew. In calm confidence that nothing could baffle the love of the Father, John abbreviates the process with a simple clause of purpose. It was all providential.

Observe v. 20. It seems clear that the Gnostics, whose dangerous teaching is never far from John's anxious thought, claimed, and perhaps practised, a special 'anointing'. A Gnostic document says, in the obscure language the heretics affected: 'We alone of all men are Christians, who complete the mystery at the third portal, and are anointed there with speechless anointing.' Probably the sectaries had adopted some of the rituals of the pagan 'mystery-religions', and were in the habit of exalting their ritual over the simplicities of John's flock. 'Fear not,' says the apostle, 'your anointing is real.'

Note that 'all' in the best manuscripts is the subject of 'know' not the object. 'You all know (the truth),' not, 'You know all things.' The RSV is correct, the AV(KJV) wrong. The former reading, designed by John as a riposte against the self-styled 'enlightened', is a rebuke to sacerdotalism. We are all 'priests of God', equally open to the Spirit's insight.

The next verse underlines this fact. John's approach is simple. He has warned his friends against antichristian falsehood, not because they lack intelligence, but because they possess the truth, and because every species of falsehood is alien to the truth. The *Cambridge Greek Testament* aptly says: 'Many of us think we can put the truth into people by screaming it into their ears. We do not suppose that they have any truth in them to which we can make appeal.'

712 : John's Last Word

1 John 4

The movement of John's theme has been likened to the windings of the river Maeander near which he lived. But like that same stream, for all its intricacy and turning on its course, it has beginning, progress, and safe exit to the sea. A little patience is sometimes needed to follow it, but no great literature ever yielded its best to the hasty and impatient reader.

The transition from v. 6 to v. 7 may seem abrupt, as if an unpleasant subject had been summarily dismissed, but the links are there for the finding. The power to love, no less than the faith which confesses Christ (4.2), mutually aid, and are both given by the Spirit of God. The antichristian spirit is selfish, exalts man, and divides the Church.

Such a quest was the tenor of John's ministry. Jerome's story is well known: 'Saint John the Evangelist, living in Ephesus in his extreme old age, when he was with difficulty carried into the church by his disciples, had no strength for longer exhortation, but could only say: "Little children, love one another." At length, the disciples and brethren who were there, wearied by the repetition, said: "Master, why do you always say this?" He replied in words worthy of himself; "Because it is the Lord's command and if that alone is done, it suffices".' It suffices, because God is love supremely, and only those who are partakers of the divine nature by faith can truly love.

In v. 8 John makes the third of his great pronouncements about God. 'God is spirit' (John 4.24); 'God is light' (1.5), and now, 'God is love'. Of the three great truths the last is chief. It shows the Spirit to be personal, and it fills His glory with a warmth and life which brings it near to the heart of man. The idea has conquered the world, and even coloured some non-Christian thinking. The savagery, the terror, the cruelty of pagan theologies, have been banished. Indeed, a subtlety of temptation today lies in the attitude which presumes on the love of God and forgets God's justice and stern condemnation of sin. Fitzgerald's Omar touches the note in a quatrain from his vision of the Potter's Shop: The Pots speak and:

Said one—'Folks of a surly Tapster tell
And daub his Visage with the smoke of Hell;
They talk of some strict Testing of us—Pish!
He's a Good Fellow and 'twill all be well.'

All of which is far removed from the mighty truth of John's
immortal sentence. The love of God is the love of Christ, and
when that is said all is said.

713 : John's Faith
1 John 5

In the fourth verse John sums up his Apocalypse, which we shall
soon read. 'Faith is the victory'. The word *pistis*, which is the
commonest word in Greek for faith, occurs nowhere else in the
Epistles and Gospel of John, in spite of the pervasive presence
of the idea. In its Classical Greek form the word for victory, curiously enough, occurs nowhere else in the New Testament. But
it is not such peculiarities of vocabulary that make the wonder of
the verse. It is the profundity of the thought that faith is victory.
Once faith is born in the Christian's heart, he becomes forthwith
invincible. If a man grasps with full confidence the truth of v. 5,
that the living God burst into human history in Christ, and in
Christ wrought his salvation, nothing can destroy him.

Like the vase, in which roses have once been distilled,
You may break, you may shatter the vase, if you will,
But the scent of the roses will cling to it still.

Consider the audacity of such a statement. An effort of the
mind is required to catch the fresh strength of a saying as it first
fell from lips or pen. John, the fisherman from Palestine, wrote
these words at the end of the first century of the Pax Romana.
Rome ruled the world in which the apostle lived, Rome the
mighty conqueror, whose word was law around the circle of the
Inland Sea. If victory was the prerogative of any man, it belonged
to the prince by the Tiber, whose legions were thrusting north
through the lakes of Cumberland, manning the banks of the
Rhine and the Danube, and holding the fierce Parthians behind
the Armenian mountains. Rome was supreme.

But Rome was doomed. Already in the cryptic language of the
strange book he had sent from Patmos, John had told of her
defeat, and how the victory was theirs in whom Christ dwelt,

who, out-living and out-dying their persecutors, were to aid in the fulfilment and fruition of the plans of the living God. Faith, 'the title-deeds of things hoped for and the evidence of things not seen' (Heb. 11.1) was to prove a mightier force than the swords of the legions, and all the power of the Empire.

Questions and themes for study and discussion on Studies 704–713

1. Where in the Gospels is the family of the Lord mentioned?
2. What, in the Christian sense, is love?
3. What is the function of the pastor?
4. What echoes of the Fourth Gospel do you detect in 1 John 1?
5. What other writings in the New Testament has the problem of false teaching prompted?
6. Is sin clearly enough defined in modern preaching?
7. When does a Christian cease to be useful?
8. How should heresy be dealt with in the local church?
9. What is the wrath of God?
10. In what sense is faith the victory?

714 : John's Exile

Revelation 1.1–9; 4.1–6

We return a little down the years to an earlier time in John's ministry. He was a prisoner on Patmos. It was probably during the time when Domitian, that execrable creature who ruled Rome in the eighties of the first century, was putting pressure on the authorities in Ephesus to persecute the Church.

It may actually have been for the safety of an aged and respected member of the city that John was sent across to Patmos. The Romans called such removal 'relegation', and, if the guess is correct, the old bishop would enjoy the freedom of the island, provided he abstained from subversive activities. There is no evidence that he was under harsh duress in a labour camp. At any rate he kept in touch with the churches of his 'diocese', and wrote letters to them carefully couched in allusive, poetic language, which only the recipients would understand. His whole book, written perhaps on some vantage point, is interwoven with poetic imagery based on the island's common scenery, as every visitor to Patmos realizes. As the sun slopes, all the sea to the west can be awash with gold (4.6), as John saw it when he pictured the saints beside a glassy sea. The sea in fact, filled his mind. Its sounds are everywhere, as they are all through the Greek islands of the Aegean. Christ's voice was for the writer 'like the sound of many waters' (1.15), something universal heard everywhere, speaking over and through all other sounds.

And sometimes the mood might change. The sea, like the moving mass of mankind, is capricious, cruel. John saw 'a beast rise out of the sea', with a name of blasphemy on his head.

This, in his first meaning, was Rome and her Emperor, who demanded worship from men as a test of loyalty. Perhaps John had looked down on the land-locked harbour between the hills, which almost cuts the island in half. Perhaps he had seen some great galley of Rome loom over the horizon and come in under heavy sail, or with her three banks of oars flashing.

He might have looked east and discerned low down the pale blue coast of Asia where his beloved people endured the stress of persecution. It bore heavily and hard upon the folk of Smyrna, the ruins of whose town lie somewhere deep below the streets of modern Izmir. The old leader would have gladly stood by the persecuted community, but the sea lay wide and decisively between him and them.

In his poem he pictured, as many yearning souls have pictured, a happier age, a quieter and more gentle world. 'And there shall be no more sea' (21.1), he wrote, no more cruel separation, no forced parting, no gulf fixed between men and women who should be together. The phrase becomes poignant in its context.

715 : Christ in Glory

Revelation 1.10–20

It seems almost too audacious to set this flashing vision of the glorified Christ among the characters of Scripture, but in the context of this book's poetry it must be done. Some of the symbolism is not clear to us because much apocalyptic literature is lost. Though not biblical, it provided a store of symbols. For example, the rabbis seem to have used *aleph* and *tau*, the A and Z of the Hebrew alphabet, just as the first and last letters of the Greek alphabet are here used, to express comprehensiveness, and all-embracing communication. God has said all He has to say in

Christ. He comprehends all history and remains God's last word to man. And consider the golden lampstands. If John wrote during Domitian's persecution, after A.D. 81, the seven-branched candlestick had already lain with the Jewish loot in Rome's Temple of Peace for over a decade. But in Zechariah's day, six centuries before, the lovely piece of furniture was already a symbol (Zech. 4). The seven churches uphold the light of God's presence, but are inseparable from a central Christ (13). We know of churches at Troas, Hierapolis and Colossae, all in Asia, so why John chose the particular seven is not clear, save that the sacred number was a symbol for perfection.

This does not exhaust the echoes of the chapter, and it is not intended here to do so, but consider the audacity of faith which saw all the future, not in Caesar, but in the blameless Galilean who had died in Jerusalem, and had risen again. Only the stark fact of that triumph over death could explain a confidence so superb. The writer was suffering for his faith.

And bear in mind that the one who could write down the blazing imagery of this divine person, struggling like Ezekiel in his opening chapter to catch the transcendental in human speech, had known the Son of Man. He had also seen Him gasp away His life upon the cross, and in the murk of dawn had raced to the tomb to find it empty. That was half a toilsome century before. What utter conviction of faith invincible was this!

716 : The Ephesians

Revelation 2.1–7; Acts 20.17–35

We have met the Ephesians before in this series. In fact we know them better than most of the congregations of the early Church. They had been well-taught by Paul, Timothy and John, and could recognize impostors, and stand firm against those who sought to soften their loyalty. They belonged to an ancient city. Ephesus was already ten centuries old when Paul hired the school of Tyrannus in which to preach. It was a fine city. To stand today on the marble street and look along its length to the great curve of the theatre set in the side of the hill, is to gain a deep impression of the wealth and ability of those who built and adorned the city of Artemis.

The little group who followed Christ in the pagan capital of Asia had much to contend with. The temple of Artemis drew pilgrims and tourists from the whole world, and we have seen how sensitive entrenched heathendom and its commercialized religion was to any assault from dissident groups. Ephesus was dependent upon the industries which flowed from the worship of the goddess, and the violent and scornful proletariat was not tolerant of the church. Hence the strength of the liberal movement of the Nicolaitans, who sought to ease the confrontation.

Ephesus held some of the weariness of an ancient community. The great thesis of Sir William Ramsay was that the spirit of a community finds, for good and ill, a subtle expression in the tone and outlook of the Christian community in its midst. He showed how a deep understanding of the seven churches of these two chapters, gave some idea of the reasons for their faults and excellencies. And the Ephesian congregation showed some marks of the venerable city in which it lived. It had grown a little battle-weary, and the valiant old man on Patmos feared that they might not continue to fight on.

A new infusion of life was needed. There are coins of Ephesus which show a date-palm, a tree sacred to Artemis, as a symbol of her gift of life and fruitfulness. To those prepared to strive, John promised: 'I will give him to eat of the tree of life.' A generation later according to Ignatius, the Ephesians were running well. As late as A.D. 431 a notable episcopal council was held there. But the decline set in. The harbour filled with silt. The Turks came with blight and ruin. The candlestick fell.

717 : The Smyrnaeans

Revelation 2.8–11; John 16.1–4

Persecution was falling heavily on Smyrna, and the enduring church needed their leader's word. Youthful Smyrna was Ephesus' rival, and to Smyrna's brave church was promised a 'crown of life'. The Christians of Smyrna would fasten on the words with satisfaction, for it was the sort of poet's tag on which cities preen themselves. Athens was 'violet-crowned', until men tired of Pindar's adjective. Of Auckland, where these words are written, to its citizens' delight, Kipling wrote, 'last, loneliest, loveliest, exquisite, apart'. In such fashion the simile of a crown dominates all praise of Smyrna. Aristides calls the 'Golden Street', which ringed Mount Pagus with lovely buildings, 'the crown of Ariadne in the heavenly constellation'. Apollonius of Tyana, amid praise for Smyrna, says rhetorically that it is greater charm 'to wear a crown of men than a crown of porticoes'.

'I have been there,' wrote Freya Stark, of Mount Pagus' crest, 'sometimes to walk in the morning, with Ionia on one side and Aeolis on the other, spread below; and nearby, in a shapeless depression, the stadium where Polycarp was burned, and have thought of that old bishop, how he would describe his intercourse with John, and with the rest of those who had seen the Lord ...' Under 'the crown of Smyrna', Polycarp was not the only Christian who won 'a crown of life'.

Polycarp was born perhaps in A.D. 64, and suffered martyrdom in 155, in a persecution in which Jews joined the pagans. He claimed to have served Christ all his ninety years of life. Polycarp forms a link between the Apostolic age and the end of the second century, when those whom he taught were still active.

Smyrna, which still lives as the vigorous port of Izmir, won from John unstinted admiration. Its congregation was the salt of Asia. The church, purged by suffering, continued to stand through succeeding centuries. Smyrna was among the last cities to be submerged by Islam, and it was such delaying actions in the East which allowed the West time to arise from the torpor of the Dark Ages. Fidelity is fruitful beyond its own generation. For the menaced and the persecuted, the Resurrection, real, historical, factual, was and is an enduring anchor of the soul.

718 : The Pergamenes

Revelation 2.12–17; 20.10–15

Pergamum, royally situated, round a great acropolis, with a view of far ranges, the sea, and the purple peaks of Lesbos, had been a seat of government for four hundred years. It was a capital city in pre-Roman days, and when the last of her kings, seeing the shape of emerging history, bequeathed his kingdom to the Romans in 133 B.C., Pergamum became the chief town of the new province of Asia. It was natural that the first temple of the imperial cult—that worship of the emperor on which the Christians looked with deep abhorrence—should be located here. A temple to Rome and Augustus was erected in Pergamum in 29 B.C., and thus 'the worship of the Beast' came to Asia. But other cults beside that of Rome were endemic. There was the worship of Asklepios, the god of healing, whose symbol was a serpent coiled round a bending sapling. The emperor raises his right hand in the exact gesture of the Nazi salute.

The letter is addressed to those who dwell 'where Satan's throne is', and Christians must have found something peculiarly satanic in the town's pre-occupation with the serpent image. Pausanias, the Greek traveller, who wrote many descriptions of ancient cities, spoke of Asklepios as 'sitting on a throne with a staff in his hand, and his other hand upon the head of a serpent'. The church in Pergamum found the surrounding symbolism of paganism quite diabolical. There was also the magnificent throne-like altar to Zeus, which stood royally on the crag dominating the city, and which is now in the East Berlin Museum. The altar commemorated the defeat of a Gallic invasion of Asia, under the imagery of the legendary struggle between the gods and goddesses of Olympus and the giants. The giants, in accordance with Pergamum's prevailing obsession, are represented as a brood of Titans, with snake-like tails. Zeus, to whom the throne-like altar was dedicated, was called 'Zeus the Saviour', and the title would impress Christian minds as blasphemous. They must have called the great altar 'Satan's throne', and so put the phrase in the Apocalpyse. It helped embattled Christians, under the shadow of arrogant paganism and facing a hostile world, to know that One remembered 'where they lived'. It helps still.

719 : Jezebel of Thyatira

Revelation 2.18–29

In the letter to Thyatira, under another figure of speech from the Old Testament, the Nicolaitans appear again. Thyatira was a centre of commerce. More trade guilds have left traces at Thyatira than those of any other Asian city. Inscriptions mention wool-workers, linen-workers, dyers, leather-workers, tanners, potters, bakers, slave-dealers, and bronzesmiths. The dyers have left one mark which suggests the geographical breadth of Thyatiran trade. They brewed a red dye, probably the modern Turkey-red, from the madder root, which grows abundantly in the district. The ancient purple was a colour nearer scarlet than blue, and it was this dye that the business-woman, Lydia, was selling 500 miles away in Philippi in A.D. 52. In that year Paul arrived and found 'a certain woman named Lydia, a seller of purple from the city of Thyatira' (Acts **16**.14).

Whether Lydia still lived when John wrote is not known. It is odd that two women of Thyatira should appear in the New Testament, one the gracious hostess of Paul, the other, 'Jezebel', the target of another apostle's scorn.

Jezebel, Ahab's consort, was the seal of a trade alliance with Phoenicia, and there is no doubt that Ahab's Israel derived immense wealth from business conducted with the busy heathen on the coast. The oil and wheat of Israel went down to Tyre (Ezek. **27**). The wealth of the world flowed back. Ahab was rich. He built an ivory house in Samaria, the foundations and the broad steps of which can still be seen. But prosperity is not always good for a nation. With Tyrian goods came Tyrian gods. With Jezebel came Baal. It is possible, therefore, that the choice on Carmel involved more than theology. When the people chose Yahweh they precipitated an economic depression. A break with Jezebel was a break with Tyre.

The woman in Thyatira, a clever woman with a gift of speech who professed to interpret God's will, offered, as Jezebel did, prosperity at the price of compromise. As a Nicolaitan, she believed in establishing a compromise with society. In Thyatira, in fact, it must have been commercial ruin not to do so. Anxious men must have longed for some formula of conduct by which they could maintain both their livelihood, so dependent upon their membership of the guild, and their allegiance to Christ. Was the hard choice Christ or poverty? 'No,' said Jezebel. 'Keep your heart intact. Learn "the deep things" of religion, and you will see that even behind pagan worship lives an acknowledgement of the Most High God. Go to the sacrifice but think there of Christ. Attend the feasts, but set an example of purity and moderation.' 'Look,' answers John, 'I set her on a dining couch, and her vile associates with her, and they shall have opportunity to enjoy—great tribulation, unless *they* repent, for she has shown that *she* cannot repent.'

720 : The Lesson of the Nicolaitans

2 Corinthians 6

The solemn lesson to be learned from the compromising group which we have followed for some distance, from Corinth to

Thyatira requires a last word. These 'characters of the New Testament' fall under fierce condemnation. And yet how strong was the temptation to confront a hostile world less harshly. It still is, and it is only unbalanced characters who actually enjoy unpopularity and persecution.

Was John, then, too harsh? Sir William Ramsay answers the question well. 'The historian,' he writes, 'must regard the Nicolaitans with intense interest, and must deeply regret that we know so little about them ... And yet at the same time he must feel that nothing could have saved the infant Church from melting away into one of those vague and ineffective schools of philosophic ethics except the stern and strict rule laid down by John. An easy-going Christianity could never have survived; it could not have conquered the world; only the most convinced, resolute adherence to the most uncompromising interpretation of its own principles could have given the Christians the courage and self-reliance that were needed. For them to hesitate or to doubt was to be lost.'

The cost was heavy—in loss, in physical and mental suffering. In Nero's Rome, unpopularity begat persecution. Ephesus revealed a reaction as savage. In Bithynia, State repression followed the hostile protest of resentful paganism. In these studies we have traced the first attempts of Christians to live at peace with paganism; we have read the warnings of Paul, and seen how, in disregard of those warnings, a group emerged who abused the noble doctrine of liberty and mingled Christ determinedly with Belial. As the New Testament closes, the long years of State persecution had opened. They were to cleanse and purify the Church. But the Church could never have survived the impact of those years had there not been in her midst a body of men and women who literally 'counted all things but loss for Christ'. We bow the head before those who bore all the human heart finds it most difficult to bear, to preserve the faith unsullied, unadulterated, undamaged and intact.

Professor Butterfield's words still stand: 'We are back for the first time in the earliest centuries of Christianity, and those centuries afford some relevant clues to the kind of attitude to adopt.'

Questions and themes for study and discussion on Studies 714–720

1. How did John turn misfortune to advantage?
2. Need one interpretation of a prophecy exclude another?

3. How does a church grow weary?
4. How does a church grow strong?
5. The Church and 'Satan's Seat' today.
6. How does surrounding society get into the Church?
7. Today's Nicolaitans.

721 : The Sardians

Revelation 3.1–6; 18.1–8

Sardis, ancient capital of Lydia, old realm of Croesus the Rich, fell out of history. Some ruins lie round and under a great crumbling crag, the old acropolis, in the Hermus valley, and a small village called Sart is nearby. Once it was a road junction, straddling trade-routes, a mingling-place of cultures. Its crag, where temples and palaces stood, a great spur of mountain, was seemingly impregnable, dominating the surrounding country.

And yet it seems that the mighty strength of the city on the ridge bred over-confidence, and twice in history the acropolis was taken, and a war ended, by men scaling the heights, 'like thieves in the night', and storming the walls by a surprise attack. 'It was a city,' wrote Ramsay, who found the key to the character of Sardis in her history, 'whose story blazoned forth the uncertainty of human fortunes, and the shortness of the step which separates over-confident might from sudden disaster. It was a city whose name was synonymous with pretensions unjustified, promise unfulfilled, appearance without reality, confidence which heralded ruin.'

If Ramsay's thesis holds, and John's stern letter suggests as much, the city's Christians, like their community, had not used great advantages well. Preoccupied with their own affairs, they had not recognized the resourcefulness of the foe. How the majority had failed is not clear. It is a few only who had 'not defiled their garments'. Columns of a temple to Cybele stand on the valley floor, and hers was an Asiatic cult, with perverted sexualities, full of wild excitement, clashing cymbals, blaring horns and obscene mutilations. Perhaps some form of Nicolaitanism had corrupted the church with compromise in this regard. 'Defiled garments' suggests some unworthy conduct. The emperor-cult was also rife at Sardis, and the city had built a temple in honour of Tiberius at the time of the great Asian earthquake.

Those who held true were to 'walk in white', like generals in a triumph. We know no more of the Sardian church. A cross cut here and there into the stone suggests that the goddess' temple was used at one time for Christian worship, but the rest is silence.

722 : The Philadelphians

Revelation 3.7–13; Matthew 28.16–20

Philadelphia, whose name means 'brotherly love', was founded in the middle of the second century before Christ, and named by its founder, Eumenes of Pergamum, in honour of his loyal brother Attalus. The city was an outpost of Greek culture in Asia, but had little history until the great earthquake of A.D. 17 brought a catastrophe. Tacitus, the Roman historian, writes: 'The same year twelve cities of Asia collapsed because of an earthquake which took place at night, a calamity the more serious because it fell without warning. Escape into open country was no help because people were swallowed up by the gaping earth. Great mountains crumbled to rubble, and plains were thrust up into hills ...' Telling of Tiberius' bounteous earthquake-relief, Tacitus lists Philadelphia.

The trouble was that there was no end to disaster. The city was near the faultline, on the edge of a volcanic district named 'the Burntland', from the masses of scoria debris which strewed the countryside, and seems for a long time to have been subject to demoralizing earth tremors. Strabo, the geographer, writing in A.D. 20 said; 'Philadelphia is full of earthquakes ... its very walls are unreliable, but daily fall apart.' Escape to the surrounding countryside was a common experience, and many would live for long periods in tents on the safer ground. Hence the letter: 'I will make him a pillar in the temple of my God, and he shall go out thence no more' (12). The Philadelphian church was a tormented congregation, its poor homes ruined, its life in jeopardy.

In gratitude to Tiberius the city took a new name. It called itself Neocaesarea, but the old name reasserted itself. The Philadelphians tried unsuccessfully to write upon themselves 'the name of their god' (12).

When Eumenes founded Philadelphia he chose a notable situation. South-east from the Hermus Valley, a long vale runs into the plateau of Asia Minor, a main line of communication between Smyrna and Lydia, and Phrygia. Hence the phrase 'I have set before thee an open door which none can shut'. Philadelphia was the keeper of the gateway to central Asia Minor, a city conscious of its mission as a centre of Hellenism, and aware of its frontier position. In such a city a missionary church was natural. That role was to be strikingly illustrated in later centuries when Rome had fallen, and Constantinople, her surviving successor, was facing the pressure of Islam, rolling in from Asia. Gibbon, in chapter 64 of his great *Decline and Fall*, almost echoes John's praise of long before. Until the exchange of minorities between Turkey and Greece in 1922, there was still a Christian witness there.

723 : The Laodiceans

Revelation 3.14–22; Isaiah 1.1–18

Laodicea was no natural fortress. The low swell of ground on which its fortifications stood, could have presented no great problem for an invader, and as a strong-point Laodicea had a disastrous weakness. The water-supply came by a vulnerable aqueduct from springs six miles away to the north. A place with its water so exposed to enemy action could scarcely stand a siege. Under Rome, Laodicea grew in commercial importance. Cicero travelled that way in 51 B.C. on his way to Cilicia, and the fact that he cashed drafts in Laodicea shows that the city was already a place of financial importance. There were manufacturers too. The valley produced a glossy black wool, and the strain of sheep bred for the trade was to be traced until the nineteenth century. The wool was the basis of a textile industry.

Laodicea had a medical school. The names of its physicians early appear on coins, and there is also the device of the serpent-wreathed rod of Asklepios, the god of healing. It was probably the medical school of Laodicea which developed the Phrygian eye-powder, famous in the ancient world.

Hence the scornful imagery. The black garments exported all over the Mediterranean world, the famous eye-ointment, the city's wealth, all are there, forming a structure for the writer's reproaches.

It is possible that the letter quoted the very words of some civic inscription. In A.D. 60 a terrible earthquake 'prostrated the city'. The phrase is that of Tacitus, who wrote fifty years later. The Roman Senate again gave vast sums to devastated Asian cities, but the historian records that Laodicea refused all such aid. She rose again, writes Tacitus, 'with no help from us.' The proud fact would undoubtedly be recorded on stone.

In prosperity men too commonly decay, and the Christian community of the city had become infected with the spirit of the place. The city on an open high-road may have learned the arts of compromise in the school of history, and now she was 'neither cold nor hot'. So, too, was the church which found a place in the self-confident, easy-going community.

Whatever the cause, ease, wealth, prosperity, the pervading spirit of the place, the life of the church-community was at a low ebb. It is curious that such a state should accompany an absence of enemies or persecution. Opulence and a facile environment have not normally been the stimuli of human progress. The pressure of hard and difficult conditions has been rather the prerequisite of achievement. Physically at ease, Laodiceans had grown indifferent to the call to work and strive for excellence. They remain a warning for an age of affluence.

724 : The Christians of Hierapolis

Colossians 4

Whether or not Philip ended his days in Hierapolis, churches clustered in the broad and fertile Lycus Valley. First came Colossae, and further east, six miles apart on either side of the valley plain, lay Hierapolis to the north, and Laodicea to the south. There is nothing to be seen of Laodicea, though the humped irregular ground under the fields suggest that a task awaits the archaeologists. Hierapolis, from whose locality Laodicea drew its water, was a spa, and abundant remains of market place and cemetery, suggest that it was rich and well patronized.

Paul ordered an interchange of letters between Laodicea and Colossae, and John must surely have included Hierapolis in his strictures on Laodicea, or he would not have used the illustration of the lukewarm water. To stand in the oatfields of Laodicea and look north, is to see the white cliff at Pummakale, where Hierapolis stood. The silica-laden water has spilled over from hot springs, and in a series of beautiful white natural basins, it runs to the valley below. Any New Zealander knows the geology of such a site, for the Rotorua spa demonstrates similar phenomena. The lukewarm chemical-laden water is also just such an emetic as John describes. Those who knew the place would recognize the imagery. Here in the broad, prosperous valley were affluent Christians, a sickly brew, neither sturdily Christian nor frankly pagan, and disgustingly burdened with alien admixture.

Psa. **119.**113 says, as Moffatt renders it: 'I hate men who are half and half', and it was the rugged Elijah, using the very verb of that verse, who told Israel scornfully to be one thing or the other, and not go limping along in impossible compromise (1 Kings **18.**21). Something like that had happened, it seems, to two Lycus Valley congregations, or Laodicea would not have been addressed in a word-picture derived from the geology or geography of the neighbouring thermal spa. We say goodbye to the congregations of John with this sad picture of easy-going worldliness. The letter from Patmos must have come as a shock.

Questions and themes for study and discussion on Studies 721–724

1. How can a church be caught sleeping?
2. What 'open doors' are we prone to overlook today?
3. Is the Laodicean attitude still with us?
4. Why is 'lukewarmness' useless?

725 : The Four Horsemen

Revelation 6.1–8; 9.13–21

No one interpretation of this book of poetic prophecy precludes other modes of exegesis. The visions are fixed to no dates, and can have multiple fulfilment. The seven churches were real churches. They are also typical churches, and are found functioning today.

So with the Four Horsemen. As always the shortest path and the surest to meaning and understanding is to ask what John had in mind when he first wrote, and it seems clear that the struggles between Rome and Parthia, that great, unsolved problem of the north-eastern frontier, are prominent in John's mind.

Parthia was the successor state of the Persian Empire, and her mounted bowmen had struck heavy blows at Rome. Here, surely, was a vision of the Persian Shah, now represented by the Parthian monarch, who always wore white. A common title of the kings of the East was 'the Conqueror'. Mars, or Ares, god of war, follows in the guise of a swordsman on a crimson steed. Perhaps he has no particular nationality. The Parthians were bowmen, the Romans were men of the sword. Perhaps this is the clash of armies in some eastern Armageddon, with the most certain sufferers those whose land was trampled into infertile mud, and drenched in blood as defender clashed with raider.

A third horseman follows close behind (5). The horseman is famine, and his horse is black like the emaciated corpses by the stricken roadway. Famine follows war and breakdown. A denarius a quart was twelve times the usual market price for wheat, the vital commodity of life. In the midst of such starvation oil and wine remain mockingly unharmed. They are not dependent on a yearly sowing neglected in times of trouble. The vines and olive trees are not so easily trampled by the passing hosts. Last in the vision comes a pale or livid horse, the colour of a corpse long dead (8). The picture is strife among hungry multitudes, disease stalking abroad, the very beasts slinking into abandoned and undefended villages to rend the weak and the dying. The dreadful portrait of the rider on the pale horse is an inclusive vision. All the ills of his predecessors, after war's cumulative fashion, are summed up in him. He is general chaos . . . Such vision found widening fulfilment over the coming five centuries. Like the world today, Rome lived behind frontiers of fear. Nor has the moral law changed, nor the judgement which follows rejection of God. The four horsemen, like Satan, are 'characters of Scripture' which we shrink from meeting. None the less, they ride forth.

726 : The Martyred

Revelation 6.9–17; Psalm 79.5–10

The martyred dead must surely find a place among the characters of this book. The opening movement of the chapter presented in poetic language an all too familiar sequence of social breakdown and disaster. The latter half (9–17) takes the scene poetically to heaven, in order to link the catastrophes of earth to the divine judgement which permits them. The 'souls under the altar' call for God's retribution on sin, cruelty and murder. It is easy for the comfortable and secure to comment adversely on the cry of the agonized, but let it be boldly said that, although the Christian is bidden pray for his enemies, there is nothing wrong in committing the hardened and determined persecutor to God's judgement and mercy, and to beg for an end to man's wickedness to man.

Judgement is sure, and it is pictured under the sixth seal in the imagery of Nature's violence, and of political anarchy. We saw such use of the terrors of earth and sky in Amos, Joel, Isaiah and Ezekiel. This was familiar symbolism to those whose whole education was their ancient Scriptures. Nor has scientific explanation robbed the earthquake of its terror, or the plunging meteor of its majesty and might. The poet seeks language adequate to bring to minds habituated to the picture-language of the East the fact which still stands true—'it is a fearful thing to fall into the hands of the living God', as the writer to the Hebrews remarked. And here, in fact, another Character, One who has haunted our every page enters the scene. Before perfect Goodness, in the presence of Intelligence and Strength quite unimaginably mighty, how pathetic is the strutting of captains and kings, how feeble the little bombastic words of man, how pathetic his claims to eminence, and how ridiculous his self-assertion (15–17)! And in the light of Eternity how transient is evil! But if Christian men endure, their sufferings are not in vain. They become part of the meaning of the Cross. They fuse their sacrifice with Christ's. As Lowell wrote a century ago:

> *Careless seems the great Avenger; history's pages but record*
> *One death-grapple in the darkness 'twixt old systems and the*
> *   Word:*
> *Truth forever on the scaffold, Wrong forever on the throne,—*
> *Yet that scaffold sways the future, and, behind the dim unknown,*
> *Standeth God within the shadow, keeping watch above His own.*

727 : The Redeemed and Their Lord

Revelation 7

The strange catalogue of the sealed remnant of the tribes must be read in the light of the fact that the Church regarded the whole Christian community as the new Israel (Rom. 2.28f; Gal. 6.16; Phil. 3.3). Nor, in a book of symbolic language, can the numbers be taken literally, as some interpreters have often striven to do. The number twelve has significance in both Testaments. The square, twelve times twelve, multiplied a thousandfold, represents a perfect multitude, a generous rather than a niggardly total. In v. 9 the 144,000 merge with the multitude beyond all counting. These are they whom we have been meeting throughout this series of studies—they and their posterity.

The beautiful description of the reward from God's hand for those who came triumphantly out of great tribulation is one of the tenderest passages in the book. There is no need at all to limit the reference to any one tribulation, or to a great and final tribulation. There has been no generation, from the first century until today, when at least one portion of the Church has not faced, for the testimony of Christ, persecution and suffering which its victims must have looked upon as the ultimate in horror. John's word of comfort is for them all, and in such spirit those who suffer for the Name have always used it.

It was the thought of Christ's own sacrifice (14), which nerved and strengthened the conquerors to go through the fires and emerge to victory. It is to a sharp consciousness that they were treading a path which He had trod before, that the 'overcomers' owe their power to endure. Calvary again takes its place as the heart of Christianity. And see v. 17. It is the Lamb which 'shepherds' them, for the Lamb of this imagery is also the Good Shepherd, and the image of His guidance and care is one which runs from end to end of the Bible. Grief, in that final day, will end, for there is no sorrow there. Note, too, that the apostle speaks of tears. The Lord was no hard Stoic; He wept at Lazarus' tomb. There is no virtue in proud unwillingness to weep. It is the task of Christlikeness to take away the tears of others, or to share them, as Jesus did. And how truly John saw God in what he had seen of Christ.

728 : The Dark Invaders

Revelation 9

The reference to the river Euphrates, which was the lamentably insecure demarcation of the north-east frontier of the Empire, adds a strong likelihood to the suggestion that the plague which was unleashed against the eastern provinces was an inroad of mounted Parthian bowmen. The vast numbers mentioned (16) must be read in the context of apocalyptic poetry, for the whole population of Asia at the time did not amount to 200,000,000, the figure mentioned. Perhaps in the prophetic telescoping of time, the insight of the writer had in view the whole coming pageant of history's later catastrophes. All the riders from the untamed steppes, and the distant Gobi pasturelands, whence Hun, Mongol and Turk were yet to pour, are envisaged in one scene and moment of prophetic vision pouring in—a murdering, trampling multitude flooding through that one, wide disastrously gaping frontier. The sanguinary campaign of A.D. 58 to 62 against the Parthians must have filled the more exposed lands of the Middle East with tales of barbaric power beyond the Mesopotamian rivers. Plutarch, who wrote in the early years of the next century, spoke of the coloured and fearsome appearance of the Medes and Scythians, horse-riding tribes associated with the wild raiders, but there is no need, in such a context of apocalyptic imagery, to insist upon an allegorical meaning for every detail, much less to see a literal prophecy of arms and explosive weaponry, fortunately not known at the time when the words were written. It is the general impression which must be assessed, and that is one of stark and exotic horror. An ordered society is overrun and trampled by a foreign host. At the same time, it is possible to see historic fact in such details as those of v. 19. The Parthian bowmen were adepts at turning in the saddle of a galloping horse, and loosing a final volley of shafts as they withdrew at full speed from a rallying enemy. Hence the proverbial 'Parthian shot'. For all the storm of catastrophe, the evil society under attack and menace does not repent. The choice of Barabbas presses hard. They had chosen Caesar and rejected Christ.

729 : The Beast

Revelation 13.1–10; Daniel 7

Chapter 13 of the Apocalypse is another illustration of the fact that no single interpretation of that strange book excludes the others. The vision of the Beast is poetry of the sort which the modern world, bemused by the imitators of T. S. Eliot, finds familiar. Let it also be granted that the chapter admits of historical interpretation for it is possible to set John's imagery in a context of history. And for those who find a 'futurist' interpretation attractive, there is the patent fact that the present century knows well enough the Beast that has cursed the past, the tyrant who demands the allegiance of hand and head. He would be optimist indeed who should say that the world has seen the last of the grisly procession.

The Beast came out of the sea, and that is an image in Scripture for the agitated mass of mankind which, as Victor Hugo put it in a strange poem, casts up grim creatures in times of crisis. 'The wicked,' said Isaiah, 'are like the tossing sea, for it cannot rest, and its waters toss up mire and dirt' (Isa. 57.20). And hear George Adam Smith's rendering of the same prophet's earlier word: 'Ah, the booming of the peoples, like the booming of the sea ... like the rushing of many waters they rush ...' John sees, like some galley of the imperial fleet showing sail, then dark hull, then pagan figurehead over the western horizon, rise up the Animal, first crowned horns, then head, then feet.

This most mysterious character of Scripture is a composite creation. Leopard, bear and lion, all of which strong beasts lived in Palestine, united to give it the symbols of cruelty, agility, craft, speed and power. It was Rome to which the East, along with its visible heads, the emperors, gave worship in temple and shrine, for Rome's rough hand had brought peace. Men, weary of war, worshipped Rome, and gave Rome and her princes 'names of blasphemy', the divine titles of the emperors common enough in John's own Ephesus.

Not counting Domitian under whom he suffered, and who still lived, there had been seven emperors, from Augustus to the short-lived Titus, or ten if the few weeks of Galba, Otho and Vitellius, the victims of the Year of the Four Emperors, A.D. 69, are counted. That was the year Nero died, and Rome bled in multiple civil war, almost wounded to death, but 'recovered of her deadly wound'.

730 : The Second Beast

Revelation 13.11–17; Romans 13.1–7; Matthew 13.24–30; 1 Peter 2.13–17

The second Beast, the other composite character in this chapter, rose out of the land, a fierce Animal with a deceptive look of suavity. This surely is the religious hierarchy of Asia, and perhaps the local Roman governors, who could be coerced into the rigid application of the law. The law was on the books, and if the authorities saw fit to put John out of the way, they were also empowered to persecute with severity. A generation after this letter was written, Pliny, the humane governor of Bithynia, was told by Trajan, a just and able emperor, that the law was the law. The correspondence survives and illustrates v. 15. The governor describes his procedure: 'Those who denied they were, or had ever been, Christians, who repeated after me an invocation to the gods, and offered adoration, with wine and frankincense, to your image, which I had ordered to be brought for that purpose, together with those of the gods, and who finally cursed Christ—none of which acts, it is said, those who are really Christians can be forced into performing—those I thought it proper to discharge. Others who were named by an informer at first confessed themselves Christians, and then denied it; true, they had been of that persuasion, but they had quitted it, some three years, others many years, and a few as much as twenty-five years ago. They all worshipped your statue and the images of the gods, and cursed Christ.'

For those prepared to accept the writ of the authorities and in the same act repudiate Christ, a certificate could be issued, perhaps a seal and an official's signature on a document of repudiation. Nineteen such documents were discovered in 1904 and 1907 at the site of Theadelphia in Egypt. This is what the Aurelian family signed with appropriate witnesses: 'To the superintendents of offerings and sacrifices at the city. From Aurelius . . . son of Theodorius and Pantonymis of the said city. It has ever been my custom to make sacrifices and pour libations to the gods, and now also I have, in your presence in accordance with the commandment, poured libations, made sacrifice, and tasted the offerings, together with my son Aurelius Dioscuros and my daughter Aurelia Lais. I therefore request you to certify my statement.'

It is a sad document but illustrates the work of the second Animal.

731 : Man of Sin

Revelation 13.17, 18; 2 Thessalonians 2

Grim régimes, in past centuries and ours, have known this apparition, the Beast clothed in authority that stamps a mark on head and hand, and denies a man a right to live unless he bows and worships. Things had changed in Rome since Paul bade Christians obey and act as good citizens should (Rom. 13.1–7), and since Peter bade men honour the Emperor (1 Pet. 2.13–17). Caesar-worship had changed it all. Rome was out to crush the faith and to demand the soul of man.

Hence the image of the seal. There is evidence of branding and tattooing of slaves. There was also a red seal bearing the emperor's name and effigy, which was used in documents of exchange. It was a sign of contract and in the metaphor of the chapter suggests acceptance of the Animal's law and authority.

And what of the last enigma: '. . . his number is six hundred and sixty-six'? Note first that some good manuscripts give 616, not 666. In both Greek and Latin the letters of the alphabet had numerical value, and the fact was commonly used to build puzzles. Among the wall scratchings from Pompeii is an election notice in which the vowels are exchanged for numbers, and another inscription speaks of a girl called Harmonia. 'The number of her name,' it says, 'is 45.' The key to the puzzle seems to be that Harmonia suggests the nine Muses, and 45 is the sum of all the digits from 1 to 9.

The churches of Asia probably knew the key to 666 or 616, but it was early forgotten. In Greek 616 adds up to 'Caesar God', but 666 is not so simple, and much ingenuity with spelling has been employed to fit the number to 'Nero Caesar', or 'Caius Caesar'. It is also plausibly suggested that 666 falls short of the perfect trinity 777 in all counts, and thus presents a grisly picture of the power and baseness of Antichrist. The subject remains open for ingenuity. After all, the writer warns his readers: 'Behold, here is wisdom.' Perhaps some papyrus scrap, still undiscovered, some inscription under a Turkish doorstep or embedded in a wall, contains an answer to John's cryptogram.

But the vision abides among the dark shapes which form the characters of this part of Revelation—a thing of horror which has been seen and could be seen again.

Questions and themes for study and discussion on Studies 725–731

1. Do the horsemen still ride?
2. Lowell's verse (Study No. 726).
3. How does the modern Christian 'overcome'?
4. The fragility of ordered society.
5. The Beast today.

6. How is Christ still repudiated?
7. 'Caesar-worship' in its modern guise.

732 : Rome in Triumph

Revelation 17

Rome was a personality in John's day, a dark 'character of the Bible'. Apart from personification which made the Babylon of the New Testament a person of evil, a blood-drunken woman throned on her seven hills, Rome was worshipped, along with the emperor, in temples of the Caesar cult. John's searing denunciation of the evil creature was a lone voice. Rome had given peace to those who accepted her stern rule, and war-weary men saw her as the only hope as the frontiers bent under the pressure of an alien and uncivilized world.

Quotation can proceed until the final break-down. Here, for example, is the Greek rhetorician Publius Aelius Aristeides. He writes of Rome in the middle of the second century:

'You have made one single household of the whole inhabited world. Before the establishment of your empire, the world was in confusion, upside down, adrift, out of control: but as soon as you Romans intervened, the turmoil of factions ceased, and life and politics were illuminated by the dawn of an era of universal order ... so that today the earth and all that dwell therein are endowed with a clear and comprehensive security.'

Claudian of Alexandria writes with no less enthusiasm at the turn of the grim fourth century:

'Rome alone has taken the conquered to her bosom, and has made them to be one household with one name—herself their mother, not their empress—and has called her subjects citizens, and has linked far places in a bond of duty. Hers is that large loyalty to which we owe it that the stranger walks in a strange land as if it were his own; that men change their homes; that it is a pastime to visit Thule and to explore mysteries at which once we shuddered; that we drink at will the waters of the Rhone and the Orontes; that the whole earth is one people.'

Or hear a Gaul, Claudius Rutilius Namatianus, writing astonishingly in A.D. 416, six years after Alaric's sack of Rome:

'You made one fatherland for varied races, and under your

rule it was advantage for those who willed it not to be taken, and in offering the conquered a share in your own law, you made a city of what was once a world.'

By this time the Empire had surrendered, too late to save herself. The capital had changed to Byzantium in the East, and it was there, Constantinople as he now named it, that Constantine established Christianity as the official cult. The Roman Peace had its vast advantages. During its high noon Christianity was established. Then the Empire turned on the force which might have changed her life. Christians must have felt bitterly lonely in the midst of the chorus of adulation and of praise. Christians feel lonely still in the midst of the praise for the world of collapsing values today. But the laws of history stand.

733 : Rome in Ruin

Revelation 18

The tone changes. This chapter is less apocalyptic in its imagery, but Rome is still a personified reality. It required a bold prophet to see beyond the two centuries of prosperity and peace within the bounds of Empire which lay ahead and write this grim 'taunt-song'. The deluded world laments its overturned idol. The merchants bewail its passing. Perhaps in some Asian port John had watched the galleys loading their cargoes, redolent of the wealth sucked from a subject world by the Beast by the Tiber. There was 'merchandise of gold and silver and precious stones, of pearls and of fine linen, and purple and silk, and scarlet cloth, and vases of ivory, and costly wood, and of brass, and iron. There was cinnamon, and perfumes, and ointments, frankincense, and wine and oil . . . fine flour, and wheat, and horses, sheep, chariots, and slaves, AND SOULS OF MEN.'

The climax was bitter, and came last to the watcher's lips as he turned away from the loading dock. The Seer knew that, unless all history lied, Rome would pay for the last-named cargo in blood and ruin. And he seemed in the foresight of his vision to see the port of Ostia in the ruin in which it stands today, its warehouses hollow shells, Rome under the smoke of her burning and the voices of her music stilled. So Nineveh had lain of old under Nahum's contempt, and Tyre under Ezekiel's scorn. And here now was an audacity of prophecy to outdo them all. The Seer

839

saw a vast world empire doomed for persecution's sake, consigned to nether Hell because she had drunk the blood of the ones who had wished her well and who had spoken the words which might have saved her.

How that prophecy turned into dark fact is a matter of history. The fall of the Roman Empire is a horror which has, until today, held the fascinated imagination of the world. Rome had her opportunity, as the peoples of a wider global society have today. In the fateful generation which lay between Nero and Domitian the voice of Christianity became clear and vocal. Rome could have made her saving choice. But Rome, like a vicious person chose evilly and paid the price, over four centuries of revolution, tension, tyranny and final dissolution. So it happens with nations —and with men.

734 : The Conqueror

Revelation 19

It is important to place this imagery of the mounted Conqueror in its proper context of thought. John is not reverting to the Jewish notion of a warlike Messiah marching to free the nation or people of His choice from the bondage of the oppressor. Those who walked with Christ had expected such a consummation, even in the days when they were with their Master in His lowliness. It is clear from the Gospel narratives that they looked upon those days as a time of preparation and disguise, out of which the Conqueror of their dreams and expectations would, at the proper moment, arise. Even after His resurrection they could still ask: 'Lord, will You at this time restore the Kingdom to Israel?' (Acts 1.6). John had been sufficiently instructed in the nature of the Kingdom, and the reality of his Lord's Messiahship, not to imagine that the discarded misconception of a militaristic, nationalistic kingdom could in any way be revived.

We are reading the language of poetry, and the imagery of soldiering for Christ was used by Paul in writing to Ephesus, and in his last word to Timothy. It is found in many hymns. John is merely summing up the whole message of his book. He has seen the dawning of God's triumph over evil. The 'many waters' is an image from the opening vision of the book. The noise of the sea, driven by the north wind is seldom absent from the Aegean islands. God's voice in John's rich imagination sounded like the unending roar or murmur of the surf, but rose at times to the crash and roll of the thunder. So, in John's vision, was the utterance of God, always speaking for those who listen, but at times rising in the din of storm.

And now the glorified Christ rides forth to final victory. It is a demonstration of the old exile's indomitable faith that God and good will prevail. He is showing us that all evil must die, that sin contains the certainty of its own destruction, that tyranny is doomed, and judgement sure upon rebellion. 'Wherefore, let us this day, take up the whole armour of God, that we may be able to stand in the evil day, and having done all to stand' (Eph. 6.13). We are a vanguard of the host. A vital skirmish may be ours.

735 : The Dead

Revelation 20.11–15; 22.11; 2 Corinthians 5.10; John 3.18, 36

The awesome scene of the Great White Throne shows the ultimate ordering of justice in the similitude of a mighty court before a Judge who never errs. There is a strangely terrible saying in 22.11 which suggests that it is part of our human responsibility to carry into eternity the choice we make in time. We carry our own condemnation. 'Time present and time past,' said T. S. Eliot, 'are both perhaps present in time future.' Choose evil now and that choice is projected into another life. Choose death now, and death abides our lot. Dante, amid the sombre horrors of his poem, touched the edge of that truth: 'And I looked and saw a whirling banner which ran so fast that it seemed as if it could never make a stand, and behind it came so long a train of people that I should never have believed death had undone so many. And I saw and knew the shade of him who from cowardice had made the great refusal, and with certainty I perceived that this was the worthless crew that is hateful to God and His enemies, wretches who were never alive . . .'

Such was the poet's judgement on uncommitted lives. They followed a banner of swirling mist and had never really lived. Like the hand on Belshazzar's wall, we write our own doom. If the verb for 'perish' in John 3.16 is taken, as it can equally be, in the middle voice rather than the passive, that famous text can read '. . . that whoever believes in him should not destroy himself but share the life of God'.

841

At the great assize which John pictures the sentence of condemnation, self-chosen and self-willed is merely confirmed.
Condemnation is mere confrontation with self.

> *I sat alone with my Conscience,*
> *In a place where time had ceased,*
> *And we talked of my former living,*
> *In the land where the years increased,*
> *And the ghosts of forgotten actions*
> *Came floating before my sight,*
> *And things that I thought were dead things*
> *Were alive with a terrible might.*
> *So I sit alone with my Conscience,*
> *In the place where the years increase,*
> *I seek to remember the Future,*
> *In the place where time shall cease.*
> *For I know of a future judgement*
> *Whatever that judgement be;*
> *That to sit alone with my Conscience*
> *Will be judgement enough for me.*

736 : 'I Jesus'

Revelation 22

The vision is over. The book is ended. John has seen his Master
again arrayed as he had never seen Him before, save in that
brief transfiguration flash of another world on the slopes of
Hermon, almost a lifetime before. The island of exile resumed its
daily shapes and colours—the two harbours almost cutting its
mass in half, the small white town huddling by the sheltered
water's edge, the vine-clad and olive-clustered slopes, the vast
sweep of the sea, gold in the sloping sun.

His Lord, he knew, had always been with him. Such indeed had
been His promise, and the last of the Lord's men knew that, in all
life's experience, that promise had held true. He was still with him
at the book's end, as at its beginning, with him for evermore.

We who have moved during these studies through the Bible,
looking at the men and women who made it, whose sins and
sorrows, joys and virtues fill its pages, are conscious of that other
presence. There was Another with the three young men in the '

furnace (Dan. 3.25), 'and the form of the fourth was like the Son of God'. It is typical.

Foreshadowed in the Old Testament, a reality in the Gospels, a risen Lord in the story of the Church and in the experience of the writers of the New Testament, the Other in the story has always been at hand. Was there ever One so to dominate the writings of men? The writings only? He dominates the life. He is the supreme Character of Scripture. He is the Christian's ever-present Lord, his Word, his Will, all life's 'magnificent obsession'.

'Behold, I come quickly' ... And the promise holds when the fight is hard with foemen 'leaning on our shield' and 'roaring on us as we reel', when the way is dark and His purpose elusive, when earthly hopes fade, friends fall by the way, and likewise when the sun is on the road and 'heaven above a softer blue'. 'Even so come, Lord Jesus. Make haste to save us.'

And the grace of our Lord Jesus Christ be with you all. Amen.

Questions and themes for study and discussion on Studies 732–736

1. Why was John so lonely a voice?
2. Do the rules of history still work?
3. Is the Second Coming preached enough?
4. Why is lack of committal so deadly?
5. How do *you* sum up all these studies?